**MANAGING
THE DATA-BASE
ENVIRONMENT**

A *James Martin* BOOK

MANAGING

THE DATA-BASE ENVIRONMENT

JAMES MARTIN

PRENTICE-HALL, INC., Englewood Cliffs, New Jersey 07632

Library of Congress Cataloging in Publication Data

Martin, James
  Managing the data-base environment.

  Includes bibliographical references and index.
  1. Data-base management. I. Title.
QA76.9.D3M368   1983   001.64'42   82-16622
ISBN 0-13-550582-8

Managing the Data-Base Environment
James Martin

Editorial/production supervision by *Linda Mihatov*
Jacket design by *Karolina Harris*
Manufacturing buyer: *Gordon Osbourne*

Printed in the United States of America

10 9 8 7 6 5 4

ISBN 0-13-550582-8

PRENTICE-HALL INTERNATIONAL, INC., *London*
PRENTICE-HALL OF AUSTRALIA PTY. LIMITED, *Sydney*
EDITORA PRENTICE-HALL DO BRASIL, LTDA., *Rio de Janeiro*
PRENTICE-HALL CANADA, INC., *Toronto*
PRENTICE-HALL OF INDIA PRIVATE LIMITED, *New Delhi*
PRENTICE-HALL OF JAPAN, INC., *Tokyo*
PRENTICE-HALL OF SOUTHEAST ASIA PTE. LTD., *Singapore*
WHITEHALL BOOKS LIMITED, *Wellington, New Zealand*

TO CORINTHIA

A data base is a shared collection of interrelated data designed to meet the needs of multiple types of end users.

The data are stored so that they are independent of the programs that use them. A common and controlled approach is used in adding new data and modifying and retrieving existing data.

The objective of data-base technology is to speed up computer application development, reduce application maintenance costs, and provide end users with the data they need for doing their jobs as efficiently as possible.

Data-base technology will become the backbone of most data processing.

*The move to a data-base environment is not just a change in software; **it is a change in management**. Unless an appropriate change in management occurs, the major benefits of data-base operation will not be realized.*

This change must be understood not only by the managers in question but by the systems analysts, programmer teams, end users, and department managers who are affected.

A major responsibility of management at all levels in a computerized corporation is to ensure that the data structures they need come into existence and are compatible.

BOOK STRUCTURE

CONTENTS

PART **VI** IMPLEMENTATION CONSIDERATIONS

PART **VII** THE VIEW FROM THE TOP

PREFACE

Data-base technology is a foundation stone of much future data processing. It will be essential for the computerized corporation of the future and requires good management. The intent of this book is to explain this.

At present, data-base technology is not achieving the benefits and successes touted by the salespeople. Techniques used in many organizations contain the seeds for considerable future difficulties and anxiety.

In this book, clear techniques for the management of existing and future data bases are described. The move to a data-base environment requires a fundamental change in management. How well the data-base environment is managed will affect the profitability of many corporations in the future.

This book is the latest in the integrated set of data-base books published by Prentice–Hall. Watch this space—there is more to follow!

James Martin

MANAGING
THE DATA-BASE
ENVIRONMENT

A *James Martin* **BOOK**

PART **I** INTRODUCTION

1 EXECUTIVE CHALLENGE

INTRODUCTION A task of executives of all types in the years ahead is to assist in the building of computerized corporations.* In the age of microelectronics, fast response to customers, fast reaction to problems, and fast response to information needs will be increasingly vital for competitive survival.

Data-base usage is the key to flexible employment of computers and their transmission networks. How well the data-base environment is managed affects executives in all areas of a corporation.

CORPORATE MEMORANDUM:

. . . .Data management is primarily a business function. Decisions as to what data is important to the business, who is responsible for it, and how it is to be organized and used, can realistically be made only by business managers. The present DP community can support this function, but cannot manage it outright. . . .

SUCCESSES AND FAILURES There is now much experience in the use of data-base systems. Some installations have gained great benefits from the data base approach. In others, data-base techniques have been a failure, or disappointing.

A few years ago I was involved in a series of meetings at IBM where we were going through postmortems of data-base systems that had failed or had

---

*We will use the term "corporation" to refer to organizations of all types, including those such as government departments or universities which are not necessarily a corporation.

not worked as expected. It dawned on me during those meetings that the people there were saying the same thing over and over again. There were the same reasons for failures and the same reasons for successes.

About that time my book *Principles of Data-Base Management* [1], was in the page-proof stage, so I decided to put an epilogue at the back of the book which listed the reasons for failure, and alongside those the reasons that have made data-base installations particularly successful.

Ever since then I have been observing data-base installations. Both the technology and the perceptions of what data bases should accomplish have changed somewhat. In this book I will indicate what actions are likely to make a data-base installation succeed and what are likely to make it fail or be disappointing.

Often we find that there are partial successes. An installation has done some things right but not everything. It is desirable to succeed in *all* the different areas. In other words, get the whole act together.

WHAT IS A DATA BASE?

A data base is a collection of data that are shared and used for multiple purposes.

The term *end user* implies the *ultimate user* of a data-base facility, not an interim user such as a programmer programming functions for the end users. Data-base end users are a diverse cross section of humanity: accountants, engineers, administrative managers, civil servants, shop-floor foremen, department heads, budget controllers, professionals, actuaries, the president, and his aides.

Any manager, planner, or professional whose job will be changed in the future by data-base systems should understand the principles of data base, and become involved.

Any single user does not perceive all the types of data in the data base, only those that are needed for his or her job.* A user may perhaps perceive only one file of data. That file always has the same structure and appears simple, but in fact it is derived from a much more complex data structure. Other users see *different* files derived from the same data base.

A data base is thus not only shared by multiple users, but it is *perceived* differently by different users (Fig. 1.1).

You might think of blind persons confronted with an elephant. One person touches its leg and perceives it as being like a tree trunk. One touches its tail and perceives it as being like a rope. Another touches its tusks, and so on. Similarly, different data-base users perceive different *views* of the data. Someone has to design and manage the entire elephant. In doing so he must make sure that he meets the diverse needs of many users. In other words, all relevant user views must be derivable from the data base. This is a complex

---

*In the future I will use "his" and "he" as an abbreviation of "his or her" and "he or she."

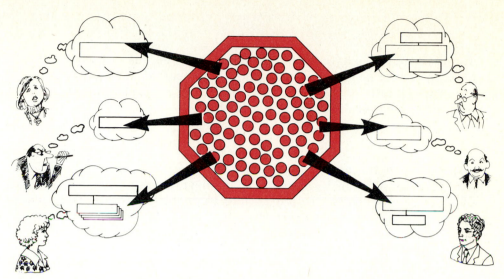

Figure 1.1 A data base is a shared collection of interrelated data designed to meet the needs of multiple types of end users. It can be defined as a collection of data from which multiple different end-user
views can be derived. The data are stored so that they are independent
of the programs that use them. A common and controlled approach is
used in adding new data and modifying and retrieving existing data.

task. The technical aspects of it can be largely automated. If this is done, the
most difficult part of the task is understanding the data needed by the users,
representing them in the data base, and ensuring that they are indeed used
appropriately. This is complicated by the fact that different users use different names for the same data item, and sometimes the same name for data
items which are really different.

For computers to work correctly, a high degree of precision is needed
in representing the data they use.

It is up to user departments to ensure that the data they need are truly
represented in a corporation's data bases, correctly defined, appropriately
organized, and protected from harm or invalid use. The data-base designer
needs the user departments' help in understanding their data needs.

There is one story after another in data processing of management not
being able to obtain the information they need from their computer system.

In one instance when a large American bank went bankrupt, a wave of
concern went through the boardrooms of other banks. Top management in
one bank compiled a list of urgent questions that it wanted answered immediately about the situation in the bank. All the data to answer these questions
were in computer disc storage. But DP management could not answer the
questions. To do so would have needed files reorganizing and programs writing. That would have taken many weeks.

> *CORPORATE SYSTEMS PLANNER:*
>
> The computer files have become a nightmare. There is just a quagmire of maintenance problems. DP have not only incurred the wrath of management because of slow response and excessive costs, but they are totally bogged down in maintenance problems.

New, unanticipated requests for information are increasing, as end-user managers realize the potential value to them of the data that are stored. Much future growth can be expected in the data requests from management as they better comprehend the potential of computers. However, to the data-processing manager without appropriate data bases, these requests can be a menace. Even if he had the staff to handle them, it would take months and then be far too late.

The concept of data base, if it works as intended, should enable the DP department to be more responsive to such requests. However, for this to happen, the right data structures must be created, and this requires close co-operation between the data-base designer and the end users' management.

It is proving a very complex and lengthy operation to build up such data bases, and with current hardware it is expensive to search them sufficiently quickly to give fast answers to unanticipated queries.

The striving for flexibility, however, is vital. In many corporations, systems (of accounts, organization, methods, responsibilities, and procedures) have been more of a hindrance to change than physical plant and unamortized capital investments. For some, retraining the whole labor force would be easier than changing the system. Quite frequently, the computer has contributed to the inflexibility by dressing hallowed procedures in a rigid electronic framework. The computer has been hailed as one of the most versatile and flexible machines ever built, but in many corporations, because of the difficulty and cost of changing the programs and data bases, it becomes a straitjacket which precludes change and even constrains corporate policy. The comment is often heard: "We cannot do that because change is too difficult with our computer system."

One of the most difficult tricks that we have to learn is how to introduce automation without introducing rigidity. The computer industry is only now beginning to glimpse how that can be done. Data-base techniques are an important part of the answer.

CONSTANT CHANGE One of the most important characteristics of data processing is the planning for constant change. Dynamic restructuring of the data base must be possible as new types of data and new applications are added. The restructuring should be possible without having to rewrite the application programs, and in general should cause as little upheaval as possible. The ease with which a data base can be changed will have a major effect on the rate at which data-processing applications can be developed in a corporation.

It is often easy for a systems analyst to imagine that the data structure he has designed for an application represents its ultimate content and usage. He leaves some spare characters in the records and thinks that these will accommodate any change that will occur. Consequently, he ties his data to a physical organization which is efficient for that particular structure. Time and time again he is proven wrong. The requirements change in unforeseen ways. The data structures have to be modified, and consequently many application programs have to be rewritten and debugged. The larger an installation's base of application programs, the more expensive is this process.

FAILURE

The decade ahead is likely to be an era of great invention in the techniques for storing and organizing data, and many of the new techniques will be highly complex. The greater the rate of introduction of new techniques or modified data organizations, the greater is the need to protect the application programs and programmers from them. This is one of the main reasons why we need data-base systems rather than merely file systems without the data independence.

However, many data-base installations have failed to lower maintenance costs and failed to respond to end users as needed. The reason is not so much a flaw in the technology as a failure to use appropriate design and management.

A data-base management system can only bring its intended benefits when used within the context of appropriate management. It does not relieve the need for formal data management; its effective use demands it. It requires more advanced planning, better communications, and a reliance on both technical and business-oriented skills.

In short, it presents a new set of management challenges.

DELUSIONS

There are several common misconceptions about data-base systems which need clarifying.

First, a data base, or data-base management system, does not necessarily imply a "management information system." There is no direct relationship between the terms. In their initial use, most data bases should be thought of merely as a way of storing data for conventional applications and making those data more easily accessible to end users. Data-base techniques are justified by giving faster application development, lowering the cost of maintenance, and enabling much end-user data to be obtained without programming. They permit the data-processing department to be responsive.

Management information is an important by-product of some data bases. It is sometimes the primary reason for data-base use.

A second delusion is that a data-base system is sometimes described as containing all the data items in a corporation or a division. Typical comments on the subject from journals such as the *Harvard Business Review* include the following misconception: "If the company had maintained all its computer-readable data in a single pool or bank—in a so-called 'data base'—and if the company had structured this base of data so that a program for virtually any feasible use could have been run from this data base, then it would have been a matter of sheer expertise and flair for a good, experienced programmer to concoct a program that pulled the desired information together" [2]. And "The data-base concept structures EDP activity in such a way that all of a company's computer-readable data are merged in a single pool, which is used to run both routine programs and programs written in response to ad hoc requests" [2].

Any attempt to implement so grand a notion is doomed to disaster before it begins. One of the reasons for data-base techniques is that files or data bases that were separate can later be combined. In this way larger collections of data can be built up with a subsequent drop in data redundancy and increase in data-base interrogation capability. However, to begin with the notion that the data base will serve everyone who uses data is asking for trouble.

Related to the delusion noted above is the notion that an organization will have *one* data base. In reality it is likely to have many data bases, eventually perhaps hundreds. Many different data bases may be used on the same data-base system, but they will be both physically and logically separate. They should be built with a common data description language, common dictionary, and common design policies because linkages between them will be forged in the future. The data-base management system should be common to all, but the data bases themselves entirely separate.

INFRASTRUCTURE A better way to think of data-base systems is that they form an infrastructure which will allow better use of data processing in the future. If the principles of this book are followed, they force clear thinking about data. A clearly defined representation of the corporate data, modeled in a relatively stable form, will steadily grow. This data modeling should keep well ahead of the implementation of specific data bases. The implementation will be such that the data representation can change and grow without usually forcing the rewriting of application programs. The programs will not have to be rewritten when better hardware is installed.

At today's state of the art, then, most corporations should not talk about a corporate-wide data base but rather a *corporate-wide organizing principle* which forms the structure for data-base development. An essential of this principle is that the data descriptions and data dictionary be standardized throughout the corporation.

INCREMENTAL GROWTH

The growth that the infrastructure permits should have two characteristics. First, it should be planned, insofar as is possible. Although planning is desirable, it must be recognized that a data base will inevitably be used in ways that were not anticipated when it was designed. Second, the plan should involve small incremental steps, one application or one improvement to be implemented at a time on each data base.

The first applications selected for use with a data base should involve three characteristics. First, the data base should not be too complicated. Second, the application should be one that is clearly cost-justifiable. And third, *the management of the user departments should give full support and cooperation.*

As the data in a corporation are defined and modeled (as described later), more separate data bases come into existence. When more data bases exist, more projects are undertaken using these data bases. Many such projects using the data bases will be relatively short in duration—not more than a few months. Many of the incremental steps will be very short to implement, such as the production of a new type of report from an existing data base.

After several years of stage-by-stage buildup the overall data-base systems will begin to look impressive if they were appropriately directed toward overall goals. To be successful the data-base management system used must provide a high level of data independence, so that growth of data structures can continue without rewriting programs.

Unfortunately, although this stage-by-stage buildup is the best formula for success, an organization-wide all-embracing implementation sometimes appears more attractive to systems analysts or to management. Few projects for a grandiose data-base-to-end-all-data-bases have met with other than bitter disappointment. If grandiose plans are needed, they should be for a standardized corporate-wide framework within which data bases evolve and interlink a stage at a time.

Great cities are not built in one monolithic implementation. They grow and evolve and are the sum of many smaller pieces of work. If their structure can be planned so that the piecemeal implementations fit into an overall design, they will be more workable cities. However, circumstances change and the best-laid plans of an earlier era go astray so that new plans must be made. The growth of corporate data bases is a little like the growth of a city. In a decade or so's time, many corporate data bases will be complex and expensive to maintain, like New York City. But like New York, they will have to go on working.

Unlike a city, however, data structures can incorporate a large amount of logical planning. We can build data structures which are relatively stable even though the applications that use them are changing. The better the planning, the better the ultimate payoff of data-base environment.

A LONG JOURNEY   A corporation setting out to build a comprehensive set of data bases has a long journey ahead of it. However, the sooner it is done the better.

The early stages of the journey should be individual systems for well-defined purposes. It is generally better to start with *operations systems* for well-specified applications rather than general-purpose *information systems,* and to select those operations systems that appear to offer tangible reward. The information systems arise, in part, as a by-product of the operations systems.

There is a *major* difference, however, between a route that gives the best short-term results irrespective of the final goal and a route that is planned to lead eventually to a comprehensive goal while being profitable, insofar as possible, in the short term.

Different systems and applications in a corporation will necessarily evolve separately because of the high level of complexity involved and the limited span of the minds of implementers. It is essential to ensure that they *can* evolve separately, implemented by teams with localized knowledge, because only in that way can they be closely tailored to the needs of the persons who will use the systems; only in that way can the high level of initiative and inventiveness of the local implementors be fully utilized. Nevertheless, it is desirable that, insofar as possible, the data-processing designers have a *master plan* for the future evolution of data bases in their organization. Centralized control is necessary to ensure an adequate measure of compatibility between the systems. Without such advanced planning the systems become more difficult (and in many cases have proved virtually impossible) to link together. They incur high costs for program or data conversion. They are often more difficult for the terminal operators to use because different terminal dialogue structures are used for different systems. They are much more cumbersome in the data-base planning, and more expensive in application of resources and in telecommunication costs. The linking together of separately designed and incompatible systems has proved to be extremely expensive in practice. In many cases the magnitude of the programming effort has been comparable to that when the systems were first installed.

Unfortunately, the adherence to a neatly conceived master plan has rarely been achieved in reality. The state of the art is moved by unpredictable tides, and their pressures are strong enough to distort the best-laid plans. A certain machine or software package suddenly becomes available. One approach works and another fails. Natural selection takes over, and we have a process of evolution dominated by the survival of whatever is the most practical.

The master plan, then, must not be too rigid; indeed, *it is absolutely essential to plan for uncertainty*. It must be permissible for different systems to evolve in their own ways. As they evolve they should employ data that have been defined and modeled *independently of specific applications*. The corporate *logical* data models described in Part III are the foundation of separate data-base evolution.

REFERENCES

1. James Martin, *Principles of Data-Base Management,* Prentice-Hall, Englewood Cliffs, N.J., 1976.

2. Richard L. Nolan, "Computer Data Bases: The Future Is Now," *Harvard Business Review,* September–October 1973. (An excellent article, highly recommended, like all Nolan's writing.)

2 DATA BASE IS A CHANGE IN MANAGEMENT

INTRODUCTION   It is important to distinguish between *file systems* and *data-base systems.*

FILE SYSTEMS   Much data processing uses *files* rather than data bases. A file environment has many problems. Figure 2.1 illustrates a file environment. There are many files of records, some on tape and some on quickly accessible media such as disc. The records contain data items, shown as circles in Fig. 2.1. When a program is written for a new application or a variation of an old application, there may be a file that contains the required set of data items. Often, however, there is not, and a new file has to be created.

Suppose that a new user request needs a file with data items A, F, and H. These data items do not appear together in the existing files in Fig. 2.1. Other files must be sorted and merged to obtain the new file, but this will not be straightforward if, as with the marketing problem above, the existing files do not have the required sets of keys. There may not be an H data item for every pair of A and F data items.

PROBLEMS WITH FILE SYSTEMS   There are three problems about the organization of data in *files* as in Fig. 2.1. To understand them the reader should imagine hundreds or thousands of files rather than the seven in Fig. 2.1.

First, there is a high level of redundancy. The same type of data item is stored in many different places. The different versions of the same data items may be in different stages of update. In other words, they have different values. This may give the appearance of inconsistency to users. A manager

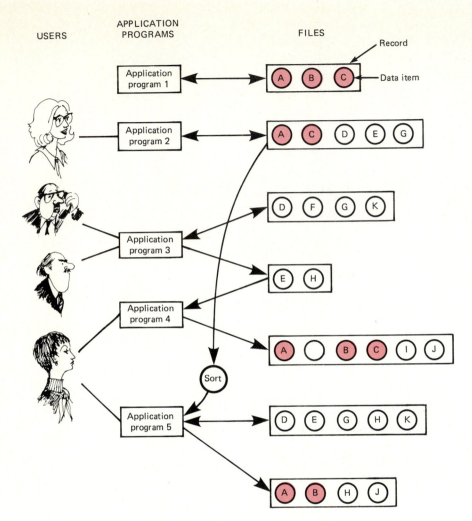

Figure 2.1 A file environment. For each new application a programmer or analyst creates a new file. A large installation has hundreds or thousands of such files with much redundancy of data.

obtains a report saying one thing and a terminal inquiry says something different.

With multiple copies of the same data item, it is difficult to maintain consistency or to ensure integrity of the data items.

Second, a file system is *inflexible*. Requests for information that require data items to be grouped in different ways cannot be answered quickly. Most ad hoc queries from a user employing a generalized query language cannot be answered. Although the data exist, information cannot be provided relating to those data. The data cannot be processed in new ways without restructuring.

One sometimes hears the protest from management: "We paid millions for that computer system and we cannot obtain the information we want from it."

Third, it can be expensive to make changes to a file system.

Suppose that application program 3 in Fig. 2.1 has to be changed in such a way that its record $\boxed{\text{E} \quad \text{H}}$ has to be modified. Unfortunately, application program 4 uses this same record; therefore, application program 4 has to be modified. Many other application programs may also use the same record (Fig. 2.2) and all have to be changed.

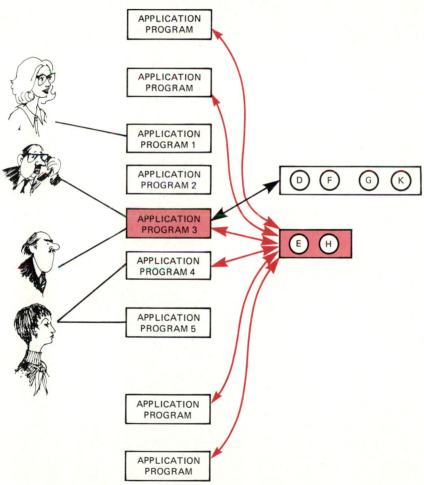

Figure 2.2 One file becomes used by multiple applications. When an application is changed (application program 3 above) and its file has to be restructured, all the programs which use that file have to be changed. A seemingly trivial change in a file environment can set off a chain reaction of other changes that have to be made.

A seemingly trivial change in a file environment sets off a chain reaction of other changes that have to be made. This upheaval is expensive and the necessary programmers are doing other work. Sometimes the modifications are difficult to make because the applications were not adequately documented.

As time goes on this problem becomes worse because more and more programs are created. More programs have to be changed whenever a file is changed.

MAINTENANCE   Computer data in an organization are no more a static entity than are the contents of the organization's filing cabinets. The details of data stored, and the way they are used, change continuously. If a computer system attempts to impose an unchangeable file structure on an organization, it is doomed to the types of pressure that will result in most of the programming efforts being spent on modifying existing programs rather than developing new applications.

Figure 2.3 shows how programming costs have tended to change in organizations. The total programming costs in a typical organization have grown, becoming a higher proportion of the total data-processing budget. However, the programming time spent on new applications has fallen steadily. The reason is that the effort to maintain or modify the existing programs becomes greater and greater. It is often thought by systems analysts and data-processing managers that existing programs that work well can be left alone. In reality, however, the data they create or use are needed for other

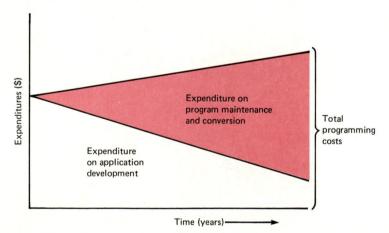

Figure 2.3 New application progress is often deferred by the rising cost of modifying existing programs and files. Some corporations now spend more than 80% of their programming budget just keeping current, and only 20% forging ahead.

applications and almost always needed in a slightly different form. New data-item types are added. New record types are needed with data-item types from several previous records. The data must be indexed in a different way. The physical layout of data is improved. Data bases for different applications are merged, and so forth.

The term *maintenance* is used to refer to the rewriting of old programs to make them conform to new data structures, new operating systems, terminals, and other system changes. Maintenance, if not consciously controlled, tends to rise as the number of programs grows. In some corporations it has risen to the disastrous level of 80% of the programming budget.

END-USER EXECUTIVE:

For one system to make a change, it requires many other development areas to get involved in the change. We had what we thought was a *very* simple change to increase our file and we were able to change our individual system in two days, but the coordination with other systems took five months. It didn't necessarily take five months' worth of time on their part but they each had their priorities and they were more concerned with doing their job than trying to take care of our problem.

DP MANAGER:

The frightening thing is that it's going to get even worse. We've got terrible problems today in terms of high maintenance costs, inconsistent data, inability to respond to management's needs, poor service. . . . But they're going to get much worse because government is increasing its demands; regulatory agencies are asking for more information, stricter audits, better privacy safeguards; the unions make settlements without any comprehension of their effects on DP.

One of the main objectives of a data-base system is that the data should be usable in new ways without setting off a chain reaction of difficult modifications to other programs. A program may be modified, changing in some way the data it uses, without disturbing other programs that use the same data.

An old file environment is like a bowl of spaghetti. Every time you pull one piece of spaghetti it shakes all the others in the bowl. As time goes by it becomes steadily worse because the number of pieces of spaghetti increases and they become more interwoven.

MEMO FROM TOP DP EXECUTIVE:

One of our lines of business recently determined that its consolidated functions system, originally designed around fewer than a dozen key files, now has almost *900 distinct files* used by about 600 programs. An inventory has been built of the *five* most important files, but there is no central inventory of the remaining 895 or so, nor any set of procedures that assures consistent updates.

Information available on the situation in other areas is not specific, although several have systems at least as extensive and complex.

. . . We have problems of *strategic* significance but do not know their extent.

The maintenance difficulties of file systems grow geometrically with the number of applications produced.

The intent of a data-base environment is to *insulate each program* from the effects of changes to other programs. And all programs should be insulated from the effects of reorganizing the data.

Data-base systems attempt to lower the maintenance costs by separating the records which the programmers perceive from the records which are physically stored. You might think of the programmer as perceiving a *make-believe* record—a record that does not exist in physical reality. The data-base management software derives this record for the programmer from the collection of data which are physically stored. Figure 2.4 illustrates this.

In Fig. 2.4, when programmer 2 changes his record structure, his new record structure is derived from the data base by the data-base management system. The change made by programmer 1 does not force programmers 2 or 3 to change *their* records.

Of course, we do not call them anything as unrespectable as "make-believe records." The records shown in Fig. 2.4 are called *logical records.* Each program refers to logical records, not the physical records which are stored in magnetic pulses on the discs or other storage media.

DATA-BASE MANAGEMENT SYSTEMS
The data-base management system is the entity that provides programmers or end users with the data they ask for. Like a conjurer pulling different-colored handkerchieves out of a hat, it derives its users' *make-believe* records from its store of data. It finds out what *physical* records contain the data in a given request, has a means of locating those records, and from them derives the logical records that were asked for.

All the major computer manufacturers provide data-base management systems—with names such as IMS, IDS, DMS, and IDMS (I in these names

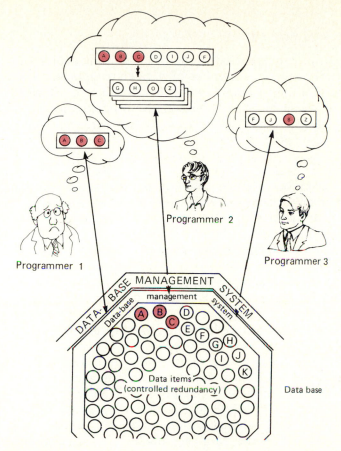

Figure 2.4 The programmers can live in blissful ignorance of how the data are really stored.

stands for Information or Integrated, D for Data, M for Management, and S for System). Independent software companies have also provided data-base management systems with names such as **TOTAL, ADABAS, IDMS**, and **SYSTEM 2000**.

This book can be understood without knowing in detail how these products work. The reader can obtain more easy-to-read details of the technology from the author's *Principles of Data-Base Management,* [1] and *Computer Data-Base Organization* [2].

DATA
INDEPENDENCE

A data base is intended to make data independent of the programs that use them. The data descriptions are no longer embedded in the application programs.

With a data base, either data or programs can be changed without causing the other to have to be changed. The data can be easily reorganized or their content added to. Old application programs do not have to be rewritten when changes are made to data structures, data layout, or the physical devices on which data are stored.

This independence of data is essential if data are to become a general-purpose corporate resource. In the past, data structures have been devised by a programmer for his own use. He writes a program to create a file of data. Usually, when another programmer needs the data for another purpose they are not structured in the way he wants, so he creates another file. Hence the duplication in Fig. 2.1.

Data independence is one of the most important differences between the way data are organized in data bases and the way they are organized in the file systems of computers that do not use data-base management software. The programmers can each have their own logical data structure, as shown in Fig. 2.4, and can program in blissful ignorance of how the data are really organized. When the data-base organization is changed, *the old programs still work.*

This facility makes the data-base software complex. However, without it, new application development can be immensely time consuming and prohibitively expensive because it makes it necessary to rewrite existing programs or convert existing data. The total number of person-years that a corporation has invested in application programs grows steadily. The original programmers are long since gone, and it is too late to complain that their documentation is inadequate.

The greater the number of programs, the more horrifying the thought of having to convert them or their data, so there is increasing reluctance in the DP department to respond to the latest needs of the end users.

tion of DP professionals devoted to maintenance activities, high cost and poor success in developing new systems for improving management information, and a variety of difficulties with inaccurate, inconsistent, and untimely reports, and the difficulty of supplying ad hoc information.

It should be emphasized that these problems arise not so much for lack of available technology as they do for lack of understanding of what changes in management process and accountability need to accompany any move toward sharing of common data—the primary problems are of a management rather than a technical nature. Once the symptoms described earlier materialize, they tend to compound fairly rapidly.

Another important feature, shown in Fig. 2.5 at the bottom, is the data-base interrogation software. This enables some users of the data to interact directly with the data base without application programs having to be written. Instead, the user employs a dialogue at a terminal, or possibly fills in a form, to express his needs.

Data-base dialogues for end users are becoming increasingly important. They enable information to be extracted from computers, and reports and listings generated *without* programming. Increasingly, end users will interact directly with the data-base systems. This is discussed in Chapter 25.

PRINCIPLES OF A DATA-BASE ENVIRONMENT

Box 2.1 summarizes the problems that are typical in an old-established *file* environment. To avoid these problems, Box 2.2 states principles of managing a data-base environment. It is important to recognize that they represent a change in management structure. *Data base is a change in management, not merely a change in software.*

In a well-managed data-base environment, data are recognized to be a corporate resource together with other resources, such as cash, people, plant, and equipment. Data are sufficiently important to merit specialized and high-level management attention. Like other resources it is necessary to:

1. Plan for data.
2. Establish a consistent approach to managing data.
3. Acquire data.
4. Maintain data.
5. Deploy data where needed.
6. Dispose of data when no longer needed.
7. Protect data.
8. Inventory data and know the effect of data changes.
9. Maintain records of the use of data.

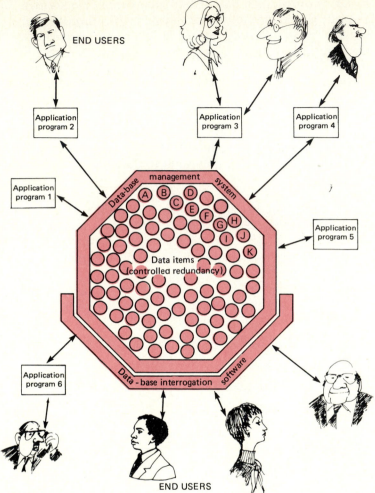

Figure 2.5 Application programs derive their logical records from the data base, and end users gain direct access to the data base with high-level data-base languages (Chapter 25).

All computer installations do 3, 4, and 6 above. Some installations do 7, although often poorly. Many installations do 5, badly, in that users often cannot obtain the data they need when they need it. Many installations, even multimillion-dollar ones, do not do 1, 2, and 8 in any formal sense.

In a well-designed and well-managed data-base environment the data are relatively stable, although the ways of looking at and using them may change rapidly.

BOX 2.1 Problems that are typical in established file installations

- High proportion of DP professionals devoted to maintenance activities.
- High cost and slow speed in developing new systems.
- Inability to respond quickly to necessary changes.
- Inability to provide ad hoc management information.
- Inconsistent definition of similar data items across applications.
- Steadily worsening proliferation of separate files.
- Increasing proliferation of inconsistent values of redundant data.
- The greater the number of programs, the worse the problem of converting them when data change, so the greater the reluctance to respond to requests for such change by end users.
- Difficulty in maintaining inventory and control of data.
- Cost of redundant storage.
- Cost of repetitive data entry.
- Lack of overall management of the data resource.

BOX 2.2 Principles in managing the data-base environment

- Data in a corporation should be managed directly and separately from the functions which use those data.
- Data descriptions should *not* be embedded uniquely in the programs which use those data. Instead, data should be designed by a separate data administrator.
- Data should be treated as a primary and vital resource in their own right, independently of current machines and systems.
- It is necessary to use standard tools and facilities throughout a corporation for managing its data.
- User departments should be given tools for specifying and extracting the information and reports they need directly from the data bases (with security and privacy control).
- Data-processing management methods need to be changed when a data-base environment is employed.
- Many corporations have data management problems of strategic significance, but do not know their extent. To deal with these problems, a high level of management needs to be involved in the data-base strategy.

The reader should contrast in his mind the bowl of spaghetti described earlier in which the number of pieces of spaghetti are steadily increasing, with the idea of a relatively stable data base from which users can exact new views of the data when they need them. The managers of the bowl of spaghetti have an application backlog of years. They are becoming increasingly frightened to change the data structures because of the chain reaction of problems that this causes. For every new application, therefore, a new file is created. By contrast, the data-base environment provides end-user management with high-level languages for querying the data, searching them, generating reports, creating their own temporary subfiles, and generating applications.

As we indicate in Chapter 3, not every data-base environment has achieved this degree of success. Indeed, data-base systems, like file systems, can plunge into trouble if they are not designed and managed appropriately.

The attempt to introduce a separate management entity for planning and managing the data resource has met with various problems, which will be described later. Not the least of the problems is that the move to a data-base environment brings changes in jobs and removes control of files from people who had previously had control.

DATA ADMINISTRATOR:

There's a very high level of change coming. It's going to change life everywhere, in many, many different ways, not all of which we can even predict. But we can be prepared for the fact that there will be a high level of changes.

END-USER EXECUTIVE:

I see a lot of headaches, agony, and bloodshed over the next three years—maybe longer.

Because of the change, and alarm about change, the move to data base is often accompanied by some aggressive corporate politics. The concerns and fears of end users have to be dealt with in an appropriate manner (Part V of this book).

SYSTEMS ANALYSIS   The traditional methods of systems analysis focus on the flow of transactions and the functions to be carried out. Data are treated as an integral part of the individual systems that are designed. It is often designed as a *by-product* of the function analysis. The Deltak video course on structured analysis states: "Defining the data flows pretty much defines the files. All you have to do is add organizational information like Sequential-by-Date."

Building applications on top of existing data bases is almost an inversion of this.

PROCESS-CENTERED VERSUS DATA-CENTERED APPROACH

We can contrast a process-centered approach of systems analysis and a data-centered approach.

The *process-centered approach* is concerned primarily with processes and data flows. A process is often drawn as a circle and the data flow as an arrow. The files or data bases are treated as an important but secondary component.

The *data-centered approach* treats the data as a separate resource—a foundation stone on which applications are built. The processes are important but must employ data that are in the data base. Part of the systems analysis must determine what ought to be in the data base; this is sometimes called *data analysis.*

We could regard the whole of data processing as a succession of changes to data. A snapshot of a system or organization at any instant in time will reveal only a data structure. A process is, technically, a series of data changes, including changes to data in working storage and input/output data.

Designing a stable, well-documented, and largely nonredundant structure of data in the long run provides a simpler and cleaner form of data processing than embedding separately designed data into hundreds of processes. Attaching logic, such as integrity checks and decision tables, directly to the data structures so that this is shared by multiple processes can further simplify the overall processing.

ADVANTAGES AND DISADVANTAGES

The data-centered approach has the following advantages.

1. It avoids the problems with file proliferation, maintenance, data redundancy, and inconsistency, described above.

2. Once appropriate data bases are in place, some types of applications can be created quickly with high-level data-base languages.

3. End users having direct access to the data bases can create their own reports and applications often without the slow steps of formal systems analysis, and often without waiting for action by the DP department.

The data-centered approach has the following disadvantages.

1. The data bases must be well designed. Although not inherently difficult, the technology of good data-base design is often not understood. It is discussed in Part III.

2. The data-centered approach implies sharing of data. This needs different management from the management of separate files.

3. There are sometimes conversion problems in moving from the traditional process-centered approach to the data-centered approach. Some of these are human problems caused by users losing control of data they previously "owned."

4. The data-centered approach is often more difficult to manage in its early phases, mainly because of pressures to take quick alternative solutions or to maintain the status quo. However, once set up, the data-centered approach is easier to manage than a process-centered approach with excessive file proliferation.

The data-centered approach, with data strictly separated from processing, is undoubtedly the best in the long run if it is done well. However, it does not come into existence without firm management, at a suitably high level, knowing what they intend to achieve. Poor design, loose management, ill-defined objectives, or management easily pushed from its objective by corporate politics, can wreck the data-centered approach. Too often management has not understood the issues clearly.

The data-centered approach does not mean that structured analysis as commonly practiced is inappropriate. On the contrary, the two approaches work together very well. When the structured analysis work identifies data that should be stored, these should become part of the data that are *synthesized* into a data-base structure as described in Part III. The resulting database structure should be designed to be as stable as possible and implemented in such a way that end users can have an appropriate degree of freedom in using the data.

COEXISTENCE   The data-centered approach and process-centered approach can, and often should, coexist. Some applications may use files rather than data bases for machine-efficiency reasons. Some installations put some of their data into data-base form but not all their data. Some programs make *calls* on both files and data bases. The systems analysis process may employ data bases where they already exist, and supplement them where they do not exist with either files or new input to the data-base synthesis process.

> *INTERVIEWER:*
>
> Do you use structured analysis?
>
> *DATA ADMINISTRATOR:*
>
> Yes.

INTERVIEWER:

Do you find it fits in well with data base?

DATA ADMINISTRATOR:

Oh, it fits in beautifully. Structured analysis makes us break everything down and group it together. So it really did merge well with data-base design.

REFERENCES

1. James Martin, *Principles of Data-Base Management,* Prentice-Hall, Inc., Englewood Cliffs, N.J., 1976.

2. James Martin, *Computer Data-Base Organization,* 2nd ed., Prentice-Hall, Inc., Englewood Cliffs, N.J., 1977.

3 FOUR TYPES OF DATA ENVIRONMENT

INTRODUCTION   There are four types of environments of computer data. It is important to distinguish clearly among them in order to discuss management of the data-base environment. Box 3.1 summarizes the four types of environment.

They have a major effect on management at all levels in an enterprise, including top management. An efficient corporation ought to have a substantial foundation of Class III and Class IV data. These, however, are only likely to be pervasive and successful if there is top management support for them, as we shall see.

FILES   A Class I environment is that of *files*. A separate file is designed for each, or most, applications. Often a direct result of structured analysis, the data are embedded in the function. This has the problems discussed in Chapter 2 and summarized in Box 2.1.

SUBJECT DATA BASES VERSUS APPLICATION DATA BASES   As we look back on years of data-base case histories, we can observe two types of approach: *application data bases* and *subject data bases*. It is quite clear which has given the best results *in the long term:* subject data bases.

Subject data bases relate to organizational *subjects* rather than to conventional computer *applications*. There should, for example, be a *product* data base rather than separate *inventory, order entry,* and *quality control* data bases relating to that product. Many applications may then use the same data base. The development of new applications relating to that data base becomes easier than if application-oriented data bases had been built.

BOX 3.1 The four types of data environment

Class I Environment: Files

A data-base management system is not used. Separate files of data are used for most applications, designed by the analysts and programmers when the application is created.

Examples of software: VSAM, BDAM, DMS

Characteristics: simple; relatively easy to implement

A large proliferation of files grow up with high redundancy leading to high maintenance costs.

Seemingly trivial changes to applications trigger a chain reaction of other changes and hence change becomes slow, expensive, and is resisted.

Class II Environment: Application Data Bases

A data-base management system is used but without the degree of sharing in a Class III environment. Separate data bases are designed for separate applications.

Examples of software: TOTAL, IMS, IDMS, IDS

Characteristics: easier to implement than a Class III environment

A large proliferation of data bases grow up with high redundancy like a file environment. High maintenance costs.

Sometimes more expensive than a Class I environment.

Does not achieve the major advantages of data-base operation.

Class III Environment: Subject Data Bases

Data bases are created which are largely independent of specific applications. Data are designed and stored independently of the function for which they are used. Data for business subjects such as customers, products, or personnel are associated and represented in shared data bases.

Examples of software: IMS, IDMS, IDS, ADABAS

Characteristics: thorough data analysis and modeling needed, which takes time; much lower maintenance costs

Box 3.1 (*Continued*)

Leads eventually (but not immediately) to faster application development and direct user interaction with the data bases.

Requires a change in traditional systems analysis methods, and in overall DP management.

If not managed well it tends to disintegrate into a Class II (or sometimes Class I) environment.

Class IV Environment: Information Systems

Data bases organized for searching and fast information retrieval rather than for high-volume production runs. Employs software designed around inverted files, inverted lists, or secondary key search methods. New data-item types can be added dynamically at any time. Good end-user query and report generation facilities.

Examples of software: IBM's STAIRS, ICL's CAFS, STATUS, the relational data bases of NOMAD, MAPPER, SQL, QBE, and various other fourth-generation languages

Characteristics:

- Often easy to implement
- More flexible and dynamically changeable than traditional data-base systems
- Should often coexist with a Class III environment
- Low maintenance

Typical *subjects* for which data bases are built in a corporation are:

- Products
- Customers
- Parts
- Vendors
- Orders
- Accounts
- Personnel
- Documents
- Engineering descriptions

Some applications use more than one subject data base. The programs make *calls* to multiple separate data bases. For example:

SUBJECT DATA BASES

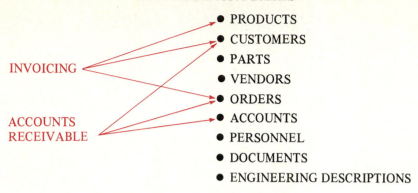

SUBJECT DATA BASES

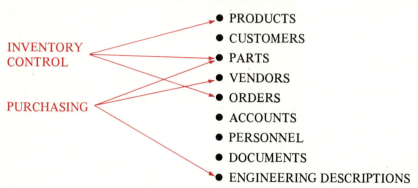

By using *subject* data bases rather than *applications* data bases the eventual number of data bases is far lower. A corporation builds up a very large number of applications but does not have a large number of operational *subjects*. If *files* are designed for specific applications the number of files grows almost as rapidly as the number of applications, and results in the great proliferation of redundant data found in a typical tape library today. Application-oriented data bases can also proliferate rapidly. Using *subject* data bases, however, the number of applications grows much faster than the number of data bases.

**CLASS II
ENVIRONMENT**   A Class II environment is one of application data bases rather than subject data bases. The systems analysts tend to create a separate data base for each new application as they do with file systems. Because data-base management systems are used, there is some degree of data independence, but proliferation of redundant data grows as with file systems and has most of the problems listed in Box 2.1.

It is sometimes said that a data-base management system is used like a file access method rather than as a true data-base system.

CLASS III ENVIRONMENT

A Class III environment is one of *subject* data bases. When a collection of such data bases have been built, they represent the data resource we discussed in Chapter 2—data independent from specific applications.

The types of data represented do not change very frequently, whereas the functions that use the data do. Therefore, it makes sense not to embed the data in the functions as in a Class I environment.

DISINTEGRATION

Many data-base installations have set out to create a Class III environment and have had problems. A new application comes along and for some reason a new data base is created for it rather than using the existing subject data bases.

It is easier and quicker to create application data bases than doing the overall design that is needed for subject data bases. However, as the years go by installations that do this end up with almost as many separate data bases as they would have had *files* if they had not used data-base management. They do not then achieve the advantages of data base described in Chapter 2. The use of data-base management in such installations has not reduced the program maintenance cost as it should.

Too often the attempt to create a Class III environment disintegrates into Class II. This may be due to poor management or to poor subject data-base design.

Sometimes end users or analysts want their own data base for reasons of pride, politics, or because it is easier. Management is not strong enough to enforce the principles of the Class III environment, or possibly does not understand them or their significance.

Sometimes the analyst needs a new view of data which cannot be derived from the existing data bases. Consequently a new data base is created. This happens over and over again until there is a proliferation of data bases. The cause of this is usually inadequate design in the first place. The principles of data analysis, data modeling, and stability analysis described in Part III have not been followed.

DATA ADMINISTRATOR:

They brought in IMS and didn't manage it well. So, what happened, they ended up with as many data bases as they have files, with the same information being redundant throughout those data bases. The end effect is that they have a big expensive access method as opposed to a data-base manager.

INTERVIEWER:

And that really means they've got the same maintenance problem as they had when they had files.

DATA ADMINISTRATOR:

Or a larger one, because the layer of complexity that you add to a program because of the data-base management system is more complicated to change.

TOP DP EXECUTIVE:

There seemed to be all manner of short-term expedient reasons for accommodating new functions by giving them a new data base. Or even files. This was self-defeating. It brought back the redundancy that the data-base approach was supposed to avoid. Now the problems of adding new applications are immense.

DATA-BASE ADMINISTRATOR:

The problem with it is it takes a lot of planning. Someone else is going to do that planning. You take something away from the analyst and the programmer. Some analysts resent that or they don't like it. So they still wanted to design their own data and management allowed them to do so, instead of being tough.

So you have an analyst design a data base. And then you have an analyst on a similar application and his office is designing a data base. And they're designing the same thing.

Because of the analyst not wanting to lose his art of design, I suppose that a company allows it to happen until they get into a big mess and then they try to get out of it by giving that responsibility to a data-base administration group.

INTERVIEWER:

But by that time, you've got a quite horrible conversion.

DATA-BASE ADMINISTRATOR:

Right. By that time, it is really bad. And it's a matter of changing a lot of programs because their logic is probably going to be based on that little specific data base. Now they need a bigger data base, a different structure, so those programs are going to change.

INTERVIEWER:

So you're faced with rewriting the application programs even though you're in data base?

DATA-BASE ADMINISTRATOR:

That's right. And management gets upset and they are mad at the vendor. And really they brought it on themselves by not managing it from the beginning.

TOP DP EXECUTIVE:

The salesman told me it would reduce program maintenance costs. We can look back on five years of data-base usage now and in practice it hasn't reduced our program maintenance costs by one cent.

It is extremely important that management understand the difference between a Class II and Class III data-base environment, and understand how the Class III environment should be designed and managed so that it does not disintegrate into a Class II environment (or worse, Class I).

It is important to understand this at the start, not when it is too late.

DATA-BASE ADMINISTRATOR:

There's a lot of after-the-fact management of data bases.

CLASS IV ENVIRONMENT

Data-base dialogues for end users are becoming increasingly important. They enable information to be extracted from computers, and reports and listings generated *without* programming. Increasingly, end users will interact directly with the data-base systems. There is a growing diversity of user-friendly languages with which a user or analyst can query data bases, search them, associate separate data, and generate reports.

Figure 2.5 suggests that a corporation's data are stored in a large reservoir in which the users can go fishing. Although this figure forms a useful way to explain data-base concepts to management, it is nevertheless a naive view of a data base—in some cases dangerously naive. The data items inside the octagon of Fig. 2.4 have to be organized in such a way that they can be found and accessed with sufficient speed. The organizing introduces many complexities into data-base design. The structuring problems can be sufficiently great that a designer may sometimes elect to employ separate data-base systems, even though they contain much of the same information.

The fields in a data base are arranged into groups called records or segments, and a single READ instruction results in one such record or segment being read into the computer's main memory. Many data-base inquiries refer to *one* record, for example "Display purchase order 29986," or a small number of records "Display the account of R. V. AGNEW" or "Display details of the armaments on the ship INTREPID." Others, however, require the data base to be searched, for example, "Display all British ships within 48 hours sailing time of the Falkland Islands carrying antiaircraft missiles with a range greater than 300 miles and defense capability against the Exocet missile.

Queries that cause searching can take much more machine time. If there are too many of them, they take too much machine time, slow down the main work of the system, and give unacceptable response times.

Some data-base languages for end users are powerful and easy to use, but they enable end users to take actions often unwittingly, which cause expensive searching of data bases.

Some data-base software is specifically designed to permit the data bases to be searched efficiently. Spontaneous queries of a diversity of types can be handled quickly. The software employs data structures that are appropriate for this, such as inverted files, inverted lists, or multiple efficiently designed secondary indices. In some cases special hardware is used to make the data searching fast.

We describe this as a Class IV environment—a system designed for flexible information retrieval.

Information retrieval systems are often separate from the production data-base systems which produce the daily paperwork and do the routine data processing. They are often easier to install and easier to manage. They use different software. A Class II or III environment uses software such as IMS, IDMS, TOTAL, and IDS. A Class IV environment uses software such as SQL, QBE, FOCUS, NOMAD, RAMIS II, NATURAL, and STAIRS. The end-user language for interrogating the data base is often closely interrelated to the data structures. Some software can handle either a Class III or Class IV environment, or both at the same time, but one or the other is handled without the highest efficiency.

An information retrieval system often contains some of the same data as a related production system. Why should they be separate? Primarily for reasons of efficiency. We will discuss this in more detail later. An information system needs its data to be organized differently from a production system. Often it contains only a subset of the data. An information system could be highly inefficient if it contained and had to search the vast mass of data kept in a production system. On the other hand, the production processes could be disrupted by many end users entering queries that trigger searching operations.

It is important in discussing data-base management to distinguish between Class III and IV environments. They have different problems, are managed differently, and both need to fit into the overall planning of a corporation's data resources.

MIXTURES

An ideal situation is a mixture of Class III and Class IV, and most of our comments in the rest of the report will be oriented to this. However, most corporations have substantial existing Class I and Class II environments. It is almost always necessary that these coexist with the Class III and Class IV environments. Conversion of Class I, and sometimes Class II, to Class III environments is often necessary.

There are good reasons in certain cases for using files rather than a shared data base. These include the following:

- A *very* high transaction volume is to be processed with fast response times (as on airline reservation systems). Data-base systems do not give good enough machine performance in some such cases.
- *Very* large files must be processed in different ways using different keys. Sorts are necessary in a file system to accomplish this. It would be too inefficient with existing data-base management systems.
- The data are *highly* volatile with a *very* rapid rate of creating new records and deleting old ones. Again data-base systems have efficiency problems.
- Application software has been purchased which uses files rather than data bases.

Although there are certain cases where files are desirable rather than data base, usually an analyst's determination to use files is not based on sound technical judgment but on lack of understanding of the long-range objectives of data base, or resistance to a data-base environment for personal reasons.

DATA-BASE ADMINISTRATOR:

I had one problem that was very large. The analyst I was working with absolutely did not want to give up his right to design his files. He did not want to give up his right to backup and control the recovery of his files.

INTERVIEWER:

Was he justified?

DATA-BASE ADMINISTRATOR:

No. Data base was the best solution. But he was adamant. He made it a personal issue.

INTERVIEWER:

What happened?

DATA-BASE ADMINISTRATOR:

It went on for months. Eventually it got to a higher level of management and he was moved to a different area.

It is necessary for management to distinguish among the four types of environments, and their trade-offs, and build an appropriate mixture of facilities into the strategic planning for data bases.

4 MEASURES OF SUCCESS

How should we judge whether the use of data-base management is a success or not? What are the objectives of good data-base systems?

The overall objective is to assist the enterprise in question meet its goals. In a corporation the predominant goal is usually profitability. The data-base environment needs to affect the bottom line in the corporation rather than be something esoteric that is happening without any effect on the balance sheet.

To achieve this, a data-base system needs to provide better information for decision making, improve the systems' responsiveness to requests for information, and improve productivity in the corporation, especially productivity within the DP department.

Figure 4.1 gives a hierarchy of goals of data-base usage. The relative importance of the goals lower in the hierarchy ought to be judged by their effect at the top the hierarchy. In some enterprises, such as government departments, schools, hospitals, and social institutions, the predominant goal is not profit. Whatever it is, the data-base environment should be judged by its overall contribution to the main goals of the enterprise. It ought to be understood and judged by businessmen (or enterprise managers) rather than only by technicians who perceive a limited technical goal.

In its early days data-base management was concerned mainly with lowering maintenance costs, as discussed in Chapter 3. This is still a very important objective, but other objectives have a major effect on the overall business goals:

- Faster application development
- Direct end-user involvement in application creation, resulting in applications of more immediate value to end users
- Quick retrieval of up-to-date management information

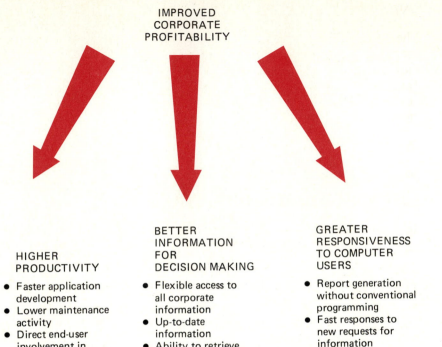

Figure 4.1   Overall objectives of data-base usage.

- Flexible access to information that improves the decision making of executives
- Generation of reports and screen displays without conventional programming
- End-user capability to extract information and create new types of reports when they need them

**SPEED IN MEETING
END USERS' NEEDS**   Some end-user executives perceive that the main goal of data-base technology is to meet their information needs quickly.

INTERVIEWER:

In the experience you've been gaining in doing this job, what do you think are the most important criteria for judging the success of the data bases you're involved with?

END-USER EXECUTIVE:

The speed and accuracy with which you can provide data to the end user. For so long in the development cycle, the end user has waited for months and years before the data necessary for him to do his day-to-day business were available. Using a data-base type of technology, if you can provide quick, accurate information to the end user, he will view data base as being a very successful tool.

INTERVIEWER:

So speed in responding to the end user's need. . . .

END-USER EXECUTIVE:

Speed and accuracy.

Data-base management can speed up *conventional* application development, but not by a very dramatic factor. The major change comes when data-base systems permit computers to be used without conventional programming, by means of report generators, query languages, application generators, and high-level end-user languages in general.

The following interview is typical and relates to application development using conventional programming:

INTERVIEWER:

Has data base significantly increased your application development productivity?

DP MANAGER:

In the beginning, it doesn't seem to do that. In the beginning, there's a learning curve on the part of the people in development. It is a new thing. They do have to learn it. It does take them longer. It interjects techniques of how to install the products they develop that they're not familiar with.

So, in the beginning it takes longer. We have noticed that the second or third time around a particular analyst group goes through the process, they do it much faster.

Some comparative cost studies said that it cost us this much money to develop it under a previous access method and now it costs this other amount of money under data base, and data base is less. The basis for that seems to be that when there is a data base out there that they can use, it's much simpler for them to plug into it.

Twenty to forty percent is a typical range of reduction in application
programming time when data bases become fully operational.

Once the data bases are in place, usage of the data can swing away from
programming in languages of the level of COBOL to higher-level nonprocedural languages which obtain results much faster. There are now many such
languages on the market. Every major vendor of a data-base management system has one or two, but there are many others, often better, from independent software vendors.

More important, perhaps, with high-level languages, the end users themselves can create the reports and procedures they want. This can greatly
increase the number of persons involved in application creation and so further
speed it up. The end users often have a much better understanding of their
own needs than does the DP department. They do, however, need substantial encouragement and education.

type of capability and he does his own reports, modeling, forecasting, whatever he wants to do with those particular data.

INTERVIEWER:

So the user is in effect acting as a programmer in order to create his own data from the data base?

DATA-BASE ADMINISTRATOR:

From the aspect of writing reports and procedures, yes he is. From the aspect of actually creating the files, that's a capability that we are still restricting to the data-base administrative function—to prevent the proliferation of data files throughout the division.

Many data-base installations have *not* achieved a high level of end-user interaction with the data bases. There are some problems that have to be solved in connection with this—particularly machine performance problems. These are discussed later in the book. In installations where extensive end-user interaction is taking place, it can be impressive and has increased the value of computing substantially.

BANK EXECUTIVE:

It's given the portfolio managers control over their accounts. They can monitor across accounts very easily and keep track at all times of what's going on. But the decision-analysis and decision-making capabilities have provided them with something they've just never had before. They would sit there with a *Wall Street Journal* and an *S&P Guide* and a pencil and a piece of paper and maybe a calculator and it would take them hours or even days to do the kind of thing they can do now in just a couple of minutes. And the customers have been very, very responsive to this system because they're able to ask for information and to get results back much more quickly than they can anywhere else. . . .

END-USER MANAGER:

They can create "what if?" situations. Many times they will be working with a given set of customer orders and want to find what machine shop schedules will meet the conflicting demands. There are functions within the system that allow them to "filter"—choose the individual constraints that meet a varying set of criteria. The end users have the ability to change these.

> But it's never set in concrete. Anything can go wrong and often does, so you have to reschedule often to meet the new criteria. Then somebody phones and says this is urgent or that is urgent. So they rerun "what if?" situations to see what they can do.

A high level of end-user involvement should be regarded as a measure of success in managing the data-base environment.

The extent to which data-base use has speeded up application development, especially through high-level languages and report generators, should also be regarded as a measure of success. In some installations there is a remarkable reluctance among programmers to condone anything higher level than COBOL.

CHANGE IN SYSTEMS ANALYSIS
The data-base environment requires a change in systems analysis methods.

Part III of this book describes the processes of data analysis and design of stable data-base structures. Once the data-base structures are in place, end users in some installations, or the technical staff who assist them, create reports, queries, and some types of applications *without any formal systems analysis.* With high-level data-base languages much time is saved not only in avoiding programming, but also in avoiding formal system analysis, specification, and documentation. This welcome speeding up is generally practical only if much thought has gone into the analysis and design of the data bases themselves.

DATA ADMINISTRATOR:

One application was the generation of a four-year plan with 28 different reports. This was completed in 10 days. The data used resided in several compatible data bases with a total of 400 million bytes of financial data.

CORPORATE SYSTEMS PLANNER:

The more the system is used, the better it becomes. We keep adding to the data structures. A macro library contains stored user procedures. This is continually growing as new tools and user-written programs are added. The more exposure occurs to different business problems, the greater the capabilities become. The users don't spend months writing specifications. Most new applications are done in a few days.

Although formal specifications are not written for user applications, the data representation is highly formal, and should be thoroughly documented with a data dictionary and data modeling software.

SLOW DATA-BASE GROWTH   The goals we are describing can be achieved when an appropriate set of subject data bases are in operation. This takes time—in some installations from two to four years. There is a learning curve to be climbed, especially with highly complex software such as IMS and other powerful data-base management systems.

As the number of subject data bases grows, the number of applications that they can be used with grows disproportionately, as shown in Fig. 4.2. Eventually, most new applications can be implemented rapidly because the data are available and the software provides tools to manipulate them.

This should be the goal of data-base management, but it is usually not achieved quickly. In the first-year application, development is usually slower because the first data bases have to be designed and installed and the new methods have to be learned.

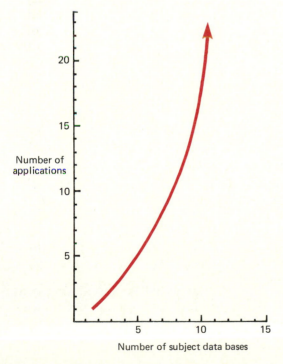

Figure 4.2 As the number of subject data bases grow, the number of applications using them grows disproportionately. Eventually most new applications can be implemented rapidly because the data are available and the software provides tools to manipulate them. This curve was taken from a corporation with five years of subject data-base development.

Management therefore needs to understand that *data-base systems have a long-term payoff.* The full return on the data-base investment does not come in the first two or three years. With careful project selection data-base systems can be made to be profitable in the first year or so, but the big payoff comes later. While working toward the larger payoff it is important to prevent the Class III environment disintegrating into Class II, or even Class I, which may give more immediate results but miss the long-range payoff.

An exception to these comments about slow startup is found in some Class IV environments where an information system is installed quickly and relatively easily. Some minicomputer information systems are easy to implement, and are in successful operation remarkably soon after installation. Sometimes, though, they draw their data from *existing* data-base systems.

DP EXECUTIVE:

We've got 24 Microdata Reality data-base systems in different user locations.

INTERVIEWER:

Why so many?

DP EXECUTIVE:

They're cheap. They're easy to implement, we get them working in a week, and the users love them. It's data processing like it ought to be. The users can do anything they want in them but they can't foul up the data in the big systems.

CURVES REPRESENTING GOALS

Figures 4.2 to 4.9 give a set of curves showing desirable objectives in data-base development. The extent to which these curves are followed can be regarded as a measure of success in data-base operation.

BETTER CONTROL

Sometimes the goal of data-base installation is to achieve better control of data than is possible with separate files. In some organizations the worsening proliferation of incompatible files takes them dangerously close to chaos.

There is often a high level of inconsistency between the values of the same data in different files, and this inconsistency is perceived by management or end users.

OTHER GOALS

While the goals and measures of success discussed above are the most important ones for most organizations, there are other objectives of data-base management.

- To lessen redundancy and lessen the storage requirements
- To lessen off-line storage operations
- To increase the accuracy and integrity of data
- To provide tight security and privacy control

RECENTLY HIRED DP EXECUTIVE:

Why did we change to data base?
     We had no option! The business was slipping out of control. There was no correlation between the different tape systems. There were 260 files all with financial information updated at different times. There had been major errors in assessing the overall cash position. And the situation was rapidly getting worse.

SYSTEMS ANALYST:

Large customers could not tell how much money they had in the bank. They have many time deposits all coming due at different times, on-call deposits, numerous different account numbers for the same customer. No one statement contained more than a portion of the customer's cash position. All the data was on-line but we couldn't tie it together. Incidentally, some of it was in data-base form, but it had been designed like a collection of separate systems with no integration. The thing that finally put the management heat on it was that two big customers moved to a different bank with better account management.

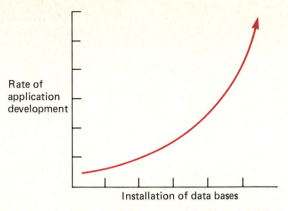

Rate of
application
development

Installation of data bases

Figure 4.3 When appropriate data bases are installed, this should increase the rate of application development. This happens for several reasons: (1) When the data base exists, the programmer does not have to spend time designing the data he used, and should not have to write data descriptions in his program. (2) Query languages, report generators, and data-base application generators enable applications to be created without conventional programming. (3) Reports and information can be generated when needed without conventional systems analysis. (4) Maintenance activities are greatly reduced, as shown in Fig. 4.4.

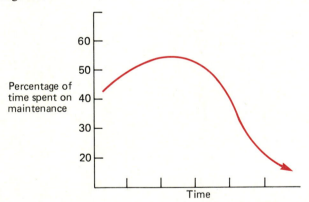

Percentage of
time spent on
maintenance

Time

Figure 4.4 The proportion of time spent on maintenance activity has grown to 50%, 60%, and as high as 80% in some installations. It is desirable to pull this curve down to 20% or lower if possible. This has been achieved in Class III and Class IV data-base environments (see Chapter 3) but not in Class II.

Good data-base software will not lower maintenance activity *by itself*. Good management is also needed. Subject data bases must be built which are *stable* as described in Part III. Programmers and end users must be made to conform to the formats in the data dictionary and data models. The modeling process must keep well ahead of application development pressure.

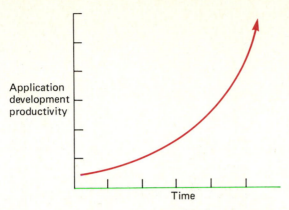

Figure 4.5 As computers continually drop in cost and programmers increase in cost, programmer productivity becomes increasingly important. However, we should no longer say merely *programmer* productivity because greater productivity results from application development without programming. This is being accomplished with report generators, query languages, and high-level data-base end-user languages. An objective of data-base development should be to employ such facilities to the fullest extent possible.

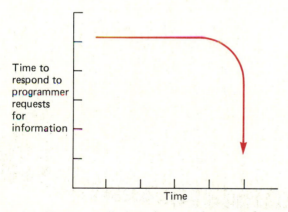

Figure 4.6 Many installations have a three- or four-year backlog of applications waiting to be developed. The computer industry is filled with horror stories about managers not being able to obtain information when they need it even though the data in question are on-line. An objective of data-base development should be to reduce the time taken to respond to new requests for information.

Note the shape of this curve. We are not saying, reduce the time to respond to management needs by 10% or 20%; we are saying, change it from many months to half an hour or so. This should be a major objective of data-base implementation. It requires both high-level query software and careful system design, sometimes with distributed processing.

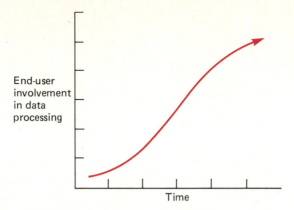

Figure 4.7 A major objective of data-base development should be to increase end-user involvement in data processing. First, users should be intimately involved in defining the data they need and assisting the data administrator to create data models which will be stable, as discussed later. End-user involvement is critical to successful data modeling. Second, they should be involved in creating the information reports and documents they need, and in updating their own data and keeping them accurate. They should be encouraged to take the initiative about how they use data and computers, but to do so within the framework of the overall data administration.

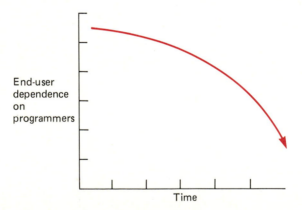

Figure 4.8 An objective should be to make end-user departments increasingly reliant on their own capability to extract and process information from the central data bases, and to build their own subdata bases. Dependence on the DP Department, with its lengthy backlogs, to do all their programs for them should decrease. In some cases user departments should do their own report generation or programming in languages such as SQL, NATURAL, FOCUS, or IDEAL. Sometimes they should use contract programmers.

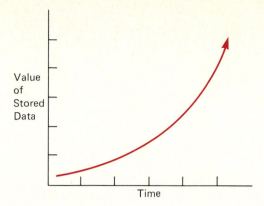

Figure 4.9 The value of the data stored in a corporation increases if the data can be used for making better management decisions. They should be easily available, via networks, to the people who need them, and should be easily processible with high-level data-base languages.

Data become more valuable when they are timely, available when needed, well summarized, and presented with the utmost clarity, often with graphics. This should be an objective of data-base development. It often requires information systems which are separate from production systems, but planned with a common data modeling facility.

5 THE NEED FOR TOP MANAGEMENT INVOLVEMENT

THE NEED FOR TOP-LEVEL PLANNING

It would be unthinkable to build a battleship without an overall plan for the entire ship. Once the overall plan exists, separate teams can go to work on the components.

Corporate information engineering is not much less complex than building a battleship, yet in most corporations it is done without an overall plan of sufficient details to make the components fit together.

The overall architect of the battleship cannot conceivably specify the detailed design of the guns, electronics, or other subsystems. These have to be developed by different teams working autonomously. But imagine what would happen if these teams enthusiastically created their own subsystems without any coordination from the top.

The DP world is full of inspired subsystem designers who want to be left alone. Their numbers are rapidly increasing as minicomputers proliferate and end users learn to acquire their own facilities. In many cases they are doing an excellent job. However, the types of data they use overlap substantially and this is often not recognized. The subsystems need to be connected together, but often this cannot be done without conversion. Conversion, when the need for it becomes apparent, is often too expensive to accomplish and so incompatible systems live on, making it difficult or impossible to integrate the data that management need.

In the late 1960s the dream emerged of a totally integrated corporate data base. This was completely unworkable. The task of building one database system for a corporation is unthinkably complex. It is far beyond the capability of any one team to design it, and even if it could be designed, machine performance consideration would make it unworkable (except in small corporations).

Good system design avoids excessive complexity. Corporate information systems ought to be composed of discrete modules, each of which is simple enough to be efficiently designed, completely understood by its design team, low in maintenance costs, and susceptible to high-productivity development methods (such as the use of high-level data-base languages). But the modules must fit together and they will not do so unless designed with planning from the top.

We have stressed that much of the information in distributed systems and minicomputers is used by other people in different locations from that minicomputer—in different parts of the organization. Data in one subsystem are also needed by other subsystems. And yet in many organizations each subsystem designer is independently creating his own data.

An organization needs top-level planning, with appropriate design tools, to pull the act together.

THE COMBINATION OF TOP-DOWN PLANNING AND LOCALIZED DESIGN

Corporatewide planning of data bases is vital, but corporatewide design of an integrated data base is impractical. What is needed is bottom-up design of individual subsystems with maximum encouragement for local initiative in creating such subsystems, and a methodology for top-level planning of the data resources which these systems use—like the building of a battleship.

To build a computerized corporation it is essential to have both top-down planning of data, and localized design of data bases in multiple user areas.

A computerized methodology is needed for both, and the two methodologies need to be compatible so that one feeds the other. Top-down planning can be done with varying degrees of detail. It may start as a coarse summary of the resources needed. To be useful, more detail is needed.

The author's book *Strategic Data-Planning Methodologies* (SDPM), [1] describes various methodologies for top-down planning and discusses experience achieved with them.

CONSISTENCY OF INFORMATION

A major objective of top-down planning is to achieve consistency of information.

Inconsistency results from the historical evolution of computer usage that usually occurs without overall planning. Data can be inconsistent in four ways:

> *Field definition.* Different parts of the organization do not agree about the definitions and meanings of a field.
>
> *Field structure.* The same field is structured differently in different places (different lengths, binary versus decimal, different code structures, etc.).

Record structure. Records with the same key are differently structured in different places.

Time of update. Data may be processed monthly, weekly, daily, or interactively in different subsystems, making different copies of the data have different values. Managers often perceive inconsistent data.

The dangers of inconsistency are much greater now that the computers are becoming cheap and widespread, so that many departments will have their own computer. Distributed processing and small end-user computers greatly increase the need for corporatewide strategic planning of information resources.

Incompatible data in separate files or systems can prevent, or make difficult, the integration of data to generate the information required by management.

DECOUPLED PROJECTS   Subsystem designers, and sometimes end users, are often concerned that if they have the design of data imposed on them from elsewhere, they will lose their freedom to be creative. In practice, installations where the data-base function has been well managed have demonstrated that the opposite is true. Procedure designers are given *stable* data structures and tools with which they can extract data in many forms quickly. The ease and speed of creating new procedures with high-level data-base languages leads to much more creativity in changing and inventing procedures. *Without* good data-base management the ability to change systems increasingly bogs down in maintenance problems and problems with incompatible data.

The data models that result from good data administration are a foundation stone on which new procedures can be created quickly by small teams— most often by one person. *Strategic planning of data permits separate design projects to proceed by themselves. Each project can be reasonably coherent and decoupled from other projects.* The separate projects can be small and easy to implement. Yet they are integrated by using data that are centrally defined.

TOWER OF BABEL   The languages and software for creating commercial DP applications are really improving and will continue to do so. *Nonprocedural* languages and facilities now permit many applications to be created without conventional programming, and in some cases permit them to be created by end users. The image of a computerized corporation of the near future which the reader should keep in mind is one in which *many* different people are creating and adjusting the electronic procedures. They have user-friendly software which enables them to do this *rapidly.* Cheap computers are spreading and there is a terminal on most desks. The challenge for both DP and corporate management is: How do you control this environment? The most important aspect of control is coordinating the data that are used. If this is not done, there will be a Tower of Babel effect.

To build data processing throughout an enterprise without coordinated planning of data would be like running a telephone system without a common directory.

If every person creating DP procedures invents his own data and designs and defines them himself, a high price will be paid for the resulting chaos. Many systems will have to be changed later or taken out of use. Higher man-

"If this is what they can do as a beginning, then nothing that they resolve to do will be impossible for them. Come, let us go down, and there make such a babble of their language that they will not understand one another's speech." *Genesis* 11: 6, 7.

P. Breughel, the Elder, "Turmbau zu Babel," 1563
Kunsthistorisches Museum, Vienna

Figure 5.1 With cheap computers and user-friendly languages, if everyone designs his own data, it will be like the Tower of Babel. A high price will be paid in lack of management information, inability to improve procedures, and future maintenance costs.

agement will not be able to extract the data they need for higher-level control or decision making. Many of the improvements in procedures and management that ought to result from a terminal–network–data-base environment will not occur.

SENIOR
MANAGEMENT
INVOLVEMENT
In many cases the attempt to create corporatewide planning of data has come from the DP department itself. This is often not too successful for two reasons. First, the DP executives do not have enough authority to make everybody conform to the data definitions and representations. Second, DP professionals do not fully understand the business (although they sometimes think the contrary). It is desirable to involve senior management themselves in the information planning process.

IBM's manual on its Business Systems Planning (BSP) methodology states: "A BSP study should not be started unless a top executive sponsor and some other executives are committed to being involved in it. The study must reflect their view of the business, and the success of the study depends upon their providing the business understanding and information requirements to the team. Most of the input will come directly or indirectly from these executives" [2].

INTERVIEWER:

You've seen data base evolve over about eight years in your organization. What do you think is the single most important ingredient for success?

DP EXECUTIVE:

Top management. Top management has got to understand what's going on and how it affects the future of the organization. If you don't have somebody at the top pulling the pieces together, everybody's going to charge off in their own direction. You might as well have an orchestra with everyone playing a different symphony.

There are many reasons why top management involvement is needed in top-down data-base planning. These reasons are listed in Box 5.1.

We examined case histories of top-down planning done *with* top management involvement and sponsorship and *without* it. The difference is far greater than is often generally realized. The planning done *without* senior management involvement is DP looking outward. However good as analysts, they usually do not have the business experience that is needed to understand the subtleties of information requirements. When they create a top-down plan, although it may be ingeniously conceived, it is often not accepted by senior management, and has often become the basis for bitter political arguing.

The primary payoff from executive involvement is solid management support for the data systems that will eventually be developed. The detailed

BOX 5.1   Why top management involvement is necessary for data-base success

- Information is an extremely vital corporate resource. It affects productivity, profitability, and strategic decisions.

  Any resource that important needs planning from the top.

- Where a *technical* group has planned corporate information resources it has generally been unable to have the perspective of businessmen or to understand the overall corporate information needs.

- The best-laid plans of data-base designers have crashed on the rocks of corporate politics. Data-base plans tend to create political problems, often severe ones, and various factions will oppose them.

  Often these problems can be solved only when top management has made it clear that it believes that data base is the way of the future, and has signed-off on a corporate information systems plan.

- Productivity in DP development is vital.

  An appalling waste of development resources results from redundant uncoordinated application development, and excessive maintenance and conversion activity. A top-down corporatewide information architecture is needed to lessen these.

- Budgets need to be set for data-base development independently of application development.

- Class 3 and 4 data bases need to be planned, rather than Class 1 (Files) or Class 2 (Application Data Bases). This needs a view from the top.

- Orchestration is needed to make the various efforts fit together. Multiple *incompatible* fragments of data bases cause excessive conversion costs and prevent senior management from obtaining the information they need.

- An infrastructure needs to be planned for distributed systems. The separate data-base systems should be linked by a common network.

- Standardization is necessary to achieve agreement about the definitions of data items. Corporatewide standards are needed for use of a common dictionary and common modeling tool.

BOX 5.1 *(Continued)*

- A set of software packages is needed which provides not only data-base management but also data communications, and as far as possible, automation of application development. It is when all these components work together that the fullest advantages of data base are realized.

- A formally structured corporatewide view of information processing is needed in order to set DP priorities.

- The methodologies described in the following chapters need the involvement of senior management and staff from user departments working with an overall directive from the top.

- Some of the methodologies for top-down data planning reveal anomalies, waste, and inefficiencies in the *corporate* organization and methods. In many cases top-down data analysis has led to the reorganization of procedures and to corporate restructuring, independent of DP.

data modeling is more likely to succeed, represent the enterprise correctly, be used, supported, and understood.

The second payoff is more subtle but in some cases has been very powerful—the effect on the enterprise of having a fresh picture of itself. Having such a self-perception evolve, clearly charted, and unaccompanied by preaching about how the enterprise "ought" to do things is often a more effective force toward organization restructuring than an army of management consultants who are explicitly trying to "change agents."

DATA-BASE EXECUTIVE:

When we adopted the plan three years ago we did not go to the top management because we felt that, at that time, they were not quite ready because it was so new in concept and they would be very concerned.

INTERVIEWER:

If you look back on that experience now, do you think it was a mistake not to go to top management in the beginning?

DATA-BASE EXECUTIVE:

It was a catastrophe! It seemed intuitively obvious to us that the plan was right, but nobody else saw it that way. The whole thing has been a political nightmare.

COMMUNICATIONS GAP   In many corporations there is poor rapport between DP management and top management. There are a variety of reasons for this: DP use of jargon, management incomprehension and fear of DP technology, DP failing to fulfil the promises of an earlier age (especially information systems for top management), and top management failing to understand the need for their involvement. Too often senior management regards the data administrator as a technician who lives down in the bowels of the earth.

DP CONSULTANT:

I can remember when the data-base administrator, who was a senior analyst before he became a DBA, went to the MIS director and said "I want to understand the corporate needs so that I can take those into account in my planning." The MIS director said "It's none of your business." In fact, that company still uses data base in an application-by-application manner, although it paid lip service to the idea of data base being corporatewide seven years ago.

INTERVIEWER:

Did you have the capability to really communicate with top management to explain the trade-offs to them?

DP EXECUTIVE:

No.

INTERVIEWER:

What do you think would make that possible?

DP EXECUTIVE:

It needs credibility, in terms of what you are talking about, and some real-life examples that they can relate to in hard quantifiable terms. So the experience of installing the product and starting to work on it, even if it is in some degree bottom-up, then gives you the wherewithal to go to the management team and make presentations that say, "OK, now look. Here's where we have been, and here's where we see the direction going. Based on this experience I can make some real predictions. I can give some deliverable items and we can move ahead in that direction." I think if you can do that, they will give you resources.

INTERVIEWER:

But that's going to take much more time because you've got to spend three years getting some experience before you can then go to top management.

DP EXECUTIVE:

That's been our experience, about two to three years.

In an organization with little or no data-base experience it is not a good idea to wait for three years, gaining experience, before approaching top management. Top-down planning is needed from the start and as part of this process top management must be given realistic expectations about the time scale.

If there is a communications gap between DP and top management, several actions can help to bridge that:

- A consulting firm is brought in which specializes in strategic data-base planning.
- IBM is asked to initiate a BSP study.
- Top management is shown video tapes on the subject, such as those of Deltak.
- Top management is asked to read this book.
- Top management is asked to attend a short seminar on the subject.
- It is stressed to top management that corporate or organization changes often result from a top-down examination of corporate data usage.

Top management is likely to be turned off completely by technical talk about data structures. They are likely to be sceptical about vague promises of better management information. There are, however, certain aspects of the subject which are likely to turn them on.

Senior management takes an active interest in decisions about how the corporation *should* be run:

- Changes in organizational procedures, structural changes, or corporate reorganization are usually suggested by the entity analysis methodologies.
- Most senior managers perceive some areas where they would like better information. Sometimes they have not had an opportunity to articulate this and to be heard.
- Senior management is often concerned about officework productivity. Most corporations waste money because of redundant procedures or procedures that could be eliminated. A detailed charting of activities that use similar data can help to clean up anomalies in organization methods.

- Most senior managers perceive problems in today's DP operations or have their own ideas about what they would like accomplished. The business systems planning methodology is particularly effective at highlighting these.

- DP responsiveness, or speed of new application development, is sometimes perceived as a problem. Management cannot obtain new reports when they want them. One large bank in New York indicated to the author that it had a seven-year backlog of applications. Thorough data-base planning and implementation ought to greatly increase DP responsiveness and the speed at which new reports can be generated.

- To be competitive top management has to build a highly computerized corporation in the near future. The basis for this is corporatewide analysis of data.

CORPORATE POLITICS   The move to a shared data-base environment often worries or antagonizes end users. A user sometimes has to be told that data which he has regarded as his own will now have to be shared, or derived from a data base maintained by others. The user may regard the data-base approach as an invasion of his own carefully protected turf.

We stress that reorganization of procedures or corporate restructuring should often go hand in hand with the data-base approach, and that needs senior management involvement.

Often management or users receive their information from different sources once the data bases are operational. This may upset older, established employees who used to provide this information.

DATA ADMINISTRATOR:

We had one accountant who was quite determined not to allow me to dig in and understand what his systems were providing. He felt that he could satisfy all the report requirements of his users. It was his prerogative to supply the data *in his manner.* This gave him some status which I think he was afraid of losing. He's still bent out of shape by the idea of users being able to step up to a terminal and gain access to the kind of information that he used to provide.

In many corporations, politics have left in ruins the attempt to move to a data-base environment. Throughout the short history of data base the main reason for failure has been human problems, not technical problems.

There is the world of difference between a situation in which DP is trying to pioneer data base on its own, and a situation in which top management understands, endorses, and visibly supports the move to data base. It makes a big difference if top management is saying: "We have to build a computerized corporation. That has to be a data-base corporation. I want you *all* to understand that and help as fully as possible."

The emphasis on avoidance of disruptive politics needs to be an ongoing one because, left alone, it will soon reassert itself.

PROGRAMMER:

Once data-base implementation was under way, management left everything "to run on rails." As often as not, it ran *off* them.

DATA-BASE   Another reason for top management involvement
CHARGE BACK   is the budget needed for data-base development. It
                       is expensive to develop the data bases that a corporation needs. The payoff is a long-term one and the costs should not all be borne by the first applications, or the first user department.

DATA-BASE EXECUTIVE:

When we discussed the plan with the end users, they would feel, "Gee! It's going to cost so much money."

We're faced with the question: "Who's going to pay for that?" The end users feel that they already have a system that's working and they don't want to pay the cost of rewriting it under the data-base umbrella.

INTERVIEWER:

So this concern about who pays for things is a major inhibiting factor in evolving from a file environment into a data-base environment?

DATA-BASE EXECUTIVE:

In the past they paid just as much, and possibly even more, under the file systems. *But they knew what they were paying for.*

With data base, especially at the beginning, startup time, they think they are paying for a system that's not totally their own.

INTERVIEWER:

So what do you think is the right way to deal with that problem?

DATA-BASE EXECUTIVE:

We have to come out with a better charge-back system and also we have to come out with some kind of research and startup budget. We have to go to top management and have a total commitment and show them the total picture. In fact, we have to go to them with an information systems architecture. This is what we are trying to do.

We have given them a plan with detailed costs and milestones for all that we want to implement in the next two to three years.

We didn't want them to just imagine how much the cost would be. I think that in the past, with MIS, we never identified the total cost.

We justify the cost in terms of reduction of maintenance costs, which are big, and speeded-up application development.

If a company is oriented to a long-term planning horizon, it may be ready to accept a data-base approach which requires a three- or four-year involvement. If it has a very short term approach to its business and is trying to squeeze the maximum profit in sales out of every year, anybody who presents a multiyear project is not going to be too well received.

Maximizing return on DP investment in the short term requires different actions from maximizing it over a three- or four-year period.

One of the world's fastest-growing computer service corporations developed hundreds of millions of dollars worth of business per year installing customer applications which minimized immediate costs. To achieve this end they strictly avoided data-base techniques. However, the costs of maintenance on these applications rose until it was consuming 80% of the service corporation's manpower. The objective of minimizing *immediate* DP costs results in high maintenance costs *in the long term,* and prevents the development of data bases that should give fast inexpensive application creation when they are complete.

DP EXECUTIVE:

The problem is that the corporate executive today has to deliver today's profits. And a major data-base expenditure is going to pull right out of the today's profit line.

INTERVIEWER:

Do you see a solution to that problem?

DP EXECUTIVE:

First of all, we have to educate senior management. That they ought to be willing to take a little bit of an expenditure in today's dollars in order to get a maximum return in tomorrow's dollars. But if the government would come around to looking at a data base or any kind of a major information systems expenditure, as a capital item, then we could look at it as any other major capital expenditure in the corporation.

Data-base expenditure is a type of cost that ought to be capitalized. Like the installation of a major piece of capital equipment, it is designed to last for many years. If the designers succeed in creating stable data structures— then the data base has a life span of at least five years and probably ten or more. It will last as long as a major piece of production machinery with a similar ratio of maintenance costs. To charge such a cost to this year's users does not make sense, especially as it takes some years to develop the applications to utilize data bases fully.

SELECTION OF FAST-PAYBACK PROJECTS

Having said that, there *are* opportunities to obtain fast payback from data bases in certain applications. When a top-down plan is created, it is desirable to look for those systems with which results can be quickly demonstrated. Often those quick results from higher-level data-base languages such as NATURAL, IDEAL, SQL, etc.

DATA-BASE EXECUTIVE:

Our own experience is that management has to get a sense of some immediate payback. So an opportunity to deliver something—and in fact delivering it—is critical. The undertaking should not be so ambitious as to seem mystical.

IMPLEMENTATION PRIORITIES

An important part of strategic planning is to select implementation priorities. A corporate-wide view of the needed systems should be developed in such a way that priorities can be rationally set. The subsystems implemented first should be those which solve immediate problems, have fast payoff, or are quick and easy to implement.

Multiple systems with these characteristics can be implemented if they are designed to be building blocks in an overall corporate-wide plan.

MULTIPLE SUBSIDIARIES

Some corporations have multiple subsidiaries. If these are miscellaneous corporations which have been taken over, they may be entirely differently structured. If they are spin-offs, for example foreign subsidiaries of a parent corporation, they may be similar in structure.

It is often desirable that the data bases of the subsidiaries be at least partly compatible with those of the parent.

When a methodology for strategic design is first employed, it is usually done in one corporation, or division, or factory, at a time. The team implementing the methodology becomes familiar with it and skilled, and is then in a good position to extend it to other parts of the organization. This should be done with top management directives.

It is sometimes the case that spin-off corporations, or separate factories in a larger corporation, can use essentially the same types of subject data bases encompassing similar entities.

Management should be concerned with common application development. To what extent can an application developed in one location be used in the others? An examination of the top-down data-base plans, if they are done with enough detail, can help to reveal this.

DP EXECUTIVE:

There are international operations in many countries. They are modeled on the domestic one but they all have their own idiosyncrasies. We found that the domestic entity analysis and supergroups were largely transferable if we accepted that some time was necessary to accommodate local differences.

At the detailed modeling level the differences are much more severe, so each country maintains its own model. However, the identical documentation technique and charting of the models enables the head office to see where common application development is likely to be useful and workable.

DP PRODUCTIVITY   DP productivity is a concern in many organizations. It is becoming a more important concern as computers drop in cost. The cost of a computer is often much less than the cost of the programmers, and analysts, who keep it busy. Computers are plunging in cost, while programmers' and analysts' salaries are going up. Senior management often perceive DP productivity problems in terms of how long it takes to develop the new applications that are needed.

Many authorities advocate that DP productivity be attacked by using structured programming and structured analysis. These help a little. However, certain *major* causes of low DP productivity are *not obvious* and will not be corrected by *structured versions of the same procedures.* They include the following:

- There are multiple versions of similar paperwork in different departments. Each requires different application programs and maintenance. If the procedures were replanned, they could be similar enough to utilize the same programs. To perceive this and plan the solution needs a top-down analysis of data requirements.

- A seemingly trivial change sets off a chain reaction of program modifications, as discussed earlier. This was one of the main reasons for the development of database management systems. To solve the problem fully needs top-down planning of *subject* data bases.

- Much of the logic in today's programs is redundant, with many different programmers writing routines that ought to be the same.

- Time-consuming program coding could be lessened with data dictionary techniques.

- Most of today's commercial programs are written in languages such as COBOL and PL/1. In typical installations the rate of program creation varies from 7 to 40 lines of code per day. High-level data-base languages permit much faster development of many (but not all) applications. One line of code in such languages is often equivalent to between 10 and 40 COBOL statements.

- End-user languages are permitting users to create their own queries and generate their own reports and graphics, provided that appropriate data-base facilities are accessible.

- Slow and laborious systems analysis procedures can be avoided for certain types of transactions, and speeded up for others, if appropriate data bases already exist. Relatively fast analysis of data-base events can generate structured English programming specifications.

Good strategic data-base planning should aim to attack these areas and maximize future DP productivity.

REFERENCES

1. James Martin, *Strategic Data-Planning Methodologies,* Prentice-Hall, Inc., Englewood Cliffs, N.J., 1982.

2. "Business Systems Planning," *Information Systems Planning Guide,* IBM Corporation, White Plains, N.Y.

6 WHO DOES WHAT?

INTRODUCTION
The major difference between data-base operation and file operation is that a high degree of sharing of data takes place. This has several effects. It means that the design and management of data spans multiple departments which may previously have kept their data to themselves. It raises questions in the end users' minds about who owns the data, whether the data are private, and whether anyone could harm or invalidate the data. It means that users from separate departments must cooperate, first at a high level to determine what data resources are needed, and second at a low level to define the data items and data structures.

LEVELS OF DATA SHARING
The sharing of data takes place at several levels, as shown in Figs. 6.1 to 6.3.

At the lowest level (Fig. 6.1) the same data item (field) is used in multiple records or documents.

At the next level (Fig. 6.2) the same files or data-item groupings are used in multiple applications.

Multiple groups of data items are organized into data bases. One system may contain several separate data bases. One such data base might contain all the data about customers, or all the data about parts, and so on. At the highest level of sharing (Fig. 6.3) each complete data base may be used by several departments, divisions, or other organizational entities.

DATA-ITEM DEFINITION
For all levels of sharing, agreement must be established on the definitions and representation of each data item.

Figure 6.1 The same data items are used in multiple records and documents.

The types of data items that are used in a corporation have to be given names and must be defined. Many corporations are in the process of building a *dictionary* specifying and standardizing the types of data items in their corporate data bases. In a payroll application the data items have names such as GROSS MONTHLY PAY, FEDERAL INCOME TAX DEDUCTION, EMPLOYEE NAME, and SOCIAL SECURITY NUMBER. In a purchasing application they have names such as SUPPLIER NUMBER, SUPPLIER NAME, INVOICE DATE, QUANTITY ORDERED, and so forth. As the desire to analyze the corporate activity develops—a natural by-product of computer usage—more elaborate data items are needed, such as QUANTITY OF DELIVERIES LATE YEAR-TO-DATE FROM THIS SUPPLIER. Large cor-

Figure 6.2 The same files or data groupings are used in multiple applications.

porations have more than 10,000 data items, with the number still growing rapidly.

Different computer applications, serving different departments of the corporation, can share many of the same data items—an employee's name, a part number, a customer order—and the details of these need not be separately recorded for each different department that uses them (as they have been in the past). They can be recorded once in a standard fashion and the data organized in such a way that they can be used for many different purposes.

The standardization and definition of this large number of data items is a lengthy operation and is made longer because different departments often define the same item differently or disagree about its precise meaning. Many corporations have not yet reached the stage of standardizing the corporate data items, but this is an essential step toward building up the data bases they will eventually need.

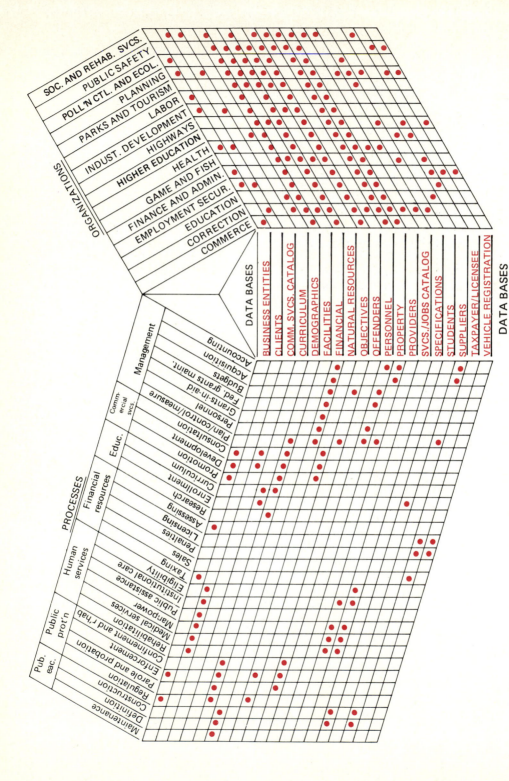

Figure 6.3 An efficiently planned set of data bases may be shared by multiple processes and multiple organizational groups. It should therefore cut across political boundaries. This example is taken from a local government study [1].

> *CORPORATE HEAD OFFICE DOCUMENT:*
>
> Common records at each location will increase our effectiveness in . . . interpreting and assisting with another plant's problems . . . transferring or promoting personnel to other locations . . . transferring product responsibilities . . . exchanging product information . . . starting up new plants . . . Will be of great significance to new people joining the company . . . It will be easier for personnel to exchange information when that information has a common meaning . . . Other areas of interplant communications will be substantially improved . . . faster, more accurate communications . . . faster response to changing conditions . . . shorter lead times . . . improved performance at lower cost . . . will result.

The difficulties of linking together or integrating the data base, and of standardizing the data items, can be particularly acute in a corporation with several divisions or plants, which have each evolved their own ways of keeping accounting, engineering, sales, production, or other data. In some corporations the struggle for standardization of computer-processible data will go on for many years.

DATA MODELING

Data items do not exist in isolation but are associated with one another. Maps need to be drawn of which data items are associated with which others, and what types of association these are. Such maps give an overall representation of the data that are needed to run an organization. They are referred to as *data models.*

Modeling the data is fundamental to successful data-base operation. In many data-base installations it has not been done adequately and consequently, the full advantages of data base are not achieved. This subject is discussed further in subsequent chapters.

Data definition and modeling go hand in hand, and are independent of any one application, any current implementation, or any specific computer or software. They are fundamental to the process of understanding the data in a corporation.

DATA ADMINISTRATOR

The person who presides over the process of defining and modeling the data is called a *data administrator.*

To accomplish the task the data administrator needs to work closely with the end users. The best way to do this is to set up a *user group* for the creation of a particular data base. The users, systems analysts, and the data administrator create separate views of the data that are needed. An individual view might relate to a document, an inquiry, a report, or an application of the data. The separate views are synthesized into a common data model from which any of the views can be derived.

The model and the definitions of data are reviewed periodically with the user group. There is usually substantial argument about the definitions of data. Agreement needs to be established about common definitions and data structures before the data can be put into a shared data base which can serve multiple users as effectively as possible.

Particularly important in modeling is to create a model which is *stable* so that old programs do not have to be rewritten when the data are employed in new ways. Tools and techniques are available for stable data modeling.

DATA-BASE DESIGNER

The task of physically designing the data base is different in nature from the task of data modeling, and is often done by a different person. Physical data-base design is concerned with the machine and data-base software. Data modeling is concerned with what data are needed to make the business function.

We will refer to the person who does the physical data-base design as the *data-base designer*. He needs to be a skilled technician who understands the subtleties of the data-base management system, and how to obtain good performance from it.

Often the term "data-base administrator" is used instead of "data-base designer." Some installations distinguish between their *data administrator* and *data-base administrator*. These terms, however, are so close that they have often caused confusion and sometimes have been used interchangeably. To avoid this confusion the term "data-base designer" is used exclusively in this report for the physical designer. It is important for success to distinguish between the *data administrator* and *data-base designer*. They need quite different talents.

LOGICAL AND PHYSICAL DATA

The form in which the data are actually stored does not necessarily resemble the form in which they are presented to the application program. The end user's or application programmer's view of the data may be much simpler than the actual data and tailored to his own application. The data structure that the user or application program employs is referred to as a *logical structure*. The data structure, which is actually stored on tape, discs, or other media, is called a *physical structure*. The words "logical" and "physical" will be used to describe various aspects of data, *logical* always referring to the way the programmer or end user sees it and *physical* always referring to the way the data are recorded on the storage medium. The programmers' views illustrated in Fig. 2.4 are logical (make-believe views).

The difference between logical and physical records had a humble beginning. When records were first stored on tape, the *gap* between records was lengthy compared with the records themselves. The gaps wasted much space, so it was economical to have long physical records. Many logical records were therefore grouped into one physical record. The software separated

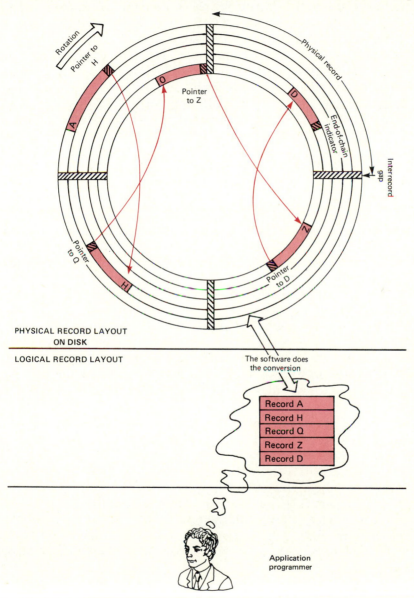

Figure 6.4 An example of the difference between logical and physical records.

them when they were presented to an application program and combined them when they were written on tape.

Today the differences between logical and physical data can be much more complex. The linkages among data are often different in the programmer's view and in the physical organization (for example, the linkage between a factory *part* record and a record for the *supplier* who supplies that part). We use the terms *logical relationship* and *logical data description* to describe the programmer's view. *Physical relationship* and *physical data description* describe actual ways in which data are stored. It is a function of the software to convert from the programmer's or user's logical statements and descriptions to the physical reality and back again.

Figure 6.4 shows an example of different logical and physical structure. Physical records on a disc contain logical records which are *chained* together; that is, a pointer in one logical record links it to another. The programmer requires a file of logical records in the sequence of the chain. He does not necessarily know about the chain. The software presents his program with logical records in the required sequence. Other programs may be given records in a different sequence. Many different types of data structures are possible.

The data model that the data administrator creates is entirely a logical structure of data. The data-base designer converts this *logical* structure into *physical* structures. The end users generally need not be concerned with the physical structures.

THE DESIGN PROCESS   Figure 6.5 summarizes the design process.

The *data administrator* collects the data requirements expressed by end users and systems analysts, and synthesizes these to create a *logical* model of the data needed to run given activities. The model and definition of data items should be reviewed by a carefully selected committee of end users (labeled "end-user group" in Fig. 6.5) to achieve agreement on the definitions and to ensure as far as possible that no important data have been forgotten.

The data modeling process is fundamental to building a corporation automated with networks and data bases. It can be done independently of specific data-base design and should keep well ahead of the implementation of data bases for particular applications. Many corporations have not done the data modeling adequately, with the result that their data-base implementation degenerates into something more like *file* implementation than true data-base management. This causes problems like those discussed in Chapter 2.

The *data-base designer* creates specific data bases with specific software, implementing a selected part of the data model. He assists the programmers in efficient use of the data base. He monitors the resulting system and times the data base physically to achieve the best performance he can.

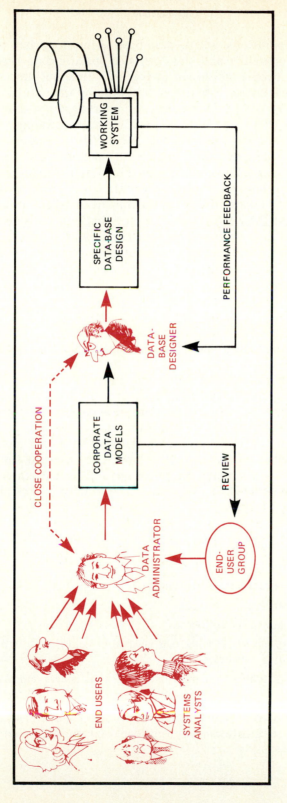

Figure 6.5 The data modeling and data-base design process.

In many corporations where data-base technology has been a major success, the data modeling and the design of specific data bases have been done by different people, as shown in Fig. 6.5. In some successful installations the modeling and data-base design are done by the same person.

The personality and skills needed for creating corporate data models are different from those needed for specific data-base design. The data administrator needs skill with people and the ability to understand the business. The data-base designer needs skill with machines and software, and a knowledge of the complex mechanisms of the data-base management system.

The *end-user group* of Fig. 6.5 is particularly important. This team of end users should be carefully chosen from the different areas represented by the model. It has the vital task of ensuring that end users needs in general are met in the modeling process. It is up to end users to ensure that the data bases being created do in fact contain what they need and will need in the future. We discuss this process in subsequent chapters.

THE VIEW FROM THE TOP

Many corporations have a top-level steering committee which makes decisions about major computer purchases and projects. Top end-user management participate in this process.

Often the steering committee does not plan the data-base requirements, but it is becoming increasingly important that this should be done. We will refer to the top-level data-base planner as the *data strategist.* He should create a corporatewide plan for what data resources are needed.

Figure 6.3 illustrates one such plan. This illustration includes only data bases. In fact, an organization is likely to have many existing files. It will also have collections of data for specific purposes, such as certain end-user information systems. These need to be in the overall data resources plan.

The plan should include:

- Files (Class I environment)
- Application data bases (Class II environment)
- Subject data bases (Class III environment)
- Information retrieval systems (Class IV environment)
- Old files that have to be converted
- Old (badly designed) data bases that have to be converted—often narrowly conceived application data bases
- Files in small distributed systems which relate to data bases elsewhere

Increasingly, the data storage in a corporation is *distributed;* it exists at multiple geographical locations. The top-level plan should be concerned with

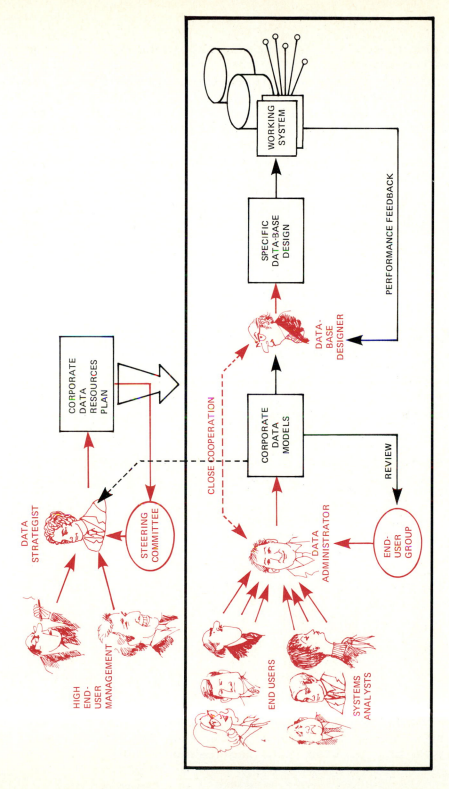

Figure 6.6 Top-level planning directs the data-base development process.

what data bases exist at different sites, and to what extent they share the same data structures.

Figure 6.6 illustrates the high-level planning of data resources.

In some organizations the persons shown as *data administrator* and *data strategist* in Fig. 6.6 are the same person. Large organizations may have one data strategist with a view of the whole organization, and multiple data administrators, each handling different areas.

One finds several different ways of dividing up the tasks shown in Fig. 6.6, although the division in Fig. 6.6 may work the best. Particularly important is the end-user involvement illustrated in Fig. 6.6.

DATA DISTRIBUTION

Increasingly now, data are distributed among multiple locations. This raises new design and management questions.

- Where should the data be located?
- How should integrity be maintained with synchronized copies of the data?
- What conflicts could occur in updating the data, and how are such conflicts avoided? (See Ref. 2.)
- Who designs the data?
- Who enforces compatibility of data structure among different locations?

We will assume that an individual is responsible for these concerns and refer to him as the *data distribution administrator.* This may be a separate function, or it may be an extension of the data administrator's function.

In a large organization there may be several data administrators for different portions of the data. Data distribution administration may need to span these. It needs the authority to enforce its decisions in multiple locations, so it may be a high-level function. It may report to the top-level corporate DP management, or be a function of the top-level data strategy group.

The conventional data administration function will design the logical models of the data used, and the data distribution administrator will ensure that they interlink appropriately between separate sites.

RESPONSIBILITY BREAKDOWN

Figure 6.7 shows a suggested breakdown of responsibilities.

The *data-base designer* is perceived as being a skilled technician concerned with the data bases at one location, and the subschemas that are derived from them. Some of these subschemas may be used as *file* structures in peripheral machines connected to that location.

	USER GROUP	PROGRAMMER AND SYSTEMS ANALYST	DATA BASE DESIGNER	DATA ADMINISTRATOR	DATA DISTRIBUTION ADMINISTRATOR	TOP LEVEL DATA STRATEGIST	AUDITOR	SECURITY OFFICER
TOP LEVEL DATA STATEGY								
Planning corporatewide file and data base strategy				C		PRIME		
Planning what corporate data resources are needed.						PRIME		
Planning responsibilities and job descriptions.						PRIME		
Determining data base standards and design techniques.						PRIME		
Data base software evaluation and selection.			C	C	C	PRIME		
Selection of a data dictionary and modelling tool				C		PRIME		
Control of corporatewide dictionary maintenance				P		PRIME		
DATA ADMINISTRATION								
Data analysis.	P	P		PRIME				
Field definition and design.	P	P		PRIME				
Logical model design.			P	PRIME				
Stability analysis.	C	C		PRIME				
Logical model validation.	P	P		PRIME			P	P
Planning what subject data bases are to exsist.				PRIME	P	P		
DATA DISTRIBUTION ADMINISTRATION.								
Data distribution analysis.				P	PRIME			
Deciding what data structures should reside at what locations.				P	PRIME	P		
Distributed recovery/integrity planning.					PRIME		P	
Conflict analysis.					PRIME		P	
Enforcement of compatibility of data structure between different locations.				P	PRIME	P		
DATA BASE DESIGN								
Design of schemes used in one data base system.			PRIME	P				
Physical data base design for that system			PRIME	C				
Integrity/recovery planning for that system.			PRIME				P	
Performance analysis.			PRIME					
Subschema file design (including subschema files at peripheral locations)	C	P	PRIME	P			P	
Planning the data base's compatibility with existing files.			PRIME	P				
INDEPENDENT FILE DESIGN								
Design of files which do not use data base systems.	C	PRIME				P		
AUDITING & SECURITY								
Audibility design.	C	C	C	P	P	P	PRIME	P
Security stategy and design.	C	C	P	P	P	P	P	PRIME

Key PRIME ═ PRIME RESPONSIBILITY
P ═ PARTICIPATING RESPONSIBILITY.
C ═ CONSULTING WHEN NECESSARY

Figure 6.7 Suggested responsibilities for data-base design and management.

The data-base designer needs to have a close relation with the *data administrator* who models the data, and with the *data distribution administrator* if he is a different person. The data base designer is concerned with performance, and for performance reasons may occasionally want to deviate from the data administrator's structure. He may sometimes find it desirable to split a data structure into two structures which run on different machines.

Most corporations will continue to have independent *files* (as opposed to data bases) for some applications. The use of files rather than data bases may be one of the concerns or decisions of the top-level data strategist. Where independent files are used, a systems analyst may design and control them in the conventional way.

The most common reason for using files is that they already exist, often in large quantities, and the reprogramming needed to convert them to data base is too expensive at the present time. New data bases must then coexist with the old files. This is a concern for the data administrator who must ensure that there are suitable bridges, where needed, for data to pass from one to the other. This may affect his logical model design.

The *data strategist* is seen as creating the organization-wide strategy for the use of data. He must form a clear view of the corporation's future information requirements, and must steer the evolution of data facilities so that the requirements become realizable. A set of data bases is needed which provide for the most rapid, high-productivity application development, using higher-level data-base languages (Chapter 9) where possible and which provide the information systems needed by all levels of management.

If possible within the organization management structure, the data strategist should be responsible for the selection of what types of data-base management system are used (CODASYL, DL/1, Relational, etc.) in order that the logical data descriptions of different systems can be compatible. In some organizations the top data-base management has created standards for data-base design, such as the use of *third normal form* (Chapter 12) or *canonical data structures* (Chapter 14). This should be done and should be linked to design tools which enforce the best form of logical data modeling.

The data strategist should ensure that a common data dictionary and common data modeling tool is used throughout the organization. In a large corporation the task of trying to clean up and unify the definitions of data used goes on for years. The data administrators are very much involved in this.

The data administrator's responsibilities in Fig. 6.7 are the same as in a nondistributed environment, or in an environment with simple peripheral storage devices connected remotely to a central data-base system. In an organization with multiple host computers, each with a data base, there will be multiple data-base designers, each with his own sphere of activity. This sphere may include peripheral remote storage units. The *distributed data administrator* acts as a bridge between the separate data-base designers.

SECURITY AND AUDITABILITY

The strategy for auditability and security is centrally planned in some organizations. Only a small proportion of the data in most organizations needs very tight security control. Many transactions do not need tight audit control. A central authority should decide which data need a high measure of protection, and what constraints this places on the design of distributed systems.

Figure 6.7 suggests that the primary responsibility for the security and auditability of data should reside with a professional security officer and auditor, respectively. The data strategist may work with these people. Most of this cast need to participate in making a system secure and auditable.

Both security and auditability are of more concern in a data-base environment than in a file environment because of the higher level of sharing. Security and auditing are complex subjects because there are so many ways that security can be violated. They need highly professional design. This usually means design by central authorities. Chapters 32 and 33 discuss these subjects.

POLITICS

The plan in Fig. 6.3 did not work out as shown in practice because it encompassed too many organizations that were politically separate (listed at the top right). The plan used needs to be implementable in practice with the human organizations involved, and needs to have top management commitment to the implementation effort.

Sensitivity to the way separate divisions or suborganizations are managed is needed. In some cases they will remain inevitably separate and the plan should take this into account. In other cases the plan has been needlessly torn apart by end users pulling in opposite directions or opposing the data-base approach. This situation requires strong direction from the top—a suitable mix of user education, top-level directives, and sensitivity to the personalities involved. This is one reason why top management needs to understand and endorse the data-base approach.

If top management is clearly saying, "This corporation is going to be run with data bases, and all user managements are expected to help," this directive solves many problems!

REFERENCES

1. From a systems study for the state of Arkansas prepared by the Information Systems Planning staff of the Office of the Information Systems Executive Committee, State of Arkansas, 1974.

2. James Martin, *Design and Strategy for Distributed Processing,* Prentice-Hall, Inc., Englewood Cliffs, N.J., 1981.

PART  **SOFTWARE**

7 CHOICE OF SOFTWARE

The choice of data-base management system (DBMS) is clearly an important decision. Some corporations make lists of desirable DBMS properties and rank the available products against each item on the list.

DP PRODUCTIVITY There are certain DBMS properties which are much more important than others. Sometimes the most important ones are ignored in the choice or given little attention. The main purpose in moving to a data-base environment is to achieve faster, more flexible, application development and low maintenance costs. The primary criteria for DBMS selection ought to relate to its effects on DP productivity.

Fast, flexible, application development is effected mainly by the languages that link to the DBMS—query languages, report generators, graphics generators, application generators, fourth-generation programming languages, and packages for specific application areas. With appropriate languages of these types applications can be created in a tenth or less of the time it takes with COBOL or PL/1.

Although this is perhaps the most important single selection criterion for data-base software, many DP executives have selected a DBMS with *no* high-level languages, on the basis that it is CODASYL, that it comes from a chosen mainframe, or that it ranks well on a selection criteria list which is largely unrelated to DP productivity. It is sometimes assumed that all DBMS applications will be programmed in COBOL—an assumption that defeats much of the purpose of moving to a DBMS environment.

One typical large corporation spent several person-years on selecting DBMS:

From the Executive Summary of the
DBMS Selection Report

The selection study was conducted by a working group consisting of four members from Group Data Processing and three members from Corporate DP Support under the guidance of a review group.

The following tasks were performed:

1. Formation of review and working groups
2. Preparation of a task list
3. Preparation of selection criteria
4. Market survey for DBMS packages
5. Weighting of the criteria
6. Package study
7. Vendor presentations
8. User visits and interviews
9. Package scoring
10. Follow-up discussions on package futures

Candidate DBMS were scored numerically against the selection criteria. All packages were subjected to extensive analysis based on:

- Their ability to meet our basic requirements
- Their ability to maintain the data base's integrity through all failures
- Their ease of use
- Their flexibility
- Their operating efficiency
- The amount of support that could be expected from the vendor
- Their special features and costs, which we categorized under general items

Among the selection criteria listed above there is no mention of DP productivity, high-level data-base languages, speed of application development, minimization of maintenance costs, or the distinction between production systems and user-driven systems. The selection criteria, such as operating efficiency, integrity through all failures, ease of use, flexibility, and vendor support are of basic importance. But if we match this corporation's selection list against the curves in Chapter 4, which are the measures of success of data-base management, there is almost no correspondence.

It is often the case that one knowledgeable person is better than a committee at selecting a DBMS. It is, however, a major responsibility and the choice may be much criticized in the future. Executives wanting to protect themselves politically sometimes pass this choice to a committee.

SELECTION CRITERIA   Box 7.1 provides a list of DBMS selection criteria.
No one DBMS provides good answers to all the criteria in Box 7.1. No one DBMS environment needs everything in Box 7.1. If a using organization employs Box 7.1 to assist in selecting a DBMS, it should first go through the list and decide what items are important to it. Some of the items are expensive, such as nonstop operation and geographical data independence, and the organization can function without them.

BOX 7.1   DBMS selection criteria

Development Languages

- What high-level languages are available for the DBMS for application development? (These may be available from separate software vendors.)
- What improvement in development productivity has been experienced when using these languages?
- How easy are the languages to use?
- Specifically which development language or languages would be chosen in conjunction with the DBMS in question?

End-User Languages

- What languages for end users can be employed with the DBMS—query languages, report generators, graphics generators, application generators, very-high-level programming languages,* statistics packages, and so on? (Again these may be available from separate software vendors.)
- How easy are they to learn and use?
- How flexible are they in searching and joining data?
- What is the quality of the reports that are generated?
- Specifically what end-user languages would be chosen in conjunction with the DBMS?

Data Structures

- Can the DBMS handle all types of data structures (e.g., all complex structures)? Can it handle them all efficiently?

*A separate checklist may be examined relating to very-high-level languages [1].

(Continued)

BOX 7.1 *(Continued)*

- Can the DBMS handle variable-length records or variable-length data items?
- Can data be searched efficiently on any data item?
- Can the system handle text data?
- Can data be searched or accessed by alphabetic identifiers with phonetic synonyms (e.g., Smith = Smythe)?

Flexibility

- Can new data items be added to an existing record without the programs which use that record having to be changed?
- Can new data items be added dynamically, or must an offload/reload occur?
- Does the DBMS allow alternative keys—the retrieval of records by more than one identifier?
- Does alternate key usage incur high overhead?
- Can alternative keys be added dynamically?
- Can secondary keys be used on any data item?
- Can secondary keys be added dynamically (while other users are employing the data base)?
- Can the DBMS accommodate growth? Is an offload/reload necessary to increase the size of the files?
- Can new associations between records be added without forcing the rewriting of existing programs?
- Can new associations between records be added dynamically (i.e., while the data base is in use)?

Security and Privacy*

- Does the DBMS have record-level, or data-item-level, security protection?
- Are the security controls powerful and unlikely to be bypassed?
- Can sensitive data be enciphered?
- Does the DBMS give a hierarchy of locks for different types of personnel?

*Further lists of features for security are given in the author's book *Security, Accuracy, and Privacy in Computer Systems* [2].

BOX 7.1 *(Continued)*

- Are there good facilities for a security officer?
- Can audit trails be made automatically?
- Are the internal auditors satisfied with the system's auditing facilities?

Restart and Recovery

- Is there automatic protection of data when a transaction aborts?
- Is there a clear *point of commitment* in transaction processing and the ability to *back out fully and automatically* if an abort occurs prior to the commitment?
- Are there automatic system restarts after a crash or power failure with complete protection of data?
- What is the mean time to recover following a crash?
- Are there means of recovery after a media failure or bad data written on the media, based on archives and activity logs?
- What is the mean time to recovery following a media failure? How automatic is the recovery?
- Can restart be performed at a task level, or does the entire system have to be restarted?
- What is the frequency of transaction aborts, system crashes, and media failures on a typical system? Do the recovery times provide high-enough system availability?
- Can the system be on the air 24 hours per day?
- Are there good system controls to prevent operator errors causing failures, particularly unrecoverable failures?
- Can the system give nonstop operation when a storage unit fails by duplicating critical data on a separate storage unit and providing automatic recovery after the failure?
- Are data-base restart and recovery procedures integrated with those of the teleprocessing system?

Integrity

- Can the system use automatic range checks and accuracy controls?
- Are there tight concurrency controls to prevent errors occurring when more than one transaction are concurrently updating the same data?

(Continued)

BOX 7.1 *(Continued)*

- Is there a potential for broken pointers, chains, indices, associators, and so on? Is there tight protection from such a possibility?

- Can data-item modification be done under very tight security controls to correct data errors found in data items? Is any such change automatically logged for auditors?

- Are there tight system controls to prevent operators from accidentally damaging data, loading wrong media, and so on?

- When the updating, deletion, or creation of certain data items has necessary consequential actions, does the DBMS take any steps to enforce these consequential actions?

- Are there controls on statements that can be made with the query language(s) to warn about queries which have semantic disintegrity?

Requirements Relating to Other Software and Hardware

- Does the DBMS operate on the computers or minicomputers that are likely to be employed?

- Does the DBMS work with the latest releases of the chosen operating system(s)?

- Does the DBMS work with the chosen terminal's teleprocessing monitor or network architecture?

- Does the DBMS support the storage devices that are likely to be employed, including hierarchies of storage devices, large solid-state cache memories, and so on?

Performance

- For specified transaction applications, how many transactions per second can the DBMS handle?

- How long do specified batch runs take?

- For specified applications, what are the mean and standard deviation response times?

- How do the performance figures vary as the data bases become large?

- Are there limits on the size of data bases that can be handled?

- How fast can searching operations be carried out?

- How badly does the addition of secondary indices or other search mechanisms degrade the performance of updating operations?

BOX 7.1 *(Continued)*

- How does the addition of many terminals affect performance?
- How do performance figures vary when complex data structures are used?

Efficiency

- Is it multithread? That is, can it process more than one transaction simultaneously or are transactions processed serially?
- Are input/output operations overlapped?
- How much extra storage space is needed for pointers, secondary indices, directories, inverted files, and so on?
- What storage load factors are normal (storage load factor = user data stored/total storage space)?
- Is data compression and compaction used?
- How much main memory is used in different circumstances?
- What is the region size? Excessive region-size requirements degrade operating system performance.
- What is the working set size (average number of active pages used)? Excessive working set size increases paging overhead.
- Does it support a back-end processor, or hardware search, join, or indexing mechanisms?
- Does it support automatic data storage between different levels of storage media?
- Is it designed to utilize a large solid-state buffer or cache memory effectively?
- Does it precompile, optimize, and store access modules for use with high-level query or relational operations?
- If automatic navigation is used, how does it optimize this?
- Does access degrade over time due to data inserts, area splits, chain length growing, and so on?

Monitoring

- What facilities exist for monitoring the performance of the data base?
- What facilities exist for monitoring and reporting on the use of the data base?

(Continued)

BOX 7.1 *(Continued)*

Ease of Use

- Is the documentation complete, clear, and easy to understand?
- What training courses are provided? How good are they?
- Is the DBMS easy to install and maintain?
- Is the DBMS operator-friendly? What special operations training is needed?
- What testing aids are provided? Can multiple test files be supported?
- Is the DBMS easy to use by programmers? Is its data manipulation language good, effective, and easy to learn?
- Can nonprocedural statements using the data base be included in conventional programs and compiled?
- Does the DBMS have a comprehensive set of utilities to assist in management?
- Is it easy for the data administrator to make changes in data structures—for example, to add new data items or new secondary indices?

Standards and Portability

- Are data-base structures represented in a standard way (e.g., using the CODASYL approach)? Unfortunately, this is not always an advantage because relational structures offer greater flexibility on some systems.
- Can application systems using the data base be moved:
  (1) To another computer using the same architecture?
  (2) To another computer using a different architecture?
  (3) To a peripheral distributed computer?
- If the choice of DBMS would tend to lock the user into that DBMS or that vendor, is the lock-in acceptable? Is it likely to be fully supported in the future? Will it provide the growth that may be needed? Will the DBMS and vendor be at the leading edge of technology evolution, including evolution that migrates data-base features to hardware for greater efficiency?

Data Dictionary*

- Does the product have a built-in data dictionary?
- How comprehensive is it?

*Desirable features of data dictionary systems are listed in Box 8.1.

BOX 7.1 *(Continued)*

- Is it an active or passive dictionary? How active?
- Does the dictionary produce clear reports for data administration purposes?
- Is the dictionary interactive? Does it have a good user dialogue?
- Does the dictionary generate the data used by programmers?
- Does the dictionary drive the high-level data-base languages?
- Does the dictionary assist end users in employing the data base?

Teleprocessing

- What teleprocessing monitor is supported? Is this integrated with the data-base operations?
- What network architecture is supported?
- How many terminals can be active at once?
- Are local area networks supported?
- Are recovery operations integrated with the teleprocessing facilities?
- Is the distribution of data supported?

Distributed Data*

- Are distributed data-base operations supported?
- Is the distribution vertical (hierarchical) or horizontal (fully generalized) distribution?
- Is it a *fully* distributed data-base system; in other words, can users or programmers refer to data by their logical name without needing to know where they exist geographically?
- Can data be moved from a centralized to a distributed environment without application programs having to be rewritten?
- Can data be reorganized geographically without affecting application programs which use those data?
- Can a single query relate to data in multiple locations?
- What utilities and tools are provided for reorganizing distributed data?
- What integrity controls are used with distributed data?

*Distributed data are discussed more fully in the author's *Design and Strategy for Distributed Data Processing* [3].

(Continued)

BOX 7.1 *(Continued)*

- Are two or more versions of the same data kept synchronously up-dated? If so, how is recovery and resynchronization achieved after failures?

Design Tools

- Is there a tool for assisting in achieving the best physical layout of data, selection of access method, optimization of indices, and so on?
- Is the physical design tool linked to automatic monitoring of system usage patterns?
- Are there design tools that will predict response times and capacity requirement as the traffic or file sizes grow?
- Is there a logical design tool to assist in achieving stable logical data structures (Chapter 15)?

Automatic Optimization

- Does the system determine and use the optimum access strategies for complex queries or automatic navigation?
- Does the system automatically reorganize the indices or other access mechanisms?
- Does the system assist in physical reorganization and layout of the data?
- Does the system handle inserts of new data efficiently?
- Does the system support automatic staging between different levels of storage media: for example, staging from mass storage to disc and from disc to large solid-state storage?
- If automatic staging is used, is it linked to the functioning of the DBMS?

Vendor Support

- Does the vendor have a reputation for giving excellent support?
- Does the vendor have local representatives familiar with the product?
- Does the vendor offer a full range of good training courses?
- Does the vendor seem committed to future releases, enhancements, and evolution of the product?

BOX 7.1 *(Continued)*

- How many systems are installed? When data-base machines (as opposed to software) become predominant, will the vendor be able to handle this evolution?
- Is the vendor financially sound?

Costs

- What additional costs are likely for add-on products, including utilities, languages, data dictionary, testing aids, auditing aids, and so on?
- What additional costs are likely for maintenance and support?
- Might the vendor raise rental or maintenance costs in the future as users become committed to the product?
- What added hardware costs does the product use incur—main memory, machine cycles, added storage unit accesses?
- What is the personnel cost to support the product?

Future

- What are the vendor's plans for future evolution of the system?
- How will the vendor support the evolution toward hardware or hardware-assisted data-base systems?
- Does the vendor have plans for back-end processors, data searching hardware, hardware-assisted indexing, intelligent relational machines, and so on?
- Does or will the vendor support both heavy-duty and user-driven DBMSs? Will these use integrated support facilities, automatic extraction, and passing of data between them, and a common data dictionary?
- How will the vendor support the evolution toward distributed data-base facilities?
- What are the plans for improving performance?
- Does or will the vendor support nonstop operation?
- What are the plans for future application generators, better query languages, graphics support, and very-high-level data-base languages?
- Does the vendor have a sound overall product migration path?

If the different criteria are given weights in the selection process, those weights should relate to the broad overall objectives, particularly to the measures of success plotted in Chapter 4.

TRAPPED IN A DBMS

In practice, organizations become trapped into continuing use of a DBMS once they have made a major commitment to it. Often they do not expect to be trapped. The reason for the entrapment is that it is too expensive to change; too many programs would have to be rewritten.

Not only do user organizations become trapped, manufacturers of the DBMS also become trapped. So many customers depend on an old DBMS that the manufacturer has to keep supporting and improving it, rather than switching to a better but incompatible form of DBMS. Many billion dollars per year are being spent by IBM's customers, for example, on analysis and programming of applications that employ IMS. IMS cannot be replaced by a different form of DBMS unless intricate conversion aids are made to work fully.

Because of this entrapment, new forms of DBMSs often come from new vendors. Most *relational* data bases that *do* have most of the properties in Box 7.1 come from organizations other than the major mainframe vendors. Some customers are reluctant to use them, for fear of becoming locked into a product that is not from an established vendor.

The initial choice of DBMS is thus more critical to future maintenance problems than is often realized when that choice is made. Should organizations delay the difficult decision? Probably not, because the move to data base is a change in DP management which encourages the cleaning up of the data in the enterprise. The sooner this is done, the sooner the benefits will be felt, and the benefits of a well-designed data-base environment are great.

MAINTENANCE

Maintenance has become a crippling problem in old data-processing installations. A major objective of data-base management is to lower the maintenance burden.

This needs to be tackled in two ways. First, make the applications that use the data base easy to change. This can be done by developing them in the highest-level languages—nonprocedural languages where possible [1]. Second, ensure that changes to the data structures can be made without forcing the rewriting of existing application programs.

If future maintenance costs are to be minimized, a data base needs to be as *stable* as possible. By "stable" we do not mean that its structure will never change. We mean that *when changes in the data structure occur, they can be made without having to modify applications that already use the data base.* The data administrator can take many actions which help to create stable data structures. These are a vital aspect of managing the data-base environment and are discussed in Part III of this book. In addition, the choice of data-base management software has a major effect on stability.

DBMS PROPERTIES DESIRABLE FOR REDUCTION OF MAINTENANCE COSTS

Certain properties are desirable in data-base managements systems if maintenance is to be minimized. These are listed in Box 7.2.

Many data-base management systems have some but not all of these properties. Some have the first four properties but do not have the ability to dynamically create new associations among data, to carry out automatic navigation, or to perform relations algebra operations.

Some of the properties in Box 7.2 are expensive in machine cycles. They are desirable for low-traffic applications but are too expensive for high-traffic applications. Some are desirable for small data bases but not for very large data bases.

Earlier, we distinguished among classes of data environment. A Class IV environment may employ a data management system which has all the properties listed in Box 7.2 except perhaps the last two. Such an environment is better than the other classes with regard to maintenance. Why are the other classes still used? For two reasons: first, machine performance—machine cost or response-time considerations, and second, to protect the large investment in existing programs which employ a given data base of file management system.

BOX 7.2   Properties of data-base-management software that minimize application maintenance costs

- *Field sensitivity*. New data items (fields) can be added to data-base record structures without necessitating change in the logical record structures that an application program uses. In other words, the record structure seen by the application program can include *some* but not necessarily *all* of the data items in a data-base record.

- *Ability to represent all data structures.* All patterns of associations between records should be representable [i.e., all plex (network) structures as well as hierarchical structures].

- *Ability to dynamically create new access paths.* It is sometimes necessary to build a secondary index on an existing data item, or to otherwise create new access paths, without affecting programs that already use the data base.

(Continued)

BOX 7.2 *(Continued)*

- *Automatic generation of programmers' data from a dictionary.* The programmers can be prevented from inventing their own data descriptions if all the data descriptions they need are automatically generated from the data base. This lessens incompatibility problems which result in future maintenance costs.

- *Ability to dynamically change associations among records.* In some data bases rigid associations between records are set up when the system is created: that is, there are pointer linkages between records which represent hierarchical structures, CODASYL *set* structures, and so on, and these cannot be changed without changing the application programs that use them.

    It is desirable to be able to add new associations between records without disrupting old programs.

- *Flexible query facilities and report generators.* The ability to extract and associate data is needed so that the data can be displayed or correlated in the ways most valuable to end users. This requires a user-friendly language.

- *Application generators.* A language is needed with which applications can be generated from the data base, preferably without programmers, and easily modified, as required.

- *Automatic navigation.* The high-level data-base languages should be able to navigate through the data base automatically, to produce the required results without a program which states how to progress a step at a time from one record to another. The commands of a relational algebra offer this capability. It is desirable that data-base systems be able to execute such commands automatically.

- *Hardware/software independence.* It is desirable that the data-base application programs should still work when the computer, storage units, operating system, or other hardware or software components are changed.

- *Distribution independence.* It is desirable that if the data are distributed on distant machines in a different fashion, the old applications using the data still function correctly.

- *Data-base-management-system independence.* It is desirable that if a change is made to a different data-base management system, the old applications should still function correctly. This property often does not exist in a complete form, although migration to improved versions of the same data-base management system is made possible.

HIERARCHICAL RECORD STRUCTURES

A data-base management system needs to be able to represent *any* logical data structure. A variety of associations occur among records.

A SUPPLIER record, for example, may have multiple ORDER records associated with it. We can draw the association between the SUPPLIER and ORDER records as follows:

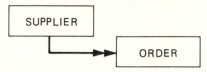

The ➤ on the line entering the ORDER record indicates that there can be many ORDER records for each SUPPLIER record.

One order may be for many parts. We may want to go from a SUPPLIER record to the ORDER records for that supplier and examine what line items for parts are on the order. We need the following data structure:

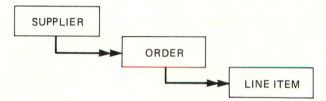

We refer to this as a hierarchical structure of data (also called a tree structure).

Each record in the hierarchy (except for those at the top) is associated with *one* record in the next higher level of the hierarchy.

PLEX STRUCTURES

The association between records may not be strictly hierarchical. For example, we may want to add a PART record to the structure, showing what orders there are for that part, and perhaps also a quotation record showing the prices and delivery times that suppliers have quoted for each part:

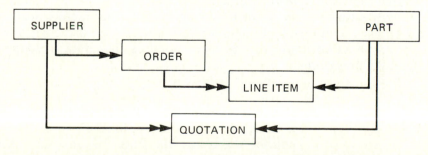

A structure of records more complex than a hierarchical structure (like that above) is called a *plex structure*. Many data that we need to represent are plex-structured.

REPRESENTATION OF DATA STRUCTURES

A DBMS must be able to represent these associations among records. There are various ways in which it can be done.

Three main approaches to representing such structures exist, referred to as:

- The hierarchical approach
- The network approach
- The relational approach

These approaches are described in more detail in the author's book *Computer Data-Base Organization* [4]. Here we summarize them briefly.

Figure 7.1 shows a plex structure and Figs. 7.2 to 7.4 show how it is represented with these three approaches. The fields shaded red in these diagrams are the primary keys that uniquely identify each record.

The first approach breaks the plex structure up into hierarchies. It uses pointers to link the hierarchies together. The red dashed lines in Fig. 7.2 represent these pointers. A hierarchy (tree structure) of records can be represented simply by the sequence of laying out the records on the surface of a disc or other storage medium [4]. A record is then physically close to the records with which it is associated in the hierarchy. A record and its associated records can be accessed together quickly. To move from one hierarchy to another in Fig. 7.2 takes longer.

The network approach is the basis of the CODASYL data-base management systems [4]. Records are grouped into two-level hierarchies called *sets*. The sets can overlap to form networks (plex structures). In other words, a record can be part of more than one set.

Figure 7.3 shows a network representation of the structure in Fig. 7.1, using four sets. Associated records in a set can be stored in physical proximity so that they can be read together.

All early data-base management systems used either hierarchical or set structures. They employed pointers to interlink the records. They could represent any data structure by means of pointers. The data structure had to be carefully preplanned.

RELATIONAL DATA BASES

The third major way of representing data structures is the relational approach. This avoids using pointer structures like Figs. 7.2 and 7.3. All data are represented as records without pointer linkages. Instead, the records con-

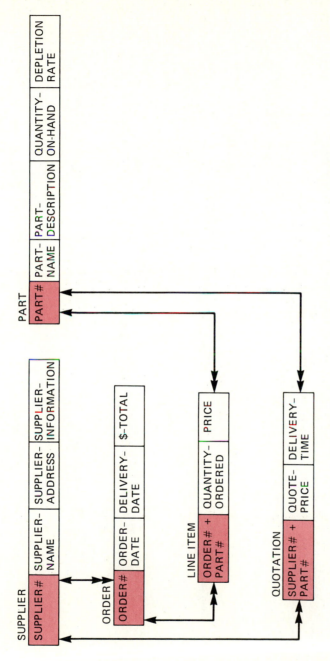

Figure 7.1 A plex structure of associations among records. This can be represented with a hierarchical approach (Fig. 7.2), a network approach (Fig. 7.3), or a relational approach (Fig. 7.4).

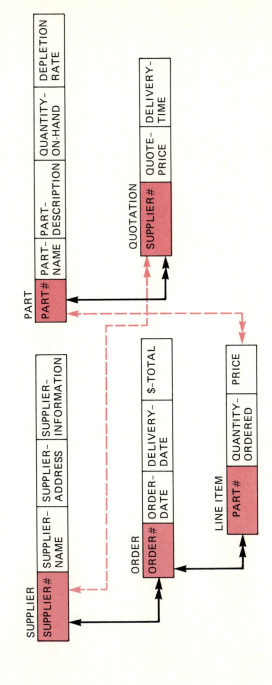

Figure 7.2 A hierarchical (tree structure) version of the data structure in Fig. 7.1.

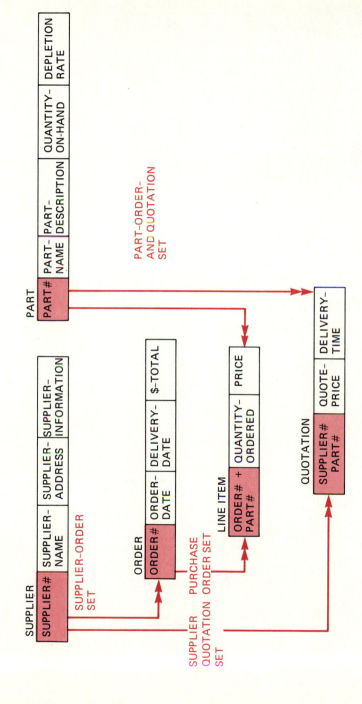

Figure 7.3 A network (CODASYL) version of the data structure in Fig. 7.1.

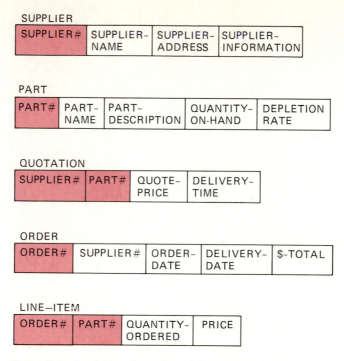

SUPPLIER

SUPPLIER#	SUPPLIER-NAME	SUPPLIER-ADDRESS	SUPPLIER-INFORMATION

PART

PART#	PART-NAME	PART-DESCRIPTION	QUANTITY-ON-HAND	DEPLETION RATE

QUOTATION

SUPPLIER#	PART#	QUOTE-PRICE	DELIVERY-TIME

ORDER

ORDER#	SUPPLIER#	ORDER-DATE	DELIVERY-DATE	$-TOTAL

LINE—ITEM

ORDER#	PART#	QUANTITY-ORDERED	PRICE

Figure 7.4   A relational version of the data structure in Fig. 7.1.

tain data items which allow the necessary associations to be made. This approach gives simple tabular structures of data which are easy to describe mathematically.

Figure 7.4 shows a relational version of Fig. 7.1.

In order to follow the associations between records, some redundant data items are placed in the records. For example, in Fig. 7.4, it is necessary to go from the ORDER record to the SUPPLIER record to find the supplier name and address when printing an order. To do this, the data-item SUPPLIER# is placed in the ORDER record.

To find the orders for a given part, in Fig. 7.2 or 7.3 the DBMS would follow the pointer linkage from the PART record to the LINE ITEM record. In the relational data base no such pointer linkage exists. Instead, there is an index on the PART# data item of the LINE ITEM record. The LINE ITEM record contains the ORDER# so that the relevant ORDER records can be examined.

A relational DBMS should provide the capability to build an index on any data item. It should also have the capability to add a new data item to an existing record without changing the programs that use that record—in other words, have the field sensitivity property listed in Box 7.2. These two capabilities make it possible to change the data structure when needed. With most pointer-linked data-base systems it is difficult or impossible to change the pointer linkages—the basic data structures—without changing the programs that use those data structures.

A relational data base thus represents data structures in a highly flexible fashion. They can be changed by adding new data items to the records. With some relational DBMSs this can be done dynamically while users are using the data base.

To be worth calling a relational data base the software ought to have a set of commands which are the equivalent of a relational algebra [4].

A logical file of records is referred to as *a relation*. A relation is a two-dimensional array of data—a table. Figure 7.4 shows five relations. The reader should imagine many instances of each record type in Fig. 7.4, forming five tables of data. The relational algebra has commands that manipulate entire relations.

For example, a relation may be *projected* by one command. We might ask for a projection of the PART relation in Fig. 7.4, which contains only PART NAME and QUANTITY-ON-HAND. Sometimes a projected relation contains fewer records than the original relation because duplicate records in the result are included only once.

Two or more relations may be *joined* by one command. For example, we may request a join of the QUOTATION and SUPPLIER relations to form a table which lists PART#, QUOTE PRICE, DELIVERY-TIME, SUPPLIER-NAME, and SUPPLIER-INFORMATION.

A considerable amount of machine activity is necessary to project or join relations. Some machines have been built which give hardware assistance in performing relational operations. It is likely that major *data-base machines* of this type will exist in the future.

PROPERTIES OF A RELATIONAL DATA BASE

A relational data base should thus have three properties:

1. It represents data in flat-file form, as in Fig. 7.4, without pointer structures.

2. New data items and data-item indices can be added to existing records without forcing the rewriting of programs that use the previous version of those records.

3. The equivalent of a relational algebra exists for automatically creating projections and joins of logical files of records.

If a DBMS does not have these properties, it probably ought not to be regarded as a complete relational DBMS. It is easy to meet the first property without the others and claim that the data are in relational form, but this is of little value.

AUTOMATIC NAVIGATION Using a programming language such as COBOL or PL/1 the programmer *navigates* through the data base. He accesses one record at a time and follows the pointer links of Fig. 7.2 or 7.3, one at a time. He instructs the computer what to do a step at a time.

Some data-base systems can be programmed with a higher-level language. Suppose, for example, that we wanted to produce a report from the data structures in Figs. 7.1 to 7.4 which lists PART#, QUANTITY-ON-HAND, QUANTITY-ORDERED, and DELIVERY-DATE.

Using a conventional programming language, this would mean navigating among the PART record, LINE ITEM record, and ORDER record. The whole report might take 50 or so lines of code in COBOL. With the NOMAD language, which employs a relational data base, the report can be generated with one line of code:

LIST PART# QUANTITY-ON-HAND QUANTITY-ORDERED DELIVERY-DATE

The software uses a dictionary to locate which record contains each of these data items. It then executes a relational *join* to produce the required combination of data items.

The result could be sorted to put at the top of the report the parts with the greatest risk of running out. Items with lower values of (QUANTITY-ON-HAND/DEPLETION-RATE) should be higher on the report. The user adds another line of code:

ORDER BY (QUANTITY-ON-HAND/DEPLETION-RATE)

These operations would require much "navigation" if done with a conventional program which tackles them one record at a time. Using higher-level data-base commands, the navigation is automatic. A wide variety of different data-base languages employ automatic navigation. Fairly complex software is needed in the DBMS to handle automatic navigation efficiently. Some DBMSs do not have this capability.

Automatic navigation, and the languages that employ it, save much programming. They also save much maintenance work because they generate error-free code and are easy to change. Perhaps more important, they enable end users and systems analysts to obtain results without programmers, and this changes the entire management of application development.

With certain data-base systems, high-level statements that provide automatic navigation can be included in conventional programs. Statements of DEC's DATATRIEVE language or IBM's SQL, for example, can be inserted into COBOL or PL/1 programs.

The compiler translates the SQL statements into compact routines in machine language. These precompiled routines may access many records in an optimized sequence. They are called whenever the COBOL or PL/1 program is executed.

It is more efficient to use precompiled, optimized routines for automatic navigation, but more often the high-level statements are entered interactively by end users and are interpreted rather than compiled.

Automatic navigation is most commonly associated with relational data bases. It should not be thought of as a property of relational DBMSs only. Some pointer-linked or CODASYL DMBSs also have automatic navigation. Automatic navigation leads to high flexibility of data-base use, so the flexibility of creating new access paths which a relational DBMS provides is important.

WHICH IS BEST?   There can be endless arguments about which is best: the hierarchical approach or the CODASYL approach. Thousands of data-base installations of each type now exist. Experience with the better data-base management systems indicates that there is little to choose between them. Both work well. There can be differences in machine performance depending on how well the data usage paths fit the data structuring approach, but averaged over all typical commercial usage, the two approaches are about equivalent.

Because of this, data-base systems should be judged by the languages for application creation rather than by which internal structure they use. We should ask: Are the development aids and languages powerful? Can we obtain results quickly? Can we modify (maintain) those systems easily and inexpensively? Do the applications so created give good machine performance?

There is a huge difference between different systems in their capability to dynamically change data structures and usage. We believe data-base systems should be regarded as being of two categories: those designed for dynamic change and those designed for high-volume prespecified use.

The relational approach has succeeded in giving data systems which are highly flexible and dynamically changeable—more so than most hierarchical or CODASYL DBMSs. However, as always, greater flexibility extracts a price in machine performance. In some cases the price is high.

Relational systems *can* be designed to give good machine performance for systems which are carefully prestructured and which limit flexibility. However, most of the fastest DBMSs at the present time are the hierarchical or CODASYL systems. Many corporations are using hierarchical or CODASYL data bases for their heavy-duty computing in conjunction with relational systems for decision-support or user-modifiable computing which employs flexible, user-friendly languages.

MACHINE PERFORMANCE

We indicated in Chapter 3 that there are various mechanisms which can be used for automatic navigation—searching, joining, or the equivalent of following pointers. Unfortunately, all of the mechanisms that give efficient searching, joining, and so on (at least with storage units which are partially mechanical) *substantially degrade the performance of simple updating of the data.* When a field is updated on which there is a secondary index, the index also has to be updated. The same applies to other mechanisms for searching and joining.

Secondary indices, inverted lists, and so on, take up much more storage space than do primary indices—often 10 times as much. The reason is that data are often stored in the sequence of their primary key; they cannot be stored in the sequence of secondary keys. The sequencing makes possible powerful index compression techniques which can be applied to the primary index. In some systems the secondary indices, inverted lists, and so on, take up more storage than the original data. Long accesses are needed to update these indices or lists.

The transaction rate varies enormously from one type of data base to another. Large banking systems process 100 transactions per second at their peak periods. Some decision support systems have fewer than 100 transactions per day. Most systems with very high transaction volumes process the transactions in a way that is entirely prespecified. Most decision support systems deal with unanticipated queries, and unanticipated requests to examine or process the data in new ways. Most decision support systems benefit greatly from automatic navigation. Most prespecified systems do not need it.

PRESPECIFIED VERSUS USER-DRIVEN SYSTEMS

The requirements for DBMSs thus tend to fall into two groups, shown in Box 7.3. We will call them prespecified systems and user-driven systems. Prespecified systems have large transaction volumes following preplanned usage paths. Efficiency of operation is gained at the expense of not being able to dynamically change the data structures and having limited ability to search and join them. User-driven systems are much more flexible, being able to respond to users' changing requirements. The users often need to search and join the data, and to examine them in new ways. With very high transaction volumes or very large data bases, these more flexible mechanisms tend to be too expensive.

Prespecified systems can employ high-level languages for application generation using prespecified data structures. Such languages should result in the compilation of optimized blocks of machine language code. User-driven systems require user-friendly languages which enable users or analysts to obtain results quickly and to modify these results dynamically. The languages for user-driven systems result in data being interactively searched, joined, and sometimes sorted. These operations may be saved for batch runs on the prespecified systems. The languages for user-driven systems may have the capability to add new data items to existing records or to modify the associations between records.

Data bases designed for prespecified operations commonly use COD-ASYL data structures like Fig. 7.3 (IDMS, Burroughs' DMS II, Univac's DBMS 1100, Honeywell's IDS II) or hierarchical structures like Fig. 7.2 (IBM's DL/1 and IMS, TOTAL, Hewlett-Packard's IMAGE).

Data bases designed for user-driven computing commonly employ relational structures like Fig. 7.4 (IBM's SQL and QBE, Univac's MAPPER, NOMAD, ORACLE).

There are exceptions to this. A relational system can be designed to be efficient with prespecified operations (Tandem's ENCOMPASS, DATACOM). A pointer-linked DMBS can be designed to have secondary indices and

BOX 7.3 Requirements for data-base management systems tend to fall into these two categories, which to a large degree are incompatible

Prespecified Systems	User-Driven Systems
● Almost all accesses are prespecified.	● Many accesses are not prespecified.
● Multiple prespecified applications are supported.	● There are diverse unanticipated user requests.
● The transaction volume is high, so access efficiency is primary.	● The transaction volume is low, so access efficiency is not as important.
● There is not a major use of secondary indices. They may be important to a limited extent.	● Secondary indices, or other methods of searching and joining the data, are used extensively.
● Automatic navigation is of limited use.	● Automatic navigation is of great value and is used extensively.
● Most queries are primary-key queries.	● Queries with multiple secondary-key retrieval are important.
● There is little or no need to dynamically change the data structures.	● New data-item types and new secondary indices need to be added to existing records while they are in use.

flexible end-user languages. Some DBMSs are hybrids giving efficient high-volume operation with predefined usage paths *or* flexible operation with secondary key retrival (ADABAS, SYSTEM 2000).

USING TWO TYPES OF DATA BASES   *The choice that is best for most enterprises is to have two types of data bases, one chosen for efficient operations in heavy-duty computing or the other chosen for user-driven systems.* The data base used for processing the claims in an insurance company should be different from that used by actuaries. The data base used for customer transactions in a bank should be different from that for investment planning. The data base used for high-volume production of routine documents should be different from that used for decision support and analysis.

These two types of users tend to be fundamentally incompatible. The mechanisms giving the flexibility needed for user-driven computing and the pointer linkages and data structures good for high-volume prespecified computing limit the flexibility of user-driven computing.

It is often desirable that the same data should be in both, often derived, as we shall discuss, from the same overall data model. It would be useful if both had the same dictionary. Often, this is not the case. There could be a bridge between the dictionaries of the separately structured systems.

OTHER CRITERIA   Other criteria in Box 7.1 which are not discussed in detail in this chapter are very important: for example, integrity, security, restart and recovery after failures, prevention of damage to data, data dictionary facilities, distributed data, and vendor support. These are discussed later in the book.

REFERENCES

1. James Martin, *Application Development Without Programmers*, Prentice-Hall, Inc., Englewood Cliffs, N.J., 1982.

2. James Martin, *Security, Accuracy, and Privacy in Computer Systems*, Prentice-Hall, Inc., Englewood Cliffs, N.J., 1973.

3. James Martin, *Design and Strategy for Distributed Data Processing*, Prentice-Hall, Inc., Englewood Cliffs, N.J., 1981.

4. James Martin, *Computer Data-Base Organization*, 2nd ed., Prentice-Hall, Inc., Englewood Cliffs, N.J., 1977.

8 USE OF DATA DICTIONARIES

The role of the data dictionary is vital. Most data items are used by multiple applications, multiple end-user groups, and now with distributed systems multiple computers. Without a dictionary there will be no coordination. The same data item will be represented differently in different places and defined differently by different users.

---

*CHAIRMAN OF A UNIVERSITY DEPARTMENT OF
INFORMATION SYSTEMS MANAGEMENT:*

It is my contention, backed up by sad experience and horror stories, that data-base management needs a dictionary more than the data-base system. All too many industrial and government users have found that their data-base system was relatively useless until they implemented a good data dictionary system [1].

Even if an organization does not use a data-base system, it ought to employ a data dictionary. It is likely to move the data-base operation at some time in the future, and this will be much easier if the data representations are coordinated, have agreed-upon definitions, and are catalogued in a generally available fashion. We have stressed that a major task in building a computerized corporation is to clean up the representation of data. The same data item should not have different bit representations in different places and be defined differently by different users. Rather than cleaning up the mess in data representations, many corporations are making it worse and worse by allowing every systems analyst (each claiming to use structured methods) to create his own data representations.

USES OF THE DATA DICTIONARY   A data dictionary has three categories of uses: (1) to inform people about data, (2) to help control the definition and representation of data, and (3) to indicate what programs are affected when changes are made to data structures or representation.

```
DATA

DATA BASE       HUMAN RESOURCE

THE HUMAN RESOURCE DATA BASE CONTAINS THE INFORMATION RELATED
TO PERSONNEL, PAYROLL, SKILLS, AND BENEFITS. IT IS MAINTAINED
BY THE VARIOUS SUBSYSTEMS THAT MAKE UP THE HUMAN RESOURCES
APPLICATION SYSTEM. IT IS USED FOR REPORTING BY THESE SAME
SUBSYSTEMS AS WELL AS THE MANAGEMENT REPORTING SYSTEM AND
ACCOUNTING REPORTING SYSTEM.

   AREA          PAYROLL

   THE PAYROLL AREA CONSISTS OF THE PAYROLL MASTER FILE AND
   CONTAINS INFORMATION REGARDING ALL PAY UNITS. IT IS MANAGED
   BY THE PAYROLL DEPARTMENT.

      FILE          PAYROLL--MASTER

      THE PAYROLL MASTER FILE CONTAINS A RECORD FOR EACH EMPLOYEE
      INCLUDING ACTIVE EMPLOYEES, TERMINATED EMPLOYEES, AND
      SUSPENSIONS.

         RECORD          PAYROLL

         THE PAYROLL RECORD CONTAINS EMPLOYEES NUMBER,
         HIS/HERS PAY CODE, AND RATE OF PAY, WHICH ALSO INCLUDES
         TAX INFORMATION

            KEY          PAYROLL.NUMBER

            THE EMPLOYEE NUMBER KEY IS USED TO RANDOMLY ACCESS
            PAYROLL RECORDS FOR IDENTIFICATION AND TAX REPORTING
            PURPOSES. ONCE ENTERED, AN EMPLOYEE NUMBER
            SHOULD NOT BE MODIFIED.

            FIELD          PAYROLL.ACTIVITY-CODE

            THE EMPLOYEE ACTIVITY-CODE ELEMENT CONTAINS THE EMPLOYEE
            NUMBER AND EMPLOYEE PAY CODE AND STATUS CODE

            FIELD          PAYROLL.EMPLOYEE-CODE

            EMPLOYEE CODE IS ONE CHARACTER FIELD THAT CONTAINS THE
            EMPLOYEES' PAY TYPE. IT SHOULD CONTAIN "H" FOR HOURLY
            OR "S" FOR SALARY. THIS IS USED FOR PAY RATE AND YEAR-TO-DATE
            INFORMATION
```

Figure 8.1   A verbal description of the use of fields, keys, records, data bases, and so on. This illustration is from ADR's dictionary for their **DATACOM** relational data base.

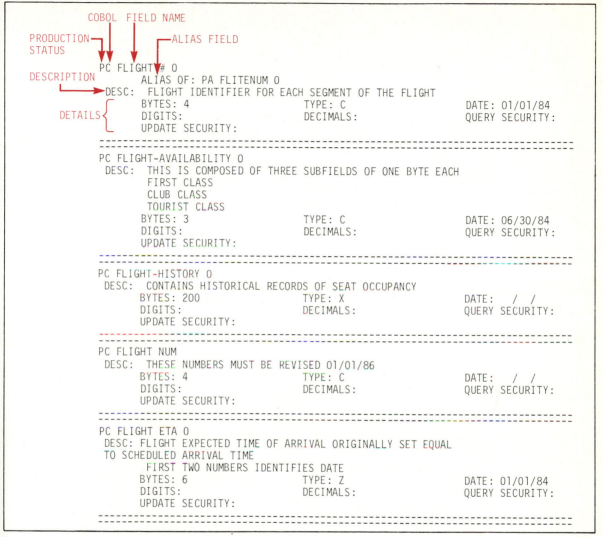

Figure 8.2 The user of the IBM DB/DC data dictionary requests a list of all data items (elements) with production status, where the subject code is COBOL, and the data item name includes the character string 'FLI':

In an organization without a dictionary, or without tight data administration, a great proliferation of data develops over the years. The same data types are often represented incompatibly in many places. It can be difficult to find out where required data exist.

As well as helping to *find* data, the dictionary is essential to *gain control* of data. It enables the many programmers, analysts, and now users who create files or data bases to use the same data formats.

INFORMATION CENTER EXECUTIVE:

We spend 25% of our manpower just trying to find the data that our end users ask for. The firm has never implemented a data dictionary.

The dictionary provides a vital tool for involving users in discussions about definitions of data. This is often one of the most difficult aspects of managing the data-base environment.

Figures 8.1 to 8.3 illustrate a data dictionary in use.

```
LIST OF SELECTED MEMBERS
     MEMBER NAME                   TYPE      USAGE CONDITION AC ALT REM OWNER

     EMPLOYEE-CODE                 ITEM      7   SCE ENC YES YES YES PERSONNEL
     EMPLOYEE-DATE                 ITEM      1 *     DUM YES YES YES
     EMPLOYEE-HISTORY-RECORD       GROUP     1   SCE ENC YES YES YES
     EMPLOYEE-HISTORY-REPORT       FILE      2   SCE ENC YES YES YES
     EMPLOYEE-MASTER-RECORD        GROUP     1   SCE ENC YES YES YES
     EMPLOYEE-REPORT               FILE      2   SCE ENC YES YES YES
     EMPLOYEE-REPORT-HEADER        GROUP     3   SCE ENC YES YES YES
     EMPLOYEE-REPORT-RECORD        GROUP     1   SCE ENC YES YES YES
     EMPLOYEE-TRANSACTIONS-FORM    GROUP     2   SCE ENC YES YES YES
     PM1                           ITEM      2 *     DUM YES YES YES
     PM2                           ITEM      2 *     DUM YES YES YES
     PM3                           ITEM      2 *     DUM YES YES YES
     PM4                           ITEM      2 *     DUM YES YES YES
     PM5                           ITEM      1 *     DUM YES YES YES
     P1-ERS                        SYSTEM    0   SCE ENC YES YES YES
     P1I01                         MODULE    2   SCE ENC YES YES YES
     P1P01                         PROGRAM   1   SCE ENC YES YES YES
     P1S01                         PROGRAM   1   SCE ENC YES YES YES
     P1S01TSORT                    FILE      3   SCE ENC YES YES YES
     P1U01                         PROGRAM   1   SCE ENC YES YES YES
     P1U02                         MODULE    1   SCE ENC YES YES YES
     P1U02MEMP                     FILE      5   SCE ENC YES YES YES
     P1V01                         PROGRAM   1   SCE ENC YES YES YES
     P1V01WVAL                     FILE      2   SCE ENC YES YES YES
     P2-EHS                        SYSTEM    0   SCE ENC YES YES YES
     P2P01                         PROGRAM   1   SCE ENC YES YES YES
     P2U01                         PROGRAM   1   SCE ENC YES YES YES
     P2U01TEMP                     FILE      3   SCE ENC YES YES YES
     REPORT-PAGE                   ITEM      1   SCE ENC YES YES YES
     REPORT-TITLE                  ITEM      1   SCE ENC YES YES YES
     STANDARD-DATE                 ITEM      4   SCE ENC YES YES YES
     TRANSACTION-CODE              ITEM      4   SCE ENC YES YES YES
     TRANSACTION-RECORD            GROUP     4   SCE ENC YES YES YES
     UPDATE-CONTROL-RECORD         GROUP     1   SCE ENC YES YES YES
     UPDATE-CONTROL-REPORT         FILE      2   SCE ENC YES YES YES


     LIST CONTAINS        11 ITEMS
                           7 GROUPS
                           7 FILES
                           2 MODULES
                           6 PROGRAMS
                           2 SYSTEMS
                           6 DUMMIES
                          35 MEMBERS IN TOTAL
```

Figure 8.3 The user of the MSP data dictionary requests a list of data items, groups, files, or any other components of the data base which are new or changed. (Courtesy of MSP.)

COMMITMENT

Perhaps the most important purpose of a dictionary is to enforce the use of data representations which are centrally standardized and defined. This mode of working removes some responsibility from the programmers and analysts. It makes demands on the end users to agree on the meaning of data items. In short, it requires *discipline* which will be enforceable *only if there is a strong enough and high enough level of management commitment.*

Managing the use of a data dictionary encapsulates most of the problems of managing the data-base environment itself. To succeed fully, it requires:

1. A data administration function operating as described in Chapter 2

2. User involvement as described in Part V

3. Top-down planning as described in Chapter 5

4. An effective method of planning and introducing change into data-processing systems

5. A suitably strong and high level of management commitment

SPAN OF CONTROL

Should a data dictionary address all the computerized data in a corporation?

Ideally, the answer is "yes." In practice, this is *very* difficult in large corporations which have multiple factories and locations. A few large corporations have attempted it, some with success, some without. In a small corporation one common data dictionary can be both practical and very valuable.

As with the entire data administration process, a suitable span of control needs to be selected for the use of a dictionary. If the span of usage is too small—for example, one project or a small group of applications—it will lessen the value of employing the dictionary. The span of control might be one factory of a multifactory corporation. Often, however, applications or records are moved from one factory to another and in this case there should be a commonality of the data represented in dictionaries in the separate factories. It would be much easier if they all employ the same dictionary. Good dictionaries have tight security features which prevent one department or division from seeing the data representations of another, where this is desirable.

To achieve common dictionary use over a large span, a suitably high level of management commitment (and understanding) is needed.

A problem of choice of dictionary arises if more than one type of data-base management system is used within the dictionary span of control. Where multiple types of DBMSs are used (due perhaps to lack of farsighted planning), it is often desirable that *one* dictionary describe their data because data are passed between one DBMS and another. There is much to be said for a DBMS-independent dictionary. However, there is a strong argument against this—data dictionaries are now being built into DBMSs. As this integration of the dictionary and DBMS occurs, the dictionary becomes an *active* facility instead of a *passive* recording system; it drives certain DBMS functions, assists in the usage of the DBMS, and enforces correct representation of data by programmers.

CORPORATE DICTIONARY MANAGEMENT   The data dictionary, together with the corporate entity models described later, is a corporate resource. It enables the information needs of the corporation to be charted and catalogued, and harmful redundancies removed. Cleaning up the data needed to run a corporation, defining them correctly, and understanding their functions are important activities over and above DP activities.

The strategic planning and functional analysis of corporate information requires the involvement of senior end-user management. Management needs to be involved in charting the corporation. This involvement often leads to reorganizing parts of the corporation.

Because this activity is important, business-oriented, and to a large extent independent of DP, some corporations have set up a staff function at the highest level for developing data dictionary control and doing strategic planning and functional analysis of corporate information. This activity has a major long-range payoff in the lengthy evolution of a computerized corporation.

Unfortunately, in most corporations the use of dictionaries has grown up from groups with a much narrower focus and lower level of authority. Most dictionaries are related to specific data bases or sets of projects. This does not achieve the more important objective of corporate information planning.

Worse, in some corporations the dictionary has been seen as an overhead item with an ill-defined payoff, and is sometimes dispensed with when budget cuts are sought.

SOURCES OF DICTIONARIES   There are several possible sources of dictionaries:

1. A dictionary can be kept manually with a card index system. This is inadequate for today's data-base environment.

2. Some corporations have written their own data dictionary software. This is highly undesirable, for several reasons. First, good dictionary software is much more complex than is generally realized. Second, it is cheaper to buy a dictionary. Third, the dictionary and data-base management software ought to be tightly integrated.

3. A dictionary may be acquired that is independent of any data-base management system. Such dictionaries are available from independent software houses. DBMS independence is attractive, but to obtain an independent dictionary is often not a good

decision because of the intimate interlinking of the dictionary and the DBMS. The trend toward having these products tightly integrated will increase.

4. A *passive* dictionary which *uses* one particular DBMS but which can store information about the data in other DBMSs may be obtained. Most such dictionaries come from the DBMS vendor.

5. An *active* dictionary may be used which is tightly coupled to a particular DBMS. The active coupling provides advantages, which we describe below, sufficiently great that all good DBMSs in the future are likely to have built-in, integrated, dictionaries which drive the DBMS and its high-level data-base languages.

DATA STORED   Figure 8.4 shows some of the types of items about which a dictionary stores information. The relationships between them are complex enough to require the use of a data base. Data-base management systems thus support their own dictionaries.

The items on the right-hand side of Fig. 8.4 are maintained by the data administration staff. The items on the left should be maintained by the project teams.

A variety of different views of dictionary data bases will be needed for different uses. Figure 8.5 shows some examples. The first two examples are for programs which show where a given data item is used and what data a given program uses. The third example relates to the origination and use of the data and might be employed by the systems analysts in examining the flow of data in a data-processing organization.

The user asks which files and programs use the data-item DEPARTMENT:

```
                    WHICH FILES USE DEPARTMENT.

THE FOLLOWING USE ITEM DEPARTMENT
    FILES           EMPLOYEE-MASTER
                    EMPLOYEE-HISTORY-MASTER
                    EMPLOYEE-HISTORY-LIST
                    EMPLOYEE-LIST
                    EMPLOYEE-TRANSACTIONS
                    EMPLOYEE-TRANSACTIONS-SORTED

                    WHICH PROGRAMS USE DEPARTMENT.

THE FOLLOWING USE ITEM DEPARTMENT
    PROGRAMS        CALCULATE-GROSS-EARNINGS
                    EMPLOYEE-HISTORY-REPORT
                    EMPLOYEE-MASTER-UPDATE
                    EMPLOYEE-REPORT
                    EMPLOYEE-HISTORY-UPDATE
                    EMPLOYEE-VET
```

In some cases project teams are geographically dispersed but need to use the same data structures. In this case a central data administration function is needed with user representatives from various project locations. A

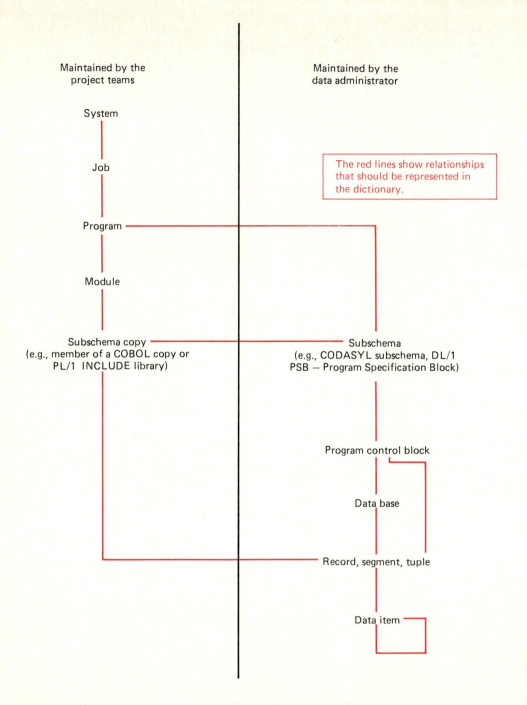

Maintained by the
project teams

Maintained by the
data administrator

System

Job

The red lines show relationships
that should be represented in
the dictionary.

Program

Module

Subschema copy
(e.g., member of a COBOL copy or
PL/1 INCLUDE library)

Subschema
(e.g., CODASYL subschema, DL/1
PSB — Program Specification Block)

Program control block

Data base

Record, segment, tuple

Data item

Figure 8.4 Some of the items in the dictionary may be maintained by
the project teams and some by the data administrator, as shown here.

(1) Where is a given data item used?

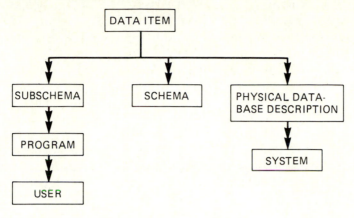

(2) What data does a given program use?

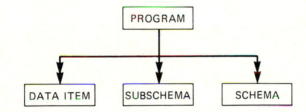

(3) Produce a matrix of data-item origination and usage.

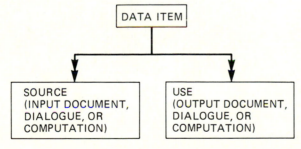

Figure 8.5 A variety of subschemas of the data dictionary will be used for different purposes.

dictionary system with terminals is desirable so that staff at the dispersed locations can all use the dictionary.

GENERATION OF PROGRAMMERS' DATA

A particularly important feature of data dictionaries is the capability to generate the programmers' views of data—to generate the Data Division statements of COBOL, the data descriptions of PL/1, or data descriptions of a data-base language such as MARK IV. They will also generate the control blocks and parameters required by DBMS programs: for example, the PSBs of IMS/DL/1, the DBGENs, DCBs, format buffers, and so on, of IDMS, ADABAS, SYSTEM 2000, TOTAL, and others.

This automatic generation of data for programs has two advantages. First, it enforces the correct use of data. The programmer cannot, by design or accident, deviate from the required data representations. Second, it saves time and money. One large corporation studying its COBOL programs found that 46% of the lines of code were in the Data Division. Often the programmer takes as long to write a Data Division line of code as any other line of code. Automatic generation of the Data Division saves the programmer coding and debugging time. It also removes some of his documentation tasks. This saving alone is sufficient to pay for the dictionary in most installations.

Figure 8.6 illustrates automatically generated source code.

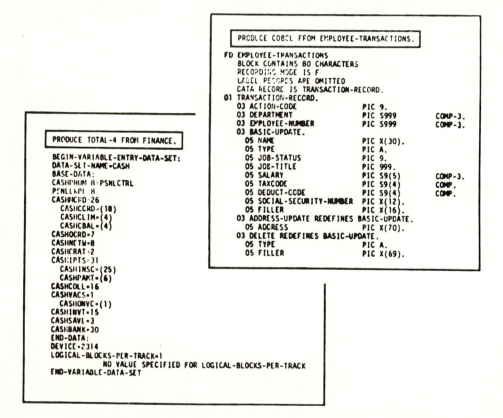

Figure 8.6 Typical *source language* generation by a data dictionary. Source language for the DBMS user facility MARK IV, and for a COBOL program, generated by MSP's DATAMANAGER. (From Ref. 2.)

**CHOICE OF
DICTIONARY**
The choice of a data dictionary system is critical. Systems differ considerably in their capabilities. Box 8.1 lists desirable features of a data dictionary system.

A data dictionary provides information about data which is itself kept in a data base. Most data dictionaries employ a data-base management system for handling these data. Most data dictionaries are therefore associated with a particular data-base management system. Most major data-base management systems have their own data dictionary provided by the DBMS vendor. Some independent dictionaries, created by software houses, employ *one* DBMS; a few do not employ a DBMS but provide their own means of filing and retrieving the information. The latter often interface to more than one DBMS.

An important criterion for dictionary selection is: Should it be able to handle the data for multiple types of DBMS? Most dictionaries can describe the data for multiple types of DBMS, but few can generate the programmers' views of data and the data-base control blocks from these multiple types.

Most dictionaries that are designed for one DBMS have the ability to *describe* data used by other DBMSs. For example, IBM's DB/DC dictionary is designed to work with IMS data bases, but its *extensibility* feature enables it to be employed for other types of information, including the data in files and other vendors' data bases. It cannot generate other vendors' data-base control blocks.

BOX 8.1   Desirable features of data dictionary systems

Group 1. Passive Features

- Supports definitions of all types of data items, data grouping, and data associations.
- Permits information to be stored about the data associations.
- Permits long data-item names (some dictionaries restrict the name to too short a length).
- Permits aliases (synonyms) to be recorded, and indicates where one data item is really the same as another which (for historical reasons) may be represented differently.
- Permits homonyms to be recorded (different data items that have been given the same name on different projects) and indicates on which projects they are used.
- Gives support for file systems as well as data base (including the old files).

(Continued)

BOX 8.1 *(Continued)*

- Gives support for different types of DBMS so that a multiple-DBMS environment can be supported.
- Supports the definition of process entities (systems, programs, modules, projects, transactions, etc.).
- Supports the definition of usage entities (users, terminals, department, company, etc.).
- Supports a teleprocessing network, allowing the network to be reconfigured dynamically.
- Automatically captures the data in existing programs.
- Prints attractively formatted, easily comprehensible reports of all aspects of dictionary usage.
- Displays dictionary information interactively.
- Has an elegant, easy-to-use, interactive dialogue for its users.
- Is suitable for use by end users as well as DP professionals.
- Provides KWIC (Key Word in Context) indices to help in searching for information in the dictionary.
- Usage for both *production* and *test* data, with on-line updating of data definitions being prohibited for production data.
- Supports the definition of security levels and authorization details saying who can do what with the data.
- Built-in security so that the data in the dictionary cannot be tampered with.
- Supports distributed data-base systems, showing what data are kept at each location, and what type of distribution is used (replicated data, partitioned data, copies synchronized or nonsynchronized, etc.).

Group 2. Generation of Data Descriptions

- Generates COBOL Data Division code, or the equivalent for other languages.
- Supports a diverse set of languages (or all languages employed in an installation).
- Generates the control blocks and parameters used by DBMS programs; for example, the PSBs of IMS, the DBGENs, DCBs, format buffers, and so on, of IDMS, ADABAS, SYSTEM 2000, TOTAL and others.
- Generates the items listed above for multiple DBMSs so that a multi-DBMS environment can be supported.

BOX 8.1 *(Continued)*

- Generates screen or report formats for high-level-language features.
- Supports query languages, report generators, dialogue generators, and application generators.

Group 3. "Active" Features

- *Enforces* the use by programmers of data definitions that are in the dictionary.
- Selective enforcement. Enforces the use of dictionary definitions for some projects and not others.
- Automatically converts data items to the same formats before adding or otherwise manipulating them in combination. This implies a tight combination of dictionary and DBMS (as in IBM System 38, for example).
- Sharing of dictionary and DBMS tables for operational efficiency.
- Integration of the dictionary with the DBMS user languages and sometimes direct interaction with the language user.
- Used in the *interpreter* or *compiler* of data-base languages.
- Inserts labels of data items, columns, or chart axes into reports generated by users.
- Assistance to the end user in understanding what is available to him in the data base.
- Enforcement of auditor's rules.
- Enforcement of privacy and security rules.
- Support of distribution of data which enables one machine to locate and utilize data that reside in different machines.
- Automatic measurement of accesses to data and compilation of statistics of data accesses.

Note: Some of the active features imply tight integration of the dictionary and DBMS. This prevents the dictionary being DBMS-independent, which is otherwise a desirable feature.

ACTIVE AND PASSIVE DICTIONARIES

Most early data dictionaries were *passive*. They provided useful information about data but did not participate actively in the handling of transactions. Later, some dictionaries became more intimately involved with the DBMS so that they could *enforce* standardization. Data could be represented and accessed only in the manner described in the dictionary. This prevented programmers from breaking the rules, but it also helped the programmers. In some systems a programmer could be more casual in references to the data. For example, IBM's System 38 is a data-base machine with a built-in dictionary. The DBMS and the dictionary are inseparably intertwined and use the same tables. The programmer makes a symbolic reference to data and the DBMS–dictionary combination checks this, converts it, and accesses the data. The programmer may say "Add A to B" when A is a binary data item and B is decimal. The dictionary detects this difference and the two data items are automatically converted to the same representation before adding.

Where the dictionary plays an active role in enforcing correct data representation and/or usage, or assists in converting data, it is called an *active* dictionary and contrasts with conventional passive dictionaries. Increasingly in the future, dictionaries will be an integral part of the DBMS and play a valuable *active* role. In advanced systems, all accesses to data flow through the dictionary. The dictionary both controls the usage of data and assists in the processing, query answering, and report and screen generation.

DESIRABLE DICTIONARY FEATURES

The desirable dictionary features listed in Box 8.1 are broken into three groups. The first group comprises the *passive* features of defining and cataloguing data. In addition to cataloguing data, a data dictionary is often used to catalogue and describe programs, modules, projects, users, or other such entities which relate to the DP function. The dictionary can show which projects use which programs, and so on.

The second group relates to the automatic generation of programmers' data descriptions, control blocks, and so on. It is this group which gives the most tangible payoff in using a data dictionary. The dictionary cost can be justified in the saving of programmers' time. The less tangible justification of gaining control of data corporatewide may in the long run have a larger payoff but is more difficult to quantify.

The third group relates to the *active* features of a dictionary—used for enforcing standards, driving high-level data-base languages, and possibly controlling access to data in a distributed environment. The use of active, integrated dictionaries represents a higher level of automation and will be an essential part of future data-base software and hardware (as on the IBM System 38). Many installations, however, are not ready for the enforced control represented by an active data dictionary, so a desirable feature may be the ability to make this enforcement optional. It may be enforced on some projects and not others.

GOOD FOR END USERS

Most early data dictionaries were designed for DP professionals, not for end users. Such dictionaries produce reports full of information useful for programmers but incomprehensible to end users.

As we describe later, the dictionary should play a major role in communication with users, to help obtain agreement about the definitions and uses of data items. Good end-user human factoring is highly desirable.

Dictionary output differs greatly in its comprehensibility. Good report design, screen design and interactive dialogue design are important features.

DRIVING THE DATA-BASE LANGUAGES

One of the most important aspects of data-base use is the very-high-level languages that employ data bases. Some of these, as described in Chapter 25, are designed for end users; some, as described in the next chapter, are designed for systems analysts to create applications or prototypes; some are designed to enable programmers to create applications in a small fraction of the time they would take with COBOL or PL/1. These languages enable a major payoff to be derived from data-base technology. Increasingly, they are being linked to an *active* data dictionary.

The dictionary stores users' names for data and associates them with the internal data-base names. In some cases there are multiple names or aliases for one data item. In some user languages the user keys in English-like statements and the language processor attempts to associate the words used with the data-base names so that the statements can be processed. Coded indications of the meaning or semantic properties of user words are stored in the dictionary.

Some dictionaries which are integrated into data-base languages store report formats and screen formats. Some store column heading names for data items. A user of the language NOMAD can write

    LIST BY INVNUM QOH LPD SRQ;

where "INVNUM," "QOH," "LPD," and "SRQ" are users' abbreviations for data.

The system will create an attractively formatted report with column headings labeled INVENTORY NUMBER, QUANTITY ON HAND, LAST PURCHASE DATE, and STANDARD REORDER QUANTITY. It can do this because it makes intelligent assumptions about the report format, and column headings for data items are stored in the data-base dictionary together with the users' names for these data items, such as "INVNUM," "QOH," and so on.

INTEGRATED DATA DICTIONARY

The dictionary, then, is becoming increasingly integrated with both the DBMS and the data-base languages. The term *integrated data dictionary* is used for this.

Figure 8.7 shows Cullinane's diagram of its data-base product line. Sig-

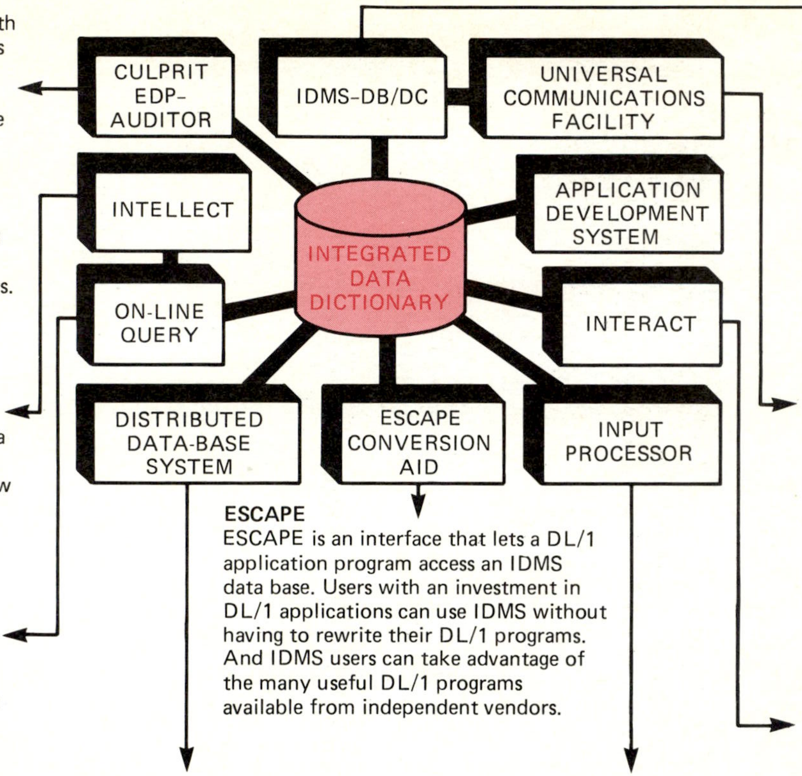

Report Generator

CULPRIT can be used to produce complex reports quickly, easily, and with a bare minimum of coding. It can access virtually any file structure including conventional files or data bases. CULPRIT is economical. It can produce up to 100 reports with a single pass. CULPRIT can be used as a powerful stand-alone facility or as part of a fully integrated data-base management system from Cullinane. EDP AUDITOR combines the capabilities of CULPRIT with a special Library of Audit Routines.

INTELLECT

This sophisticated English language inquiry system is designed for use by those in top management who have no background in computers, but have a need for timely information. Operating with a large, flexible dictionary, this new system has an outstanding ability to respond to conversational questions.

On-Line Query

On-Line Query is an interactive information retrieval system. Fully integrated with IDMS, it requires no programming in order to be immediately useful upon installation. It provides managers and user departments with a powerful, easy-to-use set of English commands that allow instant access to selected information stored in the data-base.

Data Communications

IDMS-DC is a data communications system designed specifically for use in the data-base environment. Fully integrated with IDMS, IDMS/DC gives faster response time, more economical use of memory, and greater simplicity of use than a nonintegrated TP monitor can. IDMS/DC provides a powerful recovery facility, mapping support, storage protection, and other data integrity features.

Universal Communications Facility

Applications developed with IDMS/UCF will run under any TP monitor without modification. With IDMS/UCF, programmers don't have to know the characteristics of the TP monitor they are using or may use. Applications will execute equally well through terminals connected to CICS, SHADOW II, Intercomm, Westi, Task/Master, and others.

On-Line Program Development

INTERACT is an on-line system for program development, remote job processing, text editing, and word processing. It offers a powerful command repertoire, fast terminal response time, and economical CPU requirements.

ESCAPE

ESCAPE is an interface that lets a DL/1 application program access an IDMS data base. Users with an investment in DL/1 applications can use IDMS without having to rewrite their DL/1 programs. And IDMS users can take advantage of the many useful DL/1 programs available from independent vendors.

Input Processor

IDMS input allows programmers, as well as nontechnical end users, to develop application programs in an IDMS batch environment. This new product comes with its own simple language, making it easier and faster to program with IDMS input than with traditional programming languages.

Distributed Data Base

Cullinane's Distributed Database System allows multiple IBM computers to share a common IDMS data base. It supports applications programs at remote sites and allows them to access a central data base with complete user transparency and full data integrity.

Central diagram nodes: UNIVERSAL COMMUNICATIONS FACILITY, APPLICATION DEVELOPMENT SYSTEM, INTERACT, INPUT PROCESSOR, IDMS-DB/DC, INTEGRATED DATA DICTIONARY, ESCAPE CONVERSION AID, CULPRIT EDP-AUDITOR, INTELLECT, ON-LINE QUERY, DISTRIBUTED DATA-BASE SYSTEM

Figure 8.7 Cullinane's IDMS data-base management system and its languages are driven by an *active* data dictionary. This is a highly complex facility which is fully integrated into Cullinane's data-base product line. Cullinane's advertisements draw the dictionary at the center, not the DBMS. This full integration of the data dictionary is a mainstream trend in DBMS evolution. (From Ref. 3.)

nificantly, the dictionary is drawn at the center with all the software described above linked into it. Even the data-base management system, IDMS, is shown as being peripheral to the dictionary, and Cullinane refers to it as a *dictionary-driven* DBMS. This dictionary is active and fully integrated with the DBMS. It enables the IDMS teleprocessing system to be reconfigured dynamically without bringing the system down and disrupting operations. It is integrated with the various query, report generation, and application development facilities of IDMS.

A dictionary that is fully integrated into a data-base product line becomes very complex. The Cullinane dictionary, for example, has *many* CODASYL sets managed by its own IDMS.

INDEPENDENT OR INTEGRATED DICTIONARY?

Should you use an independent dictionary or a dictionary that is linked to a particular DBMS?

As dictionaries become increasingly *active* and integrated into the DBMS and its languages, so it becomes increasingly desirable to use *them* rather than an independent dictionary. The main argument for an independent dictionary is that it can handle data for many different DBMSs.

If a corporation uses IDMS, it is highly advantageous to employ IDMS's integrated dictionary. The same argument is true for most other well-designed DBMSs. Users of IBM's IMS should use its own DB/DC data dictionary, and so on.

These data dictionaries are also designed to catalogue information about data that exist in files and systems other than their own DBMS. Good dictionaries, even though integrated into a particular DBMS, can be used as independent systems to define and catalogue all data resources, whether manual or automated, file or data base, and to catalogue program, project, and system resources.

A problem in the choice of dictionary arises when a corporation has two or more major DBMSs, each with its own integrated dictionary, and wishes to have a common corporate-wide dictionary. In this case one of the following compromises is necessary.

1. Use the integrated dictionary of each DBMS and make sure that data items that are stored with more than one DBMS are represented the same way. This solution may well result in a loss of control.

2. Employ the dictionary of the most widely used DBMS in the corporation and store in it details of data managed by the other DBMSs. This is less than ideal because control blocks and parameters needed by the other DBMSs' programs cannot be automatically generated.

3. Use an independent dictionary that supports all the DBMSs. This would have been a good solution before the days of active integrated data dictionaries. With these more

valuable dictionaries it is perhaps the worst solution because *none* of the data bases can use their in-built dictionary.

Of the three compromises, the author favors the second in cases where the dictionaries are not active, and the first where there is a major use of separate DBMSs covering different areas of the organization, or DBMSs each with active dictionaries.

Where it is desirable to have *one* dictionary it is also desirable to have *one* type of DBMS, at least for Class II and III operations. This becomes increasingly so as the dictionary evolves into an active resource which drives the DBMS and facilities such as those in Fig. 8.7. Some organizations that in the past allowed multiple DBMSs to be used are now limited in the tightness of dictionary control they have achieved. Nevertheless, there is a strong argument for a separate Class IV data management with its own active dictionary. An automatic bridge between the dictionaries would be useful.

The choice of dictionary and the facilities that are linked to it need to be a part of the strategic top-down planning of the data-base environment.

CONTROL OF CHANGE

The introduction of changes into data-processing systems can be a problem because many different programs or users may be affected by a change. The dictionary helps to control changes, and may indicate whether the data and other items it catalogues are in *test* status or *production* status.

When a programmer wants to add a new data item or change an existing one, he requests permission. The request may be forwarded by the local manager with responsibility for data, and if he agrees, to the central data administrator. The data administrator will decide whether he concurs with the change, examining the data to ensure that they do not duplicate or conflict with existing data. If the change appears to be acceptable, he will determine whether it affects other data users (Fig. 8.8). If not, he will enter the change in the dictionary as a change "concurred" with. If the proposed change affects other users, it will be passed to the affected users to see whether they agree, and the change will be entered into the dictionary as "proposed."

Where there is argument or the users disagree with the proposed change, the data administrator must help resolve the situation—a process not shown in the lines at the top of Fig. 8.8.

Once a change is entered as "concurred," program testing which the change necessitates will commence. Once the change is tested and proven, the data administrator will enter it into the dictionary as "approved," together with a date of acceptance.

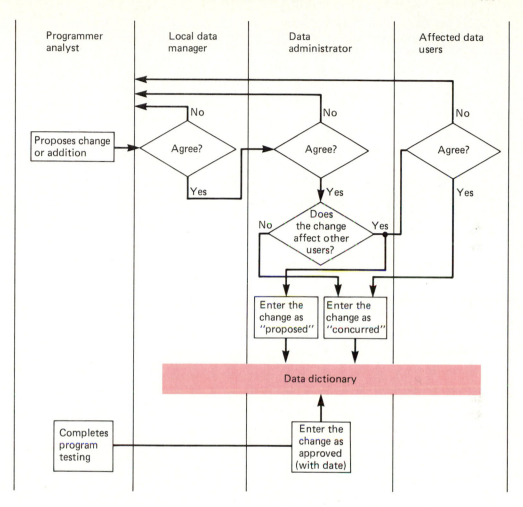

Figure 8.8 Use of a data dictionary to control changes.

IMPLEMENTATION AND RESPONSIBILITIES   Figure 8.9 shows the various responsibilities in setting up and operating a data dictionary. The split between data administration and project responsibilities is important.

Installing the dictionary should be treated and controlled like any other major DP project. It must be a project of high priority and status.

The operation of the dictionary can be approached in phases. The early phases may use *passive* dictionary features but not yet use *active* ones.

KEY: P = Prime responsibility
       S = Secondary responsibility

	Data administrator	Project development	Operations	Clerical support	End users	System programming function
Installation and maintenance of the dictionary	S					P
Running the dictionary (restart, recovery, etc.)	S		P			S
Establishing standards, procedures, and setup	P	S				
Entry and maintenance of data definitions (right-hand side of Fig. 8.1)	P	S		S	S	
Entry and maintenance of program and project data (left-hand side of Fig. 8.1)	S	P		S		
Linkage to the data modeling tool	P				S	
Library management	P	S	S	S		S
Security administration	P		S			S
Defining requirements for dictionary reports and queries	P	S				
Establishing keyword-in-context reports	P	S			S	

Figure 8.9   Responsibility for operations using the dictionary.

The operation may start by taking on *existing* data-base definitions of data. It may then expand into taking on project information—programs, modules, jobs, and so on. The data in existing files may then be added. This usually requires redefinition of data, and conversion of programs, so it may extend over a long period.

The data dictionary should be linked to the data modeling tool. Keyword indexing should be added to the information in the dictionary.

When the dictionary operation has settled down, all new projects should be controlled by the dictionary. At this point *active* control may be used.

Converting to dictionary operation means that some installation *standards* have to be modified. The dictionary is a valuable tool in helping to clarify and enforce standards relating to data.

The programmers will become dependent on the dictionary and its standards. This may cause some resistance among programmers, but it is important for managing and controlling a data-base environment. High-speed turnaround from the dictionary is necessary so that program testing is not slowed down. Appropriate management of the programmers and project staff is needed in conjunction with the introduction of the dictionary, and a high-enough level of DP commitment to dictionary operation is vital for this.

SECURITY

A particularly important feature of a data dictionary is that it should preserve a high level of security over its contents. It would clearly be harmful if unauthorized persons could alter any of the data descriptions or other entries. A person disagreeing with a data description might be tempted to do that.

Control of unauthorized reading or printing of the contents is also necessary. If a person were planning to subvert or manipulate a computer system, a natural starting point would be the data dictionary. A wide variety of security techniques are available on modern computer systems. They need to be applied thoroughly to the data dictionary. Some dictionaries have tight security and some do not.

SUMMARY

The use of a data dictionary is essential for good management of a data-base environment. It can greatly benefit an enterprise, *but only if it is done well* (see Box 8.2).

The installation of a dictionary should be regarded as a project in its own right. Eventually, all the shared data in an enterprise should be represented in a dictionary. Deciding the span of usage of one dictionary should be part of the top-down strategic planning of the corporate information resources.

Information engineering is so important to corporate management that it should transcend the DP operations. There is thus a strong argument for dictionary maintenance being a corporate function controlled externally to the DP department.

BOX 8.2   Benefits of using a data dictionary system

● **Achieving Commonality of Data Representation**

The dictionary is the basis for ensuring that the same data items are represented in the same way in different programs.

● **Achieving Agreement About Data Definitions**

The dictionary is the basis for documenting and achieving agreement about the definition of data items.

● **Trustworthy Documentation**

The dictionary is a common source for data about programs, jobs, modules, data bases, records (tuples, segments), and data items. It provides a body of information about data which can be trusted by all users.

● **Automatic Generation of Programmers' Data Descriptions**

The programmer's description of data, for example, the Data Division of COBOL, can be generated from a (good) data dictionary.

● **Reduction of System Development Costs and Lead Time**

Because centrally maintained data definitions are available, systems analysts and programmers do not have to spend time designing or arguing about these data. Programmers do not have to write data definitions. Often more than a third of the lines of code in a COBOL program are Data Division lines, and these usually take as long to write as the main program. Duplication of effort is reduced. This benefit alone will usually pay for the data dictionary software.

● **Enforcement of Data Standards**

When programmers' data descriptions are generated from the dictionary, this enforces correctness. It saves debugging problems and gives better-quality results.

● **Avoidance of Redundancy**

Data redundancies often occur because a systems analyst creates a data item without realizing that it already exists elsewhere. Such redundancies waste space and create update and integrity problems because of a potential lack of consistency. They also waste the analyst's time. Use of a dictionary reduces the chances of unintentional redundancy.

● **Detection of Old Redundancies**

In most installations many old data redundancies exist. A data dictionary can help to detect these, and document them. Some may be re-

BOX 8.2 *(Continued)*

moved as the data-base systems evolve. Some dictionaries access the data descriptions of existing programs as input, and create sorted lists of the data items to assist in detecting redundancies.

- **Better Control of Changes**

    The impact of a proposed change can be seen without reliance on individual memory or the scanning of paper documentation. The dictionary displays all affected programs, records, and transactions. Without a dictionary there are often failures to anticipate the impact of changes. These failures cause expensive reprogramming and severely affect projected costs and schedules.

- **Reduction in Data Analysis Effort**

    Some installations report a reduction in data analysis effort due to the availability of central data definitions.

- **Identification of Synonyms**

    All names used for a data item are documented together.

- **Identification of Homonyms**

    Use of the dictionary indicates when two different data items accidentally have the same name.

- **Documentation of End-Users' Business Names**

    User departments give many data items their own special names. These may be overlapping or confusing. The dictionary can document them.

- **Aid to Communication**

    Different people often have different ideas about the meaning of data items. The dictionary acts as a focal point for discussing these and standardizing meaning. It helps overcome semantic misunderstandings among programmers, analysts, data administrators, and different classes of end users.

- **Aid to Parallel Project Development**

    Multiple projects using the same data can proceed simultaneously with confidence that they are using the latest version.

- **Reduction of Administrative Effort**

    The task of administering the documentation for many hundreds of

(Continued)

BOX 8.2 *(Continued)*

changing data items, records, and programs is of such magnitude that it is difficult to carry out, and is often not done adequately. A dictionary lowers the administrative costs.

- **Assistance in the Design of Distributed Data**

    Documentation of which data items are in which distributed machines, and whether they are replicated data or another form of distributed data.

- **Aid to Auditors**

    It can help external auditors, internal auditors, system reviewers, and others to gain an understanding of the systems to be audited. It provides data standards against which the audits are to be performed. Without a dictionary it is very difficult for outsiders to understand quickly the data base and its uses.

- **Aid to Security and Control**

    The dictionary can indicate who is authorized to make changes to data or who "owns" data. This can aid in controlling the use of data.

- **Aid to Performance Measurement and Tuning**

    The dictionary may gather statistics of the accesses to data of different types.

- **Aid to the Use of High-Level Data-Base Languages**

    High-level data-base languages, the most promising key to DP productivity, link, in some cases, directly to data dictionaries. The information in the dictionary enables substantial results to be achieved quickly. This *integrated* data dictionary may generate forms, displays, column headings, and so on.

- **Aid to End Users**

    A dictionary can clarify for the end user what types of data he can display, the meaning of data fields, and possibly the types of reports he can see. It may equate end-user names for the data with the internal data-base names. It may equate several such *aliases* for certain data items. An *integrated* data dictionary is needed which links to the end-user language.

REFERENCES

1. Edgar H. Sibley, Foreword to Henry C. Lefkovits, *Data Dictionary Systems,* Q.E.D. Information Sciences Inc., Wellesley, MA 02181.

2. Manuals and information on Datamanager are available from MSP, 71 Gloucester Place, London, W1H 3PF.

3. Manuals and information on all Cullinane's products are available from Cullinane Database Systems Inc., 400 Blue Hill Drive, Westwood, MA 02090.

9 HIGH-LEVEL DATA-BASE LANGUAGES

Particularly important in the choice of a data-base management system is the software that uses it for application creation. This software is sometimes a major reason for moving to a data-base environment. It can greatly speed up the development of applications, and ease their maintenance. Sometimes a data management system is introduced as a by-product of employing the language. A nonprocedural language may be selected and the data management system comes with it.

A major reason why the data base's languages and application generators can be relatively simple is that the data are predefined in a data dictionary linked to the computer or interpreter.

SEVEN TYPES OF SOFTWARE   High-level data-base languages fall into seven categories:

1. Simple-Query Facilities

These have existed since the earliest disc storage devices. They enable stored records to be printed or displayed in a suitable format.

2. Complex-Query Languages

These are data-base user languages which permit the formulation of queries that may relate to multiple records. The queries sometimes invoke complex data-base searching or the *joining* of multiple records: for example, "List all U.S. ships within 500 miles of the Straits of Hormuz carrying crew-members with experience in desert combat." Because of the searching and joining, only certain data-base systems are appropriate for on-line use of such languages.

Many data-base user languages now exist. They differ greatly in their syntax and structure. Some are marketed by vendors of their host data-base management systems; others are marketed by independent software houses.

Many query languages permit users to enter and *update* data as well as query. With some, users can create their own files.

3. Report Generators

These are facilities for extracting data from a data base and formatting it into reports. Good report generators allow substantial arithmetic or logic to be performed on the data before they are displayed or printed.

Some report generators are independent of data-base or query facilities. Others are an extension of data-base query languages. Ideally, an end user should be able to start by learning to make simple data-base queries and should steadily extend his skill to data manipulation and report formatting. The report generator should be an extension of the query language; many are not.

4. Graphics Languages

Graphics terminals are dropping in cost and give a particularly attractive way for certain types of end users to display and manipulate data. Software for interactive graphics is steadily improving. It can enable users to ask for data and specify how they want the data to be charted. They can search data bases and chart information according to different criteria. Like report generators, some graphics packages allow considerable arithmetical and logical manipulation of the data.

5. Application Generators

These contain modules that permit an entire application to be generated. The input can be specified, its validation, what action it causes to happen, details of that action, what arithmetic and logic is performed, and what output is created. Most application generators operate with data bases.

Some applications can be generated only partially. They require certain operations that the application generator cannot create. It is still useful to employ the generator provided that it has an *escape* mechanism which permits inclusion of routines written in a program language.

Some application generators are designed to create heavy-duty applications in which efficient coding and data accesses are needed because of the high transaction volumes.

6. Very-High-Level Programming Languages

A new crop of programming languages have come into existence which enable programs to be written with an order-of-magnitude fewer lines of code than COBOL, FORTRAN, or PL/1, and permit much faster application development. Some of these are data-base languages designed to operate with particular data-base management systems. Software A.G.'s NATURAL, for example, works with the ADABAS data-base management system. CIN-COM'S MANTIS works with TOTAL and DL/1. Some of the new languages employ a data management system especially created for them. This is the case with NCSS's NOMAD, for example.

With high-level languages such as NOMAD the user does not have to specify every detail of procedures that are used. He can say LIST, TITLE, INSERT, AVERAGE, SORT, SUM, and so on. He need not describe in code the format of a report or screen. The interpreter selects a reasonable format and the user can adjust it if he wishes.

Cost studies have indicated that the cost per line of code is typically $10 in the United States (although it varies from $5 to over $300) and that this cost is largely independent of the language. A COBOL program often has 20 to 40 times as many lines of code as the same application written in a very-high-level language.

7. Parameterized Application Packages

Packages can be purchased for running certain applications. These pre-programmed packages are increasing in number, diversity, and quality. They often require a considerable amount of tailoring to fit the organization which installs them and are designed with parameters that can be chosen to modify their operation. This parametorization is the key to success in many cases. As the marketplace for packages grows, they tend to be built with a richer set of parameters so that they have wider applicability.

Some application packages are written to operate with a data-base management system: for example, IBM's comprehensive production control system, COPICS. Figure 8.7 shows a typical set of data-base languages linked to a data-base management system.

SUITABLE FOR END USERS? There are many types of software in the categories listed above. Most vendors of such software claim that it is "designed for end users." In many cases this claim is questionable because the software requires more skill and training than most users will acquire. In many cases the software should be used by systems analysts who work with the end users.

Some of the software is excellent for end users. Some of the best data-base query and update facilities can be employed by users who have never touched a terminal before: for example, VIDEOTEX sets, IBM's QUERY-BY-EXAMPLE, and Cullinane's ON-LINE ENGLISH.

We might classify something as "suitable for end users" if typical end users can learn how to use it and obtain valuable results in a two-day training course and they don't forget how to use it if they leave it for several weeks. (The *would* forget codes and mnemonics.) End users could not adapt fully to

	Suitable for End Users	Suitable for DP Professionals
Simple-Query Facilities		
Complex-Query Languages		
Report Generators		
Graphics Languages		
Application Generators		
Very High-Level Programming Languages		
Parameterized Application Packages		

Figure 9.1 Categorization of facilities for application creation without conventional programming.

IBM's application generators DMS or ADF (discussed in this chapter), for example, in a two-day course. With these criteria we can categorize the software for data-base application development with the matrix in Fig. 9.1.

The reader might like to fill in Fig. 9.1 with software with which he is familiar. There is scope for argument about which compartment in Fig. 9.1 certain facilities fit into. Many fit into more than one. For example, a good data-base language might be *both* a complex query language *and* a report generator. A language might be categorized as suitable for end users *and* suitable for DP professionals, because the users can learn (in two days) to use *some* of its facilities, but not all.

A desirable property of a language is that it should be *easy to start to use it,* but that the user can continue to learn more about it and improve his skills for a long time. Languages with this property should be taught in subsets. If a language has a beginner's subset which can be well learned in *one* day, many users will cross the threshold from being mystified outsiders to being initiate members of the club.

Facilities for end users are discussed in Part III.

ESCAPE FEATURE   Application generators are not capable of generating *all* applications. Sometimes they lack the capability to generate particular logic or algorithms which are needed. Too often a generator is rejected for this reason. An important feature of a generator is the capability to associate with it modules of logic written in programming languages. This is sometimes called an *escape* feature. Where possible, it is desirable that the user of the generator can also use the language to which the escape is made.

In some cases a programmer is required to handle the escape language but if the programmer is part of the DP department doing conventional coding, the problems with programming backlog affect the use of the generator.

Ideally, then, the products in Fig. 9.1 should be integrated as much as possible. The query language should support the creation of reports and graphics, and be the basis of an application generator. A high-level programming language should be available both for use in its own right and for *escape* from the application generator. Most products in existence today do not yet have this degree of integration. Computer manufacturers and software houses have often created separate languages for data-base query, report generation, graphics, application generation, and high-level programming.

At present, several query languages and report generators are suitable for end users, but many application generators are not. Application generators *can* be designed for end users and some good ones exist.

There is *much* software of these types on the market.

ON-LINE OR OFF-LINE?	A further categorization of the software in Fig. 9.1 can indicate whether it is on-line or off-line. Some query languages, report generators, and application

generators operate interactively at a terminal; some operate off-line, with the users or systems analysts filling in forms or coding sheets.

The use of forms gives the user time to think about what he needs. In some cases he may fill in the forms at home or away from his office.

Nevertheless, on-line operation can be much more satisfactory if it is well designed psychologically. It can lead the user to do what is required a step at a time. It can check the user's input as he creates it. It can make tutorial explanations available on-line and can assist if the user presses a HELP key. On-line operation can generally be made much more versatile than off-line operation. When the product types in Fig. 9.1 are integrated, on-line operation can make a wide range of features available to the user.

FOURTH-GENERATION LANGUAGES	The high-level languages are sometimes called *fourth-generation languages*. There have been four generations of computer languages:

First generation:	Machine language; no assemblers, compilers, or interpreters
Second generation:	Assembler language

Third generation: COBOL, FORTRAN, PL/1, BASIC, etc.

Fourth generation: Languages that automate many of the basic functions which had to be spelled out in third-generation languages, and which can obtain results with an order-of-magnitude less coding than COBOL

Fourth-generation languages were created for two main reasons: (1) so that nonprogrammers could obtain results from computers, and (2) to speed up greatly the programming process. Some fourth-generation languages are nonprocedural. Some are procedural but results can be obtained with an order-of-magnitude fewer lines of code than with COBOL or PL/1. Many contain both procedural and nonprocedural statements. A proliferation of such languages has emerged, differing widely in their syntax and capability. There are no standards yet. New language ideas are emerging too rapidly. Most fourth-generation languages link into a data-base system. Some allow users to create their own personal data base. Some create and employ relational data bases because these provide more powerful and flexible user commands than do traditional data bases. Some fourth-generation languages are very user-friendly and users become competent at obtaining useful results after a two-day training course.

With most fourth-generation languages a user does not have to specify how to do everything. Instead, the compiler or interpreter makes intelligent assumptions about what it thinks the user needs. For example, it may automatically select a useful format for a report, put page numbers on it, select chart types for graphics display, put labels on the axes or on column headings, and ask the user in a friendly, understandable fashion when it needs more information. Where a language makes intelligent default assumptions, these assumptions are likely to become steadily more intelligent as the language evolves and improves. An assumption behind such languages is that a relatively large amount of computer power can be used for compiling or interpreting.

Now that we have the term *fourth-generation language,* it is likely that every new language will be called "fourth generation" by its advertising copywriter. Some new languages, however, have the characteristics of third-generation languages. For language to be worth calling "fourth generation," it should have the following characteristics:

1. It is user-friendly.

2. A nonprofessional programmer can obtain results with it.

3. It employs a data-base management system directly.

4. Procedural code requires an order-of-magnitude fewer instructions than COBOL.

5. Nonprocedural code is used where possible.

6. It makes intelligent default assumptions about what the user wants, where possible.

7. It is designed for on-line operation.

8. It endorses or encourages structured code.

9. It is easy to understand and maintain another person's code.

10. Non-DP users can learn a subset of the language in a two-day training course.

11. It is designed for easy debugging.

12. Results can be obtained in a tenth of the time required with COBOL or PL/1.

Many new languages have these properties, but many also have the characteristic that they cannot create all types of applications. They are not general-purpose. That is a price which we may have to pay for the great productivity improvements that fourth-generation languages bring. In this case we have to *select the language to fit the application*. This is repugnant to some programmers and purists. But it is a vitally important fact that languages of limited scope are enabling users to obtain the results they need *fast,* whereas the traditional programming process in COBOL or PL/1 was not.

Fourth-generation languages need data bases, and often make it easy for end users to create their own data bases. If this happens in an uncontrolled fashion, it will be a formula for chaos in data. As the powerful new languages come into widespread use it is essential to link them into the overall data administration control.

FOURTH-GENERATION LANGUAGE ENTHUSIAST:

The end users have gone crazy with LINK. You should just see them. They get results so fast. It's like a nine-year-old child with a machine gun.

NONPROCEDURAL LANGUAGES
Fourth-generation languages can be categorized as *procedural* or *nonprocedural.* Some combine procedural and nonprocedural facilities.

Some of these languages are referred to as *nonprocedural languages.* "Procedural" and "nonprocedural" is a useful and much used language distinction. A procedural language specifies *how* something is accomplished. A nonprocedural language specifies *what* is accomplished but not in detail *how.* Thus languages such as COBOL and PL/1 are procedural. Their programmers give precisely detailed instructions for how each action is accomplished. An application generator whose users fill in forms to tell it what to do is nonprocedural. The user merely says *what* is to be done and is not concerned with the detailed procedure for *how* it is done.

Most query languages, report generators, graphics packages, and application generators are nonprocedural. However, some high-level programming languages are now acquiring nonprocedural capabilities. NOMAD, for example, is a high-level language with which some end users obtain fast results from a computer. Most professionals would call it a programming language because it has IF statements and DO loops. However, results can be obtained with brief nonprocedural statements such as

LIST BY CUSTOMER AVERAGE (INVOICE TOTAL).

This is a complete "program." It leaves the software to decide how the list should be formatted, when to skip pages, when to number pages, how to sort into CUSTOMER sequence, and how to compute an average.

The compiler or interpreter of nonprocedural languages thus makes intelligent assumptions about what it thinks the user wants. If the assumption is not correct, the user can adjust the results. The use of nonprocedural languages sometimes progresses by stepwise refinement of the results. The intelligent assumptions that the software makes will, no doubt, become more intelligent as the software is further improved.

APPLICATION GENERATORS

Data-base applications consist of a succession of events that create, retrieve, update, or delete data-base records. The records are often designed and associated independently of any one application (using techniques which we discuss later). A data entry dialogue is needed for creating and updating the data. Reporting or output printing routines are needed. Validity and accuracy checks are needed. Appropriate action must be taken when any machine failures occur. Apart from those operations the logic of the application is often fairly simple and easy to create.

Data-base application generators may provide software for data entry, software for creating output, software accuracy and validity checks, restart and recovery after failures, and a simple means of creating the application logic.

Application generators differ widely in how well human-factored they are. We will illustrate this by contrasting IBM's two main generators, DMS (Development Management System [1]) and ADF (Application Development Facility [2]). Good human factoring is important because it encourages use of the generator by the analysts who work with the end user and understand their applications, rather than by programmers.

The increase in productivity, or in application development speed, that has been achieved with application generators is spectacular. They clearly have a vitally important role in the future of data processing and will greatly change the system analysis process. Some DP professionals are remarkably reluctant to recognize this. It took the DP profession 10 years to swing from assembly languages as the main form of programming to widespread use of COBOL and PL/1. It is dismal to reflect that it might take 10 years to swing from COBOL and PL/1 to application generators and other high-level facilities. The slowness of the swing and the reluctance to recognize what is happening will do great damage in many corporations.

HEAD OFFICE DP EXECUTIVE OF A LARGE MULTINATIONAL CORPORATION:

Reluctance to move to the new techniques is a major problem in many of our installations around the world. The only solution we can see is to enforce early retirement of the DP managers.

DESIRABLE PROPERTIES OF HIGH-LEVEL DATA-BASE LANGUAGES

Box 9.1 lists desirable properties of fourth-generation languages and software from obtaining results from data-base systems.

The remainder of this chapter discusses two application generators from IBM.

BOX 9.1 Desirable properties of fourth-generation languages

- How rich are its functions?
  - Simple query
  - Complex query
  - Report generator
  - Graphics generator
  - Application generator
  - High-level programming
- Are there intelligent default assumptions if details are unspecified?
- Is it easy to design and change screen formats?
- Can it also be used as a development language?
- Can it generate?
  - compares?
  - logic operations?
  - Boolean algebra?
  - conditional clauses?
  - loops?
  - subroutines?
- Is it on-line or off-line?
- Is it suitable for end users, systems analysts, or programmers?
- Is the language syntax good for maintenance? (With some it is easy to understand another person's code; with others it is difficult.)

(Continued)

BOX 9.1 *(Continued)*

- Does it use a standard DBMS, its own simple DBMS, or files?
- Is it DBMS-independent?
- Is file design automatically provided for?
- What support facilities does it have?
  DBMS
  Concurrency controls
  Security
  Logging and audit tools
  Recovery and restart
  Dynamic data base
    modification
  Data dictionary
  Procedure library
  Terminal driver
- Is multithread operation supported?
- Dialogue ease of use. Is is easy to learn? Is it easy to remember?
- Does it force the operator to remember mnemonics, formats, or fixed sequences?
- Is it self-teaching, with computer-aided instruction or effective responses to HELP requests on all its functions?
- Is it easy to install? Can it be installed without systems programmers or does it require complex systems programming?
- Is it operating system independent?
- Is it terminal independent?
- Does it have its own terminal driver?
- How good is the quality, appearance, and richness of the reports, displays, or graphics?
- Can it store catalogued procedures? Can these be parameterized?
- Does it use color?
- Can it operate at different levels of verboseness in its dialogue?
- Does it have simple obvious-to-use sign-on procedure?
- Does it have good, clear documentation?
- Is is easy to debug? Does it have good testing tools?
- Does it give clear self-explanatory error messages?
- Can new data be added dynamically (while other users are employing its data base)?

BOX 9.1 *(Continued)*

- Can the data-base structure be changed dynamically (while other users are employing its data base)?

- Can new secondary indices (or other search mechanisms) be added for any field? At any time?

- Can data be automatically extracted from an existing data base or file system and rebuilt for this system?

- Can data be moved from this system to a separate file or data-base system?

- Does the organization selling it give good service and support?

- Does it employ a dictionary?　　　Active or passive dictionary?
　　　　　　　　　　　　　　　　　Is it linked to a major DBMS
　　　　　　　　　　　　　　　　　　　dictionary?
　　　　　　　　　　　　　　　　　Can it use aliases?
　　　　　　　　　　　　　　　　　Does it store or generate
　　　　　　　　　　　　　　　　　　　column heading or report
　　　　　　　　　　　　　　　　　　　and chart labels?

- Can it generate good security and privacy locks?

- Can it generate good auditing features? Automatic audit trails
　　　　　　　　　　　　　　　　　　Accuracy controls
　　　　　　　　　　　　　　　　　　Logs of usage

- Can it be used for accurate data entry operations?

- Does it have good protection from system crashes?

IBM'S DMS

IBM's DMS, Development Management System, is a tool for generating interactive applications using DL/1 data bases. Often complete applications are generated with it; sometimes it is used in conjunction with routines programmed in COBOL, PL/1, Assembler Language, or RPG II (Report Program Generator II).

It is not usually employed by end users. It forms a valuable tool for the systems analyst and can entirely change the systems analysis process when it is employed efficiently. Often, the systems analyst creates a complete application. Sometimes he creates a demonstration or *prototype* which needs to be tuned by a DMS expert or to have programmed routines written to supplement it. In either case the systems analyst works with the end users, shows them his results, and refines the results repeatedly until the users are happy with them and use them efficiently.

The systems analyst should be expected to learn DMS very thoroughly

and become slick in using it. He should be able to create screens and dialogues very quickly. It is very easy to make adjustments to an application
which do not involve non-DMS programs. This enables a systems analyst to
keep the users happy, making changes for them when this can improve the
way they use the system. In some corporations the analysts make such
changes in one hour. This is very different from an environment in which all
changes are resisted, and where those which *are* made, wait in a queue for
programmers for months.

DMS uses a "fill in the blanks" technique that makes it possible for on-
line applications to be developed with little or no programming. Preprogrammed facilities are selected for functions such as data entry, inquiry,
update, dialogue processing, and message switching.

The application creator describes data files, display screens called
"panels," and the application processing, either *interactively* through a
terminal or *off-line* through the use of a series of forms. With the interactive
facility, the user is prompted through each stage of the application definition. Specifications are validated to reduce errors. A HELP facility is provided which gives additional information and explains data to be entered.

DMS provides the ability to perform calculations and editing of data.

DMS FUNCTIONS   Figure 9.2 lists the main functions of DMS.
                         The standard data-base functions such as in-
quiry and update are provided. A data routine function provides the capability for directing messages or displays to another terminal in the network
or to a printer. Program control allows the user to call another program or
return to another program.

Data fields may be edited for validity using such techniques as table

- Data-Base Operations
  - Inquiry
  - Update
  - Amend/Insert
  - Deletion
  - Search/Browse
- Data Routing
- Program-to-Program Control
- User Processing
- Data Validation
- Calculation Functions
- Application Generation Through Forms
- Restart/Recovery
- Audit Control
- Security and Integrity

Figure 9.2   Functions of DMS.

lookup, comparing one value with a field, and so on. The user has the capability to select editing where it is needed and also to alter the sequence of processing as a result of any errors that are encountered.

The calculation functions provided with DMS enable the user to perform arithmetic and simple logic operations.

The systems analyst can build an end-user dialogue employing multiple screen panels which are logically linked. He can capture data from a set of logically linked panels and construct from this logical file records or a data-base path involving up to four files or data bases. The updating or creation of the data records occurs after the last panel of the set is processed.

Users who are in distributed locations may generate and test applications at a central point.

Restart and recovery functions are provided which allow the user to save data and instructions previously entered, in the event of a system failure.

Audit procedures are available in DMS. A log is kept, in some detail, of all terminal errors; this allows auditors to check for inconsistencies.

Security is provided at various levels, such as password protection at the terminal level. Integrity controls are provided which allow the user to verify the contents of records. Search requests can be accommodated which produce listings of keys or records.

In general, systems produced with DMS:

- Are easier to design
- Avoid most of the need for programming
- Are easier to test
- Are self-documenting
- Are much easier to maintain

In some cases DMS is used to *convert* existing batch applications to an on-line environment. The existing files or data bases of the batch system can be used for this.

The cost of recreating an existing application in DMS is often less than the cost of maintaining that application for a year. Once it exists in DMS form, it is relatively cheap to maintain. DMS and other such application generators therefore offer a way out of the maintenance trap which is such a burden in many installations.

USE OF DMS   With DMS the systems analyst can specify the screens that will be used in an interactive dialogue, how the user may respond in the dialogue, and how the responses are processed.

Suppose that he designs an opening menu such as that shown below. From this the user can select one of the four applications shown.

```
                                                              MENU

                        **** MENU ****

        1   CREDIT MANAGEMENT

        2   ORDER ENTRY

        3   PURCHASING

        4   INVENTORY CONTROL


           *** KEY A 1 2 3 OR 4 TO SELECT APPLICATION. ***
           PRESS THE ENTER KEY.
```

PANEL DESCRIPTION FORM   To create this panel the systems analyst fills in the Panel Description Form shown below. He fills in a similar form for each panel he wishes to create.

The screen layout he enters contains all the fixed data, such as headings, titles, and so on, exactly as they will appear on the screen, as shown on p. 153.

The analyst may now define the first panel displayed if the end user selects the *credit management* application. This panel is shown below.

The end user may key "1" and fill in the CUSTOMER NO. if he wishes to inquire as to credit status. The results are displayed in the upper half of the panel. He may change any of these data by keying "2" and entering the new data. See the panel on p. 154.

SUPERVISORY COMMANDS   The systems analyst must specify how the end user may respond to a panel and specify the processing that will occur for each response. He specifies this in the Response Specification Cards portion of the Panel Description Form. The four possible responses, 1, 2, 3, and 4, are entered in the form shown at the bottom of p. 154.

The code after each response is called a *Supervisor Function Code.*

DMS/CICS/VS Panel Description Form

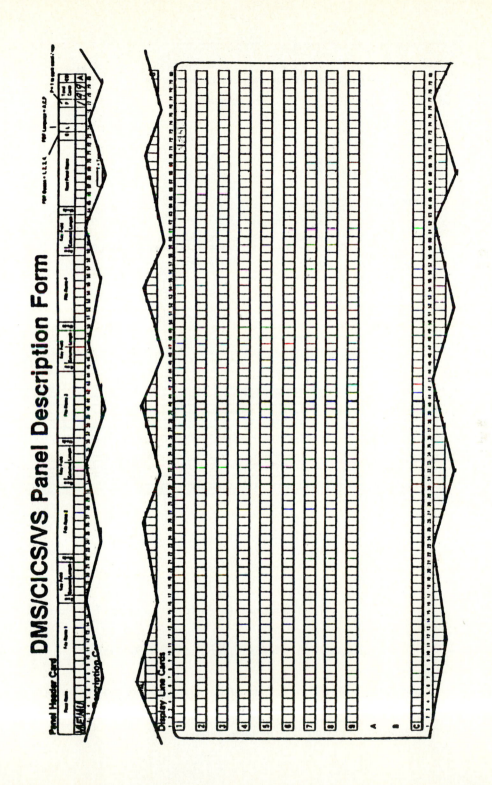

153

```
                  *** CREDIT MANAGEMENT SYSTEM ***               PANELA

     CHANGE                              CURRENT

                    NAME:
                    ADDRESS:
                    CITY:
                    STATE:
                    ZIP CODE:
                    CR STATUS:


          *** ENTER CUSTOMER NO.:

             KEY  1  TO INQUIRE CREDIT STATUS.

             KEY  2  TO CHANGE A CUSTOMER RECORD.
                     ENTER DATA UNDER "CHANGE" ON LINE TO BE UPDATED.

             KEY  3  TO CLEAR AND RE-ENTER DATA.

             KEY  4  TO RETURN TO MENU.
```

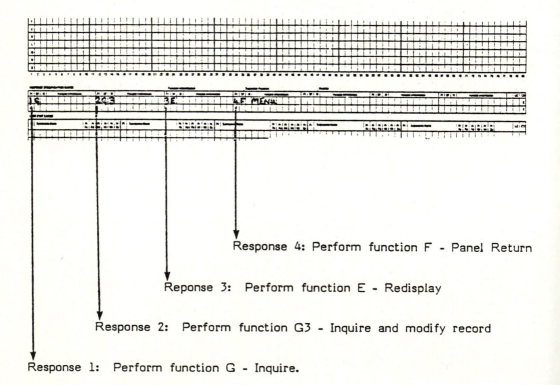

Response 4: Perform function F - Panel Return

Reponse 3: Perform function E - Redisplay

Response 2: Perform function G3 - Inquire and modify record

Response 1: Perform function G - Inquire.

There are five classes of these codes: *display control, file and data-base operations, data routing, program control,* and *system services.* Each code is one character, and it may be followed by a modifier character.

The Supervisor Function Codes are shown in Fig. 9.3.

After the Supervisor Function Codes on the Response Specification Card the systems analyst could enter variable information, such as the name of a panel, the number of panels skipped in a PAGE FORWARD or PAGE BACKWARD (codes C and D), a record or data-base identifier, and so on.

The *display control* functions enable the systems analyst to specify routes through the panels he designs. He can thus build a dialogue.

The *panel overlay* function produces a named display at the terminal without retaining any information from the preceding display. The *panel link* function similarly produces a named display but saves the calling panel so that it can be brought back together with any variable information that may have been entered. The *redisplay* function redisplays the current panel—

SUPERVISOR COMMANDS:

Class of Function	Function Code	Function Name
Display control	A	Panel overlay
	B	Panel link
	C	Page forward
	D	Page backward
	E	Redisplay
	F	Panel return
File and data-base operation	G	Inquiry/inquiry for update
	H	Record add
	I	Update/delete
	J	Search DMS/CICS/VS indexed files
	K	Set sequential/end sequential
	L	Cursor key select
	M	Selector-pen key select
	N	Copy
	P	End inquiry level
Data routing	Q	Data route
	R	Send/get message
	S	Send/get image
Program control	T	Call user program
	U	Return to calling program
	V	Reset/delete communication fields
	W	End transaction
System services	X	Load PF key or edit mask table
	Z	Set time, date, operator ID
	>	User supervisor function

Figure 9.3 DMS commands are of two types: *supervisor commands* and *arithmetic and logic commands,* shown in Fig. 9.4.

but in its original form, without any data that the operator may have entered. The *panel return* function redisplays the starting panel of the dialogue or a named panel, and deletes all panels saved since the start of the dialogue.

The *data base* functions permit data retrievals, adds, deletes, updates, and searches. Sequential or random-access operations may be carried out. Single-key and multiple-key retrieval can be specified. Copies of data can be made. DMS/CICS files may be used, or DL/1 data bases.

The *data routing* functions provide the capability to send panel images from one terminal to another. Panels can be printed. Messages can be queued and stored as in a message switching system. Either complete panels may be transmitted or data extracted from panels.

The *program control* functions allow the systems analyst to invoke programs. With the *call user program* function a user response to a panel may call a specified program. Information from the panel will be passed to the program as specified. Sometimes a panel operation is called by a program. The *return to calling program* function extracts required information from the panel and returns control to the program.

The *system services* functions permit such operations as the use of function keys on the terminal devices, setting the time and date, and allowing users to define and code their own supervisor functions.

CALCULATION AND LOGIC COMMANDS

DMS uses two types of commands: the *supervisory commands,* shown in Fig. 9.3, and *calculation and logic commands.*

Figure 9.4 lists the calculation and logic commands. With these commands, calculation can be specified and the sequence of application flow can be altered according to conditions: for example, if a counter reaches zero or if the result of subtraction goes negative.

DMS FORMS

Some entire applications that use a previously existing data base are created merely with a set of Panel Description Forms. Many applications, however, require two other forms.

DMS provides three forms for application creators to fill in (Fig. 9.5). These are:

- The Panel Description Form
- The File Description Form
- The Data Transfer Form

Command Name	DMS Symbol/Code
Add	+
Subtract	−
Multiply	*
Divide	/
Move remainder	MVR
Move right	MOVER
Move left	MOVEL
Compare	COMP
Test display field	TEST
Set a field attribute	SET
Search a table	FIND
End of processing	EXIT
Operation complete	OPCOMP
Terminate a browse	TRMBR
Execute a new function	NEWFI
Terminate a transaction	TERM
Terminate with a dump	TERMD
Write an error message	WMSG
Redisplay	RDISP
Write no erase	WNOER
Call user subroutine	CALL
De-edit	DEDIT

Figure 9.4 DMS calculation and logic commands.

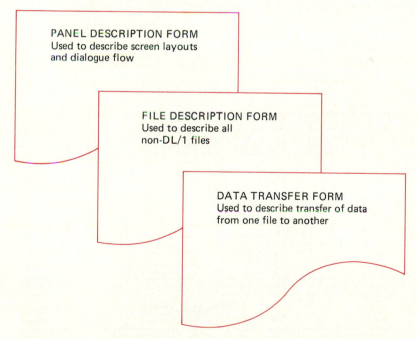

PANEL DESCRIPTION FORM
Used to describe screen layouts
and dialogue flow

FILE DESCRIPTION FORM
Used to describe all
non-DL/1 files

DATA TRANSFER FORM
Used to describe transfer of data
from one file to another

Figure 9.5 Applications are created with DMS by filling in these three forms. Many applications can be created with only the Panel Description Form if the data base they use already exists. Figure 9.6 shows the Panel Description Form.

DMS/VS
DMS/CICS/VS Panel Description Form

1 **Panel Header Card**

Panel Name | File Name 1 | Key Field (Row, Column, Length) | File Name 2 | Key Field | File Name 3 | Key Field | File Name 4 | Key Field | Next Panel Name | O | L | C/E | Total Cards | CD A

2 **DL/I Description Card**

PSB Name | DBD1 Name | PCB No | DBD2 Name | PCB No | DBD3 Name | PCB No | DBD4 Name | PCB No | Optional PSB Name | CD 2 | CD A

3 **Display Description Card**

PF Key Equivalents 1 2 3 4 5 6 7 8 9 10 11 12 | CD | Display Line Cards | CD B

Display Description Card

PF Key Equivalents 13 14 15 16 17 18 19 20 21 22 23 24 | CD 2 | CD B

4 **Display Line Cards**

1 2 3 4 5 6 7 8 9 A B C D E F G H I J K L M N O P Q R S T U V W X Y Z . (+) ; / , ?

5 **Response Specification Cards**

Variable Information | LC | CD C

6 **User Exit Cards**

Subroutine Name | LC | CD D

7 **Data Definition Cards**

Segment Name | Command Codes | Pre Segment Read User Exit Name | Post Segment Read User Exit Name | Pre Segment Write User Exit Name | Qualification Statement 1 3 5 & 7 | Qualification Statement 2 4 6 & 8 | Reserved | LC | CD

DATA FIELD: Data Field Name | Row | Column | Length | FO | V | A | R | CD E

* No. of forms per pad may vary.

1. The panel leader card contains the panel name, the file names associated with the panel, and the next panel name. The reset panel name is useful when a sequence of panels is required, for example, in a menu.

2. The DL/1 description card specifies the data bases to be accessed. With this entry the user can also specify that the panel is still in test mode, if required. Dumps can be provided; trace tables are used to assist in debugging.

3. The display description card indicates specific characteristics of the panel and the features of the IBM 3270 terminal that is required, for example, the model for which the panel is intended, and the cursor position when the panel is displayed.

4. The display line cards define the static data, such as headings, titles, and narrative that is required for the screen. It is intended to be an exact image of the screen that is required.

5. The response specification cards define the processing to be undertaken from the operator's response, for example, return to main menu, display another panel, call a user program, and so on. DMS commands are shown in Figs. 9.3 and 9.4.

6. User exit cards define program exits.

7. The data definition cards define the display fields and identify the file and communication. Data can also be entered by the operator for updating files or transmission to other terminals.

Figure 9.6   Panel Description Form.

FILE DESCRIPTION FORM

The File Description Form describes DMS files. It is not used if the application employs a DL/1 data base rather than files.

Information is entered into the header card describing the file name, its organization (key sequenced VSAM, ISAM, etc.), record size, blocking factor, and the key field.

Subsequent cards define all fields in order of sequence.

If a file is used in multiple applications, it need be described only once to DMS.

DATA TRANSFER FORM

The Data Transfer Form is used to record additions and deletions and field-by-field transfers of data from one file to another.

This form enables the systems analyst to use data from files in *existing* applications. A utility is provided to aid in converting the files of off-line applications to DMS files.

GENERATOR HUMAN FACTORING

If an application generator such as DMS is well human-factored, it is reasonable to expect systems analysts to learn it and use it. Programmers need be involved only to code exit routines for functions that the generator cannot handle. It is highly desirable that such a facility be used by the systems analysts because they work directly with end users and can rapidly modify their design as the end users react to their prototype, and as they think of new features they want included.

Some application generators are powerful or versatile in what they can create but are not well human-factored. More training and practice is needed in coding them. Systems analysts do not learn them easily. They tend to become tools for programmers rather than for analysts. If this causes the analyst to become once again a middleman between the programmer and the end user, it removes much of the value of application generation.

Often a hybrid person is used, who is referred to as a programmer-analyst. The job of the analyst, however, ought to be concentrated on the applications and the end users, not on complexities of coding.

There is a marked contrast between DMS and IBM's other major application generator, ADF (Application Development Facility). Whereas DMS is easy to understand and use, ADF requires complex coding rather like JCL (Job Control Language). DMS is commonly used by systems analysts. ADF is suitable mainly for programmers and systems programmers. Programmers *do* find it easy to learn.

ADF has improved application creation productivity very much in some installations. As with DMS, it is not uncommon to find productivity improvements of 1000% over conventional use of COBOL or PL/1. Some corporations quote speeds of application creation 10 to 50 times those of conventional programming, whereas others have had much less successful results. The best results are achieved by highly skilled ADF specialists—ADF "acrobats."

A case quoted by John Deere, Inc., is typical of a person who makes himself highly skilled with ADF. A new employee, inexperienced in programming, achieved *twice* the productivity of the COBOL team on his first application, *32 times* that of the COBOL team on his second application, and *46 times* on the third [3].

Although ADF is clearly a major aid to productivity, of all the software mentioned in this book it is among the worst in terms of human factoring. There is no basic need for such a situation. It is rather like trying to fill in your income tax return with Roman numerals. ADF is a powerful product designed by programmers for programmers. Some organizations have abandoned ADF while others have built up a team with high expertise and achieved impressive results. It has sometimes been abandoned because of its human factoring and sometimes because it is limited in the screen dialogues that it can create, and these may be perceived to not fit the application.

When application generators are difficult to code they are often used by programmers rather than analysts. This is undesirable. It ought to be the analysts who are creating applications and prototypes, and rapidly modifying them as the end users interact with them and make suggestions. Wherever possible, it should be the aim of the computer industry to end the analyst's role as a middleman and requirements-writer.

HOW ADF WORKS   ADF is an application generator which runs under the IMS/VS data-base management system. It provides several skeletal IMS application programs and additional modules of code and data. Applications are created by directing the skeletal programs to execute application functions. This is done by means of *rules* which define aspects of the application.

Code modules perform application functions that are common to many IMS applications. These common modules are combined selectively with the skeletal IMS application programs under the direction of the rules. During the execution of ADF the precoded modules access the rules to customize their behavior.

ADF is summarized in Fig. 9.7.

Figure 9.8 shows the five main groupings of modules available from ADF:

- *Menus* that identify the user department at sign on. *Function selection* using the function keys of the 3270 terminal. *Transaction selection* will identify the types of transactions or data that will be accessed.

- The *key selection* prompts for keys to records or segments for retrieval from the data base.

- Tables of parameters called "rules" specify the IMS applications desired.
- Preprogrammed modules of code can be invoked by the user for such functions as
  - Accessing the data base
  - Screen formatting
  - Data entry validation
- During execution, the modules access sets of rules to customize the result.
- Functions not supported by ADF can be programmed with conventional procedural code, or a combination of code and rules.

Figure 9.7   How ADF works: basic elements.

- The *transaction driver* is a module that controls the flow of logic to process a transaction.
- The *screen formatter* works with IMS to format screens. The call handler allows DL/1 calls to the data base if this facility is chosen. The *auditor* has the logic to analyze the data base and the data being entered. The *message generator* informs the terminal user about conditions during processing.

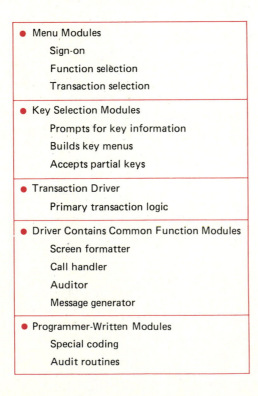

- Menu Modules
    - Sign-on
    - Function selection
    - Transaction selection
- Key Selection Modules
    - Prompts for key information
    - Builds key menus
    - Accepts partial keys
- Transaction Driver
    - Primary transaction logic
- Driver Contains Common Function Modules
    - Screen formatter
    - Call handler
    - Auditor
    - Message generator
- Programmer-Written Modules
    - Special coding
    - Audit routines

Figure 9.8   ADF module functions.

- Finally, the *interface to programmer-written modules* is provided for operations that need special processing, such as complicated calculations or audit routines.

Figure 9.9 specifies what the programmer-analyst is required to define to ADF. The screen formats require analyst definition, what data are to be displayed, and where.

- Format and content of screens
- Structure and content of data base
- Data to encode/decode selected fields
- Information to validate data
- Format of messages and routing information
- Security information

Figure 9.9　The ADF analyst-programmer defines the following functions.

The structure of the data base requires a definition indicating its contents, keys, and segments. The analyst also provides information to ADF to enable it to encode data entered in the data base and decode it when the data are retrieved. For example, a state code can be held in the data base as a two-digit code, but when displayed it can show the full name. Validation criteria are also required when data are entered into the data base. The format of messages is required and, if necessary, routing information to other terminals or departments. Security information is also required from the analyst, to allow ADF to decide who can retrieve, add, update, or delete transactions to the data base.

From these specifications ADF will provide:

- Screens for identification and sign-on of procedure users
- Screens to locate and retrieve data
- Screens that display the data for retrieval, update, and addition or deletion of segments

ADF RULES　　　　These are two type of rules with ADF:

- Static rules
- Dynamic rules

Static rules are created by the ADF rule generator, which processes descriptive statements supplied by the programmer. They control the con-

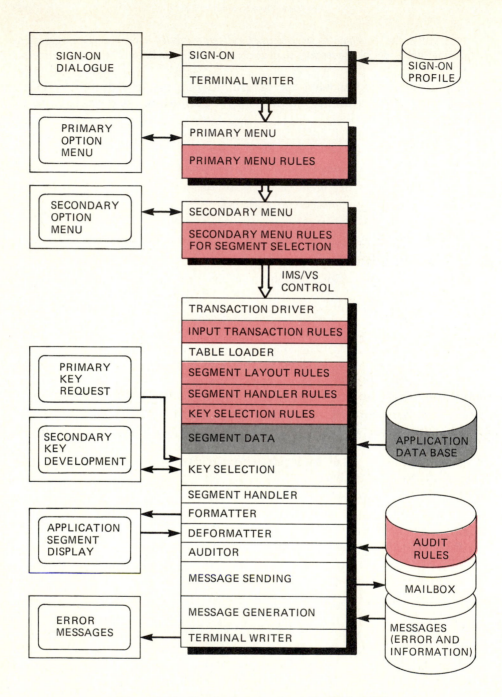

Figure 9.10 Standard processing with IBM's ADF.

tents of terminal screens, which fields are to be displayed, and where they are positioned.

Dynamic rules can be entered to ADF from a terminal using ADF-supplied routines. The Dynamic rules control such functions as sign-on profiles and the coding and encoding of selected fields. They also control the auditing and verification of data entering the system. Dynamic rules are stored in a Dynamic rules data base and are accessed by ADF.

Figure 9.10 illustrates the flow of control during a typical standard ADF transaction.

1. The user enters his identification. IMS/VS dispatches the ADF *Sign-on/Option Menu Controller* to process the opening of the application. This verifies the user's authorization. The *Sign-on Profile* data base contains the authorization profiles.

2. The *Primary Menu* function formats the data for the display of the opening menu. This is displayed on the user terminal. The user selects an application and control is passed to an appropriate module.

3. The *Secondary Menu* function receives control and formats another menu display. This menu is based on the user's authority profile, the processing option selected, and the response to the primary menu. The user's response to the secondary menu determines which *transaction driver* is dispatched to IMS/VS control. Both the primary and secondary menus employ rules specified by the application analyst.

4. The *transaction driver* is composed of a number of modules which are common to all transactions. The driver loads the *input transaction rules* associated with the user's processing requirements. These were, again, specified by the application analyst.

Other functions and associated sets of rules are shown in Fig. 9.10.

CODING SAMPLE

Following on p. 166 is an example of the coding of ADF. It will be seen that it is more difficult than the form filling needed for DMS. Even so, it is less flexible than DMS, with which the user can create any layout for his display panels.

SUMMARY

Data-base application generators are a giant step forward in achieving results from data processing. They are achieving 1000% improvement in productivity over conventional programming in which everything is coded in COBOL or PL/1. Some organizations have achieved higher gains than this. Good generators can be used for most but not all commercial DP applications, sometimes with the help of specially programmed subroutines.

The best generators enable maintenance changes to be made in an hour

```
*******************************************************************************
*     APPLICATION DEFINITION INPUT STATEMENTS FOR PARTS DATA BASE
*******************************************************************************
SYSTEM    SYSID=SAMP,DBID=PA,                        RULE ID CHARS
          SOMTX=OR,                       DEFAULT SECONDARY OPTION CODE
          SIGNON=YES,                     REQUEST FOR SIGNON SCREEN
          POMENU=(A,B,C,D,F,H,I),         REQUEST FOR PRIMARY MENU
          PCBNO=1,                        PCB NUMBER FOR DATA BASE
          SDBNAME='ASSEMBLY PARTS',       DEFAULT DATA BASE NAME
          SHEADING='S A M P L E   P R O B L E M',   GENERAL HEADING
          SFORMAT=DASH,                           SCREEN FORMAT
          PGROUP=ZZ,                              PROJECT GROUP
          ASMLIST=NOLIST                          GENERATE OPTIONS
*******************************************************************************
*     APPLICATION DEFINITION INPUT FOR ROOT SEGMENT
*******************************************************************************
 SEGMENT LEVEL=1,ID=PA,NAME=PARTROOT,LENGTH=50,
         SNAME='PART SEGMENT',SKSEG=18
   FIELD ID=KEY,LENGTH=17,POS=1,KEY=YES,NAME=PARTKEY,
         SNAME='PART NUMBER',DISP=YES,REL=YES
   FIELD ID=DESC,LENGTH=20,POS=27,SNAME='DESCRIPTION',DISP=YES,REL=YES
*******************************************************************************
*     APPLICATION DEFINITION INPUT FOR INVENTORY SEGMENT
*******************************************************************************
 SEGMENT ID=IV,PARENT=PA,NAME=STOKSTAT,KEYNAME=STOCKEY,LENGTH=160,
         SNAME='INVENTORY',
         SKLEFT='INVENTORY         UNIT       CURRENT ',
         SKLEFT='LOCATION          PRICE       REQMNTS ',
         SKRIGHT='  ON       TOTAL    DISBURSEMENTS    ',
         SKRIGHT=' ORDER     STOCK    PLANNED  UNPLANNED'
   FIELD ID=W,LENGTH=2,POS=1,KEY=YES,TYPE=DEC,SNAME='00',DISP=NO,
         COL=1,SLENGTH=2
   FIELD ID=AREA,LENGTH=1,KEY=YES,SNAME='AREA',DISP=YES,COL=3
   FIELD ID=INVD,LENGTH=2,KEY=YES,SNAME='INV DEPT',DISP=YES,COL=4
   FIELD ID=PROJ,LENGTH=3,KEY=YES,SNAME='PROJECT',DISP=YES,COL=6
   FIELD ID=DIV,LENGTH=2,KEY=YES,SNAME='DIVISION',DISP=YES,COL=9
   FIELD ID=FILL,LENGTH=6,KEY=YES,SNAME='FILLER',DISP=NO,COL=11
   FIELD ID=PRIC,LENGTH=9,POS=21,TYPE=DEC,DEC=2,SLENGTH=9,
         SNAME='UNIT PRICE',DISP=YES
```

or so, for most but not all changes. The application can therefore be adjusted constantly to the users' needs.

They enable systems analysts to create prototypes, try them out with the users, and adjust them until the users are satisfied. Often the prototype becomes the final application. Prototyping by analysts replaces the laborious and inadequate writing of requirement documents and program specifications. It therefore completely changes the development cycle and the job of systems analysts.

Some generators can employ existing data bases. They therefore provide a means of converting old applications to generator form, or of converting batch applications to on-line operation. The applications then become relatively easy to maintain. For some systems this is the best way out of the maintenance trap.

Several characteristics are needed in good application generators for DP professionals.

● They should be versatile so that as large a range of applications can be generated as possible.

- Some generators are too limited in scope. They should be well human-factored so that all systems analysts can use them without feeling that they are being reduced to the role of a coder. Some generators look as though they are designed by programmers for programmers.

- They should be able to use existing data bases. A major form of future application creation will be: first create the data bases, then generate applications which use them with high-level data-base languages.

- They should be able to convert existing applications to generator form in order to make them interactive or to lessen their maintenance costs.

- They should permit most maintenance changes or changes to prototypes to be made in an hour or so.

- They should have compilers which give efficient code. Sometimes they produce better code than COBOL or PL/1 because the preprogrammed modules of code that the generator selects are tightly coded in Assembler Language.

REFERENCES

1. *Development Management System/Customer Information Control System/ Virtual Storage: General Information Manual,* IBM Manual No. GH20–2195–2, IBM, White Plains, NY, 1980.

2. *IMS Application Development Facility, General Information Manual,* IBM Manual No. GB21–9869–1 IBM, White Plains, NY, 1980.

3. Holtz, D. H., *ADF Experiences at John Deere,* D303–SHARE 50, Denver, CO, March 6, 1978.

PART **III** DATA ADMINISTRATION
AND DESIGN

DATA ADMINISTRATOR:

Going in and building a data base is like having the first child in the house. At some point during that first year, I suspect that all of us want to drown the poor little rascal.

Well. Persevere! It has its ups and downs! There are good days and bad days.

All the benefits don't come at once, all the trust doesn't come at once, all the cooperation doesn't come at once. So I think the primary message is to persevere and have patience. And recognize that it only comes a step at a time.

10 BUBBLE CHARTS

One of the factors most critical to the success of a data-base environment is the overall *logical* design of the data bases. This is done by the *data administrator* and he needs a substantial amount of help from the end users.

End-user management should be prepared to give as much help as they can to the data administrator and take an interest in the models of data he is creating. It is clearly in their best interests to do so. If the models do not represent their data well, their department will not reap the advantages of the data-base environment later.

BUBBLE CHARTS In order to communicate with the data administrator, the end users should be able to draw representations of data structures, and to understand the diagrams of the data administrator.

Data-base professionals use very complicated words. To involve end users, we must communicate in simple words. Using the bubble charts described in this chapter, we could explain the basic ideas of data structures to a child of 10.

Bubble charts provide a way of representing and thinking about data and the associations between data items. They explain the nature of data very simply so that end users can be taught to use them, draw them, and think about their data with them.

As we shall see in Chapter 11, bubble charts drawn by end users can form a vital input to the data-base design process.

DATA ITEMS

The most elemental piece of data is called a *data item*. It is sometimes also called a *field* or a *data element*.

It is the atom of data, in that it cannot be subdivided into smaller data types and retain any meaning to the users of the data. You cannot split the data item called SALARY, for example, into smaller data items which by themselves are meaningful to end users.

We will draw each *type* of data item as a bubble:

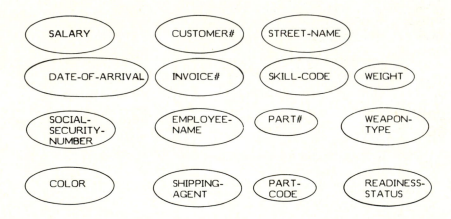

A data base contains hundreds (and sometimes thousands) of types of data items. Several thousand types of data items are used in the running of a large corporation.

In order to computerize the activities of a corporation, the data items it uses must be defined, catalogued, and organized. This is often difficult and time consuming because data have been treated sloppily in the past. What is essentially the same data item has been defined differently in different places, represented differently in computers, and given different names. Data items which were casually thought to be the same are found to be not quite the same. In one insurance company the term POLICY NUMBER was widely used, but as the data bases were being defined it was found that it was used with a dozen different meanings in different places. If a simple term such as POLICY NUMBER causes this problem, think of the problem with some of the more subtle terms.

The data administrator has the job of cleaning up this confusion. Definitions of data items must be agreed upon and documented. Much help from end users is often needed in this process.

ASSOCIATIONS BETWEEN DATA ITEMS

A data item by itself is not of much use. For example, a value of SALARY by itself is uninteresting. It becomes interesting only when it is associated with another data item, such as EMPLOYEE-NAME. Thus:

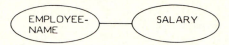

A data base, therefore, consists not only of data items but also of associations between them. There are a large number of different data-item types and we need a map showing how they are associated. This map is called a *data model.*

SINGLE AND DOUBLE-HEADED ARROWS

There are two types of links that we shall draw between data items: links with a single-headed arrow and links with a double-headed arrow.

A single-headed arrow from data item A to data item B means that *at each instant in time, each value of A has one and only one value of B associated with it.* There is a one-to-one mapping from A to B. If you know the value of A, you can find the value of B.

There is only one value of SALARY associated with a value of EMPLOYEE# at any instant in time; therefore, we can draw a single-headed arrow from EMPLOYEE# to SALARY, thus:

It is said that EMPLOYEE# *identifies* SALARY. If you know the value of EMPLOYEE#, you can find the value of SALARY. The single-headed arrow notation is consistent with the notation of mathematical logic, in which A→B means A *identifies* B.

A double-headed arrow from A to B means that *one value of A has zero, one, or many values of B associated with it.* This is one-to-many mapping from A to B.

Whereas an employee can have only one salary at a given time, he might have zero, one, or many girlfriends. Therefore, we would draw:

For one value of the data item EMPLOYEE#, there can be zero, one, or many values of the data item GIRLFRIEND.

We can draw both of the situations above on one bubble chart, thus:

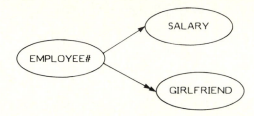

This bubble chart *synthesizes* the two previous charts into one chart. From this chart we could derive either of the two previous charts.

The two previous charts might be two different user views, one user being interested in salary and the other in girlfriends. We have created one simple data structure which incorporates these two user views. This is what the data administrator does when building a data base, but the real-life user views are much more complicated than the illustration above and there are many of them. The resulting data model has a large number of data items.

By the way, we need to build privacy controls into a data model. We do not want *any* person who feels like it finding out about our salary and girl-friends! Privacy is discussed in Chapter 32.

MANY OCCURRENCES OF DATA ITEMS   The bubble chart shows data-item types. There are many occurrences of each data item. In the example above there are many employees, each with a salary and with zero, one, or many girlfriends. The reader might imagine a third dimension to the bubble charts, showing the many values of each data item, thus:

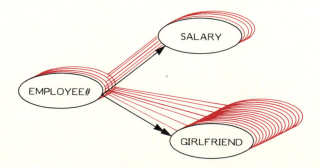

Between any two data items there can be a mapping in both directions. This gives four possibilities for forward and reverse association. If the data-item types are MAN and WOMAN, and the relationship between them represents *marriage,* the four theoretical possibilities are:

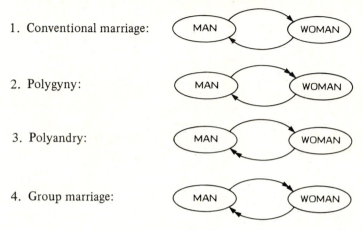

1. Conventional marriage:

2. Polygyny:

3. Polyandry:

4. Group marriage:

The reverse associations are not always of interest. For example, with the data model below we want the reverse association from DEPARTMENT# to

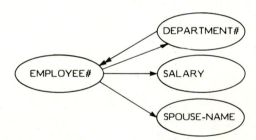

EMPLOYEE# because users want to know what employees work in a given department. However, there is no arrow from SPOUSE-NAME to EMPLOYEE# because no user wants to ask: "What employee has a spouse named Gertrude?" If a user wanted to ask "What employees have a salary over $25,000?", we might include a double arrow from SALARY to EMPLOYEE#.

DATA-ITEM GROUPS Between N data items there are $N(N - 1)$ possible associations. A large data base has more than a million *possible* associations between data items. It would be impractical to handle all of them, so the data items are arranged into groups, and we refer

to associations between groups. This cuts to a reasonable number the number of associations we are concerned with.

The data-item group is given different names in different data-base management systems—"record," "segment," or "tuple." We will refer to the record, segment, or tuple as a *data-item group*.

We will draw the data-item groups as a bar containing the names of the data items. thus:

SUPPLIER#	SUPPLIER-NAME	SUPPLIER-ADDRESS	SUPPLIER-DETAILS

This data-item group represents the following bubble chart:

We use both single- and double-headed arrows to link the data-item groups. They have the same one-to-one and one-to-many meanings.

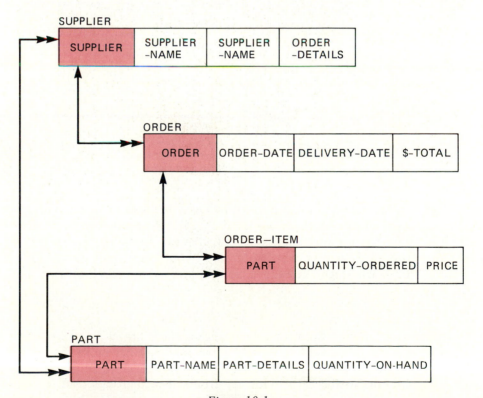

Figure 10.1

Thus, in the structure in Fig. 10.1 there are several suppliers for one part, many outstanding orders for one supplier, several order items on one order, and so on.

1:1, 1:M, AND M:M LINKS

A single-headed arrow (one-to-one) between bubbles or records is called a *1 association*. A double-headed arrow (one-to-many) is called an *M association*.

Describing the arrows at both ends of a link, we can have a 1:1, 1:*M*, *M*:1, or *M*:*M* association between two data items or records, as between MAN and WOMAN above.

As we will see, later there can be problems associated with *M*:*M* associations. Group marriage gets you into trouble.

Sometimes we do not know, or do not need to know, the reverse association on a link. In this case we refer to the link as a *lone 1* or *lone M* link.

KEYS AND ATTRIBUTES

Given the bubble chart method of representing data, we can state three important definitions:

1. Primary key
2. Secondary key
3. Attribute

A primary key is a bubble with one or more single-headed arrows leaving it. Thus in Fig. 10.2, A, C, and F are primary keys.

A primary key may uniquely identify many data items.

Data items that are not primary keys are referred to as *nonprime attributes*. All data items, then, are either *primary keys* or *nonprime attributes*.

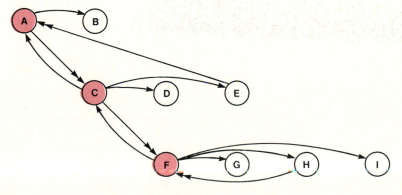

Figure 10.2

In the diagram above, B, D, E, G, H, and I are nonprime attributes. Often the word "attribute" is used instead of "nonprime attribute." Strictly, the primary key data items are attributed also. EMPLOYEE# is an attribute of the employee. Primary keys will be colored red in our diagrams.

We can define a nonprime attribute as follows:

A nonprime attribute is a bubble with no single-headed arrows leaving it.

A *secondary key* does not uniquely identify another data item. One value of a secondary key is associated with zero, one, or many values of another data item. In other words, there is a double-headed arrow going from it to that other item.

A secondary key is a nonprime attribute with one or more double-headed arrows leaving it.

In Fig. 10.2, E and H are secondary keys.

For emphasis the following box repeats these three fundamental definitions.

A *primary key* is a bubble with one or more single-headed arrows leaving it.

A *nonprime attribute* is a bubble with no single-headed arrows leaving it.

A *secondary key* is a nonprime attribute with one or more double-headed arrows leaving it.

DATA-ITEM GROUPS   In the bubble chart that results from combining many user views, the bubbles are grouped by primary key. Each primary key is the unique identifier of a data-item group. It points with single-headed arrows to each nonprime attribute in that data-item group.

The data-item group needs to be structured carefully so that it is as stable as possible. We should not group together an ad hoc collection of data items. There are formal rules for structuring the data-item group, which we discuss later.

OPTIONAL LINKS   Sometimes the link is optional. For one value of A there may or may not be one value of B. We will draw this with a zero by the arrowhead, thus:

There is no need to put a zero on a double-headed arrow because this already means that *zero,* one, or many values of the data item at the head of the arrow are associated with one at the tail.

Later, when we discuss the grouping of data items into records or data models, we will treat an optional link *to an attribute* as though it were at one link. The zero really means that the attribute could have a null value which is conceptually no different from an actual value.

When the optional link points to a primary key the situation is different. It means that an entire record may or may not exist. For example, an EMPLOYEE may or may not be assigned to a PROJECT. We therefore retain the zero on single-headed links between primary keys or data groups.

ENTITIES AND ATTRIBUTES

We will refer to items about which we store information as *entities.* An entity may be a tangible object such as an employee, a part, or a place. It may be nontangible, such as an event, a job title, a customer account, a profit center, or an abstract concept.

Box 10.1 summarizes what entities are.

An entity has various *attributes* which we may wish to record, such as color, monetary value, or name. Often in data processing we are concerned with a collection of similar entities such as employees, and we wish to record information about the same attributes of each of them. A programmer commonly maintains a *record* about each entity, and a data item in each record relates to each attribute. Similar records are grouped into *files.* The result, shown in Fig. 10.3, is a two-dimensional array.

Inside the box in Fig. 10.3 is a set of data items. The value of each data item is shown. Each row of data items relates to a particular entity. Each column contains a particular type of data item, relating to a particular type of attribute. At the top of the diagram, outside the box, the names of the attributes are written. The leftmost column in the box contains the data items that *identify* the entity. The entity in this example is a person, an employee. The attribute referred to as the entity identifier in this case is EMPLOYEE NUMBER.

Such a two-dimensional array is sometime referred to as a *flat file.* The use of flat files dates back to the earliest days of data processing, when the file might have been on punched cards. Each card in a file or deck of cards such as that in Fig. 10.4 might contain one record, relating to one entity. Certain card columns were allocated to each data-item type, or attribute, and were called a *field.* When magnetic tapes replaced decks of cards and discs replaced magnetic tapes, many programmers retained their view of data as being organized into flat files. No matter how the data are stored in a data base, the software must present the data to the application program in flat-file form if that is the way the program is written.

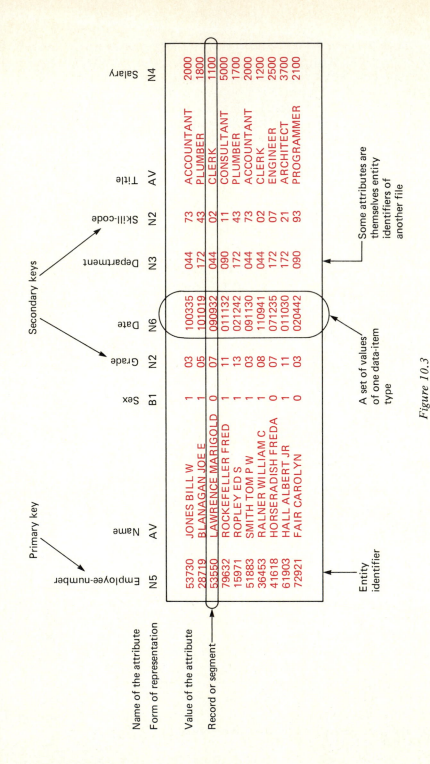

Figure 10.3

180

BOX 10.1 Entities

An entity is something (real or abstract) about which we store data.

Examples of entities are: CUSTOMER, PART, EMPLOYEE, INVOICE, MACHINE TOOL, SALESPERSON, BRANCH OF-FICE, SALES TV AREA, WAREHOUSE, WAREHOUSE BIN, SHOP ORDER, SHIFT REPORT, PRODUCT SPECIFICATION, LEDGER ACCOUNT, JOURNAL POSTING ACCOUNT, PAY-MENT, CASH RECEIPT, DEBTOR, CREDITOR, DEBTOR ANALYSIS RECORD.

The name of each entity should be a noun, sometimes with a modifier word. An entity may be thought of as having the properties of a noun.

An entity has various *attributes* which we wish to record, such as color, monetary value, percentage utilization, or name.

The term *entity* is used as shorthand for *entity type* or *entity instance.* Similarly, the term *record* is a shorthand for *record type* or *record instance;* similarly with data item, attribute, and other words describing data.

An *entity type* is a named class of entities which have the same set of *attribute types:* for example, EMPLOYEE is an entity type.

An *entity instance* is one specific occurrence of an entity type: for example, B. J. WATKINS is an instance of the entity type EMPLOYEE.

In this book, when we say *entity,* we mean *entity type;* when we say *record* we mean *record type;* and so on. Usually, the meaning of this shorthand is clear.

For each entity type we have at least one record type. Sometimes this is called an *entity record.* The EMPLOYEE record, for example, is an entity record containing data about the entity EMPLOYEE.

Often, more than one record type is needed to store the data about one entity type. This is often because the data are normalized (a process of breaking data into separate records which each have a clean structure—described in Chapter 8).

An entity usually has a data item that uniquely identifies it. For example, EMPLOYEE NUMBER is the *unique identifier* of the EMPLOYEE entity. This data item is used as a *primary key* of the entity record.

(Continued)

BOX 10.1 *(Continued)*

When there are multiple records relating to one entity, the unique identifier consists of more than one primary key joined together (concatenated). For example, the EMPLOYEE HISTORY record has two data items as its primary key: EMPLOYEE NUMBER and DATE.

Some records contain information about a relationship among entities. For example, SUPPLIER and PART are entity types. Their unique identifiers are SUPPLIER# and PART#. A record with both of these primary keys is used to store details of a part being supplied by a supplier: for example, its price and delivery time. This is sometimes called *intersection data.* The SUPPLIER-PART record has two primary keys—SUPPLIER# and PART#—to identify it uniquely. Such a record may be referred to as an *intersection entity record.*

An *entity chart* shows the entity records, including those with more than one primary key, and the associations between entity records. It does not show the data items in these records because it is intended to be an overview, produced relatively quickly. Details of the data items are determined later with detailed data modeling.

An entity identifier and its attributes are drawn on a bubble diagram as follows:

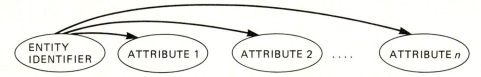

A data-item that appears as an attribute in one place can be an entity in another place. The EMPLOYEE entity in Fig. 10.3, for example, has DEPARTMENT as one of its attributes, but DEPARTMENT itself is an entity. It would be drawn on a bubble chart as shown in Fig. 10.5.

Furthermore, many attributes are not identified by any single entity. They need more than one entity to identify them. For example, the *price* of a *part* is an attribute which may not be identified by the entity PART alone. Different prices are charged for the same part by different suppliers and may also depend on the *time* of quotation.

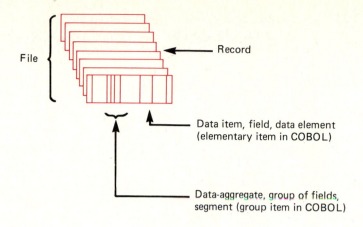

Figure 10.4 A flat file, showing the wording commonly used to describe the application programmer's view of data. Most checks of punched cards are flat files.

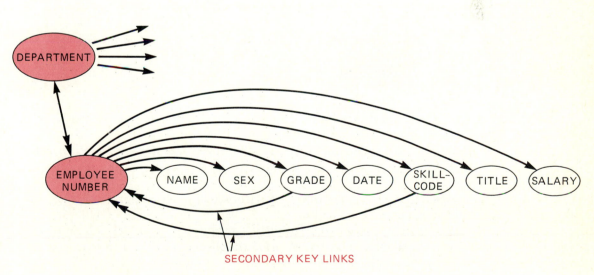

Figure 10.5 A bubblechart of the data in Fig. 10.3, assuming that DEPARTMENT is a separate primary key.

CONCATENATED KEYS   Some data items cannot be identified by a single data item in a user's view. They need a primary key (unique identifier) which is composed of more than one data item in combination. This is called a *concatenated key*.

Several suppliers may supply a part and each charge a different price for it. The primary key SUPPLIER# is used for identifying information about a *supplier*. The key PART# is used for identifying information about a *part*. Neither of those keys is sufficient for identifying the *price*. The price is dependent on both the supplier and the part. We create a new key to identify the price, which consists of SUPPLIER# and PART# joined together (concatenated). We draw this as one bubble:

The two data items from which the concatenated key is created are joined with a "+" symbol.

The concatenated key has single-arrow links to the keys SUPPLIER# and PART#. The resulting graph is as follows:

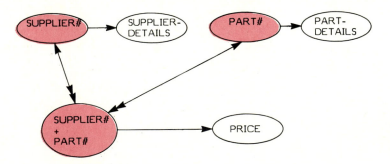

By introducing this form of concatenated key into the logical view of data, we make each data item dependent on one key bubble.

Whenever a concatenated key is introduced, the designer should ensure that the items it identifies are dependent on the whole key, not only on a portion of it.

In practice, it is sometimes necessary to join together *more than two* data items in a concatenated key.

For example, a company supplies a product to domestic and industrial customers. It charges a different price to different *types of customers;* the price also varies from one *state* to another. There is a *discount* giving different price reductions for different quantities purchased. The *price* is identified by a combination of CUSTOMER-TYPE, STATE, DISCOUNT, and PRODUCT, thus:

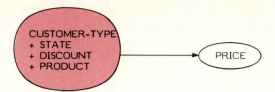

The use of concatenated keys gives each data-item group in the resulting data model a simple structure in which each attribute is fully dependent on the key bubble and nothing else:

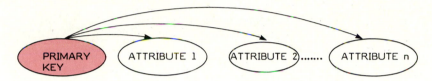

MULTIPLE ASSOCIATIONS BETWEEN DATA ITEMS

On rare occasions it is necessary to have two associations between the same two bubbles. Suppose that we have a data item called PERSON and a data item called DOG, and we want to represent which dogs a person owns and also which dogs a person has been bitten by. We would draw

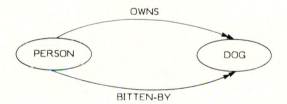

Because there are two links between the same two data items, the links are labeled.

Situations like this requiring labeled associations can usually be avoided by introducing an extra data item type, thus:

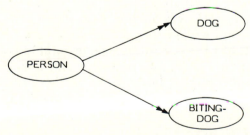

A single-headed arrow may go from both of the DOG data items above to PERSON, to show who owns what dog. The owner of the biting dogs may then be traced.

It is recommended that labeled associations be avoided, where possible, but they cannot always be avoided.

LOOPS

Occasionally, a data item points to itself. For example, some employees manage other employees. This is drawn as follows:

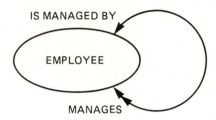

This is called a *loop.* A loop may occur with primary keys, or the records identified by those keys. It is usually desirable to attach labels to the loop as shown above.

LEVELS OF PRIMARY KEYS

Some of the primary keys themselves identify other primary keys; that is, they have single arrows going to other primary keys. For clarity the diagram of the data structure is often drawn with the single arrows between primary keys pointing upward whenever possible. This is normally done in a tree structure representation of data. The record at the top of the tree is called the *root record,* and its primary key is a *root key.*

We can define a root key as follows:

A root key is a primary key with no single arrows leaving it to another primary key.

In a tree structure there is one root key. Structures more complicated than a tree structure (called *plex* or *network structures*) may have more than one root key.

In Fig. 10.2, data-item A is the root key. In Fig. 10.1 there are two root keys, SUPPLIER# and PART#.

The definition of root key is not fundamental to understanding data as are the definitions of a primary key and secondary key. It is, however, *useful* when planning the physical organization of the data to know which are the root keys and root records.

The primary keys, or records they identify, can be arranged into levels. The highest level is the root key, and we will call this depth 1.

A depth 2 primary key has a single-arrow link to a depth 1 primary key.

A depth 3 primary key has a single-arrow link to a depth 2 primary key but no single-arrow links to a depth 1 primary key.

A depth N primary key has a single-arrow link to a depth $N-1$ primary key but no single-arrow links to a depth M primary key, where $M < N-1$.

The primary keys with the greatest depth in a data structure have no single-arrow links entering them.

Levels can be indicated on a drawing by positioning the data-item groups with different amounts of offset. The depth 1 groups are the leftmost and the deepest groups the rightmost, as shown in Figs. 10.1 and 10.2.

11 DATA MODELING

LOGICAL DESIGN · A data base contains a large number of types of data items. These data-item types have to be associated into a data-base structure. How do you organize them into a logical structure? What is the best logical structure?

This question is vitally important because that logical structure is the foundation stone on which most future data processing will be built. Not only will conventional programs be written to use the data base but, increasingly, higher-level data-base languages will be used which enable users to extract the information they need from the data base directly, and sometimes to update the data bases. The future corporation will be managed with data-base resources, networks to access the data bases, and end-user software for employing and updating the data.

If the logical structures are designed badly, a large financial penalty will result. A corporation will not be able to employ the data bases as it should, so productivity will suffer. The data bases will constantly have to be modified, but they cannot be modified without much application program rewriting. The end users will not be served as they need, and because of this many will try to create their own alternatives to employing the data base.

After the first decade of data-base installations, it became clear that many of them were not living up to the publicized advantages of data base. A few rare ones had spectacularly improved the whole data-processing function and greatly increased application development speed and productivity. Time and time again the difference lay in the design of the overall logical structure of the data.

One of the arguments for using data-base management systems is that they greatly reduce such maintenance. We have indicated that data-base techniques have often not succeeded in lowering maintenance costs because a need is felt to create new data bases as new applications come along. The reason for this lies again in the logical structuring of the data.

The following chapters discuss formal techniques for structuring the data in such a way that maintenance costs are minimized. They have worked very successfully in installations that have used them. They are concerned with how the data items are grouped into records, segments, or tuples, and how these are linked into data-base structures. Any data-base installation that does not structure its data in such a form before doing the physical design is throwing money down the drain. It is condemning itself to large future maintenance costs and the inability to respond to many users' needs.

DATA ADMINISTRATION

The task of designing the logical structure of data is done by a *data administrator*. He works with the systems analysts and end users of data to find out what data are needed for their operations. The data items are defined and catalogued in a *data dictionary*. The data structures needed for different users are determined and are synthesized into the data-base structure.

A data base can be defined as a collection of data from which multiple different end-user views are derived. The task of designing a data base is then to capture the end-user views and synthesize them into a data-base structure (Fig. 11.1).

However, the resulting structure needs to be as stable as possible. If it has to be changed in certain ways in the future, it will force the rewriting of application programs. This is expensive, sometimes so expensive in practice that it is never done and so vital data-base uses are postponed.

A key to success in data structuring is for the data administrator to involve the end users as fully as possible. The users should be asked to think about the data they need for running their function, to participate in defining the data items, and to check the output from the data modeling process.

It helps greatly if selected end users can draw the data structures they need. To do this they need to learn the material of the preceding chapter, and to practice drawing the bubble charts described. Experience has shown that after minimal training, users are capable of developing views of the data that relate to their jobs.

The author's book *An End-Users' Guide to Data Base* [1] describes in nontechnical words the basic information that end users need in order to help as they should in the data administration process. This book forms the basis of end-user training on data base in some corporations.

DATA MODELS

A data model is a logical representation of the data structure which forms a data base. It shows the data-item types and the associations among them. It represents the inherent

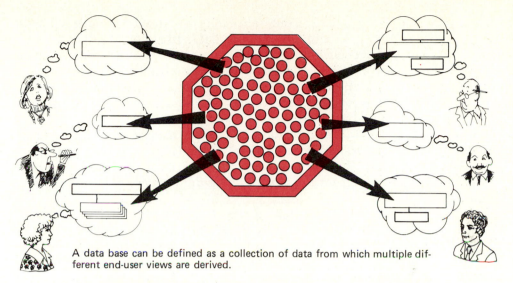

A data base can be defined as a collection of data from which multiple different end-user views are derived.

The task of designing the data is then to capture the end-user views and synthesize them into a data-base structure:

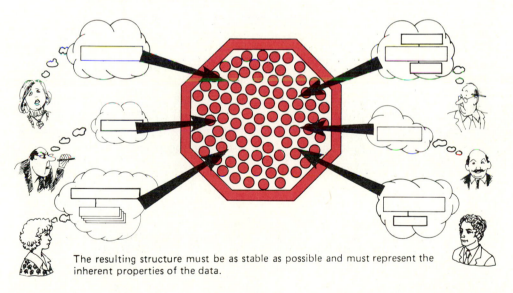

The resulting structure must be as stable as possible and must represent the inherent properties of the data.

Figure 11.1

properties of the data in a fundamental way which is independent of the physical representation of the data and of the data-base management system used.

The bubble charts of Chapter 10 are simple forms of data models. *The data model is independent of computers or software.* It represents clear thinking about the nature of data.

SCHEMA The word *schema* is also used to mean a logical representation of data. It is commonly used in a way that is *not* independent of the software used. We talk about a CODASYL schema, for example, meaning a structure of data which although it is logical, not physical, groups the data into the sets which are used by a CODASYL data-base management system. This structure would not be used in a hierarchical data-base management system (such as IMS, DL/1, TOTAL, IMAGE, SYSTEM 2000) or a relational data-base management system (such as SQL, DATACOM, NOMAD, or Tandem's DBMS).

We will employ the word *schema,* then, to mean *a version of a data model which is oriented toward a particular DBMS approach to representing logical data.*

Sometimes the word "schema" *is* used to mean a software-independent representation of data. The term *conceptual schema,* for example, is used to refer to a representation of the properties and structure data which is independent of how we implement the data base. We prefer to use the word "model" for this because the word "schema" usually implies a type of software structure.

THREE REPRESENTATIONS OF DATA Effective data-base design goes through the three stages illustrated in Fig. 11.2. First, logical models are created of the data needed to run a corporation. These should usually be *subject* data-base models. They are designed to represent the inherent properties of the data in as stable a fashion as possible. They are *independent of the software or hardware* that is used. They are a statement about the data needed to run the corporation—documented, precise, clear thinking about these data.

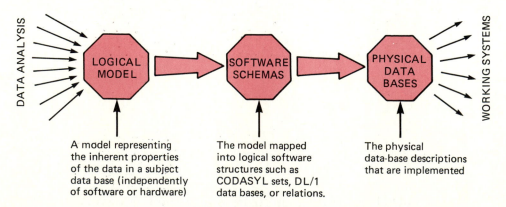

Figure 11.2 Data-base administration and design progresses through these three data representations (see Fig. 19.1).

When data bases are implemented the models are translated into the logical structures that a particular data-base management system is designed to handle. For CODASYL-based data-base management systems they are represented as *set* structures. For IBM's IMS or CICS they are represented as DL/1 structures. For relational data bases they are represented as tuples.

The data-base designer designs *physical* representations of these logical structures (the right-hand octagon of Fig. 11.2). He designs the physical layout of the data and selects the access methods.

The physical data-base design will change when usage patterns of the data change, or when the hardware is upgraded. The logical software schemas should not change if the data-base management system has *thorough* data independence. In fact, it often *does* need to change to achieve better machine performance (a criticism of today's generation of data-base management systems).

The model, however, is entirely independent of current software, implementations, and usage volumes. The models of corporate data can, and should, be created long before data bases employing those models are actually implemented. That is important because the data models will be a corporate resource that will remain valuable long after the software representations of data have changed.

THE END-USER COMMITTEE

A technique that has proved highly successful is to form a team of users who have expert knowledge of their own data, as discussed in Chapter 3. The team is composed of selected users who meet periodically with the data administrator who will think about the data structures needed in their area. The data administrator, with the help of systems analysts, feeds the user views of data into a data modeling process and at the same time into a data dictionary. The output of the dictionary and data modeling process are then given to the user committee.

Normally, there will be much argument about the definitions of data items and about which data items are standard. It is the task of the data administrator to resolve these arguments.

The following comments are from an end-user committee in a large insurance company trying to model the subject data base for policyholder data:

MEMBER OF END-USER GROUP:

We are a very large group representing many departments, with key people in each department. In order to analyze the data dealing with policyholder information, we are trying to make sure that this information is organized so that we can produce the various products that each department deals with. And to make sure that we're able to give management the information they need.

It was kind of amazing that we're all working for the same company but when a particular term was mentioned, that there were three or four different definitions of that term, and that each department was using the term to mean something else. So we started by coming up with some unique definitions of each term and then we spent an awful lot of time trying to understand the relationship of each item to other items.

We've just gone through this over and over and over again to assure a good logical organization.

The task of designing data bases involves cleaning up the data that are used in a corporation. This is usually a formidable task because for decades the data have evolved in an uncontrolled fashion. When computers were first used for inventory control they revealed what a mess the stores were really in. The mess had to be cleaned up before computerized inventory control worked. Similarly, data-base design reveals what a mess the data in an organization are in.

Our field personnel were just going absolutely nuts; they were upset; the schedule was falling behind; it affected another system that didn't need to fall behind, but had to. The answer was very simple. Over the 50 years that we have been writing group business we wrote anything and everything. Standardization did not exist; it was a you-pick schedule for everyone, all a little different. I think when you have a highly automated system and you're coming from a very uncontrolled environment the process of picking up data elements and converting them has got to be slow, painful, laborious; I don't think there's any alternative and that's got to be sold up front. It wasn't, I don't think, in this case.

It is a long and tedious job to clean up the discrepancies. But doing so is essential to building the foundation stone of future network data-base systems.

In the insurance company above the field CLAIM ADDRESS had different meanings:

For example, there's the physical address of the claims office itself and then there are the addresses of the people that will receive the benefits directly. It seemed that somewhere along the line in our structure that didn't come through very clearly, and we had to find out the hard way, by kind of locking horns to find out that that was a conflict.

Often the conflicts are much more complicated:

There is a conflict in the definition of a plan. What is a plan? Particularly for people who go back over five years, the definition of a plan will vary. If you took 20 people, I think you would have 20 different ones. It's only been the people who have been exposed to a couple of the more recent systems who would have a relatively consistent definition and even then, if you dig beneath the plan level and get into the benefit level, you'd find differences there.

Twenty different people with different definitions. That must take quite a bit of resolving in the user's group.

I think you'll find that the user group will have to spend a great deal of time on definition. Just based on that, I personally am quite thankful that there are such animals as data dictionaries.

END-USER ITERATIONS

When the users look at the resulting design, they often suggest changes. It is desirable that these changes be made quickly so that the users can see their effects on the overall design.

If the modeling is done by computer, changes can be made quickly. The effects of these changes need not be inserted into the official data model until they have been examined by the systems analysts and users. This fast automated response to suggested changes enables the data-base design process to be highly interactive, which is what it should be. The data administrator can experiment with various forms of user requirements quickly and easily. In particular, he should think about future needs to determine how data models serving future applications fit in with what is being done today. The impact of proposed systems on the existing data base can be evaluated quickly.

When the data administrator has to do *manual* designs, the process is slow, tedious, and error-prone. The result is usually not an optimal structure. Because it is so tedious and time consuming, the data administrator repeatedly avoids redoing the design. But repeated redesign is often very important in clarifying the nature of the data. *The more thinking, iteration, and interaction with the users that goes on before a data base is implemented, the better the final product will be.*

In many cases with *manual* data modeling the data administrator hardly dare show his model to the users because so much work has gone into it and he knows they will change it.

A computerized data modeling tool and a data dictionary permit this iteration and enforce clarity of thinking about the data. We believe that they are *essential* tools for the data administrator. We have observed in installations beginning to use them a sharp change in the conceptual clarity and quality of the design process. We discuss these tools in Chapter 15.

CLEAR REPRESENTATION

Many data-base designers have flip charts on sheets of paper with arrows straggling wildly out of control from one block to another. Pointers to pointers to pointers. A bird's nest of linkages, frequently patched, often incomplete, almost impossible for a third party to check. This type of confused diagram leads to bad data-base design and prevents effective communication with users. A good modeling tool should draw clear diagrams of data-base structures. Changes should be simple to make and when made, the tool should implement redrawing of the diagrams. These diagrams can be given to analysts and users to check, think about, and provide feedback for redesigns. Together with the data dictionary, they form the basis for that communication link with user departments without which data-base installations will not be truly successful.

SYNTHESIS

The data modeling process takes many separate user views of data and *synthesizes* them into a structure that incorporates all of them, as illustrated in Fig. 11.1.

The synthesis is done in such a way that redundant data items are eliminated where possible. The same data item does not generally appear twice in the final result. Also, redundant *associations* are eliminated where possible. In other words, a minimal number of lines connect the bubbles in the resulting bubble chart.

The synthesis process is a formal procedure following a formal set of rules. Because it is a formal procedure it can be done by a computer. This eliminates errors in the process, provides formal documentation which is a basis for end-user discussion, and permits any input view to be changed or new views to be added and immediately reflects the effect of the change in the resulting data model.

There is *only one* data model which is a minimal nonredundant synthesis of any given collection of user bubble charts.

As a simple illustration of the synthesis process, consider the four user views of data shown in Fig. 11.3. We want to combine those into a single data model.

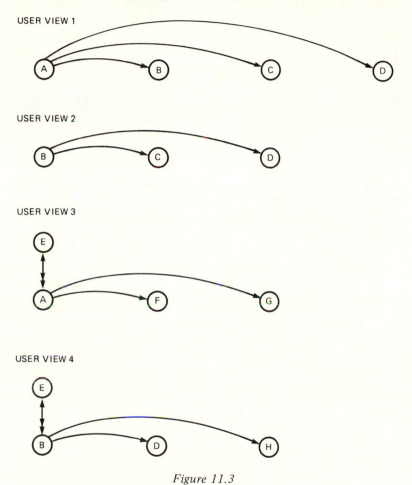

USER VIEW 1

USER VIEW 2

USER VIEW 3

USER VIEW 4

Figure 11.3

To start, here is view 1:

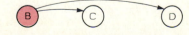

We will combine view 2 with it:

None of the data items above appear twice in the result:

There are, however, some redundant links.

> A identifies B; A—►B.
> And B identifies C; B—►C.
> Therefore, A *must* identify C.
> Therefore, the link A—►C is redundant.

Similarly, A identifies B and B identifies D; therefore, A *must* identify D. Therefore, the link A—►D is redundant.

The redundant links are removed and we have

Now the third view:

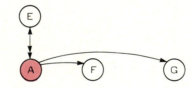

This contains three data items: E, F, and G. When it is merged into the model, we get

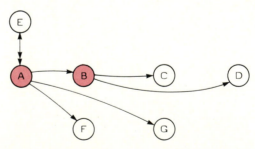

There are no new redundancies, so we will merge in the fourth view:

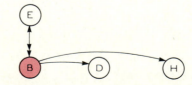

This adds one new data item to the model, H:

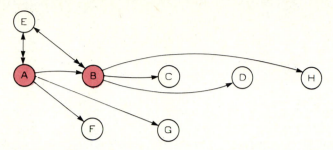

There is now one redundant link.

A identifies B; B identifies E; therefore, A *must* identify E. We can remove the single-headed arrow from A to E (we cannot change the double-headed arrow from E to A):

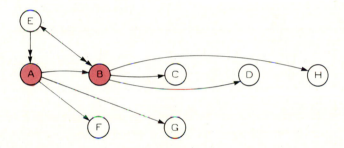

In this resulting structure there are two *primary keys:* A and B. (A primary key is a bubble with one or more single-headed arrows leaving it.)

We can associate each primary key with the attributes it identifies:

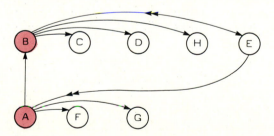

On each linkage between primary keys it is desirable to put the reverse linkage. We should therefore ask: Is the link from B to A a double-headed arrow or a single-headed arrow link?

Suppose that it is a double-headed arrow link.

The diagram on p. 200 draws the logical data-item groups (records, segments, tuples) that result from this design.

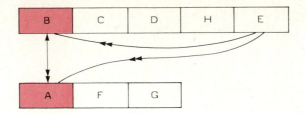

E, here, is a *secondary key* pointing to both A and B. In old punched-card or batch-processing systems, secondary keys, such as E, were the *sort* keys. In on-line systems secondary-key paths such as those from E to A or B are followed by such means as pointers or indices.

Chapter 14 discusses this synthesis process further. Before that we should describe the concept of *third normal form*.

USES OF DATA MODELS

Data modeling in practice is used in three different ways:

1. Application Data Base

The data required for a specific application or group of applications are synthesized from the available documents and user views.

2. Subject Data Base

The broader operation of building subject data bases is carried out, synthesizing all useful data about a "subject" such as customers, vendors, and so on.

3. Overall Corporate Data Model

The data needed to run an enterprise are defined in a data dictionary and data model, a step at a time. The resulting overall data model is sometimes called a *conceptual model* (or *conceptual schema*). The model is often too broad to form a data base itself. Subsets of it are partitioned and become implementable data bases, as shown in Fig. 11.4.

Application-data-base and subject-data-base models are converted directly into schemas for implementation. The overall corporate data model is not converted directly into a schema; only extracts from it become schemas. Instead, it becomes a standard for defining the corporate data. It has various uses in the strategic planning of data systems.

Many existing systems do not conform to the model. They were built before the model was created. As systems come up for redevelopment they are converted to conform to the model and associated data dictionary. (As data-base usage becomes mature it can be cheaper to redevelop than to continue maintenance of old systems.) The model thus becomes a goal toward

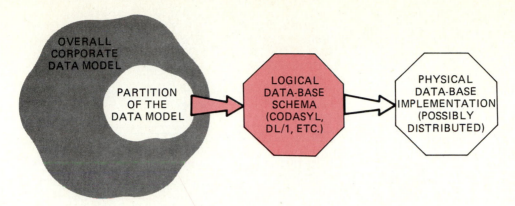

Figure 11.4 The overall corporate data model is much broader in scope than any specific data base. Multiple data-base schemas may be derived from it for individual data-base implementations. Because they are derived from a common model, data can be interchanged among them.

which DP works. In eight years or so, most applications become redeveloped to conform to the model.

ENTITY-RELATIONSHIP MODEL

The application-data-base and subject-data-base models need to be complete because they are used for application creation. The overall corporate data model may be a summary model not showing all the attributes.

A summary model may contain only the primary keys and the links among them. Attributes are not included. This is sometimes called an *entity-relationship model* [2]. It shows the entities in the enterprise and the relationships among them.

An entity-relationship model can be created much more quickly than a model that attempts to include every data item. The latter could take years to build and quick results are needed for strategic planning.

Glancing ahead, Fig. 37.9 shows an entity-relationship model for a small- to medium-sized corporation.

It is desirable to have a tool which automates the data modeling process (discussed in Chapter 15). With such a tool, an entity-relationship model can be created first, and more detail can be added to it steadily. The attributes associated with each primary key are added when those details are worked out. The tool can print either an entity-relationship model, or a complete model, or extracts from the model that are relevant to a particular application or data-base-schema implementation.

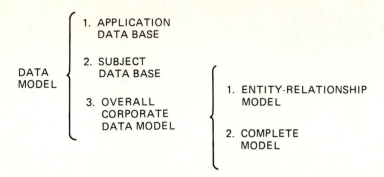

Figure 11.5   Categories of data model.

It may be desirable to print all the primary keys or entity records which are associated with a given entity or group of entities. This is sometimes called a *neighborhood*. The neighborhood chart or submodel may be used in planning the procedures that will use that data base. We can draw *logical access maps* on top of the submodel chart in order to plan the procedures. These are illustrated in Chapter 20.

Figure 11.5 summarizes the categories of data models.

REFERENCES

1. James Martin, *An End-Users' Guide to Data Base,* Prentice-Hall, Inc., Englewood Cliffs, NJ, 1981.

2. *How to Do Optimal Logical Data Base Design,* a manual on DATA DESIGNER, Data Base Design Inc, 2020 Hogback Road, Ann Arbor, MI 48104.

12 THIRD NORMAL FORM

An issue of concern to data-base designers is what data items should be grouped together into records, segments, or tuples. There are many different ways in which the hundreds or thousands of data items can be grouped, and some ways are better than others. Some will lead to subtle problems in the future.

As we have stressed, most data bases change constantly. New data items and new associations between data items are added frequently and new usage patterns occur. As we change the data base, we must preserve the old user views of data so as to avoid having to rewrite programs. There are, however, certain changes in data associations or usage which could force modification of programs. For example, we may have to split a record (segment) into two, or change the key that is used for certain data items. Such changes can be extremely disruptive. If the grouping of data items and keys is well thought out originally, we can make such disruption unlikely.

Normalization is a formal approach which examines data, and groups the data items together in a form that is better able to accommodate future business change, and to minimize the impact of that change on application systems.

Data exist in real life as groups of data items. They exist on invoices, waybills, tax forms, driving licenses, and so on. These groupings are often not in a normalized form. Not surprisingly, systems analysts have often implemented computer records that are also not normalized. However, data that are not normalized can lead to various subtle problems in the future.

Experience has shown that when computer data are organized as described in this chapter (i.e., in third normal form), the resulting data structures are more stable and able to accommodate change. Each attribute relates to its own entity and is not mixed up with attributes relating to different entities. The actions that create and update data can then be applied with simple structured design to one normalized record at a time.

This chapter and Chapters 13 and 14 are concerned with the best grouping of data items into records, segments, or tuples. The ideas in these chapters are a fundamental part of a systems analyst's understanding of the data. They are important for the design of stable data structures that will minimize the probability of future disruption. They may be tedious for some readers to grasp but fortunely, can be automated in the design process.

FIRST, SECOND, AND THIRD NORMAL FORMS

Third normal form is a simple, relatively stable grouping of data items into records (segments, tuples, or whatever the basic data-item group is called). Its purpose is to find those groupings of data items least likely to give maintenance problems—least likely to change in ways that force application program rewriting.

The basic simplicity of data in third normal form makes the records easy to understand, and easier to change, than other ways of organizing a data base. It avoids some of the anomolies that arise with other data structures.

At the time of writing only a small porportion of existing data bases are in third normal form. Some corporations have several years of experience of operation of third-normal-form data structures. There is no question that they have greatly benefited from this type of design, especially when it is combined with the steps given in the following chapters.

Reacting to the perceived benefits, some corporations have incorporated into their data-base standards manuals the requirement that all data-base structures be in third normal form. Usually, this form of design is better in terms of *machine* requirements as well as in logical structuring, but this is not always the case. Sometimes the physical designer finds it desirable to deviate from third normal form. A compromise is then needed. Which is preferable: somewhat better machine performance or better protection from maintenance costs? Usually, the potential maintenance costs are much the more expensive.

We suggest that the data-base standards manual should say that all data will be *designed* in third normal form, but that the physical implementation may occasionally deviate from third normal form if the trade-off is fully explored and documented.

To put data into third normal form, three steps may be used (first described by E. F. Codd [1]). It is put into *first normal form,* then *second normal form,* then *third normal form.* Box 12.1 summarizes these.

The basic ideas of this normalization of data are simple, but the ramifications are many and subtle, and vary from one type of data-base usage to another.

It is important to note that normalization describes the *logical* representation of data, not the physical, There are many ways of physically implementing the data.

First normal form refers to a collection of data organized into records which have no repeating groups of data items within a record. In other words, they are flat files, two-dimensional matrices of data items, as shown on page 206.

BOX 12.1   Conversion to third normal form

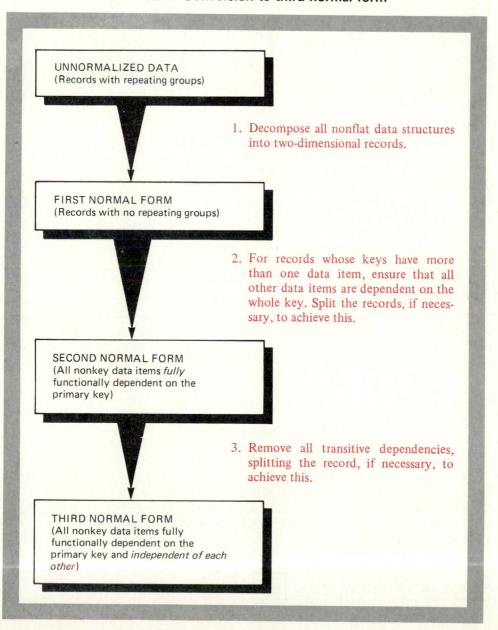

UNNORMALIZED DATA
(Records with repeating groups)

1. Decompose all nonflat data structures into two-dimensional records.

FIRST NORMAL FORM
(Records with no repeating groups)

2. For records whose keys have more than one data item, ensure that all other data items are dependent on the whole key. Split the records, if necessary, to achieve this.

SECOND NORMAL FORM
(All nonkey data items *fully* functionally dependent on the primary key)

3. Remove all transitive dependencies, splitting the record, if necessary, to achieve this.

THIRD NORMAL FORM
(All nonkey data items fully functionally dependent on the primary key and *independent of each other*)

PART#	SUPPLIER#	SUPPLIER-NAME	SUPPLIER-DETAILS	PRICE
1	1000	JONES	x	20
1	1500	ABC	x	28
1	2050	XYZ	y	22
1	1900	P-H	z	30
2	3100	ALLEN	z	520
2	1000	JONES	x	500
2	2050	XYZ	y	590
3	2050	XYZ	y	1000
4	1000	JONES	x	80
4	3100	ALLEN	z	90
4	1900	P-H	z	95
5	1500	ABC	x	140
5	1000	JONES	x	140

Such a flat file may be thought of as a simple two-dimensional table. It may, however, contain many thousands of records.

Most programming languages give programmers the ability to create and refer to records that are not *flat;* that is, they contain repeating groups of data items within a record. In COBOL these are called *data aggregates.* There can be data aggregates within data aggregates—repeating groups within repeating groups.

The following COBOL record contains two data aggregates, called BIRTH and SKILLS.

```
RECORD NAME IS PERSON
    01      EMPLOYEE# PICTURE "9(5)"
    01      EMPNAME TYPE CHARACTER 20
    01      SEX PICTURE "A"
    01      EMPJCODE PICTURE "9999"
    01      SALARY PICTURE "9(5)V99"
    01      BIRTH
    02          MONTH PICTURE "99"
    02          DAY
    02          YEAR PICTURE "99"
    01      NOSKILLS TYPE BINARY
    01      SKILLS OCCURS NOSKILLS TIMES
    02          SKILLCODE PICTURE "9999"
    02          SKILL YEARS PICTURE "99"
```

PERSON

EMPLOYEE#	EMPNAME	SEX	EMPJCODE	SALARY	BIRTH			SKILLS	
					MONTH	DAY	YEAR	SKILLCODE	SKILLYEARS

BIRTH causes no problems because it occurs only once in each record. SKILLS can occur several times in one record, so that record is not in first normal form. It is not a *flat*, two-dimensional record. To *normalize* it, the repeating group SKILLS must be removed and put into a separate record, thus:

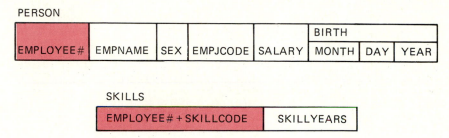

The lower record has a concatenated key EMPLOYEE# + SKILLCODE. We cannot know **SKILL YEARS** (the number of years of experience an employee has had with a given skill) unless we know EMPLOYEE# (the number of the employee to whom this refers) and SKILLCODE (the skill in question).

In general a nonflat record is normalized by converting it into two or more flat records.

If the normalized records above were implemented in a CODASYL, DL/1, or other nonrelational data-base management system, we would not repeat the field EMPLOYEE# in the lower record. A linkage to the upper record would imply this key:

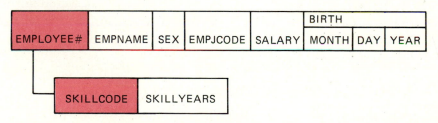

A relational data base *would* employ a separate SKILLS record (relation) with a key EMPLOYEE + SKILLCODE; it thus avoids pointer mechanisms in the logical representation of data.

In much of this chapter we are concerned not with how the physical implementation is done, but with the overall *logical* representation of data. We need to analyze and chart an enterprise's information resources and how they are used. We draw the lower record with its complete concatenated key so that it can stand alone and the key uniquely identifies the data in the record.

The important reason for normalization is that it gives a clear simple data structure which is necessary for many of the subsequent stages in information engineering.

CONCATENATED KEYS

Employee number and skillcode in the example above are both entities. To identify the number of years an employee has had a skill, we need to refer to both entities and use a key which combines the two entity identifiers. The same is true with a line item on an order. We need both ORDER NUMBER and PRODUCT NUMBER to identify it.

Some records need more than two entity keys to identify them.

We use the term *normalized record* to refer to these records with concatenated keys as well as to records with a single data-item key. The attributes we store in them should be dependent on the complete concatenated key, just as SKILL YEARS is dependent on EMPLOYEE# and SKILLCODE.

FUNCTIONAL DEPENDENCE

In attempting to lay out the relationships between data items, the designer must concern himself with which data items are dependent on which other. The phrase *functionally dependent* is defined as follows:

Data item B of a record R is functionally dependent on data item A of R if, at every instant of time, each value in A has no more than one value in B associated with it in record R [2].

Saying that B is functionally dependent on A is equivalent to saying that *A identifies B*. In other words, if we know the value of A, we can find the value of B that is associated with it.

For example, in an employee record, the SALARY data item is functionally dependent on EMPLOYEE#. For one EMPLOYEE# there is one SALARY. To find the value of SALARY in a data base you would normally go via EMPLOYEE#. The latter is a key that identifies the attribute SALARY.

Consider the record for the entity EMPLOYEE:

EMPLOYEE#	EMPLOYEE-NAME	SALARY	PROJECT#	COMPLETION-DATE

The functional dependencies in this record are as follows:

EMPLOYEE#	is dependent on EMPLOYEE-NAME
EMPLOYEE-NAME	is dependent on EMPLOYEE#
SALARY	is dependent on either EMPLOYEE-NAME or EMPLOYEE#
PROJECT#	is dependent on either EMPLOYEE-NAME or EMPLOYEE#
COMPLETION-DATE	is dependent on EMPLOYEE-NAME, EMPLOYEE#, or PROJECT#

EMPLOYEE# is not functionally dependent on SALARY because more than one employee could have the same salary. Similarly, EMPLOYEE# is not functionally dependent on PROJECT#, but COMPLETION-DATE is. No other data item in the record is fully dependent on PROJECT#.

In the preceding chapter we drew one-to-one associations as single-headed arrows. A functional dependency may be drawn as a single-headed arrow:

$$\text{EMPLOYEE\#} \longrightarrow \text{SALARY}$$

When we remove *redundant* associations while synthesizing data, as in the example at the end of the preceding chapter, it is associations that are functional dependencies which we remove.

Functional dependencies are the single most important input to the data-base design process apart from the data items themselves. Some notations for drawing data-base structures *cannot represent functional dependencies;* they draw a line with no arrowhead on it when there is really a functional dependency. Such notations are best avoided.

Using this notation, we can draw the functional dependencies in the EMPLOYEE record as follows:

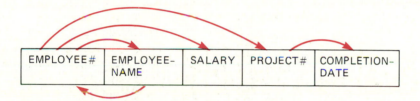

A data item can be functionally dependent on a *group* of data items rather than a single data item. Consider, for example, the following record, which shows how programmers spent their time:

PROGRAMMER–ACTIVITY

PROGRAMMER#	PACKAGE#	PROGRAMMER– NAME	PACKAGE– NAME	TOTAL– HOURS– WORKED

TOTAL-HOURS-WORKED is functionally dependent on the concatenated key (PROGRAMMER#, PACKAGE#).

The functional dependencies in this record can be drawn as follows:

PROGRAMMER#	PACKAGE#	PROGRAMMER– NAME	PACKAGE– NAME	TOTAL– HOURS– WORKED

FULL FUNCTIONAL DEPENDENCY   A data item or a collection of data items, B, of a record R can be said to be *fully functionally dependent* on another collection of data items, A, of record R if B is functionally dependent on the whole of A but not on any subset of A.

For example, in the record above, TOTAL-HOURS-WORKED is fully functionally dependent on the concatenated key (PROGRAMMER#, PACKAGE#) because it refers to how many hours a given programmer has worked on a given package. Neither PROGRAMMER# alone nor PACKAGE# alone identifies TOTAL-HOURS-WORKED.

TOTAL-HOURS-WORKED, however, is the *only* data item which is fully functionally dependent on the concatenated key. PROGRAMMER-NAME is fully functionally dependent on PROGRAMMER# alone, and PACKAGE-NAME is fully functionally dependent on PACKAGE# alone. The arrows above make the dependencies clear.

SECOND NORMAL FORM   We are now in a position to define second normal form. First a simple definition:

Each attribute in a record is functionally dependent on the whole key of that record.

Where the key consists of more than one data item the record may not be in second normal form. The record above with the key PROGRAMMER# + PACKAGE# is not in second normal form because TOTAL-HOURS-WORKED depends on the whole key, whereas PROGRAMMER-NAME and PACKAGE-NAME each depend on only one data item in the key. Similarly, the following record is not in second normal form:

PART#	SUPPLIER#	SUPPLIER-NAME	SUPPLIER-DETAILS	PRICE

There are a few problems that can result from this record not being in second normal form:

1. We cannot enter details about a supplier until that supplier supplies a part. If the supplier does not supply a part, there is no key.

2. If a supplier should temporarily cease to supply any part, the deletion of the last record containing that SUPPLIER# will also delete the details of the supplier. It would normally be desirable that SUPPLIER-DETAILS be preserved.

3. We have problems when we attempt to update the supplier details. We must search for every record which contains that supplier as part of the key. If a supplier supplies many parts, much redundant updating of supplier details will be needed.

These types of irregularities can be removed by splitting the record into two records in second normal form, as shown in Fig. 12.1. Only PRICE is

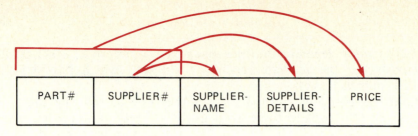

PART#	SUPPLIER#	SUPPLIER-NAME	SUPPLIER-DETAILS	PRICE

An instance of this record:

PART#	SUPPLIER#	SUPPLIER-NAME	SUPPLIER-DETAILS	PRICE
1	1000	JONES	x	20
1	1500	ABC	x	28
1	2050	XYZ	y	22
1	1900	P–H	z	30
2	3100	ALLEN	z	520
2	1000	JONES	x	500
2	2050	XYZ	y	590
3	2050	XYZ	y	1000
4	1000	JONES	x	80
4	3100	ALLEN	z	90
4	1900	P–H	z	95
5	1500	ABC	x	160
5	1000	JONES	x	140

To convert the above records into second normal form, we split it into two records, thus:

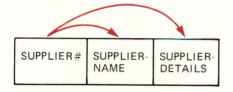

SUPPLIER#	SUPPLIER-NAME	SUPPLIER-DETAILS

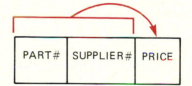

PART#	SUPPLIER#	PRICE

An instance on the above pair of records:

SUPPLIER#	SUPPLIER-NAME	SUPPLIER-DETAILS
1000	JONES	x
1500	ABC	x
2050	XYZ	y
1900	P–H	z
3100	ALLEN	z

PART#	SUPPLIER#	PRICE
1	1000	20
1	1500	28
1	2050	22
1	1900	30
2	3100	520
2	1000	500
2	2050	590
3	2050	1000
4	1000	80
4	3100	90
4	1900	95
5	1500	160
5	1000	140

Figure 12.1 Conversion to second normal form.

fully functionally dependent on the concatenated key, so all other attributes are removed to the separate record on the left, which has SUPPLIER-NUMBER only as its key.

Splitting to second normal form is the type of splitting that natural data-base growth tends to force, so it might as well be anticipated when the data base is first set up. In general, every data item in a record should be dependent on the *entire* key; otherwise, it should be removed to a separate record.

Figure 12.1 illustrates the splitting of the record above into second-normal-form *normalized records.*

CANDIDATE KEYS   The *key* of an normalized record must have the following properties:

1. *Unique identification.* For every record occurrence the key must uniquely identify the record.

2. *Nonredundancy.* No data item in the key can be discarded without destroying the property of unique identification.

It sometimes happens that more than one data item or set of data items *could* be the key of a record. Such alternative choices are referred to as *candidate keys.*

One candidate key must be designated the *primary key.* We will draw the functional dependencies for candidate keys which are not the primary key *underneath* the record, thus:

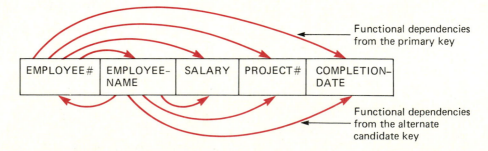

In this illustration EMPLOYEE-NAME is regarded as a candidate key—an alternative to EMPLOYEE#. This is not generally done in practice because two employees *might* have the same name. Only EMPLOYEE# is truly unique.

The possible existence of candidate keys complicates the definitions of second and third normal forms.

A more comprehensive definition of second normal form is:

A record R is in second normal form if it is in first normal form and every nonprime data item of R is fully functionally dependent on each candidate key of R [2].

In the EMPLOYEE record above the candidate keys have only one data item, and hence the record is always in second normal form because the nonprime data items *must* be fully dependent on the candidate keys. When the candidate keys consist of more than one data item, a first-normal-form record may not be in second normal form.

THIRD NORMAL FORM   A record that *is* in second normal form can have another type of anomoly. It may have a data item which is not a key but which itself identifies other data items. This is referred to as a *transitive dependence*. Transitive dependencies can cause problems. The step of putting data into *third normal form* removes transitive dependencies.

Suppose that A, B, and C are three data items or distinct collections of data items of a record R. If C is functionally dependent on B and B is functionally dependent on A, then C is functionally dependent on A. If the inverse mapping is nonsimple (i.e., if A is not functionally dependent on B *or* B is not functionally dependent on C), then C is said to be *transitively dependent* on A.

In a diagram C is transitively dependent on A if

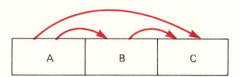

Conversion to third normal form removes this transitive dependence by splitting the record into two, thus:

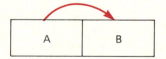 

The following record is not in third normal from because COMPLETION-DATE is dependent on PROJECT#.

EMPLOYEE

EMPLOYEE#	EMPLOYEE-NAME	SALARY	PROJECT#	COMPLETION-DATE

A few problems might result from this record not being in third normal form.

1. Before any employees are recruited for a project the completion date of the project cannot be recorded because there is no EMPLOYEE record.

2. If all the employees should leave the project so that the project has no employees until others are recruited, all records containing the completion date would be deleted. This may be thought an unlikely occurrence, but on other types of files a similar danger of loss of information can be less improbable.

3. If the completion date is changed, it will be necessary to search for all records containing that completion date, and update them all.

A simple definition of *third normal form* is:

A record is in second normal form and each attribute is functionally dependent on the key and nothing but the key.

A more formal definition which incorporates candidate keys is as follows:

A record R is in third normal form if it is in second normal form and every nonprime data item of R is nontransitively dependent on each candidate key of R [2].

Figure 12.2 shows the conversion of the EMPLOYEE record above to third normal form.

The conversion to third normal form produces a separate record for each entity-normalized record. For example, Fig. 12.2 produced a separate record for the entity PROJECT. Usually, this normalized record would be needed anyway. We need data separately storing for each entity.

STORAGE AND PERFORMANCE   The concept of third normal form applies to all data bases. Experience has shown that the records of a CODASYL system, the segments of a DL/1 system, or the group of data items in other systems can benefit from being in third normal form.

Objections to third normal form are occasionally heard on the grounds that it requires more storage or more machine time. A third-normal-form structure usually has more records after all the splitting described above. Isn't that worse from the hardware point of view?

Not necessarily. In fact, although there are more records, they almost always take less storage. The reason is that non-third-normal-form records usually have much *value* redundancy.

Compare the records in Fig. 12.1. Here records not in second normal form are converted to second normal form by splitting. It will be seen that the lower red part of Fig. 12.1 has fewer *values* of data written down than the red part at the top. There are fewer values of SUPPLIER-NAME and SUPPLIER-DETAILS. This shrinkage does not look very dramatic on such

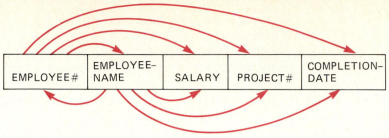

An instance of this record:

EMPLOYEE#	EMPLOYEE-NAME	SALARY	PROJECT#	COMPLETION-DATE
120	JONES	2000	x	17.7.84
121	HARPO	1700	x	17.7.84
270	GARFUNKAL	1800	y	12.1.87
273	SELSI	3600	x	17.7.84
274	ABRAHMS	3000	z	21.3.86
279	HIGGINS	2400	y	12.1.87
301	FLANNEL	1800	z	21.3.86
306	MCGRAW	2100	x	17.7.84
310	ENSON	3000	z	21.3.86
315	GOLDSTEIN	3100	x	17.7.84
317	PUORRO	2700	y	12.1.87
320	MANSINI	1700	y	12.1.87
321	SPOTO	2900	x	17.7.84
340	SCHAFT	3100	x	17.7.84
349	GOLD	1900	z	21.3.86

To convert the above record into third normal form we split it into two records, thus:

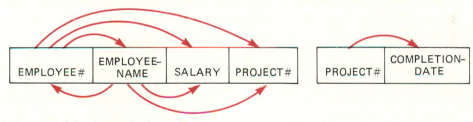

An instance of the above pair of records:

EMPLOYEE#	EMPLOYEE-NAME	SALARY	PROJECT#
120	JONES	2000	x
121	HARPO	1700	x
270	GARFUNKAL	1800	y
273	SELSI	3600	x
274	ABRAHMS	3000	z
279	HIGGINS	2400	y
301	FLANNEL	1800	z
306	MCGRAW	2100	x
310	ENSON	3000	z
315	GOLDSTEIN	3100	x
317	PUORRO	2700	y
320	MANSINI	1700	y
321	SPOTO	2900	x
340	SCHAFT	3100	x

PROJECT#	COMPLETION-DATE
x	17.7.84
y	12.1.87
z	21.3.86

Figure 12.2 Conversion to third normal form.

a small illustration. If there had been thousands of suppliers and thousands of parts, and many attributes of both, the shrinkage would have been spectacular.

Again, compare the red parts of Fig. 12.2. Here a record is converted to third normal form by splitting. The number of *values* of data shrinks. There are fewer values of. COMPLETION-DATE recorded after the split. Once more, if there had been many employees, many projects, and many attributes of those projects, the shrinkage would have been dramatic.

Conversion to third normal form almost always reduces the amount of storage used, often dramatically.

What about machine time and accesses? Often this is less after normalization. Before normalization many aspects of the data are tangled together and must all be read at once. After normalization they are separated and so a small record is read.

Also, because there is less value redundancy in third normal form, there is less duplicated updating of the redundant values. Suppose that project x slips its completion date (which it does every week!). In the record at the top of Fig. 12.2 the completion date has to be changed seven times; in the third-normal-form version it has to be changed only once. A similar argument applies to SUPPLIER-NAME and SUPPLIER-DETAILS in Fig. 12.1. The argument would have more force if the examples had hundreds of employees, thousands of suppliers, and many attributes that have to be updated.

DEVIATIONS FROM THIRD NORMAL FORM There are, however, exceptions to this. On rare occasions a designer may consciously design non-third-normal-form records for performance reasons.

We recommend that data models *always* be designed in third normal form, but that the physical data-base designer be permitted to deviate from it if he has good reasons and if the data administrator agrees that no serious harm will be done.

In some cases third-normal-form records are split for machine performance reasons, as illustrated in Fig. 12.3. The result is two groups of attributes with the same key type. In the upper example the attributes used for high-volume computer runs are separated from those with infrequent use in order to speed up the high-volume access. In the lower example in Fig. 12.3 attributes stored for the weekly batch run are not needed for normal on-line operations. They are stored separately so that the on-line data base is smaller.

Only in extreme cases are such actions worth taking. They are not done by the designer of the *logical* data base, but separately by the *physical*-data-base designer.

In another example a record has a lengthy attribute, say CONTRACT DETAILS. Only some applications require CONTRACT DETAILS, so the attribute is replaced by a short code or pointer which points to where CONTRACT DETAILS is stored in a separate logical file.

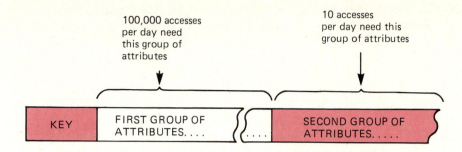

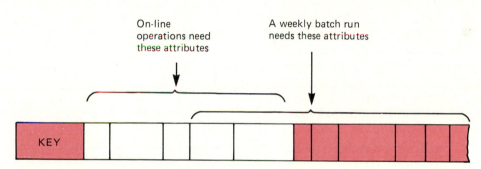

Figure 12.3 Third-normal-form records are sometimes subdivided for physical implementation to achieve smaller on-line data bases or better performance with high-volume runs.

Again only 10% of the records of a certain record type have a given group of attributes. The logical file or relation is therefore split into those which do have this group and those which do not.

SEMANTIC DISINTEGRITY

A further reason for using third normal form is that certain data-base queries can run into problems when data are not cleanly structured. A query, perhaps entered with a data-base query language, can appear to be valid, but in fact have subtle illogical aspects sometimes referred to as *semantic disintegrity*. When the data are in third normal form, rules can be devised for preventing semantic disintegrity or warning the user about his query. These rules are given in the author's book *Computer Data-Base Organization* [3].

If data are *not* in third normal form, no set of rules can be devised which safely warn against semantic disintegrity. Because of this, ambiguities arise or wrong results appear when relational JOIN operations are performed.

Because of this ambiguity or disintegrity problem, some organizations have created query languages or other data-base facilities which cannot perform a relation JOIN. This is harmful because often a join operation is needed. A better solution is to enforce rules relating to third-normal-form design.

SUMMARY   The concept of third normal form applies to all data bases. Experience has shown that the records of a CODASYL system, the segments of a DL/1 system, or the group of data items in other systems can benefit from being in third normal form. Relational systems and fourth-generation languages benefit strongly from third-normal-form data.

We believe that the ability to spot that a record is not in third normal form should be part of a systems analyst's instinct when he deals with data. He may sometimes choose to allow a record or segment to be stored *not* in third normal form, but when this is so, he should at least know what he is doing, understand his reasons, and understand the possible consequences when new data items and association are added. A record not in third normal form may occasionally be used for performance reasons.

A record in third normal form has the following simple structure:

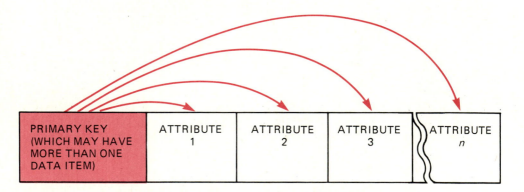

The key may be concatenated, using multiple data items. There are no hidden single-headed-arrow associations in the record (no transitive dependencies). If they key is concatenated, all data items are dependent on the entire key.

We can give a loose definition of third normal form, which has the advantage of being easy to remember:

Every data item in a record is dependent on the key, the whole key, and nothing but the key.

If a systems analyst remembers this definition (understanding that it is not rigorous like those earlier in the chapter) he can quickly spot and modify records which are not in third normal form. He should be familiar enough with this, that alarm bells go off in his mind whenever he sees records which are not in third normal form.

This clean, simple, data grouping is easy to implement and to use. There may be complications in store in the future if more complex record structures are used.

For the data-base administrator, third normal form is an aid to precise thinking. A data base in third normal form can grow and evolve naturally. The updating rules are straightforward. A third-normal-form record type can have records added to it or can have records deleted without the problems that could occur with non-third-normal-form record types. Consequently, third-normal-form structuring gives a simple view of data to programmers and users, and makes them less likely to perform invalid operations.

Figure 12.4 gives a simplified illustration of the three steps in achieving third-normal-form structures.

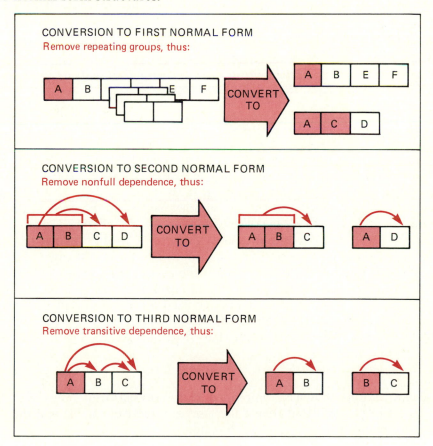

Figure 12.4 Simplified illustration of the three steps in conversion of data to third normal form. Figure 12.5 gives an illustration with real data.

A SUGGESTED EXERCISE

Probably the best way for a data-processing user to become convinced of the value (or otherwise) of normalization is to take a section of his files and write down what third-normal-form records would be used to represent them. A group of systems analysts should then list all the plausible changes that might occur to the files as data processing evolves in the years ahead, and see how many of these changes would necessitate restructuring the records in such a way that previously written application programs would have to be changed. Compare this with what reprogramming would be needed if the same changes were applied to the existing records.

In examining existing data bases it has been my experience that time and time again they are not in third normal form. This spells trouble for the future. Unless it was the conscious policy of management to create third-normal-form structures, the design has been far from these principles.

PROBLEMS WITH UNNORMALIZED DATA

Data that are not fully normalized can cause all manner of problems, many of which are subtle and quite unforeseen by the analysts who design the system.

DATA ANALYST:

The users won't say "You violated third normal form" or "You have the same data with different names in two data bases." They'll say: "We have this problem. The totals on these reports don't match." The commanding officer threw out two reports and wouldn't look at them again. He said they didn't make sense.

They often bypass the problem. They tie a knot in their handkerchief. They say: "Be careful not to do this because it'll cause that." They describe the symptoms of the problems, not the causes.

I listen to the problem and go and check thoroughly. Ninety-nine times out of a hundred there's a conceptual error, usually in the data-base structure or conditions for updating it. Sometimes it's an error in the processing logic. More often than not, though, the error is in the data model.

Organizations that have employed third-normal-form design for years *have* found in practice that their data bases are relatively stable and that this *has* greatly reduced the cost of maintenance.

Third-normal-form data also clarify the design of applications. The techniques for designing data-base applications, discussed in Part IV of this book, are all built on third-normal-form data. Without this clear thinking about data, application design is more difficult and prone to subtle unrecognized problems.

LEAD MIS DESIGNER:

The data model and the function breakdown go hand in hand. I look at the organization, I'm talking to all these managers, and information is pouring at me in all directions—and there's zero coherence. But when you talk to enough people and see enough about the organization, the key information entities start to recur. Stage by stage I build the data model that's needed.

INTERVIEWER:

In third normal form?

LEAD MIS DESIGNER:

Oh, absolutely! It must be.

A data base *implemented* in third normal form is capable of being used in new ways quickly. This is important in achieving the flexibility-of-use goal in data-base design. New query facilities, report generators, and high-level languages are steadily increasing our capability to derive new results quickly from existing data bases. Much of this power is lost if the data are not correctly normalized.

AN EXAMPLE OF NORMALIZATION   Consider an ORDER record with the following unnormalized structure:

ORDER   (*Order number,* order date, customer number, customer name, customer address ((product number, product name, quantity ordered, product price, product total)), order total.)

Applying the three normalization steps to this example is illustrated in Fig. 12.5.

Application of the *first-normal-form* rule (remove repeating groups) creates two records: ORDER and ORDER-PRODUCT. The primary key is made up of *Order#* and *Product#.* (ORDER-PRODUCT is in fact the ORDER LINE ITEM record that we discussed above.)

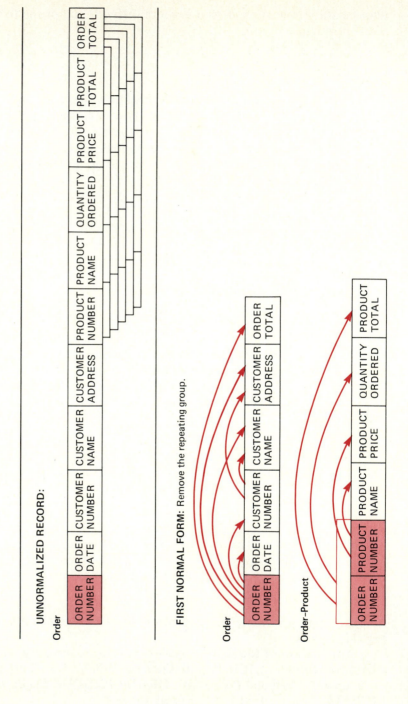

UNNORMALIZED RECORD:

Order

| ORDER NUMBER | ORDER DATE | CUSTOMER NUMBER | CUSTOMER NAME | CUSTOMER ADDRESS | PRODUCT NUMBER | PRODUCT NAME | QUANTITY ORDERED | PRODUCT PRICE | PRODUCT TOTAL | ORDER TOTAL |

FIRST NORMAL FORM: Remove the repeating group.

Order

| ORDER NUMBER | ORDER DATE | CUSTOMER NUMBER | CUSTOMER NAME | CUSTOMER ADDRESS | ORDER TOTAL |

Order–Product

| ORDER NUMBER | PRODUCT NUMBER | PRODUCT NAME | PRODUCT PRICE | QUANTITY ORDERED | PRODUCT TOTAL |

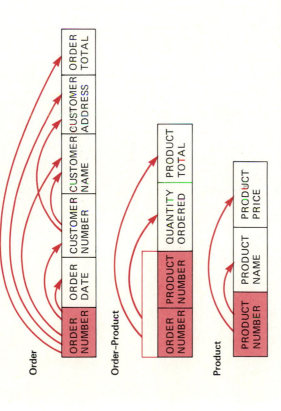

SECOND NORMAL FORM: Remove attributes not dependent on the whole of a (concatenated) primary key, as in the ORDER-PRODUCT record above.

Figure 12.5 Illustration of the three stages of normalization.

THIRD NORMAL FORM: Remove attributes dependent on data item(s) other than the primary key, as in the ORDER record above.

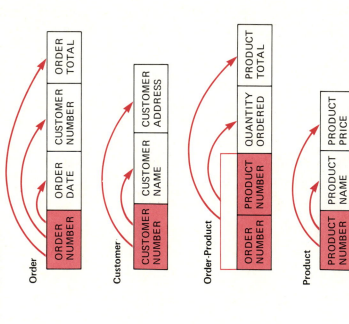

Figure 12.5 (Continued)

Second normal form removes the product name from the ORDER-PRODUCT record into a new record: PRODUCT. Product name is wholly dependent on product number; it is only partially dependent on the primary (combined or compound) key of ORDER-PRODUCT: *Order# + Product#*.

Third normal form removes the customer details from the ORDER record to a separate CUSTOMER record. Customer name and address are wholly dependent on customer number; they are not dependent at all on the primary key of ORDER (i.e., *Order#*). (A customer will not change his name and address with each new order . . . unless he doesn't intend to pay for it!)

The four resulting records—ORDER, CUSTOMER, ORDER-PRODUCT, and PRODUCT—in Fig. 12.4 are in third normal form. Normalization has, in fact, produced the four records we discussed earlier, which we intuitively felt were necessary to accommodate business change more readily.

The CUSTOMER and PRODUCT normalized records would be needed for other purposes and created by other analysts. We need to synthesize the data that result from multiple normalization processes, as discussed later in the book.

END-USER PARTICIPATION   This book stresses strongly the need for end-user participation in the design of data. Users know their own data instinctively, whereas DP analysts are much less familiar with it.

REFERENCES

1. E. F. Codd, "Further Normalization of the Data Base Relational Model," in *Courant Computer Science Simposia: Data Base Systems,* ed. R. Rustin, Prentice-Hall, Inc., Englewood Cliffs, NJ 1972.

2. James Martin, *Principles of Data-Base Management,* Prentice-Hall, Inc., Englewood Cliffs, NJ, 1976.

3. James Martin, *Computer Data-Base Organization,* 2nd ed., Prentice-Hall, Inc., Englewood Cliffs, NJ, 1977.

13 FOURTH NORMAL FORM

(This chapter may be omitted on first reading of the book.)

INTRODUCTION

A further step of normalization is sometimes described as fourth normal form. Many data administrators have ignored this, being content to stop at third normal form, and regarding fourth normal form as too esoteric. Certain combinations of data items in third normal form can, however, contain anomalies which require a further normalization step. This step is concerned with *multivalued dependencies*.

MULTIVALUED DEPENDENCIES

Most attributes are functionally dependent on a primary key. For example, AGE is functionally dependent on EMPLOYEE:

EMPLOYEE ——————▶AGE

For certain attributes, however, there may be more than one value associated with a primary key. For example, an EMPLOYEE may have more than one SKILL:

EMPLOYEE ——————▶SKILL

This is referred to as a *multivalued dependency*. One value of a data item X identifies not one but several values of a data item Y. If you know the value of EMPLOYEE, you can find the values of multiple associated skills.

One multivalued dependency can be recorded in a flat file as in the following example:

EMPLOYEE	SKILL
JENKINS	ACCOUNTANT
JENKINS	COBOL PROGRAMMING
JONES	NUCLEAR ENGINEER
JONES	STATISTICS
JONES	COBOL PROGRAMMING
JUNG	PHYSICS

If, however, a multivalued dependency is recorded in a flat file which also contains functional dependencies (i.e., single-valued dependencies), redundancy exists. For example:

EMPLOYEE	AGE	ADDRESS	SKILL
JENKINS	27	xxxxxxxxxx	ACCOUNTANT
JENKINS	27	xxxxxxxxxx	COBOL PROGRAMMING
JONES	39	yyyyyyyyyy	NUCLEAR ENGINEER
JONES	39	yyyyyyyyyy	STATISTICS
JONES	39	yyyyyyyyyy	COBOL PROGRAMMING
JUNG	45	zzzzzzzzzzzz	PHYSICS

Here, when an employee's age or address changes it will have to be changed in several records.

This anomaly can be avoided by placing the multivalued dependency in a separate record from the functional dependencies, thus:

EMPLOYEE	AGE	ADDRESS
JENKINS	27	xxxxxxxxxx
JONES	39	yyyyyyyyyy
JUNG	35	zzzzzzzzzzzz

EMPLOYEE   SKILL

JENKINS	ACCOUNTANT
JENKINS	COBOL PROGRAMMING
JONES	NUCLEAR ENGINEER
JONES	STATISTICS
JONES	COBOL PROGRAMMING
JUNG	PHYSICS

In practice the *physical* implementation of this in some systems uses a nonflat file in which a record can be of variable length and can contain multiple values of a data item like SKILL without also containing redundant values of items like AGE and ADDRESS, which are functionally dependent on the key.

FOURTH NORMAL FORM

The term *fourth normal form* is used when discussing anomalies caused by multiple dependencies. These can occur within the key of a record that is in third normal form.

Suppose that an employee can be assigned to several projects concurrently. Also suppose that he can have several skills. If we record this information in a single relation, all three attributes are needed to make a tuple unique, so the entire tuple is a key, thus:

EMPLOYEE-PROJECT-SKILL

EMPLOYEE #	PROJECT #	SKILL-CODE
1	3	A
1	3	B
1	3	C
1	7	A
1	7	B
1	7	C

In this example there are no attributes which are not part of the key, so the relation could be said to be in third normal form.

There is much redundancy in the relation above. If we add a new project to employee 1, we have to add several new tuples. We can remove redundancy if we split the relation into two relations, thus:

EMPLOYEE-PROJECT

EMPLOYEE #	PROJECT #
1	3
1	7

EMPLOYEE-SKILL

EMPLOYEE #	SKILL-CODE
1	A
1	B
1	C

Now a new project can be added by the addition of one tuple.

This view is said to be in *fourth normal form.* Fourth normal form avoids anomalies such as the above which are caused by more than one multivalued dependency in a relation.

As with conversion to second or third normal form, conversion to fourth normal form usually lowers the amount of data that are stored. In the example above the non-fourth-normal-form version contains 18 data items and the fourth-normal-form version contains 10.

This fourth-normal-form view would be created by the canonical synthesis process. We would employ user views saying: "What projects does an employee work on?":

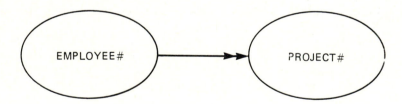

and "What skills does an employee have?":

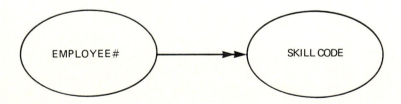

The canonical synthesis process would not group the three data items into one key.

DEFINITIONS OF FOURTH NORMAL FORM

Fagin [1] defines fourth normal form as follows:

A relation R is in fourth normal form if whenever a nontrivial multivalued dependency X———▶▶Y holds for R, then so does the functional dependency X———▶A for every column name A of R.

X and Y in this definition may refer to single data items or to grouped (concatenated) data items.

The multivalued dependency (A, B)———▶▶C holds for every record with exactly three data items, A, B and C. In other words, for each value of the pair A and B, there is a set of values of C. This is called a *trivial* multivalued dependency and is of no interest.

The definition above says, in effect, that a *record should not contain more than one nontrivial multivalued dependency*. If it contains EMPLOYEE#———▶▶PROJECT#, then it should not also contain EMPLOYEE# ———▶▶SKILLCODE.

If it contains EMPLOYEE#———▶▶PROJECT#, then every other data-item in the record should be functionally dependent on EMPLOYEE#; that is, EMPLOYEE#———▶A for each data item A other than PROJECT#.

Note that if a record is in third normal form and it has a concatenated key like EMPLOYEE# + PROJECT#, then all data items are identified by the whole of this key and none by EMPLOYEE# alone. EMPLOYEE#———▶A does not exist.

In general, it is desirable to go further than Fagin's definition and avoid mixing any dependency (function or multivalued) with a multivalued dependency. This avoids the problem with the (EMPLOYEE, AGE, ADDRESS, SKILL) record illustrated above.

Another definition of fourth normal form is also concerned with solving the same problem [2]:

A record is in fourth normal form if and only if it is in third normal form and no part of a concatenated key is unrelated to any of the remaining data items in that key.

The problem in the record above containing EMPLOYEE#, PROJECT#, and SKILLCODE arises from that fact the PROJECT# and SKILLCODE are unrelated. They need to be split into separate records.

KEYS THAT CANNOT BE SPLIT

A concern with both of the definitions of fourth normal form above is that sometimes concatenated keys are needed which cannot be split as above because they are required to *identify* other attributes.

Consider a situation in which the PRICE of a product is functionally dependent not on PRODUCT# alone, because different types of customers are charged different prices, and different prices are charged in different countries.

We have

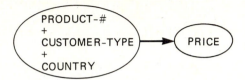

A given product is marketed only to certain customer types, so we have the multivalued dependency

$$PRODUCT\# \longrightarrow\!\!\!\!\rightarrow CUSTOMER\text{-}TYPE$$

Also, a product is marketed only in certain states, so we have another multivalued dependency $PRODUCT\# \longrightarrow\!\!\!\!\rightarrow COUNTRY$.

Using either of the definitions above, the following record would not be in fourth normal form:

PRODUCT#	CUSTOMER-TYPE	COUNTRY

It could be regarded as *all key,* and is similar to the examples of non-fourth-normal-form records in the literature on the subject [1–3]. It would be split, as before, into

PRODUCT#	CUSTOMER-TYPE

and

PRODUCT#	COUNTRY

Now, however, we need the three data items in one record because PRICE is functionally dependent on a concatenation of them. We are therefore forced to use

PRODUCT#	CUSTOMER-TYPE	COUNTRY	PRICE

To accommodate concatenated keys which are necessary, we would add to Fagin's definition of fourth normal form as follows:

A relation R (or record) is in fourth normal form if and only if it is in third normal form, and should there be no nonprime data items, the following applies: Whenever a nontrivial multivalued dependency $X \longrightarrow\!\!\!\!\rightarrow Y$ holds for R, then so does the functional dependency $X \longrightarrow A$ for every data item A of R.

In other words, if a record is all key, it cannot have more than one multivalued dependency.

PRACTICAL STEPS

In data-base practice the concept of fourth normal form has caused much confusion. This is partly because of the confusion over defining fourth normal form and partly because of the abstruse style with which papers on the subject have been written.

In practice a simple rule can be given for the creation of a logical model of data:

If a multivalued dependency is employed and is necessary, avoid mixing it with other dependencies in the same logical record unless this intermixing is necessary to build a concatenated key on which other attributes are fully functionally dependent.

Concatenated keys should be brought into existence only where their use is *necessary* for the identification of other data items.

The canonical synthesis process described in Chapter 14 gives a clear, easy-to-use set of steps for creating data bases which are in third and fourth normal forms.

Most of the examples of non-fourth-normal-form data in the literature would not have come into existence if canonical synthesis were used, because they are unwanted and unnecessary combinations of data items. In commercial practice examples of non-fourth-normal-form data are rarely encountered, and are easy to avoid.

REFERENCES

1. R. Fagin, "Multivalued Dependencies and a New Normal Form for Relational Databases," *ACM Transactions on Database Systems,* Vol. 2, No. 3, September 1977.

2. J. Stewart, "Relational Data Bases," Part 3, *Computer Weekly,* November 9, 1978.

3. C. J. Date, *An Introduction to Database Systems,* Addison-Wesley Publishing Co., Inc., Reading, MA, 1975.

14 CANONICAL SYNTHESIS

INTRODUCTION   Chapters 12 and 13 were concerned with the relations between data items in a record. This chapter is concerned with the association of data items to form an entire data base or model of data.

CANONICAL SCHEMA   It is desirable to step away from the current software for a moment and ask the question: Are there any inherent properties in the data which should lead to data items being grouped and groups being interconnected in a particular structure? The design procedure described in this chapter makes such structures clear. We refer to them as *canonical structures*. To be inherently stable, and be able to evolve naturally to meet the needs of new applications, a data model should have a canonical structure. This gives it the best chance of surviving future changes. It minimizes the risk of having to rewrite application programs because of data-base changes.

The ideas of canonical structuring are important in the design of data bases using today's software. They provide a design technique which the data-base administrator can and should apply in designing the schemas.

Both the ideas of third normal form and the ideas of canonical structuring are an aid to clear thinking about data. The systems analyst should make himself sufficiently at ease with both sets of ideas to apply them freely.

We will define a canonical model as *a model of data which represents the inherent structure of that data and hence is independent of individual applications of the data and also of the software or hardware mechanisms that are employed in representing and using the data.*

A DESIGN PROCEDURE

A procedure is described in this chapter by means of which a canonical model can be derived, starting from a number of end-user views of data supplemented by the views of the data administrator. *The records in the resulting structure are in third normal form.*

As we have stressed, most data bases will be changed frequently as new applications are added and new user views incorporated. It is therefore of value if the procedure can be an incremental one to observe the effect on an existing data base of incorporating new data.

The canonical form of data that we derive in this chapter is independent of whether the data will eventually be represented by means of hierarchical, CODASYL, relational, or other structures. An additional step in deriving a workable schema is to convert the canonical form of the data into a structure that can be supported by whatever software is being used. This is a relatively straightforward step.

The process of canonical synthesis creates the *logical model* of data shown in Fig. 11.2. This model is then converted into a logical representation (schema or schemas) that the software can handle, and this is represented physically (Fig. 11.2).

In first deriving the canonical form of the data, we will ignore the question of machine performance. Infrequently used linkages between data will be treated in the same way as linkages of high usage. The resulting minimal data structure will then be reexamined to distinguish between the high-usage and low-usage paths, or paths that are used in real-time operation and batch operation. It will often be necessary to deviate from the minimal structure because of constraints in the software that is used.

The synthesis process can be done largely automatically with a tool that produces third-normal-form structures and good documentation. Such a tool should be used on a corporatewide basis to design, clarify, unify, and document the corporation's data structures. The tool can be used in conjunction with a data dictionary as discussed in Chapter 15.

APPLICATION OR SUBJECT DATA BASES

Canonical synthesis is valuable with either *application* data bases or *subject* data bases.

Generally, we recommend the use of *subject* data bases, but application pressures sometimes demand that application data bases be built. Also, some application areas can be isolated from the use of data elsewhere without doing any harm. When this is the case it can simplify the development and control of that application area.

In doing *application*-data-base design the data administrator collects all the views of data he can relating to that set of applications, and synthesizes them.

In doing *subject*-data-base design he usually starts in the same way but then tries to create a structure representing the inherent properties of the data independently of any one application. This is a bigger task and needs assistance from many types of end users. It takes multiple reiterations in which the data administrator and the users examine the data to determine whether the model meets their needs now and, as far as they can anticipate, in the future.

CANONICAL RECORD STRUCTURE

A user view, or data-base model, can be represented by a bubble chart, as discussed in preceding chapters.

The simplest grouping of data items is a record consisting of one key which identifies *n* attributes:

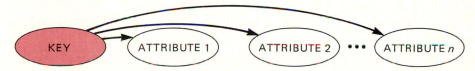

The record has no transitive dependencies and if a concatenated key is used, this key is regarded as one data item. The key completely identifies the attributes. Such a record is in third normal form. We will refer to this as a *canonical* record structure (or *canonical* segment structure where "segment" is the word used for a data-item group).

COMBINING BUBBLE CHARTS

The procedure we describe takes any number of user views of data and combines them into a minimal set of canonical records with the requisite links between records.

We will represent the user views, or application views of data, by means of bubble charts and will combine them, a step at a time, eliminating redundancies as at the end of Chapter 13. We will not include every possible link between the data items, only those which end users or application programs employ. The procedure is tedious to do by hand but is easy to do by computer.

ELIMINATION OF REDUNDANCIES

Where single arrows are used, we can eliminate those which are redundant. In the following grouping of data items, the arrow from X to Z is probably redundant:

If we know that X———►Y and Y———►Z, this implies that X———►Z (i.e., there is one value of Z for each value of X). In other words, X identifies Y; Y identifies Z; therefore, X identifies Z.

Why did we say that the arrow from X to Z is "probably" redundant? Is it not *always* redundant?

Unfortunately, we cannot be absolutely sure unless we know the meaning of the association. As we have illustrated earlier, it is possible to have more than one association between the same two data items:

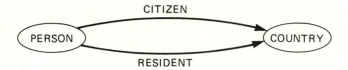

Therefore, before we delete X———►Z we must examine the meaning of the associations to be sure that X———►Z is *really* implied by X———►Y and Y———►Z.

In the following case we could not delete it. An employee has a telephone number:

The employee reports to a manager:

The manager also has a telephone number:

Combining these, we get

It would not be valid to assume that EMPLOYEE———►TELEPHONE# is redundant and delete it. The employee's telephone number is different from the manager's and we want both:

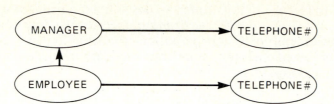

Because TELEPHONE# is an attribute, we can have a separate data item with this name associated with both EMPLOYEE and MANAGER. The problem in the example above is really caused by inappropriate naming of the data items. A manager *is* an employee, and should be handled by a loop, as at the end of Chapter 10.

The same pattern of associations could have occurred if all the data items in question had been keys.

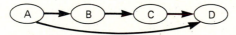

In this case the links between the three key data items would be left as shown. Nevertheless, the situation when we have

and cannot delete X———▶Z is the exception rather than the rule. We have trouble in the case above because of muddled thinking: MANAGER and EMPLOYEE are really the same type of data item—a manager is an employee. We will use the rule that single-arrow redundancies can be removed, but each time we use this rule we must look carefully to ensure that we have a genuine redundancy.

Sometimes redundancies can be removed in longer strings of links. Thus, in the case

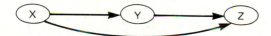

A———▶D is a candidate for removal.

**COMBINING
USER VIEWS**
In the procedure that we recommend, the first user view is drawn as a bubble chart. The other user views are then added to it one at a time. As each new user view is added, the combined diagram is inspected to see whether any single-arrow links can be removed, as illustrated above.

CANDIDATE KEYS　　In Chapter 10 we defined a primary key as *a node with one or more single arrows leaving it.*

There is one exception to this definition—the situation in which we have more than one *candidate key*; more than one data item identifies the other data items in a group, thus:

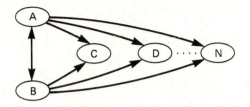

A and B in this case are equivalent. Each identifies the other; hence both identify C, D, . . . , N. There is redundancy in this diagram. We could remove A——►C, A——►D, . . . , A——►N. Alternatively, we could remove B——►C, B——►D, . . . , B——►N.

The designer might decide that A is the candidate key that he wants to employ. A, for example, might be EMPLOYEE# and B, EMPLOYEE-NAME. The designer then deletes the links B——►C, B——►D, . . . , B——►N:

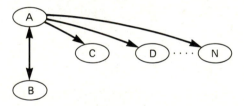

Candidate keys are not as common as this example or those in Chapter 12 might suggest. EMPLOYEE-NAME would not normally be represented as identifying EMPLOYEE# because two employees could have the same name. EMPLOYEE# is the unique identifier. Occasionally, there is a genuine A◄——►B relationship which should be left in the graph: for example, EMPLOYEE#◄——►SOCIAL SECURITY#. The designer must make a decision about which redundant links are deleted.

TRANSITIVE　　The input views to the synthesis process should
DEPENDENCIES　　contain no *hidden* primary keys. In other words, there should be no *transitive dependencies*.

The following purchase-order master record contains a transitive dependency:

ORDER#	SUPPLIER#	SUPPLIER-NAME	SUPPLIER-ADDRESS	DELIVERY-DATE	ORDER-DATE	$-TOTAL

ORDER# is the key. It might be tempting to diagram this record as

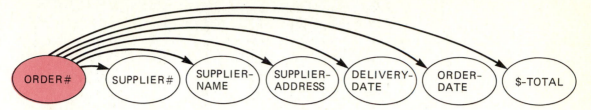

However, SUPPLIER-NAME and SUPPLIER-ADDRESS are identified by SUPPLIER#. The record is therefore better diagrammed as in Box. 14.1.

BOX. 14.1   Avoidance of hidden transitive dependencies in the representation of user views of data

The record below, taken from a user's view of data in Fig. 10.2, contains a hidden transitive dependency:

ORDER#	SUPPLIER#	SUPPLIER-NAME	SUPPLIER-ADDRESS	DELIVERY-DAY	ORDER-DATE	$-TOTAL

It might be tempting to diagram it thus:

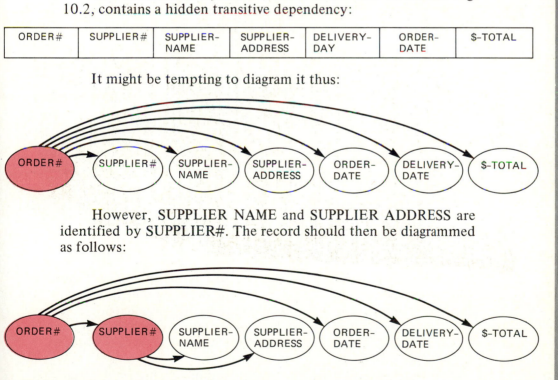

However, SUPPLIER NAME and SUPPLIER ADDRESS are identified by SUPPLIER#. The record should then be diagrammed as follows:

This process of removing transitive dependencies is essentially equivalent to the conversion to *third normal form* discussed in Chapter 12.

In the design technique discussed in this chapter, transitive dependencies will be removed from user views when they are diagrammed, making all the user's attributes directly, not transitively, dependent on a key. This is done before they are fed into the synthesis process.

CONCATENATED KEYS   Some data items may not be identified by a single data item in a user's view. For example, several suppliers may supply a part, and each charge a different price for it. The key SUPPLIER# is used for identifying information about a *supplier*. The key PART# is used for identifying information about a *part*. Neither of those keys is sufficient for identifying the *price*. The price is dependent on both the supplier and the part. Therefore, we create a new key to identify the price, which consists of SUPPLIER# and PART# joined together (concatenated). We draw this as one bubble:

The concatenated key has single-arrow links to the keys SUPPLIER# and PART#. The resulting graph is as follows:

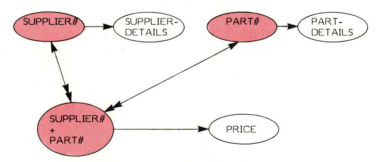

By introducing this form of concatenated key into the logical view of data, we make each data item dependent on *one* key data item.

Whenever a concatenated key is introduced, the designer should ensure that the items it identifies are dependent on the whole key, not on a portion of it only. Concatenated keys enable us to represent all records (segments) in the simple canonical form with one *key* bubble.

In practice, it is sometimes necessary to join together *more than two* data items in a concatenated key.

For example, a company supplies a product to domestic and industrial customers. It charges a different price to different *types of customers,* and also the price varies from one *state* to another. There is a *discount* giving different price reductions for different quantities purchased. The *price* is identified by a combination of CUSTOMER-TYPE, STATE, DISCOUNT, and PRODUCT.

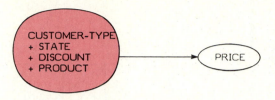

When the modeling process encounters a concatenated key such as this, it automatically makes the component fields of the key into data-item bubbles in their own right in the model. In other words, it explodes the concatenated key thus:

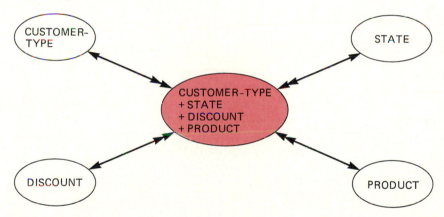

Some of these data items might become keys themselves: for example, PRODUCT; others may remain attributes.

In the final synthesis those that remain merely attributes may be deleted because they already exist in the concatenated key. They are deleted if they are not used as a separate data item.

INTERSECTION DATA

In some types of data-base software data items can be limited to the *association* between data items. A part, for example, may be supplied by several vendors; each charges a different price for it. The data item PRICE cannot be associated with the PART record alone or with the SUPPLIER record alone. It can only be associated with a combination of the two. Such information is sometimes called *intersection data*—data associated with the association between records.

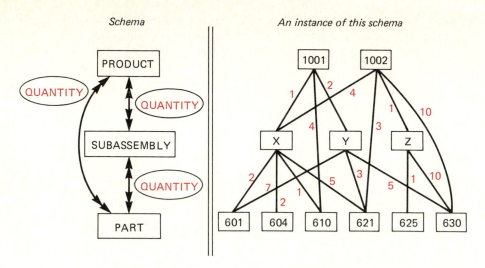

Figure 14.1 Bill-of-materials data base. In this illustration there is much intersection data. Extra records (segments) can be created to store intersection data, as in Fig. 14.2.

Figure 14.1 shows a more complex example of intersection data. Products made by a factory are composed of subassemblies and parts. In the factory data base are records called PRODUCT, SUBASSEMBLY, and PART. These records are different in composition. They might be linked as shown in the schema of Fig. 14.1. Associated with each link is a number that tells how many of a given part are in a given subassembly or product, and how many subassemblies are in a product. For example, product 1001 contains 1 of subassembly X, 2 of subassembly Y, and 4 of part 610. In general, a structure something like that in Fig. 14.1 gives a *bill of materials* showing a breakdown of the products for manufacturing purposes.

M:M ASSOCIATIONS   It is necessary to be cautious with links that have double-headed arrows pointing in both directions: *M:M* associations. There are two possible problems with them.

The first relates to physical representation. There are various straightforward ways of representing a 1:*M* association. Commonly, the association A◄──►►B is represented by the child records, B, following their parent, A. A_1 is followed by its associated B records, then A_2 is followed by its B records, and so on. Alternatively, a chain of pointers may be used, linking each A record to its associated B records. These simple methods cannot be used with the *M:M* mapping A◄◄──►►B. Instead, there may be a file of A records and a file B records, and separate information showing how they are related.

Two examples of intersection data:

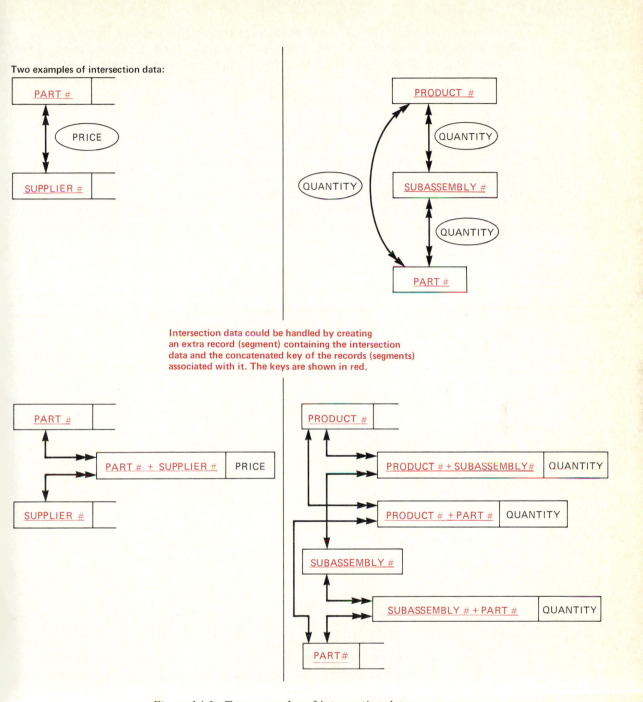

Intersection data could be handled by creating an extra record (segment) containing the intersection data and the concatenated key of the records (segments) associated with it. The keys are shown in red.

Figure 14.2 Two examples of intersection data.

The second problem (the one that concerns us here) is that in practice when an *M:M* association is used there will usually be *intersection data* associated with it sooner or later. If there are no intersection data to start with, they are likely to be added later *as the data base evolves.* If intersection data are associated with records having keys A and B, those data are identified by a concatenated key A + B. Figure 14.2 shows two examples of intersection data and how they might be handled.

Because of the likelihood of adding intersection data, it is usually best to avoid an A◄──►B link in a schema and instead create an extra record having the concatenated key A + B when the data base is first implemented. This avoids later restructuring and consequent rewriting of programs.

Canonical structuring is an attempt to achieve the most stable data model, so it avoids any *M:M* mappings between primary keys. Furthermore, it should be designed so that such a mapping will not appear in the future as the data base evolves.

MAPPING
BETWEEN
PRIMARY KEYS

To avoid this problem, when the design procedure gives a mapping *between keys* in one direction, we will add the equivalent mapping in the opposite direction. In other words, the line between keys has arrows drawn in both directions. If we then have an *M:M* mapping between two keys A and B:

and the path in either direction might conceivably be traversed, we introduce a third key A + B as follows:

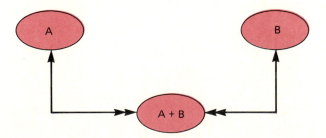

Because we use this procedure the canonical model we create will have no *M:M* links between keys unless the association could *never* be used in one direction.

INTERSECTING ATTRIBUTES   A problem which sometimes exists in the synthesized structure is that an *attribute* may be attached to more than one primary key. In other words, it has more than one single-headed arrow pointing to it. This is sometimes called an intersecting attribute. It cannot remain in such a state in the final synthesis. An attribute in a canonical model can be owned by only one key.

Box 14.2 illustrates an intersecting attribute and shows three ways of dealing with it. There should be no intersecting attributes on the final canonical graph.

BOX 14.2   **Reorganization of intersecting attributes**

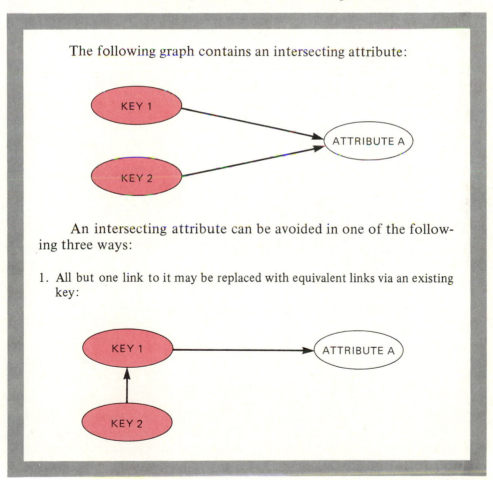

The following graph contains an intersecting attribute:

An intersecting attribute can be avoided in one of the following three ways:

1. All but one link to it may be replaced with equivalent links via an existing key:

(Continued)

BOX 14.2 *(Continued)*

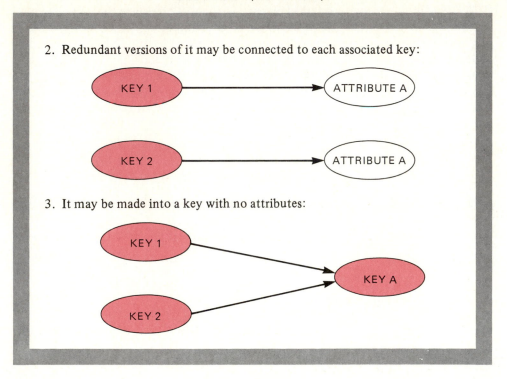

2. Redundant versions of it may be connected to each associated key:

3. It may be made into a key with no attributes:

ISOLATED ATTRIBUTES

An isolated attribute is an attribute that is not identified by a primary key. It is a bubble with no single arrows entering or leaving it, although there will be double-arrow links.

An isolated attribute should be treated in one of the following ways:

1. It may be implemented as a repeating attribute in a variable-length record.
2. It may be treated as a solitary key—a one-data-item record.

Often, it results from an error in interpretation of the user's data, so the meaning related to it should be carefully checked.

RECORD SEQUENCE

In certain user views the *sequence* in which the data are presented to the application program, or displayed on a terminal, is critical. However, the canonical model does not indicate the sequence in which records are stored. *In general, it is undesirable to state a record sequence in the canonical model because different applications of the data might require the records in a different sequence.*

In a data base of book titles, for example, one application might want a logical file of book titles in alphabetical order, another might want them ordered by author, another by Library of Congress number. The different sequencing can be indicated by secondary keys—bubbles with a double-arrow link to BOOK-TITLE.

When the canonical schema is converted to a physical representation, it is necessary to state the record sequencing. This is a statement that should be part of the physical, rather than the logical, description of data. Some *logical* data description languages require statements about the order of records. This information must then be added when the canonical model is converted to the software logical schema. The enthusiasts of *relational* data bases stress that the sequencing of the tuples should not be part of the *logical* data description.

AUTOMATING THE PROCEDURE   Box 14.3 summarizes the procedure for canonical modeling.

           This procedure is tedious, but as we have stressed, tools exist for automating it (discussed in Chapter 15).

BOX 14.3   Procedure for canonical data-base design

1. Take the first user's view of data and draw it in the form of a bubble chart—a graph with point-to-point directed links between single data items, representing associations of the two types: 1 and *M*.

   Where a concatenated key is used, draw this as one bubble, and draw the component data items of the concatenated key as separate bubbles, thus:

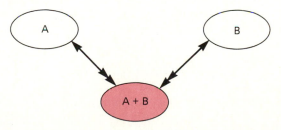

   Check that the representation avoids hidden transitive dependencies. Where a concatenated key data item has to be used, ensure that all single-arrow links from it go to data items which are dependent on the

(Continued)

BOX 14.3 *(Continued)*

full concatenated key, not merely part of it. In other words, ensure that the representation of the user's view is in third normal form.

Otherwise, draw only the associations that concern this user.

2. Take the next user's view, representing it as above. Merge it into the graph. Check for any synonyms or homonyms, removing them if they appear.

3. In the resulting graph distinguish between the attribute nodes and the primary-key nodes. (A primary-key node has one or more single-arrow links leaving it.) Mark the primary keys in some way (e.g., red color).

4. For each association between keys, add the inverse association if it is not already on the graph. If this results in an *M:M* link between keys, determine whether the inverse association would ever be used in reality. If it could be used at any time in the future, replace it by introducing an extra concatenated key incorporating the key data items that were linked.

5. Examine the associations and identify any that appear redundant. For any associations that are candidates for removal, check carefully that their meaning is genuinely redundant; if so, remove them.

6. Repeat the previous four steps until all user views are merged into the graph.

7. Identify the root keys. (A root key is a primary key with no single arrow leaving it to another key.)

For pictorial clarity the diagram should be rearranged with the root keys at the top. The single-arrow links between keys should point upward where possible. The links between primary keys may be marked in color.

8. Observe whether the graph contains any isolated attributes. An isolated attribute is a node with no single-arrow links entering or leaving it (only double-arrow links). An isolated attribute could be treated in one of three ways:

   (a) It may be implemented as a repeating attribute in a variable-length record.
   (b) It may be treated as a solitary key—a one-data-item record.
   (c) It may be the result of an error in interpretation of the user's data, in which case the error is corrected.

9. Adjust the graph to avoid any intersecting attributes (an intersecting attribute with more than one single-arrow link entering it). An intersecting attribute can be avoided by:

BOX 14.3 *(Continued)*

(a) Replacing one or more links to it with equivalent links via an existing key.

(b) Duplicating the data item in question.

(c) Treating it as a solitary key—a one-data-item record.

10. Redraw the data items arranged into groups (records, segments, tuples), each having one primary key and its associated attributes. A group may now be drawn as a box. The boxes may be offset from the left to indicate their "depth" under the root group.

11. Identify all secondary keys. (A secondary key is an attribute with one or more double-arrow links leaving it.) Draw the secondary-key links between the boxes.

12. To make the resulting model as stable as possible, apply the steps referred to in Chapter 17 on stability analysis.

13. The unconstrained "canonical" model may now be converted into the more constrained schema associated with a particular software package. It is generally a simple step to convert the canonical model into a CODASYL, DL/1, or relational schema. Some software, however, has constraints that would require a major deviation from, or splitting of, the canonical view. Some software will simply not be able to handle it.

    In converting the canonical model to a particular software schema, performance considerations associated with high-usage and fast-response paths should be examined. We suggest the following steps:

(a) Mark all paths which are used in interactive systems and which need fast response time.

(b) Estimate the number of times per month each user path will be traversed. Add up how often each association will be traversed (in each direction when applicable).

(c) Estimate the length of each group.

(d) For each M association, estimate the size of $M;$ that is, how many values on average are associated with one value, or how many "child" groups are associated with a "parent" group.

    The information above may affect the choice of structure and may cause the designer to modify the schema. In some cases a group may be split because it contains a mixture of frequently used and rarely used data, or is too long. In some cases a schema will be split to avoid complexity.

14. With the software schema designed, return to the original user views and ensure that they can be handled by it. In some cases the performance cost of handling a particular user view is sufficiently great that it is worthwhile completely modifying that user view.

If these tools are not available, the designer may compromise by identifying the primary keys in all the input views and building a linkage between these by hand. He then adds the attributes which these keys identify. The tool saves him time, enforces discipline, helps avoid errors, and provides documents which form the basis of vital communication with end users.

Either way, the designer tackles one input view at a time, checks that it appears correct in its own right, has it merged into the model, and inspects the results. When the program deletes an apparently redundant association, it should ask the designer if he considers it to be *genuinely* redundant. Each time a programmer or user wants to add new data types or use the data base in a new way, the data-base administrator can enter the new user view and see what effect it has on the existing data base.

It is desirable to consider the effect of different data structures on machine performance. To do this, the frequency of use of each user's view should be estimated. From these estimates the frequency of traversing each association path may be added up—again a tedious task that should be automated. A graph showing frequency of traverse of each link may have a major effect on how a designer converts his canonical model into a working software schema. As well as showing the frequency of traverse, the graph should show which associations are used interactively with fast-response requirements.

We will discuss performance considerations later.

HUMAN INTELLIGENCE   Even if the synthesis process is automated, there are several steps that require intelligent human understanding of the meaning of the data. The input must be carefully examined to ensure that the correct keys are used for all data items, and transitive dependencies are removed. When links are removed because they appear to be redundant, the data administrator must check that this reflects the true meaning of the links.

SHIPPING EXAMPLE   Now we will examine an example selected to illustrate how intelligent human attention is needed to the *meaning* of the links when they are candidates for deletion.

The application relates to the movement of cargo by sea. A company operates a fleet of cargo ships which visit many ports. Box 14.4 shows views of the data which various application designers require. The example is *highly* simplified from reality. For ease of tutorial diagramming, many *attributes* have been combined or omitted, and the number of views is small. A real bill of lading typically contains about 65 data items, not the 15 shown here. The final result is shown in Fig. 14.3. This example contains 32 data items; in a real shipping company more than 600 data items may be involved. This example can be synthesized by hand. In real life it would be far too complicated to do by hand. A computerized synthesis tool is needed.

BOX 14.4 Shipping example: seven input views

Input View 1

Information is stored about each ship. The key is VESSEL#.

VESSEL#	VESSEL -NAME	TONNAGE	DETAILS	COUNTRY-OF- REGISTRATION	OWNER	VOYAGE#

Input View 2

A ship stops at many ports. It is necessary to print its itinerary.

VESSEL#

PORT	DATE-OF- ARRIVAL	DATE-OF- DEPARTURE

Input View 3

A shipper may have many consignments of goods in transit. These are given a consignment identification number. A list can be obtained, when requested, of what consignments a shipper has in shipment.

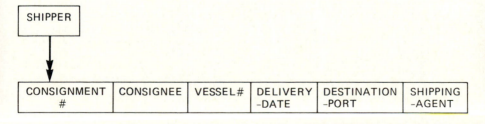

SHIPPER

CONSIGNMENT #	CONSIGNEE	VESSEL#	DELIVERY -DATE	DESTINATION -PORT	SHIPPING -AGENT

BOX 14.4 *(Continued)*

Input View 4

The fourth user view is the bill of lading. A bill of lading relates to a given consignment of goods. Large containers are used for shipping the goods. A bill of lading relates to goods in one container. If a shipper's goods fill more than one container, a separate bill of lading is used for each container.

BILL-OF-LADING#	SHIPPER	CONSIGNEE	CONSIGNMENT#	SHIPPING AGENT
	WAYBILL-DATE	SAILING-DATE	CONTAINER#	ORIGINATION-PORT
	DESTINATION-PORT	TOTAL-CHARGE		

ITEM#	NO-OF-PIECES	COMMODITY-CODE	WEIGHT	CHARGE

Input View 5

A shipping agent wants a list of what containers he has in shipment, and what consignments of goods they contain:

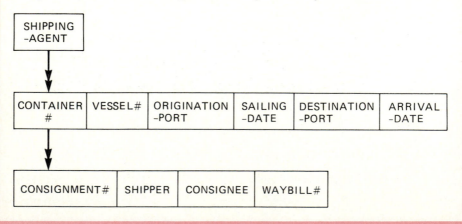

SHIPPING-AGENT

CONTAINER#	VESSEL#	ORIGINATION-PORT	SAILING-DATE	DESTINATION-PORT	ARRIVAL-DATE

CONSIGNMENT#	SHIPPER	CONSIGNEE	WAYBILL#

BOX 14.4 *(Continued)*

Input View 6

Details of the containers are required.

CONTAINER #	OWNER	TYPE	SIZE	VESSEL –NAME	DESTINATION –PORT	ARRIVAL –DATE

Input View 7

When a vessel stops at a port a list is required of what containers are to be loaded on it. Details of the container size, type, and handling instructions are needed for loading purposes.

Similarly, a list of what containers should be taken *off* the vessel is needed.

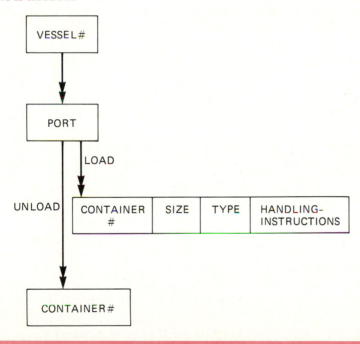

CLARIFICATION OF USER VIEWS

Before attempting to synthesize the views in Box 14.4, we need to clarify their structure. As is often the case, they are drawn loosely in Box 14.4 (although not as loosely as often in real life!). The drawings of Box 14.4 contain various traps for the unwary. Some of them are incorrect representations of data. Before reading further we suggest that the reader examine Box 14.4 looking for misrepresentations of data. We gave Box 14.4 to one senior systems analyst and after trying for a week he was unable to find some of the misrepresentations in it.

To clarify the input views, they should be drawn as bubble charts. The data administrator or analyst needs to ask the following question for each data item that is synthesized into a data model: "On what is it functionally dependent?" In different words, "What data item (or items) identifies it?" The single-headed arrow links between the data items *must* be correct.

Box 14.5 shows the redrawing of the input views.

Input view 1 appears simple, but VOYAGE# should not be in the same data group as the other data items. A vessel can go on many voyages. A double-headed arrow is needed from VESSEL# to VOYAGE#, as in Box 14.5.

In input view 2 we need to ask: What identifies DATE-OF-ARRIVAL and DATE-OF-DEPARTURE? The stopping of a ship at a port. Is VESSEL# + PORT an adequate key? If you know VESSEL# + PORT, does that identify DATE-OF-ARRIVAL? Not completely, because the vessel stops at the same port many times. VESSEL# + PORT + DATE-OF-ARRIVAL would be a complete key for identifying the itinerary records. In practice, the shipping company gives each voyage a number. The itinerary entries can therefore be identified by VOYAGE# + PORT. VOYAGE# identifies VESSEL#. The view is redrawn as shown in Box 14.5.

Input view 3 is straightforward except that we need to ask whether DESTINATION-PORT is the same as PORT in view 2. It is. Again, is DELIVERY-DATE the same as DATE-OF-ARRIVAL in view 2? The data administrator decides that these are different dates. DATE-OF-ARRIVAL is the scheduled docking date of the vessel, and DELIVERY-DATE is the estimated date of delivery to the customer.

In input view 4 there is a hidden transitive dependency. CONSIGNMENT# identifies CONSIGNEE, SHIPPER, SHIPPING-AGENT, CONTAINER#, ORIGINATION-PORT, DESTINATION-PORT, and SAILING-DATE. This is indicated for the bubble chart for that view in Box 14.5.

It is necessary to ask: Does CONSIGNMENT# always identify CONTAINER# or could one consignment be sent in more than one container? It is decided that if a consignment is split into two or more containers, a different CONSIGNMENT# is used for each container.

Both ORIGINATION-PORT and DESTINATION-PORT are the same as PORT in view 2. We have to decide how to handle these in the synthesis process.

BOX 14.5 Bubble charts for the loosely drawn input views in Box 14.4

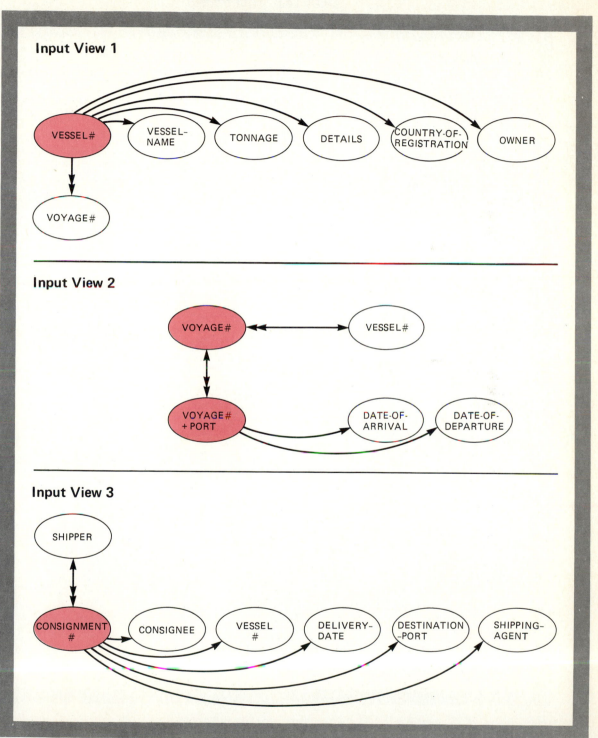

(Continued)

BOX 14.5 *(Continued)*

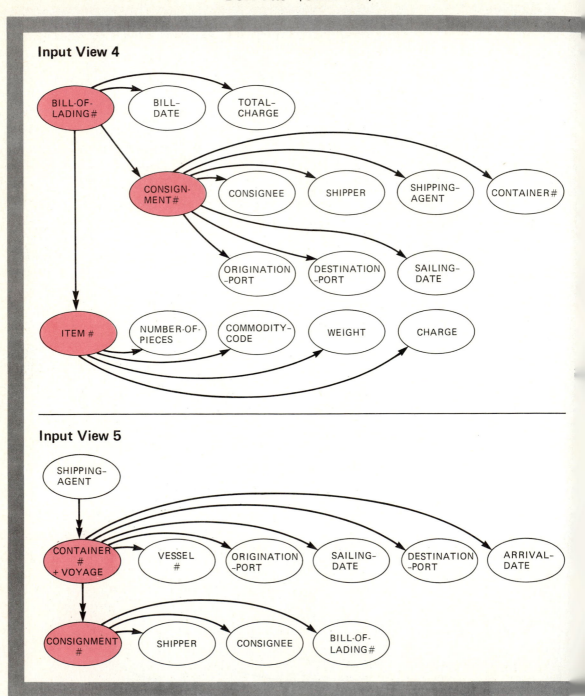

Input View 4

Input View 5

BOX 14.5 *(Continued)*

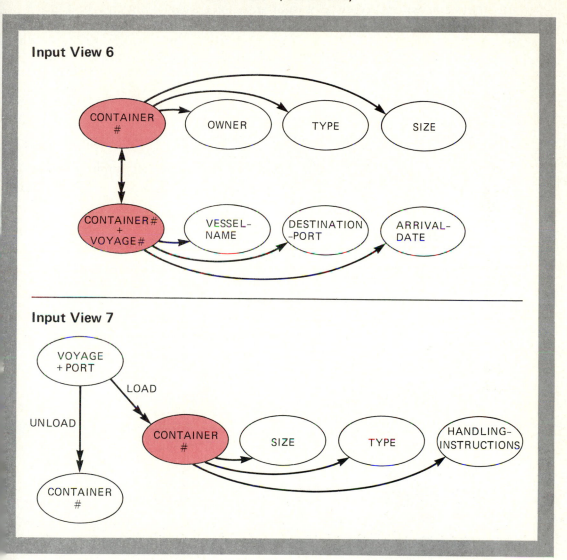

Input View 6

Input View 7

View 5 contains the data item WAYBILL#. It is realized that this is called BILL-OF-LADING# in view 4. It is therefore changed to BILL-OF-LADING#.

There is another problem in view 5. CONTAINER# does not, by itself, identify any of the data items that are linked to it. The same container can go on many voyages. To identify VESSEL#, SAILING-DATE, and so on, we need a concatenated key CONTAINER# + VOYAGE#. Box 14.5 shows this.

View 6 mixes up two types of data. Some data are properties of the container, regardless of where it is. Some are properties of the container on this particular voyage. View 6 is split into data items identified by CONTAINER# and data items identified by CONTAINER# + VOYAGE#, as in Box 14.5.

View 7 also has a problem. A vessel stops at the same port many times. We need VOYAGE# + PORT to identify what containers are to be loaded and unloaded.

THE SYNTHESIS PROCESS

The following diagrams illustrate the synthesis of the data views in Box 14.5.

The bubble chart for the first input view is straightforward:

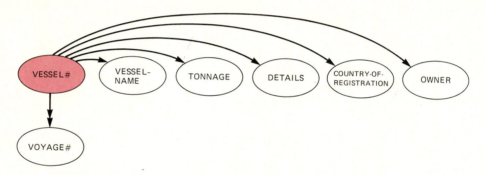

The second input view is now added, using the same bubbles for vessel and voyage:

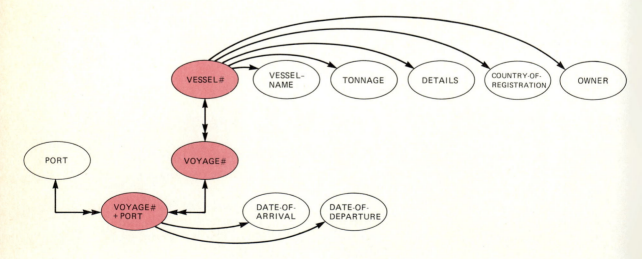

The synthesis process automatically explodes a concatenated key into its components, so PORT appears as a separate bubble.

The third input view is now added:

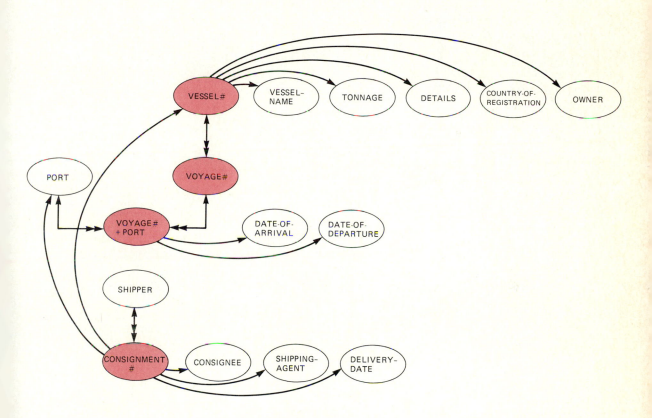

DESTINATION-PORT is really the same data item as PORT in the previous chart. So these are combined. This makes PORT an intersecting attribute. We could take action at this stage to avoid the intersecting attributes. However, we should leave them until the remaining input views are merged into the graph, because they might disappear.

The fourth input view is now added:

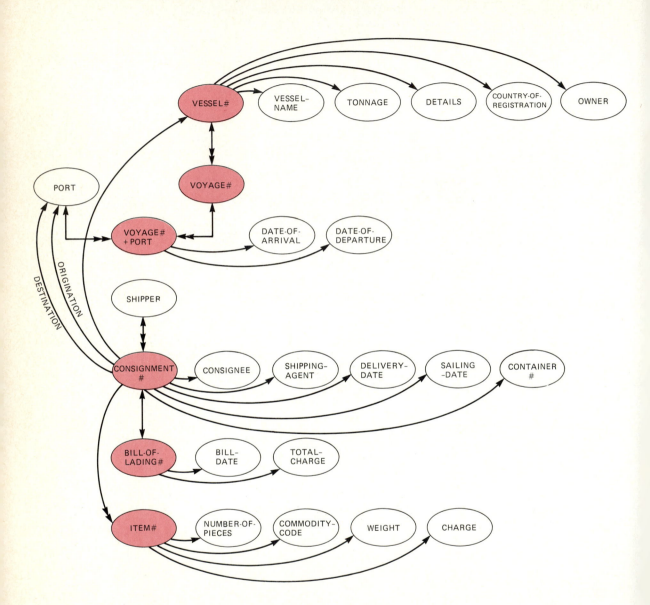

There are now two associations between CONSIGNMENT# and PORT. It is acceptable to draw multiple links between the same two data items. When this is done, the links must be labeled to indicate their meaning.

Now the fifth input view is merged into the model. This view has no new data items but adds several new links.

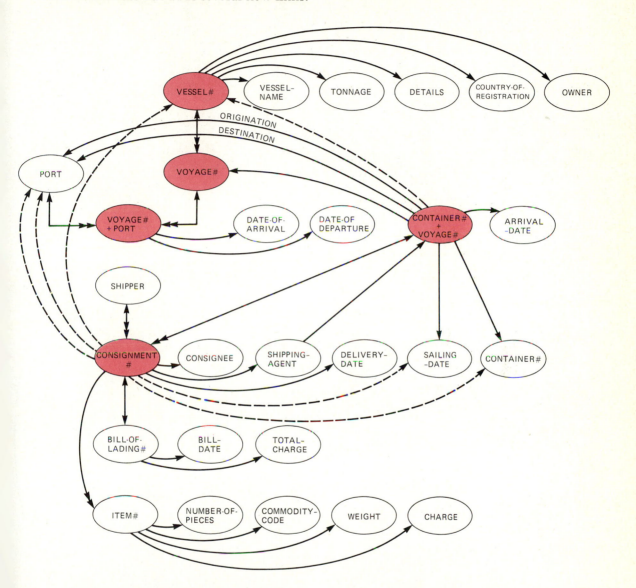

The six links shown as dashed lines are made redundant by the new links added. The data administrator checks that those are genuine redundancies, reflecting the true meaning of the data.

Input view 6 introduces some new data items, identified by CON-TAINER#. This is shown on page 264.

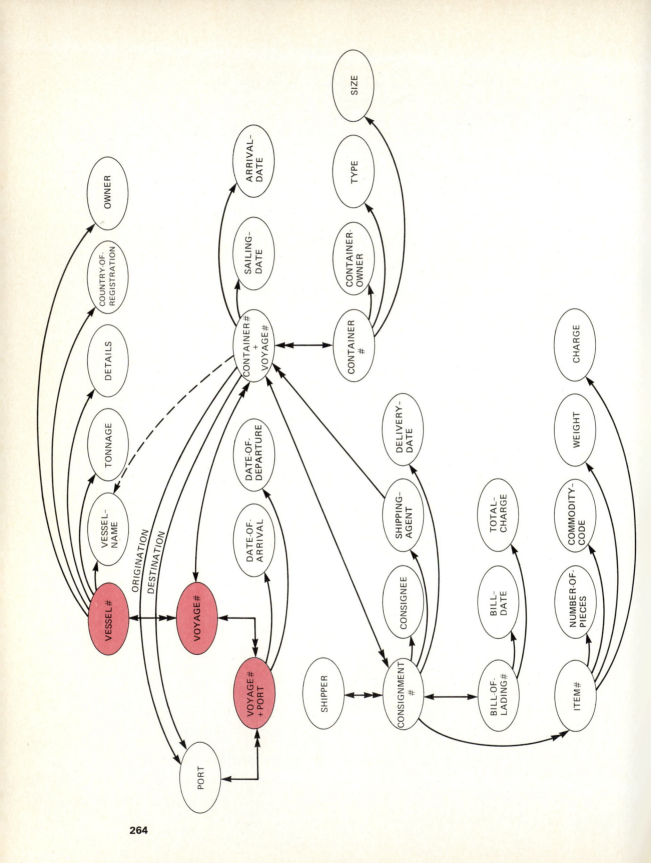

OWNER

COUNTRY-OF-REGISTRATION

SIZE

TYPE

DETAILS

ARRIVAL-DATE

CONTAINER-OWNER

TONNAGE

SAILING-DATE

CONTAINER # + VOYAGE #

CONTAINER #

VESSEL-NAME

ORIGINATION

DESTINATION

DATE-OF-DEPARTURE

CHARGE

DELIVERY-DATE

WEIGHT

DATE-OF-ARRIVAL

SHIPPING-AGENT

COMMODITY-CODE

VESSEL #

VOYAGE #

CONSIGNEE

TOTAL-CHARGE

NUMBER-OF-PIECES

VOYAGE # + PORT

SHIPPER

CONSIGNMENT #

BILL-DATE

BILL-OF-LADING #

ITEM #

PORT

264

There is a data-item-naming problem. CONTAINER# identifies a data item called OWNER. But VESSEL# also identifies a data item called OWNER. They are clearly not the same data item. Therefore, their names should be changed. This is a *homonym* problem. The term "homonym" refers to two data items which are really different but by accident have been given the same names.

Their names are changed to VESSEL-OWNER and CONTAINER-OWNER.

CONTAINER# + VOYAGE# points to VESSEL-NAME rather than VESSEL#, which is used as the vessel primary key. This is taken care of automatically because there are already links from CONTAINER# + VOYAGE# to VESSEL# and VESSEL# to VESSEL-NAME, so CONTAINER# + VOYAGE# to VESSEL-NAME is deleted.

Seventh input view is shown on page 266.

CANDIDATE KEYS   There is a single-headed arrow in both directions between CONSIGNMENT# and BILL-OF-LADING#.

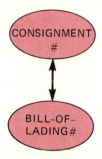

This means that CONSIGNMENT# and BILL-OF-LADING# are functionally equivalent. Either are *candidate keys* for the identification of SHIPPER, CONSIGNEE, SHIPPING-AGENT, DELIVERY-DATE, BILL-DATE, and TOTAL-CHARGE.

When confronted with candidate keys in the bubble chart, the data administrator needs to ask: *Are they likely to remain functionally equivalent?* If the candidate keys are A and B, could there be some view of data in the future in which A would identify a data item that B does not identify? Or could there be two values of A that are identical when the equivalent values of B are not identical?

In our shipping example, the data administrator might decide to use BILL-OF-LADING as the primary key of SHIPPER, CONSIGNEE, SHIPPING-AGENT, and DELIVERY-DATE. CONSIGNMENT# is a candidate key, sitting like an attribute in the record which uses BILL-OF-LADING as its primary key.

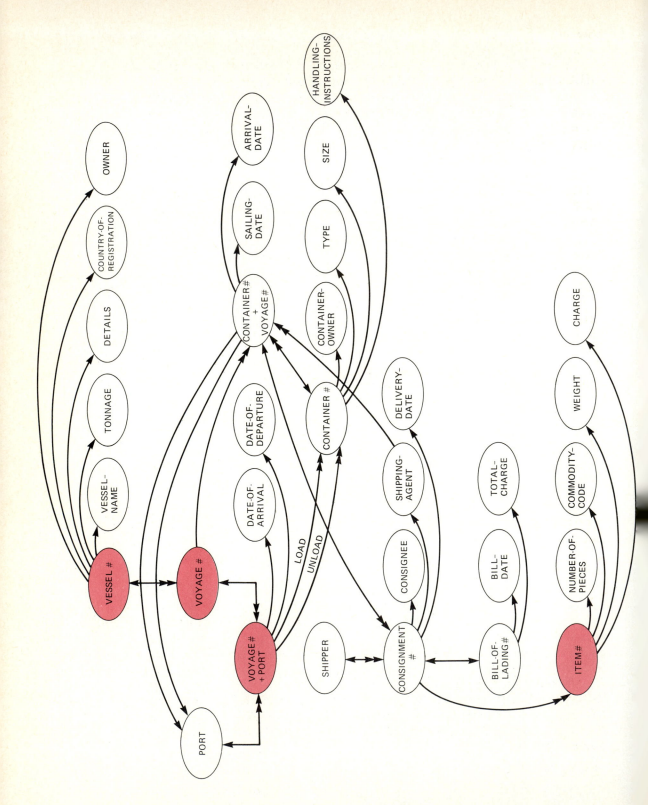

266

If CONSIGNMENT# is likely to be *not* functionally equivalent to BILL-OF-LADING# in the future, it should be separated out now.

If it is entirely functionally equivalent, then the broader organizational question should be asked: Why is it necessary? Could not the procedures and paperwork be reorganized to use BILL-OF-LADING# instead? In most organizations there is much redundant paperwork that should be reorganized.

COMPONENTS OF CONCATENATED KEYS

When a concatenated key is used, the synthesis process automatically explodes it into its component data items and puts these into the bubble charts as discussed earlier. If these are not themselves used as keys which identify their own attributes, they do not need to have a separate existence in the final bubble chart. In our example this is the case with PORT and VOYAGE#.

The data administrator needs to ask: Should PORT or VOYAGE# be a primary key in its own right? Will this data base ever need to store information about ports or voyages, separate from that identified by PORT + VOYAGE#?

If the answer is no, then PORT and VOYAGE# do not need to exist separately from the concatenated key PORT + VOYAGE#.

In this textbook illustration we can answer "no" to the question, terminate the separate existence of PORT and VOYAGE#, and draw the diagram in a more conventional fashion as in Fig. 14.3.

In practice, the answer would rarely be "no."

In Fig. 14.3 ORIGINATION-PORT and DESTINATION-PORT have been added as attributes of CONTAINER# + VOYAGE#.

SECONDARY-KEY PATHS

The red links with double-headed arrows in Fig. 14.3 are *secondary-key paths*. A variety of different software and hardware methods exist for following secondary-key paths.

In the batch processing world a secondary key is a *sort* key. The logical files may be sorted by SHIPPER or by SHIPPING-AGENT.

In the world of CODASYL data bases the secondary key is called a *search* key. It has been implemented by means of chains through the data, ring structures, and multilist structures. These tend to be rather slow and are often too slow for interactive systems. Interactive systems often employ a secondary index. IBM's IMS employs secondary indices.

In machines designed for data-base activities the hardware may assist in secondary-key accesses. This is the case in IBM's System 38.

There are various ways to provide hardware assistance in secondary-key activities.

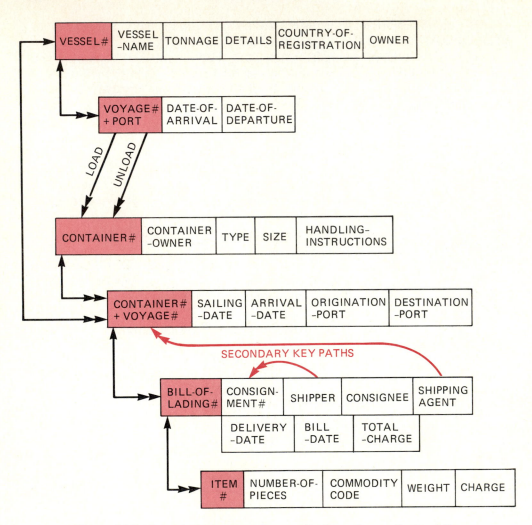

Figure 14.3 Canonical structure that results from the synthesis of the data in Box 14.5. PORT and VOYAGE# have been made attributes of CONTAINER# + VOYAGE#. PORT is represented as two attributes: ORIGINATION-PORT and DESTINATION-PORT.

SOFTWARE SCHEMA   The model of Fig. 14.3 is represented as a CODA-SYL schema in Fig. 14.4 as DL/1 (IMS) data bases in Figs. 14.5 and 14.6, and a relational data base in Fig. 14.7.

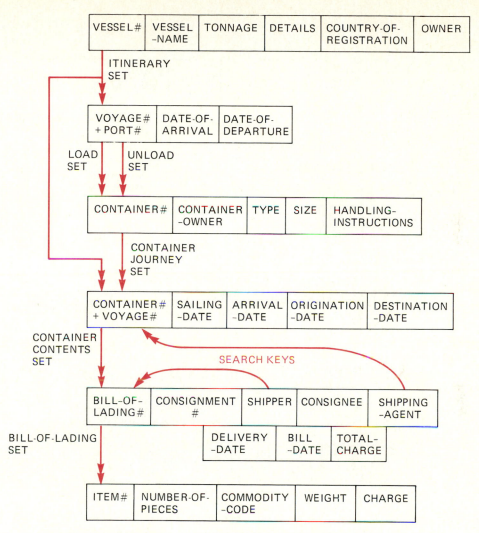

Figure 14.4 CODASYL representation of the canonical model in Fig. 14.3.

A secondary-key path from **SHIPPER** and **SHIPPING-AGENT** can be represented with secondary indices in either CODASYL, DL/1, or a relational structure.

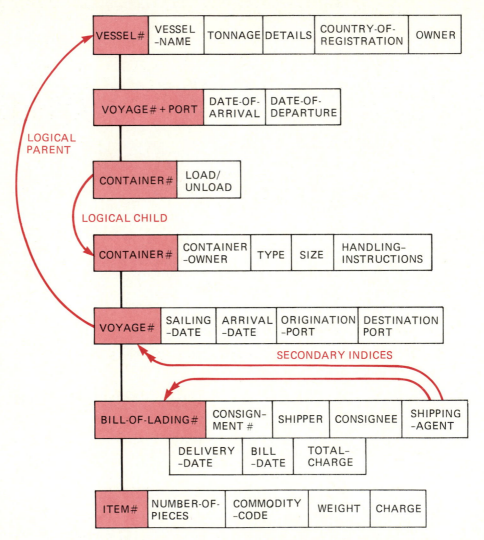

Figure 14.5 DL/1 representation of the canonical model in Fig. 14.5 using two hierarchies. Figure 14.6 gives a version of this representation adapted to give better machine performance.

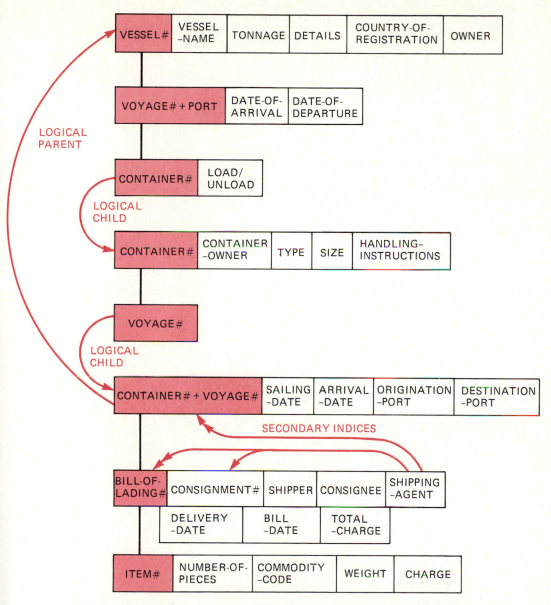

Figure 14.6 Another DL/1 version of the model in Fig. 14.3. Most of the transactions are for the bottom hierarchy and do not need information in the segment identified by CONTAINER#. This segment is therefore made a separate physical data base.

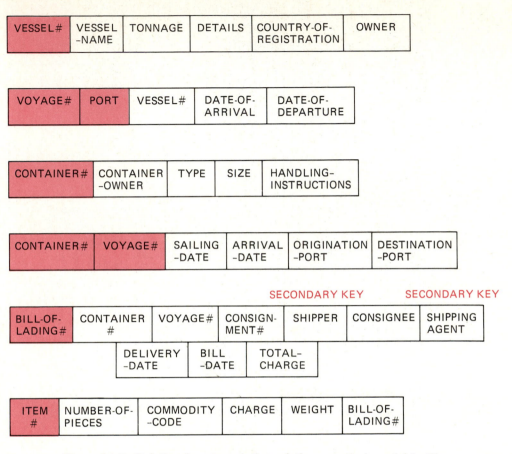

Figure 14.7 Relational representation of the canonical model in Fig. 14.3. An optimal physical structure used to implement this schema could be similar to that used to implement the schemas of Fig. 14.4 or Fig. 14.6.

VALIDATION

When a software schema is created in this way, it should be validated by returning to the original user views and checking to see whether each view can be handled satisfactorily. If some of them cannot, this may indicate either that the user views were misinterpreted in the design process, or that the software does not contain adequate facilities for handling a canonical structure.

When the software is not adequate, it is usually possible to back away from the canonical structure by introducing redundancy. Some software, for example, cannot handle the secondary keys of Fig. 14.3. Additional records, sets, or segments may be added to avoid the need for secondary-key mechanisms. In general, however, such deviation from the canonical structure may cause the future needs for program conversion that we seek to avoid.

ADJUSTMENTS TO THE MODEL

When converting the canonical model to a working data-base schema, the data-base designer might make various adjustments. The reasons for adjusting the model are as follows:

- Adjustments are made to fit the capabilities (or lack of capabilities) of the software data-base representation. In IMS, for example, a segment cannot have two logical parents; a logical child cannot itself have a logical child.

- Adjustments are made for machine performance reasons.

- Adjustments are made because the working data base takes a narrower view of the data. It may be decided, for example, not to store data about the part.

It is important to ensure that the adjustments are not made with too narrow a viewpoint so that they cause maintenance problems later.

MACHINE PERFORMANCE ADJUSTMENTS

The model in Fig. 14.3, for example, breaks naturally into two hierarchical structures, as shown in Fig. 14.5. However the bill-of-lading information is used very frequently, whereas the information about the container is used infrequently. The designer therefore decides to separate the data identified by CONTAINER# into a separate physical structure as shown in Fig. 14.6.

Whereas a canonical data structure is not concerned with machine performance, a DL/1 or CODASYL structure needs to take into consideration which are the frequently used paths or paths used in fast-response operation. It may also need to take into consideration the lengths of records (segments). Inasfar as these considerations are necessary, it could be said that DL/1 and CODASYL data descriptions (and those of most other data-base software) are not completely machine independent.

We discuss performance considerations in Chapter 18.

ELIMINATION OF UNWANTED ENTITIES

PORT and VOYAGE# were eliminated in the example above because it was decided that the data base in question would not store information about them.

Figure 14.8 shows another example. In the canonical diagram at the top of the figure, EMPLOYEE#, CITY, COUNTY, and STATE are keys. COUNTRY would be if it had any attributes. A canonical design tool would show one-item data groups with the keys CITY, COUNTY, and STATE, and another with the key COUNTRY. The designer, however, does not want to store information about cities, counties, states, or countries. He wants these data items merely as information about where the employee lives. Therefore, he uses the data group at the bottom of Fig. 14.8.

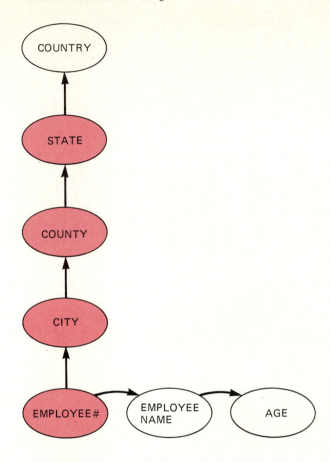

Figure 14.8

REASONS FOR DEVIATION FROM CANONICAL FORM

Box 14.6 lists reasons for deviating from canonical form. The deviations that *split* data may improve performance but give redundant update problems. The deviations that *combine* data may result in non-third-normal-form records. The side effects of these deviations should be thoroughly explored, particularly the future maintenance costs. Data-base designers commonly fail to anticipate the maintenance problems that will result from non-third-normal-form data.

BOX 14.6   Reasons for deviating from canonical form

1. Software limitations make it necessary to modify the structure, often by adding redundant records, sets, or segments.

2. Redundant fields may be added to reduce the number of required accesses or the following of complex paths.

3. Records may be combined to reduce the number of accesses or reduce the depth of a hierarchy. Where this aggregation produces non-third-normal-form data, careful thought is needed about future maintenance consequences.

4. A record may be split because it is excessively long, and performance can be improved by dividing it.

5. A data base may be split to avoid excessive complexity or size, or to improve machine performance.

6. Frequently used or fast-response paths may be separated from infrequently used paths to improve machine performance.

7. A hierarchy of records (segments) may be split because it is too deep.

8. A hierarchy or other structure may be split because a heavily used path enters at the middle rather than at the top.

9. A normalized record may be split because some data items in it are used by one application area and others by a different application area. The relationship from the key to the attributes in the two groups may be of a fundamentally different nature semantically.

10. A data base may be split for security reasons.

11. A data structure may be split to improve the efficiency of secondary-key (search) operations.

12. In certain applications high availability may be exceptionally critical. The data for those applications may be isolated from the overall schema so that if a failure occurs relating to other less critical data, it does not knock out the critical applications.

13. The data may be split into several distributed data bases. Distributed data need to be designed with a common modeling process.

SUMMARY   A canonical data-base structure is a minimal non-redundant model. Its records are in third normal form (and fourth normal form). It can be derived by a step-by-step procedure of combining the user views of data. It is sometimes referred to as a "conceptual schema."

When implemented with an appropriate data-base management system, it will provide the best protection from the future that can be reasonably expected. In the future the requirements for, and usage of, data will change, and in most cases such change can be accommodated by incremental growth of a canonical model, without drastic restructuring.

It is recommended that a data-administrator design a canonical model and then a data-base designer represent it in the software structure of his choice, carefully examining the performance considerations, and adapting the model to give appropriate software schemas.

A canonical model can be represented as a network (CODASYL), hierarchical (e.g.,IMS), or relational data-base system. When optimal access methods are designed to handle a canonical structure the similarity between these three approaches is often more striking than the differences. The canonical model should form a DBMS-independent means of representing data.

A large canonical model may be kept, updated, and designed by computer, to represent overall the data which are the foundation of a computerized enterprise. This model is too large and all-embracing for any one data base. It is partitioned into the data bases which are actually implemented. Submodels are extracted from the overall model and converted into an implementable data-base schema. These submodels are also used *to design the procedures that employ the data base.*

The overall model should form the basis for data bases in different machines, including small end-user machines. It should be employed to stop the spread of incompatible data as applications become easier to generate and machines become cheaper to install.

15 DESIGN TOOLS

SIX TOOLS
Data-base design tools fall into two classes: those concerned with the physical design and performance of individual data-base systems, and those concerned with logical structuring, coordination, and documentation.

The former are strongly dependent on the data-base management system software and hardware. The latter can be independent of them.

The tools needed are as follows:

For Data-Base Design:

- *Physical design aids* for estimating machine performances, throughout and response times, selecting access methods, determining hardware requirements, and organizing the data.

- *Measurement aids* for measuring the utilization system bottlenecks—CPU, memory, channels, access mechanisms.

- *Saturation testing aids* for flooding the system with transactions to measure its capacity and balance its facilities so that it can handle the highest throughput.

- *Monitoring aids* to measure input volumes from end users, types of transactions, response times, and rates of growth.

For Data Administration:

- A *data dictionary* which catalogues the data types and where they are used, and generates the programmers' data descriptions.

- A *modeling tool* which synthesizes the optimal third-normal-form structures, documents them, assists in data-base design, and creates corporate-wide models of the data.

PHYSICAL DESIGN AIDS Most data-base management systems have tools associated with them for estimating machine performance, throughput, and response times. These assist in selecting access methods, determining hardware requirements, and laying out data on discs.

It is desirable to check the existence of such tools when selecting the hardware and software. The case histories of data base are filled with stories of computers not powerful enough to do the intended work, or runs that took several times longer than anticipated.

DATA-BASE DESIGNER:

When we were selecting the data-base management software, we asked whether it could handle large data bases and the answer was "yes." We asked if it could handle complex data bases and again the answer was "yes." But we weren't smart enough to ask: Can you handle large, complex data bases? So, consequently, ability to get good performance on-line as well for some of the off-line processing is very difficult.

With large data bases, very long runs, or very large traffic volumes, it is especially important to do the design calculations before purchasing or programming the system. An amazing number of installations do not do them and this is asking for trouble.

Some of the biggest data-base disaster stories relate to installations of machines that could not do the job for which they were purchased. In one large and prestigious bank a computer was purchased with a data-base management system. For two years programs were written and tested, and the machine was installed. There was no possible way in which it could handle the volume of work. It was far too small. Bitter legal recriminations followed, the customer blaming the manufacturer. In fact, both were at fault because no realistic design calculations had been done.

Data-base design calculations are difficult to do without assistance from the software vendor. Without a model of the data-base management system's performance, it is difficult to estimate how many accesses are needed, how long the accesses are, or how many machine cycles are used. When selecting a data-base management system, a customer should ask whether or not it comes with good design tools and systems engineering help in using the tools.

MEASUREMENT AIDS After a system is working, much more precision can be achieved in predicting its future behavior. It is desirable to have tools for measuring its behavior.

278

Often the transaction volume on a system is increasing and it is necessary to know what throughput it can handle. Aids should be available for *saturation* testing. The system and data base are operated with a simulated stream of transactions. The volume of this stream is steadily increased until an overload occurs. Measurements are made of the channel usage, CPU usage, and main memory usage. Adjustments are made to achieve as balanced a system as possible so that overload on one system component does not knock out the system while other components are still underloaded.

Saturation testing is best carried out with two computers. One computer generates transactions and sends them to the computer under test. The volume is steadily increased and the pair of machines produce a set of reports for studying the conditions when saturation occurs. Sometimes two computers are not available, so one computer must generate transactions and feed them to itself for processing. If the transactions arrive on telecommunications links, these links will be temporarily *wrapped around* so that the machine can transmit transactions to itself. Well-designed software is needed for performing saturation testing. A would-be vendor of data-base management software should be asked whether such tools exist for the combination of hardware and software in question.

Saturation testing needs to be done well ahead of the time when the system becomes overloaded. It takes time to expand the system or replace the processing unit.

MONITORING AIDS   We have stressed the growing importance of direct end-user involvement with data-base systems. Users should be able to formulate and enter their own requests for information, generate their own reports, and so on. However desirable, this activity can be unpredictable. There is a danger that DP management does not know how much of it is occurring, and this has sometimes played havoc with machine performance.

When a high level of end-user activity takes place, the system should have the capability to *monitor* it. The data-base designer needs to know how many end-user transactions are occurring, of what types, what response times they are receiving, and how fast the transactions are growing.

The monitoring aids often give design feedback which causes the data-base designer to make adjustments in the data structures, access methods, or transaction priorities.

On some systems end-user activities have increased by a large amount over a short period and have swamped the system. The result is either delays in other system activity or else poor response times or poor system availability to the end users. This can be highly frustrating. We will discuss it further in Chapter 18. Often the best solution is *distribution* of data-base facilities.

DESIGN TOOLS FOR END USERS

The second class of tools is important for both the data administrator and the end users. The data dictionary and the logical modeling tool both have input which comes from an understanding of the users' data needs and definitions. Both create output which becomes formal documentation of the data and which should be reviewed by the end users to make sure that it represents their needs correctly.

There are many data dictionaries on the market. Data modeling tools are less common. Both should be regarded as important for success in database installations. The illustrations in this chapter are from two of them, which are designed to work together: The IBM IMS DB/DC Data Dictionary [1] and DATA DESIGNER, a modeling tool [2].

DATA DICTIONARY

A data dictionary, as discussed in Chapter 8, is a tool which lists all data items that are used, their definitions, how and where they are used, and who is responsible for them.

```
                    ***** DB/DC DATA DICTIONARY REPORT  *****          03/02/79
DICTIONARY DATA BASE : SEG
SEGMENT NAME :   TC EMPLOYEE-PAYROLL-RECORD 0
  SECONDARY NAME:
                    TA PAYRDATA 10
                    TA EMPLDATA 20
  ATTRIBUTES EFFECTIVE AS OF 02/28/79
   LENGTH :   00095
   NUMBER OF DATA ELEMENTS: 009
DATA ELEMENT NAME                          STARTING POS BST LEVEL
TC PERSONNEL-DATA 0                          00001       0        NOT USED IN DBD
TC NAME 0                                    00001       0        NOT USED IN DBD
TC AGE 0                                     00061       0        NOT USED IN DBD
TC SEX 0                                     00063       0        NOT USED IN DBD
TC PERSON-NUMBER 0                           00064       0        NOT USED IN DBD
TC PAYROLL-INFORMATION 0                     00074       0        NOT USED IN DBD
TC PAY-RATE 0                                00074       0        NOT USED IN DBD
TC FICA 0                                    00082       0        NOT USED IN DBD
TC TOTAL-PAY 0                               00088       0        NOT USED IN DBD

  DESCRIPTION:
     003    THE EMPLOYEE-PAYROLL-RECORD CONTAINS
     006 TWO TYPES OF DATA: PERSONNEL DATA AND
     009 PAYROLL INFORMATION.  PERSONNEL DATA
     012 CONSISTS OF NAME, AGE, SEX, AND PERSON-
     015 NUMBER.  PAYROLL INFORMATION INCLUDES
     018 PAY-RATE, FICA, AND TOTAL-PAY.
     021
     024    THERE IS ONE EMPLOYEE-PAYROLL-RECORD SEGMENT
     027    FOR EACH SALARIED EMPLOYEE.
     030
SEGUSER1:
SEGUSER2:
SEGUSER3:
SEGUSER4:
SEGUSER5:
                 * * *  END-OF-REPORT  * * *
```

Figure 15.1 Reports for a personnel application from the IMS DB/DC Data Dictionary [1]. (Copyright by International Business Machines Corporation.)

```
          *****  DB/DC DATA DICTIONARY REPORT  *****          03/02/79
DICTIONARY DATA BASE : DTE
DATA ELEMENT  : TC PERSONNEL-DATA 0
 ATTRIBUTES
  TYPE: C
  LENGTH :  00073
SEGMENT NAME                         STARTING POS BST LEVEL
TC EMPLOYEE-PAYROLL-RECORD 0            00001       0         NOT USED IN DBD

 DESCRIPTION:
    003   THE PERSONNEL-DATA FIELD IS PART OF
    006 THE EMPLOYEE-PAYROLL-RECORD.  IT CONTAINS
    009 NON-FINANCIAL INFORMATION ABOUT AN
    012 EMPLOYEE:
    015
    018    NAME
    021    AGE
    024    SEX
    027    PERSON-NUMBER
 DTEUSER1:
 DTEUSER2:
 DTEUSER3:
 DTEUSER4:
 DTEUSER5:
                  * * *   END-OF-REPORT   * * *
```

Figure 15.1   (Continued)

In a distributed environment the dictionary ought to be accessible via terminals so that the same definitions are available to all locations.

Figure 15.1 shows sample entries in a data dictionary used in a personnel example. Data items such as those in Fig. 15.1 are employed by different types of users for different purposes. There is sometimes considerable debate at the data-base user group meetings before common definitions are agreed upon.

When data at geographically dispersed sites are used via a communications network, the fields at all locations should be in the dictionary. It is helpful when the same dictionary can be used for an entire corporation or corporate subsidiary or division. The dictionary helps to enforce agreement on the definition of each data item and its bit structure.

A major problem in creating data models that serve multiple users is that different users mean different things by the same term. Also, data items that are really the same are given different names by different users. The data administrator has to try to resolve this.

MEMBER OF END-USER COMMITTEE:

There was an amazing difference of opinion about what the various terms meant. For example, what is a policyholder's name? What is a renewal? It's very surprising that if you went to five different departments within the group division, you'd probably get five different answers to each of those questions.

INTERVIEWER:

Even simple terms like POLICYHOLDER'S NAME. Why would there be any argument about that?

MEMBER OF END-USER COMMITTEE:

Well, for example, the Experience Rating Department will look at a case in total and may use the corporate name. But some of the people in my area may be dealing with a division of this giant corporation and it may have a different policyholder name on the billing address. Perfectly legitimate in both cases, but what we're trying to do is put them together and say: Can we reach a consensus? We recognize that there's going to be a time when there will be a conflict. Sometimes it'll be legitimate, sometimes it won't be. In that case, I personally feel it's our responsibility to—I don't mean force the issue, but explore in depth enough to make sure that the person or persons who are taking minority opinions are really listening.

The data administrator must create definitions which the various end users agree to. The data dictionary helps him to avoid having different data items with the same name (homonyms) and the same data items having different names in different places (synonyms). In some cases the same data item does have different names for historical reasons, and the dictionary informs its users of these *aliases.* The dictionary is a vital tool for enabling different users to agree about the definitions of the data needed to run a computerized corporation.

In an installation with multiple files the same data item name has often been used for many data items which are really different. For example, PRICE in one file may be the catalogue price of a part. PRICE in another file may be a price lower than the catalogue price which is charged to a given customer. PRICE in another file is the quotation price of a supplier. And so on. In a shared data-base environment these data items must be defined and given different names. The dictionary is a tool for resolving and documenting such problems.

The dictionary says how data items are arranged into the records, segments, or tuples of a data base. It may indicate where data reside geographically, and what data are replicated at different locations. It indicates which programs read the data, and which update them. It should indicate who is responsible for the accuracy of the data, who updates them, and who can read them.

The dictionary user can request a variety of reports from it. A designer at one location can ask to see where else his data are used. A data administrator faced with the prospect of changing a certain data item can ask what programs use that data item.

Sometimes installations argue about whether the cost of a dictionary is justifiable. In practice, the cost of *not* using a dictionary has been enormous, causing installations great maintenance efforts. As mentioned in Chapter 8, the dictionary ought to pay for itself by generating the programmers' data.

DATA MODELING TOOL

The data modeling tool does the data synthesis which we described in the preceding chapters. It does it in a formal (canonical) fashion. The modeling tool should create data in optimal third normal form, thereby helping to avoid large future maintenance and conversion costs.

The bubble charts showing data, which the systems analyst or end user draws, can be fed into the tool one at a time. The tool synthesizes them into the model structure. It draws the resulting structure and produces various reports.

The output of the modeling process should be studied by concerned users, together with dictionary output, to ensure that the data bases being designed do indeed meet their needs.

The data model created by the tool serves as a basis for the task of physical-data-base design. The synthesis process can show the frequency of usage of the various usage paths through the data base. This enables the designer to make decisions about how the data should be grouped into the structures (CODASYL sets, DL/1 physical data bases, pointers, etc.) that the data-base management system employs.

Figure 15.2 shows reports and plots from a data model created by DATA DESIGNER. As new views of data are fed into DATA DESIGNER it adjusts the model as necessary.

The data model description and the data dictionary listings together form a fundamental representation of the data needed to run an organization. As the networks and data bases used in running an organization build up, so the data which they employ or *will employ in the future* should be thought about and represented in this formal way.

In most corporations different computers have been used without coordinating their data structures and different files have been created by different programmers and analysts. To build a successful computerized corporation with data bases and networks, the data have to be cleaned up sooner or later. The same data-item type has to be represented in the same way in different files, different applications, and different machines. Definitions of data items have to be agreed upon. The data items should be structured into cleanly thought out data models.

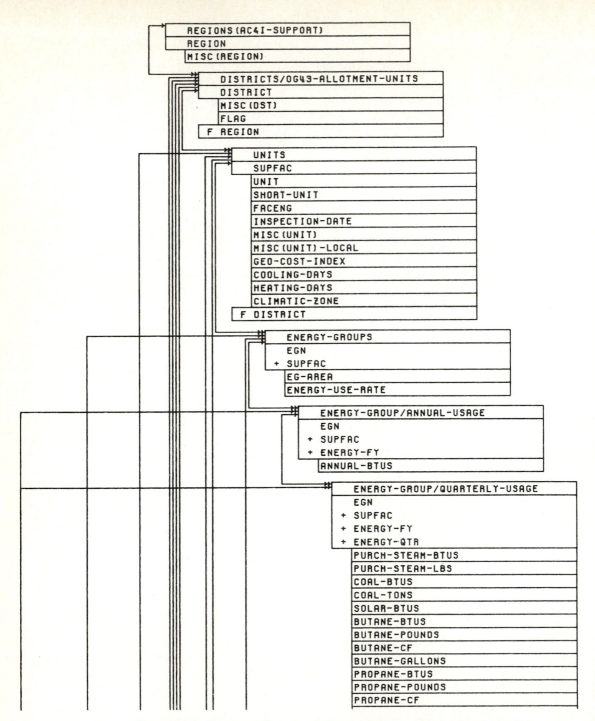

Figure 15.2 Portions of a canonical model of data used in the United States Coast Guard, produced by the DATA DESIGNER synthesis tool [2]. Reproduced with permission from a data model developed by Lt. Patrick Higbie.

```
23 ENERGY-GROUP/QUARTERLY-USAGE (EGN+ENERGY-FY+ENERGY-QTR+SUPFAC)
   Attributes:
      1   (PURCH-STEAM-BTUS)
      2   (PURCH-STEAM-LBS)
      3   (COAL-BTUS)
      4   (COAL-TONS)
      5   (SOLAR-BTUS)
      6   (BUTANE-BTUS)
      7   (BUTANE-POUNDS)
      8   (BUTANE-CF)
      9   (BUTANE-GALLONS)
     10   (PROPANE-BTUS)
     11   (PROPANE-POUNDS)
     12   (PROPANE-CF)
     13   (PROPANE-GALLONS)
     14   (NAT-GAS-BTUS)
     15   (NAT-GAS-CF)
     16   (NAT-GAS-POUNDS)
     17   (NAT-GAS-THERMS)
     18   (ELECTRIC-BTUS)
     19   (ELECTRIC-KWHS)
     20   (OIL-BTUS)
     21   (JP-5-GALLONS)
     22   (FUEL-OIL-#6-GALS)
     23   (FUEL-OIL-#2-GALS)
     24   (FUEL-OIL-#1-GALS)
     25   (QUARTERLY-BTUS)
   Links involving ENERGY-GROUP/QUARTERLY-USAGE (EGN+ENERGY-FY+ENERGY-QTR+SUPFAC)
      1 <<--> ENERGY-GROUP/ANNUAL-USAGE (EGN+ENERGY-FY+SUPFAC)

24 ENERGY-GROUP/ANNUAL-USAGE (EGN+ENERGY-FY+SUPFAC)
   Attributes:
      1   (EGN)
      2   (ANNUAL-BTUS)
   Links involving ENERGY-GROUP/ANNUAL-USAGE (EGN+ENERGY-FY+SUPFAC)
      1 <<--> ENERGY-GROUPS (EGN+SUPFAC)
      2 <-->> ENERGY-GROUP/QUARTERLY-USAGE (EGN+ENERGY-FY+ENERGY-QTR+SUPFAC)

25 ENERGY-GROUPS (EGN+SUPFAC)
   Attributes:
      1   (ENERGY-USE-RATE)
      2   (EGN)
      3   (EG-AREA)
   Links involving ENERGY-GROUPS (EGN+SUPFAC)
      1 <-->> SHORE-FACILITIES (RPFN+SUPFAC)
      2 <<--> UNITS (SUPFAC)
      3 <-->> ENERGY-GROUP/ANNUAL-USAGE (EGN+ENERGY-FY+SUPFAC)

26 ECV-PEOPLE (EMPLOYEE#)
   Attributes:
      1   (MISC(PEOPLE))
      2   (YEAR-REPORTED)
      3   (ACADEMY-CE)
      4   (YEAR-GROUP)
      5   (NON-ECV-JOB)
      6   (ANNUAL-SALARY)
      7   (RK/GRADE)
      8   (EDUC/REG)
      9   (EMPLOYEE-NAME)
     10   (MIL/CIV)
   Links involving ECV-PEOPLE (EMPLOYEE#)
      1 <-->> OG43-PROJECTS (DISTRICT+PFSR-SERIAL)
      2 <-->> ECV-BILLETS (BILLET#)

27 EPA-IDENTIFIED-HAZARDOUS-WASTES (EPA-HAZ-WASTE#)
   Attributes:
      1   (EPA-HW-NAME)
   Links involving EPA-IDENTIFIED-HAZARDOUS-WASTES (EPA-HAZ-WASTE#)
      1 <-->> HAZARDOUS-WASTES (LOCAL-HW#+RPFN+SUPFAC)
```

Figure 15.2   (Continued)

```
28 FACTYPES/PROPERTY-CODES (FACILITY-TYPE)
   Attributes:
     1  (PROPERTY-CODE)
   Links involving FACTYPES/PROPERTY-CODES (FACILITY-TYPE)
     1 <-->> SHORE-FACILITIES (RPFN+SUPFAC)

29 GROUPS-AND-SECTIONS (G/S#)
   Attributes:
     1  (GROUP/SECTION)
   Links involving GROUPS-AND-SECTIONS (G/S#)
     1 <<--> OPERATING-DISTRICTS (OPDST)
     2 <-->> USERS (OPFAC)

30 REAL-PROPERTY-INSTALLATIONS (GSA-CONTROL#)
   Attributes:




     1  (INSTALLATION-NAME)
     2  (STREET-ADDRESS)
     3 GSA-REGIONS (GSA-REGION)
     4  (INSTALLATION)
   Links involving REAL-PROPERTY-INSTALLATIONS (GSA-CONTROL#)
     1 <-->> SHORE-FACILITIES (RPFN+SUPFAC)
     2 <<--> STATES/CONTINENTS (STATE-CODE)
     3 <<--> DISTRICTS/OG43-ALLOTMENT-UNITS (DISTRICT)
     4 <<--> COUNTIES/COUNTRIES (COUNTY-CODE)
     5 <<--> CITIES/TOWNS (CITY-CODE)
```

Figure 15.2   (Continued)

APPLICATION PRESSURE

When an application is needed there is usually a high level of pressure to complete it quickly. Over and over again one observes the application pressure being so great that there is no time to complete the data modeling and definition process. Usually, this process takes much longer than expected.

The modeling tools help to speed up the process and to formalize it to ensure that it is done well.

Even *with* such tools the application pressure is often too great. Corners are cut. Data bases are implemented for urgent applications, ignoring all other applications of the same data. This will ultimately cause high maintenance costs. Sooner or later the data will have to be cleaned up and converted, and that will mean expensive reprogramming.

What is the answer? The answer is to *keep ahead* with regard to the modeling process. Defining and cleaning up the data needed in an organization should be an ongoing activity independent of current application pressures. When those pressures arise, if the data have already been designed the implementation can proceed more quickly. In fact, if data bases already exist containing those data, this should substantially speed up the implementation, especially if higher-level data-base languages can be used.

It is often the case that many separate conflicting views need to be derived from a common data-base structure.

DATA ADMINISTRATOR:

We report to ourselves, we report to the government—various levels of the government—we report to various industry groups. And every one of those wants to look at the data in a slightly different way. So we do have to suffer some very complex data structures.

Such structures are automatically generated by the synthesis tool. The tool produces various reports which the data administrator and end users can study.

The data synthesis tool needs to work in cooperation with the data dictionary. The output of both should be reviewed with the end-user committee. Some corporations use DATA DESIGNER without employing a separate dictionary.

DATA ADMINISTRATOR:

We identify each individual view, code them, put them into DATA DESIGNER, and go through a series of mergers. I think the first time we tried it, we had about 12 views and we merged them all together and were faced with a staggering number of discrepancies. So we started by taking two and merging those, and then two more, and so on. Then we take the output of the package, circulate it for initial review, and once that's begun to settle down a bit, convert it into a data dictionary format for the final review and verification.

We go through two iterations with the user group.

First we show them the output of DATA DESIGNER. At that point it consists of a series of segments or records, the keys, and the contents. We're missing, at that point, the detailed definitions of the items. We circulate that for preliminary review, just to make sure that we've got the same list and that the names are familiar to people.

For the second iteration we come back with the data dictionary containing the detailed business definition of each segment or record, and each item, and ask that those be verified as well.

INTERVIEWER:

Do you feel that the design tools are essential for this?

DATA ADMINISTRATOR:

Absolutely. I'm not at all sure how one would cope without some sort of software tool.

When the user committee inspects the output of the modeling tool, they should ask certain important questions about it. These are described in the next chapter. The purpose is to help create a data base that is as stable as possible.

To build a computerized corporation, corporate-wide documentation is needed of the data definitions and data models that are used. The output of the data dictionary and data modeling tool form documentation. This documentation should be created in such a way that it is comprehensible and usable by end users and management at all levels. A major responsibility of management in a computerized corporation is to ensure that the data structures it needs come into existence and that they are compatible with the overall data structures of the organization.

REFERENCES

1. Information manuals on DATAMANAGER available from MSP Inc., 131 Hartwell Avenue, Lexington, MA 02173.

2. Information on DATA DESIGNER available from Data Base Design Inc., 2020 Hogback Road, Ann Arbor, MI 48104.

16 HOW TO SUCCEED WITH DATA MODELING

SIX RULES FOR SUCCESS   Thorough data modeling is, perhaps more than anything else, the key to long-term success in developing a data-base environment. It is the foundation stone on which everything else will be built. Too many installations have ignored it or done it badly, and one can observe them steadily disintegrating from a Class III environment to something less effective. To do data modeling carelessly is in the long run throwing money down the drain.

There are several cardinal rules for achieving success in modeling:

- Involve the end users at every step in the data modeling process.

- Employ canonical synthesis, preferably with an automated design tool, or otherwise ensure that the model is in optimal third normal form.

- Ensure that the users understand and review the data models and data definitions.

- Apply the stability analysis steps listed in the following chapter when the data models are being created and reviewed.

- Respond *rapidly* to all end-user criticisms and suggestions about the data models. Fast redesign feedback is essential to keep the end users interested.

- Manage the physical implementation so that deviation from the data models is controlled everywhere.

DATA ADMINISTRATOR:

There are many, many last-minute changes before the user meetings. I remember once we accepted a set of changes, reproduced the output, and were ready. We started at three o'clock in the afternoon and were ready for a meeting the following morning at nine o'clock. Those are the sorts of time constraints that one runs under. It's essential to automate the modeling process.

Data definition and modeling is a fundamental process essential to building a computerized corporation. It should proceed independently of specific applications, and throughout the entire organization the same dictionary and modeling tool should be used if possible.

CODING THE BUBBLE CHARTS

To present a user view of data to the data modeling tool, that view must be encoded. This can be a simple process. The bubble charts of the previous chapters can be translated directly into code and keyed into a terminal.

When DATA DESIGNER is used, each entry normally refers to one data item on a bubble chart [1]. Each entry consists of a code character and comma followed by a name, thus:

```
K, EMPLOYEE#
1, EMPLOYEE-NAME
1, AGE
```

The code character (K and 1 above) is called a *modeling command.*

Code K is used for indicating the data item at *the start of a bubble-chart arrow* (K stands for *key*).

The data item at the other end of the arrow is indicated with a code 1 if it is a *one-to-one* association (a single-headed arrow), and a code M if it is a *one-to-many* association (a double-headed arrow).

Thus

is coded

```
K, EMPLOYEE#
1, EMPLOYEE-NAME
1, AGE
```

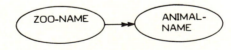

is coded

```
K, ZOO-NAME
M, ANIMAL-NAME
```

is coded

K, ZOO-NAME
1, LOCATION
M, ANIMAL-NAME

The data item labeled K can have a list of data items associated with it without its name being repeated. The list may not contain another K data item.

To code two arrows in a string, two K data items are used, thus:

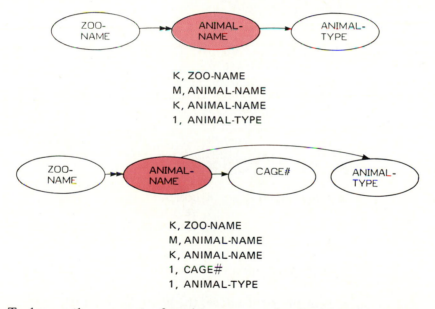

K, ZOO-NAME
M, ANIMAL-NAME
K, ANIMAL-NAME
1, ANIMAL-TYPE

K, ZOO-NAME
M, ANIMAL-NAME
K, ANIMAL-NAME
1, CAGE#
1, ANIMAL-TYPE

To lessen the amount of typing, a name that is the same as in the previous entry need not be repeated, thus:

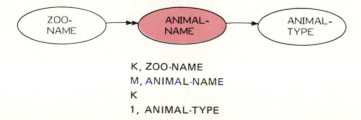

K, ZOO-NAME
M, ANIMAL-NAME
K
1, ANIMAL-TYPE

A concatenated field is represented with one of the data-item entries above, followed by one or more data items with a C code (C stands for *concatenated*).

Thus

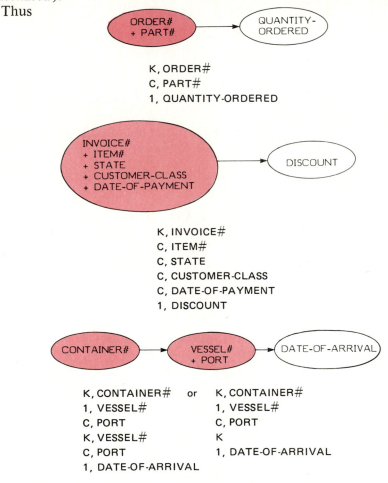

K, ORDER#
C, PART#
1, QUANTITY-ORDERED

K, INVOICE#
C, ITEM#
C, STATE
C, CUSTOMER-CLASS
C, DATE-OF-PAYMENT
1, DISCOUNT

K, CONTAINER#   or   K, CONTAINER#
1, VESSEL#   1, VESSEL#
C, PORT   C, PORT
K, VESSEL#   K
C, PORT   1, DATE-OF-ARRIVAL
1, DATE-OF-ARRIVAL

In the example on the right above, the blank K field picks up the value of the entire concatenated field (the entire bubble), not just part of it.

Using this simple form of coding one user view after another can be fed to the data modeling tool. It synthesizes them into a structure designed to be stable (a canonical, third-normal-form structure). It prints reports and draws diagrams such as that in Fig. 15.2 describing the resulting model.

INPUT TO THE MODEL

Each input data item should be checked to make sure that no data item already in the model has the same name but a different meaning.

In some cases an input data item may already exist in the model under a different name—SAILING-DATE, DATE-OF-DEPARTURE. In some cases it may exist in a slightly different form—ETD, EXPECTED-TIME-OF-DEPARTURE, may incorporate the intended SAILING-DATE. Avoiding these situations is part of the process of cleaning up the data.

In some cases the input data can be simplified. For example, they contain DATE-OF-VOYAGE, but this already exists in effect as the first of many dates in the voyage itinerary. There may be no need to have VOYAGE# identifying DATE-OF-VOYAGE when VOYAGE# + PORT already identifies DATE-OF-DEPARTURE.

It is a help to have conventions for naming the data items. This can improve the uniformity of the names, and often help to avoid the situation where the same data item has different names in different inputs.

CAUTION WITH CONCATENATED KEYS Certain cautions are necessary in creating *input* to the modeling process.

First, caution is needed with concatenated keys.

There is a big difference between

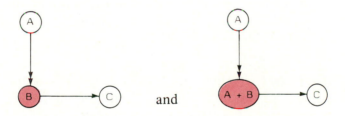

and

It would be incorrect to draw the following:

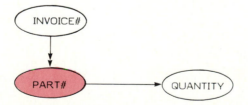

If you know the value of PART#, you do not know the value of QUANTITY. PART# alone does not identify QUANTITY. To know the value of QUANTITY you need to know both INVOICE# and PART#. QUANTITY therefore needs to be pointed to by a concatenated key, IN-VOICE# + PART#. The following is correct:

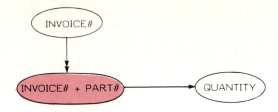

On the other hand,

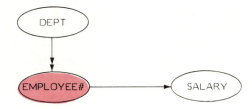

is correct, because EMPLOYEE# does (by itself) identify SALARY.

Compare the coding for the two examples above:

K, INVOICE#	K, DEPT
M, PART#	M, EMPLOYEE#
C, PART#	K, EMPLOYEE#
K	1, SALARY
1, QUANTITY	

REVERSE MAPPING BETWEEN KEYS   DATA DESIGNER, or the modeling process in Box 14.3, wants to know the reverse mapping on any links *between primary keys*. If the user does not enter this, DATA DESIGNER will ask for it. It will be faster for the user always to enter it on any input view.

For example, in the following case:

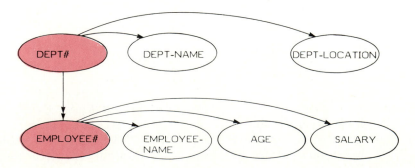

DEPT# and EMPLOYEE# are primary keys. The reverse mapping between them should be entered:

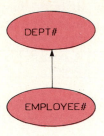

DEPENDENCE ON THE WHOLE KEY

When attributes are drawn the user should make sure that they are identified correctly by the primary key which points to them (as above) but also that they are dependent on the *whole* of a concatenated key. Thus the following is incorrect:

PART-DESCRIPTION is identified by only a portion of the concatenated key: PART#. Therefore, a separate key PART# should be drawn:

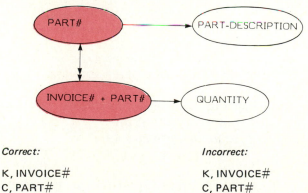

Correct:

K, INVOICE#
C, PART#
1, QUANTITY
1, PART#
K, PART#
1, PART-DESCRIPTION

Incorrect:

K, INVOICE#
C, PART#
1, QUANTITY
1, PART-DESCRIPTION

When a data-item group is entered, there may be a hidden primary key in the group. One item entered as an attribute may in fact identify some other data item in the group.

ORDER#	DATE	SUPPLIER#	SUPPLIER-NAME	SUPPLIER-ADDRESS	DELIVERY-DATE	TOTAL

There is a hidden primary key in this record. SUPPLIER# identifies SUP-PLIER-NAME and SUPPLIER-ADDRESS. It is therefore not sufficient to draw

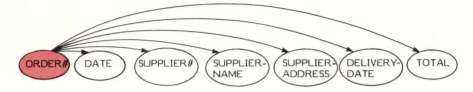

The links from SUPPLIER# to SUPPLIER-NAME and SUPPLIER-ADDRESS should also be drawn:

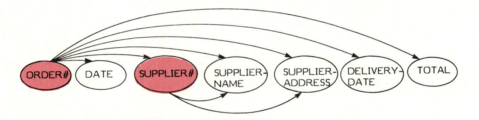

These two extra links make the links

ORDER# ⟶ SUPPLIER-NAME
ORDER# ⟶ SUPPLIER-ADDRESS

redundant. The modeling process will automatically remove them, so the creator of the input need not worry about this.

In brief: *Watch out for hidden primary keys!*

When preparing data for the synthesis process, users and analysts have sometimes worried about how complex one user view should be. They have sometimes had difficulty deciding where one user view starts and where it ends.

The answer is: It doesn't matter.

The modeling process combines them into a synthesized structure. A complex user view can be entered as multiple separate user views and the end result will be the same. It is often a good idea to do this because it lessens the likelihood of making an error.

For example, the following bubble chart represents the data on the bills that I receive from a nearby hardware store:

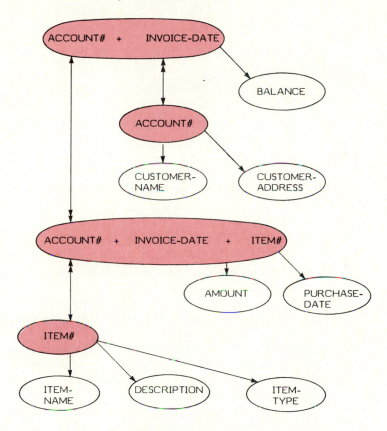

This could be entered in three separate pieces, as follows:

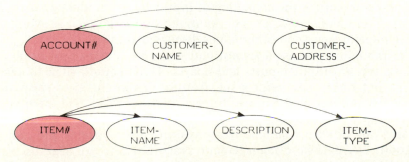

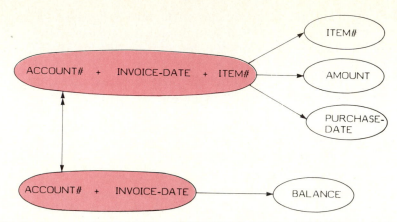

In both cases, ACCOUNT# + INVOICE-DATE + ITEM# would be auto-matically linked to its component data items: ACCOUNT#, INVOICE-DATE, and ITEM#.

ACCOUNT# + INVOICE-DATE would similarly be linked to AC-COUNT# and INVOICE-DATE. The resulting model would be the same in each case. INVOICE-DATE could be deleted as a separate data item because it is already in the concatenated key.

The synthesis process combines the *functional dependencies*. The input could be entered one functional dependency at a time. This approach gives a low probability of errors in the input.

SUMMARY

Box 16.1 summarizes the steps desirable to create stable data bases.

Step 1 of Box 16.1 refers to the overall strategy of determining what data bases are needed. This is discussed later in the book. To model any one data base it is necessary to decide what types of users are affected and find key individuals to represent each type of use.

Step 2 summarizes the software selection, discussed in Chapter 7.

Step 3 summarizes top-down planning concerns, discussed later in this book.

Step 4 summarizes the collecting of inputs to the modeling process.

Step 5 summarizes concerns in doing the synthesis, such as avoidance of transitive dependencies and other issues discussed above.

The modeling process does not end when the design tool produces an impressive set of output reports and charts. These should then be taken to the users and scrutinized with a set of questions intended to show up any potential instabilities in the model (step 6 of Box 16.1). This step is called *stability analysis* and is discussed in Chapter 17.

Part 7 of Box 16.1 summarizes physical considerations and considera-tions about the data-base management system. These are also discussed in Chapter 17.

BOX 16.1   Steps in creating stable data bases

The data models are a foundation stone on which so much will be built. The foundation stone needs to be as stable as possible (i.e., it should not change in ways that force application programs to be rewritten). The following steps are needed to achieve this:

1. Strategy

- Determine what data bases are to be designed—subject data bases, isolated application data bases, or information system data bases.
- Ensure that the data administrator reports at a high enough level in the enterprise.
- Determine all possible types of end users of a given data base.
- Establish user teams with key individuals who are highly knowledgeable of each type of use of the data base.

2. Software Selection

- Select a DBMS which has as many of the properties in Box 7.1 as possible. The DBMS for routine heavy-duty computing will often be different from the DBMS for ad hoc decision support and information retrieval.
- Make it a corporate strategy to prevent proliferation of incompatible DBMSs, understanding that organizations become locked into use of their DBMS.
- Select DMBS report generators, query languages, and application generators which will give the fastest application development and maintenance. This should be one of the most important criteria in DBMS selection.
- Select a data dictionary (today, usually the data dictionary that is built into the DBMS itself).
- Select a data modeling tool which together with the dictionary becomes the basis for a corporate-wide standard.

3. Top-Down Planning

- Determine what top-level requirements for information are likely to exist.
- Determine the entities in the enterprise about which data should be stored.
- Create an overview entity chart.
- Cluster the entities into groups each of which form the basis for detailed data models (subject data bases, entity supergroups).

(Continued)

BOX 16.1 *(Continued)*

4. Input to the Data Modeling Process

- Capture all documents that will be derived from a data base or will serve as inputs to the data base.

- Determine by discussion with the end users what types of data they want to obtain from the data base, now and in the future.

- Determine from the systems analysis process whether any new record or document requirements are emerging.

- Examine any existing data bases, files, or dictionaries which relate to these data.

- Plan whether existing files or data bases will coexist with the new data base or be converted. If they will coexist, plan the bridge between the old system and the new.

- Employ a data dictionary to document a description of the meaning of each data item.

5. Creating the Data Model

- Employ canonical synthesis, preferably with an automated design tool, or otherwise ensure that the model is in optimal third normal form.

- Inspect each input to see whether it can be simplified.

- Do any of the input data items already exist in the model under a different name or in a slightly different form?

- For each input data item, check that no different item in the model has the same name.

- Employ naming convention standards for selecting data-item names.

- Be sure that concatenated keys are correctly represented in the input to the synthesis process.

- Be sure that all attributes entered as input are dependent on the *whole* of the key that identifies them.

- Be sure that the data groups entered as input contain no transitive dependencies (see Box 14.1).

- Question the validity of all links that represent business rules, as opposed to the natural inherent properties of the data (see Chapter 17). Could these rules be changed in the future?

BOX 16.1 *(Continued)*

6. Inspecting the Output of the Data Model

- With the user group, review the data dictionary to ensure that all users agree about the definitions of data items.

- With the user group, review the model to ensure that their data requirements can be derived from it.

- With the user group, brainstorm the possible future uses of the data. For any uses that the model does not serve, create new input to the synthesis process.

- Examine every attribute field in the model to determine whether it could possibly become a primary key in the future (Chapter 17)—a simple step, often not done, which can avoid much grief later.

- Complete the reverse mapping of any links between keys to identify any possible *M:M* links (◄◄───►►). The synthesis tool will create an extra concatenated key in the model to take care of any future intersection data (see Box 17.1). This can be changed if no intersection data are possible.

- Examine any links which the synthesis process had deleted, to ensure that they are truly redundant.

- Examine the effect of exploding any concatenated keys, to see whether the resulting single-field data items need to exist separately in the data base.

- If candidate keys exist in the resulting model, check that they are in fact likely to remain candidate keys in the future.

- Check the treatment of any intersecting attributes to ensure that it is the best of the three possible treatments (Box 14.2). Could the intersecting attribute become a primary key in the future?

- Inspect any cycles in the modeling output. Check whether a further link should be added to break the cycle.

- Convert the model to the logical software schema and validate it by checking that every input view can be derived from the software schema.

- Use fast (computerized) redesign after any changes are made, to maintain the interest of the users.

(Continued)

BOX 16.1 *(Continued)*

7. Physical Considerations

- For each usage path on the model, add up the volume of usage and indicate whether it is batch or fast-response usage. This should be done by the modeling tool.

- For each A ——▶▶ B link, determine how many values of B on average are associated with one value of A.

- Use the data above for selecting the optimum representation of the model in the software (Chapter 5).

- Does the DBMS permit new attributes to be added to an existing data-item group without causing the programs which use that data-item group to be rewritten? (If not, it should be argued that that is not the right DBMS.)

- Does the DBMS permit secondary-key links to be added to an existing data base without causing the existing programs to be rewritten? (If not, it should be argued that it is not the right DBMS.)

- Does any secondary-key path have a high usage volume? If so, this may suggest that the model be split into separate data bases for machine performance reasons.

REFERENCE

1. *How to Do Optimal Logical Data Base Design,* a manual on DATA DESIGNER from Data Base Design Inc., 2020 Hogback Road, Ann Arbor, MI 48104, 1982.

17 STABILITY ANALYSIS

STABILITY   The objective of data modeling is to create data bases which are as stable as possible, and from which diverse end users can automatically derive information they need.

The data-base structures will change in the future, but an objective of their design should be to *minimize those types of change that will cause existing application programs to be rewritten.* As we have stressed, it is expensive to rewrite programs—often so expensive that it is avoided or postponed. Achieving the objective stated above has a major influence on the *effectiveness* of data processing in all areas [1].

Box 16.1 reviewed the overall steps in making data bases as stable as possible. In this chapter we are concerned with steps 6 and 7 of that box, which relate to the output of the data modeling process.

THINKING ABOUT   When the output from the modeling process is
THE FUTURE   reviewed, this is the time to think about the future. If future requirements can be understood at this stage, a better logical design will result with a lower probability of expensive maintenance later.

The users, systems analysts, and data administrator should examine the output and ask themselves: How might these data be used in the future? Any potential future use should be incorporated provisionally in the model to see whether that use causes changes in the structure of the data-item groups.

Sometimes end users are better than DP professionals at thinking about the future because they know their possible applications better. This is not always the case. Sometimes imaginative systems analysts, or a data administrator, are best at thinking up future uses for the data.

Often the best way to implement this step is with a user group meeting with the users, analysts, and data administrator all trying to brainstorm future uses of the data.

DATA ADMINISTRATOR:

When we verify a model we ask the users to sort of play games with it. Think of things that might happen that haven't happened. Think of things that weren't in the inputs to the model. Let's say that we have a major supplier and his factory burns to the ground and we need some information; can we get it? We find that if it's a good model, it answers many questions that we hadn't thought about. If that's true, then changing programs to get that information is probably going to be relatively cheap.

INTERVIEWER:

Do product changes imply that you cannot get a logical model which is absolutely stable?

DATA ADMINISTRATOR:

Certainly. We can respond to the product changes, I think, a little bit, if we have control. The people who would be responsible for developing products would be represented in the user group. So we can migrate to a new product, if you will, and make sure that the model responds to it in a controlled fashion.

INTERVIEWER:

So you feel that you've got plenty of time where you're introducing your own products.

DATA ADMINISTRATOR:

We've got the luxury of a little more time.

INHERENT PROPERTIES OF DATA

The intent of the data model is to represent the *inherent* properties of the data. If it does this, it has a better chance of being stable.

There are two types of inherent characteristics of the links on the bubble chart: those which are *naturally* inherent, and those which represent *business rules.*

The *naturally* inherent characteristics include such properties as: a branch office can have *many* salesmen; an employee has *one* pension record; a supplier can supply *many* parts; a part has only *one* description.

The *business rules* include such properties as: a particular policyholder will be sent all his bills on the same day regardless of how many policies he has; a given flight number is always the same type of plane; a person may have two addresses, but not three.

The data administrator should distinguish between the *naturally* inherent properties and the *business rules*. In the case of the latter he needs to determine how feasible the assumed rule is. Could it change? Should the data base be set up so that the policyholder bills *could* be sent out on different days? Should TYPE-OF-PLANE be identified by FLIGHT-NUMBER or FLIGHT-NUMBER + DATE? Often the data structure can be set up so as to anticipate changes in the rules.

DATA ADMINISTRATOR:

We try to anticipate certain types of changes. We sometimes place things in the model that take into account not precisely how we do the business today, but how we might do business in the future.

DATA ADMINISTRATOR:

Legal changes are a menace. Recent examples are: federal maternity legislation and age discrimination legislation, which come down upon us pretty rapidly. It doesn't allow us much time to expand and in many cases they're effective last month. We have to move quickly.

But even here the attempt to anticipate does help. Some of the legislative changes are anticipated. State-by-state changes follow a certain pattern; we can be responsive to that. We can look ahead and we can say: We've had three states that have done this; we know some more will; let's plan for it.

INCOMPLETE MODELS   It takes a long time to complete the data models in a large corporation. The published model at any time may be less than complete. The data administrator may have identified the keys that are used but not yet all the attribute data items.

DATA ADMINISTRATOR:

The actual published model that we have is really a subset of a larger model that we're working on right at the moment. We know what the major relationships are, I think. We know what the keys are. We know the relationships between the records. But we might not know the content in as much detail as we would like. We tend to use terms like reserves, knowing that there are 14 of them, that they probably are all at this level. It's not to say that one of those reserves might not wind up somewhere else, but our experience has been that they tend to stay put.

We may not be able to work out every single facet of a record, so we take our chances and go on.

DATA ANALYST:

We had one problem which dragged on for months. The users needed to see their information a different way. The analysts seemed bewildered by it. What was wrong was that an important connection in the data model had been left out. We fidgeted and fiddled around and tried to make it work, but to no avail. The data model was wrong.

JOB-ORDER# is a cost accounting key, but there were two levels of job order. One was the type of job order that the managers used to manage a piece or work. The other type of job order was one that we had to collect costs against for reporting to the government. The problem with this second type of job order was that you could only have one job order for one contract. The government would give a contract and many pieces of work would be done under it, but to report to the government we had to give one job order for multiple jobs.

All that we had to do was to create an EXTERNAL-JOB-ORDER that had a one-to-one association with CONTRACT#. Even though the contract can have multiple *real-work* job orders, it can only have one job order for collecting costs against this external system.

So we added a small relation with a concatenated key and about three fields. We had the whole thing working in a day once the data model was modified.

HIDDEN KEYS   What forces program rewriting is a change in the basic structure of a record. The most common cause of this is that a data item which is an attribute in the record *now* becomes a primary key *later*. It is easy to spot any such data items in the output of a data modeling tool.

The data administrator, systems analysts, and user committee should examine each attribute data item in turn and ask: Could this possibly be used as a primary key in the future? If data items are found which are potential future primary keys, the decision should be made whether to make them primary keys *now* by giving the modeling tool new input views. If they are made into primary keys now, this will possibly save future redesign with extensive program rewriting.

Let us reexamine our highly simplified model of data for a shipping company. For convenience it is reproduced again in Fig. 17.1.

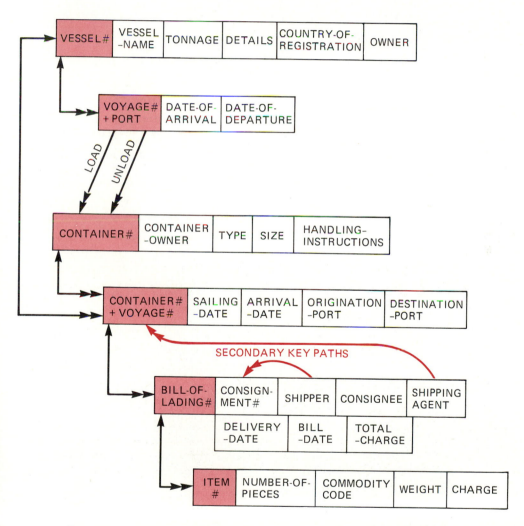

Figure 17.1   Canonical structure for the shipping example developed in Chapter 14.

We can take each data item which is not by itself a primary key and ask whether it could be used as a primary key in the future:

VESSEL-NAME:	This is equivalent to VESSEL#. VESSEL# is used to identify vessels, so there would never be *a separate record* with VESSEL-NAME as its primary key.
TONNAGE:	No. This would not be used as a primary key at any time. (It could conceivably be used as a secondary key—but that does not matter.)
DETAILS:	No.
COUNTRY-OF-REGISTRATION:	No.
OWNER:	Possibly. This deserves discussion. Would future applications use data about the vessel owner?
PORT:	Possibly.
VOYAGE#:	This has already been deleted as a stand-alone primary key on the assumption that it will not by itself identify anything.
DATE-OF-ARRIVAL:	No. (Although it may be used as a secondary key.)
DATE-OF-DEPARTURE:	No. (Although it is likely to be used as a secondary key.)
CONTAINER-OWNER:	Possibly. This deserves discussion.
TYPE:	No.
SIZE:	No.
HANDLING-INSTRUCTIONS:	No.
SAILING-DATE:	No.
ARRIVAL-DATE:	No.
ORIGINATION-PORT: **DESTINATION-PORT:**	PORT might be a primary key, as indicated above. ORIGINA-TION-PORT and DESTINATION-PORT would probably not be keys in addition to PORT.
CONSIGNMENT#:	It has been decided that this is functionally equivalent to WAY-BILL#. This assumption needs careful examination.
SHIPPER:	Probably. Information not shown in Fig. 17.1 is likely to be stored about the shipper. Another record should therefore be introduced at this stage with a primary key: SHIPPER. There should be discussion about what information about the shipper might be stored.
CONSIGNEE:	Probably. Information not shown in Fig. 17.1 is likely to be stored about the consignee. Another record should probably be introduced with CONSIGNEE as a primary key.

SHIPPING-AGENT:	Possibly. This should be discussed.
DELIVERY-DATE:	No.
BILL-DATE:	No.
TOTAL-CHARGE:	No.
NUMBER-OF-PIECES:	No.
COMMODITY-CODE:	No.
WEIGHT:	No.
CHARGE:	No.

The data administrator, systems analysts, and end-user group should examine each data item in this way. It is generally easy to spot those which might become primary keys in the future. If they are made primary keys now, that will prevent having to restructure that data and rewrite the programs using it in the future. It could save much money and disruption.

The modeling process will automatically take care of this if views of data using the key in question are fed to it.

DICTIONARY CHECK

When the checks above are taking place, the dictionary definitions of the data items should be used in conjunction with the model. Users should double check that they really represent the true meaning of the data as they are employed by the users.

INTERSECTION DATA

With a good data-base management system it is possible to add new *attributes* to an existing record without forcing the rewriting of application programs, provided that there is no change in primary keys. It is possible, however, that a new attribute might be needed which relates to an existing *link* rather than to a single key. This is *intersection data,* which we illustrated in Fig. 14.2.

If a 1:M link ($\longleftarrow\!\!\!\longrightarrow\!\!\!\rightarrow$) exists between the primary keys, new data can be identified by one or other of the existing primary keys. They can therefore be added to an existing record.

If an M:M link ($\longleftarrow\!\!\!\longleftarrow\!\!\!\longrightarrow\!\!\!\rightarrow$) exists between the primary keys, intersection data cannot be identified by either of the primary keys alone. They need a concatenated key. This is illustrated in Box 17.1.

The synthesis process should detect any M:M links between primary keys and automatically create a concatenated key which combines them, deleting the M:M link. This is illustrated in the bottom half of Box 17.1.

BOX 17.1 Intersection data

The following are examples of intersection data:

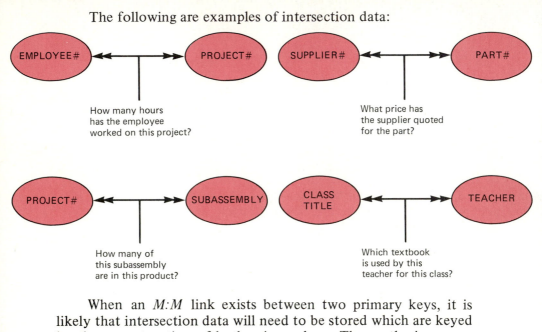

When an *M:M* link exists between two primary keys, it is likely that intersection data will need to be stored which are keyed by the concatenation of both primary keys. The synthesis process automatically creates these concatenated keys, as follows:

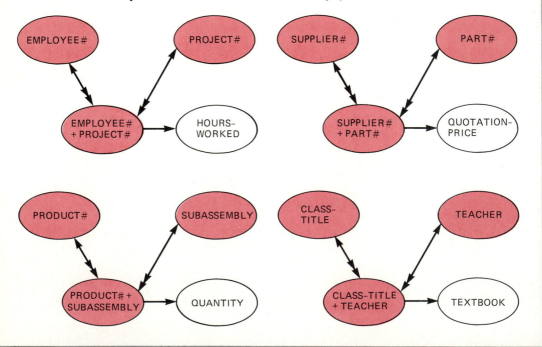

Suppose, for example, that a college data base was created that recorded information about classes and information about teachers. It contained the following *M:M* link:

It did not consider textbooks.

Sometime later it is necessary to record what textbooks are used. However, the textbook for a class is selected by the teacher. It cannot therefore be identified by the primary key CLASS-TITLE alone. It is identified by the concatenation of CLASS-TITLE and TEACHER:

In anticipation of such changes the modeling process should automatically change each *M:M* link between primary keys and insert the appropriate concatenated key:

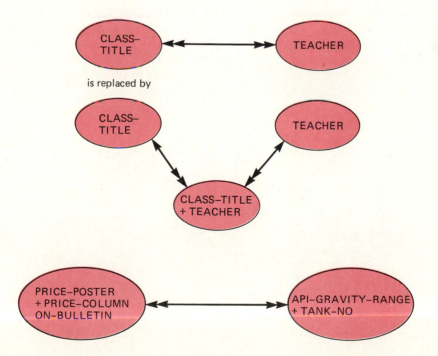

is replaced by

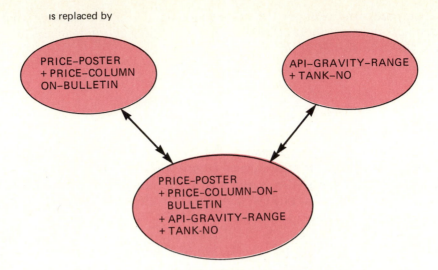

In some types of systems lengthy concatenated keys result. Some have as many as eight or nine concatenated data items. (These should usually be handled by a relational data base separate from the production data base.) In implementing the model a data administrator might decide that *nothing* will *ever* be keyed by the concatenated key. In this case he might avoid using that key in the data base if the data-base management system allows that option. Usually, however, there will indeed be some future requirement to employ the concatenated key.

When the input views are synthesized, the result may contain some links between primary keys which contain arrows in one direction only.

For example, the synthesis process might give

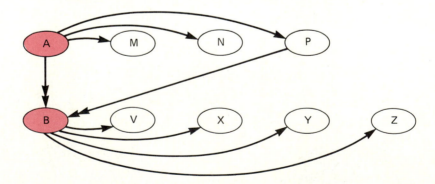

It is then necessary for the designer to ask what the type of association is from B to A. If it is a double-headed arrow, a new concatenated key would be created, A + B:

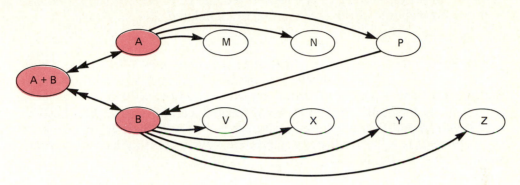

Occasionally, there is no interest in the reverse link or in possible concatenation, but for safety the possibility should be examined.

LINKS THAT ARE DELETED

The synthesis process automatically deletes links which *appear* to be redundant, as in the example at the end of Chapter 11. The designer should check all deleted links to make sure that they are *truly* redundant.

For example, in the case

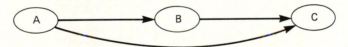

the synthesis process will automatically delete A———►C. The designer should ask: Is A———►C the same *in meaning* as the path A———►B———►C?

The following would be a case in which the meaning is not the same:

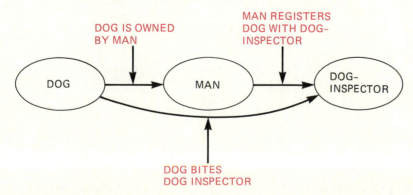

It is somewhat improbable that a link should be included as input to the data base which means *dog bites dog-inspector*. In fact, cases in which A———►C is not equivalent to A———►B———►C are rare. Nevertheless, the data administrator should check the *meaning* of all deleted associations.

CANDIDATE KEYS   The model may contain some 1:1 links. These indicate a *candidate key*. If A identifies B and B identifies A (A◄———►B), then A and B are functionally equivalent.

Any such situations should be inspected carefully and the question asked: Are A and B *really* functionally equivalent and likely to remain so in the future? It is easy to illustrate candidate keys in textbooks, but in practice they are rare because:

1. In the future A may identify a slightly different set of data items from B.
2. Two values of A may be identical, whereas the equivalent values of B are not. For example, EMPLOYEE# and EMPLOYEE-NAME, shown as functionally equivalent in Fig. 12.1, are not really equivalent candidate keys because two employees might have the same name. Only EMPLOYEE# should be used as the primary key.

The model might contain situations such as the following:

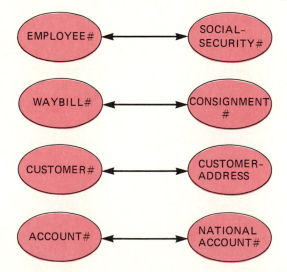

INTERSECTING ATTRIBUTES   When the model contains intersecting attributes there are three possible ways of dealing with them, shown in Box. 14.2. To decide which is appropriate the data administrator should ask: Could this attribute possibly be used as a primary key in the future? If not, the attribute should be duplicated to avoid the intersection, as in the second illustration in Box 14.2. If it *could* become a primary key, either the first or third solution should be used depending on whether a primary key path like that in the first illustration is logically correct.

CYCLES IN THE MODEL   The single-headed arrows in the model may form a cycle as in the following case:

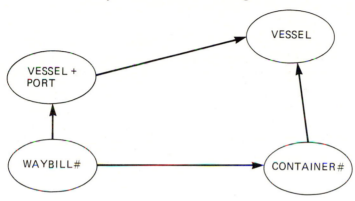

BOX 17.2   Cycles in the model

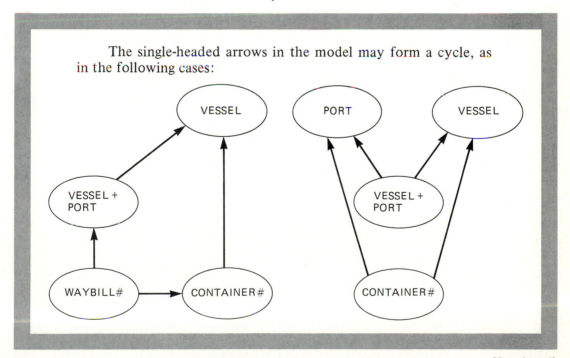

The single-headed arrows in the model may form a cycle, as in the following cases:

(Continued)

BOX 17.2 *(Continued)*

There is often a hidden redundancy in such cycles which can be broken by adding a cross-link between the data items.

For example, in both of the cases above a link from CON-TAINER# to VESSEL + PORT is needed:

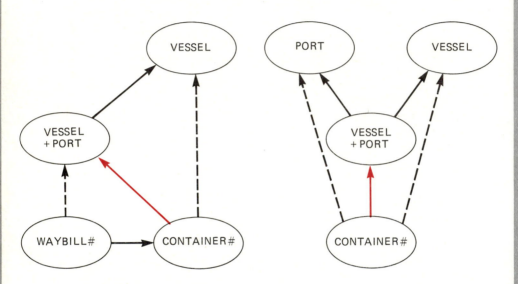

The dashed links are then redundant and automatically re-moved. A simpler structure results.

There is often a redundancy in such cycles. They can be simplified by the addition of a cross-link which causes two or more of the links in the cycle to be deleted, thus simplifying the structure. This is illustrated in Box. 17.2.

The data administrator should examine all such cycles.

VALIDATION   The data-base designer creates a logical software schema based on all or part of the model. When this is done, the designer should use the original inputs to the model and ensure that they can each be derived from the schema. The process helps to validate the design.

ADDITIONAL ATTRIBUTES

With some data-base management systems, more attributes can be added to an existing data-item group without forcing the rewriting of old programs which use that group. *This is true only if the primary key is not changed.* Adding new attributes usually necessitates major file reorganization and reloading, but the application programs can be given the same view of the data.

If a data-base management system does not allow new attributes to be added without modification of application programs, it is a risky proposition to use it.

ADDITIONAL SECONDARY KEYS

Whereas the primary keys need to be correct from the start, new secondary keys can be added in some data-base management systems without forcing changes to existing programs. This is a desirable attribute of a data-base management system. It permits the data to be searched in new ways or permits user languages that trigger secondary-key actions.

Some data-base management systems do not permit this freedom of new secondary-key access. The designer should question whether they should be used. He should ask what secondary-key paths could become important.

HIGH-USAGE SECONDARY-KEY PATHS

The synthesis process should indicate the volume of usage of the various usage paths. If a secondary-key path (drawn on the right-hand side of charts, such as that in Fig. 15.2) has a high volume of usage *and* is used interactively, that is an indication that there may be machine performance problems. If the secondary-key path is employed with batch processing, the data may be sorted before the batch is run. This is normally acceptable from the machine performance point of view except in those cases where the data base is extremely large. With extremely large data bases *and* high-usage secondary-key paths, the data may be installed as a Class I (file) or Class II environment rather than Class III.

With high-volume interaction secondary-key paths the model may be split into disjoint data bases for machine performance reasons, or may be implemented with software designed for a Class IV (information system) environment, as discussed later in the book.

DATA ANALYSIS CONSULTANT:

They mapped everything with data flow diagrams and used this technique to build their data model. They drew data flow diagrams after

---

data flow diagrams to the *n*th level and made users sign-off all the way. When the data model was used later, it didn't work in many areas. They matched their requirements against the data model and realized they were wrong with their requirements. So they invented a thing called a RAM, a requirements anomoly.

The use of structured analysis led them astray because they mapped in detail what they currently do rather than looking at the fundamental data.

At the very highest level there was a very general statement of requirements but not a very accurate one. All that the structured techniques did was to refine further what was given to them at the top, based on the premise that the starting point was accurate.

Based on our experience I think it is probably impossible to build a satisfactory data model from data flow diagrams. They can be useful if their data stores are regarded as user views for input to data modeling. The store is taken out of the procedure it's in and used as a parcel of information about data; the procedure is then discarded because the data must be independent of procedures.

DISTRIBUTED DATA

Distributed files or distributed data bases are often used. Files residing on peripheral machines should often be designed to be derivable from a central data-base system. In this case they need to be incorporated as user views in the data modeling process.

Multiple distributed data bases may be derived from a common model.

The great problem of distributed processing is the incompatibility of data on different systems separately implemented. The data modeling output and an associated data dictionary listing provide vital tools for gaining control of the distributed environment. The data-item groups used at multiple locations should be incorporated into a common data dictionary and common set of data models. These should be used for enforcing data standards among the separate locations.

A SMALL STEP AT A TIME

The data modeling in an organization needs to be broad in its scope, encompassing the old files and data bases as well as future uses of data. It needs to encompass the many locations where the data will be used.

It should not be regarded as a single task done at one time. It is often too complex for that. Rather, it should be an ongoing process done a small step at a time. The organization's data are steadily cleaned up, removing and documenting the many inconsistencies. A large and complex organization will have multiple models for different areas. It is easier to do in a small, young, organization that is growing up with computers.

The ongoing process of cleaning up, modeling, and documenting the data is an essential part of building a computerized corporation.

REFERENCE

1. *How to Do Optimal Logical Data Base Design,* a manual on DATA DE-SIGNER from Data Base Design Inc., 2020 Hogback Road, Ann Arbor, MI 48104.

18 MACHINE PERFORMANCE AND PHYSICAL DESIGN

INTRODUCTION   The physical organization of the data and access methods has a major effect on the cost, performance, and response times of a data-base system.

Some of the worst data-base horror stories relate to systems for which the physical design was done inadequately (or not done at all). One of the world's most prestigious banks had a large computer delivered for data-base operation and later discovered that there was no conceivable way that it could do the work intended for it. Only a token attempt had been made at calculating the system performance. There was no easy way out of the dilemma because the machine was purchased, not rented.

In many less dramatic cases the runs take much longer than they should because inappropriate access methods or disc layouts have been selected. More visible, the response times are sometimes much longer than expected and inadequate for the needs of the end users.

The data-base design process seeks to optimize the performance according to criteria which often conflict somewhat, as with most complex system design a careful choice among compromises is needed.

IMPLEMENTING THE DATA MODEL   The data-base designer creates the software schemas and physical designs for the data bases which are implemented, as indicated on the right-hand side of Fig. 19.1. In doing this he should work from the *data model* (such as that in Fig. 15.2) that the data administrator creates.

In a CODASYL data base he will design the set structures which are implemented, the physical layout of the data on the storage media, and the access methods for retrieving, updating, deleting, and inserting data. In a DL/1 data base he will design and code the *physical-data-base description*

321

and *logical-data-base description.* Similarly in other types of data bases, the specific data-base descriptions must be created.

In doing so the design takes into consideration the means of preserving data security and integrity, and of recovering and restarting after failures have occurred, without damaging the data.

The data-base designer often decides that in order to implement the data model efficiently or expediently, it must be split into separate data bases and, occasionally, files. He should distinguish clearly among the Class I, II, III, and IV environments.

DATA ADMINISTRATOR:

It's not realistic to expect the logical model to be mapped directly into a physical design. But it's a goal; it's a starting point that should be kept in front of the physical designers, so that the disjoint files are as few as possible and the compromises do not harm the overall concept.

Sometimes the data model is implemented on multiple machines in a distributed environment. The decision to distribute, or how to distribute, data may be made by the data-base designer or may be made by a separate *data distribution administrator* as suggested in Fig. 6.7.

Sometimes the data model is implemented on different data-base management systems. The reason for this is often to obtain an efficient *Class IV* information system working separately from the Class II or III production systems. In some cases the reason is political or is that different data-base management systems already exist serving different areas which are now linked with a common data model.

COMPROMISES   Often the data-base designer finds that compromises are desirable. He may split the data model, or implement separate file systems, for performance reasons. When he takes such actions they need to be discussed with the data administrator to see whether they might interfere with future flexibility of using the data, or might add to future maintenance costs.

---

*DATA-BASE DESIGNER FOR A SYSTEM WITH VERY
HIGH TRANSACTION VOLUMES:*

We're finding this an intricate process.

We take the logical model and mark on it the access paths. We determine the number of accesses that are required to perform the various functions that the applications want. As we collect that information we extrapolate it into preliminary performance figures.

In most of the cases, we're finding that our first-blush desires cannot be met by the hardware and software. Consequently, the intricate process starts here, where we go back to the data administrator and the application development project leader and say that this is the extent of the problem. It in fact can be represented this way physically, but we're not sure that you want that kind of performance, and usually they agree.

Then the questions become: What kind of compromises can be made; could you get this a different way; could we store this in a different form; could we off-load this file? We discuss the possibilities with them and then go back and take another cut at the physical design, again trying to predict a performance that we could expect when it's implemented. Then, we go back again, and say this is what we found this time: Is this acceptable?

We're finding we have to go through that several times.

The designer might decide to deviate from third normal form for performance reasons. He might group a non-third-normal-form collection of fields into a record because that record is used in a very high volume run. (This does not necessarily improve performance, but it can do so in certain cases.) When deviation from third normal form is suggested, the data administrator should evaluate the extent to which it will increase future maintenance costs. It is often the case that the increase in future maintenance costs is greater than the saving in machine costs. Both sides of the situation need to be evaluated.

INFORMATION NEEDED FOR PERFORMANCE DESIGN   A data model showing logical associations, such as that in Fig. 15.2, does not contain enough information to perform efficient physical data-base design. To do this the data-base designer needs three more pieces of information:

1. For each double-headed arrow showing a one-to-many association it is necessary to know *how many*. In the following case:

How many B data items are associated on average with one A data item?

This number can be written against each double-headed arrow. Thus

means that an invoice has five items on it, on average.

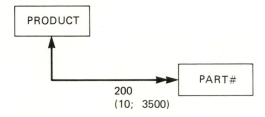

means that a product record has an average of 200 part records associated with it and that this number can vary from 10 to 3500.

The data-base designer is concerned with how the records should be laid out on the discs or other storage media. He asks questions such as: "Does a CODASYL set fit on a single disc cylinder?" or "Does the occurrence of a customer record and the

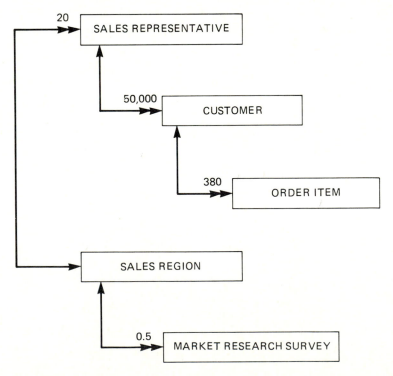

Figure 18.1   Occurrence frequencies superimposed on the data model.

associated transaction records usually fit on a single disc track?" To answer such questions he needs for each one-to-many association to know *how many*.

This information can be coded in the input views of data that are entered into a data modeling tool. Figure 18.1 shows a data model with this information printed by each double-headed arrow.

2. For each of the usage paths represented in the model (each line between bubbles) it is desirable to know how often it is followed.

When individual user views are created, the number of times per month each view is employed can be stated. The synthesis process adds up the usage of each path as it builds the data model. DATA DESIGNER, for example, prints these usage path figures in its output reports ready for the physical data-base designer.

3. Similarly, for each usage path it is desirable to know whether it is followed with *on-line* processing or *batch* processing. If *on-line*, is a fast response time required?

Figure 18.2 illustrates a data model with details of the usage paths superimposed on it.

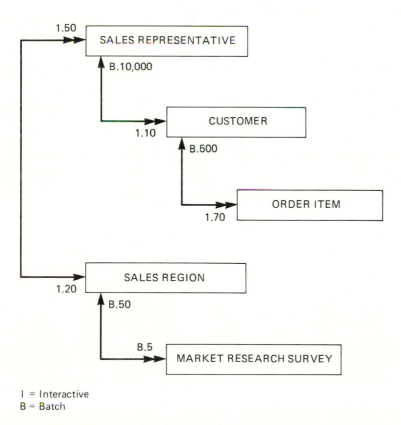

I = Interactive
B = Batch

Figure 18.2   Usage frequencies superimposed on the data model.

ALTERNATIVE STRUCTURES

If it is decided to implement a certain data model, possibly a portion of an overall corporate model, there are often multiple ways to represent it either as a hierarchical or a CODASYL data-base structure. (There is usually only one direct translation of a third-normal-form model into a relational data base.)

Figures 18.3 and 18.4 illustrate this. The simple five-record model at the top of these figures can be represented as four possible hierarchical data-base structures (e.g., DL/1, IMS, TOTAL, IMAGE, System 2000, etc.) or four possible CODASYL data-base structures (IDMS, IDS, DMS 1100, etc.). In either case machine performance considerations will usually determine which is the preferred structure.

In the hierarchical structures (Fig. 18.3), following paths *within* a hierarchy takes less machine time than following paths that span hierarchies (the red links). The data-base designer will take the paths through the model which have a high usage, first, and ensure that those are within a hierarchy. The low-usage paths can be paths that stretch between hierarchies. The paths often require a machine *seek*, whereas the paths within a hierarchy usually do not.

The record labeled ORDER + PART is the individual item on an order. The path from ORDER to ORDER + PART may be more frequently used than any other path. Therefore, the bottom two versions are ruled out. The path from PART to SUPPLIER + RULE may be much more frequently used than the path from SUPPLIER to SUPPLIER + PART. Therefore, the second of the four versions is chosen.

Given a set of usage path weights on a complex model, the best combination of hierarchies to represent that model can be selected *automatically*.

In the CODASYL versions in Fig. 18.4, the path from PART to ORDER + PART may be followed frequently. Use of this path should be in a separate set from the path from PART to SUPPLIER + PART. One of the bottom two versions is therefore selected. The paths from SUPPLIER to ORDER or SUPPLIER + PART are followed infrequently. These may therefore be in the same set, and the third of the four CODASYL versions is selected.

Whereas a canonical data structure is not concerned with machine performance, the selection of hierarchical or CODASYL structure needs to take this into consideration.

LAYOUT AND ACCESS METHODS

Having determined what set structures or hierarchies are to be implemented, the data-base designer must choose the access methods to be used.

If the records are always used one at a time in no particular sequence, a *random-access method* would be selected. The computer needs to go directly to the record in question and the term *direct-access method* (DAM) is used. The most common direct-access method uses *hashing* [1].

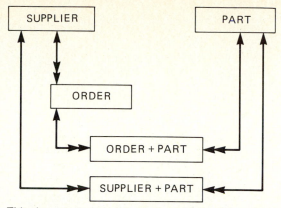

This plex structure can be represented as two hierarchical structures with links between them. There are four possible ways to accomplish this, shown below. The red lines show the links between hierarchies.

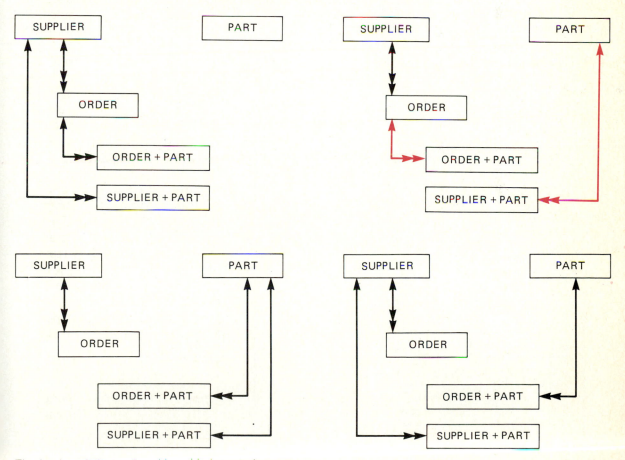

The data-base designer using a hierarchical approach must select which of these four gives the best machine performance.

Figure 18.3

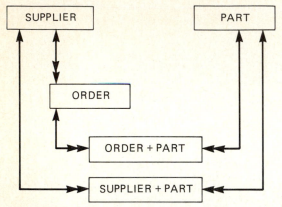

This plex structure can be represented with four possible combinations of CODASYL sets. The red lines show the sets:

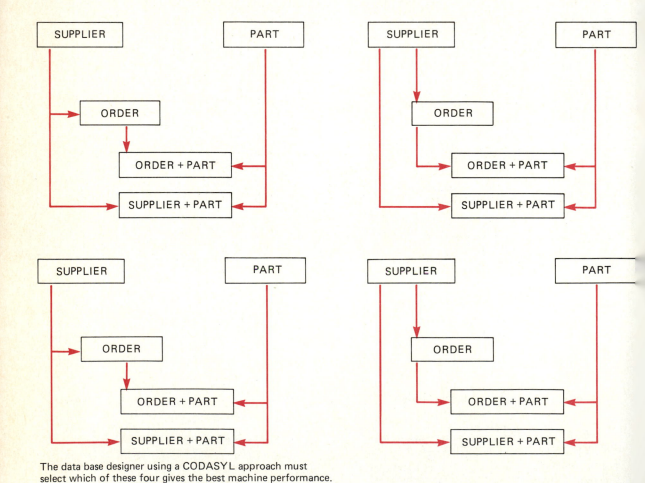

The data base designer using a CODASYL approach must select which of these four gives the best machine performance.

Figure 18.4

Some Class IV data-base management systems use *only* hashing. Hashing, or other direct-access methods, result in data being laid out on the discs in no particular sequence. This is not efficient for a high-volume batch operation. In a large batch operation, it is desirable that the data be laid out in the sequence of their primary keys. The run then progresses through the data in the same sequence as that in which they are laid out on the discs, and consequently the number of seeks are reduced. The data may be read into main memory a track (or part of a track) at a time. With direct-access methods a separate *seek* is needed for almost every record accessed.

If data are used *only* for batch processing in one particular sequence, a *sequential-access method* (SAM) can be used. Almost always, however, there is need to access *individual* records, one at a time. Therefore, a means of finding records quickly in the middle of a sequential file is needed. For this, an index is employed. We then have an *indexed sequential-access method* (ISAM) [2].

Data can be laid out in the sequence of its primary keys but then not in the sequence of any other field. It cannot in general be in the sequence of its secondary keys. If it required to access the data by a primary key, another index may be used—a *secondary index*. A secondary index is usually much bulkier than a primary index because if the records are not in sequence by the indexed field, most techniques for compacting the index are not applicable [3].

Just as records laid out in sequence may be scanned, so records not in sequence may be searched. Similar values of certain fields may be strung together with pointers forming *chain* or *ring* structures. Following chains or rings through a mechanical storage unit is very time consuming, so other means of searching are also employed [4].

We thus have five main types of access methods:

- *Sequential-access method (SAM):* useful only for sorted batch operations with no random access.

- *Indexed sequential-access method (ISAM):* in which the data are in sequence by primary key but an index is used for accessing them randomly.

- *Direct-access method (DAM):* usually hashing. The data are directly accessible without an index but are not in sequence for fast batch processing.

- *Secondary indices:* for finding records with particular values of a secondary key.

- *Searching techniques:* for searching data to answer unanticipated queries. Various searching techniques are used.

HEAVY-DUTY SYSTEMS

Some data-base systems are used for processing a mass of routine transactions. They are heavy-duty systems which process large volumes of input and produce large volumes of output; for example, the processing of orders in a mail-order house or the processing of claims in a large insurance company.

With such systems the designer knows the predominant uses of the machine. He will select the physical data-base structure, the disc layouts, and access methods that give the best machine efficiency.

Such systems are very different from data-base systems that are predominantly used for inquiry processing or for nonroutine low-volume transactions. They need different access methods and data layouts. Although the two can be combined, it often pays to separate the heavy-duty data base from the nonroutine data base or information system, even though their data are partially the same and their structures are derived from the same data model.

We have stressed the separation of the Class IV from the Class II and III environments. Sometimes the same DBMS is used for the heavy-duty and nonroutine data bases, although these are separate. They may be disjoint data bases residing in the same machine. If complex queries are to be processed in an information system, it may pay to use a separate DBMS and possibly a separate computer (now that computers are inexpensive).

It is desirable to distinguish between different types of queries. Simple queries can be efficiently handled by a heavy-duty data-base system. Complex queries often cannot.

DATA-BASE EXECUTIVE:

We analyzed the overhead associated with one of our large data-base systems. We found that 70% of the machine instructions being executed resulted from DBMS overhead. Some of our files have billions of bytes. For systems this size, processing costs amount to 6 or 7 figures per year. The overhead burden could be several hundreds of thousands of dollars.

We are restructuring the DBMS use to try to reduce processing requirements by a full 40%.

DATA-BASE QUERIES   Data-base queries can be classified into four types.

1. Primary-Key Queries

A record is accessed by means of its primary key. This can be done quickly and uses few machine cycles.

An example of a primary-key query would be "PRINT DETAILS OF THE SHIP ACHILLES." SHIP-NAME is a primary key for accessing a naval data base. A single record is looked up, and its contents are printed.

2. Single-Secondary-Key Queries

This type of query may be represented on a data model diagram as a secondary-key path. If it is anticipated, a secondary index or other mechanism may be used. It requires far more machine cycles than a primary-key query.

An example of a single-secondary-key query would be "PRINT DETAILS OF ALL SHIPS WITH A READINESS-RATING = C1." If the question was anticipated by the system designer, there may be a secondary-key index showing what ships have a given readiness rating.

3. Multiple-Secondary-Key Queries

This requires more than one secondary-key access. It can be substantially more complex and expensive in machine cycles than a single-secondary-key access.

An example of such a query might be "PRINT DETAILS OF ALL RUSSIAN SHIPS WITHIN 900 MILES OF THE STRAITS OF HORMUZ CARRYING TORPEDOES WITH A RANGE GREATER THAN 20 MILES." A secondary index to the weapons data base may be used to find which weapons are torpedoes with a range greater than 20 miles. There may be a secondary-key index showing which ships are Russian. It may be necessary to examine their records to find whether they carry those weapons. This produces a list of ships. The area around the Straits of Hormuz is then examined to find which ships are within 900 miles of that location. These ships are compared with the previous list. This requires a considerable amount of machine activity, especially if there are many ships.

4. Unanticipated Search Queries

Secondary-key queries may take place relatively quickly if there is a suitable secondary index. If there is not, then it may be necessary to search the records in question a record at a time. This is very expensive in machine time.

DEDICATED MACHINES

If a computer did nothing other than process one query at a time, a relatively inexpensive machine might be used. Even if it processed multiple similar queries at once, machine time need not be a serious problem.

Unfortunately, many systems are designed to do conventional high-volume data processing, with queries fitting in as required. A DP manager has to decide which activities have priority. Queries about Russian ships near the Straits of Hormuz may have very high priority, but ordinary commercial use of an end-user query language may not.

The end user with a language like Query-by-Example can very quickly enter a query such as the following:

EMPLOYEE	EMPLOYEE#	NAME	LOCATION	SALARY	YEAR-OF-HIRE
	A	P.	P.	<25000	>1975

SKILLS	SKILL-TYPE	GRADE	EMPLOYEE #
	ACCOUNTANT	>6	A

The user may have no concept of how much is involved in processing this query. The response time might be quite long. If this type of query is given a low priority, the response time might become degraded to a level that seems unacceptable to end users. If the necessary secondary indices do not exist and the **EMPLOYEE** or **SKILLS** records have to be searched, the time taken may be excessive.

EXPENSE   When a query initiates the searching of a data base on a large system it may be more expensive than the end user realizes. Often there is no indication of the cost involved when a data-base facility is used. The user may not know the wide difference in cost between a primary-key query and one that triggers searching operations. It would be useful if computers would tell the user the cost before they process the query, but most do not.

Sometimes user management is surprised by the charges and unable to comprehend them.

CATEGORIES OF   Figure 18.5 shows six categories of data system.
DATA SYSTEM   In its early years data-base usage employed predominently primary-key access paths. The high-volume activity of most computers is category 1 in Fig. 18.5: production data processing. Primary-key queries are used with the production systems with no problem (category 2).

Off-line secondary-key queries can be saved and processed in a scheduled batch fashion (category 3 in Fig. 18.5). This does not disrupt the production system.

Category 4 is much more disruptive of the production system. A data base designed to be efficient for high-volume production is not usually effi-

	IS THE INFORMATION PRODUCED ON A SCHEDULED BASIS BY THE SYSTEM?	
	YES SCHEDULED	NO ON DEMAND
PRIMARY KEY	① ROUTINE PRODUCTION DATA PROCESSING	② SIMPLE QUERIES
ANTICIPATED SINGLE-SECONDARY-KEY AND MULTIPLE-SECONDARY-KEY	③ COMPLEX OFF-LINE QUERIES	④ COMPLEX ON-LINE QUERIES
UNANTICIPATED	⑤ SLOW-REACTING INFORMATION SYSTEM	⑥ GENERALIZED INFORMATION SYSTEM

Figure 18.5 Categories of data systems. Categories 4 and 6 may need to be in a different computer from category 1.

cient for complex secondary-key queries, and vice versa. Category 6 is worse. The queries are not planned and may require parts of the data base to be searched.

It is often desirable that categories 4 and 6 be in a separate computer system to the category 1 high-volume production systems. End-user departments might have their own computer—either an information system or a production system. This may make sense both for performance and other reasons.

Category 5 in Fig. 18.5 is less useful. Non-predefined information requests might be satisfied by visual inspections of listings produced on a scheduled basis. Although this has been common with some computer systems, it is generally a rather unsatisfactory way of answering spontaneous requests for information.

SCHEDULING AND RESPONSE-TIME PROBLEMS

Some data-base systems have severe scheduling and response-time problems. This is especially so when secondary-key paths have high-volume usage. DP operations are tending to swing from mainly primary-key usage of data to a substantial amount of secondary-key usage.

This will be increasingly so in the future as good end-user data-base inquiry languages become popular.

Figure 15.2 shows the key paths. A large traffic figure associated with a secondary-key path is an indication of potential scheduling problems.

Given the falling cost of minicomputer information systems, it often makes sense to create functional information systems *separate* from the high-volume production systems. The secondary-key paths in the data model may indicate a need for this. The use of separate end-user data bases is discussed in Chapter 26.

Scheduling problems are generally caused by having conflicting types of activity combined on the same machine. Sometimes different forms of data-base activity conflict from the machine performance point of view. Sometimes a high-volume non-data-base activity such as sorting interferes badly with the response times of the data base.

DATA-BASE EXECUTIVE:

We have found that our design arithmetic has been pretty much correct. The machine performance has been what we predicted.

However, another problem has hit us that we didn't anticipate initially.

We were not aware of how data-base jobs are run in the data center in terms of machine allocations and scheduling. This was outside the view of the data management division. Once jobs are accepted into the data center for scheduling, then it's in the province of the data center manager. If he runs the wrong mix of jobs, then he affects the performance of any on-line operation whether it's data base or not. Sometimes he has to run big compiles or sorts alongside the on-line jobs. Then the response time goes to pieces.

Sometimes he is forced to do this because of job pressures, sometimes because another machine is down. It is difficult to manage our way out of this problem because it usually requires more hardware.

The degradation in response time that results from such scheduling problems is sometimes severe. In bad cases a 2-second response time has changed to 30 seconds or more. This is insufferably frustrating for the end users.

DP EXECUTIVE:

We made a detailed survey of the discontent in the end-user departments. Many of them were clamoring for their own machine and there were too many uncontrolled minicomputers.

We found that the biggest reason was availability. The users perceived the system as being down too often—frequently when it was vital for their work.

Often the system wasn't really down at all. It was a scheduling problem. Some other jobs were taking priority. Sometimes the response times had become so bad that the users *thought* the system was down.

EXCESSIVE GROWTH IN UTILIZATION

A critical form of performance problem occurs when a data base becomes perceived by end users as giving a particularly valuable interactive service. The good news spreads and the utilization can expand too rapidly for the system to handle. This has happened to many data-base systems, particularly when powerful end-user languages have been employed which enable the users, often unwittingly, to trigger data-base searches.

Primary-key linkages are often predictable in their usage, but *secondary-key* usage may grow suddenly and unpredictably. The data administrator can predict the forms of secondary-key usage with an appropriate modeling tool, but is often not able to predict surges in volume of their use.

Figure 18.6 shows a common pattern of growth for useful interactive systems. The value of the system is perceived slowly at first, or there is a reluctance to use it because it is strange. Users do not want to appear foolish by employing the terminal incorrectly. It represents a change in office culture and cultural changes come slowly. The system instigators are sometimes disappointed by the slow acceptance, but gradually the users find out that it does give a valuable service. They tell their associates. Leading users are seen to employ the terminals and the others want to follow suit. There is positive feedback and the utilization grows rapidly, often explosively, until the system cannot handle it.

The caption of Fig. 18.6 quotes a somewhat cynical law: "If a service is created which is sufficiently useful, utilization expands until it knocks out the system!"

The answer is often to give the users their own system. They can do what they want in their own system and pay for it. They can expand or duplicate the system if they wish. The data are organized for the activity in question, so the activity is much more efficient than if it were carried out with data organized differently, for heavy-duty production runs.

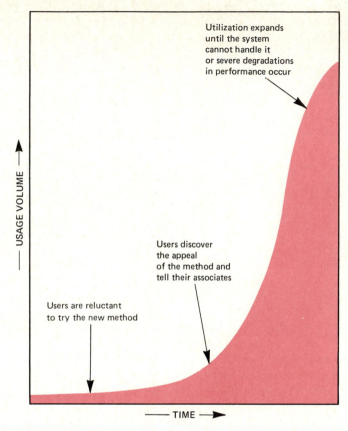

Figure 18.6 Martin's Law: "If a service is created which is sufficiently useful, utilization expands until it knocks out the system!" Many end-user services have had a growth pattern similar to this diagram.

PENALTY FOR BAD DESIGN

For each data-base access method there are many variations on how exactly the data (and indices) can be organized. How are new records inserted and old records deleted? How much free space should be left for new records? How often should the data base be reorganized? What storage devices should be chosen? Where should the data be placed on the devices? Should the indices be on a different device from the data? And so on.

These factors affect the performance in subtle, complex ways, and there are so many factors and conflicting objectives that no single algorithm can be used for optimizing the data base. Algorithms can be used for optimizing certain aspects of the design [1], but the overall design remains a heuristic process.

The penalty for bad design is higher in a data-base system than in a file system. In one well-known corporation a data-base application was programmed and, when it was eventually run, to everybody's horror it took about 60 hours. A hue and cry ensued, and a manufacturer's specialist redesigned the data base to achieve a run time of 12 hours. The system operated like this for some months while a more fundamental redesign was done which eventually brought the run time down to 3 hours.

The data-base designer needs to understand the choices that are open to him with the DBMS in question. He needs to be able to estimate the number of accesses, the length of accesses, and the queuing delays that occur, for different data organizations.

DATA-BASE DESIGNER:

This is not a very detailed analysis in the beginning. It's more a rough sizing to estimate our options. We estimate the response times for on-line applications and the run times for batch applications.

Considerable discussion of the options occurs with the data administrator before we finally cast it in concrete. Then we do a more detailed calculation for the particular system design that we have decided upon.

Sometimes the design estimates are done too late. A machine is delivered that cannot do the work for which it is intended. Again it is important to stress that enough time needs to be spent on the design of data bases before they are implemented.

Perhaps the most common data-base disaster story is that relating to inadequate design calculations.

REFERENCES

1. Physical data-base design is discussed in James Martin's *Computer Data-Base Organization,* 2nd ed., Prentice-Hall, Inc., Englewood Cliffs, NJ, 1977. Hashing is described in Chapter 21.

2. Ibid. Chapter 20 discusses index sequential organizations of data.

3. Ibid. Chapters 29 and 30 discuss index techniques.

4. Ibid. Chapters 25 to 27 discuss searching techniques using multiple keys.

19 THE DATA-BASE-ADMINISTRATION FUNCTION

INTRODUCTION   Because a data base serves many applications and many departments, it needs centralized coordination.

This chapter summarizes and discusses the various functions of data-base planning, design, and operation. They are listed in Box 19.1.

Establishing the necessary data bases is a complicated task. It is also a very critical one because so much future data processing depends on it. It ranges from physical data-base design, tuning for performance, and guidance of the programmers, to logical modeling, understanding end-user needs, top-down planning, and trying to comprehend what data will be needed in the future.

Should that be done by one person? Should it be done by committee? Or should it be split into different tasks?

We can look back on many data-base case histories now and observe what has made them successful, or unsuccessful.

CENTRALIZED   As we have commented, a typical corporation has
SERVICE   or will have thousands of types of data items, all
               of which must be organized into suitable records, segments, sets, or relations (depending on the preferred terminology and software). A single data item may be used by multiple departments in a corporation and for multiple applications. It therefore needs to be standardized in name, representation, and definition. The groupings of data items need to be organized into schemas which can best serve the widely differing uses, and the schemas must be mapped into physical organizations. Careful attention must be paid to security, accuracy, and privacy. The data must have suitable controls and must be protected from accidents, acts of God, embezzlers, thieves, and incompetents.

339

BOX 19.1   Functions of data-base executives

A. Data Strategist

1. Enterprise-wide planning of data.

2. Assessment of future information requirements.

3. Achievement of uniformity in data definitions throughout the enterprise, where possible.

4. Development of an entity-relationship overview chart.

5. Clustering entities into subject data bases.

6. Coordination of the work of separate data administrators.

7. Handling of human and political problems in the establishment of common data throughout the enterprise.

8. Education of top management in the need for strategic planning of data and enforcement of common data definitions and models.

B. Data Administrator

1. Data analysis, to determine what data should be in the data base.

2. Setting up end-user committees to be involved in data analysis, modeling, and definition.

3. Collection of end-user views and systems analysts' views of what should be in the data base.

4. Canonical data modeling (third normal form), preferably using an automated modeling tool.

5. Data item definition, preferably using an automated data dictionary.

6. Feedback of the model and dictionary output to the end-user committees, to ensure that these meet present and future needs as far as is possible.

7. Stability analysis (see Box 16.1).

8. Identification of data-item synonyms and representation of them in the dictionary. Elimination of synonyms where practical.

9. Development of appropriate reports from the dictionary, including cross-reference lists stating which programs use which data items. When changes are proposed, the cross referencing will show what has to be modified.

10. When users, programmers, or analysts require data that are not in the data base, the data administrator determines how (or whether) they can be incorporated.

11. The data definition analyst may determine what policies govern the retention of data, for example, to comply with government regulations.

BOX 19.1 *(Continued)*

12. He gives advice to programmers, systems analysts, and user departments concerning the data and their logical structure.

13. He attempts to maintain a view of the future needs and applications, so that the data base can be made to evolve in an appropriate manner.

14. He defines rules and functions to ensure validity, consistency, and accuracy of data. He may determine which users are responsible for the accuracy of which data.

15. He determines what data items or records need special security protection, and may determine which users are authorized to see, create, update, or delete data.

16. He plans for compatibility with existing data structures or for conversion of these structures.

C. Data-Base Designer

1. The design analyst is responsible for physically structuring the data and for planning the access methods.

2. He employs design tools such as mathematical models of the physical storage to help determine which methods of physical organization best meet the performance criteria.

3. He assists in the selection of which data-base hardware and software should be used, and specifies any additions to data-base software that might be needed.

4. He assists the programmers in using the data base, generates their data descriptions from the data dictionary, and conducts "walk-throughs" of their programs to ensure that they use the data base efficiently.

5. He designs the means of restart and recovery after systems outages, and the means of backup.

6. He designs the means of reconstructing data in the event of loss of records or of catastrophic destruction of entire files.

7. Using the logical model of the data base, he designs the software schemas. Certain systems analysts or programmers in the user departments may be competent file designers. The design analyst or the data-base administrator staff will work with these.

8. He specifies the techniques for monitoring the data-base performance.

9. Actual data-base performance will be correlated to the predictions of the design-tool models in an attempt to react to future performance problems before they arise.

10. Measurements of how full the file spaces are will be checked periodically so that appropriate restructuring can be carried out when necessary.

(Continued)

BOX 19.1 *(Continued)*

11. The design analyst determines when and how the physical data base needs tuning to improve its performance.

12. Viewing the data base as a whole, he determines what categories of security techniques should be used. He designs the detailed structures and techniques for maintaining privacy.

13. He designs any data-base searching strategies, or plans any use of inverted files or inverted lists.

14. He defines the rules relating to access constraints, including rules to prevent concurrent updates or interlocks, and rules to prevent excessive time-consuming search operations.

15. He determines the policies for deleting or dumping old data, or data migration.

16. He selects compaction techniques.

17. He provides advice to the systems analysts concerning data-base techniques.

18. He may determine that the data model needs splitting into separate disjoint structures. These may be in the same machine or distributed machines.

19. If the data are to be distributed, he participates in determining how this should be done.

20. He ensures that data distribution is done or controlled in a way that avoids deadlocks and integrity problems.

D. Data Operations Supervisor

The data operations supervisor deals with data problems that arise on a day-to-day basis.

1. He investigates all errors that are found in the data. He flags data that are known to be in error.

2. He supervises all restarts and recovery after failure.

3. He supervises all reorganizations of data bases or indices.

4. He cleans up any data conflicts that are found (such as data items that are different when they should be the same). When existing files are merged into the data base, data conflicts almost always show up.

5. He initiates and controls all periodic dumps of the data, audit trails, vital record procedures, and so on.

6. He ensures that the volume library is correctly controlled and maintained.

BOX 19.1 *(Continued)*

7. He exerts some control over computer scheduling when necessary for data-base reasons.

8. He supervises the transfer of files to alternative media when necessary.

E. Security Officer

The security officer may *not* report to the data-base executive. His functions vary widely, depending on the seriousness of security in the installation.

1. The security officer investigates all known security breaches.

2. He receives a listing each morning of all violations of correct security procedure which could reflect attempts to compromise security.

3. He determines who is authorized to use each locked facility or each locked data item, record, area, or file. He is responsible for the authorization tables which control the locked facilities or records.

4. No one other than the security officer can make any changes to the security authorization tables.

5. He modifies the data locks and keys whenever necessary.

6. He ensures that the machine room and volume library security procedures are complied with.

7. He conducts periodic security audits.

All these functions require centralized control. They should not be scattered to the diverse desires of application programmers, systems analysts, and department heads. Only by centralizing data-base policies can the data base be optimized for the users as a whole; otherwise, parochial, short-sighted, uninformed, or politically biased policies affect the data base. A subordinate group or single application group normally will not understand the *information economics* of the corporation as a whole. To coordinate needs of the various users, a centralized view is needed. In addition, the technical skills of measuring, implementing, and optimizing data organizations require advanced training. To give such training to subordinate groups would be too expensive and would divert attention from their main task—running their departments.

Just as one group of specialists in a corporation is responsible for all purchasing, or all shipping, so one group should be responsible for the custody and organization of data. Individual departments do not do their own purchasing, shipping, or data-base design.

Some firms are too large and diverse for data administration to be completely centralized. There are different data administrators in different divisions, locations, or factories. The extent to which these separate data administrators can use common dictionary definitions and data models differs from firm to firm depending on the uniformity, management style, and policies of centralized control. Some worldwide corporations achieve uniformity of data definitions and models, while others leave all data processing design in the hands of local executives. The ideal system seems to be coordination of data so that interoperability can be achieved, while encouraging maximum local initiative in *using* computerized data resources.

CORPORATE DIRECTOR OF DP:

We avoid the words "standards" and "compatible" because of the connotations of constraining the developers of individual systems. Instead we use the word "interoperability." That is what we are really concerned about—interoperability.

There is a strong trend in computing as a whole to *decentralize.* User departments are employing minicomputers or work stations and sometimes taking a high level of initiative in creating their own applications. It is necessary in DP to take the maximum advantage of decentralized skills, energy, and innovation.

It is easy, and therefore tempting, to create a soundly designed data model for one application area and ignore other applications. Where this is done extensively it results in multiple incompatible representations of data.

DATA ADMINISTRATION CONSULTANT:

People often look at one application area and create a good data model for it. They can easily believe that the broader picture does not matter. It does! Without a broad overview that permits data interchange, parochial data modeling can be disastrous.

In DP, as in other aspects of government and management, it is necessary to ask what should be centralized and what decentralized. Too much centralization cripples initiative. But decentralized activities are more efficient if certain types of centralized services are available.

The job of setting up the data-base *infrastructure* and controlling the evolution of data-base systems in a corporation is likely to become very important. It will be a key to the success of the corporation's future data processing. The data administrator must form a clear view of the corporation's future information requirements, and must steer the evolution of data facilities so that the requirements become realizable.

The need for data-base administration became apparent at the beginning of the 1970s, and different corporations interpreted it differently. The concept of data-base administration ranged from a service function in each installation, something like the installation's systems programmer, to the overall keeper of the corporation's data. The corporation's data are such an essential and valuable corporate resource that the custodian of the data may be thought of as being as important as the corporate accountant. Initially, the need for data administration was perceived largely by data-processing executives rather than by general management, and today the task is usually performed within the data-processing function. The realization of the need for high-level data-base strategy came later in many firms.

TASKS TO BE PERFORMED
For complex data bases the functions of data-base administration are sometimes carried out not by one person but by a group. A single person is unlikely to combine the technical expertise that is needed, the knowledge of the corporation's data, and the negotiating skills.

Let us examine the design tasks that have to be performed. The major ones are illustrated in Fig. 19.1. This figure is an expansion of Fig. 6.5.

1. Canonical Synthesis

First a logical model of the data should be created as described in previous chapters. This modeling describes in formal structures the inherent nature of the data. The person who does the modeling needs to work closely with the end users and many arguments will have to be resolved.

The data models can be created independently of any implementation of software considerations. It is desirable that this activity keep well ahead of implementation.

2. Coexistence Design

It must be decided whether existing files or Class II data bases will continue to exist or whether they will be converted to the Class III database environment. Often they will continue to have a separate existence but must be derivable from, or form input to, the new data bases. The bridge between the existing files (or data bases) and the new ones must be designed and the old data structures may have to be part of the input to the synthesis process. Chapter 30 discusses conversion. It must be planned for from the beginning.

3. Stability Analysis

The data model needs to be as stable as possible. It is a bridge between the past and the future: the past because it must take into consideration con-

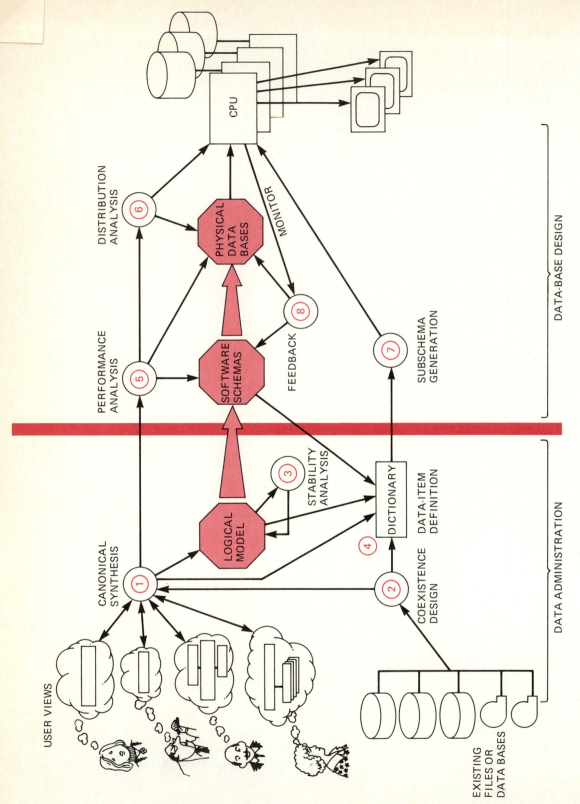

USER VIEWS

CANONICAL SYNTHESIS
DISTRIBUTION ANALYSIS
PERFORMANCE ANALYSIS

① ⑤ ⑥

LOGICAL MODEL
SOFTWARE SCHEMAS
PHYSICAL DATA BASES

③ STABILITY ANALYSIS
⑧ FEEDBACK
MONITOR

CPU

② ④ ⑦

COEXISTENCE DESIGN
DICTIONARY
DATA-ITEM DEFINITION
SUBSCHEMA GENERATION

EXISTING FILES OR DATA BASES

DATA ADMINISTRATION
DATA-BASE DESIGN

Figure 19.1 Steps in the data-base administration process.

version and coexistence of old systems; the future because the data administrator persuades the end users and analysts to think about future uses of the data, and structures the data in a fashion which is as stable as possible.

The steps described in Chapter 16 should be applied to the data model to make it as stable as possible. There is a major financial payoff in doing this well. Data bases that are unstable lose many of the advantages of data-base operation.

4. Data-Item Definition

The dictionary needs to be built up with its catalogue of data-item definitions, and details of synonyms. The dictionary listings need to be taken to the end users to ensure their agreement, and help resolve their arguments, about data-item definitions.

5. Performance Analysis

When implemented, the model or part of it has to be converted to software representation—the center octagon of Fig. 19.1. It has to be put into CODASYL sets, DL/1 hierarchies, the tuples of relational data bases, or whatever software structure is used. This may need compromises or adjustments of the logical model.

Together with this activity, the physical design needs to be done—the right-hand octagon of Fig. 19.1. The designer is concerned with machine performance. He selects access methods, works out the physical storage layout, and estimates response times and throughput.

To evaluate the alternative physical structures, the data-base designer needs three pieces of information superimposed on the logical model:

- The number of times each usage path is followed.
- Whether it is followed interactively and needs a fast response time or whether it is used in batch processing.
- For each one-to-many association (double-headed arrow), *how* many. One-to-two on average, or 1-to-10,000?

These figures should be provided as a by-product of the process that synthesizes the model. They are provided, for example, by the tool DATA DESIGNER.

Chapter 18 discusses machine performance.

6. Distribution Analysis

The data-base designer may consider distributing the data that are in the data model. This may be desirable for machine performance reasons to avoid conflicting uses of data being in the same machine. It may be desirable for other reasons. Skill is needed in designing the distribution of data to avoid integrity or deadlock problems.

7. Subschema Generation

The programmer's data descriptions ought to be generated from the data dictionary without the programmer having to code them. This saves programmer time and also ensures that the programmer is conforming to the data-base representations.

8. Feedback

Usage of the resulting computer system needs to be monitored. Changes in the physical structuring of data will often be necessary. This is the process of *tuning* the data-base system.

Sometimes the usage patterns change unexpectedly. This needs to be *detected* with the monitoring tools, and appropriate changes made in the physical design.

DIVISION OF TASKS   The skills needed to perform all the tasks in Fig. 19.1 well are often too much for one person to master (in the time available).

The tasks on the left of the vertical red line are different in nature from the tasks on the right.

The type of personality that does the left-hand tasks well is different from the type of personality well suited to the tasks on the right. The tasks on the left are concerned with applications, end users, and the nature of the data. The tasks on the right are concerned with software, computers, machine performance, design calculations, and guidance of programmers. The tasks on the left need the human skills of dealing with people and getting them to cooperate even when data-base usage may cause turmoil in their jobs.

In some organizations, one person does both of these sets of tasks. In others, they are done by different people.

The person who does the tasks on the left is the *data administrator*. In this book we refer to the person who does the software and physical data-base design as the *data-base designer*.

The overall set of tasks in Fig. 19.1 are referred to as *data-base administration*.

DATA ADMINISTRATOR'S TASKS   The data administrator is concerned primarily with the *modeling* of the data needed to run the corporation. He needs to be able to understand the business.

END-USER EXECUTIVE:

I'd describe the data administrator as a more business-oriented person. He's a person who needs to bridge the differences between the views of data and, I believe, needs to have some political capability, if not clout. He must also be very diplomatic because quite a bit of effort is spent in compromising—compromising may be a poor word—but settling disputes.

DATA ADMINISTRATOR:

I think one has to have definitely a staff temperament. One has to be able to do a great deal of digging; to have a great deal of sort of natural curiosity. And I think the most important thing for anybody that's getting into this is to recognize the direct relationship between the data structures and the way the business is run. I don't think there's a better opportunity in the world to learn how business is run than to sit down and try to organize these data.

END-USER TEAM   The data administrator needs to work very closely with the end users. This is often best done through an end-user team, as discussed earlier. Each major application area needs to be represented in the team for a given data base.

MEMBER OF END-USER COMMITTEE:

We have representation of each major functional area in the division. For instance, the people who are responsible for the collection of data from the field, people who capture the basic policy data, people interpreting those data, making sure they're accurate, releasing reports back to the field, people from the billing area premium collection areas, experience rating, accounting. So just about every major function, operating function, in the division is represented there.

They are high-level people, people who have been around for a number of years who have the business experience and understand the data needed to run their part of the operation. So, these are not, if you will, technicians, or low-level people. We've strived to seed that committee with as high a level of people as we can, those with a good knowledge of company operations, who can help to review these differences in opinions about data, resolve them, and get them accepted in their departments as well.

Selection of input is critical to the data modeling process:

DATA ADMINISTRATOR:

We selected all sorts of things. Everything from the basic paper, the actual report being produced, the actual bill, dictionaries, existing dictionaries, existing documentation, and interviews with the programmers who were actually involved in preparing that end product.

The end users play a vital role in selecting those inputs. They furnish a great deal of that material directly.

MEMBER OF END-USER COMMITTEE:

The first thing the data administrator did was he met with many individuals of each department and went through an exercise of asking various questions: What kind of information are you interested in? What kind of products do you produce? What are your responsibilities? Is this particular information necessary for your job or nice to know or whatever? He then accumulated all this information, including a picture of what each department's end product was and somehow got all of this together and built a *target.* He called that target his impression of what the logical model should be.

He then went through some exercises as to how we would be able to produce our products or retrieve information from the data base, based on this particular logical model. And that generated some discussions because many of us saw things differently than he did. Through the discussions I think we're ending up with a pretty good product.

When the user group meets, the meeting needs to be carefully planned in advance by the data administrator.

INTERVIEWER:

How does the data administrator set about controlling the meeting?

USER-GROUP MEMBER:

He has an agenda. He gives each of us an assignment before the meeting. And he makes sure that each person takes part in the conversation of the meeting.

INTERVIEWER:

What sort of an assignment does he give you?

USER-GROUP MEMBER:

Oh, a matter of thinking about many different items of information; defining them our way; thinking how those items might relate to other items; thinking how we might want to retrieve certain bits of information. Would you expect to get information out of the system this particular way or that particular way?

THE DATA-BASE DESIGNER

The *data administrator* has to be good with people and good at finding out how the corporation functions. The *data-base designer,* on the other hand, has to be good with machines and software.

The physical design needs a different type of talent from data administration. It needs a skilled technician—the type of person who reads the manuals really thoroughly and learns all the tricks of making software work and perform well. There may be different data-base designers on different projects, but one overall data administrator.

The data-base designer should assist programmers in using the data bases. He can review the sequence of calls that they use to make sure that their programs will be efficient—a formal "walk-through" of the programs.

A data dictionary should be used which automatically generates the subschemas, PSBs, or data descriptions the programs use.

COMBINATION OF FUNCTIONS

Although it usually makes sense for the data administrator and data-base designer to be different people, in some of the best installations they are in fact the same person. Such a person, however, needs a wide range of capability.

In one large bank, eight "data-base administrators" are used, reporting to the same data-base administration manager. Each does both modeling and physical design. Each works on different *subject* data bases in the bank.

MANAGER OF DATA-BASE-ADMINISTRATION DEPARTMENT:

I guess our approach (we take a lean approach) is to have the Renaissance person, so to speak. He or she is the person who can deal with what the banking issues are, conceive the functional data base logically, and go from that to the physical implementation of it.

INTERVIEWER:

Do you find it difficult to obtain and develop an individual with that range of skills?

MANAGER:

Certainly. We find ourselves devoting a good deal to the training and nurturing of these skills, and the protection of these people relative to what are the demands of the marketplace and the labor market. Those are critical challenges to the management of our organization and to me directly.

INTERVIEWER:

And that means you have to pay them a pretty good salary, I should think?

MANAGER:

Yes, and we're dealing right now with what those issues are, competitively in terms of salary. They earn more than some of the bankers.

In general, it is in small installations and installations without complex data where these jobs can be combined in one person. With highly complex installations—well, it is difficult to find the Renaissance person.

CLOSE COOPERATION   If the data administrator and data-base designer are different people, they need to work in close cooperation with one another. The data-base designer will often need to deviate from the model in some way in order to implement it.

DATA-BASE DESIGNER:

We originally started with somewhat of a naive view that we could almost take the logical model and directly map it into an IDMS schema and then a physical design. Neither the hardware nor software could handle that. We have very large files with sometimes more than one key in a record.

Once we split the model it worked fine.

A variety of compromises may be needed in implementing the data model. The model may have to be split into separate structures. Carefully designed redundancy may be introduced for performance reasons.

The model should be regarded as a desirable and necessary starting point for the physical design.

PHYSICAL DATA-BASE DESIGNER:

The model is a starting point that should be kept in front of the physical designers so that disjoint files are few and there is as little compromise as possible.

We're finding that it's an intricate process: taking a logical model, laying that alongside the access requirements in terms of the number of accesses that are required to perform the various application functions, collecting that information, and extrapolating it into some kind of performance figures. This is not a very detailed analysis in the beginning; it's more rough-sizing to see what the on-line access time will be, or, if there are off-line processes, what the run time will be.

In most cases, we're finding that there are first-blush desires that cannot be met by the hardware and software. Consequently, the intricate process starts, where we go back to the data administrator and the application development project leader and say: "This is the extent of the problem." It can be represented this way physically, but we're not sure that you want that kind of performance; and usually they agree. Then the questions become: What kind of compromises can be made? Could you get this a different way? Could we store this in a different form? Could we off-load this file? We discuss the possibilities with them and then go back and take another cut at the physical design.

The software selection has a major effect on this process. There is a trend everywhere from primary-key access to data, to secondary-key access. As this happens, data-base performance problems become more severe. With systems for management information and analysis the data structures become much more complex. The way to avoid performance problems in such an environment is often to split the data into separate structures.

Splitting the data, or otherwise deviating from the model, needs to be done with caution, because it might harm the future flexibility of the data base. The data modeler can usually perceive the potential danger but the physical-data-base designer may not be able to. For this reason the two need to work closely together.

DATA ADMINISTRATOR:

We have enormous volumes of data and enormous performance problems. The mapping of the data can sometimes be done to facilitate performance. But the danger is that some of the flexibility is destroyed.

The designer has one application that he's looking at. He's very concerned with performance and he might deviate from the model itself; might decide to split segments, combine segments, and that sort of thing in his physical design. But that might cause real problems when we get into the inquiry-type work that we plan to do two years from now.

Now a person who's worked in the modeling process, who's seen all those requests and dealt with the users, is much more likely to keep in mind not just the *immediate* needs for the data but the *long-term* needs as well.

This would be an argument for having the physical-data-base designer be the person who worked with the end users. Whether or not it is practical to employ one person for both depends on the complexity of the data and the size of the organization.

The compromise that seems to work best is to separate the *data administrator* function (left of the red line in Fig. 19.1) from the *data-base designer* function (right of the red line in Fig. 19.1), but to have the two working in close cooperation, both trained to have some understanding of the other's field.

The physical designer should be involved in decisions about conversion and coexistence design (2 in Fig. 19.1). The data administrator should be involved in decisions about whether to distribute, or how to distribute, the data (6 in Fig. 19.1).

DATA DISTRIBUTION

The splitting and distributing of data structures is becoming more economical as machines decrease in cost and small computers proliferate. Increasingly, end-users *information* systems should be separate from the *production* systems (see Chapter 26). They may be linked by networks. A network will allow end users to access more than one data-base system from their terminal. They may carry out complex accesses to their own local information system and simple primary-key accesses to production data bases to obtain details about a customer's account, a job order, and so on.

The performance analysis may make it clear that the logical model should be implemented on multiple computers. It is necessary to analyze how the data will be distributed. What data should be replicated? How will integrity be maintained? When will replicated data be updated?

In a distributed environment it is important that data in the separate machines be in the same data dictionary and derived from a common modeling process, unless the systems are entirely separate and do not contain the same data types.

The task of the data administrator thus expands. He is responsible for data models that are implemented on multiple machines. He is responsible for tying together the data at different locations to ensure that they are compatible.

We must distribute the work of the data administrator.

In geographically scattered organizations a new job is desirable—to be filled by an individual who understands the complex trade-offs and problems in data distribution, plans what data should be at what locations on a network, and ensures that a suitable degree of compatibility is maintained between the data at different locations.

GOVERNMENT OPERATIONS

Concern has been expressed about the growing overhead that data-base administration represents, but as data processing develops, like the growth of society, it becomes more complex, and more government operations are needed to prevent chaos and to enable further development. Some of the government functions are legislative, making programmers and systems analysts conform to rules that are for the benefit of the majority. The early pioneers did not need such rules, but in a data-base world they are essential. Police are needed also, to prevent violations of security and privacy. Where violations occur, or where the data are of exceptional value, data-base systems may need their own FBI.

There are administrative functions in maintaining the data definitions and schemas and in settling differences between groups who want the data defined, represented, or stored differently. The settling of such differences is often the most difficult part of the data-base administration job because of the arguments that break out about data that should be shared between departments that have not previously shared it. Department managers are understandably reluctant to relinquish full control over data about their departments. Furthermore, integration of the data base often necessitates the restructuring of earlier files and rewriting programs that use them. Departments may argue vehemently before undertaking this work.

DATA ADMINISTRATION CONSULTANT:

Given the right tools, there are no *technical* difficulties in data administration. The difficulties are *political, emotional,* and *semantic* difficulties—getting people to agree about the meanings of data.

Just as a city government organizes *services* for which its residents pay, such as transportation and sewerage, so the data-base administration organizes *services* for the application programmers and analysts which relieve them of much of the work they had to do in an earlier era. The data-base designer plans the file-addressing schemes, the physical data layout, the security procedures, and the means of restart and recovery after failures have occurred. He selects and provides data management software so that application programmers will no longer have to program such functions.

The data-base designer will be constantly concerned with performance—"tuning" the physical data structures to improve performance. The usage of the data will be monitored so that impending performance problems can be anticipated and adjustments made.

Unlike most governments in society, good data-base administration provides valuable counseling and consulting services to the data users. Application programmers can be helped with their data definitions, systems analysts can be helped to understand the structure of the data base, and user departments can be helped to understand what data can be made available to them.

These roles of legislator, diplomat, policeman, consultant, and technician are usually too much for one person—hence the need for a small team to serve the data-base administration function. Many corporations do, however, employ one person in the role of both logical modeler and data-base designer.

DAILY RUNNING OF DATA-BASE OPERATIONS

As in most data-processing functions, different talents and temperaments are needed for the *design* of operations and the day-to-day *running* of operations. The design functions in data-base administration should therefore be handled by a different person from the one who handles day-to-day control functions. The design of security procedures should be separated from the day-to-day security administration. The design of integrity procedures should be separated from the day-to-day operations for correcting file errors and ensuring that lost data can be reconstructed. The design of monitoring procedures should be separated from daily monitoring operations.

Security administration is a separate function from data-base administration for many systems in which security is a major concern. The day-to-day security operations may not be the concern of the data-base administrator.

RELATION WITH USERS

A particularly delicate and important aspect of the data administration is the relation with user groups or the groups who program specific applications.

Such groups often find it more difficult to use data in a shared data base than to have their own files which they can use in their own way. Data-base administrators must explain to them the advantages of the new methods. This task may require the art of persuasion if the groups in question find the service with a data-base system to be in some way inferior to that when they had their own files.

In a data-base environment it is often not clear who "owns" the data, so rules must be established about who is responsible for their updating. Certain users may "own" certain data items in otherwise common records. The data administrator must arbitrate and control the use of the data. Too often the conceptual clarity of shared data bases becomes clouded by political warfare. To resolve the bitter arguments that ensue, the data administrator must have considerable diplomacy and authority. It is necessary to be able to argue articulately for the right course of action.

The data administrator sometimes has to turn down a user's or programmer's request for service or for additions to the data base. In a shared data base the request may be in conflict with the needs of other users. He should explain clearly the logic of turning down a request and must have a full understanding of the user's needs. The users must have the feeling that they are talking to an unbiased and impartial authority and that the decisions being made will ultimately benefit the user groups as a whole.

There can be a delicate balance between short-term needs and long-term development. The corporate data administrator or data strategist should insist that plans for the long-term development of the data bases should be drawn up. He should maneuver the short-term implementations into directions likely to enhance the long-term prospects, or at least ensure that no further short-term decisions are made which seriously impede long-term development.

Other important aspects of the data-base administrator's relation with the users are education and documentation. The users must be educated concerning the principles and policies governing data-base design and usage. They must have available to them detailed information about what the data base contains and how it can be used. The application programmers must have access to a data-base dictionary.

BUREAUCRACY   The return on investment from successfully managed information centers (Chapter 27), user-driven computing, and decision support systems has been measured to be much higher than that from classical data processing. These uses of computers are aided by the existence of well-designed data bases, a corporatewide data dictionary and sound data models. Sometimes, however, data administration is perceived as a slow bureaucratic process which slows down or prevents the fast creation of user systems or decision support aids.

It takes a long time, often longer than expected, to create good data models. It is desirable that the fast delivery of valuable results to users not be held up while the arguments associated with data modeling are being resolved. The information center operation should link firmly to the data administrator's work, but the administrator should not prevent its delivery of needed results. A compromise is needed. The data administrator may aid the information center operation by producing quick normalized data structures for it even though the larger-scale data planning is not yet finished. He makes the data used conform to the corporate dictionary as well as he can, and aids the information center in finding the data they need quickly, even though it may not yet be in normalized, dictionary-controlled form.

The danger of information center operation, or the use of departmental computers and work stations, is that it may charge ahead without data administration. This happens too often, with the result that chaos in data spreads even more rapidly than before.

These powerful uses of computing *must* link to data administration. The data administrator *must* give them all the help he can and must be instructed to avoid slowing them down. As the data models and dictionary control become more comprehensive, it becomes easier to aid the information center and decision-support development.

A CREATIVE PARTNERSHIP

In directing the building of data models the data administrator needs to forge a creative partnership between users and DP.

CORPORATE EXECUTIVE:

The primary benefit of data modeling was that it brought users, management, and DP professionals together in a creative partnership. The value of this was immense and had untold consequences.

CHIEF OF LOGICAL DESIGN:

Based on the model (from the data design software), the end users and physical data-base designers are talking to each other without shouting. That never happened before.

PART IV

DESIGN OF DATA-BASE APPLICATIONS

20 LOGICAL ACCESS MAPS

This part of the book discusses techniques for data-base application design. It concentrates on the techniques that are unique to a data-base environment. Its contention is that good data-base management makes applications design *much* easier and faster.

DIVIDE AND CONQUER A principle of data-base application design should be: *divide and conquer.* We assume in these chapters that a thorough normalized data model exists as described in Part III. Once it exists, the building of complex applications can be reduced to relatively small projects which *enter data and apply validity checks, update data, generate routine documents, generate queries and reports, conduct audits,* and so on. Sometimes these projects use data in complex ways with many cross-references among the data.

Many such projects can be performed *by one person,* especially when fourth-generation languages are used. In this case one person can be made responsible and motivated for speed and excellence. Most of the communication problems of large programming projects disappear, and hence highly reliable code can be obtained quickly. The main communication among separate developers is *via that data model.* Figure 20.1 illustrates this.

MIS DESIGNER:

Complex integral system design needs long periods of unbroken concentration with a large amount of detail. I have to have absolute quiet for several days. I have a large table with my worksheets spread in a 180° arc around me so that I can pick stuff up, relate it, compare it, and so on. But in the middle of the table is the data model design. It's central to the whole operation.

If an important requirement of the organization is in conflict with the data model, I look at the data design and say: "Is that correct?"

I get all the facts and information, I itemize the features that are required, and I work using the data model as my blueprint. Doing this I can *modularize* a complete MIS into constituent subsystems based on the data model. Without this modularization other people couldn't implement it.

Although one person may be responsible for each of the blocks in Fig. 20.1, a team may sit side-by-side at terminals so that they can compare notes, see each other's displays, and help each other to understand the meaning of the data.

SEPARATE SMALL PROJECTS WHICH CREATE THE
DATA, UPDATE THE DATA, PROCESS THE DATA,
AND USE THE DATA

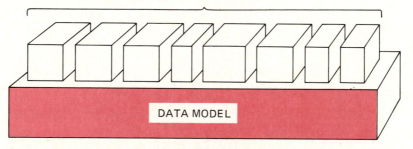

DATA MODEL

Figure 20.1 A well-designed, stable data model, with appropriate data management facilities, permits application development to be a series of separate quick-to-implement projects—mostly one-person projects. Communication among the projects is via the data model.

HIGHER-LEVEL LANGUAGES

The divide-and-conquer strategy resulting in one-person projects is made stronger by the use of higher-level data-base languages, and fourth-generation languages in general. With those one person can often obtain 10 times the results in a given time than he could with COBOL. A one-person team can replace a ten-person team. Nevertheless, *with* COBOL or PL/1, subdividing projects into small modules is highly desirable, and good data-base management assists this greatly.

Most fourth-generation languages depend heavily on a data management facility. Most techniques which have traditionally been used with

COBOL and PL/1 do not work well with fourth-generation languages. Efficient use of fourth-generation languages needs new structured techniques which are powerfully data-base oriented.

STRUCTURED TECHNIQUES

A top-quality analyst needs to be able to look at an organization, understand it and its context, and relate it to its key information entities. If these are not already in a data model, he needs to assist in creating that data model.

He then needs to be able to state the procedure *requirements.* These can usually be stated by nontechnical people. The analyst must then make the connection between the requirements, the data model, and the people who produce the programs.

The job of the analyst doing big-organization information systems has become much more complex in some cases *because fourth-generation languages make it possible to use data in more complex ways.* This increase in complexity can be handled only if there is an easy-to-use set of techniques for charting the way through the complexity.

MIS DEVELOPER:

Most fourth-generation languages are being used just as report generators. Ninety percent of FOCUS users are doing that. That is only a small fraction of the language power.

But there's a big hurdle to get over—we call it the period of pain— going from report generation to the creation of complex applications. All of our people had a big struggle getting over that period of pain. Many installations, I think, never make it. What gets us through it now is clearly representing the data before we start to design procedures, then clearly diagramming our paths and logic through the data with all the cross-references, validation checks, and so on.

The techniques that allow us to build complex systems with FOCUS are totally different from COBOL. Everything is oriented to the data structure—getting data into the data base, then getting the data validated and cross-referenced. Once the data are in, and correct, generating reports and displays is easy.

MIS DEVELOPER:

What we used to find was that training a person to get from report generation to full application development blows their mind for a while.

There is a threshhold they cannot get through. It's like flying up through clouds and then all of a sudden the plane breaks out of the clouds and the sun shines. To get through this quickly needs appropriate, ultra-clear diagramming techniques, clearly taught.

A problem with many structured techniques is that they tangle up the structuring of the data with the structuring of the procedures. This complicates the techniques used. Worse, it results in data that are viewed narrowly and usually not put into a form suitable for other applications which employ the same data.

We have stressed that the structured technique used to design the data should be separate from the structured technique used to design the procedures. Data have properties of their own, independent of procedures, which lead to stable structuring, as discussed in Part III.

This and the following chapters assume that the data are separately designed using sound techniques, preferably automated. The users or analysts who design procedures employ a data model and consider the actions which use that data model. Often the data model is designed by a separate data administrator. Sometimes it is designed by the analysts in question.

LOGICAL ACCESS MAPS   Once a data model of good quality exists, the creation of procedures which use that data becomes much easier.

A first step is to identify the sequence in which the records are accessed. This sequence can be overdrawn on the data model. We will refer to it as a *logical access map* (LAM). From the logical access map information can be created for both the physical-data-base designer and the designer of application procedures. The logical access map leads to procedure design with simple *data-base action diagrams* (DADs), which are described in the following two chapters. These, in turn, lead to structured program code (which is directly applicable to fourth-generation languages).

The complete data model is often too complex for the drawing of access sequences. Only certain entities in the data model are needed. The procedure designer specifies which entities are of concern (see Fig. 20.2).

From the data model a *neighborhood* may be printed. The neighborhood of one entity is the set of entities that can be reached from it by traversing one link in the data model. Usually, this means examining the next-door neighbors in a canonical model. Sometimes the data model may contain extra information saying that additional neighbors should be examined. The designer displays a list of such neighbors of the entities he is interested in. Occasionally, the neighbor one link away may be a concatenated entity (containing intersection data) and the design inspects the other entity type(s) in the concatenated record.

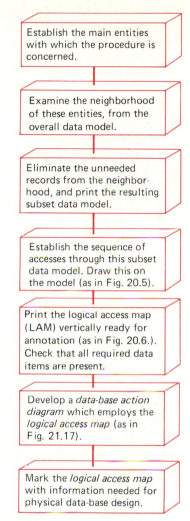

Figure 20.2   Procedure for using LAMs.

The designer examines the neighborhood. He sees the records his procedure will use, plus a few more. He eliminates those he does not want. There may be some which he would not have thought about if he had not displayed the neighborhood. There may be some which have *mandatory* links to records he has specified. For example, when a *booking* record is created, the *seat inventory* record *must* be updated.

The designer settles on the group of records his procedure will use. He then has a subset of the overall data model. Usually, this is small enough to draw on one page. A computerized tool may be available to draw it. If not, it should be drawn by hand.

The designer then makes decisions about the sequence in which his procedure uses the records. He draws this sequence, perhaps with a red pen on the subset data model. He uses a single-headed arrow to indicate that one occurrence of a record is accessed, and a double-headed arrow to indicate that multiple occurrences of a record are accessed.

LAM FOR AN ORDER ACCEPTANCE SYSTEM

Consider the design of an order acceptance application for a wholesale distributor.

A third-normal-form data model exists, as shown in Fig. 20.3. The designer knows that the application requires CUSTOMER-ORDER records and PRODUCT records. The *neighborhood* of these includes the following records:

```
CUSTOMER-ORDER
CUSTOMER
CUSTOMER-LINE-ITEM
INVOICE
PRODUCT
ORDER-RATE
QUOTATION
INVOICE-LINE-ITEM
PURCHASE-LINE-ITEM
```

The designer examines the data items in these records. The application does not need any data in the INVOICE, INVOICE-LINE-ITEM, PURCHASE-LINE-ITEM, or QUOTATION records. The ORDER-RATE record *should* be updated. The designer would have neglected the ORDER-RATE record if he had not printed the neighborhood.

The designer decides, then, that he needs five records and creates a submodel containing these records, as shown in Fig. 20.4.

Figure 20.5 shows his first drawing of the sequence in which the records will be accessed:

1. The CUSTOMER records will be inspected to see whether the customer exists and whether the customer's credit is okay.
2. A CUSTOMER-ORDER record is created.
3. For each product on the order the PRODUCT record is inspected to see whether the product can be provided as requested.
4. A CUSTOMER-LINE-ITEM record is created, linked to the CUSTOMER-ORDER record, for each product on the order.
5. The ORDER-RATE record is updated.
6. When all items are processed, an order confirmation is printed and the CUSTOMER-ORDER record is updated with ORDER-STATUS, ORDER-TOTAL, and DELIVER-DATE.

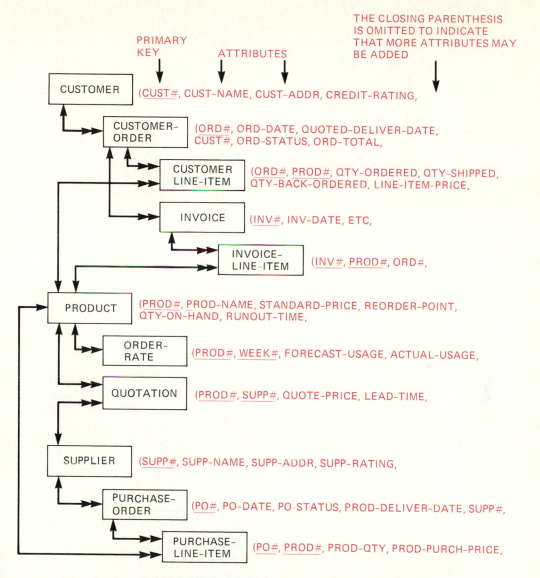

THE CLOSING PARENTHESIS
IS OMITTED TO INDICATE
THAT MORE ATTRIBUTES MAY
BE ADDED

PRIMARY
KEY

ATTRIBUTES

CUSTOMER (CUST#, CUST-NAME, CUST-ADDR, CREDIT-RATING,

CUSTOMER-ORDER (ORD#, ORD-DATE, QUOTED-DELIVER-DATE, CUST#, ORD-STATUS, ORD-TOTAL,

CUSTOMER LINE-ITEM (ORD#, PROD#, QTY-ORDERED, QTY-SHIPPED, QTY-BACK-ORDERED, LINE-ITEM-PRICE,

INVOICE (INV#, INV-DATE, ETC,

INVOICE-LINE-ITEM (INV#, PROD#, ORD#,

PRODUCT (PROD#, PROD-NAME, STANDARD-PRICE, REORDER-POINT, QTY-ON-HAND, RUNOUT-TIME,

ORDER-RATE (PROD#, WEEK#, FORECAST-USAGE, ACTUAL-USAGE,

QUOTATION (PROD#, SUPP#, QUOTE-PRICE, LEAD-TIME,

SUPPLIER (SUPP#, SUPP-NAME, SUPP-ADDR, SUPP-RATING,

PURCHASE-ORDER (PO#, PO-DATE, PO-STATUS, PROD-DELIVER-DATE, SUPP#,

PURCHASE-LINE-ITEM (PO#, PROD#, PROD-QTY, PROD-PURCH-PRICE,

Figure 20.3 Data model for a wholesale distributor. This model is not complete, but because it is correctly normalized it can be grown without pernicious impact to include such things as SALESMAN, WAREHOUSES, ALTERNATE-ADDRESSES, and so on.

367

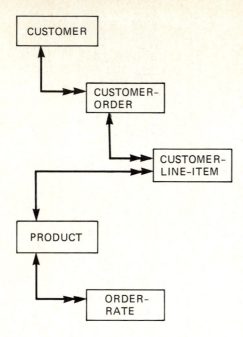

Figure 20.4 Subset of the data model in Fig. 20.3, extracted for the design of the order acceptance procedure.

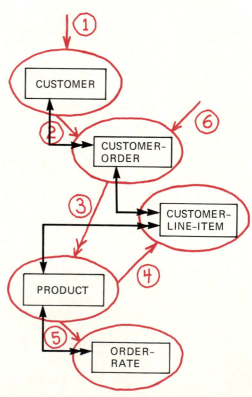

Figure 20.5 Preliminary rough sketch of the logical access map, drawn on the subset data model of Fig. 20.4.

Arrow 3 in Fig. 20.5 is double-headed to indicate that there are many PRODUCT accesses for one access to CUSTOMER-ORDER.

The designer (or computerized tool) may now straighten out the logical access map to make it easier to annotate. Figure 20.6 shows the LAM of Fig. 20.5 drawn vertically. Marked against each record are the attributes which the procedure updates or retrieves.

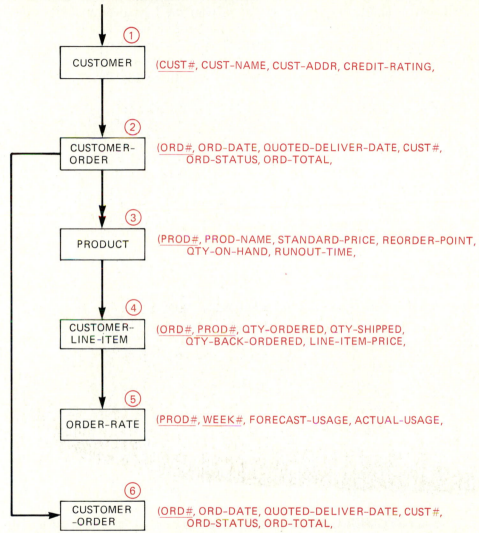

① CUSTOMER (CUST#, CUST-NAME, CUST-ADDR, CREDIT-RATING,

② CUSTOMER-ORDER (ORD#, ORD-DATE, QUOTED-DELIVER-DATE, CUST#, ORD-STATUS, ORD-TOTAL,

③ PRODUCT (PROD#, PROD-NAME, STANDARD-PRICE, REORDER-POINT, QTY-ON-HAND, RUNOUT-TIME,

④ CUSTOMER-LINE-ITEM (ORD#, PROD#, QTY-ORDERED, QTY-SHIPPED, QTY-BACK-ORDERED, LINE-ITEM-PRICE,

⑤ ORDER-RATE (PROD#, WEEK#, FORECAST-USAGE, ACTUAL-USAGE,

⑥ CUSTOMER-ORDER (ORD#, ORD-DATE, QUOTED-DELIVER-DATE, CUST#, ORD-STATUS, ORD-TOTAL,

Figure 20.6 The logical access map in Fig. 20.5 drawn vertically, with data-item details, ready for drawing the data-base action diagrams discussed in the following chapter (see Fig. 21.17). This diagram could be produced by the customer tool that assists in the data modeling process. Two accesses are shown to customer order. The first reads it; the second updates it. The update of CUSTOMER_LINE_ITEM and ORDER_RATE is done for each PRODUCT access. The update of CUSTOMER_ORDER is not done for each PRODUCT access but for each CUSTOMER_ORDER access. Access 6 is therefore drawn as shown.

PROCEDURE DESIGN

The designer now starts to be more precise about what needs to be done with the data.

Initially, the *physical* aspects of accessing the data are ignored. Because the data are properly analyzed and structured, the DBMS can assemble the required data. From the logical point of view the LAM is available as though it existed in memory just for this designer. Later the LAM will be annotated with details of numbers of accesses so that it forms valuable input to the physical-data-base designer.

For each step in the LAM the designer asks three questions:

1. *Under what conditions do I want to proceed?*
   - Valid or invalid records?
   - Data item >, =, or < certain values?
   - Errors?
   - Results of computations?
   - Matching data items in different records?

2. *What do I want to do with, or to, the data?*
   - Create, retrieve, update, or delete records?
   - Search, sort, project, or join relations?
   - Computations with the data?

3. *What other operations accompany the data-base actions?*
   - Print documents?
   - Data entry screen usage?
   - Security checks?
   - Audit controls?
   - Execution of subroutines?
   - Triggering other transactions?

In Fig. 20.5 or 20.6 the first access is to the CUSTOMER record. The designer asks: "Does a record exist for this customer?" If not, a record must be created. Next: "Is the customer's credit OK?" If it is not, the order is rejected.

The CUSTOMER-ORDER record is created regardless of validation conditions so that it is available for future reference.

The third step in Fig. 20.5 or 20.6 is to the PRODUCT record. The designer asks: "Is this a valid product? Is it discontinued? Is there sufficient product in stock?"

If there is insufficient product in stock, a backorder must be placed. This is done by a separate routine related to the routine for placing supplier orders. It will be shown on a separate LAM.

The CUSTOMER-LINE-ITEM record is created, again regardless of validity conditions, so that it is available for future reference. It will contain details of any backorder if one is placed. The CUSTOMER-LINE-ITEM records are linked to the CUSTOMER record.

The ORDER-RATE record is updated when the line item is processed.

Finally, the CUSTOMER-ORDER record is updated, with order status, order total, and the estimated delivery date. At that time a confirmation is printed for the customer.

To create the logic and control structures of the program that uses the data base we recommend the use of *data-base action diagrams,* described in Chapter 21. Glancing ahead, the right-hand side of Fig. 21.17 shows an action diagram for the procedure described above. The LAM is on the left of Fig. 21.17. The action diagram is an extension of the LAM designed to translate directly into the code of fourth-generation languages (Fig. 21.20), such as FOCUS, IDEAL, NOMAD, MANTIS, etc. It can also provide structured English for creating COBOL programs (Fig. 21.19).

The development of the LAM and *data-base action diagram* (DAD) go hand in hand.

PHYSICAL DESIGN   We have commented that the LAM gives information to the physical-data-base designer as well as to the application procedure designer.

The physical accesses may not be in the same sequence as the logical accesses of the LAM. In Fig. 20.6, for example, there are two accesses to CUSTOMER-ORDER; in physical practice there would only be one. The first creation of the CUSTOMER-ORDER record would be in the computer's main memory. This record would not be written on the external storage medium until the second reference to it in the LAM, after which it is complete.

Again, the LINE-ITEM records in Fig. 20.6 are children of the CUSTOMER-ORDER record, and so with most data-base systems would not be written physically until after the CUSTOMER-ORDER record had been written.

It is often the physical-data-base designer who makes such decisions, not the designer of the logical procedure, who draws the LAM and the DAD.

Figure 20.7 shows the LAM of Fig. 20.6 annotated for physical design. It should indicate the initial access method—primary key, secondary key, or sequential read.

COMPLEXITY   The subset data model that is used for one application usually does not become very big. It can usually be drawn on one page, and so can the associated LAM.

NUMBER OF TIMES PER DAY: 3200

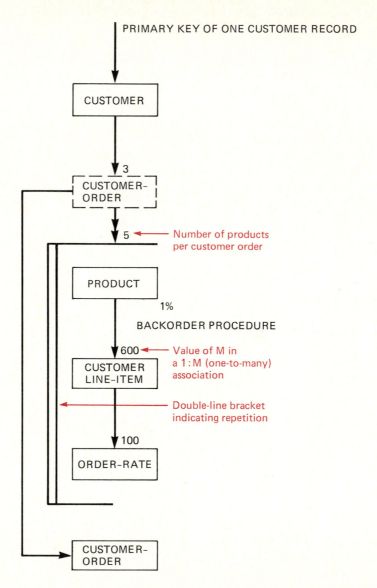

Figure 20.7 The LAM of Fig. 20.6 annotated for the physical designer.

In some corporations with highly complex data processing, the subset data models have never exceeded a dozen third-normal-form records. Most do not exceed five.

DATA-BASE CONSULTANT FOR A GIANT AEROSPACE CORPORATION:

We draw about a thousand LAMs. One had 11 normalized records. None had 10, 9, or 8. Most had between 3 and 5. The one with 11 was a very elaborate tracking mechanism for cost control and estimating. It needed budgets and actual figures for parts and people, and there was complex matrix management where an employee had a *home organization;* he might be assigned to the *responsible organization* and that could be involved with the *performing organization.*

STANDARD PROCEDURE

It is very simple to *teach* the use of LAMs. Together with DADs, described in Chapter 21, these should be an installation standard rather than a tool of certain individuals.

DATA-BASE ANALYST:

A nice by-product has been that LAMs dramatically highlight the transaction-driven nature of proper data-base systems. This concept— transaction driven—has been surprisingly difficult for many DP professionals to grasp.

DATA-BASE CONSULTANT FOR A GIANT AEROSPACE CORPORATION:

Initially, it was the data administration staff who draw LAMs. That was because the application analysts were not exposed to data-base techniques and the pressure of work was too great for them to switch to new techniques.

Once the data model settled down, the LAMs gave a very simple technique for specifying applications. Once it became successful the corporate data administration set up standards and procedures for general use of LAMs. It started with a small pocket of analysts. It worked well, so others said "I'll try it." Later we had formal procedures for LAMs, and in the future we will hold classes on their use throughout the entire company.

Figure 20.8 shows an example of a form used for logical access maps, where this has been made a formal manual procedure.

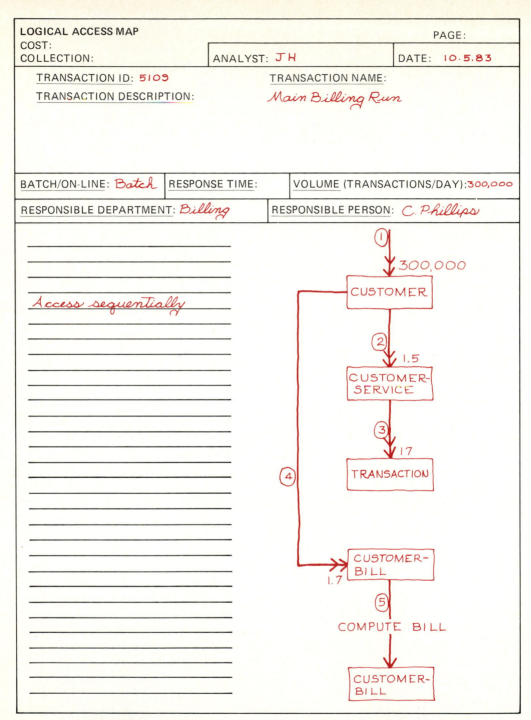

LOGICAL ACCESS MAP		PAGE:
COST:		
COLLECTION:	ANALYST: J H	DATE: 10.5.83

TRANSACTION ID: 5109   TRANSACTION NAME:

TRANSACTION DESCRIPTION: *Main Billing Run*

BATCH/ON-LINE: *Batch*   RESPONSE TIME: VOLUME (TRANSACTIONS/DAY): 300,000

RESPONSIBLE DEPARTMENT: *Billing*   RESPONSIBLE PERSON: *C. Phillips*

Access sequentially

① → 300,000 → CUSTOMER

② 1.5 → CUSTOMER-SERVICE

③ 17 → TRANSACTION

④

1.7 → CUSTOMER-BILL

⑤ COMPUTE BILL → CUSTOMER-BILL

Figure 20.8 Example of a LAM form, where a formal manual procedure is employed. Comments about the LAM accesses may be written
on the left.

The access path from CUSTOMER to CUSTOMER–BILL is separate from the path from CUSTOMER to CUSTOMER–SERVICE to
TRANSACTION, and is performed after it.

21 DATA-BASE ACTION DIAGRAMS

INTRODUCTION   Experience has shown that once a sound data model exists, the design of data-base applications becomes *much* easier. Without good data analysis and normalization, all manner of difficulties and anomalies arise.

It is necessary to have a technique for program design which employs the data model and the sequence of accesses through the data model which are drawn as in Chapter 20.

This chapter discusses a technique which is very easy to use—much easier than most structured programming techniques. It can be taught to non-DP professionals in a day. Its diagrams are easy to read and check, and are almost self-explanatory. (Glance ahead to Fig. 21.18, for example.) Psychologist Dr. K. Winter assisted in the design of this technique to make the structure diagrams as user-friendly as possible.

USER-DRIVEN PROCEDURE DESIGN   As cheap terminals, networks, and on-line data systems spread, the most efficient procedures in an enterprise should be quite different from those in offices where everything was done with paper. Also, the procedures in an integrated data-base environment should be quite different from those in an environment where each functional area has separate systems.

Most data processing in an on-line environment consists of a sequence of actions that change or use the on-line data. The flow of paper, or electronic equivalents of this paper, between departments should be largely replaced with on-line action processing. The actions must often happen in particular sequences, and certain conditions apply to their occurrence. One action changing the data may trigger other actions.

A dispatcher in a factory no longer should fill in pink forms each with 10 carbon copies which go to different areas in the factory. Instead, he enters data into a terminal. The other areas have terminals linked to the same data. Their terminals may print transactions of queue transactions for screen access. The other area staff see the changes that have been entered into the data base.

The carbon copies of the forms do not flow as they did before. Instead of using data flow diagrams to chart their movement, we need a different technique with which to explore the actions which instantaneously change the on-line data, replacing the earlier data flow, and forming the basis for new types of procedures.

One of the most exciting new directions of data processing is the development of powerful languages which enable results to be obtained without the use of professional programmers [1]. The languages vary greatly in their power and capabilities. Some are merely query languages; others are report generators or graphics generators; others can generate complete applications; some are very high level programming languages. Such languages may be employed by end users or, more commonly, by systems analysts directly aiding the end users.

Most of these languages use data-base systems of various types. The data are often designed separately from the procedures that employ the data. Designing the data is the function of a data administrator.

Often the best approach is for DP professionals to *create* the data base and build appropriate data entry routines and integrity checks, and then for end users to *employ* the data base, learning how to generate their own reports from it.

MIS DESIGNER:

We want the end users to *use* the data bases but not to set them up. Setting them up is a highly professional, complex activity, especially in an integrated environment. Once we have designed the data model, we get into a *lot* of detail about validation, checks needing cross-references, data entry controls, and so on.

Once the data are there, we want the users to use them. They love this. Once the data reflect their organization, cleanly, they want to look at it thousands of different ways. Let the user define how to *join* them and *compare* them. They love that stuff. We're not interested in it.

We found that they rarely produce a report that doesn't access three data bases—because the data are there and the tool is easy to use.

Today, unlike the era when structured techniques were first created, the user or analyst can make many procedures work on computers without employing professional programmers, by using powerful user-friendly languages: the fourth-generation languages such as NOMAD, RAMIS, FOCUS, MANTIS, MAPPER, DMS, NATURAL, IDEAL, and the various query and report generators [2].

Many of the techniques for system analysis and program design, however, were created in an earlier era before the widespread use of data-base systems, networks, cheap terminals, and fourth generation languages.

Often where end users have acquired their own ability to create and modify their own procedures, the results have been spectacular [1]. The users know their own problems and can invent, a small step at a time, procedures that improve how the work is done. Often they need to work with systems analysts who create and refine the results.

We are moving rapidly into an era of user-driven computing. The frustration felt by users in not being able to have or change the systems they need is being overcome by new techniques.

This plunge into user-driven computing can be alarming for DP managers, who sometimes perceive it as a formula for chaos. When users create their own DP procedures this process has to be managed and controlled; otherwise, confusion will slowly spread and chaotic procedures result. The necessary controls come from the data administration process, data modeling, and appropriate charting of the procedures used [3, 4].

PROPERTIES OF A USER-DRIVEN DESIGN TECHNIQUE

We need a structured technique that is appropriate for end users and analysts working with them, and is oriented toward data-base systems. The technique must be designed to encourage end users to create, change, and think about the DP procedures they need.

The technique should have the following properties:

1. It must be highly user-friendly.

2. It should be data-base oriented.

3. It should be oriented to fourth-generation languages.

4. It should employ diagrams which are clear and easy to build up. The diagrams should be easy to read and check by non-DP professionals.

5. The diagrams should be directly convertible into programs in a way that leads to bug-free structured code.

6. The technique must use sound structured techniques, capitalizing on the experience of structured design, structured programming, and structured analysis.

If we employ a technique that is appropriate for end users, systems analysts will be able to learn it easily, too. Some of the older techniques for structured design are too difficult for typical end users who *should* be creating procedures.

> *LEAD MIS DESIGNER:*
>
> To step from defining the requirements to creating the program specifications for complex MIS was a gap that was very difficult to fill. I have to cover it myself. One thing became clear; unless I chart the specifications clearly, I just spin the wheels of the programmers. They have told me this several times. I tried verbal specifications, but verbal specifications are just never any good.

Because of the rapid changes that are occurring in computer languages, and the wide diversity of approaches that exist with fourth-generation languages, the procedure design techniques should be independent of the language used.

> *LEAD ANALYST:*
>
> I write the application specifications. I have an extensive programming background in COBOL, so I can think like a programmer. However, if I infer any COBOL programming techniques, they get laughed out of the building by the FOCUS coders. So I never go to the level of saying you'll write your program this way; I say this function must be performed against the data. Action diagrams are the right level for this.

Failure to use clear methods of charting the application accesses and control structure leads to all manner of problems. Often the analysts struggle to comprehend the required procedures. The brightest ones succeed and the less bright ones do not.

> *DP EXECUTIVE:*
>
> The lead analyst was highly experienced in MIS building and could conceptualize what was needed in his head. He could keep amazingly complex procedures in his head. He was brilliant. The problem was that nobody else could understand what was in his head.

In some cases code becomes created which is poorly diagrammed, and future maintenance of that code becomes very expensive. Often the difficulties of understanding and hence changing the code lead to severe inflexibilities.

DP EXECUTIVE:

There was a whole bunch of code, many pages of it, for complex validations with cross-references to multiple records, but the code was uncharted. Nobody dared touch it! They didn't know what they might screw up.

MIS DESIGNER:

This system is so complex that I don't think we *could* have built it with COBOL and conventional structured techniques. We had 48 record types and cross-reference between records.

INTERVIEWER:

Why so many?

MIS DESIGNER:

The *account number* included a source of funds. That *source of funds* was a government sponsor. An attribute in the fund data base was *agency*. Agency was looked up in system tables. It could be a *federal sponsor* or a *nonfederal sponsor*. If it was a federal agency, we had to look down in the *fund* data base and find the *expense limits*. Some agencies want you to place a limit of $10,000 on salaries, $5000 on bills of materials, $2000 on travel, and so on. When those expenses are coming into the mill of zillions of other transactions it's very difficult to know that you may be exceeding the budget, so we go to the *category codes—expense object classification*. If it's *travel* expense, we go to the *fund number* and see if it's a *federal* agency. If so, we go to that *agency* record to find the *general ledger* number and then find the category code and thence the budget limit for travel.

Then I have to add the dollars for this transaction to the dollars that have already been expended for this source of funds to see if it exceeds the travel budget.

This is only part of it. Government bureaucracy gets unbelievable!

Anyway, you couldn't design that sort of system without an absolutely clear data model and a simple technique for charting your way through the data.

ACTION DIAGRAMS   The techniques in this and the following chapter employ data-base action diagrams (DADs). These can be used for creating procedures which are programmed in COBOL, PL/1, BASIC, and so on, or in the newer fourth-generation or nonprocedural languages. Where conventional programming is used the technique provides easy-to-read program specifications, which result in relatively fast highly reliable coding. The diagrams result in code structures that are relatively easy to maintain. Box 21.1 describes actions.

Complex systems can be broken down into multiple procedures employing the same data model. The separate procedures are each small enough for *one person* to design and create. This speeds up application creation and lessens communication problems. Communication among separate developers is mainly via the data model.

The basic premise of action diagrams is that the data lie at the center of modern data processing. This is illustrated in Fig. 21.1. The data are stored and maintained with the aid of various types of data systems software. The processes on the left in Fig. 21.1 create and modify the data. The data must be captured and entered with appropriate accuracy controls. The data will be periodically updated. The processes on the right of Fig. 21.1 use the data. Routine documents such as invoices, receipts, freight bills, and work tickets are printed. Executives or professionals sometimes search for information.

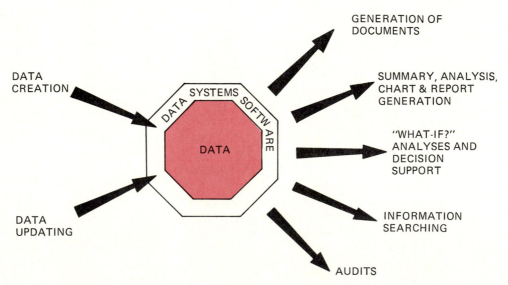

Figure 21.1   Most modern data processing is composed of actions that create and modify data, with appropriate accuracy controls, and processes that use, analyze, summarize, and manipulate data, or print documents from the data.

They create summaries or analyses of the data, and produce charts and reports. They ask "What if?" questions and use the data to help them make decisions. Auditors check the data and attempt to ensure that they are not misused.

The data in Fig. 21.1 may be in multiple data systems. It may be stored in different ways. It may be distributed. It is often updated and used by means of transmission links and terminals.

BOX 21.1   What are actions?

A *simple action* is defined as an action applied to one instance of one normalized record, which creates, reads, updates, or deletes that record.

The reader may remember these four basic types of action with the memorable acronym C.R.U.D.: Create, Read, Update, Delete. High-level data-base languages have operators which permit these four types of actions.

The action includes the necessary logic or computation. *It does not include any conditions that affect the sequence of accessing records.* Conditions are expressed separately from actions and govern the execution of actions.

Actions may be given numbers, Ax. Short numbers are used in this report for purposes of simple illustration. In practice a more elaborate numbering scheme is needed which permits new actions to be added. The first digits of an action number may be the number of the normalized record it relates to.

A simple action is drawn as a lozenge, thus:

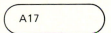

A description of the action is written in the lozenge. This should usually be a command sentence starting with a verb, such as UPDATE FLIGHT AVAILABILITY RECORD. Sometimes more than one sentence is used, giving details of the actions necessary when a single action occurs.

A *compound action* also takes a single action against the data base, but the action may use multiple records of the same type. It may search or sort a logical file. It may be a relational operation

(Continued)

BOX 21.1 *(Continued)*

which uses an entire relation. It may be a relational operation requiring a join of two or more relations [5].

A compound action is drawn as a lozenge with a double bar in it, thus:

For both simple and compound actions the name of the normalized record or relation to which the action refers is written above it.

Most of the actions in traditional data processing are simple actions. As relational data bases and nonprocedural languages spread, compound actions will become more common.

Action diagrams show the logic that controls the execution of actions in such a way that it can be converted directly into a program. The action diagram links directly to the diagram of the data structures that are employed.

Each action is shown as a lozenge, thus:

```
    ╭─────────────────────────╮
    │  READ PASSENGER         │
    │  NAME RECORD            │
    ╰─────────────────────────╯
```

The phrase describing the action is written inside the lozenge, and should begin with an action verb. A sequence of actions is shown by lozenges underneath one another in the required order, thus:

```
    ╭─────────────────────────╮
    │  CHECK FLIGHT           │
    │  AVAILABILITY RECORD    │
    ╰─────────────────────────╯

    ╭─────────────────────────╮
    │  UPDATE SEAT            │
    │  INVENTORY RECORD       │
    ╰─────────────────────────╯

    ╭─────────────────────────╮
    │  CREATE PASSENGER       │
    │  NAME RECORD            │
    ╰─────────────────────────╯

    ╭─────────────────────────╮
    │  UPDATE FLIGHT          │
    │  AVAILABILITY RECORD    │
    ╰─────────────────────────╯
```

We add information about conditions and repetition of actions to these diagrams. Glancing ahead, the right-hand side of Fig. 21.16 shows a procedure with seven actions. The red notation above each action shows which normalized record it uses. Each action corresponds to a block in a Logical Access Map (shown on the left on Fig. 21.16).

The action diagrams and data models go hand in hand. Each action relates to one normalized record. We can therefore draw the sequence of actions on a data model chart creating a Logical Access Map (LAM) as described in the previous chapter. The LAM is converted into the action diagram.

ACTION CONDITIONS   Actions are drawn from top to bottom on an action diagram in the sequence in which they are executed. Actions may be omitted when certain conditions apply. Conditions are indicated at the head of *brackets* which enclose the actions and logic to which those conditions apply, as shown in Fig. 21.2.

The condition must be satisfied before the action or actions that it refers to are executed. Thus, following action A1 in Fig. 21.2, action A2 will be executed only if the first condition is satisfied. Then action A3 is ex-

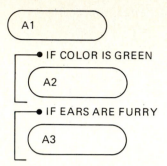

Figure 21.2   After action A1, actions A2 and A3 may occur, depending on which conditions are fulfilled. If both A2 and A3 occur, A2 occurs *first*.

ecuted (after A2 because it is drawn below A2) only if the second condition is satisfied.

BRACKETS

Actions are arranged into groups which are indicated with brackets, thus:

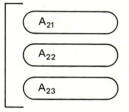

A bracket indicates a block of actions. A simple control rule applies to the bracket: You enter it at the top, do the things in it in a top-to-bottom order, and exit at the bottom. A condition may apply to an entire bracket and the bracket may contain multiple actions.

MUTUALLY EXCLUSIVE ACTIONS

If one, and only one, of several actions is to be executed, these are drawn with a partitioned bracket, as in Figs. 21.3 to 21.6. In Fig. 21.2 the brackets are not partitioned, so actions A2 and A3 could both occur. Figure 21.3 shows a similar diagram in which the bracket is partitioned; actions A2 and A3 could not both occur.

Sometimes the word ELSE is written on a bracket to indicate the opposite to a condition, as in Fig. 21.4. In the partitioned bracket of Fig.

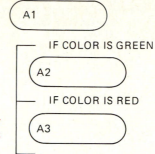

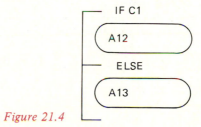

Figure 21.3 Mutually exclusive conditions are shown by a partitioned bracket. Unlike Fig. 21.2, actions A2 and A3 could not both occur.

21.4, if condition C1 is satisfied, action A12 is executed; if condition C1 is not satisfied, action A13 is executed.

IF C1

A12

ELSE

A13

Figure 21.4

A partitioned bracket is really a set of brackets, each with its own condition. However, the conditions are mutually exclusive so that not more than one of the brackets in the set will be executed.

The ELSE condition may be used after a string of mutually exclusive conditions, as in Fig. 21.5. Figure 21.6 shows an example. A new customer order is being processed. A check is made on the appropriate PRODUCT record to see whether the quantity on hand of the product is greater than the quantity ordered. If the quantity on hand is sufficient, the action CREATE LINE-ITEM RECORD is taken. If not, the bottom two actions in the bracket are taken.

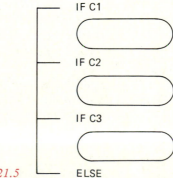

Figure 21.5

PRODUCT

CHECK QTY_ON
_HAND

— IF QTY_ON_HAND > QTY_ORDERED
CUSTOMER_LINE_ITEM

CREATE LINE_ITEM
RECORD

— ELSE
CUSTOMER_LINE_ITEM

CREATE LINE_ITEM
RECORD WITH QTY
_BACKORDERED

PURCHASE_LINE_ITEM

CREATE PURCHASE
ORDER ITEM

Figure 21.6 The action diagram is directly linked to the data model. The name of the normalized record that an action relates to should be written above the action lozenge. This diagram uses the data model in Fig. 20.3.

Whenever a condition is identified, which must be satisfied before propagation from one action to another, we should also define the action which is to be taken if that condition is not satisfied. The negative of the condition should be indicated.

NO CONDITIONS WITHIN AN ACTION

In its final state an action should not contain internal conditions relating to data access.

The validation action at the top of Fig. 21.6 removes the need to have conditional logic *within* the *CREATE LINE-ITEM RECORD* action. Each action is similarly examined to identify any conditions that govern its execution.

An important rule in drawing action diagrams is that conditions must not be allowed to conceal actions. That is, any accesses to the data base required by the evaluation of conditions must be explicitly shown on the diagram.

For example, a condition might be "IF EMPLOYEE IS FEMALE." This cannot be evaluated without examining the employee record. An action that retrieves the employee record must therefore precede the use of this condition.

LINKAGE OF ACTION DIAGRAM AND DATA MODEL   Each action is associated with one normalized record. To clarify the linkage each action lozenge may have the name of the record it uses written above it.

The action diagram in Fig. 21.6 uses the data model shown in Fig. 20.3. The names of the records are written above the lozenges. Throughout this chapter they are written in red.

Actions do not access single fields; they access records with normalized groups of fields. The construct at the top of Fig. 21.7 would be incorrect.

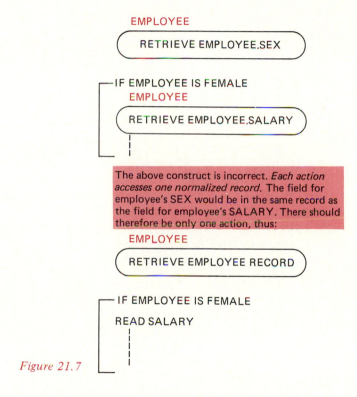

Figure 21.7

The user drawing this was thinking of individual field access rather than normalized-record access. The bottom of Fig. 21.7 shows the correct version.

PROCEDURES   A procedure is a group of steps which together accomplish some meaningful business operation such as creating a purchase order, accepting a booking, or producing an accounting document. The details of an automated procedure may be specified with an action diagram.

One bracket may be drawn around the group of operations which constitute the procedure. The procedure is given a name, and this may be indicated with a bullet on the top of the procedure bracket, thus:

A bracket with a name, like this, may represent a subroutine or subprocedure which is used in multiple other procedures. It may represent one module of a more complex procedure. It is referred to in that procedure.

When a procedure is to be designed, the relevant partition of a data model should be examined. The partition of a data model for one procedure can normally be drawn on one sheet of paper. In one large aerospace corporation 1000 procedures were created using their data models and only two required as many as 12 normalized records. Most had fewer than six.

Procedure design, then, employs a one-page partition of a data model. The user draws a Logical Access Map on it, like Fig. 20.5, and then creates the action diagram. In some cases the procedure is simple enough to be handled without an action diagram.

NESTED CONDITIONS

When a condition is nested it may give rise to one action or many. It may give rise to a subprocedure.

The testing of condition C1 in the top diagram of Fig. 21.8, for example, gives rise to the subprocedure that contains actions A31, A32, and A33 and conditions that control them.

COMPOUND CONDITIONS

More than one condition may be drawn at the head of a bracket.

When two or more conditions need to be satisfied *together* before a particular action is executed, this is indicated with the word "AND" joining the conditions. For example, where C1 AND C2

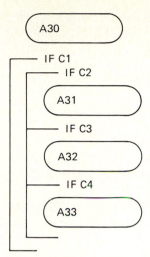

If condition C1 is satisfied, then
one of actions A31, A32, or A33 is
executed.

The same procedure could alternatively be drawn as follows:

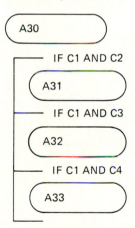

Figure 21.8   Compound conditions.

AND C3 must all be satisfied, we write

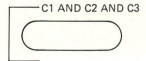

When one condition or another must be satisfied, we join these with the word "OR." For example, where C1 OR C2 OR C3 must be satisfied, we write

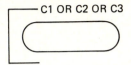

The procedures at the top of Fig. 21.8 could be drawn without two brackets by putting condition C1 on the diagram multiple times, as in the bottom drawing of Fig. 21.8.

The negation (the opposite) of a condition may be shown by drawing a horizontal bar over the condition phrase. Thus $\overline{C1}$ means condition C1 is not true.

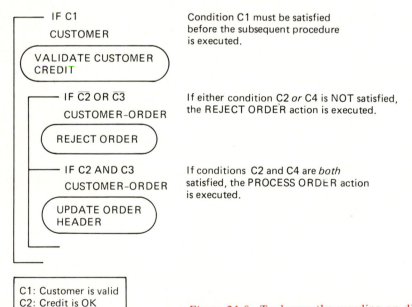

Condition C1 must be satisfied before the subsequent procedure is executed.

If either condition C2 *or* C4 is NOT satisfied, the REJECT ORDER action is executed.

If conditions C2 and C4 are *both* satisfied, the PROCESS ORDER action is executed.

C1: Customer is valid
C2: Credit is OK
C3: Account is open

Figure 21.9 To lessen the wording on diagrams, conditions used repeatedly may be coded as shown.

In Fig. 21.9 the negation of either condition C2 or C3 can give rise to rejection of the order. Thus an order is rejected if either the account is not open OR the customer's credit status is not satisfactory. The satisfaction of both conditions C2 and C3 causes the action "Update Order Header" to occur.

INITIAL CONDITIONS

Sometimes one or more initial conditions must be satisfied before a procedure can begin. This is shown by a condition on the top of the bracket as illustrated in Fig. 21.9. The first action cannot occur unless the customer is valid. Once this validity is established, the customer's credit is validated by means of an access to the CUSTOMER record.

CHECK THAT ALL NEGATIVES ARE SHOWN

We have indicated that the negative of a condition as well as the condition itself can be drawn on the procedure chart. For completeness the negatives of all conditions should be shown. A procedure chart should be visually checked to see whether this has been done. Figure 21.10 illustrates this.

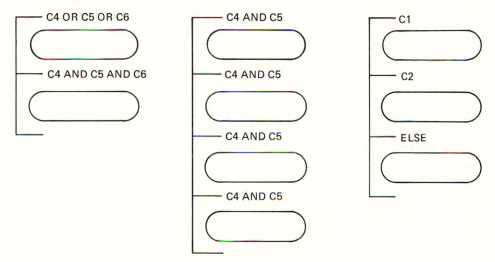

Figure 21.10 The action diagram should be checked to ensure that it shows what happens when the negatives of all stated conditions apply.

REPETITION OF ACTIONS

Some actions are executed repetitively in computer processes. This is controlled by a loop in a program. Actions that are repeated are indicated by a bracket drawn with a double line, thus:

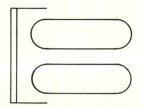

This double line looks like a "repeat" in musical notation:

Repetition brackets are just like other brackets except that the condition which controls the execution of the bracket is tested repeatedly and if satisfied the activities in the bracket are executed.

There are two types of repetition condition:

1. DO what the bracket indicates WHILE a certain condition is satisfied.

2. DO what the bracket indicates UNTIL a certain condition is satisfied (often with REPEAT-UNTIL instruction in a programming language).

The condition for the DO-WHILE bracket is tested before the bracket is entered, and the condition for the DO-UNTIL bracket is tested after the bracket has been executed.

Because of this the condition bullet for the DO-WHILE is placed at the top of the bracket; the condition for the DO-UNTIL bracket is placed at the bottom, thus:

The items in the DO-UNTIL bracket are executed at least once. They will be executed more than once if the condition is fulfilled.

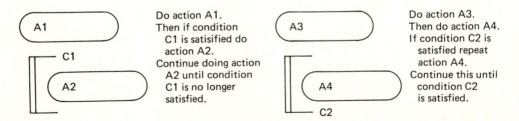

Figure 21.11 Repetition of actions (loops).

The items in the DO-WHILE bracket are not executed at all if the condition is not satisfied.

In the first diagram of Fig. 21.11, action A1 is executed first, then A2 is executed repetitively WHILE condition C1 is satisfied. If C1 is not satisfied on the first test, action A2 is never carried out.

The second diagram shows that action A3 is executed first, then action A4 is executed UNTIL condition C2 is satisfied. Action A4 will be executed at least once before condition C2 is checked.

The procedure designer can often select either construct. DO-WHILE COUNT $\leq$ 10 is the same as DO UNTIL COUNT = 11.

To make the procedure drawing as clear as possible, the words WHILE or UNTIL may be written on the drawing, thus:

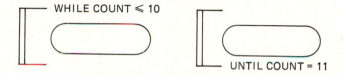

We suggest that the procedure designer *always* use DO-WHILE, unless DO-UNTIL makes the procedure significantly clearer. DO-UNTIL is sometimes used for situations such as DO-UNTIL LAST TRANSACTION IS PROCESSED. But this may be more clearly expressed as

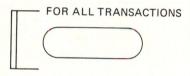

SETS OF DATA   When the actions in a bracket are repeated, the repetition is sometimes controlled by conditions; sometimes the bracket is repeated for a specified set of records.

For example, an action, A15, might be executed for all customers in Manchester:

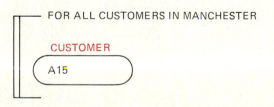

An action might be executed for all customers with CUSTOMER# between 51200 and 67000:

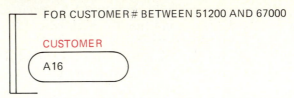

When an action or procedure is executed for all instances of a record, we may mark the bracket arrow with an asterisk:

The asterisk means "for all instances of the first type of logical record in the procedure" (if there is more than one).

Often a hierarchical or "member" relationship exists in a data base, for example:

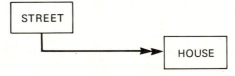

This relationship may be a **CODASYL** set or parent–child relation in a hierarchical data base such as **IMS**. It may be any one-to-many fragment of an entity chart.

A for-all notation may be applied to the link in the relationship, meaning all the lower records associated with one of the upper records—in the illustration above, all the houses in a given street. This is shown with an arrow between actions, thus:

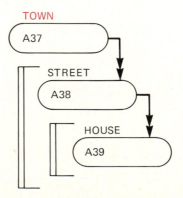

The association between actions is drawn on the right rather than the left to avoid problems in drawing when a different action intervenes, thus:

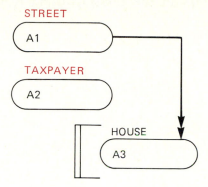

The double-arrow link could be drawn in other positions.

NESTED BRACKETS   The TOWN-STREET-HOUSE diagram above, and Figs. 21.8 and 21.9, show nested brackets. The contents of one bracket include another bracket.

A complex procedure may have brackets within brackets within brackets. Glancing ahead, Figs. 21.13 and 21.14 show procedures with the nested brackets.

The need for nesting or repetition can be determined from the drawing of the logical access map. Figure 21.12 shows a partition of a data model

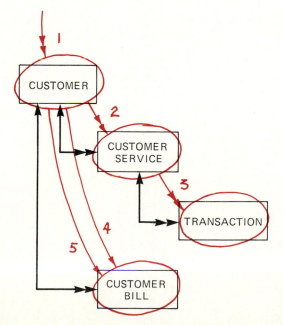

Figure 21.12 Portion of a data model required for a billing procedure, with the logical access map (LAM) for this procedure drawn on it. The same LAM is shown in Fig. 21.13, which shows how it relates directly to the DAD.

with a logical access map (LAM) drawn on it. Figure 21.13 redraws this and shows an action diagram corresponding to the LAM.

One-to-many links in the LAM result in repetition brackets in the action diagram.

ERROR SITUATIONS

In some cases, a negative condition may require an alternative action to be executed. In other cases the negative may indicate an error situation.

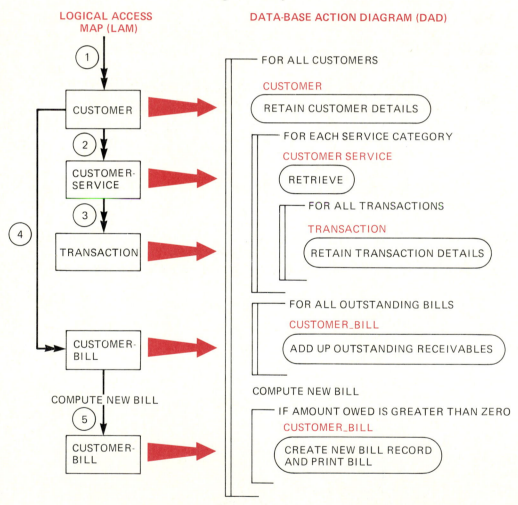

Figure 21.13 The correspondence between the logical access map (LAM) and the data-base action diagram (DAD). The five accesses in the LAM become five actions in the DAD. The double-arrow (one-to-many) accesses in the LAM become double brackets (repetitions) in the DAD.

When an error condition arises, a particular action may need to be carried out. This may be of a general nature, such as notifying someone of the presence of the negative (error) condition. Alternatively, it may represent a specific action to be carried out on that error condition.

Usually, an error condition causes data to be changed, if only the setting of a flag in a record. Where it does not cause data to be changed, it should be marked on the diagram.

TERMINATIONS   Certain conditions may cause a procedure to be terminated. They may cause the termination of the bracket in which the condition occurs, multiple brackets, or possibly the entire procedure.

Terminations are shown by an arrow going to the left from a statement of the termination condition. Thus the following shows a bracket termination:

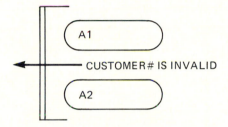

The following shows the simultaneous termination of multiple brackets:

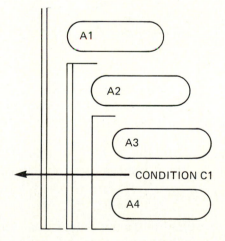

When a bracket is terminated, control passes to the item that immediately follows the bracket. The termination arrow may pass through several brackets, in which case control passes to the item that follows this group of brackets.

Caution is needed with terminations. Abrupt exits may leave some loose ends dangling. An orderly exit is needed and the designer should check that nothing is left uncompleted that should have been completed when a termination occurs.

It might be better to avoid terminations and work one's way to the bottom of the procedure chart exiting one bracket at a time. This is like banning the branching from a subroutine in structured programming. Usually, terminations can be avoided by appropriate sequencing of the bracket contents.

If a user draws a termination arrow, an analyst or programmer should check carefully that the termination is valid and that nothing that *should* be completed is bypassed by the termination.

ACTIONS WITH MULTIPLE STEPS   In some cases an action may be drawn with multiple steps in it; for example when a quantity of parts are withdrawn and depletion-rate and runout-time are calculated and updated, these operations may be shown inside the bracket. Thus:

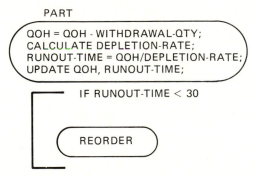

NONACTION ITEMS   It is often useful to write items on the action diagrams which are not themselves actions. Such items are written in the appropriate place in the action sequence without being enclosed in any box or lozenge.

In Fig. 21.13, for example, the item COMPUTE NEW BILL is written. An item can be written like this if it does not itself require any further access to the data base.

SUBPROCEDURES   Sometimes a user needs to add an item to an action diagram which is itself a procedure that may contain actions. We call this a *subprocedure,* or *subroutine,* and draw it with a rectangular box. "Backorder procedure" in Fig. 21.14 is an example. A sub-

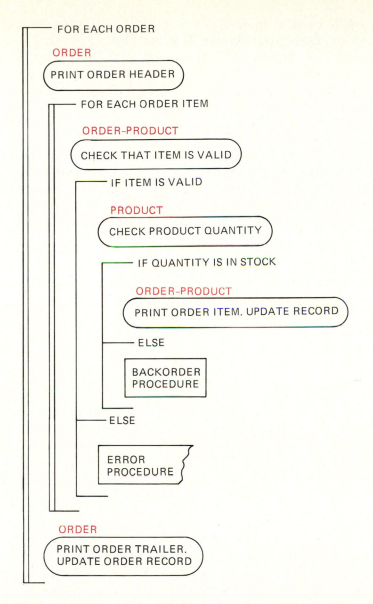

FOR EACH ORDER

ORDER

PRINT ORDER HEADER

FOR EACH ORDER ITEM

ORDER-PRODUCT

CHECK THAT ITEM IS VALID

IF ITEM IS VALID

PRODUCT

CHECK PRODUCT QUANTITY

IF QUANTITY IS IN STOCK

ORDER-PRODUCT

PRINT ORDER ITEM. UPDATE RECORD

ELSE

BACKORDER PROCEDURE

ELSE

ERROR PROCEDURE

ORDER

PRINT ORDER TRAILER. UPDATE ORDER RECORD

Figure 21.14 Subprocedures (subroutines) are represented as rectangular boxes. These are exploded into detail showing the actions they contain, in another chart. Subprocedures that have not yet been worked out in detail are shown as rectangular boxes with a wavy edge, like "Error Procedure" above.

procedure might be used in several procedures. In another chart it will be'
exploded into detail showing the actions it contains.

SUBPROCEDURES   In some cases the procedure designer has sections
NOT YET DESIGNED   of a procedure which are not yet thought out in
                           detail. He can represent this as a box with a wavy
edge. "Error procedure" is such a box in Fig. 21.14.

The use of such boxes enables an action diagrammer to concentrate on
those parts of a procedure with which he is familiar. Another person may,
perhaps, fill in the details in the boxes. This enables an elusive or complex
procedure formation problem to be worked out a stage at a time.

The use of these boxes makes action diagrams a powerful tool for designing procedures at many levels of abstraction. As with other structured
techniques, top-down design can be done by first creating a gross structure
with such boxes, while remaining vague about the contents of each box. The
gross structure can then be broken down into successive levels of detail. Each
explosion of a box adds another degree of detail, which might itself contain
actions and boxes.

Similarly, bottom-up design can be done by specifying small procedures
as action diagrams whose names appear as boxes in higher-level action
diagrams.

Structured vagueness is important because a user cannot necessarily
understand a whole procedure at once. He can design the parts of the procedure that he understands while remaining vague about how the unsolved
parts will be done. The diagrams he draws are, however, specific about the
control structure—about what will happen in what order and under what
conditions.

Action diagrams are a powerful means of creating procedures in a non-
data-base environment, especially with fourth-generation programming languages. In information engineering, however, it is important that they not be
separated from the data models because the data models provide the glue
that links together the many separately created procedures. Without tight
data administration chaos can spread rapidly in a user-driven environment.

Some items on the action diagram will themselves need further structuring in the programs that are written. The conventional techniques of
structured programming can be used for this. However, for most commercial
applications most or all of the structuring has been done when the action
diagrams are completed.

ACCESS METHODS   Data can be accessed by several basic methods. Let
                           us review how these methods are shown on action
                           diagrams.

1. *Random access by primary key:*

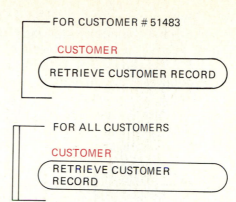

2. *Serial access:*

3. *Secondary-key access:*

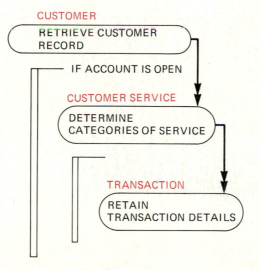

4. *Associative access* (i.e., to records associated with the **CUSTOMER** record):

CORRESPONDENCE OF LAM AND DAD   Figure 21.13 shows the correspondence of the logical access map and the action diagram. The action diagram is an extension of the LAM, adding more detail and drawing a control structure ready for program coding.

Figures 21.15 and 21.16 show another example.

Each day a report is to be produced giving details of customer orders that have not been delivered when they should have been. The procedure designer sketches an access sequence on the data model, as shown in Fig. 21.15. Figure 21.16 shows that LAM drawn as a vertical sequence, and shows the corresponding action diagram.

The action diagram can be converted directly to program code. Although it uses seven different record types it is easy to design with the technique shown in Figs. 21.15 and 21.16, and easy to translate into fourth-generation languages.

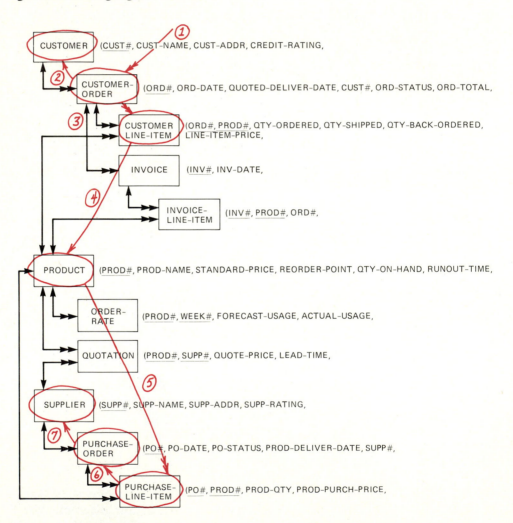

Figure 21.15 Logical access map drawn on the data model of Fig. 20.3 as a first step to designing the procedure shown in Fig. 21.16.

Sometimes an access on a LAM corresponds to two or more lozenges on an action diagram relating to the same record with different conditions applying. This is illustrated at the top of Fig. 21.16, which shows the procedure discussed in Chapter 20 for order acceptance.

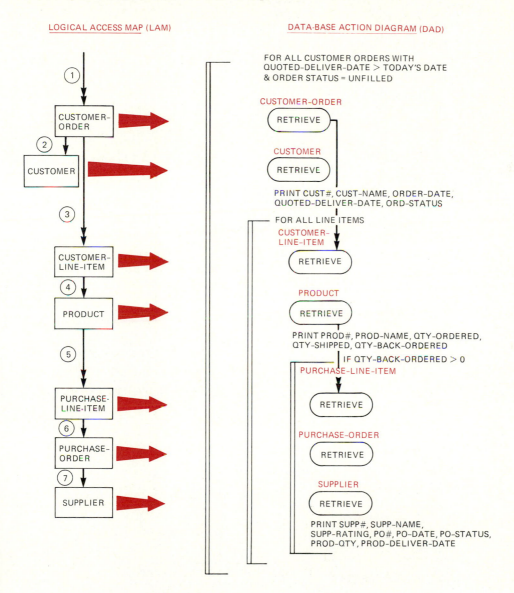

Figure 21.16 This complex query requires access to seven records. Drawing the LAM and DAD makes the procedure easy to design, given the data model shown in Fig. 21.15.

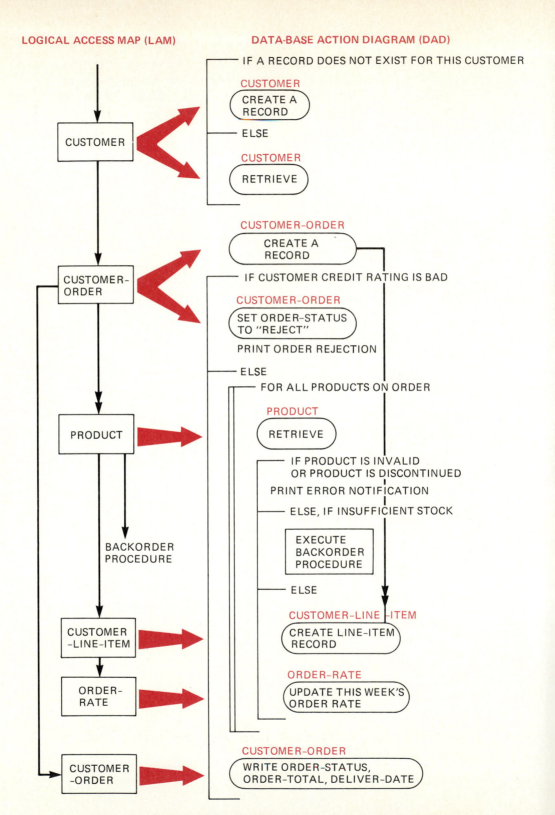

Figure 21.17 Data-base action diagram based on the LAM in Fig. 20.6.

PHYSICAL ACCESSES   We have commented that the *physical* accesses to disks or other storage units may not correspond exactly to the sequence drawn on the LAM or action diagram. In Fig. 21.17, for example, the CUSTOMER-ORDER record would not be created and then updated with separate disk accesses. Instead, it would be retained in main memory until the final update; then it would be written to disk.

With some data-base management systems the CUSTOMER-LINE-ITEM records in Fig. 21.17 would have to be written after the CUSTOMER-ORDER record, because they are its children. With others (e.g., relational DBMS) this would not be so.

The procedure designer may avoid paying attention to these *physical* questions and concentrate on the *logical* design. A data-base designer, taking the LAMs and DADs, should determine the physical design.

SUMMARY   Box 21.2 summarizes data-base action diagrams using simple actions.

BOX 21.2   Examples of action diagrams with simple actions

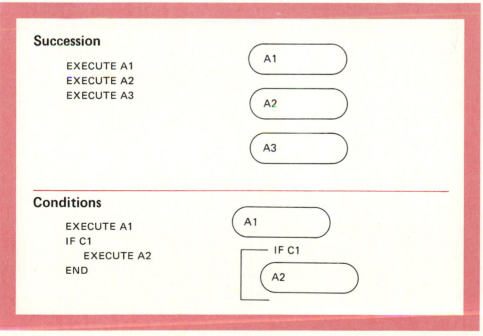

(Continued)

BOX 21.2 *(Continued)*

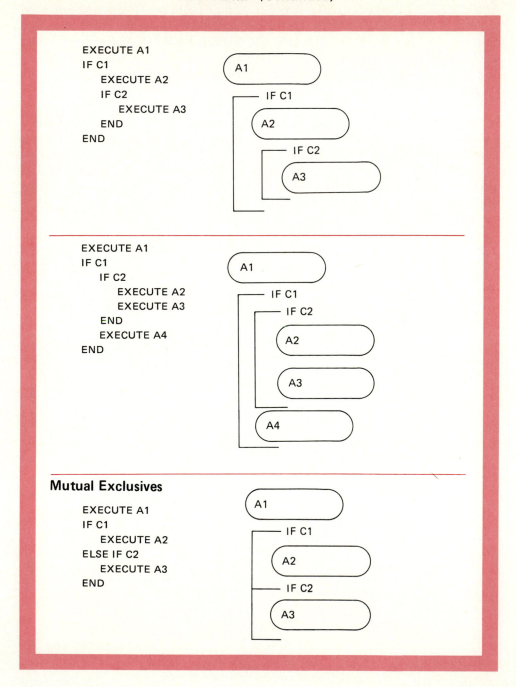

```
EXECUTE A1
IF C1
   EXECUTE A2
   IF C2
       EXECUTE A3
   END
END
```

```
EXECUTE A1
IF C1
   IF C2
       EXECUTE A2
       EXECUTE A3
   END
   EXECUTE A4
END
```

Mutual Exclusives

```
EXECUTE A1
IF C1
   EXECUTE A2
ELSE IF C2
   EXECUTE A3
END
```

BOX 21.2 *(Continued)*

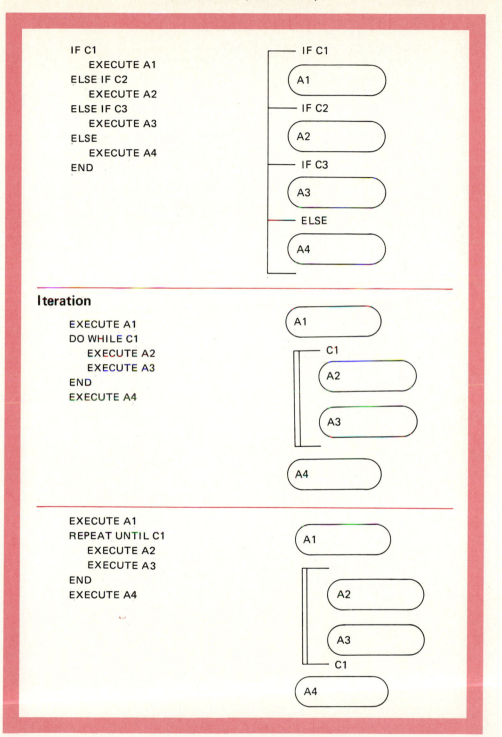

```
IF C1
    EXECUTE A1
ELSE IF C2
    EXECUTE A2
ELSE IF C3
    EXECUTE A3
ELSE
    EXECUTE A4
END
```

Iteration

```
EXECUTE A1
DO WHILE C1
    EXECUTE A2
    EXECUTE A3
END
EXECUTE A4
```

```
EXECUTE A1
REPEAT UNTIL C1
    EXECUTE A2
    EXECUTE A3
END
EXECUTE A4
```

BOX 21.2 *(Continued)*

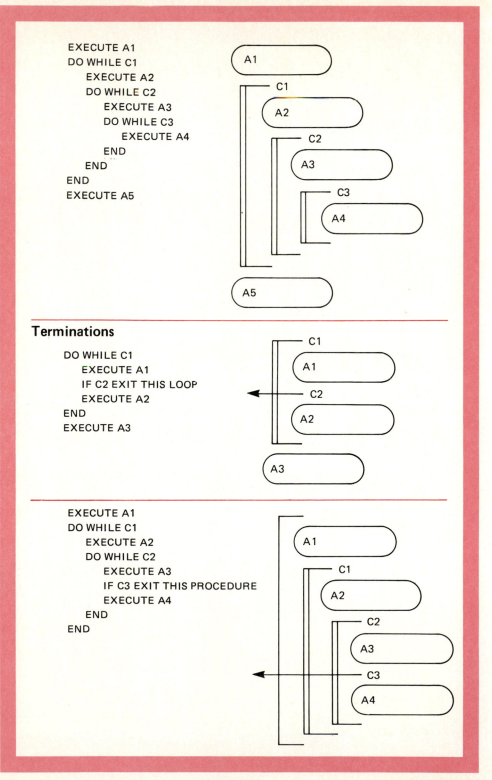

```
EXECUTE A1
DO WHILE C1
    EXECUTE A2
    DO WHILE C2
        EXECUTE A3
        DO WHILE C3
            EXECUTE A4
        END
    END
END
EXECUTE A5
```

Terminations

```
DO WHILE C1
    EXECUTE A1
    IF C2 EXIT THIS LOOP
    EXECUTE A2
END
EXECUTE A3
```

```
EXECUTE A1
DO WHILE C1
    EXECUTE A2
    DO WHILE C2
        EXECUTE A3
        IF C3 EXIT THIS PROCEDURE
        EXECUTE A4
    END
END
```

BOX 21.2 *(Continued)*

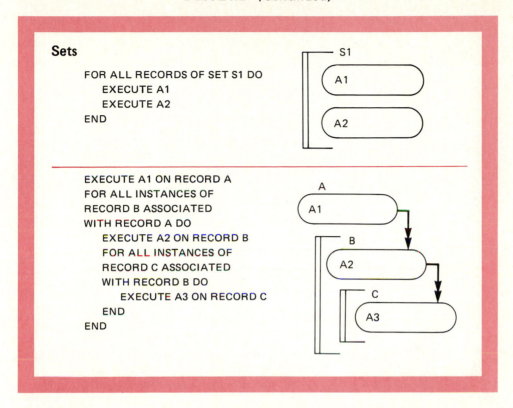

Sets

```
FOR ALL RECORDS OF SET S1 DO
    EXECUTE A1
    EXECUTE A2
END
```

```
EXECUTE A1 ON RECORD A
FOR ALL INSTANCES OF
RECORD B ASSOCIATED
WITH RECORD A DO
    EXECUTE A2 ON RECORD B
    FOR ALL INSTANCES OF
    RECORD C ASSOCIATED
    WITH RECORD B DO
        EXECUTE A3 ON RECORD C
    END
END
```

**CONVERTING
ACTION DIAGRAMS
TO PROGRAM CODE**

Action diagrams are intended to be converted directly to structured program design. This is one of their most useful and important characteristics.

They can be converted directly into one of the following:

- A user-oriented form of structured English.
- Skeleton code of a fourth-generation programming language. When this is done with languages such as FOCUS, RAMIS, NOMAD, IDEAL, MANTIS, NATURAL, and so on, results can be obtained extremely quickly.

Figure 21.18 is an action diagram for an enquiry procedure. Figure 21.19 shows it represented in structured English. Figure 21.20 shows it in MANTIS code.

The vertical red lines of Fig. 21.19 show the code indentation that are used in structured programs. It will be seen that the positions of the brackets in the action diagrams correspond exactly to the positions of the offsets in

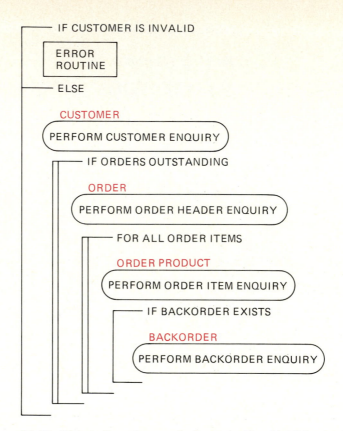

IF CUSTOMER IS INVALID

ERROR
ROUTINE

ELSE

CUSTOMER
PERFORM CUSTOMER ENQUIRY

IF ORDERS OUTSTANDING

ORDER
PERFORM ORDER HEADER ENQUIRY

FOR ALL ORDER ITEMS

ORDER PRODUCT
PERFORM ORDER ITEM ENQUIRY

IF BACKORDER EXISTS

BACKORDER
PERFORM BACKORDER ENQUIRY

Figure 21.18 This action diagram is shown in Fig. 21.19 in structure English and in Fig. 21.20 in the code of a fourth-generation language.

```
IF (CUSTOMER INVALID)
      PERFORM ERROR ROUTINE
ELSE (CUSTOMER VALID)
      PERFORM CUSTOMER ENQUIRY
      DO WHILE (ORDERS OUTSTANDING)
            PERFORM ORDER HEADER ENQUIRY
            REPEAT UNTIL (NO MORE ORDER ITEMS)
                  PERFORM ORDER ITEM ENQUIRY
                  IF (BACKORDER EXISTS)
                        PERFORM BACKORDER ENQUIRY
                  END
            END
      END
END
```

Figure 21.19 Structured English version of the procedure in Fig. 21.18. Although some analysts advocate the use of structured English, it is of little value with action diagrams. The action diagram (like Fig. 21.18) is generally easier to read than structured English.

```
IF CUSTOMER = "INVALID"
· CALL ERR-INVALID-CUST
ELSE
· DO CUSTOMER-ENQUIRY
· WHILE ORDERS-OUTSTANDING > 0
· · DO ORDER-HEADER-ENQUIRY
· · UNTIL ORDER-ITEMS = 0
· · · DO ORDER-ITEM-ENQUIRY
· · · IF BACKORDER > 0
· · · · DO BACKORDER-ENQUIRY
· · · END
· · END
· END
END
```

Figure 21.20 Code for MANTIS, and other such fourth-generation languages for data-base use, can be derived directly from action diagrams. This is MANTIS code for the procedure shown in Fig. 21.18.

the structured code. Although structured English, as in Fig. 21.19, can be derived simply from the action diagram, it is usually unnecessary because *the action diagram itself is generally clearer than the structured English.*

The control structures for the action diagram brackets represent what various third- and fourth-generation languages do with DO loops, FOR, WHILE, WHERE, IF, IF-THEN-ELSE, CASE, CASE WITH DEFAULT, REPEAT UNTIL, and other such constructions.

Just as the data model and LAM are independent of the DBMS, so the action diagram is independent of the programming language. It can be converted quickly into highly reliable code. Conversion from one language to another is relatively quick and easy if both programs are derived from the same action diagram. This aids conversion and maintenance. Some organizations change their choice of fourth-generation language, and others are concerned that some of these languages may disappear or cease to be supported. LAMs and DADs form a documentation tool that make conversion from one fourth-generation language to another easy.

REFERENCES

1. James Martin, *Application Development Without Programmers,* Prentice-Hall, Inc., Englewood Cliffs, NJ, 1982.

2. James Martin, *Fourth Generation Languages,* Savant Technical Report 25, Savant Institute, Carnforth, Lancashire, UK, 1982.

3. James Martin, *Managing the Data-Base Environment,* Prentice-Hall, Inc., Englewood Cliffs, NJ, 1982.

4. James Martin and Clive Finkelstein, *Information Engineering,* Savant Technical Report 22, Savant Institute, Carnforth, Lancashire, UK, 1981.

5. Relational joins and other operations are explained simply in Chapter 13 of James Martin's *Computer Data-Base Organization,* 2nd ed., Prentice-Hall, Inc., Englewood Cliffs, NJ, 1977.

22 COMPOUND ACTIONS AND AUTOMATIC NAVIGATION

Fourth-generation languages and high-level data-base languages permit the use of statements that relate to not one but many record instances. Examples of such statements are:

SEARCH

SORT

SELECT certain records from a relation

PROJECT a relation

JOIN two or more relations

Such an operation is called a compound action. We draw it as a lozenge with a double bar in it, thus:

Figure 22.1 gives an illustration of a compound action that is a relational *join*. In this case two relations (logical files or tables) are used: the

Figure 22.1 Compound action representing a relational join that joins the EMPLOYEE and BRANCH relations by equating the CITY data item in the EMPLOYEE relation with the LOCATION data item in the BRANCH relation.

EMPLOYEE relation and the BRANCH relation. They might perhaps look like this:

BRANCH

BRANCH-ID	LOCATION	BRANCH-STATUS	SALES-YEAR-TO-DATE
007	Paris	17	4,789
009	Carnforth	2	816
013	Rio	14	2,927

EMPLOYEE

EMPLOYEE #	EMPLOYEE NAME	SALARY	CODE	MANAGER	CITY
01425	Kleinrock	42000	SE	Epstein	Rio
08301	Ashley	48000	SE	Sauer	Paris
09981	Jenkins	45000	FE	Growler	Rio
12317	Bottle	91000	SE	Minski	Carnforth

These relations are combined in such a way that the CITY field of the EMPLOYEE relation becomes the same as the LOCATION field of the BRANCH relation, with the following result. As requested in Fig. 22.1, only the EMPLOYEE-NAME, MANAGER, BRANCH-STATUS, and CITY fields are in this relation, which results from the join:

EMPLOYEE-NAME	MANAGER	BRANCH-STATUS	CITY
Kleinrock	Epstein	14	Rio
Ashley	Sauer	17	Paris
Bottle	Minski	2	Carnforth

As required by the opening statement in Fig. 22.1, only employees whose code is SE and whose salary exceeds $40,000 are included in the result.

AUTOMATIC NAVIGATION A compound action may require *automatic navigation* by the data-base management system. Relational data bases and a few nonrelational ones have this capability. For a data base without automatic navigation a compiler of a fourth-generation language may generate the required sequence of data accesses.

With a compound action, search parameters or conditions are often an integral part of the action itself. They are written inside the lozenge on the action diagram. With simple actions the equivalent parameters would be written outside the action lozenge to control the sequence of data accesses.

SIMPLE VERSUS COMPOUND ACTION
There are many procedures that can be done with either simple actions or compound actions. If a traditional DBMS is used, the programmer navigates his way through the data base with simple actions. If the DBMS or language compiler has automatic navigation, higher-level statements using compound actions may be employed.

Suppose, for example, that we want to give a $1000 raise in salary to all employees who are engineers in Carnforth. With IBM's data-base language SQL, we would write

```
UPDATE EMPLOYEE
SET SALARY = SALARY + 1000
WHERE JOB = 'ENGINEER"
AND OFFICE = 'CARNFORTH'
```

We can diagram this with a compound action as follows:

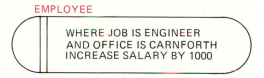

With simple actions (no automatic navigation) we can diagram the same procedure thus:

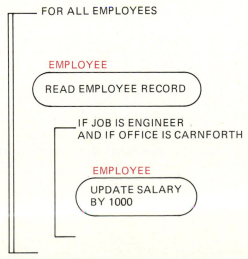

Similarly, a relational join can be represented with either a sequence of single actions or one compound action, as shown in Fig. 22.2. In this example there are multiple projects of an EMPLOYEE-PROJECT record showing how employees were rated for their work on each project they were assigned to. They are given a salary raise if their average rating exceeds 6.

For simple uses of nonprocedural coding there is no need to draw action diagrams. Results can be obtained directly by coding. For more elaborate procedures diagrams are necessary. Sometimes these incorporate both simple and compound actions.

EXAMPLES USING COMPOUND ACTIONS   Consider the process of reordering stock as it becomes depleted. We will use this to illustrate how compound actions are employed. The record structure is shown in Fig. 20.3.

As a request for parts is satisfied, the quantity on hand, recorded in the PART record, is depleted. Each time this happens the program calculates whether to create an order for more parts from their supplier.

The requests for parts are handled interactively throughout the day. The person designing the procedure decides to create a temporary file of order requisitions, to accumulate such requisitions as they occur, and then to sort them and place the orders at the end of the day. In this way an order for many parts can be sent to a supplier rather than creating a separate order each time a part reaches its reorder point.

Figure 22.3 shows the results. In the top part of Fig. 22.3, the selection of suppliers is done with a compound action. This can be represented with one statement of some fourth-generation languages. For example, in SQL it might be

```
SELECT SUPPLIER
FROM QUOTATION
WHERE RATING > 3
AND MIN (QUOTE-PRICE)
```

In the bottom part of Fig. 22.3, the order requisition file is sorted by supplier. This can also be represented by one fourth-generation-language statement:

```
ORDER REQUISITION BY SUPPLIER
```

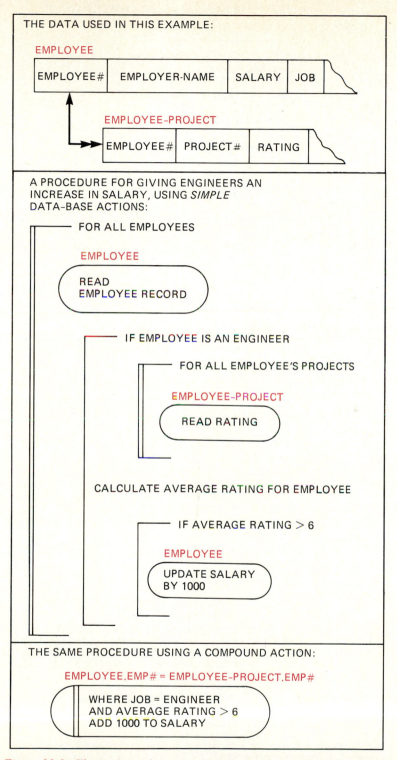

Figure 22.2 Illustration of a procedure that may be done with either multiple simple actions or one compound action.

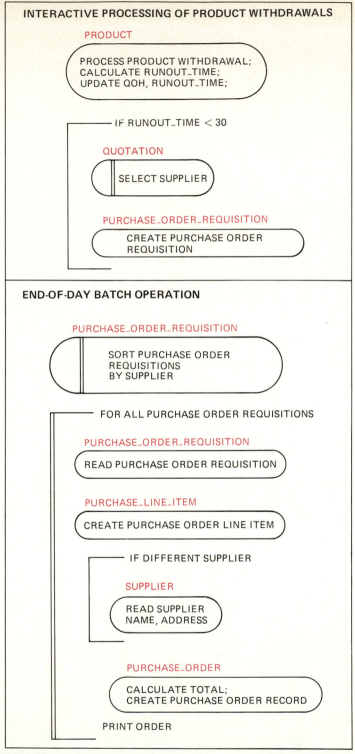

Figure 22.3 Procedures for **PRODUCT** withdrawal and reordering using the data structure in Fig. 20.3 and a temporary **PURCHASE** order requisition file. Two compound actions are used in these procedures.

The person responsible for purchasing might decide that it would be useful to have a plot of the usage rate of each part and see how it compares with the forecast usage rate.

Figure 22.4 shows the data structure and action diagram for this. Again, it can be represented simply in fourth-generation code. In NOMAD, for example, it is as follows:

```
TITLE   'USAGE RATE PLOT';
PLOT    ACTUAL-USAGE-RATE
        FORECAST-USAGE-RATE AGAINST WEEK
        FOR EVERY PART;
```

The example in Fig. 22.4 may be too simple to be worth drawing. It could be coded without drawing. In more elaborate cases it is necessary to diagram the procedure.

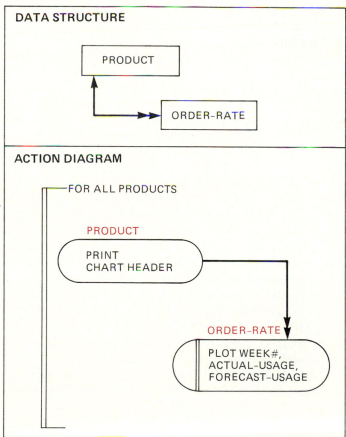

Figure 22.4 Data structure (a partition of that in Fig. 20.3) and action diagram to plot a usage chart for every product.

FOURTH-GENERATION LANGUAGES

Different fourth-generation languages or high-level data-base languages have different dialects.

It would be useful if vendors of such languages would draw illustrations of the set of control structures and compound actions which their languages employ.

A compound action is rather like a macroinstruction which is decomposed into primitive instructions by a compiler or interpreter before it is executed.

To clarify how a compound action in a language operates, the vendor might draw a diagram decomposing it into simple actions. However, this is not always useful because some compound actions are easy to understand but difficult to draw in a decomposed form (e.g., SORT).

The user could conceivably design some of his own compound actions, drawing them as subroutines composed of simple actions.

Compound actions, like simple actions, need to be converted directly into the code of very high level languages. Often the wording inside the action lozenge should resemble the resulting code, as it does in Fig. 22.1. The dialect of the language is thus incorporated into the diagram. Converting the action diagrams to code can be computer-assisted and could form part of an interactive design tool.

The software designer creating a fourth-generation language would do well to start with LAMs and action diagrams, design an easy-to-use technique for charting data-base procedures, and then create an interpreter or compiler with which code can be generated from the diagrams.

USE OF ACTION DIAGRAMS

Action diagrams are valuable both to DP professionals and to end users. They are designed to be easy to teach to end users, and easy for users to read and check. Intelligent end users with no experience of systems analysis or programming learn to create procedures quickly with them. In many cases they adapt to using this technique more quickly than DP professionals who have long experience with more clumsy techniques.

It is highly desirable that end users should have such a technique for thinking about and creating their own procedures. When they draw procedures maps a DP professional can check them for completeness. Because the action diagram is so close to the code structure it can be very quickly coded, especially with fourth-generation languages.

Many systems analysts have expressed a procedure such as that in Fig. 21.17. in a narrative form. This is often clumsy, difficult to read, and incomplete, for example:

> Retrieve the customer record and create a customer-order record. If the customer credit rating is bad, set the order-status code to "reject." Otherwise, write the order status, order total, and delivery date in the customer

order record and for each product ordered check whether the product is invalid or discontinued; if there is insufficient stock of the product, create a product backorder. Create a line-item record on the customer order until the last product ordered is reached. Update the week's order rate for that product. If a record does not exist for the customer in question, create a record.

The representation of the procedure in Fig. 21.17 is more precise, easy to check, and can be converted directly to code.

The derivation of new procedures is an evolutionary process. Techniques are needed which permit new procedures to evolve a step at a time. The techniques need to break away from the constraints of the past. Traditional DP techniques have been excessively rigid and unchangeable because of the expense of maintenance procedures. They have prevented the *evolution* of procedures. As new procedures are derived, ideally by end users who know the environment, these procedures need to be synthesized into the overall system structure.

In many enterprises a vast and wasteful redundancy grows up in the procedures that are separately programmed without knowledge of their commonality. In one corporation we found many different procurement procedures, for example, where one would suffice.

Where a data-base environment is soundly managed, common data models exist, removing much of the redundancy in data. Much procedure redundancy becomes apparent among actions that use the same data.

As the opportunities for combining procedures become clear, new integrated procedures may be designed. Clumsy paperwork procedures are replaced with simpler on-line procedures, avoiding the flow of multiple copies of documents. As procedure consolation is done throughout an enterprise, the need to restructure the departments and management often becomes clear.

New procedures may offer business opportunities that were not apparent from the limited perspective of the existing procedures. It is desirable to encourage as much imaginative thinking as possible among the users in improving their procedures.

MORE COMPLEX SYSTEMS   In some cases the use of fourth-generation languages with data models has made it possible to design more complex information systems than were designed with third-generation languages and techniques.

MIS DEVELOPER:

Fourth-generation languages with this technique are allowing us to do things much more complex than we ever did with COBOL.

The real benefit is the extra power it gives you for complex applications.

This financial system is so complex that they never succeeded in doing it in COBOL with data flow diagrams.

INTERVIEWER:

How did they operate, then?

MIS DEVELOPER:

Oh, they simply don't have these controls. They exceed the federal budget limits and they go back after the fact and back costs out.

One reason fourth-generation languages are permitting skilled DP staff to create more complex systems is that one person can create 10 times as much application logic in a given period. The challenge is to be able to conceptualize the actions and control structures that are needed.

MIS DEVELOPER:

The problem that we get into with complex systems is that the fourth-generation languages allow you so much power in linking all these data bases and doing all these strange concatenations of lookup. It allows you to conceptualize a much more complex type of system. It allows you to design the system to be much closer to what the organization needs and has never been able to have.

The level of detail, particularly in an integrated environment with multiple data bases, is much more difficult to grasp. It is much more difficult for me to design an MIS in FOCUS than it would be to design a typical application in COBOL—because we do so much more. This means that we have even more need than before for clear structured techniques which are data-base oriented.

If the developer can generate complex systems 10 times as fast as with third-generation techniques, one person can create a system that would previously have needed 10 people. Because this greatly lessens communication problems, it makes the development of more complex systems practical.

However, many users of powerful fourth-generation languages do not quickly master the full power. Many succeed only in query and report generation. The author has observed this in many installations. The solution is to provide clear data modeling and procedure design tools with which complex procedures can be simply charted. The courses teaching the language should be based on LAMs and DADs.

The most valuable fourth-generation languages ought to start out with a tool for clear conceptualization of the data and procedures, and progress from that to the generation of code.

PART **V** **END USERS**

23 THE CONCERNS OF END USERS

RESISTANCE TO CHANGE As we look back over the case histories of data base we find that more data-base failures or disappointments have been caused by human problems than by technical problems. The technology is complex and needs to be mastered. But more than this is needed to make data base succeed.

The introduction of the data-base approach brings major changes not only in the work of application development but also, often, in the jobs of end users. To succeed, the data-base planning and design must be done in very close cooperation with the end users, with a sensitive understanding of their fears.

People who have done their jobs for years tend to take their data sources for granted. What they are aware of—the documents, the printing on forms— may only be the visible part of a quicksand of data. They have developed rituals about the portion of data they know about. They are generally not aware of the processing rules in their own heads that guide what they do. When a systems analyst enters this relatively peaceful territory and attempts to make the rules explicit, the staff naturally feel alarmed and often threatened.

The rules have become hallowed rituals, insulated from change, unquestioned, and confortable like old traditions. The rituals tend to replace the broader objectives. Means are confused with ends. Often the unwritten rituals have become different from what was originally intended.

The analyst wants not only to make the rituals explicit, but to change them, to change the use and ownership of data, and often to change the reporting procedures. Sometimes the move to a data-base environment involves very substantial organizational changes.

DP EXECUTIVE:

Organizations like ours, that are solid, have been in existence for a long time, and have evolved into a very sizable expense in the data-processing end of the business, are going to face traumatic changes. The trauma is going to be in the human organizational changes. Now, I think that this is the most difficult aspect that we'll have to face and cope with for the foreseeable future.

Jobs will be performed in different ways, with different tools and information sources. Some types of jobs will be eliminated or transferred.

DATA ADMINISTRATOR:

It's going to be a long hard process for us, because you're taking away from sophisticated end users, and development areas, functions that have traditionally belonged to them.

END-USER EXECUTIVE:

In a migration to a data base of the size we're going into there's going to be a lot of stubbing of toes. The bloodshed I see is the out-and-out resentment.

As the move to data base is being planned and implemented, good communication is desirable at all levels of management involved, to explain to end users what it is all about, why it is happening, and what its advantages are. Users need to be persuaded, as far as possible, that it is to their advantage to cooperate.

END-USER EXECUTIVE:

DP management should keep the user heavily involved, and sometimes that generates conflicting priorities for the user. But I think most users understand that this is the thing of the future and we had better really understand what's going on at the front end because at the tail end it might just be too late.

Color 428

Many end users feel they need to be in control of their own data. When the data are moved to a shared environment, they feel that control is being taken away from them.

END-USER EXECUTIVE:

The billing function, for example, is being told to use data that are created by the sales organization, and this is a difficult adjustment to make.

First of all, he's aware that garbage in that data base is going to screw up his billing operation, and he's uncomfortable about that.

Second, when he wants to make a change, he has to go through a committee that he's part of rather than a leader in. And that's going to cause a problem.

Organizations are designed to be rational. If they were truly rational, data bases and information systems would fit into them smoothly like parts of a machine. In practice the individuals who comprise organizations are not like parts of a machine. They have ambitions, fears, fantasies, emotions, and above all rivalries.

The data modeling process does not take this into consideration. It associates data from different areas and different individuals into what appears to give the cleanest, most efficient data structure. It cuts across the lines on the organization chart and across informal lines of communication, which are often quite different from those on the organization chart.

In many organizations the education in bureaucratic survival causes information to be covered up, delayed, or tunneled through certain channels. The image of a corporate data base making information generally accessible is a cause for alarm.

FOUR CLASSES OF ATTITUDE

A high-level manager in a large insurance company identifies four classes of end users:

1. Enthusiastic, helpful
2. Competent but unwilling to change unless pushed
3. Unable to adjust
4. Hostile, counterproductive

END-USER EXECUTIVE:

I think in the change from any one system to another on a large scale, you've got those users who *are really enthusiastic* and those are the people who want to get on this development team. You've got those in the middle who would like to continue, they'll do a good job, but they really *don't want to get involved unless pushed.* You've got those that *will probably never be able to adjust,* because of lack of natural ability, to a new more technical environment. But I think that you've got a final group, and I hope we don't have too many, that *will be counterproductive.*

The data administrator needs help from the end users. It is useful for him to categorize them in his mind into the four classes described above. He will then go to Class I whenever possible, and avoid Classes III and IV.

END-USER EXECUTIVE:

Suppose that the development project team is asking: "How often do you use this technique?" They should be smart enough not to go to the counterproductive person. If they do, you can be sure that they're not going to get a good answer. Not one you can hang your hat on.

It often helps if a suitable level of management explains this categorization of end users to the users in question. Most will then strive to avoid being classed as III or IV. Really good management of this area could make most of them Class I.

INTERVIEWER:

What are you going to do with the ones who will never adjust?

END-USER EXECUTIVE:

It's an interesting question. Most people like that, when they see that the installation is imminent, usually make the move on their own. Meaning they're doing something productive, they know they can be productive in something, and they will usually ask for a transfer. My experience has been that those transfers can be arranged because the person is not counterproductive. I don't think that's the majority; it's not even a large minority.

Many people are comfortable with what they've got. Those are the people that management should address and try to light a spark of interest in. Perhaps they're not naturally curious, but after a time that can come with the right education.

SKELETONS IN CLOSETS

The investigations of the data administrator often reveal situations, procedures or past actions which were not what management intended, or which would be frowned on by the current regime. The data administrator should be prepared for these and must handle them with extreme tact.

END-USER EXECUTIVE:

I think one of the keys is that data modeling, and data base in general, involves an investigation of the organization itself, and our experience has been that we find a lot of skeletons coming out of a lot of closets. There are a lot of things that were done under pressure years ago in another environment altogether that, looked at in the light of today's experience and today's tools, obviously weren't the best things to do, or perhaps weren't the best things to do then, and certainly aren't valuable today. If there were some way to declare sort of general amnesty throughout the organization, while you're going through this process, people tend to react less negatively.

I think it's very important to recognize that we are looking from a different viewpoint. We're looking from five more years' experience in this industry. We're looking at it with new tools and new techniques that people didn't have. And the one thing one must not do is to get into that sort of evaluative phase: why did you do this, that wasn't the best way to do it.

The move into data base is an opportunity to forgive and forget the sins of the past. As in other walks of life, this needs to be done periodically.

END-USER EXECUTIVE:

There was one particular thing that we thought we had stopped doing. We decided to stop offering this service to policyholders, I think, five years ago. And sure enough it cropped up somewhere. They'd taken it out of one place and somebody had put together a structure and was offering it under another name. Few people in the organization were aware that that was going on.

The data models that are built may *incorporate* the data for old methods, "skeletons in closets," and services such as that above. Decisions about function do not have to be made when the data are being modeled. The data that are fed into the modeling process may incorporate the unofficial procedures as well as the official or planned ones.

END-USER COMMITTEE

The *end-user committee* that we discussed in earlier chapters is a good place to air the concerns of end users. The data administrator can address these. The committee should contain appropriate members of user management, who can in turn address the fears of their subordinates.

END-USER COMMITTEE MEMBER:

Just about every major operating function in the division is represented there. They are high-level people. People who have been around for a number of years, who have the business experience and understand the data needed to run their part of the operation. So these are not technicians, or low-level people. We've strived to seed that committee with as high a level of people as we can, with basic operating knowledge, who can help to review the differences in data representation and resolve them. And get them carried out in their departments as well.

POWER AND FREEDOM

In some areas a major effect of computers is likely to be that they can automate those parts of jobs that were easy for human beings but cannot touch the parts that were difficult. Where this is true they increase the overall difficulty human beings have in doing their work. This is seen in many walks of life in the steady spread of complexity that the modern world is bringing. Paradoxically, it is not necessarily bad for the individual concerned. His job may become more difficult, but it also becomes more interesting, more stimulating, and more fulfilling. The easy parts of his job were the dull parts, and it is now possible to dream of a world in which dull jobs are done by machines and interesting jobs are done by human beings. Unfortunately, we are some way from this world as yet.

A less fortunate aspect of computerization occurs where it is possible to automate those parts of a person's job that give him a feeling of power, achievement, or responsibility.

It is interesting to reflect on the reasons people in corporations seek power. No doubt some of them do it for the sheer enjoyment of exercising naked power. Except in a few extreme cases, however, this is probably not the main reason. Some want power in order to achieve objectives they believe in. Probably the major reason, however, stems from the need for freedom. The more power they have, the freer they are to take the actions they want—the freer they are to control their environment. Freedom of action is a basic need of capable people. How many of the younger capable employees in a corporation do you hear saying that they want to be their own boss? They would like to leave the organization and work for themselves, or they want to be left free to see a job through in their own way. It has become a cliché of youth that they want to "do their own thing." They are asking for freedom.

Centralized computers and data bases can decrease the freedom of action of junior or middle management, and for some people this can be exceedingly frustrating. The data-base system can centralize many of the important decisions. Many decisions are taken out of the hands of the local managers. If a local manager wants to alter a plan, he may not be able to do so. A central computer system may create a very unattractive environment for the local decision maker.

On the other hand, distributed systems, personal work stations, and the Information Center concept can increase the freedom of action of lower management if the managers in question can come to grips with making their local computers manipulate the information they need. The local manager in a distributed environment will "do his own thing," using his own computer, within a minimal set of rules determined by higher-level management. He will know how his efforts are measured and judged.

Chris Argyris, Professor of Administrative Sciences at Yale, has studied the effects of computers on middle management [1] and concludes that they can be similar to the effects of job specialization on lower-level employees.

A young man can start working on an assembly line with a rather high degree of commitment. But he learns very soon that if he maintained that commitment, he could go mad. So he begins to withdraw psychologically. And as he withdraws certain things begin to happen: he no longer cares about the quality of the work as he used to; he also begins to see himself as a less responsible human being.

Confronted with computers making the decisions, Argyris claims, many middle managers also lose much of their commitment.

Daily goals are defined for the manager; the actions to achieve those goals are specified; his level of aspiration is determined for him; and his performance is evaluated by a system *over which he has no influence.*

These conditions may lead managers to perform as expected. However, they will also lead to a sense of psychological failure. Those managers who aspire toward challenging work with self-responsibility will be frustrated; those who prefer less challenge will be satisfied. The former may leave, fight, or psychologically withdraw: the latter usually stay and also withdraw. In short, the manager, because of information systems, will experience frustrations that his employees once experienced when quality control engineers first designed their work and monitored their performance.

Middle managers feel increasingly hemmed in. In psychological language, they will experience a great restriction of their space of free movement, resulting in feelings of lack of choice, pressure, and psychological failure. These feelings in turn can lead to increasing feelings of helplessness and decreasing feelings of responsibility. Result: a tendency to withdraw or to become dependent upon those who created or approved the restriction of space of free movement.

COMMANDS ON USER INITIATIVE

With this in mind we can comment on good and bad uses of a data base.

Good design would leave managers or professionals a major degree of autonomy in how they use the data base. Bad design would make the managers merely cogs in a computerized machine. Good design should allow managers to operate within a set of objectives. They should have an appropriate degree of power and freedom in meeting those objectives. This includes the freedom to utilize and devise computer applications. Good data-base systems should provide users with powerful tools for generating the reports or information they need when they need them. Users should have the ability to develop their own information sources.

They may create their own files or sub-data bases, which can be separately locked. They may move data between central data bases and their own small minicomputer. If they find that data they want are not in the data base, they should be able to negotiate with the data administrator.

Rather than having no scope for initiative as Argyris describes, they should have authority and responsibility for how they employ the data bases. Indeed, a danger of end-user data-base languages and very cheap peripheral computers is that demands on local management initiative may become too great.

In some cases end users already believe that their departments should be developing their own systems.

END-USER EXECUTIVE:

I personally would raise blazes if I thought a data-processing group was going to, in effect, build a system for me. That's the old way things were done.

In such cases the difficulty may be to ensure that the data used fit in with the overall data-base plans.

RUSH TO IMPLEMENT End-user management in many areas is becoming much more sophisticated about computing. They often want their own computing resources and data. Because of this a major problem in some data-base implementations is that the end users develop systems which cut across the data-base plans.

DP EXECUTIVE:

I don't think we can prevent it; pragmatically speaking, they can be devious. They can find ways of bypassing DP's edicts. And until the higher authorities within the organization recognize this, and the potential that it has of harming the health and welfare of their organization, we're going to see more of that.

We've seen instances when the one group will ask for certain data to be included within the data base but they're not in the priority scheme. Consequently, they'll develop an alternative, which is more expensive to the company but gets the job done, because they are still responsible for getting their function performed.

They're going to do it at all costs.

Once appropriate data-base systems are in place, the best course of action for user managers is likely to be to use the data base with end-user languages, or to extract a subset of the data base for their own decision-making.

DP EXECUTIVE:

I think that they'll be stopped from building their own files as their investment in the total data base becomes greater, and the data base becomes more an integral part of the business function. As that happens, they won't want to build an incompatible system.

   We've got a critical few years to get over. In a few years' time we'll probably have very good data bases which serve the end users very well. But the danger is that in the near future, end users might rebel and build their own file systems before we've got good data-base service in place for them.

Some DP managements have a policy of *encouraging* end users who put too much pressure on them to build their own systems.

DP EXECUTIVE:

Today, where we find that we must support the business function *before* we can build a comprehensive data base, we will form a deliberate strategy to, say, take the expedient solution rather than wait your turn. We do that as a deliberate strategy today. I believe that over the next couple of years, during the transition to the data-base technology, we'll see that technique diminish.

   Encouraging separate system development as an interim pressure-relieving measure makes more sense if it is done using the corporate data dictionary and possibly also the corporate data modeling tool. If this is not done (and too often it is not), incompatible data systems result which will be expensive to fold back into the mainstream data-base development. Often they are never converted and the chaos of incompatible data prevents the desirable information systems being available.

OWNERSHIP OF DATA   A major concern of data-base end users is: "Who owns the data?" In some end-user group meetings there are endless arguments about this and about what the word "own" means in a data-base environment.

   In a *file* environment it is usually clear who owns the files. Data base is different because many types of users share the data. Who owns it in this case? Does the central data-processing department own it? Has a user who once owned his own files lost control of them?

   Much of the problem in these arguments results because the word "own" is itself imprecise in this context. There are several separate attributes to ownership. We ought to replace the question of who owns the data with the following questions:

1. Who is responsible for the accuracy of the data?
2. Who is permitted to update the data?
3. Who is permitted to read and use the data (without necessarily being permitted to change them)?
4. Who is responsible for determining who can read and update the data?
5. Who controls the security of the data?

Each data-item group or each data item can be separately controlled so that only authorized users can read it or change it. A good data-base management system has the capability to enforce tight security control of this type. The system designer must then define who is permitted to read and update the data. It is usually desirable that *only one* person or department should be able to change a given data item or data-item group. If more than one can change it, it is more difficult to control integrity. There are exceptions to this. For example, many branch banks may have access to a customer's central record and can debit or credit transactions to it. In this case careful central auditing controls are essential and must be thorough. The branch that holds the customer's account has the final responsibility for its accuracy.

In many cases one department enters a certain type of data. It creates the records and updates them. It is responsible for their accuracy. Although these data are extensively shared, no other department or individual is permitted to change them.

Good security is extremely important in this environment. The data must be effectively locked to prevent unauthorized reading and updating. There are many different ways of subverting a computer system and equally many safeguards to prevent it. A security officer is needed who applies the safeguards and enforces their use. The security officer is normally part of a central DP organization, not part of individual user departments.

Given that tight security is enforceable, who should decide *which* individual users are authorized to see *which* data, and to update *which* data? This decision is part of the overall system design. How the data are used, and who uses them, needs to be negotiated when the data bases are being planned. Some end users should be involved in this planning, especially when they have concerns about the sharing of data which they previously owned.

The central DP organization is often the *custodian* of the data. In a distributed environment there may be distributed custodians. Being a *custodian* of data is quite different from being their *owner*. A bank manager is the custodian of what is in his bank vault, but he does not own it. The DP department is responsible for safekeeping and controlling the data. The data may be *used* by any persons or departments to whom authority is given. They may be *updated* by one or more authorized persons.

The custodian of data knows what types of data items exist, but does not know their individual values. He knows that the payroll record contains a SALARY data item, but he does not know the value recorded in this data item; indeed, he is specifically locked out of that data item so that he cannot read it. However, if the SALARY data item must be expanded from six to seven digits, only the custodian of the data can accomplish this change.

Auditing the data usage may be a responsibility of the custodian, but generally auditors external to the custodian department are needed. A bank manager should be audited by authorities outside the bank.

In a simple file environment the "owner" of the data may have performed all of these functions. In the data-base environment there may be a separate:

1. Custodian of the data

2. Security authority for the data

3. Auditor of the data

4. Persons permitted to read or use the data

5. Persons permitted to create or update the data

Who exactly can do what to what data is a basic set of decisions that should be made when the system is designed. This usage of data can be repeatedly reviewed. Details of who is authorized to read and update what data items may be recorded in the data dictionary. At a minimum, details of persons permitted to create and update the data should be recorded.

SECURITY

Somewhat related to the question of ownership, users worry if data-base systems can really be trusted. Are they really secure? Or could some unauthorized user harm the data?

It is important to users to understand that computer data *can* be made highly secure. Data can be locked up in a computer as securely as money can be locked up in a bank vault. Often, however, they are not. Tight security adds slightly to total system cost and could make a system slightly less convenient to use. End users, auditors, systems analysts, and the data-base designer may all participate in determining the degree of security protection, and the specific locks that are used with the data.

With the spread of high-level data-base languages, security and auditability become major concerns. Some of these languages are designed to be very easy to use. They can be used from terminals anywhere in a corporation or even outside it if appropriate security constraints are not applied. It is clear that widespread use of powerful end-user languages (Chapter 9) would be dangerous if rigorous security and auditability controls were not in force.

The information stored is sometimes of great value to a corporation. It must not be lost or stolen. The more vital the information in data bases becomes, the more important it is to protect it from hardware or software failures, from catastrophes, and from criminals, vandals, incompetents, and people who misuse it.

Privacy and security are discussed in Chapter 32.

> **BOX 23.1   Summary of the fears of end users about data base, and a summary of its potential advantages for them.**

Fears of End Users

- Fear of change.
- Loss of control over something that they had control over.
- Fear of unofficial methods, inefficient methods, or hidden data being discovered.
- Too rapid visibility of their data.
- Loss of ability to manipulate data, maintain reserves, or hide information for their own purposes.
- Fear that they will not learn how to work the terminals well.
- Fear of losing their job and being moved to a job which they may not be as good at.
- Concerns about who "owns" the data.

Advantages for End Users in Data-Base Operations

- Information is quickly available.
- Users can do their job better.
- Boring work or drudgery is reduced.
- If user departments are judged by their bottom line, data-base usage can help them achieve the desired figures.
- Complex situations can be better organized.
- New applications can be developed faster.
- Powerful end-user languages enable users to generate their own information and applications using the data.

SUMMARY OF END-USER CONCERNS

Box 23.1 summarizes the common concerns of end users about data-base implementation. The management involved should understand and address these concerns, discussing them with the users. Too many systems designers have largely ignored the fears of the users, and too many data-base plans have failed because of lack of user support.

Box 23.1 also lists the advantages of data-base systems to end users. The advantages can be considerable, and discussion of these is desirable to generate some excitement among users and encourage them to cooperate in the traumatic period of change.

If we can draw one message from all of this it is that the most important factor in data-base implementation is *communication*. The data administrator needs to be, above all, a good communicator. There must be good communication with top management and top management must make it clear to everyone that they intend to build up the stable data-base structures that are vital for the corporation of the future. Good communication within the DP department is also vital.

Communication from the top and careful explanations from the data administrator must reach all end users. They must understand the potential benefits and the need for data modeling and compatibility. Their very substantial fears must be listened to carefully, but they should be left with no doubt that data base is the way of the future.

REFERENCE

1. Chris Argyris, "Resistance to Relational Management Systems," *Innovation,* February 1970.

24 END-USER EDUCATION

INTRODUCTION The need for end-user involvement and cooperation is vital in data-base development, but is all too often neglected. To achieve it, appropriate education is necessary for *all* involved end users.

END-USER COMMITTEE MEMBER:

We're struggling a bit. We're trying to find our legs, we're trying to position ourselves to the point where we feel we can contribute the most. Everybody's learning, it's new to all of us, it's strange. I believe to some extent we've been holding back a bit. We have that situation of many users, a lot of business background, wanting to find the best way to bring that to bear on the process and never sure of when to jump, when to hold back.

Education and communication are the key to many end-user problems. In some installations the technical staff is well trained, but education of the end users has been ignored or thought unnecessary.

DATA ADMINISTRATOR:

Our experience has been that data base is the subject about which everyone is sort of half-educated. It might be better if they knew nothing at all. But there are many, many misconceptions. I think that from the data-processing department outward through the entire organization there is an enormous amount of educating that has to be done.

FOUR PARTS TO USER EDUCATION

There are five parts needed in education of data-base end users:

1. Basic education of what a data base is, why it is important, and what the effects of data-base operation are.

2. Enough education about data modeling to enable end users to think about their own data needs, assist the data administrator to understand them, and help review the data models he creates.

3. Localized education about how the move to data base affects a particular user's working environment. This is especially important when the introduction of data base changes that environment.

4. Education in how to use terminals and end-user languages.

5. Education designed to enable more advanced users to assume responsibility for some of their own data processing.

AVOIDANCE OF TECHNICAL COMPLEXITY

Education for end users should explain the principles of data base in a manner which omits almost all of the technical jargon. There is no need to tell users about DL/1's bidirectional pointers with intersection data using physical or virtual pairing!

What the end user need to know about data base can be explained in simple terms, without oversimplifying. A major mistake that is often made is for an instructor to teach data base as though he were instructing a group of DP professionals. Often he gives the same course that the systems analysts receive or a sawn-off version of it. The users do not understand much of it; it seems too complex to them. This heightens their natural fear reaction to data base. They are afraid they will not be able to cope with it.

All acronyms—such as PSB, DML, physical DBD—should be avoided. It is necessary to use nontechnical language where possible, and communicate in a way that gains the user's interest.

END USER:

I've seen a lot of failure in this. I've seen some examples of where there have been presentations that are meant to interest people in what this is and . . . well, when you look around after an instructor's been talking for only 15 minutes and see people dozing off, you know there's something wrong.

You have people who just don't want to hear about it and you have to get through to them. A lot of users are *afraid* of a new world, and incomprehensible instruction full of jargon and difficulties which they can't understand makes them *more afraid*.

Confronted in large installations with the problem of end-user education, I wrote a short book for end users: *An End-User's Guide to Data Base* [1]. The book contains almost no technical words. I believe that the material in it should be read by *all* data-base end users.

Its substance can be taught to end users in a two-day course. It is designed to address end users' fears about data base, to explain the principles in a nontechnical fashion, and to prepare the users to cooperate fully with the data administrator in defining and modeling the data.

End users also benefit considerably from seeing the series of films made in conjunction with this book (*Managing the Data-Base Environment,* Deltak Inc., Oakbrook, IL 60521).

The Deltak videotapes on data base made by the author include the following:

1. Video journals that require no reading:

    (a) *Corporate Data-Base Strategy:* three tapes for top management
    (b) *An End-User's Guide to Data Base:* three tapes
    (c) *Managing the Data-Base Environment:* five tapes giving an overview of this book
    (d) *Application Development Without Programmers:* four tapes

2. Video courses that require reading and question answering:

    (a) *Principles of Data Base:* three tapes for beginning
    (b) *Data-Base Techniques:* a continuation of the introduction above: five tapes
    (c) *Data-Base Architectures:* five tapes

In addition to the material cited above, users need to be given some education about how the data bases in question affect their own working environment.

END-USER EXECUTIVE:

I think it's incumbent on every manager in the division to make a stab at education. We are sorely lacking in understanding, particularly as it could have a very positive benefit. Some of the people have labored with the older systems to the extent that they gimmicked and played games and heaven knows what, to get a result to a given policyholder. If they could see that they no longer need to do that and that they will have a system that is not only responsive to their current needs but will be responsive to unanticipated needs . . . if that is approached and presented that way, it would certainly lessen the fear impact. I would think that it would create some excitement: this is a new world we're going into.

There's no need to teach end users anything about data-base management system mechanisms or software. They need to know the broad principles of what such software achieves and why it is used. This can be taught without any technical words, as in *An End-User's Guide to Data Base* [1].

The users should be taught who does what, who can help them, and what their own responsibilities are. A major responsibility is to help the data administrators understand their data needs. To do this they should understand the basic principles of what data are: bubble charts, primary keys, secondary keys, concatenated keys. They should be able to take a document or a report and draw a bubble diagram to represent its data structure.

They should understand the basic ideas of data modeling and should fully understand the output of the data modeling tool used. They should be able to examine models of data presented to them by the data administrator so that they can help with the *stability analysis* steps given in Chapter 17.

Data representation and modeling can be taught employing the end user's *own* data. He can draw diagrams of his own documents or reports that he would like to receive.

The user should be familiar with the use of the data dictionary, and the need for standardizing the definitions and representations of data items in the corporation.

The users should be made familiar with the arguments about *ownership* of data. The word *ownership* should be replaced by the five different characteristics listed in Chapter 23. The users should understand the first principles of how data are made secure and private.

The user should be taught in general terms what factors affect machine performance, why unanticipated searches or multiple-secondary-key queries can take a long time, and why too many unanticipated queries play havoc with production systems. They should be told what factors can degrade their response times.

They should be taught why distributed systems are sometimes used, and what the problems are in certain types of data distribution. They may be taught how users can take control of part of their own data processing with minicomputers or possibly with time sharing.

It is desirable to generate a substantial amount of enthusiasm for the new data-base environment. This is a most important motivating factor. In installations where this is not done, the users sometimes remain hostile to the whole idea. However, it is important not to *oversell*. The difficulties of moving to data base should be explained, and the time scale. Users should not be made to expect results quicker than they can be achieved. In some cases this overexpectation has resulted in great pressures on the DP department which they cannot easily respond to. At worst it has led to discontented end-user management breaking away from the DP plans.

END-USER EXECUTIVE:

It was oversold so that a lot of managers began to think that data base was a panacea. As we find out that we've been a bit naive about how much and how quickly a data-base environment can materialize, we're starting to become concerned. It's big, it's scary, the road is dark, full of snakes; we're encountering them much too slowly in some regards. Although we feel that things will accelerate in the future, we don't know when. So there's a bit of an *unselling* job to do in terms of making management aware of that.

It may be a panacea some way down the road. It may create a more responsive data-processing environment, but we're not going to get there tomorrow. We're not going to get there without a lot of bleeding on the part of a lot of people and it's going to be a bit more costly than we might have thought at the outset.

VIDEO TAPE TRAINING　　　A particularly effective vehicle for training certain types of end users is video tape. This medium can convey important messages to people who are not likely to read or sit still for extensive training programs. Tapes are sometimes shown to end users or management in small discussion groups. Sometimes this is done at lunchtime.

Sometimes the end users themselves have taken the initiative and obtained the video tapes. And sometimes the result has been a surprise to the data-processing department.

INSURANCE COMPANY DIVISION MANAGER:

I managed to stop a major data-base project from continued progress down a doomed path since there was almost no end-user involvement. The Deltak video series *Managing the Data-Base Environment* was the vehicle I used. I showed it to key people in small discussion groups and we then compared *our* development process. The project is being reformulated—and I know it will be successful in the future.

Needless to say, the Systems Department project manager saw us as a guerilla group and almost refused to acknowledge our existence. When confronted he simply said: "I'm designing it so that it can be changed in the future. . . ." It was not an acceptable response since

> everyone who had watched the tapes was armed with a commitment to extensive user involvement.

In some cases video tapes are shown to top management in an organization, especially when top management cooperation, policy making, or clout is needed.

When video tapes are used it is generally desirable that the DP organization should have planned beforehand what messages it wants to convey with them, and how they relate to the corporation in question. These messages can then be reinforced after the showing of the tape.

END-USER EXECUTIVE:

You know, new worlds are frightening sometimes. If you just throw someone in a dark room, his fears are going to start right off the bat. But if you do that and say: by the way, it's perfectly safe and the walls are made of rubber, it takes some of the edge off. I think that's what our responsibility is as managers in this area. But first, the managers have to be educated!

DEVELOPING   Perhaps the biggest challenge in user education is
END-USER   to encourage end users to take the initiative and
RESPONSIBILITY   employ the data bases to create their own data processing. They can do this with the data-base languages discussed in Chapter 9, or they can employ staff who can program in such languages.

CORPORATE DATA-BASE PLANNER:

Getting people to think differently about where the responsibilities lie—getting the users to assume more of the responsibilities for the direction of the data-processing operation than they have in the past—is the biggest challenge we'll face for the next couple of years.

Corporations that use computing the most effectively as data-base systems evolve may be those in which good data bases and networks are in place, and users in many areas understand the potential of these for affecting how they run their departments and take the initiative in employing them.

END-USER EXECUTIVE:

I think that the education of the users into what their potential is is where it's going to happen. I believe that we have to manage their education and involve the users more in project teams, putting the responsibility for the project directly with the user, rather than with DP. Some users are going to evolve into that technique naturally. I guess natural selection is a process for doing it.

Practice with report generators and practice with data-base dialogues then become an important part of user training. The user must know what exists and what the potential of using it might be to his department. He should be involved in project teams. The business persons and department heads need to be made to *think data base*.

HIGH EXECUTIVE:

When data base started in our organization, it was just a bunch of technicians playing in a sand box. They had the latest software wonder and they made it work, but it didn't do much good.

They never bothered to spend time with end users. Upper management didn't know what was going on. The businessmen didn't know about data base and the data-base types didn't understand the business.

The trouble with data base is that it's often just a small exotic group of technical people who play with it and you don't reap the true benefits of data base until it's applied with a broad understanding of the business.

INTERVIEWER:

What's the answer?

EXECUTIVE:

Education. Communication. You have got to get it out of the sand box and into the hands of the business managers.

REFERENCE

1. James Martin, *An End-User's Guide to Data Base,* Prentice-Hall, Inc., Englewood Cliffs, NJ, 1981.

25 DATA-BASE LANGUAGES FOR END USERS

One of the most important current developments in data-base technology is the growth of high-level languages for data-base users. These languages enable queries to be formulated, reports generated, and applications created, using the data bases. In some cases they enable end users to create their own Class IV data bases.

Figure 9.1 categorized the various types of data-base user languages.

Some are designed for end users and require little or no computing skills. They do not require the remembering of mnemonics, formats, or fixed sequences of entry. End users can learn to employ them by attending a training course of one or two days.

Other data-base languages are designed for DP professionals to create results or applications much more quickly than they could with conventional programming [1]. Often they are used by systems analysts rather than programmers. The systems analysts may create a prototype or a final application. Sometimes the data-base languages need to be used in conjunction with conventionally programmed code.

We sometimes use the term "end user" as though it referred to one breed of creature. In reality, computer end users vary across the entire spectrum of humanity both in skills and in motivation. Some budget planners and production schedules work wonders with APL. But most users are frightened of terminals and do not yet dream that they could instruct computers to go to work for them. A sensitive seduction process is needed to encourage them to join the club—and many are too set in their ways to be seduced.

In the long run it is certain that much computing will be user driven. In the early days of the motor car its users employed a chauffeur. Technology improved and a chauffeur became unnecessary. Technology will increasingly improve the user interface to computers so that for many applications users will not need a computer-chauffeur.

449

INTEGRATED LANGUAGES

Although some languages fall into *one* of the seven categories in Fig. 9.1, it is desirable to have languages that are in multiple categories. Some report generators, for example, are entirely separate from query languages and some data-base query languages do not have a report generation capability. It would be preferable for a user to learn a query language with which he could steadily extend his skills and become able to create reports with useful formats. He should also be able to create business graphics. Similarly, the language should be extendable so that it is a full application generator.

Several query languages and report generators today are suitable for end users, but many application generators at the time of writing are not. As discussed in *Application Development Without Programmers* [2], application generators *can* be designed for end users and some good ones exist.

EXISTING PRODUCTS

Figure 25.1 lists some existing products of the types discussed in this book.

There is *much* software of these types on the market. Box 25.1 at the end of the chapter gives a longer list of some of the products that are available.

Not too much weight should be attached to whether a facility is listed in the "Suitable for End Users" column of Fig. 25.1 or Box 25.1. There will always be some argument about which facilities are truly suitable for end users. *Some* end users learn to employ some of the facilities on the right of Fig. 25.1 in order to obtain results faster than their overworked DP department.

EFFICIENCY

An argument often voiced *against* application generators and the other facilities of Fig. 9.1 is that they generate inefficient code and use an excessive amount of computer time. It is important to realize that this is true with some and not with others. It is an important characteristic to examine when selecting such software, but not a blanket argument against its use. *Surprisingly, perhaps, some application generators create object code which is better than the same applications programmed in COBOL or PL/1.* The reason for this is that statements in the generator language result in the use of blocks of code which have been written in assembler language and tightly optimized. These assembler blocks are better optimized than the object code which is compiled from COBOL or PL/1. On the other hand, the worst of both worlds is a generator that generates COBOL (or PL/1) source code, and this is then compiled.

Some generators also use less compile time than COBOL or PL/1. IBM's DMS (Development Management System) commonly takes a sixth of the compile time of the same functions written in COBOL. The reason for this is it generates major blocks of code *which are precompiled.*

	SUITABLE FOR END USERS*		SUITABLE FOR DP PROFESSIONALS	
		VENDOR		VENDOR
DATA-BASE QUERY LANGUAGES	QUERY-BY-EXAMPLE ON-LINE ENGLISH QWICK QWERY EASYTRIEVE ASI/INQUIRY SQL	IBM CULLINANE CACI PANSOPHIC ASI IBM	QWICK QWERY EASYTRIEVE GIS MARK IV DATATRIEVE	CACI PANSOPHIC IBM INFORMATICS DEC
INFORMATION RETRIEVAL SYSTEMS	STAIRS CAFS	IBM ICL		
REPORT GENERATORS	NOMAD QWICK QWERY EASYTRIEVE	NCSS CACI PANASOPHIC	NOMAD GIS IBM SYSTEM 34 UTILITIES RPG II RPG III ADRS MARK IV/REPORTER	NCSS IBM IBM VARIOUS IBM IBM INFORMATICS
APPLICATION GENERATORS	MAPPER RAMIS II LINK	UNIVAC MATHEMATICA INC. BURROUGHS	ADF RAMIS II DMS ADMINS II USER II ADS USE-IT	IBM MATHEMATICA INC. IBM ADMINS NORTHCOUNTY COMP. INC. CULLINANE HOS INC.
VERY HIGH-LEVEL PROGRAMMING LANGUAGES	APL (Simple functions) NOMAD (Simple functions)	VARIOUS NCSS	APL APL-PLUS ADRS NOMAD FOCUS MANTIS RAMIS II	VARIOUS STSC IBM NCSS INFORMATION BUILDERS, INC CINCON MATHEMATICA, INC

*Items are in this column if end users can learn to use them after a one-day training course. Note that what is "suitable for end users" and what is not is always open to debate.

Figure 25.1 Examples of the types of software discussed in this chapter.

451

Some generators work interpretively; some work with compiled code. As elsewhere, *compilation* can give better machine performance than interpretive operation. Compilation is desirable for repetitive operations.

Applications created for high-volume operation need to be efficient. Some application generators are designed to give efficiency with heavy-duty systems; others are designed for ad hoc operation for on-off reports or low-volume activity.

In some cases an expert on the software is needed to extract good performance from it. The expert may make an application run twice as fast by using a different data-base design. He may save more time by sorting the input or changing the operation sequence. In some cases experts on the software improve its performance by a much larger factor.

When choosing the software it is necessary to decide whether machine efficiency is a selection criterion. If its use is for a few transactions a day, machine efficiency does not matter at all. However, it is also important to use generators for heavy-duty applications as well as for low-volume ones.

ON-LINE? INTERACTIVE?

Some data-base languages are designed essentially for off-line use. The user fills in query forms, submits them to the computer center, and expects a reply in a few hours or on the following day. Some are designed for on-line use in which the user composes his query at a terminal and expects a reply in seconds or, at most, minutes. On-line use places constraints on the data-base organization in that it must be designed to give suitably fast response times. Nevertheless, on-line use can be far more effective than off-line use when the user has the capability to carry on a dialogue with the system. The system can help him to specify complex queries, and he can narrow down his search step by step until he finds the information he is looking for.

HEURISTIC SEARCHING

It is often the case that the answer to a single off-line query does not provide the information that was sought. The user needs to try a new query or adjust the previous one. Often an initial query is too broad and would result in hundreds of responses or an entire file search. Interactive operation allows the query to be modified so that it is more reasonable before the full search is executed. On some systems the user may adjust his query 20 to 30 times before he finds the information he wants.

The successive modification of queries to home in on information that is sought is sometimes referred to as *heuristic searching* of a data base.

SPONTANEITY

Executives who understand that data-base information is available to them sometimes develop many spontaneous ideas for using it. To put the data base to good use for decision

Using a conventional programming language:

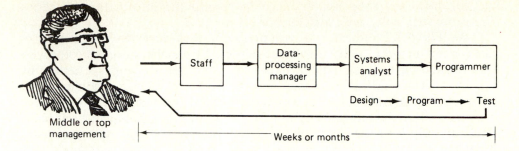

Middle or top management → Staff → Data-processing manager → Systems analyst → Programmer

Design → Program → Test

Weeks or months

Using a data-base interrogation language.

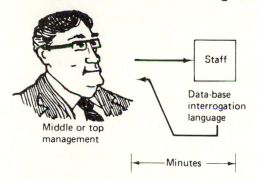

Middle or top management → Staff

Data-base interrogation language

Minutes

Figure 25.2 An executive can evaluate spontaneous ideas if he receives sufficiently fast responses to his requests for information.

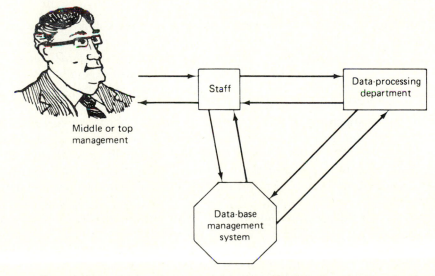

Middle or top management

Staff

Data-processing department

Data-base management system

Figure 25.3 The fact that the management staff can interrogate the data base directly takes a load off the data-processing department.

making, however, they usually need to receive the information *quickly* — tomorrow they will have a different problem.

As Fig. 25.2 indicates, a vice-president may have to wait weeks or months if a program written in a conventional language is needed to process his information request. With a data-base interrogation language usable by the information staff at terminals, he may receive the information he wants in minutes. Spontaneous ideas involving information usage are encouraged.

As indicated in Fig. 25.3, the fact that the data base can be interrogated directly by the information staff takes a load off the data-processing department.

STANDARD DATA-BASE STRUCTURE? Some end-user data-base facilities operate with standard data-base management systems such as IBM's IMS or Cullinane's IDMS. Others operate with their own special structures, often relational structures, which are separate from the organization's major production data bases.

In some cases data bases are built especially for end-user activities. These may be built by end-user departments themselves. Often they are spin-offs from an organization's major production data bases. In selecting a structure and organization for the data in such data bases the predominant concern is convenience and speed of use by end users. Often the spin-off data base has a different structure from its parent and may be built with a different data-base management system.

INFORMATION RETRIEVAL SYSTEMS Sometimes a data base is built solely for the purpose of being searched so that queries can be answered. This would be the case with *information retrieval* systems. These were originally used to store library abstracts or legal documents in such a way that users can search them rapidly to find the information they need.

After initial successes with document retrieval it became realized that *information retrieval software,* such as IBM's STAIRS, for example, was valuable for many of the types of information needed in running an organization. Some corporations load their information retrieval system periodically with data from their major production systems (which may use data bases or files).

Searching through a large amount of information in order to answer queries can take many machine cycles or disc accesses. It is desirable to find data organizations that speed up this process. Special hardware is becoming available which automates much of the searching process. An example of this is ICL's CAFS (Content Addressable File Store). Content addressing is a technique for retrieving information by its attributes and characteristics. The ICL machine searches data in 12 parallel channels simultaneously. Each channel handles data read from one disc track. Hardware units scan the data looking for field values that meet specified search criteria. When data are found that meet these criteria, they are sent through the channel to the CPU.

FORMS-ORIENTED LANGUAGES

In a common type of off-line query language the user fills in forms to indicate what he wants. Informatics' MARK IV system is of this type [3]. Figure 25.4 gives a simple example of a MARK IV query. The form that it shows can be filled in very simply and quickly and then keypunched and processed. The user employs a simple data dictionary to tell him the names of the data items he can list on his form.

MARK IV employs many different forms, including forms for defining data structures, defining transactions used to update the files, defining logical and arithmetic operations to be performed on the data items, defining in detail the layout of reports to be generated, defining tables to be used, and cataloging the processing requests.

MULTIPLE LANGUAGES

There are a relatively small number of types of data-base management systems. However, the data-base languages that use these are proliferating. Many user languages plug into IBM's IMS or Cullinane's IDMS, for example.

There is much to be said for standardizing within a corporation on one type of data-base management system for the major DP applications. An organization might adopt CODASYL, IBM's DL/1, or some other form of data-base *schema* representation as its internal standard. However, although a standard data-base management system is desirable, all manner of different end-user data-base languages may profitably employ it. The data-base language software is usually loaded and scheduled as though it were an application program. Different types of end users need different types of languages. Some of the interesting forms of data-base user dialogues come from independent software houses rather than large manufacturers, and this represents a major business opportunity for software houses in the future. Craftsmanship and ingenuity in dialogue design may be more likely to come from talented independents than from major manufacturers.

There are various data-base user languages that plug into IBM's DL/1, or IMS data bases. Mark IV in Fig. 25.4 is one of them. Another is GIS/2 (Generalized Information System) [4]. Both are intended primarily for off-line operation, although GIS is often used from terminals. Some data-base languages are intended primarily for use at terminals, for example ASI's INQUIRE using DL/1 or IMS.

MARK IV, produced by Informatics Inc., is a data-base management system which permits information requests to be specified very quickly by filling in forms. MARK IV can handle complex data bases using the DL/I language, and process complex information requests. The following is a simple illustration.

An accountant has received a request from his boss for the total year-to-date activity on one vendor's account. Taking an Information Request form, the accountant writes in a Request Name. Any name that fits ① . He writes TODAY in the Report Date box (to get *today's* date on the report) ② .

No other information is required in the heading area of the form. MARK IV provides automatic default conditions for everything left blank. In this example, MARK IV will produce a detail report, single spaced, on standard 8½" by 11" paper.

To be able to request information from a file of data, the file has been defined previously to MARK IV. The file definition provides the accountant with the names of the pieces of data which make up the file. Other qualities of the data, such as size, are also provided. MARK IV stores this definition, and a printed glossary of the names is available any time for any users of the file.

Therefore, when the accountant wants to refer to the data in the file, he just looks at the glossary for the Accounts Payable file and uses the names that were assigned to the pieces of data in the file. For instance, the piece of data which is the vendor number is called VENDOR, and since the vendor in which he is in-

terested is ABC Manufacturing (vendor number 2386), he "selects" that vendor by writing VENDOR EQ (equal) D (for Decimal) 2386 in the Record Selection area of the form. When looking at the Accounts Payable file, MARK IV will pick out only the data about vendor number 2386 ③ .

And, since only activity for 1972 is of concern, the accountant writes A (for And) INVYEAR EQ D 72 to select only the activity concerning ABC Manufacturing Company that has taken place in 1972 ④ .

If no such special selection criteria are required, then the Record Selection portion of the form is left blank. The default condition for this is that MARK IV will report on the total contents of the file.

Now that the accountant has specified the selection criteria, he can specify the data he wants to see on the report itself. He wants to see the vendor's invoice number, invoice date, invoice amount, check number, check date and amount paid. He writes the names for those pieces of data, one to a line and in the sequence he wants them to appear across the report, in the Report Specification section of the form ⑤ .

To get a total of the activity being reported, the accountant simply enters a G (for Grand) in the column marked Total on the same lines as INV–AMT and AMT–PAID. MARK IV will provide a grand total of all the INV–AMTs and AMT–PAIDs in the report ⑥ .

Finally, to give a meaningful title to his report, the accountant writes his own title in the section of the form labeled TITLE ⑦ .

④

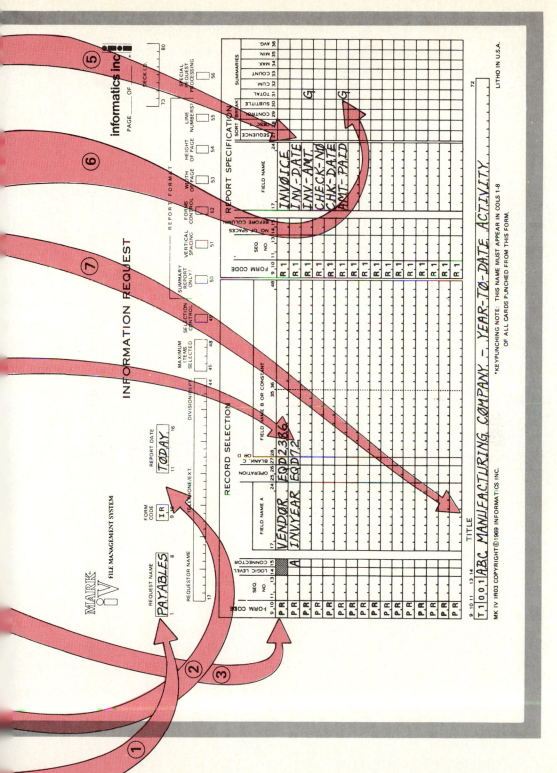

Figure 25.4 The MARK IV Information Request Form.

457

The accountant will give his filled out Information Request form to someone in the data processing organization who will have the form keypunched, put it on the computer, and deliver the resulting report as soon as it is available.

The report produced by this request is shown below:

```
04/28/72    ABC MANUFACTURING COMPANY - YEAR-TO-DATE ACTIVITY       PAGE 1
------------------------------------------------------------------------------
           INVOICE   INVOICE   INVOICE    CHECK    CHECK     AMOUNT
           NUMBER    DATE      AMOUNT     NUMBER   DATE      PAID
------------------------------------------------------------------------------
           51-03917  01/12/72       3.47  002571   02/15/72       3.47
           51-07242  01/14/72      60.43  002571   02/15/72      60.43
           51-11275  01/21/72     152.40  002571   02/15/72     152.40
           51-12336  01/27/72     104.53  002571   02/15/72     104.53
           51-14514  02/03/72      14.44  002819   03/15/72      14.44
           51-17180  02/14/72     102.42  002819   03/15/72     102.42
           51-20992  02/29/72      63.00  002819   03/15/72      63.00
           51-21541  03/02/72     189.12  002819   03/15/72     189.12
           51-23730  03/07/72      19.72  003093   04/17/72      19.72
           51-24226  03/10/72   1,092.46  003093   04/17/72   1,092.46
           51-28859  03/27/72     605.00  003093   04/17/72     605.00
           51-29331  03/31/72   5,486.00  003093   04/17/72   5,486.00
           51-31155  04/11/72      19.09
           51-33126  04/21/72     187.55
           51-34568  04/25/72      28.90

                                                              7,892.99
```

Other MARK IV forms enable the professional analyst programmer to execute more complex processing and reporting operations.

Courtesy of Informatics Inc., Canoga Park, Calif.

Figure 25.4 (Continued.)

Many data-base languages look as though they were written by programmers for programmers. Some are now beginning to emerge that are suitable for use at terminals by an end user with very little training.

DEC's DATATRIEVE language, like others, uses English-like commands. DATATRIEVE is a command interpreter that both interprets and acts on each statement received. The language is built like an extension to COBOL. It can be easily learned, but the manual [5] warns that its reader, ideally, is a programmer or data administrator.

Substantial research has been done on the psychological factors affecting an end-user data-base language, and a variety of languages have been designed in a research environment to demonstrate ease of use.

These include:

RENDEZVOUS [6]   QUEL

SQL (pronounced "Sequel")   SQUARE

INGRES [8]   CUPID [12]

QUERY-BY-EXAMPLE [9–11]   FORAL LP [13]

SEPARATE END-USER DATA BASES

All of these use *relational* data-base structures (FORAL LP uses binary relations) rather than the structures of conventional data-base management systems such as IMS, IDMS, TOTAL, and so on.

In a *relational* data base the logical structure of the data is in the form of simple two-dimensional tables [14]. These are easier to comprehend and to manipulate than the more complex structures of DL/1 data bases, CODASYL data bases, and others.

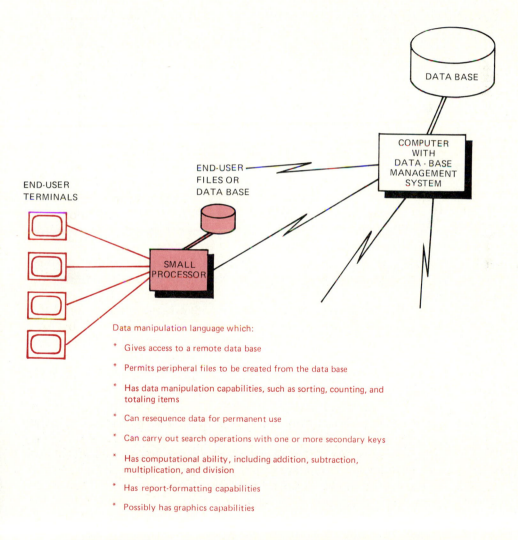

DATA BASE

COMPUTER WITH DATA - BASE MANAGEMENT SYSTEM

END-USER FILES OR DATA BASE

END-USER TERMINALS

SMALL PROCESSOR

Data manipulation language which:

* Gives access to a remote data base

* Permits peripheral files to be created from the data base

* Has data manipulation capabilities, such as sorting, counting, and totaling items

* Can resequence data for permanent use

* Can carry out search operations with one or more secondary keys

* Has computational ability, including addition, subtraction, multiplication, and division

* Has report-formatting capabilities

* Possibly has graphics capabilities

Figure 25.5 Some systems need languages that can create peripheral files from a remote data base, and allow end users to manipulate and search those files peripherally, without endangering the integrity or performance of the remote data-base system.

With distributed processing an attractive feature is the ability to create data bases for end users in a peripheral machine so that users can manipulate or search them without affecting the central data base or the workload on the central machine. The features described above may then reside in the peripheral machine, whereas the data base itself does not.

There is often concern that end users employing a data base will harm its integrity if they are allowed to modify it, and, even if not, may cause performance problems that will interfere with other processing. The performance problems may be especially severe if the users have a language that triggers *secondary-key* operations or *join* operations in a relational system.

Because of these concerns it is often good design to place the users' data manipulation activities and information systems in a peripheral computer with separate files. This separate computer handles the data manipulation language (Fig. 25.5). In some cases the peripheral computer is a small minicomputer with good data manipulation capabilities, and is relatively easy to install. Sometimes it contains a small relational data-base management system; sometimes it stores data in file rather than data-base form.

GIS

IBM's GIS (Generalized Information System) is designed for operations on a data base structured using the DL/1 data description language. The following example consists of 14 lines of GIS code. To produce the same report in COBOL would require about 250 lines of code [15].

Figure 25.6 shows a DL/1 data base and a GIS query using that data base. Suppose that a marketing manager has been conducting a new advertising campaign.

He is concerned after an intensive burst of advertising that certain warehouses may be running out of stock of product number 75438.

From the data base in Fig. 25.6 he receives monthly reports of sales and advertising expenditure. These do not tell him about the sales of the 13 days of the current month which may have been critical. He can obtain a stock status report on any product when he wants it, using a previously written inquiry program. This confirms his fear that certain warehouses may be running short. He can also check the replenishment schedule for the warehouses, and he sees that the next delivery to some warehouses is not until late next week. His staff assistant asks the data-processing manager for an urgent report showing how many days of stock are left at the current rate of sale.

The results could not be obtained sufficiently quickly using COBOL or any other conventional programming language. The GIS specialist enters the query shown in Fig. 25.6. He creates a new file, which he calls FREDFILE, and creates two new data items on it. The first, called SALERATE, shows the average rate of sale of product number 75438 over the past 13 days. The second, called DAYSLEFT, shows how many days stock are left if the item

A DL/I schema data-base description:

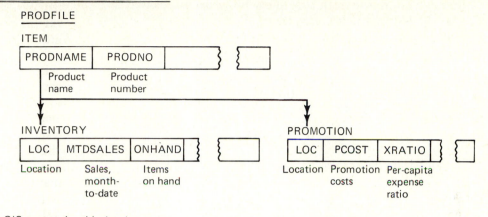

PRODFILE

ITEM

PRODNAME	PRODNO			
Product name	Product number			

INVENTORY

LOC	MTDSALES	ONHAND		
Location	Sales, month-to-date	Items on hand		

PROMOTION

LOC	PCOST	XRATIO		
Location	Promotion costs	Per-capita expense ratio		

A GIS query using this data base:

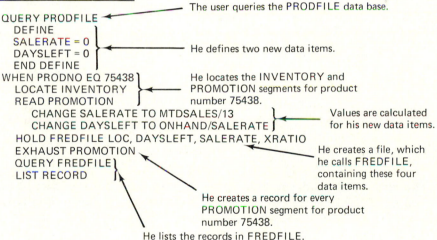

QUERY PRODFILE ← The user queries the PRODFILE data base.

    DEFINE
    SALERATE = 0 ← He defines two new data items.
    DAYSLEFT = 0
    END DEFINE
WHEN PRODNO EQ 75438
    LOCATE INVENTORY ← He locates the INVENTORY and PROMOTION segments for product number 75438.
    READ PROMOTION
        CHANGE SALERATE TO MTDSALES/13
        CHANGE DAYSLEFT TO ONHAND/SALERATE ← Values are calculated for his new data items.
    HOLD FREDFILE LOC, DAYSLEFT, SALERATE, XRATIO
    EXHAUST PROMOTION ← He creates a file, which he calls FREDFILE, containing these four data items.
    QUERY FREDFILE
    LIST RECORD

He creates a record for every PROMOTION segment for product number 75438.

He lists the records in FREDFILE.

Figure 25.6 Use of GIS.

continues to sell at that rate. The printout that results from the query in Fig. 25.6 is as follows:

LOC	DAYSLEFT	SALERATE	XRATIO
ATLANTA	3	805	4.0
BOSTON	10	512	2.7
CHICAGO	15	441	1.0
HOUSTON	20	325	0.8
MILWAUKEE	12	622	2.1
NEW YORK	3	2113	2.1
SAN FRANCISCO	25	401	0.7
ST. LOUIS	4	407	3.7

On seeing the result the GIS specialist decides to add a title to the report and sort the output to show the warehouses that are running out fastest at the top of the list. He enters:

```
QUERY PRODFILE DEPLETION REPORT FOR PRODUCT
NUMBER 75438,' PRODNAME
SORT FREDFILE DAYSLEFT
QUERY FREDFILE
LIST RECORD
```

This time he obtains the following:

DEPLETION REPORT FOR PRODUCT NUMBER 75438, BEDWARMER

LOC	DAYSLEFT	SALERATE	XRATIO
ATLANTA	3	805	4.0
NEW YORK	3	2113	4.1
ST. LOUIS	4	407	3.7
BOSTON	10	512	2.7
MILWAUKEE	12	622	2.1
CHICAGO	15	441	1.0
HOUSTON	20	325	0.8
SAN FRANCISCO	25	401	0.7

The marketing manager holds a conference and decides that some of the product should be moved from the Houston warehouse to the Atlanta warehouse, from Boston to New York, and from Chicago to St. Louis. The advertising expenditure in San Francisco is stepped up.

The GIS specialist improves his routine and his report format in anticipation of its being used again and stores it. Most decision making is rarely a one-step process. The decision maker is likely to come back with a series of refinements, a progressive reexamination of successive results. The ability to store GIS routines, report formats, and interim files and to modify them later is therefore important.*

GIS has facilities for more elaborate logical and arithmetical operations. Its output can be edited and formatted as required. The user can query many segments at once, taking different data items from each, and can create many temporary or permanent files. These files, unlike that in the example, could be very large files. It does, however, need a specialist to use it, not a casual terminal user without training.

EASY-TO-USE DATA-BASE LANGUAGES   Although languages such as GIS are easy for a programmer to use, most (but not all) end users avoid them because of their seeming difficulty. However, other query languages with equivalent data manipulation capabilities have characteristics that allow them to pass the "two-day-test" [2].

As we commented, many of the better data-base languages use *relational* data bases. Psychologists Greenblatt and Waxman [16] compared three such languages by teaching them quickly to undergraduate students and then testing their use of them. The results they achieved were as follows:

	Query-by-Example	SQL	A Relational Algebra-Based Language
Mean age of student	19.3	24.8	20.9
Mean high school average	90.8	82.8	87.4
Mean college GPA (grade A = 4.0)	3.3	3.4	2.9
Training time (hours:minutes)	1:35	1:40	2:05
Mean total exam time (minutes)	23.3	53.9	63.3
Mean correct entries (%)	75.2	72.8	67.7
Mean time per query (minutes)	0.9	2.5	3.0

The students took from $1\frac{1}{2}$ to 2 hours to learn these languages. The time to formulate a query was substantially shorter with Query-by-Example, and the accuracy slightly higher. Typical queries were of the level of complexity of the Query-by-Example query used in Chapter 3 of *Application Development Without Programmers* [2], which needed 364 lines of COBOL to program. The average time to formulate such a query was less than a minute.

QUERY-BY-EXAMPLE   It is desirable that a naive user approaching a terminal should be required to know as little as possible in order to get started. He may have to know a little more in order to use the subtleties of the language, but this also should be *minimized*.

He may approach a data base knowing very little about the names of the records or fields, or how to access them. Using Query-by-Example, I have taken a secretary who had never touched computers or terminals before, and explained in the simplest terms what a data base is. Within half an hour she was using the language, and exploring and manipulating the data stored.

The user sitting at the terminal is presented with the skeleton of a table on the screen, thus:

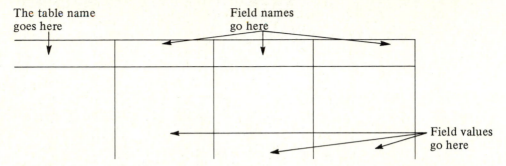

The table name
goes here

Field names
go here

Field values
go here

The user may fill in the spaces for table name, field name, or field value in order to express a query. He can also modify the data, or insert or delete new items.

P. stands for "print." If the user writes P. in one of the spaces, he wants the machine to fill in that space.

He might want to know what fields are in the EMPLOYEE record, so he types:

EMPLOYEE	P.		

The terminal may respond, increasing the number of columns as necessary:

EMPLOYEE	EMPLOYEE#	NAME	SALARY	DEPARTMENT

The SALARY field heading may not appear if the user is not authorized to see salaries.

If he wants to know what employees work in the TIN BENDING department, he types

EMPLOYEE	EMPLOYEE#	NAME	SALARY	DEPARTMENT
		P.		TIN BENDING

Their names are then listed in the NAME column.*

He may not be sure of the correct title of the TIN BENDING department, so he puts a P. in the DEPARTMENT value column:

EMPLOYEE	EMPLOYEE#	NAME	SALARY	DEPARTMENT
				P.

The terminal will then list the names of all the departments, and the user can select the one he needs.

If the user wants to know the salaries of all the employees in the TIN BENDING department, he enters two P.'s:

EMPLOYEE	EMPLOYEE#	NAME	SALARY	DEPARTMENT
		P.	P.	TIN BENDING

To obtain all the information in the EMPLOYEE record about employees in the TIN BENDING department, he can write:

EMPLOYEE	EMPLOYEE#	NAME	SALARY	DEPARTMENT
P.				TIN BENDING

The machine will then fill in the whole skeleton for the TIN BENDING department.

*The initial marketed implementation of the language did not implement all of its features.

The user may be interested in SALARY values, but he does not know which record contains salaries. He can write SALARY in the empty skeleton, and a P. in the table name position:

P.	SALARY			

It does not matter which column heading SALARY is written in. The machine displays the name of the tables, or names of several tables, which contain a field called SALARY.

Even more basic, the beginner might simply print P. in the table name position:

P.				

The machine then displays the names of *all tables that the user is allowed to see (within whatever security constraints exist).*

UNKNOWLEDGEABLE BEGINNERS It will be seen that the user can approach this dialogue from the standpoint of uncompromising ignorance. He need not even know the names of any tables or fields in the data base. Yet five minutes after first sitting at the terminal he can be making inquiries, even inquiries which would be fairly complex in other languages, such as: "List all employees with a training in cost accounting who joined the company before 1975 and are earning more than $20,000."

EMPLOYEE	EMPLOYEE#	NAME	SALARY	DEPT	YEAR OF HIRE	TRAIN-ING
P.			> 20000		< 1975	ACCOUNTING

Here he is using the operators *greater than* and *less than* (> and <). He may use any of the following inequality operators: ≠, >, >=, <, and <=. ≠ can be replaced by ⌐ or ⌐=.

The user may have more columns than he needs on the screen (especially if the width of the display exceeds the width of the screen). He may blank out some of the column headings and re-enter his request. The result omits the unwanted columns.

UPDATES

The user may be permitted to update certain fields.

The update operator is "U." If he wants to increase WEINBURG's salary to 21,000, he may type "U." and "21,000" as follows:

EMPLOYEE	EMPLOYEE#	NAME	SALARY
		FLANAGAN J E	
		SNOOK S	
U.		WEINBURG G	21000

As with any data-base user, dialogue security is important. If access to the data base is made easy, security must be made tight.

ARITHMETIC

The user can employ arithmetic operators. For example, he may want to increase WEINBURG's salary by 10%. He can do this as follows:

EMPLOYEE	EMPLOYEE#	NAME	SALARY
		WEINBURG G	20397

EMPLOYEE	EMPLOYEE#	NAME	SALARY
U.		WEINBURG G	20397 × 1.1

The machine responds by placing the updated amount in the SALARY field 22436.70.

EXAMPLES   With some of the more elaborate types of query the user gives an *example* of the results he wants. In doing so he may type a value that is not an actual value but a made-up value. He indicates that it is a made-up *example* of a value by underlining it.

To illustrate this, suppose that the user was not permitted to know WEINBURG's salary, but nevertheless wanted to update it by 10%. He would type an example of what the salary might by (e.g., 500). 500 is invented. It does not matter how far from actuality it is. The update is done as follows:

EMPLOYEE	EMPLOYEE#	NAME	SALARY
U.		WEINBURG G	500 X 1.1

The machine indicates that the salary field has been updated.

The use of examples permits many fields to be changed with one instruction. Thus everybody in the **TIN BENDING** department could be given a salary increase of $200 as follows:

EMPLOYEE	EMPLOYEE#	NAME	SALARY	DEPARTMENT
U.			500 + 200	TIN BENDING

"200" is real; it is not underlined. "500" is a guess; it is underlined.

These two types of entries, real and imaginary, can be placed anywhere in the skeleton.

Partial underlines are also permitted. For example, "WONG" or "WX" might be typed in the NAME column. This would mean that W is real, the other letters are imaginary. It would refer to all names beginning with "W." Similarly, "WENDY" is an example referring to all names beginning with "WE." If he does not know WEINBURG's initials, he might type "WEINBURG X." Similarly, "20000" means all numbers ending with "000."

MORE COMPLEX QUERIES   More complex queries are possible in which the user enters more than one row into the skeleton. The rows are linked by *examples*.

The user may have the following query: "Find the names of all employees who earn more than WEINBURG." He can guess a value for WEINBURG's salary, say 700. He than makes an entry requesting the names of employees who earn more than this value 700:

EMPLOYEE	NAME	SALARY
	WEINBURG	700
	P.	> 700

It does not matter what value is entered as the example. A user familiar with the system might enter:

EMPLOYEE	NAME	SALARY
	WEINBURG	X
	P.	> X

The user might want to ask the question: "Which employees earn more than their manager?" Using the table

EMPLOYEE	NAME	MANAGER	SALARY

the user types an example of the result that he wants—printing the names of employees who work for FRED, let us say, and earn more than 700 (also an example) when FRED earns 700:

EMPLOYEE	NAME	MANAGER	SALARY
	P.	FRED	> 700
	FRED		700

The names of employees who earn more than their manager will be printed.

The cautious user may want to check that the result is what he wanted so that he might display the salaries in question. If WEINBURG's name is in the result, he might verify it by entering.

EMPLOYEE	NAME	MANAGER	SALARY
	WEINBURG	Z	P.
	Z P.		P.

The name of WEINBURG's manager will be printed and the salaries of both of them.

The user might want to ask: "Does anyone earn more than the salaries of WEINBURG and FLANAGAN combined?" Let us imagine that WEINBURG earns 2000 and FLANAGAN earns 3000:

EMPLOYEE	NAME	MANAGER	SALARY
	WEINBURG		2000
	FLANAGAN		3000
	P.		> (2000 + 3000)

IMPLICIT AND & OR   To display all employees in the TIN BENDING department with a salary between 2000 and 3000, the skeleton is filled in as follows:

EMPLOYEE	NAME	SALARY	DEPARTMENT
	P. FRED	> 2000	TIN BENDING
	FRED	< 3000	

This request contains an AND condition:

$$(\text{SALARY} > 2000) \text{ AND } (\text{SALARY} < 3000)$$

The AND condition is implicit in the way the skeleton is filled in. Similarly, an OR condition can be implicit. For example: "Display all employees earning more than 2000 who work in either the TIN BENDING or MILLING departments":

EMPLOYEE	NAME	SALARY	DEPARTMENT
	P.	> 2000	TIN BENDING
	P.	> 2000	MILLING

LINKS BETWEEN TABLES

The query that a data user has often cannot be answered by reference to one type of record. It requires data in more than one record. With Query-by-Example it would require more than one table.

Often managers perceive their data-processing installation as being inflexible because their queries cannot be answered. The data to answer them is scattered through more than one type of record. Data-base management technology seeks to solve this problem by providing appropriate links between records. The *relational algebra* of a relational data-base system provides a powerful way of doing this [14].

The Query-by-Example user can display two or more different skeletons on the screen at once. He fills in both of them and then presses the ENTER key (or equivalent), indicating that this is one entry.

The skeletons we have shown above do not show who is the manager of the TIN BENDING department. Suppose that this information is given in a separate table, as follows:

DEPARTMENT	DEPT NAME	LOCATION	MANAGER

The user wants to know the salary of the manager of the TIN BENDING department. He enters the following query, using the example "FRED" to link the two tables:

DEPARTMENT	DEPT NAME	LOCATION	MANAGER
	TIN BENDING		FRED

EMPLOYEE	NAME	SALARY
	FRED	P.

The machine will print the salary of the manager of the TIN BENDING department.

The language is designed with the excellent principle that the thinking process the user follows is that which he would use to find the same information without a computer. Suppose that he had to answer the query with a set of printed tables. He would first look up to find who is the manager of the TIN BENDING department and then look up his salary.

Suppose that the manufacturing of a product requires operations to be done in several departments as shown in the shop floor routing record:

SHOP FLOOR ROUTING	PART#	OPERATION#	OPERATION TYPE	DEPARTMENT

One location has several departments in it, and the query must be answered: "What parts have operations performed in the location XYZ?" Using manual tables the user might look up what departments exist in the location XYZ, and then what parts have operations in those departments. With Query-by-Example he would do the same, as follows:

DEPARTMENT	DEPT NAME	LOCATION	MANAGER
	MILLING	XYZ	

SHOP ROUTING	PART#	OPERATION#	OPERATION TYPE	DEPARTMENT
	P.			MILLING

FUNCTIONS

Query-by-Example has a number of built-in functions. These are represented by mnemonics such as the following:

SUM: The sum of the values

CNT: A count of the values

AVG: The average of a set values

MAX: The maximum value

MIN: The minimum value

UN: Unique values (i.e., the values in a set excluding duplicates)

The average salary in the TIN BENDING department is found as follows:

EMPLOYEE	EMPLOYEE#	SALARY	DEPARTMENT
		P. AVG	TIN BENDING

The department whose manager has the maximum salary can be found as follows:

DEPARTMENT	DEPT NAME	MANAGER
	X P.	FRED

EMPLOYEE	NAME	SALARY
	FRED	MAX

Again the user is formulating the query in the same way that he would do it manually. He would look up the manager of each department, then look up his salary, and find the maximum salary. He could ask the machine to display the maximum salary by typing P. MAX in the salary column.

The user is not completely free of mnemonics because of the functions above. However, a beginner does need them. To avoid the need to remember mnemonics, the functions could be on specially labeled keys.

USE OF A CONDITION BOX

In addition to displaying one or more table skeletons, as described above, the user can display another two-dimensional object called a CONDITION BOX:

CONDITIONS

The user can display this condition box any time he wants. He uses it to display conditions that are difficult to express in the tables. For example, the query "Display all employees earning more than 2000 who work in either the TIN BENDING or MILLING departments" could be expressed as follows:

EMPLOYEE	NAME	SALARY	DEPARTMENT
P.	S	D	

Multiple conditions relating to one query can be listed in this way.

CONDITIONS
D = (MILLING/TIN BENDING)
S = > 2000

INSERTIONS AND DELETIONS   The Query-by-Example user can insert new entries into the tables, or delete entries (with appropriate security constraints). Insertions and deletions are done in the same style as query operations except that "I" is used instead of "P" for insertions, and "D" is used for deletions. To insert a new employee record, the user calls up the EMPLOYEE skeleton and fills it in:

EMPLOYEE	EMPLOYEE#	NAME	SALARY	MANAGER	DEPARTMENT
I.	27511	BONTEMPO C	8000	MORTON A	SYSTEMS

Similarly, an employee record can be deleted:

EMPLOYEE	EMPLOYEE#	NAME	SALARY	MANAGER	DEPARTMENT
D.	27511	BONTEMPO C	8000	MORTON A	SYSTEMS

All employees in the SYSTEMS department may be deleted as follows:

EMPLOYEE	EMPLOYEE#	NAME	SALARY	MANAGER	DEPARTMENT
D.					SYSTEMS

Similarly, the user can create a new table or add a new field to an existing table. The language permits him to create a new table from existing tables which is either a *snapshot* or a *view*. A snapshot merely contains the values of the data as they were at the time of its creation. A view is a table that will be dynamically updated to reflect changes in the base tables.

Psychologists Thomas and Gould [10] studied the behavior of subjects using Query-by-Example. They concluded that the advantages of this type of dialogue were:

- The tabular form of representation is helpful.
- The absence of keywords is helpful.
- The user has an explicit representation of the data to work with.
- The dialogue is easy for a naive beginner to learn.
- The language is "behaviorally extendable."

ON-LINE ENGLISH   It is sometimes commented that the ultimate in user-friendly dialogue would be to make the computer communicate in the user's own language. Many attempts have been made to program computers to understand English. Unfortunately, our own language is far more ambiguous than we realize. A computer can look up the words in a dictionary but still cannot resolve the ambiguities. A highly restricted version of this communication problem is the use of English to make data-base queries.

The user of data-base system may type a query in free-form English. The software scans this input to see what words it can recognize. A record or field name in the data-base dictionary may have multiple *aliases* which the user may employ to refer to it.

One such system is Cullinane's On-Line English [17], which itself has had many names. It was originally called ROBOT [18], and is sold with the name INTELLECT by the Artificial Intelligence Corporation, USA.

On-Line English queries a retrieve-only file which is created from an operational file or data base (as in Fig. 25.6 except that the user language cannot update the file). A system administrator specifies how this file is created and builds its dictionary. He can add more *aliases* to the dictionary if the users type in words that are not interpretable.

A typical query against a personal file might be:

USER: WHAT ARE THE NAMES OF ACCOUNTANTS IN NEW YORK.

TERMINAL: PRINT NAME OF ALL EMPLOYEES WITH
            CITY = NEW YORK
            AND JOB = ACCOUNTANT

The system rephrases the query so that the user can determine whether it has been correctly interpreted. It prints the number of records that must be retrieved to meet the request and then prints the answer.

TERMINAL: THE NUMBER RECORDS TO RETRIEVE IS 15
            JONES H.A.
            KENDAL C.B.
            :
            :
            :

The user may key in another question which relates to the same query.

USER: WHICH ONES EARN MORE THAN 20,000

TERMINAL: PRINT NAME OF ALL EMPLOYEES WITH
            CITY = NEW YORK
            AND JOB = ACCOUNTANT
            AND SALARY   20,000

            THE NUMBER OF RECORDS TO RETRIEVE IS 5
            JONES H.A.
            POTTER J. B.
            :
            :
            :

A vocabulary that a particular On-Line English system can use is called its *lexicon*. The lexicon contains two classes of words: those provided with the software and those entered by the administrator for this particular system. The former are called *root* words. They are words such as WHAT, WHEN, IN, COUNT, STATISTICS, ALL, HOW MANY, EVERYTHING. Every installation can use these words. The second class are words unique to a particular application, such as EMPLOYEE, TITLE, SALARY. Synonyms for these can be entered such as WORKER, PERSON, JOB, PAY.

If the software does not understand a word, it will say so:

USER: WHAT ARE THE NAMES OF ACCOUNTANTS IN POUGHKEEPSIE

TERMINAL:	I'M NOT FAMILIAR WITH THE WORD "POUGHKEEPSIE"
	IF IT'S A WORD YOU EXPECT TO FIND IN THE DATA BASE HIT THE RETURN KEY.
	OTHERWISE EITHER FIX ITS SPELLING OR ENTER A SYNONYM FOR IT.
USER:	presses the return key.
TERMINAL:	WHAT FIELD SHOULD IT APPEAR IN?
USER:	CITY
TERMINAL:	PRINT THE NAMES OF ALL EMPLOYEES WITH
	CITY = POUGHKEEPSIE
	AND JOB = ACCOUNTANT

The user may wish to see what fields are available in a given record. He could type:

USER:	WHAT FIELDS ARE IN THE CITY FILE?
TERMINAL:	

FIELDS IN THE FILE CITY

FIELD NAME	SEARCHABLE	SORTABLE	FORMAT	LENGTH
NAME	FAST	YES	ALPHABETIC	30
STATE	FAST	NO	ALPHABETIC	15
POPULATION	SLOW	YES	NUMERIC	7
:				
:				

This indicates that some fields are searchable **FAST**. This means that these fields have a search index. **SLOW** means that they do not have a search index and to find records of a given value would require a time-consuming scan of the file.

The user can sort the data on certain fields and not others.

The user can request statistics and the printing of bar graphs.

The software for On-Line English and other free English query languages (LADDER, RENDEZVOUS [6]) is complex because so many types of input wording must be interpreted.

Natural English input is attractive and fascinating to users who have not used a terminal before. It encourages them to begin. Unfortunately, it also encourages them to key in questions that the computer cannot answer. In some cases these seem to the user to be highly relevant questions. This problem is referred to in academic circles as *semantic overshoot.*

Furthermore, natural English dialogue does not impose a structure on the data as do the tabular forms of dialogue such as Query-by-Example or Univac's MAPPER. This structure is often valuable for manipulating data or

BOX 25.1 Some products of the type discussed in this chapter. This list is not intended to be complete or comprehensive. The software is changing rapidly.

Product	Query Language	Report Generator	Graphics Generator	Application Generator	High-Level Programming	Vendor	Machine Type	On-Line?	Suitable for End Users?	Data Base?
ADAM				✓		San Francisco Intelligent Machine Corp.	Own Machine			
ADMINS/11		✓	✓	✓		ADMINS Corp.	PDP/11	✓	✓	Its own files
ADPAC		✓	✓			Adpac Computer Languages Corp.	IBM		✓	
ADRS (APL-based)	✓	✓			✓	IBM	370	✓	✓	DL/1
APG	✓	✓				I.D.S.B.	DEC	✓		Its own files
APL					✓	Various	Various	✓	✓	
APL-DI		✓			✓	IBM	370	✓	✓	DL/1; IMS
APL-PLUS	✓				✓	STSC	Various	✓	✓	
ADF				✓		IBM	370/OS	✓		For IMS Applications
ASI INQUIRY	✓	✓				APP Software	370	✓		Queries IMS
ASI-ST						Applications Software Inc.	IBM			

478

(Continued)

Package					Supplier			Machine			Data base/files accessed
ASRES	✓	✓			Univ. of Georgia			360	✓		Its own files
BASIS	✓	✓			Batelle			Various	✓		Its own files
CAFS	✓				ICL Series		✓	2900	✓		Its own associative Information Retrieval system
COBOL Program Generator					Black/Prime			Prime			
COMPOSE-II	✓	✓			Compusource			Data General			Its own files
CONTEXT C-705	✓				Context System		✓	370	✓		Associative records
CS4			✓		Databaskonsult, Sweden			DEC/IBM			
DATA ANALYZER	✓	✓			Prog. Products		✓	370	✓		Its own files
DATATRIEVE-11	✓	✓	✓		DEC			PDP/11	✓	✓	DEC's files and data base
DMS	✓	✓	✓		IBM			370	✓		DL/1 CICS and its files
DMS	✓	✓			IBM			8100	✓		Its own files
DIRECT	✓	✓			Bancohio			Honeywell	✓		Its own files
Display Information Facilities	✓				IBM			S/38	✓		For S/38 DB
D.L.A.	✓	✓			E.M.I. Ltd.			Various	✓	✓	Its own files
DRS-11	✓	✓			Synoco Ltd.			DEC	✓		Its own files
EASYTRIEVE	✓	✓		✓	Pansophic			Various	✓	✓	IMS, TOTAL, ADABAS
EQUS	✓	✓			IBM			S/3, S/32	✓		Its own files.
EXTRACTO	✓	✓			Optipro Ltd.			370	✓		Its own files
FLEXTRACT	✓	✓	✓	✓	Faulkner			Various	✓		Its own files
FOCUS	✓	✓	✓		Info. Builders			370	✓	✓	Its own files
Gen. Information Systems	✓	✓		✓	IBM			370	✓		Its own DB
GENASYS					Generation Sciences			IBM			
GIS	✓	✓			IBM			Various	✓		DL/1; IMS
HARVEST	✓	✓			I.D.S.B.			DEC/IBM	✓		Its own files
IBM 3790	✓				IBM			370	✓		Its own files

BOX 25.1 (Continued)

Product	Query Language	Report Generator	Graphics Generator	Application Generator	High-Level Programming	Vendor	Machine Type	On-Line?	Suitable for End Users?	Data Base?
IBM BRADS	✓	✓		✓	✓	IBM	5110/20	✓	✓	Its own files
ICES	✓	✓				Univac	Univac	✓		Its own files
IDEA	✓	✓		✓		Data General	Data General	✓		Its own files
IDEAL	✓				✓	ADR	370	✓	✓	DATACOM / Relational data base
IIS DATA LOGGER	✓	✓				Int. Inf. Sys.	DEC	✓		Its own files
IMDOC	✓	✓				M.A.G.	370	✓		Its own files
IMS FASTON	✓	✓				IBM	370	✓		IMS
INFORMAT	✓	✓				M.R.P.	NOVA	✓	✓	Its own files
IN? QUIRY	✓	✓				Informatics	370	✓		IMS and own files
INSCI	✓	✓				Information Science	Various	✓	✓	Its own files
INSYTE	✓	✓				Remote Comp.	Burroughs	✓	✓	Its own files
INTELLECT	✓					Artificial Intelligence				
IQ	✓	✓				Man. Group	Various	✓	✓	IDS, IMS, TOTAL
IRS	✓	✓				Sigma Data	370	✓		Its own files
ISA/OAS	✓	✓				ISA Corp.	370	✓		Its own files
JPLDIS	✓	✓				Univ. of Georgia	Univac	✓		Its own files
LIRS	✓	✓				Univ. of Georgia	370	✓	✓	Its own files

Product	Supplier	Machine								Data base/files
MANTIS	CINCOM	Various	✓	✓			✓			Total, DL/1 and files
MAPPER	Univac	1100	✓	✓	✓		✓			Its own files
MARK IV	Informatics	Various	✓	✓			✓	✓		DL/1
MAXIMUS	Maximus	Data General & Eclipse								
MDQS II	Honeywell	60/66	✓				✓			Its own files
MICRODATA REALITY	Microdata	Reality	✓	✓	✓		✓			Its own files
MRS	Infopac	370	✓	✓			✓			Its own files
NCR TOTAL IQL	NCR	NCR	✓	✓	✓		✓	✓		TOTAL
NOMAD	Nat. C.S.S.	N.C.S.S.	✓	✓			✓	✓		Its own relational DB
OADS	Cullinane	Various	✓	✓		✓	✓	✓		IDMS
ON-LINE ENGLISH	Cullinane	370	✓				✓			IDMS and its own files
ORACLE	Distribution Man. Systems	PDP11	✓	✓			✓			Its own files
PRO	Business EDP Services	Burroughs	✓				✓			Its own files
QL SEARCH	QL Systems	370	✓	✓			✓			Its own files
QUERY-BY-EXAMPLE	IBM	370/4300	✓	✓			✓			Its own relational D/B
QUERY 5/3	IBM	S/3	✓	✓						S/3 files
QWICK QUERY	CACI	Various	✓	✓			✓			Its own files
RAMIS II	Mathematica	370	✓	✓		✓	✓			Its own DB
RECALL	Data Man.	370	✓	✓			✓			Its own files
REQUEST	SY. Automation	Various	✓	✓			✓			Its own files
ROBOT	Artificial Intelligence	IBM, Honeywell					✓			
RPG II	IBM	Various	✓				✓			Conventional files

(Continued)

BOX 25.1 *(Continued)*

Product	Query Language	Report Generator	Graphics Generator	Application Generator	High-Level Programming	Vendor	Machine Type	On-Line?	Suitable for End Users?	Data Base?
RPG III	✓	✓			✓	IBM	S/38	✓		For S/38 files and DB
S/34 UTILITIES	✓	✓			✓	IBM	S/34	✓		Uses S/34 files
S/38 DBMS					✓	IBM	S/38	✓		For S/38 DB
SL/1		✓		✓		Thorne	370	✓		Defines its own files
SQL	✓					IBM	370	✓	✓	Its own relational DB
STAIRS	✓					IBM	Various	✓	✓	Its own information
SYS/38 QUERY	✓	✓				IBM	S/38	✓	✓	Its own DB
T-ASK	✓	✓				Cincom	370	✓	✓	TOTAL
TCS/1700	✓	✓				Ded. Systems	Burroughs	✓	✓	Its own files
UCC/FCS	✓	✓	✓			U.C.C. Corp.	Various		✓	Its own files
USER/11		✓	✓	✓		Northcounty	PDP/11	✓	✓	Uses its own DB
WORK TEN						National Computing Industries	IBM			

generating reports. Learning more structured dialogues sometimes helps users to compose complex queries which they may not otherwise have thought of. Learning the semantics of more artificial dialogues assists users to clarify their thinking about manipulating the data. Seeing the menus of a viewdata-like dialogue helps the user to find his way through a complex mass of data. These dialogue structures help the user to navigate, tell him what is available, and prod him into taking useful action.

The user community needs both structured dialogues and natural English dialogues. *It may in the future be desirable to have end-user systems that combine the two.*

REFERENCES

1. James Martin, *Fourth-Generation Languages,* Technical Report, SAVANT, 2 New Street, Carnforth, Lancs, UK, 1983.

2. James Martin, *Application Development Without Programmers,* Prentice-Hall, Inc., Englewood Cliffs, NJ, 1982.

3. Manuals and information on MARK IV File Management System are available from Informatics Inc., 21850 Vanowen Street, Canoga Park, CA 91303.

4. Manuals and information on GIS are available from IBM Corporation, 1133 Westchester Avenue, White Plains, NY 10604.

5. Manuals and information on DATATRIEVE-11 are available from Digital Equipment Corporation, Maynard, MA 01754.

6. E. F. Codd, "How About Recently?" (English dialogue with RENDE-VOUS Version I), in B. Schneiderman, ed., *Databases: Improving Usability and Responsiveness,* Academic Press, New York, 1978.

7. Manuals and information on SQL are available from IBM Corporation, 1133 Westchester Avenue, White Plains, NY 10604.

8. C. D. Held, M. R. Stonebraker, and E. Wong, "INGRES: A Relational Data Base System," *Proc. National Computer Conference,* 1975.

9. M. M. Zloof, "Query-by-Example: A Data Base Language," *IBM Systems Journal,* No. 4, 1977.

10. J. C. Thomas and J. D. Gould, "A Psychological Study of Query-by-Example," *Proc. National Computer Conference 44,* 1975, pp. 439–445.

11. M. M. Zloof, *Query-by-Example: A Data Base Management Language,* IBM Research Report available from the author, IBM Thomas Watson Research Center, Yorktown Heights, NY 10598.

12. N. McDonald and M. Stonebraker, "CUPID, the Friendly Query Language," Proc. ACM Pacific Conference, San Francisco, 1975.

13. M. E. Senko, "Diam II and FORAL LP: Making Pointed Queries with Light Pen," *Proc. IFIP Congress 1977,* North-Holland Publishing Company, Amsterdam, 1977.

14. Relational data bases are explained in the author's *Computer Data-Base Organization,* 2nd ed., Prentice-Hall, Inc., Englewood Cliffs, NJ, 1977.

15. This example is taken from an IBM slide presentation on GIS/VS No. V20–0480, November 1973.

16. D. Greenblatt and J. Waxman, "A Study of Three Database Query Languages," in B. Schneideman, ed., *Databases: Improving Usability and Responsiveness,* Academic Press, New York, 1978.

17. Manuals on IQS (also called INTELLECT and On-Line English) available from Cullinane Database Systems, 400 Blue Hill Drive, Westwood, MA 02040.

18. L. R. Harris, "User Oriented Data Base Query with the ROBOT Natural Language Query System," *International Journal of Man–Machine Studies,* Vol. 9, 1977.

26 SEPARATE END-USER SYSTEMS

Small computers and storage are continuing to drop in cost so that it is economical for end-user departments to have their own computer and store their own data.

CENTRALIZATION VERSUS DECENTRALIZATION

It is desirable to look at the properties of data that lead naturally to local storage, or conversely to centralized storage. These are listed in Box 26.1. Even if the cost of storage dropped to zero, there would be certain data which, by their nature, ought to be stored centrally. For example, data that are being continually updated from many locations ought to be maintained at *one* location. This is done with reservation systems for airlines, hotels, and rented cars. It is done on inventory control systems, military early warning systems, and so on.

The sharing of data among multiple applications tends to lead to centralized data-base facilities. However, a large organization does not have one center of activity, but many. The computers in different factories and different offices are interconnected and may share data in a distributed fashion. Distributed data-base systems are coming into existence.

The pattern of usage and updates may determine whether data are centralized or dispersed. Figure 26.1 illustrates how different patterns lead to different placing of data. This is discussed more fully in *Strategic Data-Planning Methodologies* [1].

A predominant trend now is towards user departments employing small computers or executive work stations and keeping at least some of their own data.

USERS

UPDATES	USERS ARE IN ONE LOCATION — UP-TO-THE-SECOND INFORMATION REQUIRED	USERS ARE IN ONE LOCATION — INFORMATION PROVIDED CAN BE HOURS OLD	USERS ARE GEOGRAPHICALLY DISPERSED — UP-TO-THE-SECOND INFORMATION REQUIRED	USERS ARE GEOGRAPHICALLY DISPERSED — INFORMATION PROVIDED CAN BE HOURS OLD
INFREQUENT UPDATES — UPDATES FROM ONE SOURCE	ONE LOCATION	ONE LOCATION	DATA CAN BE DISPERSED WITH UPDATES DISTRIBUTED VIA A NETWORK	DATA CAN BE DISPERSED WITH UPDATES DISTRIBUTED BY BATCH TRANSMISSION
INFREQUENT UPDATES — UPDATES FROM GEOGRAPHICALLY DISPERSED SOURCES	DATA ARE CENTRALIZED AT THE LOCATION OF THE USERS	DATA ARE CENTRALIZED AT THE LOCATION OF THE USERS	DATA ARE CENTRALIZED, OR DISPERSED WITH UPDATES DISTRIBUTED VIA A NETWORK	DATA CAN BE DISPERSED WITH UPDATES DISTRIBUTED BY BATCH TRANSMISSION
FREQUENT UPDATES — UPDATES FROM ONE SOURCE	ONE LOCATION	ONE LOCATION	DATA ARE CENTRALIZED, OR DISPERSED WITH UPDATES DISTRIBUTED VIA A NETWORK	DATA ARE CENTRALIZED, OR DISPERSED WITH UPDATES DISTRIBUTED BY BATCH TRANSMISSION
FREQUENT UPDATES — UPDATES FROM GEOGRAPHICALLY DISPERSED SOURCES	DATA ARE CENTRALIZED AT THE LOCATION OF THE USERS	DATA ARE CENTRALIZED AT THE LOCATION OF THE USERS	DATA ARE CENTRALIZED	DATA ARE CENTRALIZED, OR DISPERSED WITH UPDATES DISTRIBUTED BY BATCH TRANSMISSION

Figure 26.1 The pattern of usage and updates may determine whether data are centralized or dispersed. A high rate of updates from dispersed sources and differently dispersed users needing up-to-the-second data is an argument for centralization.

USERS KEEPING THEIR OWN DATA   Often end users want to keep their own data for a variety of reasons.

1. They feel that they own the data and can maintain privacy. Nobody else can interfere with their data. In fact, the data can be equally private and more secure in a centralized data base (with professional security), but end users often do not perceive that.

2. They are independent of the scheduling and availability problems of the DP center.

3. They are free to develop their own applications. Often this is important because the DP center has a large application backlog and is reluctant to take on more work.

4. They can use a level of imagination and inventiveness in application development which may be lacking in the DP department. The end users understand the subtleties of their own applications and can sometimes apply a high creativity in devising the facilities they need to do a better job.

5. The user files can be simple and easy to implement.

6. Executives and staff want personal data for personal decision making.

BOX 26.1   Centralization and decentralization of data

Properties Inherent in Certain Data that Lead Naturally to Decentralization

1. The data are used at one peripheral location; they are rarely or never used at other locations. To transmit such data for storage may be unnecessarily complex and expensive.

2. The accuracy, privacy, and security of the data is a local responsibility.

3. The files are simple and are used by one or a few applications. Hence there would be little or no advantage in employing data-base software.

4. The update rate is too high for a single centralized storage system.

5. Peripheral files are searched or manipulated with an end-user language which implicitly results in inverted list or secondary-key operations. Too many end-user operations of this type can play havoc with the performance of a central system. They may be better located in a peripheral system with end users responsible for their usage and costs.

Properties Inherent in Certain Data that Lead Naturally to Centralization

1. Data are used by centralized applications such as a corporate-wide payroll, purchasing, or general accounting.

(Continued)

BOX 26.1 *(Continued)*

2. Users in all areas need access to the same data and need the current up-to-the-minute version. The data are frequently updated. Data may be centralized to avoid the problems of real-time synchronization of multiple copies with a high update level.

3. Users of the data travel among many separate locations, and it is cheaper to centralize their data than to provide a switched data network.

4. The data as a whole will be searched or *joined*. They are part of an *information system* which will provide answers to spontaneous queries from users, many of which can be answered only by examining many records. Searching or joining data that are geographically scattered is extremely time consuming. The data should be in one location.

5. A high level of security is to be maintained over the data. The protection procedures may be expensive, possibly involving a well-guarded, secure vault, and tight control of authorized users. The data are better guarded if they are in one location, with external backup copies, than if they are scattered.

   Catastrophe protection is often an argument for bicentral systems rather than for single centralized storage.

6. The data are too bulky to be stored on inexpensive peripheral storage units. The economies of scale of centralized bulk storage are desirable.

7. To make systems auditable, details are sometimes kept of what transactions updated certain data. It may be cheaper, and more secure, to dump these into a large centralized archival storage unit.

USER EXECUTIVE:

Given the problems I mentioned of conversion, given the problems of a moving target, we're wondering whether we are putting a bit too much emphasis on data base as the cure-all. Perhaps control of data base is the cure-all. Perhaps control of data can be obtained with something short of the theoretically perfect data base. On-line systems, systems that don't frustrate the users, systems that can be responsive, and allow people to be aware of something that's happening, are vital. Maybe the data do not reside in a pure form, maybe they're just in files, but they're captured and they're current, and users can employ them today.

USER INITIATIVE

On the whole the best thing that could happen in computing is for end users everywhere to take the initiative in devising their own systems. It is often only in user departments that the true computing needs are felt and can be invented.

USER EXECUTIVE:

What DP failed to comprehend was that management needed those planning reports *today*. It was absolutely urgent. It's no good producing them in one year's time. But DP was building an entire system to run against 160 cost centers. The reports could have been created quickly with RPG III or something like it. But they never were and the department managers did not get the help they needed. DP was putting so many bells and whistles on the system that it looked like it could take years.

We asked DP to help with a system that could get the planning reports out, quick and dirty, but they said that any such policy was counterstrategic. They refused to delegate any DP function. It's become like a priesthood which demands that obsolete rituals be followed. Who's surprised that department managers are setting up their own computer operation?

COMPATIBILITY OF DATA

When separate user systems are created, this needs to be done in such a way that it does not harm the use of data elsewhere in the organization.

Some end-user installations employ data that are *never* used anywhere else in the corporation. But these are exceptional. Most end users employ some data that are of value elsewhere. They use data from other data bases and create data that will be employed in other areas. Much transmission of data occurs between end-user computers and data systems elsewhere in the organization.

In such an environment it is vital that the data items have the same definition and the same bit representation in different installations. When data are passed between a user system and a data-base installation it should be compatible with that data base. The data structures employed in the user systems should be treated as views of data which are included in the overall data modeling process. The record structures that result from the modeling should be used in the peripheral installations.

In other words, the work of the data administrator needs to be distributed. The data dictionary and the data modeling process should apply to all data in all computers in the organization (with a few exceptions such as laboratory work, where the data may be genuinely unique to that location).

This is not often the case. End-user departments in many organizations have implemented minicomputer files without regard to the data needs elsewhere in the corporation. Their programmers see only the needs of their own department, and create their own data items with their own bit structure. End users need to understand that this is harmful. The data so created cannot be used elsewhere without expensive conversion. Sometimes no conversion is possible because the data items are defined differently. Furthermore, the programmers fail to extract data that would be useful from data bases elsewhere.

The end result of totally uncontrolled application development by users is data chaos, with the same data being represented in all manner of different ways in different departments.

The data administrator should help the end users in setting up their own data resources, and he needs their cooperation.

One of the most critical decisions in the planning of data processing is what activities should be centralized and what decentralized [2]. What should be done in a central DP department and what in end-user departments? A valuable pattern that is emerging is some end users exhibiting a high level of initiative and creativity in establishing their own systems, but this being done within a controlled framework which is centrally established. A good DP department should help end users to establish facilities, when they want to, which fit into the corporate networks and corporate data modeling.

SEPARATE DATA ENTRY

Many corporations have moved the data entry process from centralized keypunching areas to the end-user departments. The end users are made responsible for the entry of their own data, and for its accuracy. When mistakes are found, they must correct them.

This change has resulted in a major improvement in the accuracy of the data. When users are responsible for their own data, they are more careful.

The data being entered may reside in end-user computers or remote, shared computers. Either way the data need to be incorporated in the overall modeling process.

MINICOMPUTER DATA BASES

DP EXECUTIVE:

Our tape systems have to be very efficient in terms of file structure because of the magnitude of the files that we've got, the size of the files, volume of customers, and so on that we're dealing with.

> As we process the tapes we capture certain information and that then becomes the input to the Microdata systems. It goes into entirely separate data bases on separate machines—informational systems which are small and specialized and easy to handle.

In the early days of end-user minicomputers, these machines kept *files*, not *data bases*. Data bases originally needed the software of large computers. Now data-base management is becoming available on small computers. (Caution is needed because some small computer vendors who do not have a data-base management system falsely refer to their on-line *file* storage capability *as data base* in their sales literature.)

When end-user *file* records are designed, these records should be one of the user views in the overall modeling process. The data administrator should advise the users about the grouping of data items into records. When end-user *data bases* are used, these and the central data bases should be designed with a common modeling process.

Various problems with accuracy and conformity of updating can occur when replicated data exist at more than one location. The data administrator should establish the rules that avoid these problems.

SEPARATE INFORMATION SYSTEMS

In the 1970s most data were accessed by means of a *primary key* such as Customer Number, Job Number, Passenger Name and Flight, and so on. Increasingly, *secondary keys* came into use so that data could be accessed by more than one key. For example, jobs could be accessed by specifying which customer they were for, as well as by job number. Data bases could be queried to "List all surgical patients under 30 in the last year who have gone into coma."

The more we employ higher-level data-base languages, the more secondary-key operations, as opposed to primary-key operations, will be initiated.

We stressed earlier that this can give performance problems. Response time on some systems is poor for queries involving secondary-key actions. Response time, and often availability of systems as perceived by the terminal user, is affected by the job scheduling. Where many different types of activities take place on the same machine, scheduling becomes complex. Changes in schedules are made frequently and these sometimes affect the end user adversely. With complex queries (and sometimes less complex ones) he can perceive a sudden drop in response time from 3 seconds, say, to 30 seconds or sometimes much longer. This is extremely frustrating for the user.

This is a problem both with large computers and minicomputers. The terminal user response time on a minicomputer can suddenly go to pieces when the machine is doing compilations, sorts, and so on.

Conversely, the data-processing manager is often concerned that much high-level data-base query usage will play havoc with the performance of the system's other activities.

This is a problem of too much complexity in a single machine. The solution is to remove some of the activity into separate cheap machines. In particular, the data structures for a high level of secondary-key usage should usually not be mixed up with the data structures for production runs.

DP EXECUTIVE:

The operational needs of some of our operating departments to get data into the system, get the data we have updated, and get it accurate tend to be very high volume and need performance-oriented systems. Those are the types of data bases, if you will, that we want to keep very simple and straightforward for quick access and quick response.

However, for informational needs, for examining trends, or analyzing the data that we have, we will increasingly be spinning off data. Perhaps samples of data, not the entire data base. We put it into an environment where people can manipulate the data, even have their own copy, but not affect basic operating data that we need to run the corporation.

TOO-RAPID GROWTH

What has often happened in practice is that a centralized service has been introduced for end users which is suddenly perceived by them to be very useful. They then increase their utilization of service until the load on the central computer becomes excessive. The service then appears to degrade, giving much longer response times and sometimes being unavailable due to scheduling problems. This degradation of a service that was good is very frustrating and the users tend to be critical of the DP department.

Because of the general incompatibility of high-volume production runs and complex information system activity, it often pays to separate the information system from the production system. In some cases a minicomputer information system has been installed to provide certain types of users with specific information.

Although it may contain much of the same data, the information system should often be separate from the production system and use a separate collection of data. The reasons for the two collections of data being separate and disjointed are as follows:

1. The physical data structures used for information systems are such that it is difficult or excessively time consuming to keep the data up to date. Production systems, on the other hand, have simpler data structures which can be designed for fast updating.

2. More serious, it is very difficult to insert new data and delete old data from the information system data base except by lengthy off-line operations. Production systems have data structures into which records can easily be inserted or deleted.

3. Production systems usually have to contain the latest transactions. However, it usually does not matter if an information system gives information that is 24 hours or more out of date.

4. Production systems may handle a high throughput of transactions so that file structures permitting rapid access are necessary to cope with the volume. Information systems containing the same data usually handle a relatively small number of queries.

5. The information system may contain summary information or digested information without all the details that are in the production system.

6. End users employing an information system may want freedom from the constraints placed on machine usage by the management of a high-volume production-oriented system.

7. Powerful languages for end-user information systems are becoming available, but management of the production system does not want end users to have free access to the production data with these languages. They prefer the end users to have their own files where they can do no harm.

8. Job scheduling is complex on systems handling widely different types of transactions and jobs. Changes in the scheduling or in the job mix can play havoc with response times. A flood of queries using secondary-key operations will interfere with the production runs and their deadlines.

9. DP managers responsible for production runs are reluctant to give end users too much freedom to use high-level data-base languages because they may adversely affect performance or even damage the data.

10. End users need their own information systems to tune and adjust, to meet their own varying information needs. They should keep their own data in their own information systems.

The production system is updated in real time. Often there is on-line entry at end-user locations. The information system is updated off-line, possibly each night, with files prepared by the production system. The production system files may have a high ratio of new records being inserted and old ones deleted, but this volatility can be reasonably easily accommodated. The information system is not concerned with real-time insertions and deletions because new records are inserted off-line.

Figure 26.2 illustrates this approach. The system on the left might, for example, be a sales order entry system with terminals in branch sales offices. Its files are updated in real time, and many modifications to the data have to be made in real time. New items must be inserted into the files as they arise. The files are all structured and manipulated on the basis of primary keys

PRODUCTION SYSTEM

- Complete data

- Updated continuously

- Data accessed
  by primary keys

- Simple primary-key inquiries

- Insertions and deletions are
  straightforward but must be
  handled in real time

- Complex operating system

- Often on-line data entry

- High volume of transactions

- Complex scheduling of work

- Main design criterion: **EFFICIENCY OF HIGH-
  VOLUME PROCESSING**

INFORMATION SYSTEM

- Summary data

- Updated periodically

- Data structured so that
  they can be searched using
  multiple secondary keys

- Psychologically powerful
  end-user language

- Insertions and deletions are
  complex because of the secondary
  keys, but are handled off-line in
  periodic nightly maintenance runs

- Simple control program

- Off-line updates

- Low volume of transactions

- Scheduling problems avoided

- Main design criterion: **EASE OF USE AND VALUE
  TO END USERS**

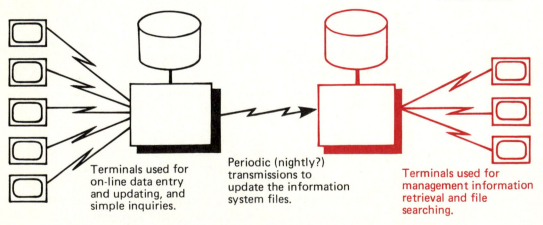

Terminals used for on-line data entry and updating, and simple inquiries.

Periodic (nightly?) transmissions to update the information system files.

Terminals used for management information retrieval and file searching.

Figure 26.2 Information systems should often be separate from production systems even though they contain much the same data, because the characteristics of their data structure and usage are fundamentally different.

such as PART-NUMBER and CUSTOMER-NUMBER. Although the files are volatile, a fairly straightforward technique can be devised for handling insertions and deletions.

The system on the right on Fig. 26.2 is designed to provide information to end users. It provides powerful end-user query languages. End users may also keep and modify their own files in it. To answer a diverse set of such queries spontaneously, the system uses special index or pointer structures. Inserting new records with these structures is complicated and time consuming because the secondary indices or pointer structures must be updated. It is therefore done off-line when the terminals are not in use. The data for the off-line updating are transmitted by the system on the left-hand side of Fig. 26.2 If this technique were not used, the volatility would be very difficult to handle.

The production system handles a high volume of transactions. A major design criterion is to maximize the efficiency of high-volume processing. Data and system structures are selected with this objective. The information system handles a very low volume of transactions compared to the production system. The design criterion is therefore not to optimize machine efficiency but to optimize the ease of use and value to the end users.

Until the late 1970s information systems tended to be centralized systems. As minicomputers became more powerful it became practical to have information systems in user departments, sometimes with very small computers.

In many cases the data stored in the information system occupy much less storage than those in the production system—they are only summary data. Therefore, a small minicomputer is appropriate. In other cases the information system storage must be very large because historical or archival data are kept.

There will be inquiries into the production system as well as the information system, but they will be mostly *primary-key* inquiries, often requesting a degree of detail that does not exist in the information system. It may be desirable that the end-user terminal connected to the information system be also linked to the production system of Fig. 26.2, or possibly to many production systems, so that managers or users can inspect detailed records of customers, bank statements, orders, and so on, when they need to.

The production system has a complex operating system, and the scheduling of jobs on it is complex. The information system may have a simple operating system or control program which handles the low volume of queries in a first-come-first-served fashion.

The main design concern with the production system is *efficiency* of high-volume operations. With the information system there is little concern with machine efficiency. The main design concerns are *effectiveness, ease of use,* and *value to end users.*

GET INVOLVED   Whatever configurations are finally used, one aspect of data processing is clear. We are leaving the age when end users could be treated as knowing nothing about it. With today's systems it is becoming increasingly important that users understand the potentials of computing in their jobs, and *become involved*.

REFERENCES

1. James Martin, *Strategic Data-Planning Methodologies,* Prentice-Hall, Inc., Englewood Cliffs, NJ, 1982.

2. James Martin, *Design and Strategy for Distributed Data Processing,* Prentice-Hall, Inc., Englewood Cliffs, NJ, 1981.

27 INFORMATION CENTER MANAGEMENT

The reader should create in his mind two vividly contrasting images of the use of computers in an enterprise. In the *first image* all application creation is done by a hardpressed DP group using COBOL, with formal systems analysis and requirements specification. Structured analysis and structured programming are used—in fact, the best of the structured software techniques. However, there is an application backlog of years, and an invisible backlog which is even greater. The users seem to be remarkably unsatisfied with the results when they get them. Top management perceives DP as a problem. End users are trying to bypass DP by obtaining their own minicomputers, but this has not been very satisfactory either.

The *second image* is one in which DP has done information analysis and data modeling throughout the enterprise and has made the data available on data-base systems. Users have terminals with which they can access these data. Some use a simple query language designed to be as user-friendly as possible. Others use a language with which they can manipulate the data, extract their own files, perform data entry, and ask "what-if?" questions. The shop floor supervisors, the expediters, the purchasing, marketing, and personnel departments all create computerized reporting and control procedures with a data-base-oriented application generator. This increases the productivity and efficiency of these departments, decreases the capital tied up in inventory, work-in-progress, and machine tools, and improves customer service. The financial staff, budget controllers, planners, and engineers create the programs they need in APL, NOMAD, FOCUS, or other high-level languages. DP operates an Information Center designed to give users the maximum help in finding the information they need, processing it or reformatting it to their requirements, and generating procedures and reports. Many DP representatives have become consultants, helpers, and instructors to the end users. Systems analysts work interactively with the end users to create their applications. Most data are on-line. Almost all users who need computing have access to terminals. The systems analysts create prototypes of applications interactively, charting complex procedures with the LAMs and DADs (see Chapters 20 to 22), which they can convert directly into code with fourth-generation languages. All such programs are based firmly on canonical data models built with computerized tools and skilled data administration. DP creates the data bases, networks, and infrastructure necessary to support this activity. End users of many types throughout the corporation are inventing how they use computers to improve their own productivity and are constantly adjusting their own applications.

The *second image* is what computing *ought* to be like. It needs support facilities creating through DP.

Today's software makes it practical for many end users to be involved with their own application generation. Whether they do it themselves or with the help of a DP specialist, it needs to be anchored firmly to stable data models and data administration controls. As discussed earlier, the existence of the data models makes application generation and procedure design much easier. The function of information centers should be to encourage and help end users to obtain the information and procedures they need, and to ensure that user-driven computing evolves within a managed framework. The primary focus of this managed framework should be the data models.

THE NEED FOR MANAGEMENT

The reasons we need to manage and control user-driven computing are as follows:

- To ensure that data entered or maintained by users are employed to their full potential rather than being in isolated personal electronic filing cabinets.
- To assist the users in attaining applications as efficiently as possible.
- To encourage the rapid spread of user-driven computing.
- To ensure that adequate accuracy controls on data are used.
- To avoid unnecessary redundancy in application creation.
- To avoid integrity problems caused by multiple updating of data.
- To ensure that the systems built are auditable and secure, where necessary.
- To link the end-user activities into the data models.

The Information Center concept is intended to provide management and support for user-driven computing.

The overriding objective of Information Center management is to speed up greatly the creation of applications that end users require. The queue for conventional development, with its long application backlog, is *bypassed*.

One DP department was required to calculate the return on investment of all DP-developed applications. The average was 37% with an average pay-back period of 30 months. This same DP department created an Information Center. This gave 100% return on investment [1]. A vice-president of the company made the following quote:

VICE-PRESIDENT:

The Information Center is our single most important productivity tool.

Sometimes Class III data bases are used, more often Class IV. Most information centers support the concept of end users developing their own applications. Some additionally use systems analysts to develop applications working in conjunction with end users, but without employing programmers or writing program specifications. In some cases programmers of fourth-generation languages work in the Information Center.

The Information Center concept should support a natural division of labor between the end users and DP staff. Each group provides what it is best equipped for. The end users know what information, reports, and decision support they need in order to do their jobs well, and usually they need results quickly. The DP support group know how these results can be obtained. The two groups work together in close partnership, balancing their resources for maximum productivity. To achieve this result the end users must be trained, encouraged, motivated, and their competence developed to a point where they can generate and manipulate the reports that they need, and perform calculations, answer "what if?" questions, perform simulations, and so on. In some cases end users have created major operations systems.

EXECUTIVE'S WORKBENCH
The terminal installed for an end user by the Information Center provides a variety of services. It has been described by the terms *executive workbench, professional workbench,* or *administrative workbench.*

Like a carpenter's workbench, the *administrative workbench* provides a set of well-organized tools. These assist the professional, manager, or their staffs to manipulate data or carry out activities such as those shown in Fig. 27.1. Display terminals are used, sometimes with color and sometimes with graphics capability.

Information Centers differ greatly in the amount of data they make available to users. Some extract data from production systems and make these available for user manipulation and decision-support activities. Some merely support the user's own data input for his own applications. Others operate major general-purpose information retrieval systems to which new data can be added whenever they are requested.

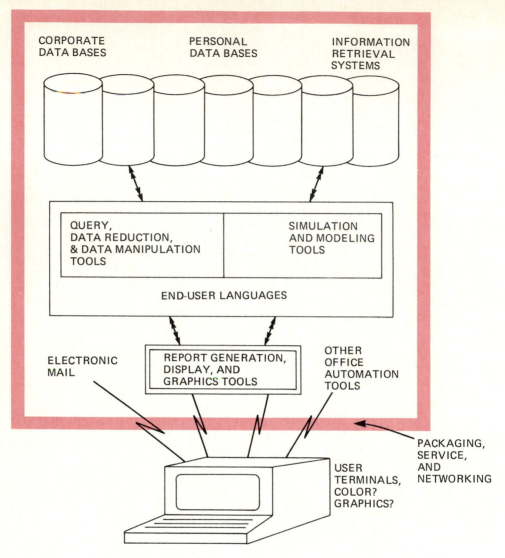

Figure 27.1 Executive/professional workbench.

Office automation (the office-of-the-future) facilities are spreading rapidly in some organizations, providing mailbox facilities, automated in-basket processing, and other services. These ought to be linked with the Information Center service. The office-of-the-future and Information Center concepts are becoming closely integrated in some organizations. Most office-of-the-future services should be regarded as additional tools for the administrative or professional workbench. Figure 27.1 illustrates the administrative workbench concept.

A particularly important facility in an executive workbench is the capability for the executive to create and adjust his own control mechanisms.

VIRTUAL FILING CABINET

In some cases the data accessible by users is perceived as though it were in an electronic filing cabinet to which they have personal access.

They have several types of reports in their *virtual filing cabinet*. They can specify the type of data they want to see, what calculations should be done on them, and how they should be sorted and presented. They may ask to see data only when they exceed certain parameters. They can determine when "exceptions" should be brought to their notice.

In some cases the data in the users' virtual filing cabinets will be derived from the master data bases (or files) which are used for the main production processes. In some cases the users will create their own personal files. Often the users will enter and maintain data that are important to their area. These data, with appropriate security, audit, and accuracy checks, are moved across to the central master data bases.

The users can transmit data from their virtual filing cabinets to other users. They can generate reports that highlight important information, and have these printed if necessary.

The concept of users' virtual filing cabinets combined with computing and report generation capability is powerful. In IBM's Yorktown Heights research laboratory this approach led to an *increase of 1300% in computer utilization* by managers and professionals, *with no system development department help* since all projects were handled by the users. A small, highly skilled support group helped the users and spread the usage of packaged tools.

In a much more spectacular example end users on the Santa Fe railroad created their own *operations* system to avoid paperwork and speed up railroad operations. This system grew until it processed more than $2\frac{1}{2}$ million transactions a day from more than 2000 terminals throughout the railroad. It had a major effect on the profitability of the railroad, allowing it to double the freight it carried without an increase in administrative staff. It permitted many changes in railroad operations and experiments in train and container usage, because the users could adapt the computer system quickly to reflect the changes.

Some DP executives and analysts are skeptical about this Santa Fe system until they see it in operation and investigate how it was created. It is a truly impressive computer system. Its development methods are now being emulated elsewhere.

INFORMATION CENTER SUPPORT

In many organizations DP executives have tried to keep end users from developing their own applications. In other organizations they have allowed it to happen, only too glad to get some of the end users off their backs. End-user development is a force that should be harnessed, encouraged, and supported to the full, but if it happens in an *uncontrolled* fashion it can store up trouble for the future because multiple versions of incompatible data come into existence, and multiple machines cannot be interlinked.

The Information Center staff should be aware of what data bases exist and sometimes sets up other data bases. It makes this information available for end users, to access and manipulate. Information Center consultants work with the end users. The consultants help users to create the decision support systems, personal computing facilities, information retrieval systems, and organizational support systems. A major reason for establishing this mode of operation has been the extreme dissatisfaction expressed by end users about the way DP has been responding to their information needs.

The consultants encourage users to employ the information facilities that already exist. They sit at terminals with the users to create the catalogued query procedures, report generation routines, or graphics generation routines. They train the users to employ these facilities.

Where more complex applications are needed, the Information Center consultants decide how they can be created, selecting, where possible, an application generator, language, or package which avoids the formal, slow, programming development cycle.

CONNECTION TO DATA ADMINISTRATION

Some Information Centers have been developed without any link to the data administration process. This is clearly disadvantageous. It is better to regard the provision of an information center as an integral part of information engineering.

The Information Center needs access, potentially, to any of the information in an organization. A center needs to comprehend fully the information resources and data models, and have access to the data dictionaries.

A well-run Information Center is in close contact with the information needs of users and management. Its knowledge of their requirements should be fed into the information analysis process.

If an Information Center is not in operation, the interviewing and involvement of senior management can seem to them like a one-way process. They make lots of statements about information needs and for a long time see no improvement in the information provided by DP. An Information Center can make this a two-way street. It can capture the types of data that management needs and make them available in Class IV data bases with good end-user languages. Providing such information to management as quickly as possible helps to clarify their real needs. The models of data become more useful and realistic.

Perhaps the biggest danger of Information Center operation, or of the spread of minicomputers and software for user-driven computing, is that multiple uncoordinated data structures will be used. The answer to this is well-controlled data administration. The data in the end users' files or Class IV data bases must be compatible, where necessary, with the data in the production data bases.

Data are often extracted from production system data bases and moved to separate Information Center data bases, as shown in Fig. 27.2. Sometimes

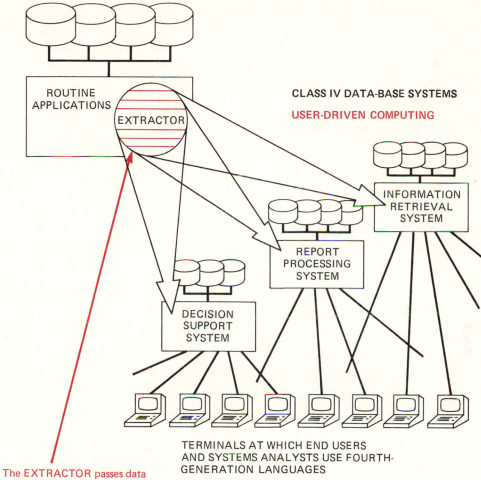

CLASS III DATA-BASE SYSTEM (or Class I or II)

**PRESPECIFIED COMPUTING
(CONVENTIONAL DEVELOPMENT CYCLE)**

ROUTINE
APPLICATIONS

EXTRACTOR

CLASS IV DATA-BASE SYSTEMS

USER-DRIVEN COMPUTING

INFORMATION
RETRIEVAL
SYSTEM

REPORT
PROCESSING
SYSTEM

DECISION
SUPPORT
SYSTEM

TERMINALS AT WHICH END USERS
AND SYSTEMS ANALYSTS USE FOURTH-
GENERATION LANGUAGES

The EXTRACTOR passes data
to the Class IV data bases.
 It works in one of the
following ways:
   1. Periodic, off-line (e.g., at night)
   2. Periodic, on-line (e.g., every hour)
   3. Operated by a trigger condition
   4. Ad hoc, or on demand
   5. Real-time

Figure 27.2 Certain data are extracted from a Class III (or I or II) system and transferred to Class IV systems.

they are moved back in the opposite direction, with suitable accuracy controls. These operations require common data administration and, ideally, the same data dictionary.

DATA COORDINATOR

If end users are given the capability to create their own files, using systems like Univac's MAPPER, for example, data-item formats and definitions should be derived from a common dictionary. Sometimes in such installations a *data coordinator* is used. This person, sometimes a specially trained end user, ensures consistency among the users' data. This data coordinator ought to report (at least for data administration purposes) to the official data administrator.

The data coordinator may have functions such as the following:

- Be aware of what data models exist and ensure that a user's data are made consistent with such models.
- Make the dictionary definitions of data available to the users.
- Where the users' data are not yet represented in data models, coordinate with the data administrator to see if the data being created can be input to the modeling process.
- Generally liaise with the data administrator about the users' data.
- Guide and encourage the users in employing data.
- Train the users.
- Move infrequently used reports or data-off-line (if this is not done automatically).
- Remove infrequently used "user views" of data.
- Establish techniques for informing users what data exist.
- Contribute to a newsletter about the systems and its available services.

CONFLICT IN SPEED OF RESULTS

There may be a conflict between the data administration process and the Information Center operation. The purpose of the Information Center is to obtain results as quickly as possible to end users. Information analysis and data modeling, on the other hand, take a long time and might delay the delivery of quick results.

Once the data models are completed and implemented, results may be obtained very quickly. Until that has been done, a compromise is often necessary. Data for a given application may be captured, possibly normalized by the Information Center analysts, and converted to the form needed by the user languages. Such data may have to be retrofitted later to the detailed models as they emerge. But the modeling process should not hold up the getting of valuable results to the users quickly.

The answer to this conflict is to get the data modeling done as soon as possible. The sooner the data models are in place, the sooner the enterprise can benefit fully from the Information Center methods.

To move rapidly into user-driven computing without data models guarantees a rapid spread of incompatible data as different users devise their own data. The mess in data will become rapidly worse.

INFORMATION CENTER ORGANIZATION

Figure 27.3 shows a type of Information Center organization which works well in some corporations. Data-processing development is split into two parts, conventional development and the information center. Both link to the data administration function, which has a vital role in standardizing the data that must pass between the two areas, and linking both areas into the information engineering processes.

The Information Center reports to the overall DP executive. Its staff consists of general consultants who work with the end users, and specialists who are expert on end-user products. These staff train and assist the end users, create applications for them, and where practicable encourage them to solve their own problems with the end-user languages.

An organization in the grip of traditional DP standards and methods can make a small beginning by initially having only a few staff using the Information Center methods. The objective should be that as the Information Center methods are demonstrated to work well, they should take over a rapidly increasing proportion of the DP development.

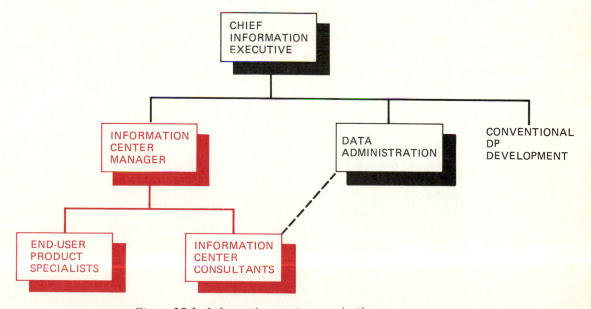

Figure 27.3 Information center organization.

The Information Center must relate closely to the data administration function, which is a vital part of conventional DP development (if it is well managed). The Information Center consultants will use the data bases, request additional data bases, and participate in all stages of the information engineering processes. The Information Center may design and operate its own data bases for decision support and information retrieval systems. The data in these will often be derived from conventional DP production-oriented data bases, and conform to the information engineering data models and data dictionary.

Sometimes an end-user application can be created partially, but not completely, with the application generators or nonprocedural languages. An important feature of these facilities is an *escape* mechanism or ability to call subroutines of conventional programming. For this purpose the Information Center may be able to call on programmers from the conventional DP group. If, however, this can be done only with a long delay because of the conventional application backlog, the Information Center may acquire some programming skill of its own.

Figure 27.4 shows a broader organization which has worked well and which is recommended.

Conventional data processing and maintenance is separated from modern technology development. Conventional DP generally refers to file systems rather than data-base systems but may include old data-base systems designed without third-normal-form data modeling. Modern technology refers to systems built with data modeling as described in this book, Class III and IV (and sometimes Class II) data-base systems, fourth-generation languages, and procedure design methods such as those described in Part IV of this book.

The name Director of Processing Systems was chosen to imply process-oriented rather than data-base-oriented design. As the information systems mature, most conventional non-data-model DP systems built with COBOL or PL/1 should be steadily replaced with modern-technology systems. Figure 27.4 shows a Director of Information Centers and a Director of Development Centers. The *information center* relates to user-driven computing. The *development center* relates to prespecified computing built with on-line development tools.

Office systems (office-of-the-future) should relate closely to Information Center systems. The Vice-President of Information Engineering in Fig. 27.4 controls both.

User departments will have systems developed for them by different groups. To avoid confusion the organization in Fig. 27.4 employs *user account representatives*. These are mature, highly paid, consultants who are assigned to specific business areas to help users obtain the systems and information they need. These representatives direct development activity to

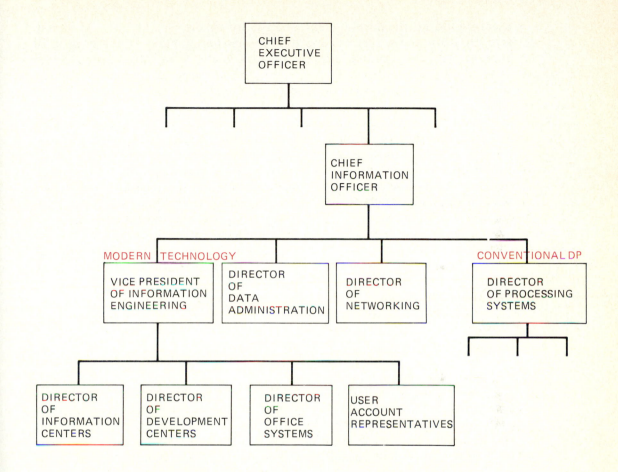

Figure 27.4 An information systems organization that has worked well.

either an Information Center, development center, office systems manager, or conventional DP. They often have to deal with problems of conventional DP systems and maintenance. Their mandate includes the general finding of solutions to user problems.

DIFFERENCES IN SCOPE   Information Centers differ greatly in their scope. Some are a small operation within a DP department, sometimes without a full-time manager. Some support *only* development by end users. Some computer vendors' proposals for Information Centers state that a basic principle is that *only* end

507

users should do the development, and the Information Center should merely give them the tools, systems and training. However, many of the most valuable Information Centers employ systems analysts or Information Center "consultants" who *do* create applications by working hand in hand with the users, but do not write program specifications for separate programmers to code. These analysts employ nonprocedural application generators or report generators which can obtain results *fast* without conventional programming. They can complete the application faster than writing programming specifications, so the traditional development cycle disappears.

Some Information Centers do no work on routine production systems, but only on ad hoc systems—information systems and decision support systems. Others are organized so that *all* application development without programmers goes via the information center (which may be called a different name). Some of the nonprocedural languages that a nonprogramming systems analyst can employ are appropriate for creating certain production systems as well as information systems, and produce suitably efficient machine code. IBM's DMS (Development Management System), for example, is used by nonprogramming analysts to create production systems.

Figure 27.5 splits application development into six categories. Some Information Centers do category 1 only. Some do categories 1 and 2. Some do categories 1 and 4, and some 1, 2, 4 and 5.

In the author's view it is desirable to support all forms of application development without programmers.

Sometimes Information Centers have been set up with the blunt insistence that the staff should do *no* application development. Often in such cases the DP department itself has used the Information Center for its own development because this is quicker than conventional techniques. This leads to another type of organization in which the Information Center provides support staff assisting both the DP department and the end users. It is gen-

	DEVELOPMENT BY END USERS ALONE	DEVELOPMENT BY SYSTEMS ANALYSTS ALONE	DEVELOPMENT BY ANALYSTS AND PROGRAMMERS
INFORMATION RETRIEVAL AND DECISION SUPPORT SYSTEMS	1	2	3
ROUTINE PROCESSING SYSTEMS	4	5	6

Figure 27.5 Some information centers support development of nonroutine systems by end users only—category 1 above. Some support categories 1 and 2 above. Some support all application development without programmers—categories 1, 2, 3, and 4.

erally better that the Information Center is separate from conventional DP so that it can fully develop the counterculture of application development by new methods. The powerful Information-Center concept will grow and evolve better if insulated from the current problems and five-brigade operations of DP.

The Information Center *should* develop applications itself so that it becomes fully familiar with the problems, and thus can better support the user development, and also because the best form of development is often users and Information Center staff working jointly on creating applications. It should, where possible, insist that users *document* their own applications, and learn how to modify (maintain) them.

The Information Center should avoid the trap of having a large number of (for example, APL) programs to maintain.

TECHNIQUES   When a demand for a new application comes up, it
ANALYST   is desirable to decide how it will be developed. Ap-
                      propriate development software should be selected.
It should be developed by the *fastest* method possible and with a procedure that will minimize future maintenance costs. This means that languages like COBOL and PL/1 should be avoided where possible.

A specialist, sometimes called a *techniques analyst* (TA) may make the decision about how a new application demand should be handled. He will know the capabilities of the different software and will decide whether the application needs conventional programming and analysis, whether it can be created by a systems analyst with an application generator such as IBM's DMS, or whether it is appropriate for end-user development perhaps with a high-level data-base language.

The techniques analyst may act as a switch, to switch an application between conventional development and Information Center development.

A major objective of the technique selection should be to avoid programming in COBOL or PL/1 wherever it can be avoided. Not only is it expensive but it results in programs that are very costly to maintain and cannot be changed quickly.

FUNCTIONS OF   Selection of the techniques or software is one of
INFORMATION   many services that should be provided by the In-
CENTER STAFF   formation Center staff. They need to train, encour-
                         age, support, and assist the end users in obtaining
the applications they need. Box 27.1 lists functions that should be carried out by the Information Center. It divides them into two groups: those performed by the analysts or consultants who work with the end users, and those performed by a technical support group or person. This follows the division shown in Fig. 27.3.

BOX 27.1 Functions that should be carried out by an Information Center

By the Consultants

- Training the users to employ the tools and create applications.
- User encouragement, education, and selling.
- Continual assistance in improving the effectiveness of end-user computing.
- Generation of applications (without programmers) in conjunction with users.
- Generation and modification of prototypes.
- Specification of changes to prototypes that may be needed to make them into working systems.
- Assistance with maintenance changes.
- Consulting on user problems.
- Debug support when something goes wrong.
- Determining whether a proposed application is suitable for Information Center development, and selecting the software and methods.
- Demonstrations of Information Center capabilities to users, including senior management.
- General communication with senior management.
- Communication with traditional DP development.
- Ensuring that the data used conform to the corporate data models.
- Close links to the data administrator(s) in defining and representing data, and evolution, if necessary, of the data models.
- Providing input to the various stages of information engineering.
- Maintaining a catalog of available applications and data bases.
- Coordination to prevent duplicate or redundant application development.
- Creating Class IV data bases, and initiating the *extraction* of data into information-retrieval facilities.
- Assisting the user in locating the data he needs. Arranging to have data converted where this is necessary.
- Assisting the user in obtaining authorization to access the required data.
- Conducting user-group meeting for users to interchange experience, and workshops to develop proficiency in better techniques and user self-sufficiency.

BOX 27.1 *(Continued)*

- Administrative assistance to help users obtain a terminal, ID, password, workspace, and so on.
- Operation of schemes for motivating users.
- Tracking the benefits to the organization.
- Promoting the Information Center facilities and benefits at all levels in the organization.

By the Technical Specialists

- System setup and support.
- Dealing with technical and software problems.
- Selection of languages and software and the versions of those which are used.
- Ongoing evaluation of software products that might be used, and their possible applications.
- Assistance in choosing techniques or software for a given application (the job of the techniques analyst).
- Selection of hardware where departmental minicomputers or microcomputers are used.
- Communication with vendors.
- Monitoring system usage, and planning future resources.
- Charge-back to users.
- Tuning or reorganizing an application for better machine performance.
- Auditing system usage and application quality.
- Ensuring that the users have the terminal they want and appropriate network access.
- Providing backup, recovery, and archiving. End-user data on peripheral systems can be included in the overall backup and recovery plan.

The size of the Information Center staff varies greatly depending on the number of users supported and whether the consultants *develop* the applications along with the users or insist that users do their own development.

Some corporations have started an Information Center with a low-level commitment and allowed it to grow. In some small operations the staff carry out all the support functions in Box 27.1; there is no division into technical and consultant staff as in Fig. 27.3. The staff play a role which is similar to that of an IBM systems engineer.

One large bank started this operation with a manager, assistant manager, two professional staff members, and a clerical coordinator. The manager was an enthusiast of the software used, had a technical background, and was chosen because he wanted to do the job. The assistant manager was an ex-operations shift supervisor with no programming or systems background. It was argued that he was going to guide users who also had no technical background, so it would be an advantage for him to have gone through the learning process relatively recently.

This Information Center (which is called by a different name) is a low-key operation with a low budget compared to the bank's overall DP budget. In other cases a much more aggressive move has been made into this form of operation with a tough executive heading it who believes that a high proportion of new application development can be done with techniques that by-pass conventional DP programming and analysis.

SELLING

The more aggressive Information Centers regard *selling* the new capabilities to end users to be of primary importance so that advanced technology can make a more rapid penetration.

In the bank mentioned above there is a department that is responsible for the services which the bank provides to its customers: a payroll service, a check reconciliation service, and so on. The bank put its Information Center in this department, arguing that people who were good at selling and supporting computer services outside the bank could also do it inside the bank. The manager of the department had experience in dealing with dissatisfied and disgruntled customers, and these talents were useful to the Information Center.

RIVALRY

Sometimes harmful political rivalry has grown up between the management of the Information Center and the management of conventional DP development. The manager of the Information Center naturally wants to satisfy as many user demands as possible and remove them from the slow conventional DP cycle. In some cases he assumes a missionary fervor about doing this. He sees conventional development as being cumbersome, expensive, and obsolete. He makes his views known about this and gains many disciples among previously frustrated end users. He advocates that instead of doing expensive maintenance on conventional programs, these should be scrapped and redeveloped with the Information Center methods where possible.

The manager of conventional development may feel attacked and in danger of losing his empire. His rival running the Information Center appears like a hero, and he does not. He may argue against the new methods. Great opposition is sometimes encountered to the setting up of, or expansion of, Information Center operation. Box 27.2 lists some of the reasons given by the opposition. Most of these are invalid compared with the major gains in productivity that can be achieved.

The solution to the rivalry lies in good overall DP management by an executive to whom both the Information Center manager and the manager

BOX 27.2 Great opposition is frequently encountered to application development without conventional programming. Reasons for the opposition are listed below. Most such reasons are invalid compared with the major gains in productivity that can be achieved.

- Programmers, systems analysts and DP managers want to continue to practice what they are good at. They are afraid that skills so laboriously acquired will be devalued.

- Conservative DP staff refuse to believe that the new methods really work.

- Seminar firms are making much money from teaching structured programming and structured analysis.

- The DP standards manual or corporate DP development "Bible" advocates conventional methods.

- A sentiment exists against "pioneering." Pioneers get killed a lot.

- There is a desire or a directive to avoid language proliferation.

- The new facilities cannot create every type of application, whereas conventional programming can.

- DP managers perceive application creation by end users as an erosion of their authority.

- Application creation by end-user groups is perceived as a formula for chaos.

- There is sometimes an anti-data-base sentiment and many of the new facilities are data-base oriented.

- Most of the new languages and facilities are not manufacturer independent.

- The new facility exists on a minicomputer or mainframe from a vendor ruled out by the corporate network strategy, or an IBM-only strategy.

- The perception exists that these facilities give much worse machine performance (not necessarily true or relevant).

- Programmers, or analysts, fearful for their jobs, manage to debunk the new facilities or methods.

of conventional DP report. The manager of conventional DP should be encouraged to use new software techniques also, and challenged to demonstrate how productivity can be increased and maintenance costs cut by combining the techniques of information engineering with the use of fourth-generation languages.

Often the manager of conventional development perceives that all *routine* operations are his territory and that the Information Center should be used only for ad hoc development such as decision support systems. The argument against this is that some case histories show successful and spectacular development of routine, transaction-driven production systems by end users. We mentioned the Santa Fe railroad, for example, where a vast system for routine operations was created entirely by end users. This system now processes more than $2\frac{1}{2}$ million transactions per day, and is constantly adjusted by the end users to improve it and adapt it to changing needs. About 1000 end users have been trained to develop or modify the applications.

A better division of responsibilities is to say that the Information Center will encourage and support all types of user-driven development that makes sense (and some does not); conventional development will support all development that involves the need for DP programmers using COBOL, PL/1, and new languages for DP programmers such as IBM's ADF, CINCOM's MANTIS, ADR's IDEAL, and HOS's USE-IT.

Because they serve the same community, often with the same data bases, it is vital that Information Center management, conventional development management, and maintenance management work closely together, and explore the most cost-effective trade-offs.

LANGUAGES SUPPORTED

Information Centers differ widely in their choice and range of languages.

Some support only one software package, such as IBM's VSPC (Virtual Storage Personal Computing) or Univac's MAPPER.

Given the *widely* varying capabilities of the software it is usually preferable, when the center becomes well established, to support more than one type of software.

What makes the Information Center possible is the software that it uses. What can make it excellent is a good choice of software.

An Information Center at the Equitable Insurance Company in New York employs the following software [2]:

● Languages to build systems:	FOCUS RAMIS	English-like languages used by managers and professionals
● Languages used for model building:	APL ADRS	(A Programming Language) (An APL report generator)

- Statistical packages: SAS   These contain many formulas
  -          SPSS   for statistical analysis

- Language for financial   FPS   (Financial Planning System)
  analysis:

- Language for querying,   QBE   (An easy-to-use query language)
  manipulating, and selecting ADI   (Giving APL programs access to
  data: data bases)
  -                        FOCUS
  -                        RAMIS

- Packages for preparing   SAS-graph
  graphs: FOCUS

Two types of color terminals are used with this Information Center. FOCUS and SAS-graph are used to display a variety of types of information in graphical form.

Some of the software needed is general purpose: query languages, report generators, application generators. Some is oriented to specify types of data such as financial planning data, project management, text processing, coordinate geometry, and so on.

Box 27.3 lists software from IBM which is used in Information Centers.

It should be noted that much of the best software for Information Center use does not come from the major computer vendors. Excellent application packages, query languages, report generators, application generators, and graphics packages are marketed by independent software vendors. In the list from Equitable above, FOCUS, RAMIS, SAS, SAS-graph, and SPSS are from independent vendors. All run with the IBM hardware and operating system.

Some organizations have many end users creating valuable results with the language NOMAD. More such software appears every month. Some of the earlier products are being constantly enhanced.

COMMUNICATION SKILLS

A particularly important skill of the Information Center staff is communicating with the end users.

Often the center is staffed by people trained as systems analysts. Their job changes fundamentally. They no longer write program specifications, draw data flow diagrams, etc. They act more as consultants, listening to the end users' problems, solving them, determining the users' needs for information, encouraging, training, and selling ideas to the end users.

It is important to train the Information Center staff in the new languages and software, but this usually comes naturally to them. Sometimes

BOX 27.3 Examples of IBM software used in Information Centers. (*Note:* Many of the best packages and end-user tools and languages are not from the major computer vendors but from independent software houses.)

Financial

Financial Planning System

Financial Analysis and Credit Evaluation

PLANCODE/I   (PLANning, COntrol, and DEcision Evaluation System: software for formulating, qualifying, evaluating, and monitoring plans)

Long-Term Debt Management System

Management Science

EPLAN—Econometric Planning Language

Forecasting and Time Series Analysis

APL Multivariate Time Series Analysis

APL Advanced Statistical Library

APL Statistical Library

Data Retrieval and Reporting

A Department Reporting System II

APL Data Interface

IMS-APL Data Link

Inter-Region Access Method

Data Extraction, Processing and Restructuring System

PL/1 File Creation

STAIRS (Information retrieval system)

Query-by-Example (QBE)

SQL—Structured Query Language, using a relational data base

Graphics Packages

Graphics Analysis Program

Graphic Attachment Support

BOX 27.3 *(Continued)*

Storage Tube and Plotter Simulation for 3277 Graphics Attachment

Plotter and Tablet Support

Graphs and Histograms

PANEL Line Art Technique

Graphical Data Display Manager

Text Processing

Document Composition Facility

APL Text Editor and Composer

Project Management

MINIPERT

Project Evaluation and Control (PECS)

Scientific/Engineering

COGO-APL Coordinate Geometry

Zeros and Integrals in APL

Continuous Systems Modeling

APL GPSS (General-Purpose Systems Simulator)

APL Decision Table Processor and Code Generator

General Cross-Assembler Generator

APL Programming Support

VS APL

APL Extended Editor and Full Screen Support

APL Computer-Aided Instruction

APL Handbook of Techniques

APL Workspace Structure Analysis

APL Data Language

Training

IIS (Interactive Instructional System)

the necessary communications skills come less naturally. A particularly valuable training for some Information Center staff has been courses on how to communicate well. Such courses should be followed by careful monitoring and guidance of their activities to help them acquire the style and techniques of a good consultant.

EARLY SUCCESS   It is generally desirable when an Information Center is established that it should be seen to be successful *quickly*. If there are no early successes, it might be regarded as an odd-ball idea or DP plaything rather than a facility that will revolutionize a major section of DP development.

The selection of the first users is particularly important. This should be a group keen to develop their own query and analysis services, and likely to cooperate well on what may be an experimental basis at first. They should have a definite business need for the new service so that there will be a strong payoff.

For this initial group the appropriate software products are selected, and data bases made available, possibly with separate Class IV data bases being extracted from established production data bases or files. A small number of users are trained and the Information Center staff work with them closely.

The initial experience with the service should be evaluated carefully both by users and DP. It may need substantial adjusting. When both parties perceive it to be working well, it can be extended to other types of users.

SPREADING THE   Eventually, when DP staff are confident of its
SUCCESS   success and capable of giving good support, the concept of Information Center operation needs to be *sold* throughout the organization.

A demonstration center should be set up and demonstrations given to all classes of users who should be employing the Information Center services. Demonstrations to senior management are particularly important. These should use *real* corporate data and be designed to show *interesting* results.

The objective of the demonstrations should be to show something of direct basic value to each area manager—something that affects how well his job is done. The demonstration content should be oriented to business results, not technical wizardry. The results-oriented data should be displayed as attractively as possible, for example on color graphics terminals. Often the data for such demonstrations need to be extracted from files or external sources and restructured to form a data base that can be manipulated with fourth-generation languages.

The author attended a demonstration in an insurance company before senior executives. Throughout almost the entire two-hour session the discussion was about business results and finances, not about computing technology. Data had been captured relating to the current concerns of the executives in question and had been converted to the relational structures which the software could manipulate. Breakdowns of expenses were analyzed; cash flows shown in color graphics; the comparative performance of competing insurance companies was analyzed. It was essential to use *real* data to generate the interest that was shown. A substantial amount of work had gone into developing the demonstrations. The persons who created the demonstrations operated the terminals and could quickly modify their nonprocedural code in order to answer the executives' questions. These top executives were fascinated to see how their business concerns could be explored: "What if the prime rate goes to 19%?" "What is the effect of holding down this budget to $600,000?" "Why did the Travelers Insurance Company do so well in this area?" And so on.

Such demonstrations can constitute a powerful form of selling. They can help to improve communication between DP and top management, which is often not good enough.

OTHER REGULATION

It is clearly necessary to control the data that are created in an Information Center, and link them to the data models of the organization. A more controversial question is whether there should be any *other* regulation.

Most end users would say no. Users usually want to be left alone to use computers in the ways that seem best to them. A charge-back scheme is necessary so that they pay for the resources used. They can then make their own decisions about the financial viability of running their own applications.

Often the DP department has thought otherwise. In some cases DP authorization is needed before end users are allowed to develop their own applications. The reasons for this include the following:

1. The Information Center should check that it has adequate computer power and resources to support the application.

2. There may be strategic reasons why the application should not go ahead. For example, there may be a larger plan to develop systems that affect the application in question, or to develop data bases to which the system will link.

3. The project may require traditional DP involvement, for example interface programming, network development, or large-volume printing. This will have to be fitted into the DP workload.

4. A check should be made that the users know what they are committing to, that their application is practical, and that no DP rescue or maintenance will be needed.

5. A check should be made that the application has no adverse security implications.

6. A check should be made that the application is satisfactory from the auditors' viewpoint.

7. If a complete charge-back is not made, with the users bearing the cost and financial responsibility, a check on the financial viability may be needed.

The problem with building up these types of controls is that they can destroy the end users' freedom to invent, which is one of the most important aspects of user-driven computing. Excessive controls can put back the bureaucracy which exists in traditional data processing. They undermine the flexibility and speed of development which is a primary objective of Information Center operation.

A compromise may be that a description of all applications is maintained by the Information Center. This is provided to auditors and other interested parties. The user departments are made responsible for cost justification, and the Information Center avoids interfering with users' decisions as far as possible.

AUDITORS

User-driven computing can be a problem for the auditors. It could increase the possibility that users could commit fraud. The auditors certainly need to know what is going on in this area.

One bank finds that the following arrangement for auditors works well. Every end-user-developed application is formally authorized. The chief auditor (who is a very powerful person in the bank) receives a copy of the authorization and a copy of any documentation that the end users produce. The end users are responsible for their own application documentation and standards are established for this. If the auditor wants to investigate the use system further, that is a matter between him and the users. The Information Center keeps out of it.

The chief auditor and his department became, themselves, major users of the Information Center. This mode of operation pleased them because it enabled them to make investigations and write checking programs without the DP organization or programmers knowing in detail what the auditors were doing or looking for. Previously they went to each branch periodically and went through the books manually looking for irregularities. Now they write programs which go through each branch's computer files in the head office. The DP manager states that the auditors created these programs *far faster* than the DP department could have [3]. The auditors can modify the programs whenever they wish, maintaining secrecy over the modifications, and this improves the thoroughness with which they can search for irregularities.

In other organizations also, the auditors ought to employ user software to improve the thoroughness of their inspections. Auditors should be one of the first customers of the Information Center.

WHO PAYS?

With user-driven computing in general it is desirable that the user should pay for the facilities he employs. Some DP organizations operate as a cost center rather than a revenue center. It is desirable that the Information Center should be a revenue center or profit center. This has several advantages:

- It causes the user departments to justify their use of computing or access to information.

- It increases the incentive of the Information Center to *sell* and to provide a level of service worth paying for.

- It is easy for users to take actions that use excessive computer time. Making them pay for the time they use seems the best way to control this.

- Sudden excessive upswings in usage are less likely to occur, so it is easier to plan and control growth.

How should the users be charged? It is difficult to find a completely fair and rational charging formula.

Some organizations have charged for terminals, connect time, CPU hours, and disc space. When users ask for certain information to be made available on an existing information retrieval system, the main extra cost is the disc space and the charge may relate to that.

Some organizations have charged a flat fee for the use of a terminal. One charged $500 per month for an Information Center terminal.

Another organization charged an arbitrary 75% of the user's current outside time-sharing rate. This encouraged the users to lessen their use of outside time-sharing and move across to the internal facilities.

It is usually desirable to make Information Center use free at the beginning. When the concept has truly caught hold, then a charge is made. Even then it may be free for two or three years to encourage new users.

It is important to make the charge simple for user management to understand and budget for.

INFORMATION CENTERS IN PRACTICE

While writing this book I surveyed the experience at a variety of Information Centers. Many of them were not called "Information Center." Other names were used, and they differed considerably in their approach,

This chapter relays some of the practical experience and consists mainly of quotations from the executives involved.

FINANCIAL ADVANTAGES To be worthwhile, the Information Center must affect the bottom line of a corporation. We formed the view that fast flexible user-driven computing can have a greater effect on corporate profits than most traditional data processing.

An Information Center executive at a large insurance company wrote the following [2]:

INFORMATION CENTER EXECUTIVE:

The potential contribution to the assets [of the corporation], from opportunities exploited by executives supported by their managers, could be in the hundreds of millions of dollars per year.

The Information Center concept has affected not only decision support and strategic planning, but also the day-to-day operations:

RAILROAD EXECUTIVE:

Since we put the techniques into place we haven't fired anybody because of them. But the freight we carry has more than doubled. That increase has been handled without any increase in staff. We couldn't have possibly handled the increase in business with our existing staff without MAPPER.

USER EXECUTIVE:

For some years I was the Production Coordinator for the Oil Consortium. The previous incumbent spent about 12 hours a day processing detailed data to find out what was going on. The information system had been designed so that information had to be available for all purposes before a single decision could be made. When a crisis arose, the coordinator was not in a position to contribute to the decision, so the job had degenerated to that of a glorified accountant.

By building an Information Center I was able to process selected key indicators quickly, interpret it and present an analysis of the situation by the time of the daily operations meeting held at 7.00 a.m. About 80% of the time nothing unusual was going on, and I was able to use the Information Center data to debottleneck production capacity. During the critical 20% of the time, I was in a position to work with operational managers on an hour-by-hour basis to balance the flow from the fields to the Abadan refinery and the Kharg Island export terminal.

The management system supported by Information Center concepts enabled the company to export an additional million barrels a month at no additional cost.

INSURANCE EXECUTIVE:

It enables us to make better decisions in cash management, and with today's interest rates that means a large financial saving.

Financial savings also results from reduced costs of developing systems:

INFORMATION CENTER EXECUTIVE:

The *saving* in development costs of the financial information system and the personnel system alone will total $6 million and cut development time in half.

Some users of the new techniques estimate that overall they can develop systems at about one-third of the costs.

More important, sometimes, they can obtain results very fast.

INFORMATION CENTER EXECUTIVE:

Users get reports on the day they ask for them, or at worst the day after. Before, it took two months. This completely changes the way they utilize information.

USER EXECUTIVE:

It enables us to spot potential troubles much more quickly. We get an overall view of supply and demand. We can spot short-term fluctuations in demand or supply problems quickly. This saves money and lets us serve customers better.

BUSINESS MANAGERS IN CONTROL

An objective of the Information Center ought to be to put businessmen more in control of how computing is used.

INFORMATION CENTER MANAGER:

Our motto is: "Put computing into the businessmen's hands." We are in business to support the business.

DP EXECUTIVE:

We tried to solve our age-old problem of turning programmers into bankers by instead turning bankers into programmers.

OPERATIONS EXECUTIVE:

An interesting by-product of the information system is that I have more feeling of control but my managers have more feeling of responsibility.

We have all the information on the projects we manage in the organization. Managers at the first level use that information to do their job; they use it as a guide on how to manage. At the same time I can look at it any time I choose. I'm not hounding them, asking them for special reports. I can generate those reports. If I look at it today and find that everything is within the parameters I'm comfortable with, I go about my business. They are operating as if they were independent entities; I rarely need to bug them at the operational level, and yet I have more control.

USER EXECUTIVE:

The Information Center has enabled senior management to participate in key decisions when they should, but keep out of them when things are going well. It provides *management distance* from the day-to-day operations.

USER MANAGER:

A lot of our people have started installing the terminals at home. When they have a problem they sometimes sit up late at night working on it.

I like to check on things at 7 in the morning (at home). If I take any actions or send messages, these are available to people two seconds later. We can start the day in good shape.

One insurance executive compares the Information Center to a military war room [2]:

INFORMATION CENTER EXECUTIVE:

Information Center adapts the military command post and war room concepts to the needs of business executives. The Information Center is built around the dynamics of business decision making. To illustrate this point we can visualize a movie of a NASA mission control center. We may first be attracted to and impressed by the computers and technical support. However, when we watch "mission control," that is, a complete mission—such as the recovery of the ill-fated Apollo 13, mobilization for a military alert, or an energy distribution crisis—rather than a still picture, attention shifts from technology to the total decision-making scene. Much frustration by executives and managers about management information systems can be traced to a misplaced and often distorted perception by systems people of information and processing needs in the real world of dynamic business decisions. Information can be systematically prepackaged so that it has the same strategic relevance and value that it *must* have in the "war room" context.

FLEXIBILITY AND RAPID CHANGE   Many executives stressed need for fast ad hoc computing as well as computing with traditional planning.

INTERVIEWER:

What do you think is going wrong with information systems in other organizations?

INFORMATION CENTER MANAGER:

I guess one thing is—studying it too long.

INTERVIEWER:

So you're saying, "Don't study it; get on with it."

INFORMATION CENTER MANAGER:

Yes. It's often delegated down to an analyst to go and study the users' needs—what they want and don't want. They do an elaborate study that gives minimal feedback, particularly if it's in the hands of someone who does not have a great deal of experience in understanding what managers may or may not want. So they're speculating about what the needs may or may not be, which is kind of what happened with the MIS direction in the early 1970s.

Instead of that, we provide the users with tools and a service. We can convert and load up any information they ask for if it's in electronic form. The time taken to get the service in action is much less than the time some people take to do a study that does not reveal the true users' needs. We add to the data available quickly as the users' needs change. The needs or perceived needs have changed all the time.

PILOT SYSTEMS

Often pilot systems are created and experimented with. Sometimes the users find them unsatisfactory and stop using them. This is not a disaster if the system is created sufficiently quickly.

DP EXECUTIVE:

If we can put something up in two weeks, it doesn't really matter if we have to throw it away and redo it in another two weeks. This is better than excessive time spent in planning and specifying when we cannot be sure what the real needs are anyway.

The main argument for this seemingly sloppy approach is that with some applications the users do not know what they really want.

DP EXECUTIVE:

We all work in different ways. You could brainstorm for years trying to find out the right way.

The best approach is to get some people using the tools and see how they feel. You adapt to some of their feelings. Sometimes they say "No. That's no good," and that's useful feedback.

One of the reasons why this is practical now is that we've been able to get these tools into people's hands within days rather than going away for two years to develop a major system and then decide.

> We put up a tool and test it on the users in a few weeks. It is better to do this than to conduct a detailed study, because the study would have taken longer.

Pilot systems reveal to end users what is possible. There is then likely to be many modifications made to the pilot to adapt it to the users' needs and ideas. Step-by-step adaptation becomes a standard pattern when building user-driven systems with very high level languages.

DP EXECUTIVE:

Once it began to gain a hold, our approach was to install pilots in every aspect of the bank. We have people in commercial banking using the system, people in trust and estates, people in international banking, people traveling from country to country.

INTERVIEWER:

How about senior management?

DP EXECUTIVE:

We have several of the senior managers who are getting involved. Others are supportive in terms of having their staff do it, and are still not personally involved. And I guess my belief is that what is most important from a firm's perspective is that senior management is supportive. And it's not necessary that they personally use the tools as long as they are getting the benefits from their organization using the tools.

TRANSITION PHASE   There is a transition phase in getting users to accept the new tools. It takes some time to overcome their apprehension, build familiarity, and advance to the stage where they are thinking creatively about how they might use the tools.

This is rather like learning photography. It takes some time to master the technicalities. Only when the photographer is familiar enough with the techniques to almost forget about them can he concentrate adequately on the creative aspects of picture making.

INFORMATION CENTER EXECUTIVE:

An individual has got to get past the stage of becoming comfortable with the tool. Once it is a habit, like the telephone, something changes.

They start to think up new ways to use it to enhance their work on how their area works. And that is infectious.

They've all got to go through the struggling transition phases, and then all of a sudden you've got everyone out there creatively thinking how to use the tools better. That's an extraordinary benefit in system development. It's light years away from what we accomplished with structured analysis.

To enable the users to forget about the mechanics and concentrate on creative uses of the systems, the user dialogue has to be very user-friendly —much more so than with many terminal systems of the past.

DP EXECUTIVE:

The old type of terminal operator used the terminal eight hours a day, was completely familiar with the system's quirks, and knew the account numbers.

Now we need to provide information to people who use the terminals just occasionally, are baffled by computer gobbledygook, and who want to go in on the first three letters of a name, or where you live, and do some searching around for information.

INTERVIEWER:

And STAIRS has that capability where IMS hasn't?

DP EXECUTIVE:

Correct. It does it very well. So it provides the capabilities we need to a much broader base of people.

GRAPHICS

Graphics give a particularly powerful way to communicate business information and understand the effects of "What-if?" questions. Some Information Centers have emphasized the use of graphics. This has had a particular appeal to their user community.

INFORMATION CENTER EXECUTIVE:

The president of the corporation likes graphs and charts. He believes that financial management and other management participate better in meetings when information is presented graphically. It enables the whole management team to participate. In 15 minutes you can get a picture of the entire situation.

Information presented graphically can enable you to spot problems quickly, and quickly understand the effects of "What-if?" questions. Graphics can highlight problem areas.

Graphics software and terminals differ greatly in their quality. It pays to select the best in order to sell the Information Center capabilities to senior management and users.

DEGREE OF COMMITMENT   Because the Information Center represents a major change in culture, both for DP and its users, the spread of the new methods is likely to be slow in most organizations. To speed it up a major senior management drive is needed.

DP EXECUTIVE:

One problem is optimism. There was a point when we thought that once the tools were in place we would have the whole organization converted in two or three years.

My current feeling is that once a firm decides to start it won't *fully* use these tools for seven to eight years.

In some cases the executive in charge of the new techniques is an aggressive senior mover-and-shaker. More often a relatively junior person is given the Information Center, and sometimes a problem person whom the DP management want to side-slip to an area where he is out of harm's way.

DP EXECUTIVE:

Our initial investment was very limited. At any time we could have abandoned the project at very little cost.

There were a number of nonconverts to the idea in the MIS Division. I wanted to avoid a long and arid theoretical discussion as to whether and how we should go ahead.

In view of the success stories we feel that a thoroughly aggressive approach is needed, and should be backed by top management. It represents a major opportunity for an adventurous forceful executive to make his name. Sometimes this has been a DP executive. Sometimes the drive has come from the end-user area. The drive needs to be linked to the overall information engineering activities.

TOP MANAGEMENT SUPPORT

Organizations that had achieved spectacular results, as opposed to a relatively small operation, often stressed that top management supported the new type of development and helped to make it a success.

USER EXECUTVE:

The president of the railroad has access to one of our terminals. When the system was built he used to be vice-president of operations. DP wasn't supporting us well enough and he knew it. So he decreed that we should have a go with this new software. DP opposed it, but he made it happen.

There was a lot of pressure on the initial end-user team. We nearly killed ourselves getting the operations going. There were divorces, nervous breakdowns. . . . If we were doing it again today with that experience, we would have far more end users involved. Spread the load. We didn't realize how big it would become.

USER EXECUTIVE:

We do lots of demonstrations of it to other firms. The computer manufacturer parades his customers through here. And the reaction is always the same. The end users love it; the DP people go bananas. They think up all sorts of reasons why it won't work in *their* shop. Sometimes we've practically had fights break out here between DP and users.

INTERVIEWER:

What's the answer to that problem?

USER EXECUTIVE:

Demonstrate it to top management.

INTERVIEWER:

You have had much more success than most in penetrating the organization with these facilities. Why do you think you've been more successful?

DP EXECUTIVE:

I guess there would be two reasons. First, I had very good support from my executive vice-president and the corporate office. I had the responsibility to assemble an overall corporate-wide picture without having to deal with many organizational levels.

Second, we chose not to package it as an office-of-the-future concept, or Information Center concept, or "we're going to automate your office." We chose to break it down into products that had some meaning to different people and implement the products. The products were like pieces of a puzzle. We hoped that we understood the puzzle and how to fit the pieces together. The users just see the products.

INFORMATION CENTER STAFF SHOULD DEVELOP APPLICATIONS

As we indicated earlier, some Information Center proposals state that the Information Center staff should *not* develop applications. The managers of some of the most successful centers disagreed vehemently with this:

INFORMATION CENTER EXECUTIVE:

It is an absolute *must* (that Information Center staff develop applications). Most end users should not do it themselves. Most don't want to. They should work jointly with the systems engineer. Most are delighted when the systems engineer takes initiative, shows them results on the screen, and then modifies the results to what they want. They have never seen this before and they often get excited about it. It's the first time I've really seen end users getting excited about DP's potential.

To work in this mode the Information Center staff need good communications skills.

INFORMATION CENTER MANAGER:

Our experience indicates that the Information Center needs a compassionate support staff, strong on communications skills, with experience to visualize the uses of the results in decision making. The support staff must be committed to assisting the professional and manager solve business problems, and feel a sense of responsibility for the outcome.

SPREADING THE TECHNIQUES

Once the techniques or pilot systems begin to succeed it is desirable to spread them as fast as possible. This can need aggressive salesmanship within an organization.

DP EXECUTIVE:

About 80% of my information comes electronically and then there is another group of people for which maybe 1% comes electronically. So one of our goals has been to get more people using the center and then people using it more completely. And the next goal for the following year will be to increase the *penetration per person* and have more things electronically transmitted to each and every individual involved.

As the user-driven systems catch hold they can reach a stage of rapid growth. As this continues, tools are needed to inform users what information and applications are available from their terminals.

INFORMATION CENTER MANAGER:

We are moving toward 5000 people in the firm using these tools. It's become a real problem to communicate change and upgrades and new functions to the users.

We think the only way is a computer-assisted tool for people to be able to educate themselves once they're over the hurdle of becoming comfortable with the basic systems.

DP EXECUTIVE:

The area of education is what, I think, we most underestimated. We expected when people saw these capabilities they would immediately respond and be delighted. But what we found is that it takes a long time to get someone trained in the whole gamut of tools we made available.

It is different from when we automated something in the past. When we automated the payroll you *had* to use it. No choice. Here there is a definite choice. We teach people how to use these tools, and after they have learned, if they haven't personally decided to adapt and use the tool, they can stop. You need an ongoing reeducation or updating process so that they know what new functions might be useful to them.

INFORMATION CENTER MANAGER:

The staff act almost like a little marketing group, where people are assigned to different areas of the organization to spend their full time helping people use the tools that are available, and being on site so that you don't have to schedule necessarily a formal meeting, but just call them over and say: "Would you help me? I'm trying to find this kind of information." That's been very successful and it's been a very useful tool for us in terms of getting feedback on what people are thinking about, what they need, and what they would like.

STAFF WITHOUT DP EXPERIENCE   Because of the change in methods from conventional DP, many managers and software vendors emphasized how bright people *who are new to DP* often achieve better results than experienced DP personnel. This is true both with management and application creation.

END-USER EXECUTIVE WHO CREATED A SPECTACULAR SYSTEM:

I think one of the reasons we succeeded so spectacularly is that nobody told us it was not possible. No one in DP would have dared to do what we succeeded in doing.

INFORMATION CENTER EXECUTIVE:

We took young people coming straight off our training program and said: "Your area is this. You will support the Trust Department. Your goal is to get more people using the tools, and get those who *are* using them using them *more*. You should locate yourself as much as possible in their area."

They had to help people use the tools, be available to answer users' questions, get users over the transition of being willing to use a terminal, and knowing how to access the information that was being made available to them.

These young people coming right out of college are doing an excellent job.

DATA ENTRY

Some Information Centers are used only for information retrieval or for manipulating data that exist in on-line systems. The end-user languages, however, can also be used for entering data. This is done on a large scale in some systems. It has the advantage of moving the data-entry process to the users, who care about the accuracy of the data.

DP EXECUTIVE:

Many users enter their own data into their own virtual filing cabinets and they are responsible for the accuracy of these data. Much of their data is used by other users or moved across to the production systems with various audit and accuracy checks.

We capitalize on capturing data at their source. There are usually so many steps in the process until a piece of data enters a computer. It comes from a customer into a salesman's hands, into some peoples' operations' hands, to some control clerks, back into the computer. There are about six layers of error potentials in there, and even if that last person keys it perfectly, it's incorrect. So that our migration is toward moving that entry back further and further until ultimately the customer can put in his own question. And the next thing is, how do you control it so that people can't mess up the files? You've got to have tight security controls and it updates the master data base only after thorough checking.

The degree of accuracy goes up exponentially as you eliminate steps in the process and deal with the person who is the most concerned that it is accurate.

AVAILABILITY To be satisfied with Information Center systems, users need high system availability. Sometimes in the systems we surveyed this had not been taken seriously enough. The users find this very frustrating and harmful to their work.

LEASING EXECUTIVE:

If somebody phones us and asks us to quote a lease for 12 jet aircraft for Yugoslavia we can't tell them to call back in four hours when the machine will be up. They need an immediate service.

The highest availability and suitably fast response time should be the rule. It is a mistake to put the Information Center operations on a backup machine which can be preempted for other work.

On the Santa Fe railroad system availability was so important that the terminals, connected to large central computers, were backed up by micro-computers providing identical screen displays which operated when the main system crashed.

The users need to be completely shielded from design considerations relating to availability, networks, physical-data-base access, or other technical matters.

INFORMATION CENTER EXECUTIVE:

The computer and the technology has got to go into the back room and disappear. People don't think about an electric generating plant or the telephone company central office as long as the service is there when you want it. The Information Center must become a service like that.

The user should have his own logical filing cabinets available when he needs them, and have tools for manipulating the data in the files, viewing them in more useful ways, asking what-if questions, investigating delays and problems, and so on. He should be able to move data from his logical filing cabinets to other people's.

HOW TO SUCCEED Different Information Center managers had different interpretations of what "success" meant. In the author's view it should mean a substantial proportion of the application development being done by end users, or Information Center consultants working with end users, and the end users being pleased with the results.

INTERVIEWER:

Having created a successful Information Center operation yourself, what advice would you give to other organizations about how to succeed?

INFORMATION CENTER EXECUTIVE:

The concept needs to be extensively sold throughout the organization, and you cannot sell it on an intellectual basis. Users must try it, get their hands on the terminals, and roll it around.

      We build pilots. We give demonstrations. We have given demonstrations to the president, to senior management, to DP personnel, and to all levels of end users. We have a demonstration center and have given so many that we are the longest running show on Broadway!

INTERVIEWER:

I'm sure that's excellent advice. What else?

INFORMATION CENTER EXECUTIVE:

Pick the most important applications. Capture data for them, and show what can be done with them. Pick the best software packages, particularly packages that give the best output—clear reports, really good graphics. Use these with the most important applications and demonstrate the results to those executives who will make things happen.

      For the Information Center to flourish fully, the data which the users need and manipulate have to be available and accessible. This requires the foundation stones of data administration to be well laid. Top-down planning of data needs to be done throughout an enterprise, as described in the last part of this book, and data must be well catalogued in a dictionary and data model. Without this planning much time will be wasted and much information will be unobtainable.

INFORMATION CENTER EXECUTIVE:

Our staff spend two-thirds of their time just trying to find data. That's because the corporation has never had a data dictionary and has never really understood data administration.

> *TOP DP EXECUTIVE:*
>
> The marketing vice-president wanted customers ranked by return on our investment so that he would know where to best place his limited resources. There was no way we could provide that information because the data needed were totally incompatible—all over the place!

REFERENCES

1. R. B. Rosenberger, *The Information Center SHARE 56 Proceedings,* Share Inc., New York, 1981.

2. Information from Jim Johnson, Operations Engineering Department, Equitable Insurance Co., New York.

3. Information from P. J. Entwistle, Chief Manager (Data Processing), Lloyds Bank Ltd., London.

PART **VI** IMPLEMENTATION CONSIDERATIONS

28 EXCESSIVE APPLICATION PRESSURE

Much data-processing development takes place in an atmosphere of semicrisis. Once management identifies the need for a certain set of applications, they want results *yesterday*.

Where appropriate data bases *already exist* it may be possible to give them results quickly. However, when developers are struggling to give birth to data bases the pressure for immediate action often plays havoc with the data-base plans. Time and time again data-base development comes apart at the seams because of excessive application pressure.

Top-down design and modeling are sometimes perceived as being luxuries that are indulged in only by those fortunate enough not to have immediate pressures. It is true not only in the data-base world but in industry in general that concentration on strategic planning is often circumvented by short-term concerns. The available money and effort tends to be spent on what will bring immediate return, rather than developing the organization for better operation in the future.

CHAIRMAN OF ONE OF THE WORLD'S LARGEST COMPUTER MANUFACTURERS:

No matter how much I say about building the company for the longer term, short-term performance is the issue that seems to take on most importance.

Concentration on immediate pressures and neglect of the long term has too often proved disastrous. The problem can be solved (at least in data-base management) by doing the strategic design while at the same time finding solutions to the urgent applications which can have a bridge to the longer-term design.

BUSINESS PRESSURES   While resistance to change is a problem with many end users, with others the problem is the opposite—they want results too fast. In some cases the benefits of data-base operation has been oversold to user management without cautionary remarks about the time scale and difficulty of data-base development. The management or educational process may have generated excitement about data base. End-user management grasp the potential advantages to their departments and want results immediately because they themselves are being pressured.

END-USER EXECUTIVE:

Our marketing people are pushing us more and more, and rightfully so, into what is called the "jumbo" or "large-case" market. These are would-be attempts to get additional policyholders such as Ford and Chrysler—that size. Obviously, policyholders like that—the ones that are very very large—they've got the clout. They've got the dollars-and-cents clout. They can apply the pressure to us. We can't afford to dawdle.

The business executives perceive such pressures as being far more real and urgent than any change in data processing.

END-USER EXECUTIVE:

There is an urgent need to improve our service *very quickly*. We recognize that emerging data-base technology may not be ideal in terms of both hardware and software. But that does not eliminate the business pressure to provide increasingly better service.

The move to data base is often not fast enough to accommodate such pressures. Data modeling almost always takes longer than expected. The conversion processes are slow and expensive. Because of the pressure, quick solutions are needed. The user departments cannot wait.

END-USER EXECUTIVE:

You've got to do something, I don't care what it is. But that's the type of environment we're in. I'm sure the marketing department would say: Isn't that a nice problem to have—that we're getting so much business? We're seeing the demand for too much too soon. We're dealing with some existing systems that are obviously antiquated. We know that. We've made starts two years ago to build the basis for the new ones, but that does not stop the cases from coming in. So that presents a problem.

Often a quick and dirty solution is to modify an old file system. In some corporations old file systems never seem to die. They hang around for years after they are formally declared obsolete, being patched and repatched, and creating offspring to meet new urgent applications. The files proliferate and various pressures prevent conversions from being completed.

Another solution is for end users to obtain their own small computer. Increasingly, as small computers drop in cost and their software improves, end-user departments are reacting to their pressures by doing this. It is becoming easier as better languages come into existence for application developments without programmers [1]. It is often quicker than waiting for the DP department to complete its data-base design.

DP MANAGER:

The application backlog has been anything up to four years, and some managers can't wait. They're much more sophisticated now than they used to be and they understand how computing can change their bottom line—and that's what it's all about. That's how *their* management judges *them*.

As discussed in Chapter 25, there are now a variety of languages that end users can employ for creating applications. They range from simple data-base query languages, through report generators, graphics packages, to programming languages like NOMAD, FOCUS, SAS and APL. Many of them plug into data-base systems, but also many are usable on non-data-base stand-alone minicomputers.

END-USER EXECUTIVE:

We had a new guy take over the plans and budgets department. He was an APL nut. He came in from the outside.

Now Plans and Budgets has a crisis once a month. Everybody works late at night getting the next month's figures out. The new guy wanted computer models. Simple models, but they needed a lot of data.

The data-base gang said: "Wait. We'll fit you into our grand design." But there was no way he was going to wait, and he would have had no control if he had depended on them, so he cut loose. It was absolutely the right thing to do.

Cutting loose may be very valuable where it obtains results faster. Sometimes, however, it is done for the sake of independence. It may be done out of fear or so that a manger can protect his own data. Some managers do it because they do not trust the DP department, and think they don't need them any more.

END-USER EXECUTIVE:

You've got a group of people who's attitude has all of a sudden become: I don't need the DP department; I don't want them anymore.

I'm not sure that I have an answer as to what should be done. My personality is such that I would use the thumper-technique I'm afraid— I think it's that serious a problem.

The data-processing industry is swinging rapidly toward distributed processing and minicomputers. This has many beneficial effects [2] but needs to have appropriate forms of management control. One of the biggest dangers is that data are represented differently in different places so that incompatibilities grow up and data cannot be exchanged between machines as they should be. This requires distributed data administration.

In short, there are sometimes expedient reasons for users to break away from a centralized data-base plan, but this needs to be carefully controlled by management.

END-USER EXECUTIVE:

Some laws have got to be laid down.

Now if the data processing department is in a bind and it is being done for purely: "I've got to produce something for a policyholder; it's essential it meets business objectives," then fine; and it's a mutually agreed upon thing. I can't build you what you want right away so that you can have one of those as an interim.

> But when they go around the back of DP, it creates far greater problems for any corporation.

CONTROLLED BREAKAWAY

When user departments do break away from the data-base planning, because it is evolving too slowly, this can be done with some measure of control. The systems that the user departments build should probably be folded into the data-base environment at some later time, or at least exchange data with it. Because of this, they should use the same data dictionary and data modeling tool. The data administrator may assist them in creating their data structures even if these are not incorporated into the overall model.

DP MANAGER:

We're trying to encourage the application development teams that are cutting loose to stay as close as possible: for instance, to use the same dictionary that the data administrator is using; to use some of the techniques that go with data base, to model it as best they can, at least to have a model. It may not be divisional-wide in view, but to the extent that data can be normalized, reduced to its simplest structure, to the extent that it's mechanized on a dictionary, certainly there's no guarantee that you can make a direct translation, but we think it will make it easier when we do come around to converting. . . .

The modeling technique described in Chapters 11 to 17 is valuable with small installations of narrow focus. In some cases it has enabled a small, *application* data base to be designed and implemented quickly.

If an end-user department is implementing a *file* rather than a *data base* system, the file may or may not be in third normal form. Better machine performance can sometimes be achieved with file systems by deviating from third normal form.

The first step in the design ought to be to put it in third normal form; then amalgamations or deviations from third normal form can be made if necessary to obtain good machine performance.

FILE SYSTEM STRATEGY

In some DP organizations there is a deliberate strategy to relieve the pressures of data-base evolution by building interim systems when the demands of end users are urgent. These may be file systems, *Class II* data-base systems, or *Class IV* systems with the new languages, with data not yet incorporated in the corporate models.

DP MANAGER:

Today, where we find that we must support the business function before we can build a comprehensive data base, we will form a deliberate
strategy to, say, take the expedient solution rather than wait your turn.
We do that as a deliberate strategy today.

INTERVIEWER:

In other words, deliberately build a file system because you can do it
quickly and that relieves the pressure from the overall building of the
integrated data base?

DP MANAGER:

That's right, yes. There are instances where that's deliberate, to accomplish our immediate need. I believe that over the next couple of years,
during the transition to the data-base technology, we'll see that technique diminish.

INTERVIEWER:

And in a few years time, are you going to want to backtrack from the
strategy by integrating the file structure which that has created into the
future data-base system?

DP MANAGER:

Yes, I believe we'll have to do that.

Although it is the intention to convert such file systems to the data-base
form later, in practice this often does not take place. The personnel costs are
too high; there is desire to avoid the upheaval of another conversion; and
there are so many needs that seem of higher priority. The incompatible
systems continue to exist.

DP EXECUTIVE:

It's all very well saying you'll convert later. But most of the time you
don't. You haven't got the personnel. Old systems never die. You're
stuck with this can of worms.

INTERVIEWER:

And its maintenance.

KEEP AHEAD OF THE PRESSURE

As more subject data bases and good stable data models are implemented, the problem of incompatible files diminishes. Users are less likely to need to cut loose and build a system with incompatible data. New applications can be built quickly on top of existing data bases.

But good data modeling, as we have stressed, takes a long time—often much longer than anticipated.

The moral of this is that *the data modeling should keep well ahead of the application pressures.* Most of the time it is done in a semicrisis atmosphere, with application pressure beating on the data administrator.

Data models are the foundation stone of much future data processing. To rush into application development with Class II or III data bases before the data modeling has been done is like building a house on the sand. It will certainly have to be rebuilt. But time and time again one sees this being done. The rebuilding is described to management as being "necessary maintenance." Management is usually not knowledgeable enough to ask why the house was built on sand in the first place.

It is not only the world of data bases that is plagued by excessive pressures for action. It is a natural human desire to "want to get the show on the road" before sufficient planning has been done.

Often, results have been promised, and so reputations are at stake.

THE SYDNEY OPERA HOUSE SYNDROME

With complex projects in many fields the desire to see something happening tends to circumvent the work of thorough design. Programmers feel a pressure to start coding before proper structured analysis and design. Some TV producers start filming before thorough scripting and planning.

One of my favorite modern buildings is the Sydney Opera House, its great white roof soaring like sails above the Sydney Bay. The concept of this building was sketched out by an architect who had not built anything like it before. The political pressures to complete the building in six years were great, just as political pressures can be great in data processing, and work began before the detailed design was done. The protests of the architect could not slow down the rush to implement.

The management had promised the end user that they would get results quickly.

DP EXECUTIVE:

It's easy to say these things in retrospect, but they rushed into the thing without any real data-base design. It wasn't true data base. They were using IMS like an access method, and then they had to keep changing it. It was all built on a trial-and-error basis. They should have backed off and done thorough data-base planning, but the pressures were always too great.

The final building was surprisingly different from the original design, just as DP systems often are.

The roof was made of concrete on steel supports and weighed 28,600 tons. It had to be raised into position a slab at a time. If the original design had been implemented, almost every concrete slab would have been of a different shape. Each had to be made in a plywood mold and there were 2194 of them, each weighing over 10 tons. This would have taken a vast amount of time and work, so the roofs were redesigned with computers to be composed of slabs of only a few different shapes. This changed the shape of the roofs, but by then 20 vast roof support columns were in place. They had to be changed. The proscenium arch and stage machinery had to be scrapped. All of this cost many millions of dollars.

DP EXECUTIVE:

They trumpeted the sales argument for data base, but in fact the pieces just didn't fit together. They eventually had to rewrite them and that cost a fortune.

INTERVIEWER:

So data base didn't reduce your maintenance costs?

DP EXECUTIVE:

Maintenance is a weasel word. What it often means is that you never did the planning.

An objective of data base is that it should greatly reduce future program rewriting. To achieve that, thorough, skilled, logical design is needed. This takes time but pays off greatly.

The estimated cost of the Sydney Opera House after the acceptance of the initial design was $7 million. In fact, it eventually cost well over $100 million. It did not open after six years as promised; it opened after 16 and even then was not finally finished. The chief contractor said it was built on a "trial and error" basis and that it was "rushed into for political reasons." He also said that it took three years off his life! In retrospect it was estimated that if it had been thoroughly designed before work began, it would have been completed in half the time and cost at least $50 million less.

THOROUGH PLANNING   The moral of such stories is that thorough planning is needed before implementation. Implementation in crisis mode or under excessive pressure always results in greater expense, and paradoxically it often results in longer implementation times.

Get the data modeling done well ahead of implementation pressures. Minimize the shortcuts that use incompatible data. Modeling the data used in a corporation should be an ongoing activity largely independent of current system implementations.

REFERENCES

1. James Martin, *Application Development Without Programmers,* Prentice-Hall, Inc., Englewood Cliffs, NJ, 1982.

2. James Martin, *Design and Strategy for Distributed Processing,* Prentice-Hall, Inc., Englewood Cliffs, NJ, 1981.

29 DATA BASE AND POLITICS

INTRODUCTION   On many occasions the proud designer of a large-scale data-base plan has presented his scheme to me. It is often impressive, logical, and well conceived. I like to return two or three years later to find out what has happened to such schemes. They almost always change, often growing as more details are filled in, sometimes being clipped of areas that prove overambitious or less profitable than the rest. But on a distressing number of occasions the plan has disappeared completely. It has crashed on the rocks of corporate politics and sunk beneath the waves without a trace.

The biggest problem confronting large data-base designs is not the technology, although that is difficult; it is the human problems and corporate politics.

INTERDEPARTMENTAL   Many organizations foster a high level of competitiveness between departments and between managers. In many ways this is healthy. It keeps managers on their toes and helps to ensure that they make the best possible demands on their management. However, in such an environment managers tend to build walls around their domains to protect them from other departments, and tend to be secretive about information.

Antony Jay, in his book *Management and Machiavelli* [1], compares corporate department heads to the barons of medieval England. England, like other countries, was frequently torn by interbaronial rivalries and jealousies even when there were great dangers threatening, or great opportunities beckoning, from overseas. The internal strife, says Jay, should be no surprise to those familiar with large corporations. Few employees of large corporations would be so naive as to say: "After all, we're all part of the same company, aren't we? Why can't we all work together instead of wasting our time on these internal wrangles?" The employees understand the strength of the interbaronial rivalries. The barons, when permitted, would build superbly strong castles. Periodically, the kings used to find it necessary to knock down some of the castles.

The DP fortress has been largely impregnable. The barons have regarded it with annoyance and forced resignment. Now with minicomputers at last it is attackable. The barons want their own data-processing and information sources.

In Jay's analogy the bricks and mortar that corporate barons build their castles with are often *withheld information* and *unreferred decisions.*

The relationship between managers and departments is far more complex than the organization chart would indicate, and the information that passes between them is not governed by straightforward rules. This is especially so in old or large corporations where managers have long since learned that in order to survive, or be promoted, certain modes of political behavior are necessary and care is needed in handling most types of information. Executives in bureaucratic organizations have a long and successful education in how to protect themselves and their departments. Computerized information systems threaten to wreck the carefully cultivated patterns.

In many organizations the education in bureaucratic survival teaches managers to hide or manipulate much information. It teaches rivalry, and mistrust. Elaborate cover-ups become a way of life. Much information is prevented from reaching other departments or higher levels of management, and much communication of information is deliberately delayed, distorted, or funneled through certain channels. The image of a corporate "information system," making information freely available to higher management, is a cause for alarm. Just as computerized inventory systems revealed the chaotic state of the stores, so advanced data-base systems may reveal to top management how much has been hidden from them. Strategic data resources planning often reveals the need for fundamental reorganizations.

**DATA BASE
TENDS TO BE
COUNTERPOLICITAL** The data administrator steps into this environment. He wants to make the data kept by different departments compatible, and organize a free and efficient flow of data. The same data items go to work for different departments. Interdepartment withholding of data has no place in the designer's scheme for maximizing the value of the data. In his view the maximum cooperation is needed. He sees corporate politics as a barrier to efficient systems design, which has to be overcome. In some corporations the barons, who are divided on everything else, have united on the fact that the information system designer is a menace. Fortunately for

them, he needs a long time to bring his plans to fruition, and he is unlikely to survive that long.

The primary difficulty in data-base design is that the overall designs which are most appealing to a systems engineer tend to be *counterpolitical*.

The synthesis process that is the key to data modeling is no respecter of politics. It freely combines the data types used in different departments to produce the most efficient structure. A design like that in Fig. 15.2 is a tight stable data model which can be converted into efficient physical-data-base structures, but it may horrify managers who guard their data jealously.

DP EXECUTIVE:

I think any corporation, given our size, has got to prepare for the fact that there are going to be some individuals in high places who are going to be resistant to the point where they will try to rally the support of their organizations against the implementation of the new system, supplying bad input. I think the senior management has got to recognize it's going to happen and has to be prepared to transfer or possibly, given the worst, terminate such an individual. But to allow that situation to go on is, in effect, I think, a cancerous growth and will ultimately do much more harm than good.

Again, the plan illustrated in Fig. 6.3 makes complete sense from the systems engineering point of view. It indicates that most of the processing in a local government organization can be done with 19 *subject* data bases. Much of the data is used by multiple government organizations, as shown by the red spots on the right-hand side of the figure. A shared set of data bases could be employed, either in a centralized or a distributed-replicated fashion. Either way the data would be of common design, and updated in one place only where possible. Unfortunately, the government organizations on the right of Fig. 6.3 almost never talk to one another. If the entire government were being designed from the beginning, Fig. 6.3 might be a good scheme, but that is not the case. The system must fit into the existing bureaucracy with its personalities, empires, and ambitions. Looking back on the local government for which Fig. 6.3 was designed, in the years that followed only a few of the organizations on the right of Fig. 6.3 used the subject data bases in the plan. Most continued with file systems or obtained their own minicomputer.

You might say: "Well that's to be expected in government; in a corporation surely it would be better because everyone works for the same firm." In practice the situation is sometimes worse in a corporation because the departments are more competitive. Departments are often run as individual profit centers and managers judged by their bottom line.

DP EXECUTIVE:

The guy who runs the factory floor is a powerful guy. If you don't get his cooperation, you're dead in the water. But you'd better understand that he's got all sorts of data which higher management doesn't know about. He's got secret reserves here and secret reserves there which he will use when somebody puts the squeeze on him. He's confident of meeting the targets that management sets because he knows things that they don't know. Now if you try to put all of that into a data base that anybody can examine. . . .

The data administrator has two options.

The first is to design the data structures with locks and security controls so that data that are sensitive to end users can still remain private. End-user management may have their own minicomputers to give them assurance of keeping their own data, but those data conform to the corporate data models. The data administrator has to build a bridge of confidence to the managers in question and may describe privacy techniques to them.

The other option is to have the support of a suitably high level of management to ensure that end users at all levels cooperate fully.

END-USER EXECUTIVE:

One person, an extremely well qualified person, was unwilling to adapt to the data-base environment. While the project was in its infancy that person was relatively sheltered. But as it became more apparent what the impact would be on his environment, this person kind of withdrew, but he withdrew taking his army with him. Literally, that left no alternative but to eliminate that position. This particular person was transferred to an area where he could be productive in doing what he could do best.

INTERVIEWER:

That can be a very tough decision for management?

END-USER EXECUTIVE:

Yes. Extremely tough and my experience has been that it's the kind that management does not want to make. They would prefer not to, and I can understand that it's a very personal touchy thing. But its got to be done. To slow the development of multi-million-dollar projects because of that is borderline insanity.

Top executives who undertand the potential value of data-base operation, and who want it to succeed, must be prepared to wield power over the barons.

The top executive should be aware that rivalries over data can cause loss of profits:

INFORMATION EXECUTIVE:

The different departments were virtually at war with one another—for all sorts of reasons: empire building, people wanting to do their own thing, personal rivalries. So the data were defined and used quite differently in different places.

Take sales forecasting, for example. Every department used its own forecasts of sales for making its own decisions.

There was a rather ambitious plant and production engineering executive. He would not make much of a reputation for himself with a low-volume production line; he needed a high production volume to justify a reputation-making, prestigious new facility. So he wouldn't hesitate to come up with a *high forecast* and lay down plant and equipment to support that high volume.

Conversely there was the material control department, which was negotiating with suppliers for bulk deliveries. The prices were linked to a broad estimate of production volumes. This figure was re-estimated each month without any agreement with the plant and production executive.

The finance department did profit planning on the basis of a *quite different forecast.* The personnel department were establishing manning levels on the basis of *yet another forecast.* And so on.

With data items like this there was anarchy. And this uncoordinated data resulted in a huge amount of waste.

You could not use one single forecast. What is needed is a probability curve. The plant and production engineering executive might work with the 95% probability level on the curve because of the great difficulty of changing production facilities. The material control department negotiating contract prices ought to work at the 80% probability level because if we did achieve higher volumes the suppliers would be delighted to provide them at the agreed price. The forecasts will be adjusted with time.

So instead of a single value we need a matrix of values, but they must be coordinated. At the moment the departments invent values of their own, and they are wildly different.

To allow this lack of coordination of data is not just bad DP management—it is bad *business* management. But it was data-base planning that revealed it.

THINKERS AND THUMPERS

The majority of decison makers in corporations tend to be at one or the other end of a scale; they tend to be organizers—people of action with little contemplation—or to be creative people with little organizing ability. One colleague who works with the military refers to them as "thinkers" and "thumpers." The thinker may be found in the operations research department or on the corporate planning staff. Sometimes he is the brain behind many aspects of the computer systems. He is bored with routine administration and cannot organize anything. His secretary has to organize *him*. However, his ideas are often brilliant and his knowledge formidable. Sometimes he has a keen vision of the future and how the corporation must change over the years ahead. The thumper, on the other hand, may never have had an idea in his life, but he can give orders and make sure they are obeyed. He can make a department shipshape and efficient and can motivate people to work well. He can see that accounts and documentation are kept efficiently. When people or organizations fail to perform well, he thumps the table. His world is one of routine. Often he has little respect for the intellectual. To him, the thinker is a necessary evil, and perhaps not even all that necessary. The thumper finds no satisfaction in contemplation of things that *could* be done or methods that *could* be used. He finds neither joy nor interest in strategic planning, but given a good plan he will charge ahead to implement it.

THE WAR OF THE PRINTOUTS

Increasingly in corporations, computer printouts are being used as weapons of politics. For the person skilled in using them they can be very effective. When a difficult moment comes in a meeting or sales situation, he says: "Let me show you something" and with a sense of drama produces a printout. The printout cannot be argued with because it comes from a computer and is suitably obscure to the opposition. There is no good means of counteracting it except perhaps another printout.

The unexpected producing of a printout is a means of establishing a case, leading the opposition into a trap, or drawing the discussion away from a problem area. It is a proven means of changing the subject at a difficult moment.

The executive skilled with printouts does not want a display terminal except to select and prepare what should be printed. He takes the printouts home, studies them, and marks them to prepare his case. He may want adjustments made in what is printed. When he wields his printout he does not want the opposition to be able to counterattack with some other action on a terminal.

As his skill improves at using printouts both to get his own way and to manage and comprehend better, he increasingly wants control of his own computing resources. He does not want to be dependent on and restricted by a central DP department.

A thumper caught in the war of the printouts may happily embrace, for a time, the expert who can give him his own armaments. He has no interest in data dictionaries, data modeling, or other aspects of data-base design. But he may join forces with a systems analyst who acts as a weapons supplier. He will be very reluctant to have his information transmitted to other computers which may be in enemy hands, or to have his data merged into a shared data base. He may be eager to extract information from other people's data bases or from centralized systems, provided that his own data can be locked and information withheld for a rainy day, when it might be needed.

THE INFORMATION POWER GAME   Some individuals regard corporate life as a constant power game. They perceive the computer as a means of increasing their own power by cornering the market for certain types of information. In some cases they can manipulate it into a form where only they can comprehend and explain it.

PUBLISHING EXECUTIVE:

We failed to use our task as a power game, being then comparatively innocent. . . . We *should* have produced a system of information so complex and ambitious that only *we* could have explained it, with the result that the executive committee would then have been obliged to consult us on publishing decisions. Instead of simplifying, we should have elaborated.

Those who play the information game know better. They not only obtain and control information, they know how to make it practically incomprehensible. Their object is to render the information at their disposal as mysterious and inaccessible as possible, so that only they can explain what (if anything) it means.

TOO RAPID INFORMATION TRANSFER   With a powerful information system, information can pass very rapidly up the chain of command. In the Vietnam war the American field commanders reportedly expressed much concern at certain times because the Pentagon and even the President were becoming involved in decisions which should have been theirs. With some corporate systems, higher management becomes similarly involved and may not know all the facts. Data that should have been the concern of a department manager have been seen by his manager first. The data are collected at their source, are processed in real time, and are then available at the display screens of the system.

The department manager does not have the time buffer that he had before, during which he could chew over the situation, find out the reasons for anything that was wrong, put it right, think up excuses, devise policy suggestions, or hide the facts. In other systems a manager's performance has been analyzed by his boss using the computer, and the first view he has seen of the analysis figures was when he was called into the boss's office to justify them.

A shop floor foreman was responsible for scheduling the sequence of work under his control. He knew everything that was taking place in his area, and people outside his area knew only what the foreman chose to tell them. With computers, each worker enters details of the status of his operations into a workstation terminal. Such information passes immediately to a computer, where it is correlated. The foreman has lost part of his control. When management wants to argue about the scheduling of a certain job, they can go first to the computer terminals or information room staff.

Similar arguments apply from the top to the bottom of a computerized corporation. Managers, who have been used to retaining control over information about the work for which they are responsible, lose the ability to withhold, delay, or manipulate the information. It passes into the all-too-accessible data bases far too quickly for them.

FEAR OF FUTURE POTENTIAL

In many cases it is not so much what a computer can do today that causes the fear of computers, but the potential, vividly expressed but not yet accomplished, of what a real-time information system will eventually do. There will be nowhere to hide. A manager's mistakes will be highly visible. Decisions that are less than optimal may be analyzed and questioned. A manager who has learned the multitude of tricks necessary for making his forecasts and budgets into self-fulfilling prophecies may be confronted with all manner of interference. When he exceeds his quota, or is well within his budget, he cannot save some of the excess for next time like a squirrel. He may have much more difficulty in setting a budget or quota which he knows he can meet because he now has to argue with staffs who have access to the information system. He had many little secrets which he could use in times of difficulty, and he fears that an all-pervading data base might prevent use of these, making everything too precise and too open. Managers who have relied on hiding the full facts in order to increase their chances of political survival fear that a computerized information system will pull the rug out from under them.

Having their own minicomputers with appropriate privacy locks may be perceived as a way for them to attempt to retain control. The data-entry devices are attached to *their* computer and they pass on what information they want.

MANAGEMENT STYLE

Many managers believe in the natural superiority of their own methods. They have their own style of managing, and if any technique comes along which is incompatible with that style, it will be largely ignored. Often the style of managing is cultivated by the corporation. It is a corporate style rather than an individual style, but the individual, in order to succeed, has assimilated the style completely.

If the general manager says: "I will not have a boob-tube in my office," then the systems analyst may have no hope of persuading any of top management to have a terminal. If certain types of decision are made by committees, it may be next to impossible to have them made by computer models. Management may have unshakable faith in the superiority of their own intuitive decisions. This is based on years of hard-won experience, and woe betide any computer specialist who challenges it.

It can be extremely frustrating, and indeed baffling, for an information scientist to find that after working for five years on a financial model of the corporation, management ignores it and continues to make financial decisions in the same intuitive way. This has happened and will go on happening because many top managers, especially older ones, have rigid confidence in their own style of decision making (usually borne out by past success).

SENIOR EXECUTIVE:

No matter how hard they have tried, the DP department has had almost no influence in this corporation on the style of management. Where the current style is "seat of the pants," it remains "seat of the pants" until there is an executive shake-up. If more mathematical analysis is called for, it does not come because the DP department has invented it. It comes because management has requested it and almost always that has been a new manager replacing the old.

Data-base systems combined with networks and distributed processing can allow a substantial degree of variance in management styles. To a greater extent than with centralized file systems, managers can run their own department in their own way.

The job of the systems analyst in this environment becomes twofold. *First,* he should assimilate himself as completely as possible into the local environment. He should live there and be the *confident* of the key local manager. He should understand that manager's style, and how best he can make use of data base and distributed systems. He should be part of the local environment rather than a visitor from head office. He should evaluate the extent to which the local staff can obtain their own information with report generators, query languages, higher-level data-base languages, or end-user programming languages.

Second, he should make sure that the corporate data dictionary is used, the data modeling procedures are followed, and the rules which are necessary for tying together a distributed system are obeyed.

FEAR OF PERSONAL INADEQUACY

Most people feel nervous about the nature of their jobs being changed, but often a new job demands the same types of abilities as the old and they feel reasonably sure that it will only be a matter of time before they have mastered it. A machine tool operator can learn to operate a new machine tool even if it uses a high level of automation. A scientist can learn a new field of research and will probably enjoy doing so. But a manager confronted with the spread of computerized decision making often feels decidedly apprehensive because he simply cannot understand what the operations research staff is talking about. Nobody has explained "integer programming" or "regression analysis" to him; he has forgotten all but the simplest of his mathematics; he simply does not know how to judge the validity of the output of a computer model. He once went to a one-day course on management science, but he cannot relate what was said to his own job and cannot understand the mess of symbols in the notes that were handed out. He doubts whether he will ever understand. He may not even want to understand. When he talks to the accountants or lawyers his management skill enables him to extract the essence from what they are saying, ask the right questions, and make judgments about the value of their advice. Not so with the operations research staff. He tries to ask the right questions but somehow seems to receive responses which are both condescending and as difficult to make judgments about as the pronouncements that triggered the questions.

NEW SKILLS

A high-level manager once asked the author to sit in on a meeting, as a personal favor, in which the senior operations research (OR) man was going to present the conclusions of a year's work. The manager pleaded: "I know I won't be able to understand what the hell he's talking about. I'd like you to listen to it and explain to me whether it makes sense and how far it would be sensible to go with it." The bearded OR man came in with flip charts. He spent the first half-hour explaining in childlike terms how one function of the corporation operated.

The manager listened with tactful patience, suppressing his growing irritation at being told information which he thought everbody knew. The OR man then switched his presentation to a mathematical analysis of the operations. His charts had partially unlabeled axes, his symbols were inadequately explained, and the purpose of his mathematics was not made clear. Only a person already familiar with the techniques in question could have followed what he was saying. The lecture ended with no clear proposal for action, and the manager said: "Well, what do you want us to do?" This triggered another burst of unclear mathematics which was cut short after 10 minutes by the manager saying he did not understand and the OR man reverting to the child's guide to how the company operates.

It was difficult to be sure whether the OR man had subconscious motives for being obscure, but there was virtually no chance at the end of the afternoon that the manager could have made a confident decision about how best to proceed. He appealed for help afterward: "It's always like that. Did you understand what he was talking about. . . ? Why can't he give a straightforward answer to my questions?"

It is not surprising that such managers produce an irrational reaction to rational systems. On the surface their reaction may be annoyance that the management scientist cannot express his views more clearly, but beneath the surface there is a fear of making decisions with the basis for the decisions not clearly understood. Worse—much worse—there is a horror that the management skills they have so arduously acquired may be inadequate in a world of computers and mathematics.

To some extent the executives in a highly computerized corporation need skills and talents different from those required before computers. The type of person best suited to decision making with computers is often unlikely to have risen through the ranks of conventional management. Conventional managers are often skilled at using intuition for judging situations and make much use of past experience, but experimentation with computer models or dialogue with an information system is foreign to both their temperament and intellect. Distributed processing and cheap personal computing is bringing the computer within range of *all* managers. New managers should now be expected to learn to use computers early in their careers, and steadily improve their familiarity and skills with them. To do this they will often need a substantial amount of help from systems analysts.

MATRIX MANAGEMENT

The question arises: To whom should the person who runs the *local* computing facilities report?

In most cases he should report to the local *user* management. They are the managers who must ultimately judge the usefulness and value of the computing facilities. They need the closest cooperation with whoever creates these facilities, and designs their applications, dialogues,

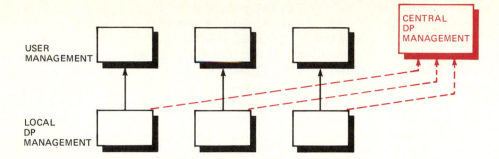

Figure 29.1 Lines of reporting: matrix management. Certain characteristics are necessary to make this work.

and printouts. User management should talk to them on a daily basis when
necessary about terminal displays or the printouts they want and the problems they foresee. To create the most effective facilities, user management
and their computer staff need to be very close. User management must feel
that *their* computer staff are on their side in the political arguments we have
described. The barons will demand unerring loyalty from their own DP staff.

This creates a conflict. We stress for many different reasons the needs
for corporatewide strategy and modeling. It must not be an ad hoc collection
of data implemented arbitrarily.

The local DP management must also report to central DP management,
as shown in Fig. 29.1, or the local data administrator must report to the
central data administrator. This situation of having two bosses is known as
matrix management. It happens elsewhere and can cause problems.

Certain characteristics are necessary in order to make the situation in
Fig. 29.1 work. First, the primary loyalty of the local DP management must
be clearly spelled out. It is shown by the solid arrows in the figure. The
barons must have no doubt about who their local DP manager *really* works
for, who judges him, and who can fire him.

Second, the characteristics of the dotted-line reporting must be spelled
out in detail. These include conforming to corporate standards, corporate
data dictionary, corporate data modeling, overall system design and distributed data administration, appropriate documentation, attendance at meetings,
memberships of committees, and so on.

Third, the dotted-line reporting should not be expected to work fully
unless there is a higher-level authority to enforce it. Both the barons and the
central DP management must report to the king. If the barons violate the
rules set by the central DP management, the latter must appeal to the king,
who has the ultimate authority over the barons (Fig. 29.2).

To make a widespread data-base environment work, then, *top management* comprehension and support is vital for political reasons as well as for
the planning reasons discussed earlier.

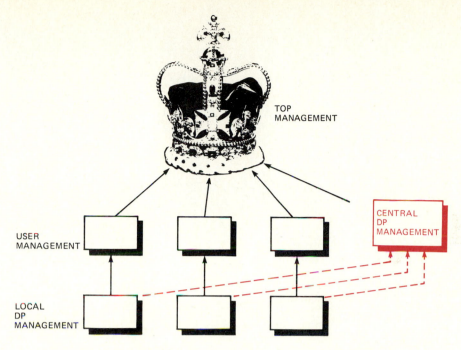

Figure 29.2 To make matrix management work, top management comprehension and support of the DDP strategy is vital.

REFERENCE

1. A. Jay, *Management and Machiavelli,* Holt, Rinehart and Winston, New York, 1978.

Could thou and I with fate conspire
To grasp this Sorry Scheme of things entire,
Would not we shatter it to bits and then
Remould it nearer to the Heart's desire!
  Omar Khayyam

30 CONVERSION

INTRODUCTION Some data administrators lie awake at night dreaming of working with a new corporation that does not yet have any data processing. Its data could be modeled correctly and cleanly from the start. A top-down plan could be implemented without problems caused by existing systems. Unfortunately, most data administrators have to live with the sins and systems of the past.

The earlier systems often use files, not data base. Their data have usually not been modeled and little or no attempt has been made to achieve data compatibility between different systems. As well as *file* systems there are often old data-base systems designed before today's principles of good data-base design were understood.

CONVERSION FAILURES What should be done with the old systems? Should they be brought into the modern world of data base and data modeling?

Unfortunately, that is often not easy to do. Much reprogramming would be needed and hundreds of person-years have been invested in the earlier systems.

Many corporations have attempted a major conversion of a file system to a data-base system and have failed. They have abandoned the attempt before it was completed. Often the reason for this is that it takes much more personnel than was anticipated; so much has to be reprogrammed. Often the attempt to convert is killed by the persons who control the DP finances. The conversion process itself creates no new *applications*. DP user management perceives a large amount of effort and expense with nothing to show for it. There is a long and serious application backlog. Management says: "Why are you spending all of this time on conversion when we desperately need you to be creating new application systems? Get on with something more useful!''

In one organization after another, the attempt to make a major conversion from files to data base has failed. This has been true in some of the most prestigious data-processing organizations. It is a piece of DP history that will doubtless repeat itself many times. Unless they were specifically designed for later conversion, you tend to be stuck with your old file systems.

END-USER EXECUTIVE:

People give a lot of lip service to how conversion is a problem. But I'm not sure the extent of the problem is completely recognized. I look at data base. Nobody can argue with it—it's like arguing with "Peace on Earth." It's a great goal and it's going to be great when we get there. However, we don't have the luxury of just starting up a new company where we can establish the environment and then start to do our business.

TWO APPROACHES   There are two approaches to evolving from the old *file* world to the new *data-base* world:

1. *Convert* the old systems to data base.
2. Allow them to continue their existence and *build a bridge* to the data-base systems.

Some old systems should probably be converted and some should continue their existence. In large installations there is a mix of these categories.

An old system exists: how should you decide whether to convert it? There are two questions that should be asked:

First, does it work?

If it works well, there is a strong argument for letting it alone. If it works inadequately, it should be revamped anyway and may be cut over to data-base operation.

Second, does it incur high maintenance costs?

If so, it is a candidate for redesign and cutting over to data-base operation.

If an application system works adequately and needs little maintenance, its conversion should probably be postponed. Expend the effort on something else; so many other applications are needed.

BUILDING A BRIDGE

If the decision is made that an old application should live on unconverted, it is often necessary to build a bridge between it and the new data-base environment.

In planning data resources, it is often unwise to assume that files will be converted easily to data-base form. A realistic appraisal is needed of the costs and difficulties of conversion, and the likelihood of completing it satisfactorily. The dismal history of uncompleted conversions should be weighed. Often system designers in the initial enthusiasm for data-base operation assume that the old systems will be converted. It is discovered too late that they will not. It is safer instead to assume that many old systems will survive, and plan a bridge that links them to the new data-base world.

DP EXECUTIVE:

We have a system that serves as an interface between the on-line data base and all the systems that were processed off-line from it—the various billing systems, and expense systems, and accounting systems. A daily tape file is fed into those systems.

Figure 30.1 shows a typical bridge. At the top is the output file from an existing application program. The data in it must update the data base, and a simple utility program is written for this. The old file records become a "user view" or subschema which must be represented in the data base. To accomplish this, some of the field formats may have to be adjusted by the utility program. There may be items in the file which would not have appeared in the data base if it had been designed by itself, but they must now be there for compatibility reasons.

The data base is updated by new programs, and from the updated version the old files are derived. The bottom of Fig. 30.1 shows this being done by another utility program. This conversion program is needed every time the old application programs are used. It may be in effect a high-speed dump which creates batch files to be run once a week or so. It may create on-line files for terminal usage. This bridge must be one of the first data-base programs to be tested to ensure that the old application programs continue to run.

In many cases an input to a data-base system must also be used to create input to a separate file system, possibly on a different machine. Such input should be entered into the system only once, and a necessary function of the data-base system is to create the required input for other operations.

A similar bridge may be used for creating files that end users manipulate

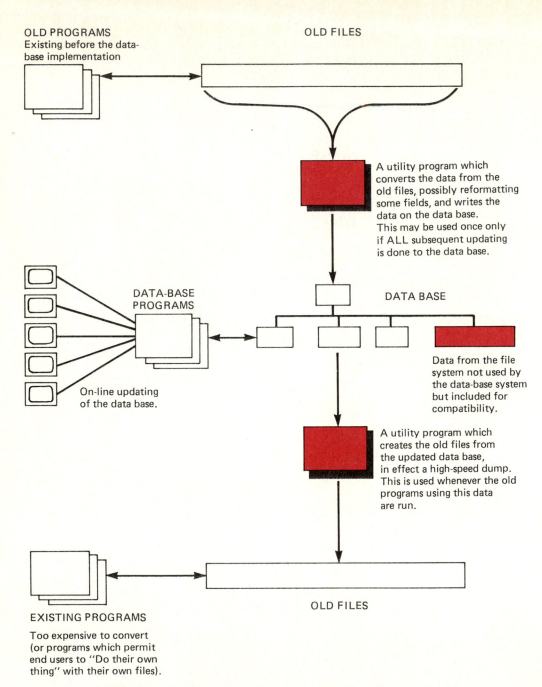

OLD PROGRAMS
Existing before the data-base implementation

OLD FILES

A utility program which converts the data from the old files, possibly reformatting some fields, and writes the data on the data base. This may be used once only if ALL subsequent updating is done to the data base.

DATA-BASE PROGRAMS

DATA BASE

On-line updating of the data base.

Data from the file system not used by the data-base system but included for compatibility.

A utility program which creates the old files from the updated data base, in effect a high-speed dump. This is used whenever the old programs using this data are run.

OLD FILES

EXISTING PROGRAMS

Too expensive to convert (or programs which permit end users to "Do their own thing" with their own files).

Figure 30.1 Bridge between the old file world and the new data-base world.

in their own way. This use of separate files keeps the end users out of the data base. Similarly, a disjoint end-user data base may be created for manipulation by a language such as Query-by-Example.

DATA ADMINISTRATOR

A lot of our systems have existing data that are of a considerable value. In developing a data base, we have to move from the old-style data files into a new data base. We generally develop a conversion aid that is tailored to that specific application and the creation of that data base, and we'll do a massive conversion with translation of the data into the new form. These are generally custom-written programs.

EXECUTIVE DIRECTOR OF SYSTEMS:

A complete overhaul of the applications programs did not seem feasible, but the division hit on the idea of a DBMS master file to serve as a sort of front end to these application programs. There was a savings of more than $100,000 annually in data preparation and data control. This limited effort brought the division into the DBMS environment and laid the basis for solid evolutionary development, including subsequent application revisions to exploit more fully the potential of the data-base environment [1].

CONVERSION MODELING

Whether old systems are *converted* or *a bridge is built,* the process needs to be taken into consideration in the *data modeling operation.*

If conversion is done, the user views employed by the old systems should be fed into the data-base synthesis process—they should be an input to the data modeling tool.

If a bridge is used, again the design of the bridge should be an input to the data modeling. The resulting model will often contain data items that would not have been included had the bridge to the old world been unnecessary. They are put into the new data bases to permit coexistence with the old systems. This is a messy but necessary compromise which the data administrator must plan.

Such planning and modeling is an essential part of evolving from the old systems to a data-base environment. The conversion programs—one might think of them as utility programs—are not difficult to write, but they have to be planned well ahead. They should be almost the first data-base programs to be tested, because the old systems must keep going.

GRADUAL CONVERSION

In long-established installations, conversion to data-base operation usually has to be a gradual process. There are too many files and programs for quick conversion, and the investment in them is high.

END-USER EXECUTIVE:

We have mounds of data; we have tons of processes and procedures. And we have the problem of all of these data which suffered from years of bad habits. We have a lot of people-conditioned bad habits, yet we want to convert all that—and at the same time we've got a moving target. We've got product changes; we've got the effect of legislative changes. It does frustrate efforts to move as quickly to the wonders of data base as management would like.

EXECUTIVE DIRECTOR OF SYSTEMS:

The problem is not unlike that of our Detroit skyline. We recently completed a magnificent new Renaissance Center along the riverfront with some of the most beautiful hotel and office structures to be found anywhere. This is exciting, but there is still a long way to go to bring the rest of the city up to Renaissance Center standards! The accumulation of history is still a huge obstacle to those who want the best of things right now.

. . . We might all wish we could somehow get rid of the old mess and start all over again. Unfortunately that old mess represents an investment in the hundreds of millions of dollars for my company [1].

What types of systems should be converted first?

There are several possible approaches to phased conversion. In some installations, data-base operation has begun at a time when most of the systems are off-line. The decision has been made that all development of all on-line systems shall employ data bases, with the off-line file systems being left alone for the time being with a bridge like that shown in Fig. 30.1.

In other installations, different types of activities can be tackled one at a time. Insurance companies refer to their different types of insurance as "lines of business." One insurance company approached the conversion problem by bringing one line of business at a time into data-base operation.

INSURANCE EXECUTIVE:

We have determined that in order to bring up applications faster, we would go with the data-base environment for all the lines of insurance that are not currently on the on-line system, and those are basically all of our commercial lines in the division. We will bring up one line of business at a time.

INTERVIEWER:

Does that mean that your files are going to continue to exist as you develop the data-base environment?

INSURANCE EXECUTIVE:

Yes. One of the problems with the amount of data that we have is that we still have to spin files off from those large on-line systems. We end up with tape volumes of 40 to 60 reels of tape that we have to process in an information type of environment, as opposed to an operational type of environment. We want to convert that operation to data base one line of business at a time.

In other installations, subject data bases have been implemented one at a time. Several banks, for example, have had a customer data base long before any other types of data base. Many programs had to make *calls* both to the customer data base and to separate *files.*

It is often relatively easy to implement separate *information system* (Class IV) data bases. Specified data are extracted from the file systems and reconstructed with the software of an information system using inverted lists or whatever means are provided for information searching.

CLEANING UP THE MESS   We have stressed that in most organizations the data are in a mess prior to the discipline of data-base techniques. Data items that are logically the same are given different names in different places and represented with different bit formats and lengths. Different data items are given the same name in different places. Data items are grouped together in any form, without any data modeling. Data bases themselves can also have this disease in a poorly controlled environment.

Much of the difficulty of the conversion process is the cleaning up of this mess. Some data dictionaries provide two functions which help in cleaning up. First, the existing data definitions can be collected (with varying degrees of automation) from the existing files, COBOL program data divisions, and directories of data-base management systems. This variety of definitions can be gathered into the data dictionary. Definitions and field formats that are more uniform can be substituted a step at a time. The data administration staff can work with the programmers, analysts, and users to select standard definitions and make modifications to programs.

The process is often slow and tedious. A small area at a time needs to be tackled. It may be relatively easy to load the definitions into the dictionary from all existing applications, but the mess revealed may be great enough to discourage even starting to clean it up.

The second valuable dictionary function is to *supply* data definitions and formats to existing programs or to the directory of a data management system. The programs can thereby be forced to use the standard definitions. One area at a time can be cut over to conform to the dictionary definitions and formats. From then on in that area, all program data definitions, all input/output area definitions, and all DBMS directory inputs will be obtained from the dictionary, thus ensuring conformity.

DISCIPLINE PRIOR TO DATA-BASE OPERATION

Conversion to data-base operation is incomparably easier if discipline has been maintained over data prior to the move to the data-base environment.

The trauma and failure rate of conversions is so great that *it cannot be recommended too strongly that both a dictionary and modeling tool be used as a corporate standard for all data, including file systems implemented long before an organization is ready for data base.* The programmers' data definitions should be generated from the dictionary.

In the long run, computerized corporations must have the discipline of data-base modeling, dictionaries, and strategic planning. The discipline ought to be in place now even in areas that are not yet ready for the data-base environment.

DP EXECUTIVE:

The file development teams all have to work from the same mechanized dictionary. This is a *corporate directive* and it applies to the minicomputer developers as well as the DP center. Furthermore, they are required to work with the data administration staff in modeling the data.

The models are, of course, a logical representation of the data. You often have to compromise from the third-normal-form structure to get performance out of a file system. But at least they start with a logical normalized view of the data and are forced to use the dictionary definitions, so when conversion to data base comes along we can do it reasonably quickly.

Nobody likes too much discipline and there was a lot of kicking and screaming when we introduced it. But in the old days before we did this, we often couldn't convert at all in practical terms.

As corporate data models become completed they cannot be employed overnight on all applications. Instead they act as strategic objectives. New applications use the data models; old applications will be converted to conform to the data models when the time comes to rebuild them. They may not be rebuilt for years, but eventually maintaining them with their old data becomes more expensive than rebuilding them new tools such as data-base application generators. Once rebuilt they are much cheaper to maintain. In a typical corporation's portfolio of applications, most will be rebuilt at some time in the next eight years. The portfolio is slowly adapted to conform to the data models, and then the information resource of the corporation is under control.

EFFECT OF DBMS ON CONVERSION   Once a data base is installed and controls a collection of applications, what effect does this have on subsequent conversion?

A major reason for moving to data base is to make application conversion easier. Different reports and query processing can be generated quickly. The ease of modifying major applications depends on whether the data-base management system has field sensitivity and other features which aid maintenance, as discussed in Chapter 7. It also depends on whether the data are correctly normalized. Good data-base installations have achieved much greater conversion flexibility.

There are, however, ways in which data-base systems make conversion more difficult. The attempt to change to a different DBMS can be difficult, and extremely difficult if that DBMS is differently structured, e.g., the change from a CODASYL to hierarchical data base.

EXECUTIVE DIRECTOR OF SYSTEMS:

Moving to a new DBMS is not unlike getting married. It takes a lot of desire, commitment, sacrifice, and investment. It involves moving to a whole new lifestyle. Once there, the return to the old lifestyle may be difficult or impossible without wrenching adjustment problems [1].

CHIEF INFORMATION EXECUTIVE:

If moving to a DBMS is like getting married, changing to a different DBMS is like divorce and remarriage—Hell!

Most DP installations change their computer every three to five years. If this is a change to a fully compatible machine, DBMS usage has no effect. If it is a change from Burroughs to Honeywell, DBMS usage makes the change very difficult and expensive. If a large number of applications are involved such a change may be prohibitively expensive.

Sometimes the change involves an upgrade in the operating system. This migration ought not to involve the DBMS, but sometimes it does. Most existing DBMSs have a poor relationship with operating systems, and this wastes machine resources. As the operating system is improved, the DBMS may be changed to work with it more efficiently. In the future we shall see DBMS

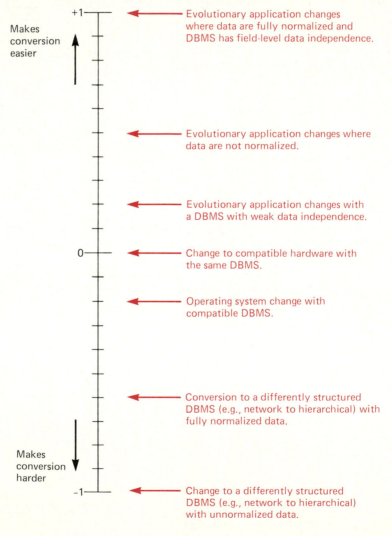

Figure 30.2 The effect of data-base use on the difficulties of conversion.

functions being tightly linked into operating systems, and into hardware, microcode, and back-end machines.

EXECUTIVE DIRECTOR OF SYSTEMS:

The presence of IMS has added substantially to the difficulty and complexity of the conversion to MVS—something close to twice as much effort as would have been involved with non-DBMS applications. The IMS conversion involves more than a new operating system. It requires the transition to an upgraded DBMS called IMS–VS. One manager sees the new package as offering many attractive new features. Another manager sees no incremental benefits at all for this particular application, but he has no choice; his present IMS software will not be supported under MVS [1].

Figure 30.2 indicates the effect of DBMS use on the difficulties of conversion. It uses a scale from +1 to –1, where 0 means no effect, positive numbers mean easier conversion, and negative numbers mean harder conversion.

Normalization and good logical design help to make conversion easier. These combined with a flexible DBMS can make a huge difference to maintenance. At the other end of the scale, an organization with thousands of applications using an ill-structured data base is effectively locked into that data base. Changing to a different data base is too expensive to contemplate.

REFERENCE

1. Mayford L. Roark, Executive Director of Systems for the Ford Motor Company, Dearborn, Michigan, "Evolution in Computer Systems," *Data Base and Sigmod Record,* Jan 1982, ACM, New York.

31 INFORMATION QUALITY

The computer with its growing storage facility is a tool *par excellence* for collecting enormous quantities of otherwise indigestible data. The collection of data, however, has little value unless the data are used to understand the world and prescribe action to improve it. Volumes of disorganized facts and figures are of little use—in industry, in government, or anywhere else. The central problem of much data processing is extracting from a mountain of facts an essence of value to human users.

Some authorities use the word *data* to refer to the mass of undigested facts and figures which computers collect, and *information* to refer to morsels extracted from this mass and processed for a specific person or persons, for a specific purpose, or to fulfill a specific request. "Information" is digested "data." The same data can be processed in a variety of different ways to produce different pieces of information which are useful in different circumstances. The key to making computers useful to management is learning how to present the right information in the right way, and this is no simple matter.

The same problem exists in all communication media. The newspaper columnist has a mass of facts available to him. He must distill from these facts an essence which captivates and informs his reader. The movie director has an infinity of subjects, perspectives, and camera angles open to him, and the film he shoots can be edited in an endless number of ways. He must choose those ways and those subjects which grip his audience. The same is true with computerized information systems, but until recently the computer has not generally been regarded as a communications medium. It is still rare to find systems analysts who think about it in this way. The communication of information is an art. Much has been said about "computer science" but little about the art of communication between machines and people. Like journalism and movies, human–computer communication must develop its own literacy and style. It is far from accomplishing this as yet, in some corporations. Many human–computer dialogues are barely fit for human consumption.

The information that can be successfully communicated, for example, to management, varies greatly with the means and style of communication, with the choice of data, and with the way the data are processed.

CAN YOU JUSTIFY AN INFORMATION SYSTEM?

Some computer systems can be cost-justified in tangible terms. It will be increasingly difficult in future systems to find tangible justification. For that matter the telephone systems of a corporation, and many other services, cannot be justified tangibly. The justification of a computer's doing the payroll depends on the number of clerks it replaces. The justification of an information system depends on the *value of the information it provides*. It becomes necessary to assess this value, rather than merely to assess cost reductions or displacements. The value of the information must exceed the cost of providing it.

Can we measure the value of information?

The answer to that question depends on what the information is used for. If it is used in an "operations system," the value of the information can usually be estimated, at least approximately. If it is a general-purpose information system, the value may be impossible to estimate in any other than the most subjective terms. It would be exceedingly difficult to estimate the value of having your telephone. Information systems will be evaluated equally subjectively. This requires end-user management (including top management) involvement in the functional analysis.

WHAT QUALITIES ARE NEEDED IN INFORMATION PRESENTATION?

To have the maximum likelihood of being valuable to its potential users, computer-provided *information* must have a number of characteristics, which are listed in Box 31.1. A manager who is given information lacking in these qualities should not accept it passively. He should discuss the matter with the data-processing manager or systems analyst.

QUALITY RATING

Having too much data can be almost as bad as having none at all. Several of my colleagues receive computer-printed listings of technical articles and reports in their fields of interest. The listings are mailed to the users periodically, and the users provide the system with a "profile" of their range of interests. The envelopes in which the listings arrive can be recognized, and many of the users drop the

BOX 31.1   Characteristics of useful computer-provided information

Computer-provided information should have the following qualities; system designers, please note.

1. It must be *accurate*. The worst criticism of some information systems is that the information is inaccurate.

2. It must be *tailored to the needs of the user*.

3. It must be *relevant* to what he requires at that time.

4. It must be *timely*. Often it must be given in response to a user's request. If it is given to him a day late, he may not use it in some cases.

5. It must be *immediately understandable*. Some computer printouts are remarkably unintelligible.

6. Its significance must be *immediately recognizable*. This is often a function of the method or format of presentation.

7. It helps if it is *attractively presented*.

8. It should be *brief*. The lengthy listings characteristic of batch processing often conceal rather than reveal information. Single significant facts should not be camouflaged by the inclusion of other less relevant data.

9. It should be sufficiently *up-to-date* for the purpose for which it will be employed.

10. It should be *trustworthy*. Management is often suspicious of computerized information sources. Management will soon lose confidence in them if occasional errors are found in the data.

11. It should be *complete*. The user should not be left feeling that he has received only part of the information he really needs. To obtain complete information, it may be necessary for the user to browse in the files or ask certain types of questions relating to the information. Human-machine dialogue then becomes a vital part of the information-finding process.

12. It should be *easily accessible*. If a terminal is difficult to use, or confusing, it will not be used.

envelopes into wastebaskets without opening them. The trouble is that the system provides too many data and the items have no quality rating. The user cannot possibly read all the literature that is listed, and he is given no way of telling which is worth reading. He finds out what is worth reading by word of mouth from his colleagues and ignores the computer listing.

What is needed is a quality rating on the input given to the system. If the reports could be classified with codes such as

E: Excellent   N: Nothing new

P: Platitudinous   B: Badly written

S: Useful survey   I: Contains new ideas

M: Highly mathematical

or better, a grading under various headings, perhaps being the mean and standard deviation of many opinions, then the information would be of value.

The reason why the *Michelin Guide* to food and hotels in France is so valuable is that it is full of quality ratings and indications of the best items on menus, and these ratings are *trustworthy*.

It sometimes seems socially undesirable to make quality judgments about technical reports or a person's work. However, because of the information deluge that computers can produce, it must be appreciated that an egalitarian attitude to information systems can be disastrous.

ACCURACY   The worst criticism of some management informa-
                                  tion systems is that they contain inaccurate data.
Inaccuracies can arise in three ways. First, the hardware, software, or transmission lines may introduce data errors. There are various effective technical controls which can prevent this happening [1].

Second, and more serious, the personnel who feed information to the system may have made errors. Human data-entry errors are more difficult to control than machine errors and are far more numerous. This is especially so when the data are entered at geographically scattered terminals. There are, however, various checks and controls that can be placed on data input [2].

Third, and still more serious, the input to some information systems becomes methodically distorted. If the system contains schedules, the users may enter deliberately pessimistic estimates. If the system is being used to judge employees in some way, the employees may learn to adjust the figures they give it. Because of complex psychological relationships between the system and its users, the information it contains may, in some cases, degenerate in quality.

One factor often works against data accuracy. The managers who use the system expect the data it gives them to be accurate and usually feel that the question of data accuracy is a technical problem to be solved by the data-processing department. The data-processing department, on the other hand, sees its job as including the design of technical controls on accuracy but thinks that if users feed wrong information into the system, that is a problem for management. In some major systems, neither side has taken responsibility for preventing input being methodically distorted, and the result has been a misinformation system that has become generally suspect.

Often, lower or middle management feels threatened by a system that makes information about their areas immediately available to their superiors. They may permit the input to the system to become distorted or take little care with its accuracy. T. B. Mancinelli, discussing experience with U.S. military information systems, compares them with corporate information systems as follows:

> The former middle management decision makers lose both authority and responsibility. No matter how much better the decision may be, lower-level management personnel are anti-computer and anti-centralization. This is understandable for they are being stripped, slowly but inexorably, of their authority, responsibility, and former decision-making powers. What are they being given in return to compensate for their loss? Mainly, more requirements to collect and submit data to the new decision makers! Is it any wonder that middle- and lower-level management personnel show little enthusiasm for data accuracy, completeness and timeliness? Especially in large organizations, middle- and lower-level management are being required, more and more, to operate strictly within the system. There is little room left for individual initiative and the important role at this level is becoming more input oriented. This represents a most serious human problem to be overcome in highly centralized automated management information systems [3].

Michael Korda [4] describes how he was assigned, early in his publishing career, to examine a book publisher's list of books over a five-year period and break the total output into several categories: "religious," "fiction," "belles-lettres," "history," "biography," and so on. This was to be done so that the executive committee could plan ahead how many manuscripts should be purchased in the different categories.

Unfortunately, it was often difficult to decide into which of the given categories a book fell. Should a work of mysticism by a Greek poet, for example, be listed under "poetry," "philosophy," "belles-lettres," or "religion"? If it was listed under more than one category, the total of books published would be wrong. Korda, who confesses complete lack of interest in the task, could either toss a coin or list it as "miscellaneous." He did the latter. Before long, half the list was "miscellaneous." There was no time to read the books to establish their category. When the list was nearing completion, the numbers in some categories seemed low, so the frustrated list maker switched some of the books to other categories. The objective was to produce a neat, interestingly colored chart, within one week. That objective was met. Because it was attractive, the chart was used for planning at the highest level for some years after.

Years later the percentages found their way into textbooks on publishing. They then assumed a far more authoritative aura. People who doubt figures in their own files, with good reason, accept them as gospel when they come back from the outside in a magazine, book, or external information system.

The problem in this case was that the categories did not make sense, and the list maker was not authorized to change them.

THE SCALE OF PROBABILITY   Information needs can be graded on a basis of how predictable they are. The degree of predictability has a major effect on the design of data-processing systems.

At the bottom of the scale in Fig. 31.1 the information in question is asked for repeatedly, many times a day, such as a branch bank officer asking for details of customers' accounts or a factory foreman asking for details of jobs to be done.

Furthermore, the nature of the information requested is known precisely, in advance of the request. It is not known which job the foreman will inquire about next, but what he wants to know about it will be anticipated precisely. As the system designers have precise knowledge of the information requests, there is no excuse for the system not responding to them in a manner that is crystal clear. The information should have all the attributes listed in Box 31.1.

Higher up the scale, the requests for information may not come quite

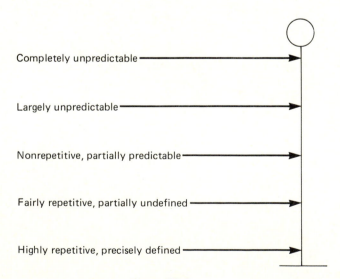

Completely unpredictable

Largely unpredictable

Nonrepetitive, partially predictable

Fairly repetitive, partially undefined

Highly repetitive, precisely defined

Figure 31.1

so repetitively. There might be one per day. There might be some variation in what is asked for, so that the computer has to compose a reply. If the information is asked for less frequently, the answer has to be more valuable to justify the cost of the system.

At the top of the scale, the information sought might be highly valuable. It might be information for a top-level corporate decision. However, the request has never occurred before. Considerable foresight would have been needed in order to anticipate it. It is quite likely that all the data needed to respond to the request will be in the data base somewhere, but possibly scattered through different record types. However, to respond, the data must be located and processed. The data can be located quickly only if they are organized in an appropriate fashion, and they can be processed only if a suitable program exists.

The books in a library illustrate the problem of locating data. The catalogue is designed to enable you to find a book of a given title or books by a given author. If, however, you ask the question "Which books have the word 'management' in their title?" the catalogue does not give a direct answer. The catalogue would have to be searched and because "management" may not be the first word in the title, all the catalogue entries would have to be inspected—a lengthy operation. The time-consuming search could be avoided by having a different type of catalogue (a KWIC index), but most libraries do not have this. Similar arguments apply to computer files. Certain types of questions can be answered only either by an expensive search through the files or by means of a special index. The question "How many books have been written about hippopotamuses?" needs either a complete search or a special index. If the special index were available, we could say that these *types* of questions had been anticipated though not their exact nature. We are halfway up the scale of Fig. 31.1.

If the library user had asked the question, "Which books discuss information systems for top management?", we would be in a much worse position. The books needed may or may not have "management" or "information systems" in the title. Some books with these words in the title would be quite irrelevant (*Greenhouse Management, Police Information Systems*). Some books on management information systems do not discuss *top* management. Searching the catalogue alone is not enough; knowledge about the books themselves is needed. If good abstracts of the books existed, the question might be answered using them. It might be answered from a set of key words describing the main themes of the book. On the other hand, it might not. It depends on whether the abstract or the set of key words is suitably composed, and many such questions would be answered only incompletely in this way. Furthermore, there is the problem of searching the abstract or key words. If this is to be other than a very long job, specially constructed directories are needed. Considering all the questions that might be asked, the directories would become massive. Already the directories to a data base occupy much more space than the data themselves in some computer systems.

"Information systems for top management" is a fairly major topic. If the user had asked, "Which books mention the Westinghouse Information system?", a much more detailed search would be necessary. Again, "information systems for top management" is a fairly well-defined topic. The user could have asked, "Which books cast light on the influence of Protestantism on the rise of capitalism?"

AN INFORMATION STAFF   The trouble with information is that it comes in an almost infinite number of varieties. We could not devise a library computer that could answer every user's question. Similarly, we cannot devise a management information system that can answer every manager's question. Top management asks the most variable and the most important questions—but they are the most difficult questions to answer.

It is the hallmark of a good manager that he asks the right questions. He constantly varies his questioning in search for the answer that is of the most use to him. He is familiar with doing this with people, not machines. However, the way to extract high-level information from future computer systems is likely to be to interrogate them at a suitable fast terminal with a variety of questions until their capability to provide the needed information is clarified. Fast searching of multiple attributes is necessary.

What can we do about the hard-to-catch nature of information? In a library there is no substitute for a really skilled librarian. If you ask a knowledgeable librarian any of the foregoing questions, she would probably come back with a reasonable answer. Similarly, in a management information system, or any other sort of information system near the top of the scale in Fig. 31.1, there is no substitute for human intelligence. The best solution to many problems results from the combination of human intelligence and computers. To provide top management with information is a formidable problem, and we cannot hope to solve it by machine alone. We need an intelligent management information "librarian" who thoroughly understands the nature of the information sources and can use the computer to process the information. In a few corporations this skill is growing in their Information Centers.

With the proliferation of corporate data bases, a vastly increased amount of data is becoming available for corporate decision making, but is still difficult to cast into the form of useful information. An important adjunct to corporate information systems is a small staff of intelligent professionals who understand the structure of the various data bases and know how to extract information from them on demand. This pliable human link is needed to bridge the gap between information users and data-base systems.

REFERENCES

1. James Martin, *Security, Accuracy, and Privacy in Computer Systems,* Prentice-Hall, Inc., Englewood Cliffs, NJ, 1973, Sec. II.

2. Ibid., Chap. 7.

3. Colonel T. B. Mancinelli, "Management Information Systems: The Trouble with Them," *Computers and Automation,* July 1972.

4. Michael Korda, *Power! How to Get It, How to Use It,* Random House, Inc., New York, 1975.

In spite of all their friends could say,
On a winter's morn, on a stormy day,
In a sieve they went to sea.
Edward Lear

32 SECURITY AND PRIVACY

INTRODUCTION   Security and privacy are important because many people in many places have access to a data-base system. The information stored in some data-base systems may be of great value to a corporation. It must not be lost, stolen, or damaged. It is important to protect the data and programs from hardware and software failures, from catastrophes, and from criminals, vandals, incompetents, and people who would misuse it.

A data base is often shared by users for whom security is of little or no importance, and other users for whom it is vital. It may be shared by users who are highly responsible with urgent business and others who are irresponsible and likely to try anything.

A shared environment is more difficult to control than a nonshared environment. Increasingly today, data are shared in data bases, and made accessible to a larger number of people via networks. A data-base, data-communication system needs tight controls. Recognizing this, the computer industry has designed hardware and software with better facilities for security than with non-data-base systems.

DEFINITIONS   *Security* refers to *the protection of resources from damage and the protection of data against accidental or intentional disclosure to unauthorized persons or unauthorized modifications or destruction.*

Privacy refers to *the rights of individuals and organizations to determine for themselves when, how, and to what extent information about them is to be transmitted to others.*

Although the technology of privacy is closely related to that of security, privacy is an issue that goes far beyond computer centers and networks. To a large extent it is a problem of society. To preserve the privacy of data about individuals, solutions are needed beyond technical solutions. Future society, dependent on a massive use of networks and data banks, will need new legal and social controls if the degree of privacy of personal information that is cherished today is to be maintained.

Data can be locked up in computers as securely as they can be locked up in a bank vault. Nevertheless, the data on many systems cannot be regarded as being highly secure because insufficient attention has been paid to the data or implementation of the security procedures.

Security is a highly complex subject because there are so many different aspects to it. A systems analyst responsible for the design of security needs to be familiar with all features of the system because the system can be attacked or security breached in highly diverse ways. Sometimes a great amount of effort is put into one aspect of security and other aspects are neglected. If a moat is seen as the way to make a castle secure, a great amount of security engineering could be applied to the moat. It could be very wide, and full of hungry piranha fish, and could have a fiercely guarded drawbridge. However, this alone would not make the castle secure. A determined intruder could tunnel under the moat. A security designer sometimes becomes so involved with one aspect of security design that he fails to see other ways of breaking into the system. It takes much knowledge and ingenuity to see all the possible ways.

TWELVE ESSENTIALS

Box 32.1 lists 12 essentials of distributed system security:

1. The users of a network must be positively *identifiable* before they use it.

2. The systems, and possibly also the network management, must be able to check that their actions are *authorized.*

3. Their actions should be *monitored* so that if they do something wrong they are likely to be found out.

4. Data, hardware, and software should be *protected* from fire, theft, or other forms of destruction.

5. They should be *locked* from unauthorized use.

6. The data should be *reconstructible* because, however good the precautions, accidents sometimes happen.

7. The data should be *auditable*. Failure to audit computer systems adequately has permitted some of the world's largest crimes.

8. The network and systems should be *tamper-proof*. Ingenious programmers should not be able to bypass the controls.

9. Transmission should be *fail-safe* so that when errors or failures occur, messages are not lost, double-processed, or irrecoverably garbled.

10. Transmissions should be *private* with some being protected from eavesdropping and tampering by cryptography.

11. Computer centers should be as far as possible, *catastrophe-proof*.

12. The system should not depend on one exceptionally vital center because it might be destroyed by fire or whatever. Such a computer center should be *replicated*. Many corporations have recently planned a second computer center.

BOX 32.1 The essence of security

System users should be

- Identifiable

Their actions should be

- Authorized
- Monitored

Data, hardware, and software should be

- Protected
- Locked

Data should be

- Reconstructible
- Auditable
- Tamper-proof

Transmission should be

- Fail-safe
- Private

Vital computer centers should be

- Catastrophe-proof
- Replicated

LAYERS OF PROTECTION The nucleus of security control lies in the technical design of the data-base management system, and network and computer systems. Without tight controls in the hardware and software, no other precautions can make the system secure.

Design of tightly controlled systems, however, is not enough by itself. Several types of protection are needed. Security can be represented by another layer diagram, as shown in Fig. 32.1. The layer of technical controls is surrounded by that of physical security. This refers to locks on the doors, guards, alarms, and other means of preventing unauthorized access, fire precautions, protection of stored data files, and so forth. It is not enough to have good hardware and software if discs can be stolen or the tape library destroyed by fire.

The next layer is that of administrative controls to ensure that the system is used correctly. The programmers and data-processing staff must be controlled so that they do not misuse the system. Controlled computer-room and program-testing procedures must be enforced. The administrative controls extend beyond the data-processing section to the user departments, scattered far across the network, the auditors, and general management.

The layers in Fig. 32.1 are not entirely separate. Physical security is not irrelevant when designing system techniques. The question of physical

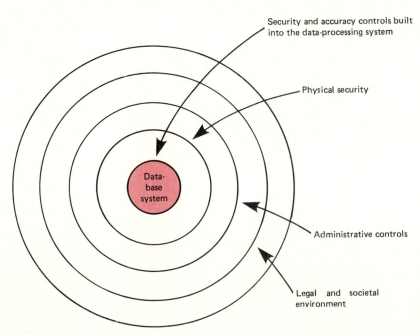

Figure 32.1 Four layers of control needed for data-base security and privacy.

security affects what transmission and system safeguards are used. The administrative procedures are very much related to the system design, especially with a real-time or terminal-based system. The auditors need to be involved in the system design, and the views of general management concerning security very much affect the system design.

The outermost layer of Fig. 32.1 is by far the most problematical. When the computer revolution has run its course, society will be very different. Many controls will no doubt have evolved, seeking to maximize the benefits and minimize the dangers of a technology of which George Orwell never dreamed. A legal framework is beginning to emerge in some countries which will relate to computers and networks.

TYPES OF SECURITY EXPOSURE

There is a wide diversity of different types of security exposure, most of them relating to the computer center, independent of networks [1]. Catastrophes such as major embezzlements have resulted in dramatic headlines, but by far the most common cause of computer calamities is human carelessness and accidents. One company reported "a $3.8 million deficiency" caused by an error in cutover. Usually, failures are less spectacular and more frequent.

Data-base languages for end users, which are easy to use, increase the dangers because far more persons can access or manipulate the data if they are not carefully protected.

Distributed systems, if poorly designed or loosely managed, could increase the probability of accidents through carelessness. Data, instead of residing in one highly secure center, may be distributed among locations with less protection. The greater complexity of a distributed system has sometimes increased the frequency of problems. Control, instead of residing in one location with one management, may be scattered.

A major exposure introduced by networks is the ease with which persons and machines can gain access to a computer center. It is necessary to prevent unauthorized access and unauthorized communication between machines.

Another exposure is that data transmitted may be seen by unauthorized persons, recorded, diverted, or even modified by tampering with the lines or switching nodes.

THREE-LEVEL ATTACK

Each security exposure must be attacked in three ways:

1. *Minimize the probability of it happening at all.* A major part of fire precautions should be preventive, and this is just as important with all other security breaches. Would-be embezzlers should be discouraged from ever beginning.

2. *Minimize the damage if it does happen.* An intruder who succeeds in bypassing the physical or programmed controls that were intended to keep him out should still be very restricted in what he can accomplish. A fire, once started, should be prevented from spreading. If the security procedures are compromised, it must be possible to limit the harm that could result. Some security designers have made the grave error of supposing that their preventive measures will always work.

3. *Design a method of recovering from the damage.* It *must* be possible to reconstruct vital records or whole files if they become accidentally or willfully damaged or lost. It *must* be possible to recover from a fire sufficiently quickly to keep the business running. If an unauthorized person obtains a security code or a file of network passwords, it must be possible to change these quickly so that they are of no use to him. It is important to attack the security problem *in depth,* and recovery procedures are vital to the overall plan. The designers of the preventive mechanisms must not be allowed to become so infatuated with their schemes that they neglect recovery techniques.

HIGHER LEVEL OF AUTOMATION   The best data-base-management-system software and hardware provides better security and recovery from failures than most *file* management facilities. To be truly secure, it is necessary to make the controls impossible to bypass without great ingenuity. An *active,* rather than passive dictionary enforces correct representation of data. A data-base-management system implemented in *hardware* or microcode rather than software prevents misuse of data by bypassing the software. A hardware implementation of a DBMS with an active dictionary and audit controls is still better. The ability to keep all sensitive data *on-line,* possibly in a mass storage system with hierarchical staging of data from a slow, cheap medium to a fast, more expensive medium, makes it difficult to steal data, lose them, or load the wrong volumes. These moves to a high level of data-base automation enhance security.

NONPROCEDURAL END-USER LANGUAGES   We have stressed that it is desirable to employ data-base languages for end users which make it as easy as possible to access and use the data, search the data base, generate reports, and sometimes update the data or create new logical files.

However, the more such power we put into users' hands and the easier we make it to access and use data bases, the more vulnerable data bases become unless the security and auditing controls are tight. Powerful end-user languages need to go hand in hand with powerful security controls.

The potential vulnerability is increased by the spread of networks. It is becoming easier to access data-base systems from remote locations. Controls are needed to know who is accessing a data base and where he is. With flexible networks he could be anywhere. Controls are needed to prevent network users seeing or, worse, changing data without positive authorization.

The authorization schemes may be linked directly to the end-user language. For example, when a user asks what logical files are available, the system will reveal *only* those which are authorized for access by that user. When a user asks what data items are in a given relation, he will be told only those he is authorized to see.

Even with such authorization controls, it is desirable to make some end-user data bases entirely separate from the master data bases. They may be separated on the same machine, but it is more secure to put the end-user data bases in a separate computer, often today a minicomputer. A user department may be allowed to access its own minicomputer with the high-level languages, but not the mainframe data bases. Data may be moved periodically from the mainframe data base to the end-user minicomputer with the various extractors illustrated in Fig. 25.6. Data may possibly be moved from the end-user data base to the mainframe data base if there are tight enough security controls.

Sometimes end users have exercised much creativity in the way they employ their own data-base systems. The nonprocedural end-user languages are increasing the scope for this creativity.

In some systems the users need to access data that are updated in real time in a master data base, as well as to use their own data-base system. The same terminal may be employed for both, with tight controls on the accesses to the master system.

PRIVACY LOCKS   The question of *who* is authorized to do *what* with a data base is vitally important. Before each operation, a computer should check that it is an authorized operation.

Authorization schemes vary from being very simple to highly complex. One of the simplest schemes requires that the user key in a *password* which only he should know. If it is an acceptable password for the program or file in question, he is allowed to proceed. The CODASYL Data Description Language uses *privacy locks* appended to the data. The privacy lock is a single value which is specified in the schema description. Data locked in this way cannot be used by a program unless the program provides a value called a *key* which matches the privacy lock. Both the lock and the key can be either a "literal" collection of bits, a variable, or the result of executing a specified procedure. It is rather like the user of a bank safe needing to know the combination that will open the safe. Unlike a bank safe, however, different combinations can be used for all different data types. The locking mechanism can be much more intricate than with a bank safe.

Figure 32.2 shows a possible sequence of events when a terminal is used, showing the variety of locks that could be applied. No one link through a network is likely to have all of these locks, but should have several.

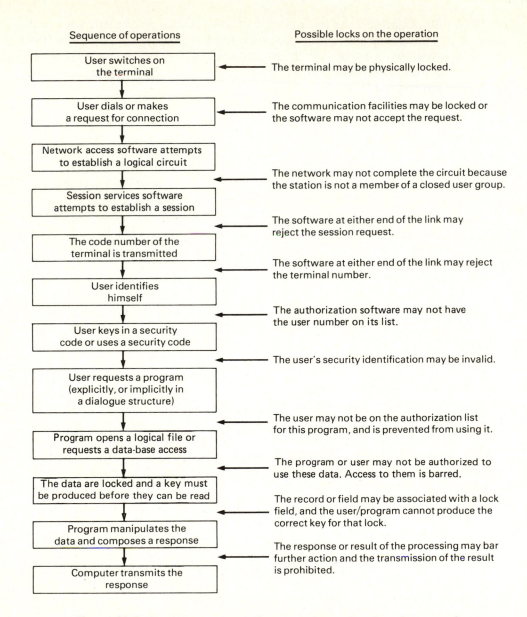

Sequence of operations	Possible locks on the operation

User switches on the terminal ← The terminal may be physically locked.

User dials or makes a request for connection ← The communication facilities may be locked or the software may not accept the request.

Network access software attempts to establish a logical circuit

Session services software attempts to establish a session ← The network may not complete the circuit because the station is not a member of a closed user group.

The code number of the terminal is transmitted ← The software at either end of the link may reject the session request.

User identifies himself ← The software at either end of the link may reject the terminal number.

User keys in a security code or uses a security code ← The authorization software may not have the user number on its list.

User requests a program (explicitly, or implicitly in a dialogue structure) ← The user's security identification may be invalid.

Program opens a logical file or requests a data-base access ← The user may not be on the authorization list for this program, and is prevented from using it.

The data are locked and a key must be produced before they can be read ← The program or user may not be authorized to use these data. Access to them is barred.

Program manipulates the data and composes a response ← The record or field may be associated with a lock field, and the user/program cannot produce the correct key for that lock.

Computer transmits the response ← The response or result of the processing may bar further action and the transmission of the result is prohibited.

Figure 32.2 Possible sequence of events when a data base is accessed, and locks that could be applied at each stage.

AUTHORIZATION SCHEMES

Locks built into systems and networks are related to authorization schemes and tables that define who is authorized to do what, or what interconnections are permitted.

The authorization tables can relate to:

1. Individual users
2. Groups or categories of users
3. Security levels (top secret, corporate confidential, etc.)
4. Application programs
5. Time of day (such as a time lock on a bank vault)
6. Terminal or terminal location
7. Network node (e.g., host computer, cluster controller, concentrator)
8. Transaction types
9. Combinations of these

Restrictions can be placed on the relationships between six different entities on a network: the users; the terminals or input/output devices that are used; the network nodes, such as host computers or terminal cluster controllers; the application programs; the data constructs—schemas, areas, records, and data items (or relations, domain and tuples)—and the volumes, such as tapes or discs, on which the data are recorded. Locks may exist on any of these relationships, and alarms may be used to bring attention to any suspected violation.

Figure 32.3 summarizes the relationships that may be locked:

1. The user himself may be identified and locked out of the terminal, or out of the node, program, data, or volume he requests.
2. A specific terminal may be considered in an insecure area and locked out of certain nodes, programs, data, or volumes.
3. A node such as a computer or terminal cluster controller may be locked out of other nodes, programs, data, or volumes.
4. A program may be prevented from accessing certain data or volumes.
5. Certain data may have a high security classification and so be prevented from being stored on any volume that has a lower classification.

The locks may be based on security classification levels, on the individual entities or groups of entities, or on time. These are indicated by the letters L, I, and T, respectively, in Fig. 32.3.

If security classification levels are used, the types of entities may each be assigned a classification, such as CONFIDENTIAL, SECRET, and so on.

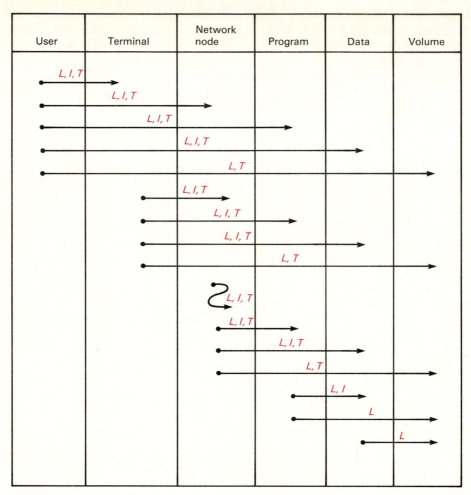

L = based on security *levels* (top secret, secret, corporate confidential).
I = based on *individual* items or persons, or groupings of these.
T = based on *time* of day (like a time lock on a bank vault).

Figure 32.3 Relationships covered by locks, alarms, and authorization tables. The column labeled "data" can be further subdivided into classes of data structure: schema, area, record, and data item (or relation, domain, and tuple).

If a user is not security cleared for SECRET information, he will not be permitted to use a terminal classified for SECRET work, or permitted to use any program data, or volume classified SECRET. SECRET data may not be transmitted to an unclassified terminal. If a volume is not labeled SECRET, SECRET data may not be written on it. And so on. As indicated in Fig. 32.3, any of the relationships may be based on such classification levels. There may be any number of levels.

Much greater precision is obtained by basing the relationships on individual users or entities. User A is only permitted to use program B, data C, and volumes D and E. Program X is only permitted to access data Y and Z. Or a certain file, volume, or program is labeled so that it can only be used by the person who created it. Some such schemes result in the need for large authorization tables. To lessen the size of the tables, the individual persons, items, or data entities can be arranged into groups, and the locks based on groupings.

Last, the system may have time locks. Like a bank-vault door, access may be permitted only at certain times of a day. A *nocturnal* intruder will not be able to access data even if he knows the necessary passwords or security codes. A terminal in a secure area on the prime shift may be classified as insecure on other shifts. If a person is detected trying to use a magnetic-strip card key on a terminal out of hours, he will immediately trigger an alarm.

ALARMS

To keep burglars out of a building or vault, the locks on the windows and doors will be backed up by burglar alarms. The locks on networks, and surveillance methods designed to detect unauthorized entry, can sound alarms. Some systems send an immediate alarm message to a security officer's terminal, and possibly ring a bell there. Some systems inform a suitable authority at the user's location. Some do both. The potential intruder may be locked out of the system, or may be kept talking harmlessly while the local security officer investigates.

The existence of alarms, but not the details of how they work or what triggers them, should be well publicized to act as a psychological deterrent.

IDENTIFYING THE TERMINAL USER

With some users of networks it is necessary to identify positively the person at the terminal. Until he is identified he should not be permitted to have access to any sensitive data or to make any modifications to the files. On other systems it is not necessary to identify the terminal user, providing the computer knows which terminal it is, because only security-cleared personnel can use that particular terminal. There are three ways in which a person can be identified.

1. *By personal physical characteristics.* For example, a device can be used for reading and transmitting a person's fingerprints or thumbprint, and the computer can have a program for identifying this. Less expensive, his telephone voice, speaking certain pre-

arranged digits or words, can be transmitted to the computer; the computer will have a program for recognizing his voice by comparing his speech against a stored *voiceprint.* Some systems have a device that measures the lengths of a person's fingers on one hand—this being a set of variables that differs from one person to another, like fingerprints, and is not too expensive to measure and encode. Physical identification schemes are likely to be the most expensive of the three ways to recognize a person.

2. *By something carried.* A terminal user can carry a badge, card, or key. He inserts the badge into a terminal badge reader or the key into the terminal itself. Magnetically encoded cards like credit cards are used for this purpose.

3. *By something known or memorized.* He can memorize a password or answer a prearranged set of questions. Techniques of this type require no special hardware. They are the least expensive of the three, and under most circumstances they can be made reasonably secure if applied intelligently. The user's identification number, however, must not be a number that might be guessed, such as his birth date or car license number.

Keys, locks, machine-readable badges, and credit cards all have one disadvantage: they can be lost. The user may fail to remove them from the terminal after the transaction is complete. If a sign-on action is used along with a badge or card, the user may forget to sign off. It may be possible to duplicate the key or badge. For these reasons, the use of the key, card, or badge is not necessarily more secure than identification of a terminal operator by a memorized security code or a sequence of questions. Keys on banking system terminals and badges in certain airline systems have been in operation for years, although nobody pretends that they would keep out an ingenious and persistent imposter, any more than an apartment lock would keep out an ingenious and determined burglar. They are better than no lock at all.

On some military systems the terminal has a small fence around it, and the operator cannot leave the area without opening a gate with the same badge or key that he uses on the terminal.

A password has been used on a number of systems to identify the user. In its simplest form, all the terminal users, or users of a given category or at a given location, know the same password; until this is typed in, the system will take no action. For any reasonable measure of security, however, it is desirable to provide each of the individual terminal users with a different security code. He must type this code into the terminal. The computer will then check what the individual using that code is permitted to do. On some systems, the user keys in his own personal identification number, followed by a security code which has been issued to him. The computer checks that he has entered the correct security code and that the transactions he enters are authorized for that individual. A table such as that in Fig. 32.4 may be used. As a result of this check, categories of authorization may be established that indicate what types of action the individual is permitted to take.

The security code must be changed periodically. On some systems, it is changed once per month. Each terminal user must take care not to let any-

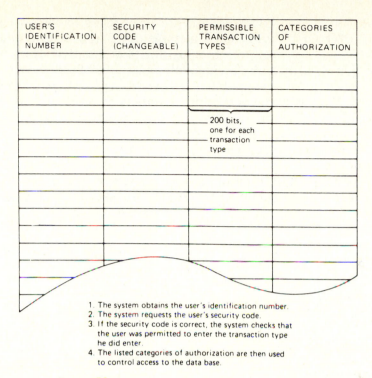

USER'S IDENTIFICATION NUMBER	SECURITY CODE (CHANGEABLE)	PERMISSIBLE TRANSACTION TYPES	CATEGORIES OF AUTHORIZATION

200 bits,
one for each
transaction
type

1. The system obtains the user's identification number.
2. The system requests the user's security code.
3. If the security code is correct, the system checks that the user was permitted to enter the transaction type he did enter.
4. The listed categories of authorization are then used to control access to the data base.

Figure 32.4   Use of a simple authorization table.

one else know his code. For example, the code for a user may be mailed in such a way that the code is on a detachable piece of card with nothing else written on it. The receiver is instructed to detach this piece of card immediately. If the card with the security code on it is lost, anybody finding it is unlikely to associate it with the correct personnel number. It must be possible to issue a user with a new security code whenever he wants it. If he feels that security has been compromised in any way—for example, by someone looking over his shoulder and seeing his security code as he types it in the terminal, he should be able to ask immediately for a new security code. On some terminals, the security code is automatically prevented from being printed or displayed as it is keyed in.

The disadvantage of the password or security code technique is that the code can be given to another person without any physical loss by the giver and without anything having to be duplicated. There is no physical evidence of the other person's possession of it. This technique must therefore be accompanied by rigorous controls and a serious attempt to catch, quickly and automatically, any person who is using another person's code. If the terminal users think that there is a high probability they will be caught if they attempt to enter the system with another person's code, they may be deterred psychologically from making an invalid entry.

MESSAGE AUTHENTICATION

Message authentication refers to steps taken to ensure that a message came from a legitimate source or goes to a legitimate destination. It is possible in a network that data might be accidentally misrouted. There have been cases of highly sensitive data being printed at the wrong location. Even the telephone network occasionally gets wrong numbers. It is possible that the misrouting could be deliberate, or that an active wiretap is being used by an intruder who wants to gain access to files.

In one message authentication scheme, the sender and receiver put unique pseudo-random numbers on the messages. Both have the same set of numbers. They may both have these numbers stored or may generate them. The receiving software compares the number on the received message with what it expects, and takes action if it is not identical.

CRYPTOGRAPHY

The safest way to have reasonable assurance that transmitted data have not been read, copied, or tampered with is to use cryptography. Cryptography can also be used to protect secret data that are stored. This means that the data are enciphered before they are transmitted or stored and deciphered before use. The enciphering process scrambles the bits so thoroughly that a person wanting the information is unlikely to be able to unscramble them.

Cryptography is not used for much stored data. It is valuable for highly sensitive or valuable data that may be vulnerable to theft.

Cryptography has been used since the ancient Chinese by spies, lovers, and political schemers. Much has been written about it since the advent of radio and data transmission, and there has been a massive expenditure on it in military and intelligence circles. There are spectacular stories from World War II about enemy codes being broken. Japanese messages planning the bombing of Pearl Harbor were deciphered and then not acted upon.

Cryptography is a fight between the person who enciphers and the perwho tries to crack the code. The subject has drastically changed its nature with the advent of computers. The enemy will use a computer to work on cracking the code, searching at high speed through very large numbers of possible transformations. However, the enciphering will also be done by a computer and an inexpensive algorithm can scramble the data in a truly formidable way. On balance, if both sides act prudently, the sender is better off than the code cracker.

Microelectronics has further changed the applicability of cryptography. Now it can be done with a microprocessor or a special cryptography chip. With this the transmission from a terminal can be enciphered without great expense.

On networks, cryptography should be an *end-to-end* process, independent of the transport subsystem. It should thus be considered a function of the control layers external to the transport subsystem. Enciphered data may be stored directly in data-base systems.

It is generally desirable for networks to interconnect many different machines, from different manufacturers. To use cryptography, two communications machines must employ the same algorithm. One machine may need to contact many different machines on the network. It would help if all cryptography on the network used the same algorithm. If the same algorithm were used by large numbers of machines, it could be implemented in the form of a cheap mass-produced LSI chip.

Would this be safe? If a mass-produced crypto chip were employed, the enemy could also use it in attempts to break the code. To make such a scheme safe, the enciphering must employ not only a suitable complex algorithm but also a *crypto key*. The key is a random collection of bits or characters which the transmitting and receiving stations use in conjunction with the algorithm for enciphering and deciphering (Fig. 32.5). If the enemy knows the crypto algorithm but not the key, it would take a large amount of work for him to break the code.

Many crypto devices use a key of 64 bits. If a code breaker attempted to decipher a message by using a computer to try out keys in a trial-and-error fashion, there would be 2^{64} possible keys to try. If an ultra-fast special-purpose computer were used for code breaking which could try out one key every microsecond, the average time taken to find the right key would be:

$$\frac{2^{64}}{2} \text{ microseconds} = \frac{2^{64}}{2 \times 1,000,000 \times 3600 \times 24 \times 365.25} \text{ years}$$

that is, 292,271 years.

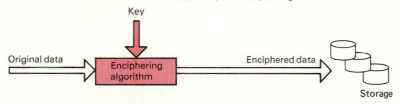

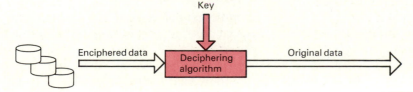

Figure 32.5 Cryptography. Both the enciphering/deciphering algorithm and the key must be sufficiently complex. Usually, only highly sensitive data, vulnerable to theft, is enciphered before storage.

A key of 80 bits would require a time longer than the age of the universe.

With such keys complete trial and error will not succeed in breaking cryptography codes. The cryptanalyst is therefore forced to find shortcuts that avoid full trial and error. Consequently, the encoding technique must do everything possible to prevent shortcuts from working; the data must be scrambled in a sufficiently complex fashion.

Most of the ciphers used prior to the development of computers can be broken by using computers. Today, however, a cheap LSI chip can execute an exceedingly complex cipher.

There are two ways to make codes uncrackable. One is sufficiently complex key usage; the other is sufficiently complex algorithms. Before computers, the safest systems used a key that was used once only. Sometimes the key was very long. Some Army Signal Corps systems used a key that occupied an entire paper tape roll 8 inches in diameter. Every tenth character was numbered so that the tape could be set up at any designated starting position. With computer storage, such a technique could employ a disc containing keys of many millions of random bits which is itself well protected from theft or copying.

A given quantity of key can be made to encode a larger quantity of data by utilizing it with a more complex algorithm. This is referred to as *key leverage*. Modern cryptographic hardware uses a relatively small key and scrambles it in association with the data in formidable ways.

DATA ENCRYPTION STANDARD

A national, and international standard for cryptography is needed in order to permit the machines of many different manufacturers to be interconnected. Such a standard is likely to be secure and practical if

1. It scrambles the data sufficiently thoroughly.

2. It uses a long enough key to prohibit trial-and-error methods of code breaking.

3. It does not add significantly to storage or transmission overhead.

4. It can be implemented on a single mass-produced LSI chip.

The U.S. National Bureau of Standards created a Data Encryption Standard (DES) [1] in 1977. It is now implemented on LSI chips costing less than $50, although the extra equipment needed to employ them is much more expensive.

The Data Encryption Standard has two modes of operation, called KAK (Key Auto Key) and CTAK (Cipher Text Auto Key). The latter is illustrated in Fig. 32.6.

In KAK mode, the input data are read into a buffer 64 bits at a time.

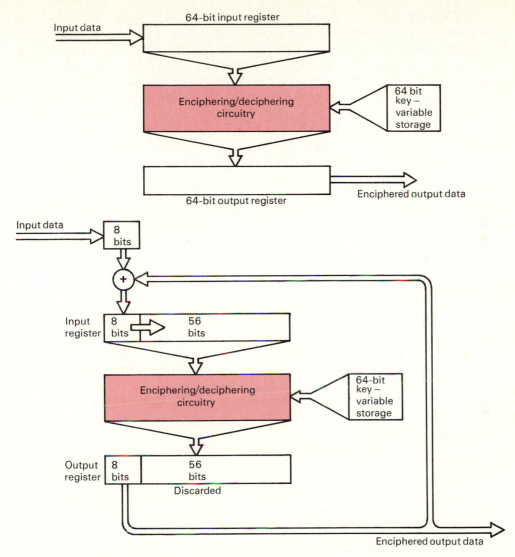

Figure 32.6 U.S. Data Encryption Standard (DES) operating in Cipher Text Auto Key (CTAK) mode. Sixty-four dummy bits are needed at start up and this degrades throughput, especially when the message lengths are short [1].

The 64 bits are then scrambled with a 64-bit key to produce 64 bits of output. The encoding operation starts with a START ENCIPHER command and then proceeds without further synchronization until the end of the data. The receiving machine knows when the data start. If a bit is lost in transmission, synchronization is lost and the data will have to be retransmitted.

CTAK mode is more complex and proceeds 8 bits at a time. It is thus convenient for transmitting a stream of 8-bit characters. The input stream enters a 64-bit register in groups of 8 bits until the register is full. Enciphering then occurs using a 64-bit key to produce 64 bits of output. Only the left-hand 8 bits of this are used. They are both transmitted and fed back to be combined with 8 bits of input as shown in Fig. 32.6. This technique is referred to as a cipher-text feedback. It increases the difficulty of attempted code breaking, but it needs a dummy 64 bits entering into the circuit to start up the operation before live data are used. It adds this much overhead to the messages sent. The KAK mode adds no extra bits to the messages.

TIME AVAILABLE FOR BREAKING THE CODE

If a cryptanalyst has a very long time available for breaking a code, he is more likely to succeed. Again, he is more likely to succeed if he has a very large amount of text to work on. The computer system should be designed so that whenever possible it minimizes the time available to the code breaker. This can be done by designing the key so that it can be changed at suitably frequent intervals.

On the other hand, some commercial data are kept on disc or tape and retain their value for a very long time. Data concerning oil drillings or mineral prospecting, for example, could be of great value to a thief, and in some cases may retain their value for years. The thief has plenty of time to break the code. In such cases an especially complex algorithm and long key may be used. If a standard algorithm must be employed, many keys may be used for different portions of the data, or the data may be enciphered more than once using different keys.

AUDIT AND CONTROL PROCEDURES

Any person contemplating an invasion of the files either through curiosity or malicious intent should be deterred by the thought that there is a high probability that the system will detect him and inform the appropriate security officer.

A log should be kept of all violations of correct procedure, for example, when a terminal user types in a security code that is not the one allocated to him or attempts to access a file for which he has no authorization. Details of these violations are printed and sent to the security officers. A branch security officer will receive a listing of all the violations that have occurred within his branch. A data owner will be sent details of all unauthorized attempts to read or change records in his data. This log of violations should be analyzed to detect any unusual activity. Most violations are accidental and caused by a genuine mistake on the part of the terminal operator. The sudden departure from the norm in this activity, however, may indicate that some user is tampering with the system, possibly exploring and trying to find a method of gaining unauthorized access. The list of violations may be printed out once a week; on the other hand, it may pay to do it more frequently on a system containing highly secure and highly sensitive information. The location security officers may be sent a list of any violations that occur each night. Then a would-be intruder will have little time to practice.

It is particularly important to maintain extremely tight security over the authorization records, passwords, file lockwords, and so on. If an imposter can change them, then most of his problems are solved. No one should be given authority to read or change these records except the file owners or the security officers. If any change is made, the appropriate data owner or security officer will be sent details of that change the following day. Such changes may be detected on a nightly run by comparing last night's authorization records and lock tables with those of tonight. If an unauthorized person has managed to make changes in them, it will be detected quickly.

It is recommended that a history be kept in which all changes made to these security records are logged, indicating who made the change and where it was made.

A SOLVABLE PROBLEM

There is much more to security than we have described in this chapter, and the reader who would like to read further on the subject should obtain Ref. 2

In general, data-base-system security should be regarded as a solvable problem. It needs to be solved at an appropriate cost for the systems in question. The systems analyst responsible for security needs the broadest possible view. Overemphasis on narrow security measures should be avoided.

- How is the use of end-user languages controlled?
- Should certain classes of end users have their own data bases separate from the master data base?
- What accuracy controls are placed on data entry?
- How will usage of data be audited?
- When errors are found in data, how will their correction be accomplished and controlled?
- What plans are made to recover from fire or catastrophic data-base destruction?
- What controls are placed on restarts after failure?
- How are changes to the data-base schemas managed and controlled?

As well as a wide-ranging systems knowledge, the manager of security needs skill in communicating with people at all levels in the organization, including senior management.

DP EXECUTIVE:

We discovered that there was need for a substantial amount of tact. She [the manager of security] was, after all, subtly implying that the senior bankers might want to rob the bank.

Several of the large computer-related crimes have been top management crimes. It is necessary to make a data-base system secure from the possibility of senior management misusing it in collusion with technical staff, as well as lower-level personnel.

The data administrator and data-base design staff need to work closely with the manager of security. Decisions that affect data-base security include the following:

- Should an *active* data dictionary be used?

- How should *active* control of data usage be measured?

- What projects and data bases (if not all of them) should be subject to active dictionary control?

- What locks should be built into data-base schemas?

- Who controls the authorization tables showing who is allowed to access, modify, create, or destroy what data?

- What special precautions are needed for locking the dictionary and authorization tables?

- Which data are especially sensitive, and how are these controlled?

- Should disjoint data bases be created for specially sensitive data?

- Should cryptography be used with any data?

THE SYSTEM'S POLICE

To maintain high security in any building or organization, police are needed. A secure computer system needs a staff responsible for the security of the data files and the control of the authorization to use these files. A security officer should be appointed who will be the sole person able to change the authorization tables or file lockword tables in the system. He will have details of what each individual is authorized to read or change on the files. He is responsible for issuing passwords or security codes and for ensuring that they are used correctly.

In a distributed environment there may be multiple security officers, possibly one associated with each computer, or one associated with each corporate division or function. In a system with terminals in scattered locations, there should be a person responsible for security in each of these locations where sensitive data are handled. A suitable person with another job, such as an office manager, can be a local security officer. He takes instructions from the main security officer. The system sends him listings of all detected violations of correct procedure that occur in his location.

When the system detects a violation of correct security procedures, it should immediately take some action. Most terminal users can be expected to make occasional mistakes. When a user's first violation is detected, the computer should ask him to reenter the data and log the fact that the violation occurred. However, if an operator who made one mistake immediately makes a second, again attempting to enter an invalid code or access an unauthorized file, this may be an indication that he is attempting to do something illegal on the terminal. The system may then immediately inform the local security officer in the hope that the culprit will be caught red-handed. This miscreant may be "kept talking" by the system, but locked out of any sensitive files, until he is caught.

A more common approach is to lock the terminal completely the moment the second violation occurs. The application programs are written in such a way that no more information is accepted from that terminal until the condition has been cleared. The only person who can clear it is the security officer for that location.

MANAGER OF SECURITY

The management of security goes far beyond the data-base environment, and needs to encompass all aspects of system design and control. There are many ways of attacking a system which do not directly involve the data base. Because there is such a great diversity of possible security breaches, both deliberate and accidental, a designer of security is needed who has wide-ranging experience and knowledge.

The designer of security needs a quite different set of skills from the persons who carry out routine policing, and usually has a quite different personality. The police in society are different from the lawmakers.

In some corporations there is an overall manager of security responsible for ongoing security design and implementation. The police or security officers may report directly to this individual or report to operations executives. Even when the security executive does not control the policing of the system, he should be immediately informed of any violations. The manager of security reports directly to the head of DP.

REFERENCE

1. *Data Encryption Standard (DES) Federal Information Processing Standard No. 46,* National Bureau of Standards, 1977. Available from National Technical Service, U.S. Dept. of Commerce, 5285 Port Royal Road, Springfield, VA 22161.
2. James Martin, *Security, Accuracy, and Privacy In Computer Systems,* Prentice–Hall, Inc., Englewood Cliffs, NJ, 1973.

33 AUDITABILITY

Some data-base systems have been unauditable. The needs of auditors were forgotten in the enthusiasm of the overall design. The spread of end-user data-base languages increases the dangers of unauditable systems use.

Are data-base systems normally likely to be a problem from the auditing point of view? No. In fact, there are certain characteristics of data-base systems which make them attractive to auditors if they are designed appropriately. However, inappropriate data-base usage with poor controls can be a nightmare for the auditor.

An auditor requires a system to have the following properties: predictability, controllability, and ease of examination and verification of what happened.

Predictability means that for every stimulus to the system one can predict its response. Inputs that would cause unpredictable responses are rejected by the system. To achieve predictability, the programs must obey their specifications and the specifications must be complete.

The more complex a system is, the more careful the design must be in order to achieve predictability. Excessively convoluted programs or systems are not predictable. Instead, the complex system must be split into subsystems each of which is simple enough to be predictable itself, and the subsystems must be interlinked in a simple precisely defined fashion.

Very complex systems run the danger of being neither predictable nor controllable unless they are divided into subsystems which are themselves predictable and controllable.

A jumbo jet is a more complex piece of engineering than most data-processing systems but it is remarkably predictable and controllable. It can tolerate many component failures. You can have the failure of an engine or even two, a landing gear control, a navigational computer, several tires, radio equipment, the oven, and the movie projector, and it will still land safely.

Similarly, a DP system can have many failures and problems but still maintain integrity of vital data. Like the jumbo's movie projector some (in fact, much) of a DP system does not need the tight controls that apply to the most vital data.

Not all applications need auditing. Some distributed facilities are used for obtaining nonsensitive information or for carrying out relatively isolated applications such as shop floor planning, engineering design, or market research. Auditing controls are necessary on any systems handling financial information, inventory data, personal data, or data that could be used for embezzlement, theft, or other crime.

To make a complex system auditable, it needs to be split into auditable subsystems. Each such subsystem needs to be small or elemental enough to be predictable. The subsystems must communicate only across predefined interfaces and only with a form and content that is precisely specified. The security controls must be such that there is no means of bypassing these predefined communication paths. The capability must exist to record the communication across the interfaces. The time, content, origination, and response must be recordable.

In some cases it makes sense for disjoint auditable modules to be on different machines. End-user departments may have their own Class IV data-base minicomputer. Separate, small on-line systems may be used for data entry. A factory shop floor, concerned about system availability, may have a different computer than the general accounting area has.

A distributed system can have certain features that help auditability. First, by its nature it is compartmental. Peripheral processors are much simpler than mainframes and easier to make predictable and controllable. The software complexity that has grown up in large mainframes and is now filtering down to small mainframes should be avoided in peripheral processors. Second, the communication paths between the processors are of narrow bandwidth. Cryptography can be used where needed to make them secure. Batches of transmission can be tightly controlled. Critical transmissions can be logged for auditing purposes.

Distributed intelligence can be employed for controlling access to systems, and for integrity checks on data entry. Distributed storage can be used for recording information which an auditor needs.

A trend in minicomputer design is to put operating system functions, storage control functions, and transmission control functions into hardware or microcode. This is very appealing from the auditor's point of view because it means that these functions are standard, predictable, and tamper-proof. Such systems are designed to prevent ingenious bypassing of storage access controls, which is always possible with *software* mechanisms.

A system with multiple computers, often minicomputers, then, can be auditable if it has simple secure nodes, and simple precisely defined communication between them. Tight controls should prevent unauthorized access to or use of the nodes. Journals should be kept of all critical actions and transmissions. The auditor should have the capability to inspect the journals, data, and programs easily.

An *unauditable* system is one in which excessive complexity exists, complex patterns of intercommunication can take place, and appropriate journals are not kept recording who does what. In some data-base systems, convoluted uncontrolled interactions build up. As the software becomes more flexible and as end-user software becomes more powerful, the capability and temptation to build unauditable systems will increase. Box 33.1 lists aspects of systems which can make them unauditable.

BOX 33.1   What makes systems unauditable?

- Higher-level languages giving end users access to data bases without adequate controls or journals.
- Lack of audit trails. It is not possible to tell who did what.
- Poor authorization control. Unauthorized persons can gain access to the system.
- Controls that can be bypassed by ingenious techniques.
- Confusion over data definitions and data representations. No data dictionary. Lack of control of homonyms, synonyms, and data representations.
- Excessive complexity so that the auditor cannot tell what happened.
- Data volumes that can be removed and tampered with elsewhere.
- Unauthorized access to a system via a network.
- Distributed data-base operations gathering or associating data from multiple nodes without adequate controls.
- Integrity problems caused by poor software or inadequate restart-recovery control.
- Unpredictable or uncertain actions taken by programs of excessive complexity. A monolithic program of 50,000 instructions is unauditable.
- Complex and unpredictable patterns of communication between the nodes.

AUDITING SOFTWARE AND HARDWARE FEATURES

To render a data-base system auditable and controllable, hardware and software features are desirable which enable the auditor to take the following actions:

1. The auditor should have access to a data dictionary and be able to check that its definitions are being followed.

2. The auditor can establish what transactions were entered, and by whom.

3. The auditor can follow the effects of a given transaction. This may involve tracing a transaction as it navigates through a data base, passes to other subsystems, or generates subsidiary transactions that affect other machines or subsystems.

4. As well as sampling routine data for routine checks, the auditor's attention should be drawn to data or transactions which are exceptional for some reason, so that the circumstances surrounding these cases can be investigated.

5. When reversals of processing or corrections of previous processing are made, the auditor must be able to check these and their accuracy.

6. The auditor must be able to check that programs at distributed locations have not been tampered with. The processing must be a reliable, repeatable process which conforms to specifications.

7. The auditor should be able to know what failures have occurred, how frequently, and what action was taken. He must ensure that the effects of failures do not cause lasting damage.

8. The auditor should check the accuracy of the data-input operations, which are often taking place on distributed machines.

9. The security and privacy controls should be as automatic as possible, with the auditor able to check their effectiveness.

10. The integrity controls and protection from the effects of machine, software, and line failures should be as automatic as possible, and the auditor should be able to check their effectiveness.

Box 33.2 lists hardware and software features to facilitate auditing control. This is a formidable list and it is desirable that as much of it as possible should be purchased in the form of standard, fully debugged products.

The best manufacturers' data-base systems contain much that facilitates auditing and control.

END-USER POWER

To some extent there is a conflict between the desire in data-base systems to allow the users to "do their own thing" and the need for tight controls and good auditing. The au-

BOX 33.2   Software and hardware features to assist in the auditing of data-base systems

1. All data are described in a data dictionary.

2. All programmers' representations of data are generated from the dictionary.

3. An active dictionary enforces correct representations of data.

4. The data are protected so that the user cannot damage them. In general, tight security controls are used.

5. Software enables the auditor to perform all terminal functions from a central location, as though he were at a remote location.

6. All end-user actions that modify data can be logged automatically with a time, date, and end-user identification. End-user *reading* of sensitive data may also be logged.

7. All data changes are automatically logged. These logs are designed to be used for reconstructing the data as well as for auditing it.

8. When data are updated incorrectly and corrections are subsequently made, these should be separately logged and brought to the auditor's attention.

9. Software permits the auditor to inspect all the logs from a central location.

10. The auditor has access to stored copies of source code, compilation listings, and symbol cross-references.

11. A flag is automatically set if the system software or control programs are modified. Any such modifications are automatically brought to the auditor's attention.

12. A list of all software modifications is automatically maintained at the auditor's location.

13. Highly sensitive portions of software may be in tamper-proof microcode. Microcoding the data-access routines could prevent the automatic logs and safeguards from being bypassed.

14. The auditor has his own securely locked records in the data bases. He can run transactions against these records to ensure that they are processed as expected. He can enter such transactions from the center as though they were entered from peripheral machines and can follow the results where more than one record or machine are affected.

15. Every user is positively identified when signing onto the system, and each user has a unique number.

(Continued)

BOX 33.2 *(Continued)*

16. Authorization tables control the users' access to data, software, application programs, and machine resources, and also control which programs can access which data.

17. The authorization tables are securely locked and accessible only by appropriate security officers and auditors. The auditor can check these tables, and all changes to them, from the central location.

18. End-user data manipulation software, report generators, and so on, are tightly controlled with user-authorization controls. Users are restricted to a certain limited view of the overall system data. Logs are kept of all accesses. Accesses to all data may be logged for billing purposes.

19. There should be an automatic log of all processor operator actions.

20. All violations of security procedures should be automatically logged.

21. All system failures, machine checks, line failures, and the like, should be automatically logged, with date/time stamps. Statistical summaries of numbers of failures, and transmission errors should be recorded.

22. The auditor should have access to all such logs from a central location. He may be able to inspect them in a last-in-first-out sequence (the most recent ones first). He should be able to correlate the failures with operator actions taken.

23. Units with removable media should be locked.

24. All removable media must have a volume and serial identification number, and their use should be automatically logged.

25. A thorough set of integrity controls should be applied to all data entry. Responsibility for accuracy of data entry should be clearly established. The auditor should have a means of checking the degree of accuracy.

26. All data entry and changes to data are regarded as temporary until a process *commitment* is made. If the process does not complete, the system automatically backs out and resets any data that have been changed.

27. Exception codes are returned to programs when errors, security violations, and failures occur. The auditor should check what actions the application programs take when these codes are returned.

28. When new records are entered, the system should check that their key is unique.

29. Teleprocessing controls should ensure that transmitted data are not damaged, lost, or accidentally double entered. The controls require tight line control procedures, and end-to-end controls on critical data involving serial numbers and batch hash totals. The auditor should ensure

BOX 33.2 *(Continued)*

that the controls are adequate. They are likely to be adequate if good end-to-end network architectures are used.

30. Counts of messages transmitted, amount totals, and hash totals may be automatically recorded for audit checking.

31. Software enables the auditor to examine all data in distributed systems from a central location.

32. When one input affects several nodes or subsystems, the flow of information across nodes or subsystem boundaries should be traceable.

33. Documentation at a central location shows what data and programs reside at distributed locations.

34. The auditor is able to examine programs in distributed machines from a central location. The software may permit him to transmit the programs to a central machine and compare them with locked and separately stored master copies.

35. Software enables the auditor to send his own programs to remote machines for testing purposes.

36. Because there is often little physical security at the distributed locations, and various employees can approach the processor, the range of operator actions at the processor may be restricted.

37. The distributed processors should be locked to prevent tampering or change of programs.

38. All distributed processors have physical locks.

39. When two processors attempt to update the same data, one of them is automatically locked from the data until the other has finished.

ditor must ensure that users are prevented from taking certain types of action, because if they did the auditor would lose control and not be able to ensure system integrity.

Some of the languages described in Chapter 25 for giving as much power as possible to end users unskilled in computing are anathema to the auditor. Their use needs to be carefully controlled with appropriate locks, logs, authorization controls, and security controls. On some systems that have been installed it is not possible to tell how a powerful end-user language was employed.

Nevertheless, the need to put more powerful resources into the users' hands is paramount. It is highly desirable to employ some of the high-level data-base languages *even though they may have inadequate controls from an auditor's point of view.* How can this dilemma be resolved?

First, the end-user software can be isolated in the end-user machine. Often it is permitted to access *only* the data in that machine.

Second, if such software *can* access data in a remote machine, it may be confined to reading that data and not permitted to modify it in any way. Appropriate security controls will be applied to the remote data, and audit trails maintained on all transmitted requests.

Third, the files or data bases used by end-user software may be created specially for that user. The end users are permitted to do whatever they want with their own data but not to invade anybody else's data. This principle is particularly important and can apply both to use of remote data and data in the user's machine. Some languages, such as IBM's Query-by-Example, do not work with a traditional data base but with a specialized one that is created from the traditional data base (or files).

Fourth, it is necessary to divide computer usage into that which must be audited because money and goods are at risk, and that which need not be audited. The former needs tight, rigorous control. The latter needs control sufficient only to prevent system harm. Many extremely valuable end-user systems fall into the latter category—information systems showing what types of customers are ordering what products, graphics systems for planning equipment layout, financial modeling systems, systems for scheduling work through the factory, portfolio management systems, cash flow and budget planning systems, and so on. Such systems can employ high-level software and Class IV data bases, and provided it is restricted in its area of use it need be only of limited concern to the auditors.

CONTROLS WITH DISTRIBUTED PROCESSORS

Many distributed processors are quite different from centralized facilities in their physical environment. They are located in conventional office space without the controlled access to the machine room that major computers have. Anyone can walk up to the machine. It is desirable that stray personnel should not be able to tamper with the distributed processors in a way that can do harm, modify programs, or damage the data.

The operating staff are likely to be less skilled and also less controlled. The distributed processors should therefore be designed to run with as little operator intervention as possible, and with as little scope for operators to take actions that might cause problems. There is not likely to be the separation of duties of DP personnel used to aid security in big systems, or the machine scheduling, input/output control section, tape and disc library controls, and so on. Sometimes the auditors want to avoid having removable discs and disc libraries at the distributed sites. If removable media *are* used, they want the disc or other media units to be lockable.

Some distributed processors have no operator's console like that on central or stand-alone systems. They are operated from a terminal. The IBM 8100 processor has a keylock with three positions: ENABLE, POWER-ONLY, and SECURE. When set to the ENABLE position, all switches on the processor are active. When set to POWER-ONLY, only the power ON and OFF switches are active. When set to SECURE, the processor may be powered down but only the key holder can turn it on. The desire to make operating procedures as simple as possible can coincide with the auditor's desire to control the actions of the distributed operators.

Many distributed processors are designed so that they can be left unattended. Some can be switched off from a central location, or by an instruction in a job stream following the last job.

The operating systems of peripheral processors may be designed so that all difficult operator actions are taken at the central machine to which they are attached. At this location there will be skilled operating staff. With this consideration there may be a substantial difference between a minicomputer designed for conventional stand-alone operation and one designed as a peripheral node of a distributed system.

It will greatly add to the security of a peripheral system if the local staff are locked out of its control programs so that no ingenious tampering can take place. They cannot bypass the auditing and security controls, especially those of the file or data-base management subsystem. The controls must not be circumventable so that records can be illicitly read or modified.

GOOD AND BAD DESIGN

Good design tends to simplify rather than complicate the overall structure of the system. A good distributed system has relatively simple nodes at end-user locations. They are easy to install and easy to operate, but cannot easily be tampered with. They have tightly controlled transmission links via a standardized flexible network. They avoid the excessive software complexity that has grown up over the years in highly generalized mainframes.

It is said that if you open a can of worms, it takes a larger can to recan them. The software of generalized mainframes has been recanned many times. Distributed processors ought to avoid this complexity and use new, simply structured software. This is true with some of the minicomputer data-base systems.

There is much to be said for having nonremovable discs for the data storage of peripheral processors. They are large enough for many locations, simplify the system operation, and improve its security.

Programs for many on-line peripheral systems may be down-line loaded from a central host. Again this improves security. The programs should reside in the peripheral system so that it can carry out useful functions when cut off from the host by failures. But the programs should be controlled and maintained centrally.

Some minicomputers now have part of their control mechanisms in hardware or microcode rather than in software. Storage management and data-base management functions are also in hardware and microcode. This improves machine efficiency and can greatly improve security. Putting critical controls into hardware or microcode ensures that they cannot be bypassed by ingenious software experts.

Transmissions of *critical* data are safeguarded by cryptography. The cryptography mechanisms are better implemented in hardware (crypto chips) than software. All critical transmissions are logged for recovery and auditing purposes.

High-level inquiry, report-generation, and data manipulation languages are provided to users to put as much capability into their hands as possible. But their use is rigorously controlled and audited where necessary. They must be prevented from accessing unauthorized data, tampering with data, or harming data by accident. Any modification of data should be restricted to data which they own, and preferably these should reside in their own machine.

The searching of data, or information system activities in general should usually be designed to take place on separate systems which are designed for this purpose. Data with a high level of secondary-key or inverted-file activities should usually be created separately from data for production runs, for reasons of improving performance, avoiding scheduling problems, and lessening the complexity of individual system nodes.

Again data with which the end users "do their own thing" should be created separately for this purpose. The users should be given powerful software and a large amount of freedom with data created for them. They should be locked out of other users' data, master files, and data for production runs.

Although it is *possible* to build distributed data systems of great flexibility, caution should be used about employing this flexibility. It can result in highly convoluted unauditable patterns of activity. Queries resulting in distributed activities are not a good idea for most commercial systems. For commercial distributed data systems, secondary-key or searching activities should take place *within one node.* Primary-key queries may employ remote machines as they are relatively simple.

Nodes may become destroyed or damaged. A system should be designed so that they can be replaced and their data reconstructed. This is usually easy with peripheral processing but may be difficult with a large central data-processing center. The concept of having *one* large centralized location should be questioned. Some DP centers are now becoming too difficult to reconstruct after a catastrophe such as fire or bombs. This can be a severe problem with *very large* data-base systems. A bicentralized or decentralized system may be preferable. Many large corporations in recent years have split a central DP location and created a second version of the facilities with appropriate network connections.

Good distributed system design then consists of discrete systems with secure interconnections between them. The subsystems are either auditable or rigorously confined to work that does not need to be audited in detail. The configuration is not vulnerable to the destruction of any one node. The subsystems avoid excessive complexity, and the overall configuration avoids convoluted interrelations between the subsystems. The end-user facilities are made as powerful and easy to use as possible. Tight security controls prevent unauthorized access and the systems are designed to prevent the controls being bypassed. Auditing of subsystems can be carried out remotely from central locations. The transport network is a discrete subsystem standardized and flexible in its interconnections. All communications across it are auditable, and adhere exactly to specified format and content.

The designer should have in his mind an image of separate autonomous nodes, each appearing to be simple to its users—the complexities hidden under the covers. The network interconnecting them is standard, flexible, and also appears to be simple, like the telephone network—its complexities hidden under the covers. The decision of what happens on end-user processors and what happens on centralized processors is carefully thought out. The pattern of transmissions between the nodes is simple. The transmissions are secure, rigorously specified, and auditable. Each autonomous node is completely auditable except where it has been decided that this is not necessary.

34 EXECUTIVE INFORMATION SYSTEMS

Probably no term in data processing has caused as much controversy as management information systems (MIS). Innumerable corporations claim to have them, universities have departments dedicated to them, MIS budgets run into millions, and yet knowledgeable critics refer to them as "myths" [1] and "mirages" [2].

One article in the *Harvard Business Review* says: "Of all the ridiculous things that have been foisted on the long-suffering executive in the name of science and progress, the real-time management information system is the silliest. . . .A company that pursues an MIS embarks on a wild-goose chase, a search for a will-o'-the-wisp" [2].

Nevertheless, one can find many examples today of executive information systems which are providing extremely valuable information, and which have become a major tool for the executive.

Why have so many attempts to create executive information systems failed? Primarily, because they have not succeeded in providing that information which the executive *really* needs. There are several reasons for this. First, the systems analysts *thought* they could identify what the executive's needs were, but in practice they did not know enough about his *true* decision-making processes. Second, the information needs of top management are mercurial. They have different problems at different times. Different executives have different decision-making styles. An information system built for one might not be used by his successor. Top management questions often cannot be anticipated. Third, most of the questions which top management asks cannot be answered directly from existing data bases. Top management does not tend to ask the data-base textbook questions which can be answered by a new juxtaposition of existing data items, such as "What percentage of sales quota did Branch Office 124 make in October?" They are more likely to ask such questions as: "Why are sales down?" or "What changes should be made to the salesman compensation plan for next year?" A staff seeking to answer these questions may well use computer programs which examine forecasts or simulate the effect of differing compensation plans using data that are derived from existing data items.

THREE APPROACHES   In order to respond to these problems, organizations have taken three types of approaches:

1. Improve the understanding of what information is needed by top management. Analyze the factors that are most critical in running the organization, determine how they can be measured, and design reports that express clearly the information related to these factors. This is the approach advocated by Rockart [3], which we will describe shortly.

2. Set up an infrastructure which enables great flexibility in meeting new requests to have data made available. The various data sources and data bases should be able to feed a generalized information retrieval system which can handle any type of information when the need for it becomes apparent.

3. Employ a top management staff group that has access to all relevant data sources and has the brilliance to move very fast in creating information reports and charts for executives when they express a need. This group should have its own Class IV data bases and employ very high level languages, such as NOMAD and APL with graphics, to process the data, build models, and answer "what if?" questions.

All three of these approaches have proven valuable, and it is generally desirable that all three should be used in conjunction.

THREE LEVELS OF MANAGEMENT   It is important in thinking about management information to distinguish between the needs of different levels of management. Three levels of activities in an organization are generally distinguished.

Level 1: Reflex actions or routine operations. Reflex actions in a living creature can be handled by low-level mechanisms that do not involve thinking in the central brain. In precomputer days, routine corporate operations were done by clerks or junior management. In a computerized corporation they may be completely automated, with human intervention occurring only when something goes wrong or something is recognized by the computers as being an exceptional circumstance needing human intervention.

Level 2: Operations involving well-defined thinking. Before computers these would have been performed by middle management and their assistants, setting operational budgets, choosing suppliers, scheduling production, and so forth. With computers they remain a human function but with the machine doing much of the work or providing well-specified information for a human being to make decisions.

Level 3: Operations involving creative thinking or strategic planning. These are the domain of top management and the corporate staff. Even in a

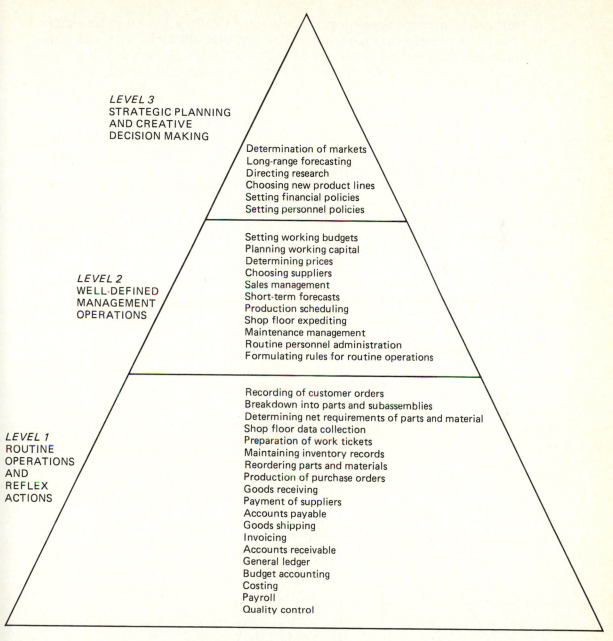

Figure 34.1 Three levels of operations. Level 1 operations can be almost completely automated. Level 2 operations can be partially automated but need management involvement. Level 3 operations require intelligent human thinking with assistance from computers.

highly computerized organization they remain eminently human tasks. The computer will help in many areas, but it is more difficult to provide computerized information or assistance at this level, for two reasons. First, the level of thinking is often complex and ill structured, and second, the needs are unpredictable.

In striving for automation it is desirable to bring as many of the operations as possible into level 1 and give as much assistance as possible to level 3. Figure 34.1 shows a breakdown of some of the main functions of a manufacturing corporation into these levels.

Much of the criticism of "management information systems" comes from persons who assume that MIS refers to top management only and that top management questions cannot be anticipated or answered in a direct way by computers alone. No matter how useful data-base systems are at levels 1 and 2, they go only part of the way needed in providing information at level 3. Part of the way, however, is better than having no computer-searchable data at all. Many of the presentations made to top management by their staff benefit greatly from accessibility to appropriate data bases.

DATA FOR THE THREE LEVELS   Data needed for the three levels differ in their structure. Data at level 1 are tightly designed for routine operations and accessed by primary keys.

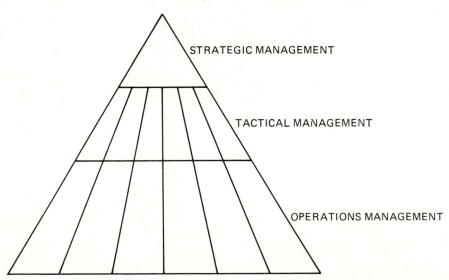

Figure 34.2 The management levels of this traditional management diagram correspond only approximately to the breakdown of activities into routine and nonroutine in Fig. 34.1. Operations management sometimes needs Class IV data bases and top management sometimes needs information from the Class I, II, and III data environments.

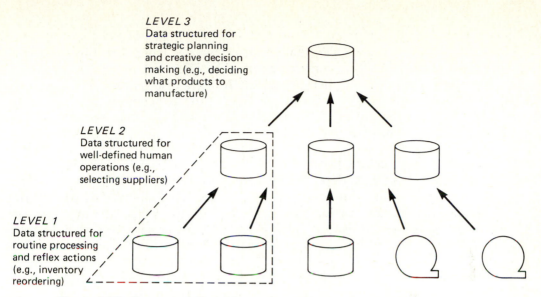

LEVEL 3
Data structured for
strategic planning
and creative decision
making (e.g., deciding
what products to
manufacture)

LEVEL 2
Data structured for
well-defined human
operations (e.g.,
selecting suppliers)

LEVEL 1
Data structured for
routine processing
and reflex actions
(e.g., inventory
reordering)

Figure 34.3 Summary information may pass from the lower-level data bases which are designed for routine operations to the higher-level data bases which are designed for nonroutine questions. In some functional areas data bases for the different levels may be combined: for example, those inside the dashed line.

Data at level 2 are often accessed by secondary keys. Usually, they are for a clearly defined purpose and can be structured for this purpose. In some cases a Class III data base used at level 1 is designed to meet level 2 needs also; for example, it may contain information to be used in selecting suppliers. Sometimes separate Class IV data bases are set up at level 2; for example, an information system for use by the personnel department. The level 2 information systems may miss out much of the detail that is recorded at level 1.

Level 3 uses Class IV data bases, and often it is not known how the data will be used. Generalized information retrieval systems are set up. Relational data bases of high flexibility are required which permit data to be analyzed quickly in diverse ways as needs arise. New types of information will often be brought into this general-purpose infrastructure at short notice.

The management of a corporation is commonly described as being of three levels, and drawn in the form of a three-level pyramid (Fig. 34.2): operations management, tactical management, and strategic management (or sometimes, operations management, middle management, and top management). The activities in Fig. 34.1 correspond only approximately to this traditional breakdown. Some routine operations have been conventionally regarded as *middle (tactical)* management. Some level 2 activities needing the ability to search data are regarded as operations management; for example, the activities of an expediter on the shop floor of a factory (Fig. 34.3). Many operations management activities could benefit from having Class IV data-base facilities.

DIFFERING EXECUTIVE STYLES To make matters worse, when one top executive replaces another he often has very different information needs. He has a different style of managing and uses information sources differently. Some are content with summary information. Some want to drop down to use level 2. Some ask for a degree of detail that can be found only in the operational files; Fig. 34.4 illustrates this.

Top management needs the data processed in some way. They need information, not raw data. Some attempts to provide this have resulted in producing summaries of operational or financial data. Cash flow, profit-and-loss figures, and costing summaries can be maintained automatically on a continuing basis. Financial models of corporations have been programmed with which the effect of different financial decisions can be tested. Top management and their aides, however, are often not content with the summary information that has been predigested for them. Sometimes they want to fish in the more detailed data base; they want the fresh fish of the operational files, not the deep-frozen fish of the summary files.

The nature of the information that management may request differs enormously. Some items are easy to obtain from the computing files, such as "Give me the total production cost of this product." Some are difficult, such as "What would be the cost of having two models instead of one model of this product?" The questions that *top* management is interested in tend to be the difficult ones. In many organizations today the majority of top management questions, if they can be answered with the computer system at all, can be answered only by the writing of a special program for the purpose possibly using a data-base interrogation language.

Top management can rarely be induced to use its own terminal with success. The lower levels of management, on the other hand, employ terminals very effectively because their information requirements, first, tend to be simpler, and second, tend to be of the type that can be anticipated; hence programs are ready to deal with them. The lower levels of management, such as production managers, store managers, office managers, and so forth, more frequently need operations systems rather than general-purpose management information systems.

Figure 34.4 shows differences in the style of operating of different executives or head office staff. Individual A is content with the planning data base that has been created. Individual B is concerned almost exclusively with financial information. She uses the financial information in the level 3 data base but usually needs the greater detail of the level 2 financial information system. Individual C is an ex-salesman, and this causes him to ask questions about sales and customers which need level 1 data. He never uses the level 3 data base.

Unfortunately for the systems analysts, when a new person fills a top-level post, the demands for information often change completely.

626

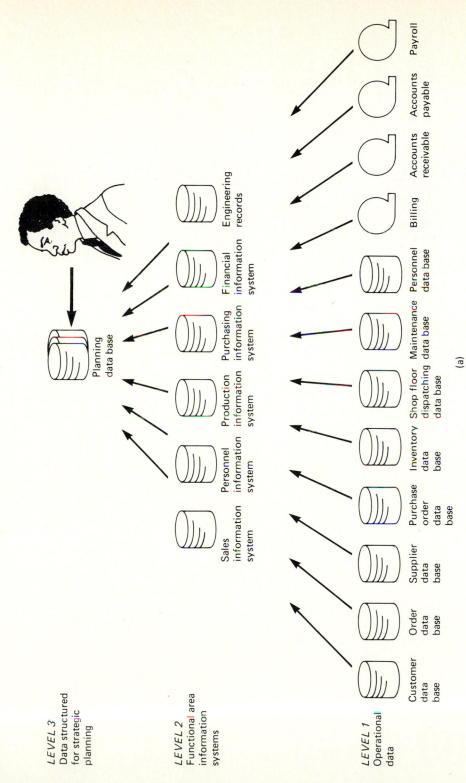

LEVEL 3
Data structured
for strategic
planning

Planning
data base

LEVEL 2
Functional area
information
systems

Sales
information
system

Personnel
information
system

Production
information
system

Purchasing
information
system

Financial
information
system

Engineering
records

LEVEL 1
Operational
data

Customer
data
base

Order
data
base

Supplier
data
base

Purchase
order
data
base

Inventory
data
base

Shop floor
dispatching
data base

Maintenance
data base

Personnel
data base

Billing

Accounts
receivable

Accounts
payable

Payroll

(a)

Figure 34.4 Different individuals in the same head office position ask for different information.

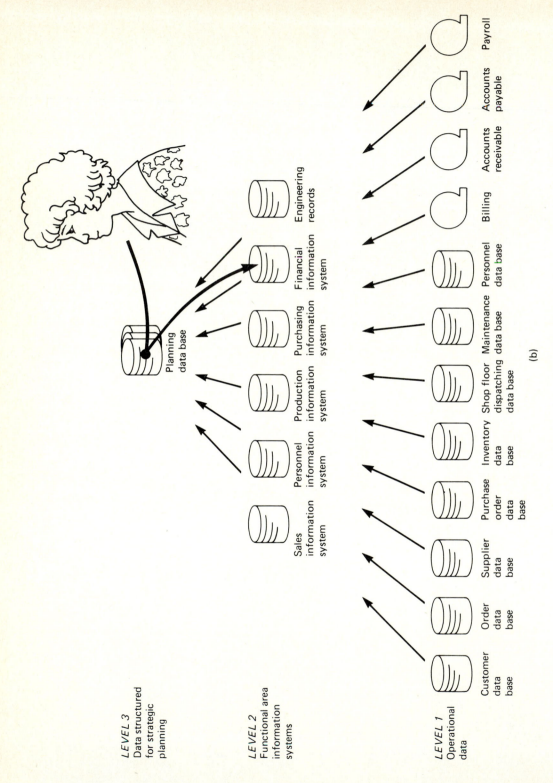

LEVEL 3
Data structured
for strategic
planning

LEVEL 2
Functional area
information
systems

Sales
information
system

Personnel
information
system

Production
information
system

Purchasing
information
system

Financial
information
system

Engineering
records

Planning
data base

LEVEL 1
Operational
data

Customer
data
base

Order
data
base

Supplier
data
base

Purchase
order
data
base

Inventory
data
base

Shop floor
dispatching
data base

Maintenance
data base

Personnel
data base

Billing

Accounts
receivable

Accounts
payable

Payroll

(b)

Figure 34.4   (Continued)

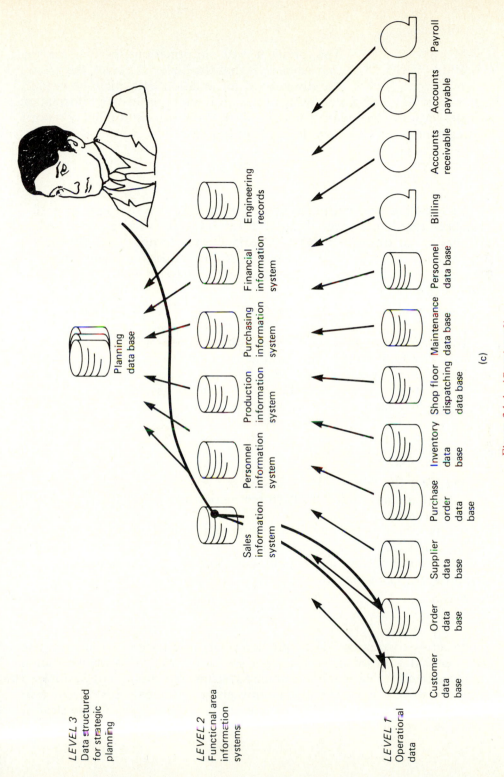

LEVEL 3
Data structured
for strategic
planning

Planning
data base

LEVEL 2
Functional area
information
systems

Sales
information
system

Personnel
information
system

Production
information
system

Purchasing
information
system

Financial
information
system

Engineering
records

LEVEL 1
Operational
data

Customer
data
base

Order
data
base

Supplier
data
base

Purchase
order
data
base

Inventory
data
base

Shop floor
dispatching
data base

Maintenance
data base

Personnel
data base

Billing

Accounts
receivable

Accounts
payable

Payroll

(c)

Figure 34.4 (Continued)

629

TOO MUCH INFORMATION   The problem with information systems for top management is that the higher the level, the greater the diversity of information that might be needed. Each area of lower-level management has an interest in feeding information to higher-level management. If uncontrolled, this results in too many reports reaching managers which they do not have time to read.

CORPORATE PRESIDENT:

I think the problem with management information systems in the past has been that they're overwhelming as far as the executive is concerned. He has to go through reams of reports and try to determine for himself what are the most critical pieces of information contained in the reports so that he can take necessary action and correct any problems that have arisen [3].

The president quoted above had 97 different computerized reports sent to him in a typical month. Almost none of them were designed specifically for him. Lower executives and staff sent them because they thought he should see "these." This is typical of most organizations. Almost none of the reports gave him anything that he could use.

CORPORATE PRESIDENT:

In my view the whole DP profession is overpaid and overrated. The systems they have built have been ineffective except for the nuts-and-bolts paperwork.

I have been inundated with reports, but there is almost nothing of value in making the real decisions I have to make to run the business. I get masses of irrelevant reports, but when I urgently need data the computer experts can't provide it.

Because it is impossible to predict what information a top executive *might* need, the information generated by lower-level management should be made accessible, preferably via on-line systems, but should not be dumped on the executive's desk. The information given to the executive needs very careful selection, and needs to be summarized and presented in the clearest possible fashion, often with graphics.

WHAT INFORMATION IS NEEDED?

What information do top executives need?

James Rude, an ex-MIS director and now a consultant to top management, says that they require the following [4]:

1. *Comfort information.* A few daily figures about the state of the business, particularly its current sales figures. The chief executive likes these figures but does not do much with them.

2. *Problem information.* Information about major crises or problems that deserve the CEO's attention. He wants daily information on these until the problem is over.

3. *Information for outside dissemination.* For example, earnings and financial data that are given to investment analysts. The CEO may wish to control the release of any such information.

4. *External intelligence.* For example, information about competitors' sales and markets; information about the economy and business environment; a model of the effects of advertising.

5. *Internal operations.* A few key figures that indicate how internal operations are going. The CEO may let the subordinate staff know that he is watching these figures closely.

Rude, like most reviewers of executive information systems, says that most of today's systems are not supporting these needs well.

CRITICAL SUCCESS FACTORS

Other authorities would argue that the list above does not represent the *most important* information for top management. The information should be generally accessible, on-line, but great care is needed in selecting what types of reports reach the chief executive's desk.

An approach advocated by Rockart [3] has been practiced with great success in some corporations. It is based on an executive's identification of those factors which he considers the most vital for the success of his organization. Rockart refers to these as *critical success factors* (CSF). The identification of critical success factors is a valuable management technique whether or not a management information system is used. It was first discussed in management literature by J. R. Daniel [5], who later became the Managing Director of McKinsey Company.

In most corporations there are a small number of factors that are vital to the success of the organization. Top management should be asked what they are: "In running your organization there are a small number of aspects of paramount importance—factors that must be done well if the operation is to succeed. Can you describe factors that are most critical for success?"

The corporate president normally finds this question interesting and relevant, and, after thinking about it, produces a good answer.

J. R. DANIEL (SUBSEQUENTLY MANAGING DIRECTOR OF McKINSEY & CO.):

In most industries there are usually three to six factors that determine success; these key jobs must be done exceedingly well for a company to be successful [5].

In a business the critical success factors relate to those aspects of the business that will ensure competitive performance. They differ greatly from one type of business to another. They differ from one time to another. The external environment can change the critical success factors. For example, the petroleum crisis changed them for the automobile industry. As a small corporation grows, it needs to shift gears and emphasize critical success factors.

One top executive may perceive different critical success factors from another. Chief executives differ in their perspective and management style. The executive information system often needs to be changed when the top management changes.

Some examples of critical success factor lists are as follows:

Automobile Industry:

- Fuel economy
- Styling
- Efficient dealer organization
- Tight control of manufacturing costs

Software House:

- Product innovation
- Quality of sales and user literature
- Worldwide marketing and service
- Ease of use of products

Prepackaged Food Corporation:

- Advertising effectiveness
- Good distribution
- Product innovation

Seminar Company:

- Obtaining the best speakers
- Identification of topics
- Mailing-list size and quality

Microelectronics Company:

- Ability to attract and keep the best design staff
- Government R&D support
- Support of field sales force
- Identification of new market needs

Life Insurance Company

- Development of agency management personnel
- Advertising effectiveness
- Productivity of clerical operations

Many corporations have a statement of organizational goals. These are quite different from the critical success factors. The goals represent long-range vision or an end point that the corporation wishes to achieve. The goals might include statements such as "maximize return on investment," "growth of 30% per year," "increase market share to 40%," "excellence of medical care" (in a hospital), and so on. Such goals say nothing about how to run the company. The critical success factors relate to the conduct of current operations and the key areas in which high performance is necessary. They give the measures which are necessary in a control system for top management. They need careful and continuous measurement and management attention if the organization is to be successful.

Critical success factors should thus be the basis of a top management control system. Certain critical success factors are likely to be common to an industry. This is true of most of those listed above.

Other critical success factors vary with the situation of a corporation within an industry. It might be a new corporation trying to carve a foothold in an established industry. In this case a critical success factor is the creation of products that are perceived by the customers as being better value, in some way, than those of the existing corporations. It may depend on searching for a gap in existing product lines or creating something that adds value to existing product lines.

New critical success factors may emerge into importance at certain times. For example, two corporations may merge and for a period a critical success factor is the integration of their product lines and sales forces. A problem may arise such as a major product line being made obsolete by competition, or software gaining a bad reputation. Recovery from these situations may be a critical success factor.

Sometimes new critical success factors arise from external causes, such as the petroleum crisis, a local war removing strategic mineral sources, a new union contract, or the effect of new legislation.

Often a chief executive's choice of critical success factors is not what an information system designer would have anticipated. For example, the following is a list from the president of a major oil company [3]:

1. Effecting organizational decentralization so that diversification can better take place in order to provide a broader earning base for future decades when petroleum supplies diminish

2. Liquidity (to facilitate acquisitions)

3. Relations with government

4. Societal image

5. Success in new ventures

PERIODIC EXECUTIVE COMMITTEE REVIEW

Studies of critical success factors at the Sloane School of Management [3,6] show them differing with time, differing with different executives, and being different for similar organizations in the same industry.

Because of these differences it is desirable that an organization's critical success factors be reviewed periodically by a top executive committee. They may be reviewed every quarter by such a committee or by the board. Regardless of computers, this is an excellent aid to management control. The controlling individual or group should periodically review what factors are the most critical for success and what pressures can be brought to optimize these factors. Achieving critical success factor objectives should be related to the bonuses or other compensation that the responsible executives achieve.

TYPES OF MEASUREMENTS

Of the critical success factors identified by top management, only very rarely do traditional financial accounting systems provide the required data. Sometimes cost accounting systems provide useful data, but often the need for improved cost accounting is revealed in the critical success factor analysis.

A substantial proportion of the data needed cannot be provided as a by-product of conventional data processing. It must be specifically collected from other sources. It may then be stored in existing computer systems. Some of the data required come from external sources.

Many critical success factors require data from multiple logical files which may be widely dispersed: for example, comparative profitability of all products, bid profit margin as a ratio of profit on similar jobs, risk assessment in contracts by examination of experience with similar customer situations. These types of measures require data-base systems and high-level data-base languages that can assemble and manipulate the requisite data.

A small proportion of the critical success factors require subjective assessment rather than being easily quantifiable. Top executives are used to this and spend much time with subjective judgments and measurements. Often objective measures can be found, but it takes considerable thought.

In some cases the discussion of how to measure a critical success factor results in several different measurements. For example, one organization needed to measure their *technological reputation with customers* [3]. They developed seven possible measures of this. A simple numeric measure was the ratio of bids made to orders received. This had other factors affecting it, such as sales aggressiveness. Most soft measures consisted of person-to-person interviews. Seven different measures were devised. Several were used for the one factor. It was decided to initiate a process of top executives interviewing the customers because this was a highly critical success factor.

In the same organization the *morale of key scientists and engineers* was considered a critical success factor because of the importance to the company of these individuals. Measures of this ranged from numeric data such as turnover, absenteeism, and lateness, to feedback from informal management discussions with employees. More formal employee assessment interviews could also be used with the manager rating the employee on a morale scale.

Some critical success factors have revealed the need to build new, often small, information systems. Today these can usually be created with nonprocedural data-base languages. This makes them quick to create and easy to modify.

CRITICAL SUCCESS FACTOR REPORTS

The process of creating this type of executive information system may begin with a DP executive or designer talking to the chief executive officer. The CEO is asked to identify the critical success factors as he perceives them. In Rockart's experience the executive time needed for this is three to six hours.

It is then necessary to devise means of measuring these factors. Some factors can only have *soft* measures; however, usually there is some means of creating numeric measures. Sometimes considerable discussion is needed of how the factors will be measured. Sometimes there is too much data and the discussion revolves around how the data should be summarized.

Next, the means of reporting the results must be derived. How summarized should the information be, or what level of detail should back it up?

For any complex set of facts there is a means of presenting them which is powerful, clear, and highlights the most important aspects of the data.

A good lecturer searches for this in creating the diagrams he uses. So does a textbook writer. The creator of an executive information system should be skilled at designing the best means of presenting information.

Some executive information should be printed, with tables of figures and graphics charts, preferably in color. The executive often takes this information home and studies it. Some executive information may be displayed on terminals. This can give more flexibility in exploring, aggregating, and charting the data. Different executives like to work in different ways and their needs must be accommodated.

It is likely that executives will want changes made quickly to the reports they receive. The reports should therefore be created with the nonprocedural data-base languages discussed in Chapter 25 so that variations on the theme can be explored quickly. A facility that creates good-quality graphics displays and allows easy manipulation of them is very useful for this. Sometimes the data for executive information systems will be stored in a Class IV data base, as in Fig. 25.6

Figure 34.5 shows a four-step approach to this type of information system. It should be noted that the last step in Fig. 34.5 is the design of

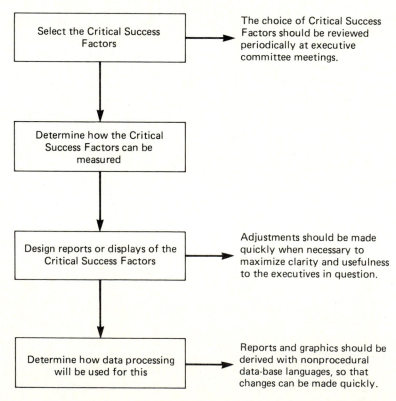

Figure 34.5   Executive Information System design using critical-success-factor analysis as advocated by Rockart [3].

the data-processing resources. Too often the opposite is true. The data-processing resources are designed first and the executive reports are created as a by-product.

CRITICAL SUCCESS FACTORS FOR LOWER LEVELS

Rockart and his associates achieved considerable success in designing information systems for chief executives. This is noteworthy because most other information systems have failed to meet the needs of the CEO.

The critical success factor method is useful also for lower levels of *general* management (i.e., management to which multiple functions report). It helps such managers decide where to focus their attention. It provides them with measures and a continuous monitoring system. Regardless of DP it is a valuable management technique. It is worth taking the time to think through the critical success factors for each general manager.

When critical success factor reports are used for multiple levels of management, often the same reports or information systems can be shared. A hierarchy of communication and reporting can be set up. A chart can be created showing the critical success factors at different levels. This helps to create a shared understanding of the management requirements. It is much more effective than merely a shared statement of the corporate goals.

In describing entity analysis earlier in the book we said that it needs the involvement of end-user management. Where management participates, corporate reorganization has often resulted, as described in Chapter 39. Critical-success-factor analysis needs ongoing input by general management. It almost always changes the setting of objectives, motivations, and compensation if done thoroughly. It is very valuable in small corporations as well as in large ones, and not all of the factors to be reported on require computers. The factors should be reviewed periodically at the board or executive committee level.

THE GIVE-THEM-EVERYTHING APPROACH

A fundamentally different approach to information systems has proven of value in some corporations. This is to make masses of data available on-line. When an executive asks for something there is a good chance that it is accessible.

TOP DP EXECUTIVE:

We are moving toward converting anything we have captured electronically, and which the user management needs onto STAIRS (an IBM information retrieval system). We have accounts payable information, savings information; I have project management data, performance information; we have expense statements, checks that have cleared for the last 42 days.

We are going across the organization and saying: "Here is an opportunity to have terminals with which you can view and access information. Is it valuable to you? What information do you want?"

We convert the information they want. Once converted for one area, it's now available for everyone else in the firm. We no longer ask: "Do we need 15 copies of this report?" We have one copy on-line.

The rationale behind this approach is that it is impossible to anticipate all the information needs of executives; therefore, you make everything available that they might ask for, on a Class IV system—a general-purpose information retrieval system.

TOP DP EXECUTIVE:

We don't try to second-guess what a senior manager needs—or what a middle manager or professional needs to do his job. We store all the information he might need, and let him do summaries, extractions, and report generation.

This is the reverse of the old MIS approach, which said: "Let's first sit down and decide what the executive needs and then let's design it."

Our internal conclusion was that when an executive has a problem, he will say, "Here's what I need." Then you generate it for him. You should not try to decide all the things you think he may need in the future. You cannot be clairvoyant enough.

This approach results in a large collection of data with large indices for information retrieval. It can be justified if those data are useful to multiple executives. Once a system is set up, the cost of adding more data to it is largely the cost of the discs. The quotations above came from a large bank which started with two disc drives and built up to 90 (at the time of writing). Each time users ask for more data to be stored, they can pay for the disc space required. On-line storage is dropping in cost rapidly. The cheaper it is, the more viable is the approach of making vast quantities of information available on-line in Class IV systems.

TOP DP EXECUTIVE:

Our approach was to go to the user area and show them what STAIRS could provide in terms of information retrieval as well as their mail. We said: "Would you like to try it?" Some did, and word got around of what it was capable. Some would come to us and say: "We would like to convert this and have access to it." We'd put it up if they could justify their application.

We put 42 days of checks on-line, for example, which needed 10 discs. It has reduced the access time of a customer inquiry from 30 or 40 minutes to seconds. In addition, if you happen to call the commercial officer rather than the operating area, he can access the data without a second phone call.

A general-purpose information-retrieval system can support all levels of management and professionals. The more people use it, the better cost-justified it is.

To achieve wide acceptance, a substantial amount of education and selling is needed. Some DP organizations send technical staff, acting like consultants, into user areas to assist and persuade the users to employ the system. These staff members determine what information should be put on the system, and generally try to solve the users' information needs.

TOP DP EXECUTIVE:

We took young people coming off our training program and said: "Your area is to support and educate the trust department in the use of these tools. Find out what data should be made available to them. Get more people using the tools and those people who do use them using them better." These young people coming right out of college are doing an excellent job.

Once a general-purpose information-retrieval system exists, it is desirable to have inexpensive terminals that can access it in most locations. These may be the same terminals that are used for office automation or electronic mail.

TOP DP EXECUTIVE:

Once we had tools and information worth using, our approach was to have terminals distributed around the bank in masses. Inexpensive terminals are important because you want them to be located on almost everyone's desk. Once you have them, you can add functions as you find meaningful solutions to information needs.

It is desirable to make users as comfortable with terminals as possible so that they can start thinking about what information they want from the terminal rather than being concerned about how to operate it.

The office terminal can provide many functions as well as information retrieval. In some corporations it is used to display mail or to act as an electronic in-basket and out-basket.

Some terminals seem particularly easy to use by non-DP staff with no special training. For example, *the viewdata (videotex)* terminals, which originated in Europe, are both attractive to use and easy to operate without training. They can also be cheap enough for widespread deployment. With such devices the office terminal will eventually become almost as familiar as a telephone. We do not think about complex operating procedures when we grab a telephone. The terminals ought to be made as common and easy to use as the telephone.

With a general-purpose information system and familiar ubiquitous terminals, the computer and complex technology can be hidden in the back room and disappear from the concern of the users. People do not think about the electricity generating plants that provide power as long as power is present when you switch it on. None of us think about the central office of the phone company as long as when we pick up the phone we receive a dial tone. Similarly, information terminals should become a generalized, easy-to-use utility.

INFORMATION SYSTEM LANGUAGES

Information retrieval systems are used differently in different organizations. Sometimes they are general centralized systems containing a diversity of different types of data. Sometimes they are special localized systems providing the information needed by one department or functional grouping of an organization.

Such systems assume much greater usefulness if the user can not only look at data and summaries of data, but can also process the data or create his own reports or charts from it. Prior to the 1980s, almost all programming was done by programmers. Recently, a variety of languages and facilities have emerged which enable end users to process their own data, as described in Chapters 25 and 26. These can greatly increase the usefulness of information retrieval systems.

INFORMATION STAFF

Critical-success-factor analysis and generalized information retrieval systems have both provided useful information sources for executives. They tend to provide quite different types of information.

Critical-success-factor analysis is extremely useful in helping executives

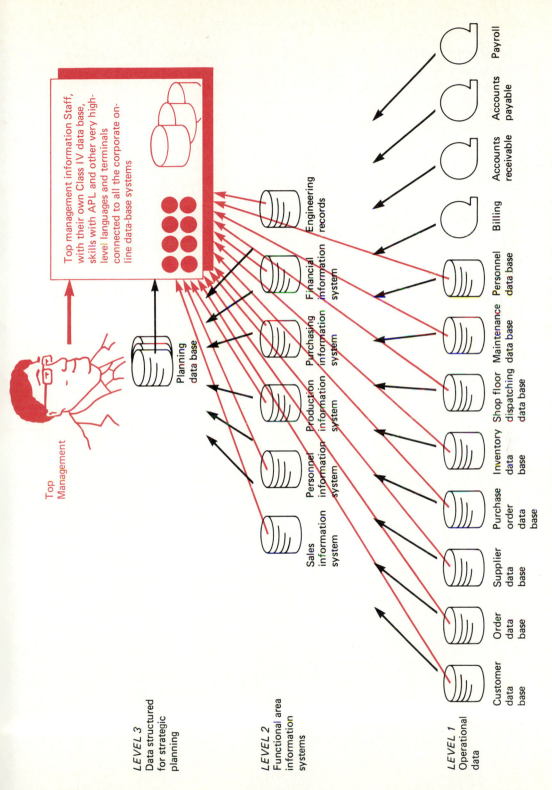

LEVEL 3
Data structured for strategic planning

LEVEL 2
Functional area information systems

LEVEL 1
Operational data

Top Management

Top management information Staff, with their own Class IV data base, skills with APL and other very high-level languages and terminals connected to all the corporate on-line data-base systems

Planning data base

Sales information system
Personnel information system
Production information system
Purchasing information system
Financial information system
Engineering records

Customer data base
Order data base
Supplier data base
Purchase order data base
Inventory data base
Shop floor dispatching data base
Maintenance data base
Personnel data base
Billing
Accounts receivable
Accounts payable
Payroll

Figure 34.6 A top management information system needs the intelligence of corporate information specialists skilled at extracting information from all the various corporate data bases, and generating programs for top management decisions very rapidly.

641

control an organization. Its more enthusiastic practitioners state that it is an indispensable part of a management control system. However, it does not attempt to provide information for *strategic* planning. Data needs for this and other top management roles are almost impossible to predict and pre-plan. New questions arise quickly and information is needed for dealing with these questions.

To deal with these unpredictable but vital needs, some corporations have a staff of information experts (Fig. 34.6). They have access to all relevant data sources. They should have their own information retrieval system or Class IV data bases, and should have the skill to create programs for providing information very quickly with program generators, report generators, graphics generators, and very high level languages.

Programmers vary over a very wide range in their skills and productivity. The best programmers can create bug-free programs 10 times as fast as average programmers. If they are trained in a language like APL which has report generation and graphics generation software, and access to data bases, they can create complex programs for showing management a range of options very quickly. With NOMAD and other nonprocedural languages, results can be obtained more quickly than with APL, in some cases, but APL is better with complex calculations and logic. The top management information staff needs both the best languages and tools available, and programmers selected because they can achieve results exceptionally fast.

Much of the information that top management needs can be generated without programmers by means of the high-level data-base languages discussed in Chapter 25. There is usually no need for efficiency of coding because the programs are not run frequently. There is need for speed in creating results, access to appropriate data bases, generation of reports and graphics of maximum clarity, and the ability to modify the results rapidly if so requested by the executives.

AN EXAMPLE OF PROGRAMMING FOR TOP MANAGEMENT

The vice-president of finance at STSC, Inc., gives a description of the use of APL for assisting with top management problems. He employed APL for the following applications:

- Pricing decisions
- Lease versus buy decisions
- Acquisition analyses
- Incentive plan design
- Capital funding decisions
- Investment scenario analyses

He discusses them in Ref. 7, from which the following extract is reproduced by kind permission of the publisher:

Pricing Decisions

Pricing has always been a challenging discipline, but given the inflation we've had to deal with in the late 1970s, pricing has never been such a delicate issue. The costs of running a business are constantly increasing. Effective pricing management, in addition to the management of productivity, is the key in maintaining satisfactory profit margins and the financial viability of an ongoing business.

Like other key business decisions, pricing decisions are complex because they depend on several factors, such as:

- *Product mix*. How will a change in price for one product affect sales for related products?
- *Existing contractual commitments*. How will a change in price affect total company revenues if some contracts (e.g., government contracts) limit price increases?
- *Product demand*. Will a price increase negatively impact demand for our product?
- *Competitive pricing*. Will a price increase result in a significant competitive disadvantage?
- *Product cost*. What does it cost to create, sell and service the product?
- *Product value*. Should the market price be independent of product cost?

All of these factors require making assumptions. The objective is to maximize revenue and profit. What happens to total company revenue if the price for product X is increased by 8 percent? If the product is new, when will the break-even point occur? What will margins be if we undercut competitive pricing by 10 percent?

Lease Versus Buy Analyses

Financial officers are frequently faced with lease versus buy decisions. Consequently, this type of application system will probably be used over and over again once it is written.

For example, you're buying a piece of equipment and you want to know the least costly alternative—owning or leasing. The choice depends on many factors:

1. The equipment's economic life to you
2. Its economic life in the marketplace (i.e., the expected value of the equipment in the marketplace when your company no longer has use for it)

3. Your ability to use the investment tax credit and accelerated depreciation

4. Who pays other ongoing costs (e.g., maintenance, insurance and personal property taxes)

5. Purchase options available during the lease term

6. The cost of funds to your company

7. The ratio of the purchase price to the pure lease price

8. Your company's required investment hurdle

Each alternative—buying or leasing—has its own projected cash flow. For example, the buy alternative may have cash flowing out of the corporation to repay debt and to pay for maintenance. It also results in cash flowing into the corporation from tax savings and from the sale of the equipment at some future date. A comparison of the present value of the cash flows of each alternative will indicate which alternative is best. If the expected market value of the equipment is difficult to predict, you can assign probabilities to alternative market values, run the model for each alternative and then graph the results.

Acquisition Analyses

Like a lease versus buy decision, the decision to acquire another company at a given price is binary—should we or shouldn't we?

The answer, to a significant extent, is derived from an analysis of the consolidation of projected financial results for both companies. If the marriage of the two companies results in cost savings due to the elimination of redundant activities, this should be factored into the analysis.

If the projected financial results of the marriage are superior to the projected results of the acquiring company alone, then it makes sense (financially, at least) for the acquisition to be pursued. Ultimately, an improvement in earnings per share must result if the acquisition is to be considered successful.

Incentive Plan Design

If your environment is dynamic (like STSC's is), incentive plan models will probably have a limited life. You'll create an incentive model for one year and then throw it away when the basic incentive algorithm becomes obsolete.

The objective here, of course, is to optimize the cost of your incentive plan, realizing that you don't know *exactly* what the financial results will be—for the company as a whole or for its various performance centers and cost centers. The controlling assumption is that the size of incentive payments is related directly to performance. You wish to fairly and competitively reward individual performance; however, total compensation should not exceed an established percentage of revenue.

Frequently, under such constraints, creating an incentive plan is a trial-

and-error process. Alternative incentive algorithms must be tested under varying assumptions. What if some performance centers exceed plan, while others fall below plan? What if the total company exceeds plan or falls behind plan? How will each of these scenarios affect the cost and the incentive value of our plan? The more you play the "what if" game, the closer you will get to the optimum incentive plan.

Occasionally, it may be necessary to create and throw away several incentive plan models in one year. *APL* offers the power and the flexibility to do this and still meet targeted completion dates.

Capital Funding Decisions

Capital funding decisions encompass some very familiar and basic decisions on how to run a business. Should we go public? Should we fund our growth with bank debt, or with a private placement of debt, or should we sell additional stock?

Of all business decisions, this is certainly one of the most complex. More debt probably means a weaker corporate balance sheet and possible restraints in the way the business is run. But, it can also mean a higher return to existing stockholders if the corporate return on investment (ROI) exceeds the cost of borrowed capital. On the other hand, more equity in the business means a stronger balance sheet and probably more flexibility in the way the business is run. But, it can also mean a lower return for existing stockholders if the new capital is put to work at a lower ROI than that which the corporation has been enjoying.

The number and combinations of "what if" possibilities here are enormous:

- What if interest rates rise? Fall? By how much?
- What if the stock market rises? Falls?
- What if our company grows 15%? 20%? 25%?
- What if additional capital is $2 million? $10 million? $100 million?
- What if our margins increase? Decrease?

The decision is made by calculating the impact of the most likely set of values for these factors on earnings per share. The alternative that results in the highest projected earnings per share is probably the best choice.

Investment Scenario Analysis

Typically, the financial planning process includes at least the following three elements:

- Goals in key results areas (e.g., earnings per share and return on equity).

- A limited number of financial resources. This includes any or all of the following:

  1. Cash flow demand internally
  2. Some limited capacity to borrow additional capital
  3. The ability to sell stock to bring in equity capital

- A list of alternative investment opportunities (e.g., new products, cost-saving programs, training, and new equipment). The return from each alternative may or may not vary directly with the amount of investment in that alternative.

The problem then is to decide how much money, if any, to allocate to each investment alternative. This usually involves an iterative process using a number of "what if" questions. What if investment in product A is increased at the expense of product B? What if all funds are invested in opportunities D and E and all others are dropped? What will the result be on the corporate balance sheet, on the company's revenue growth rate and on earnings per share in each case?"

These applications are typical of computing for senior management. Management of a tightly controlled corporation today ought to use computer models for setting and maintaining the corporate direction. They should be indispensable for top management. But *much* greater speed and flexibility are needed than with the traditional DP development cycle. Appropriate data bases should be in place and very high level languages should be used for manipulating the data. Color graphics and charts for management should be manipulated to explore "what if?" questions.

THREE INGREDIENTS FOR EXECUTIVE SUPPORT

We have indicated three types of approach to executive information systems that have achieved success. The type of success is different with the three approaches. It is desirable that all three should be ingredients of a comprehensive executive information system. Figure 34.7 summarizes this.

Box 34.1 lists keys to successful executive information systems.

Box 34.2 summarizes the various approaches that are used to provide executive information systems. Methods 4 through 8 may be used in conjunction with the information staff of method 8 tying together these separate approaches. No one method of Box 34.2 by itself provides all that is required.

BOX 34.1   Keys to successful executive information systems

- A critical success factor analysis, as developed by Rockart [3], to determine what are the most important information needs of top executives.

- A board or top executive committee that uses critical-success-factor reporting and reviews the factors periodically. This type of control should be used at all levels of general management in a coordinated fashion.

- Management of the corporate data-base environment with thorough data administration and modeling.

- The capability to extract data from the various Class III data bases and restructure them in executive data bases when needed.

- An infrastructure for generalized information retrieval for management, which is fully flexible, and to which new types of data can be added very quickly when executives ask for them.

- The use of very high level languages with which the data in the executive data bases can be extracted and manipulated. These languages should be used by nonprogrammers [8] and employed by executive staff to respond very quickly to the executives' needs.

- The use of business graphics hardware and software with which the most meaningful color charts can be created quickly in conjunction with the very high level data-base languages.

- Executive staff who are expert with languages (such as advanced forms of APL) for modeling financial and other data. Their expertise should include the ability to change the models very quickly to answer "what if?" questions.

- One or more staff who are expert on the multiple data bases and information sources that are accessible.

- Corporate wide data networking, with strategic planning for distributed systems so that data can be moved easily from one system to another [9]. The executive staff terminals should be able to access not only the executive data bases but also detailed records in operations data bases.

- Use of a strategic data planning methodology [10] which provides an updatable chart of the organization's data and how they should be organized.

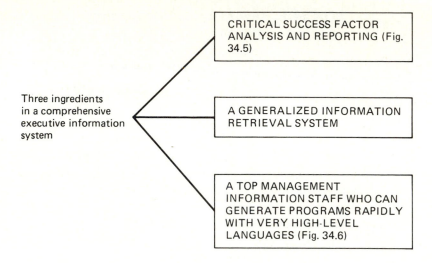

Figure 34.7 Putting together the success stories that can be found in executive information systems indicates that comprehensive support should have these three ingredients.

BOX 34.2   Summary of approaches to executive information systems

1. By-Product of Production Systems

Attention is focused primarily on production systems such as invoicing, purchasing, manufacturing control, and material requirement planning. Information by-products of these systems are made available to interested executives. They may be summaries or exception reports.

This does not focus on top management's real needs. It tends to result in a proliferation of reports and lists reaching the executive, too numerous to read and of little relevance. Often they are ongoing periodic reports started by a request for information for

BOX 34.2   *(Continued)*

some particular circumstance in distant past. Nobody dares to kill an established report. This is the most common approach and it has been of little value to chief executives.

2. Total Study

An all-embracing study is performed of a corporation's entire information needs. The most common method of this type is IBM's BSP (Business Systems Planning). This and other forms of corporate-wide top-down planning are valuable in organizing DP resources [10] but have rarely been of much use in satisfying top executive information needs.

3. Anticomputer

This school of thought believes that the information needs of top management are unpredictable, ever-changing and usually subjective, and therefore computers cannot help. Its proponents point out the uselessness of the results produced by the methods described above.

Much of the information needed by top executives is non-computerizable. Nevertheless, all of the approaches described below have proven very valuable in different corporations.

4. The Key Indicator Method

A set of key indicators of the health of the business is selected. Data are gathered on each of these and summary reports created. Exception reports are generated for indicators that fall outside a predetermined range. An executive may be given summary reports or exception reports, or may be able to display the key indicators on terminal screens. Some of the more elegant systems use graphics and/or large-screen displays in the board room.

Some top executives find these systems very valuable. Often, however, they provide only financial data.

5. Critical Success Factors

General managers are asked to identify the factors they consider most critical to the success of their organization (as described in this chapter). Measures are devised for these critical success fac-

(Continued)

BOX 34.2 *(Continued)*

tors and reports designed. It is then determined how DP can help to create the reports. The choice of critical success factors is reviewed periodically.

This is an excellent management technique, regardless of computers. It forms a basis for perhaps the best type of information system for management control, but it does not provide strategic information.

6. Generalized Information Retrieval System

A general-purpose on-line information retrieval system is set up. Many different types of data are loaded into it when management or other users ask for them. The system should permit the data to be searched and displayed easily. Reports and charts can be generated.

Key indicator and critical-success-factor information can be among the mass of other data that are stored. The system is paid for by its service to functional management, and it sometimes helps answer the unanticipated questions of general management. Increasingly in the future, larger amounts of data are likely to be available on-line. The proponents of this method say that it is impossible to second-guess what information management will need, so they recommend establishing a structure that can handle new types of information quickly.

7. Financial Models

Financial models are very important to some top management. They run or adjust the models to estimate the effect of various decisions. They use them to set budgets, sales targets, and so on. As each month's figures become available, they can be fed into the models, which provide a tight financial control mechanism.

8. Information Staff

A staff of information experts deals with top management's needs for information. It ranges from one person to a group of several specialists. The staff has access to all (or most) on-line data in the organization and may also have its own Class IV data base. It has the capability to generate new reports or charts from the data bases, and can create management information programs very quickly with fourth-generation languages.

BOX 34.2 *(Continued)*

> The group may maintain financial models, marketing models, or other models. It has the capability to do the computation needed to assess new situations, such as a merger, very quickly.
>
> The information staff may employ methods 4 to 7 above, integrating them into an overall capability.

REFERENCES

1. J. Deardon, "MIS Is a Mirage," *Harvard Business Review,* January–February 1977.

2. J. Deardon, "Myth of Real-Time Management Information," *Harvard Business Review,* May–June 1966.

3. J. F. Rockart, "A New Approach to Defining the Chief Executive's Information Needs," Center for Information Systems Research, M.I.T. Alfred P. Sloan School of Management, Report CISR No. 37, WP No. 1008–78.

4. J. Rude, "Interview with William Dougherty President, North Carolina National Bank Corporation," *MIS Quarterly,* Vol. 1, No. 1, March 1977.

5. J. R. Daniel, "Management Information Crisis," *Harvard Business Review,* September–October 1961.

6. G. G. Mooradian, "The Key Variables in Planning and Control in Medical Group Practices," Master's Thesis, Alfred P. Sloan School of Management, Cambridge, Mass, 1971.

7. R. C. Fick, "What If: The Making of a Vice President of Finance," in A. J. Rose and B. A. Schick, eds., *APL in Practice,* John Wiley & Sons, Inc., New York, 1980.

8. James Martin, *Application Development Without Programmers,* Prentice-Hall, Inc., Englewood Cliffs, NJ, 1982.

9. James Martin, *Computer Networks and Distributed Processing,* Prentice-Hall, Inc., Englewood Cliffs, NJ, 1981.

10. James Martin, *Strategic Data-Planning Methodologies,* Prentice-Hall, Inc., Englewood Cliffs, NJ, 1982.

PART **VII** THE VIEW FROM
THE TOP

35 ORGANIZATION OF TOP-DOWN PLANNING

Chapter 5 stressed the need for top-down planning of data in an enterprise. Ideally, the top-down planning should take place before the design of individual data bases.

It might be objected that the structure of this book is inappropriate: the Top-Down Planning section should appear *before* the section on Data Administration and Design. In practice, the majority of data-base installations are plunging into implementation without top-down planning. The ordinary DP analyst or manager feels that he can influence the design of individual systems but that top management planning is beyond his sphere of influence. That is why this section of the book appears last, not first—so that the ordinary reader does not feel unable to take action as he reads the book.

While most ordinary DP managers feel unable to take action on top-down planning of data, most top management are unaware of the need for it or not persuaded of the value of the effort.

INTERVIEWER:

You have much data-base activity. Why is there no attempt at top-down planning of data?

DP EXECUTIVE:

We tried to do that. We beat our heads against that particular wall for two years. The problem is that people don't like to do planning. They like to implement. It is just too difficult to make those sorts of plans work in this corporation. Everybody wants to solve their own pressing problems and do so with minimum overhead. They resent the head-office planners and think of them as unnecessary bureaucrats. The strategic data planning efforts were scrapped.

VALUE OF TOP-DOWN DATA PLANNING

The main purpose of top-down planning is to make the separately implemented data systems link together. Some important users need to access data in multiple systems and cannot do so if the data are incompatible. Some systems need to interchange data. As small computers proliferate it becomes increasingly important that their data should be compatible, derived from a common data dictionary and data model. Incompatible data in separate files or data bases can prevent the integration of data needed to generate information needed by management.

One of the most persuasive arguments for top-down planning is the costs incurred by organizations that have failed to do it. They include the costs of maintenance and retrofitting systems so that they work together. They include costs of being unable to offer new services when needed or to extract information that has become vital for management.

Two-thirds of the DP staff in U.S. government installations are working on maintenance. The ratio is similar in commercial installations. More than $20 billion per year is being spent on maintenance. There are multiple reasons for maintenance, but a large proportion of maintenance work would be avoided if systems used compatible data with data management systems, report generators, and other high-level data-base languages. The cost of top-down planning is small compared to the costs of maintenance incurred by not doing top-down planning.

The U.S. Department of Defense (D.o.D.) built many systems in the 1970s, some of them spectacular. There was inadequate overall planning of their data and requirements for operating together. D.o.D. devised an operation called ABIC (Army Battlefield Interface Concept) for migrating the separate systems into a form in which they could work together. The costs of the conversion of data and consequent reprogramming were enormous.

One large bank decided there was an urgent need to give each corporate customer a summary of the cash that was in its various accounts. Competitive banks had started to provide this service. However, different analysts had created the programs for the different types of accounts and each designed his own data. It was more than a year before the customer service could be initiated.

Industry is full of horror stories about corporations having data-base systems being unable to pull together vital information from the data bases.

ORGANIZATION FOR THE STUDY

An appropriate organization needs to be set up for conducting the strategic planning study.

The first prerequisite is a person who understands clearly what methodology will be used, and preferably has experience with it. Much time is wasted, results are poor, and the planners are discredited when they make up the methodology as they go along. Often there is nobody in the organization with strategic data planning experience, so help from an outside consultant is needed. The consultant should be selected only if he brings a formal, proven methodology, like those in the following chapters, preferably computerized.

COMPANY SECRETARY:

I feel that it is imperative to have an outside consultant, as far too frequently an in-house team is inclined to look at the way things have been done or are being done, not how they want them in the future. A consultant without the blinkers of past history in the company is well equipped to overcome this problem.

It is definitely not desirable to hand over the entire planning task to consultants, so the leader of the planning effort should be *within* the corporation and should be able to update the plan on an ongoing basis after its initial creation and acceptance. He needs training in the methodology. We will use the term *information resources planner* for the leader of the planning effort.

The planning ought to be done by a *small* nucleus team with strong leadership. The team will need much assistance from the user areas of the corporation. Key individuals from user areas need to be selected. Some of these participants should be senior managers. The form of participation differs from one methodology to another. Sometimes the user managers are interviewed. Sometimes users are trained to contribute information from their area. We will refer to these participants as *user analysts*.

Figure 35.1 illustrates the nucleus group and its input from senior end users.

In one medium-sized corporation the top-down planning was done very effectively by a team consisting of the DP manager, head systems analyst, financial director, chief accountant, operations manager, and customer services manager. This group was taught and guided by an outside consultant.

Where senior management or end users are involved, skill is needed in presenting the concepts to them in nontechnical language.

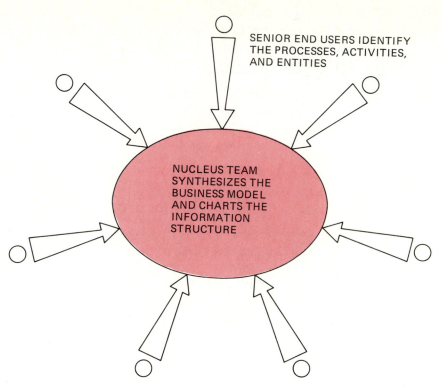

SENIOR END USERS IDENTIFY
THE PROCESSES, ACTIVITIES,
AND ENTITIES

NUCLEUS TEAM
SYNTHESIZES THE
BUSINESS MODEL
AND CHARTS THE
INFORMATION
STRUCTURE

Figure 35.1   A nucleus team of perhaps four people, with strong leadership, creates the top-down plan. To do so they need input from senior end users who have been trained to participate.

MANAGER CORPORATE PLANNING:

Initial meetings were held with senior management and users to familiarize them with the concept, and later a more formal session by the consultant to introduce the detailed approach and methodology. This formal session was not a success. Essentially, it was a technical approach at too senior a level or a too technical delivery for the audience. Nevertheless, once we began the working sessions involving the users on a regular basis, the whole project gained momentum and acceptance. A war-room was set up and a coordinator appointed. In addition, two business analysts have been assigned to the project to assist users in the techniques at the formal user-group sessions.

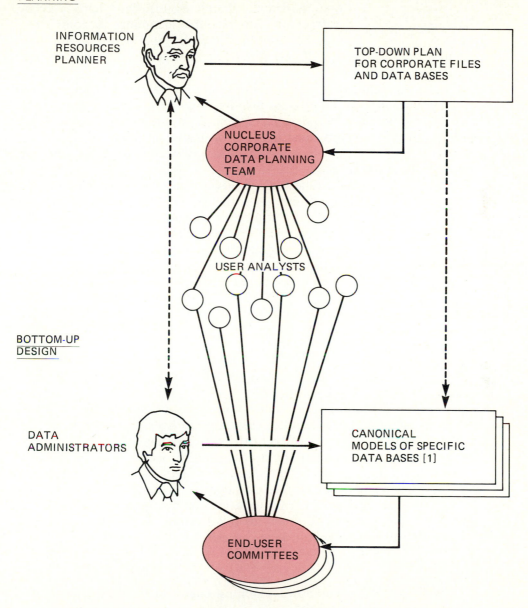

Figure 35.2 Top-down planning by the information system planner and corporate data planning group needs to guide the data modeling of the data administrators. The computerized data modeling tool should be an integral extension of top-down planning tool so that one process feeds and cross-checks the other [2].

INFORMATION RESOURCES PLANNER

The top-down planning needs to be controlled by one individual. Some organizations have a committee for data resource planning. A committee may be desirable for review and feedback, but, like data administration, the overall design needs to be the responsibility of one strong, competent individual.

In some cases that individual is responsible for planning data resources alone; sometimes he has the broader responsibility of planning information systems. The information resources planner must have the ear of top management, and top management must sign off on his plans. Where this has not been the case, the plan has often caused bitter political controversy, and has never been fully implemented.

Figure 35.2 shows the relationship between the top-down planning of the information resources planner and the detailed bottom-up planning of the data administrator(s). The top-down planner has a corporate-wide perspective and decides what data bases or other data resources the corporation needs. The data administrator does the data analysis and synthesis for each data base that needs to be created, as described in Chapters 6 to 13.

Both need help from end users, but somewhat differently. The information resources planner needs help from every functional area but not at a fine level of detail. The data administrator needs user committees looking at one subject data base at a time in fine detail, attempting to make them as stable as possible.

Both need a computerized tool. There are too many examples of database plans and designs done by hand which are coarse-grained, sloppy, difficult to modify, and consequently do not represent the true needs. Designers without computerized tools look for shortcuts to avoid detail that is too time-consuming to handle. They resist making necessary modifications to the charts they draw because of the extreme manual effort.

The computerized tool for top-down planning needs to be compatible with the tool for bottom-up design. They can feed each other and cross-checks can be applied to each other's designs. In both, the design must be updatable when necessary. Much information for bottom-up design will be collected as a by-product of the work for top-down design. It can be fed into a design tool ready for the bottom-up synthesis.

TIME SCALE

Top-down planning ought to be completed in six months.

In the case histories studied when writing this book, most were completed in six months but only when there was clear direction and a firm methodology. When a firm methodology or firm management of the process was lacking, the attempt at top-down planning could ramble on for much longer and sometimes became discredited and disregarded. Because of the ongoing pressure to develop applications, top-down planning needs to be tackled quickly and decisively.

Often, the effort is "90% complete" after six months. The remaining 10% involves subtleties and uncertainties about where to stop. It is important that the results are made *usable* after six months, even if some of the subtleties are unresolved.

If the detailed data-base modeling and design process is delayed until the top-down plan is complete, and data modeling itself takes a long time, the total delay may be so great as to defeat the objectives of rapid application development.

Some of the methods described in this book produce a coarse-grained plan. Looking ahead, the chart in Fig. 36.3 took only a few weeks to create. It was not perfect but it provided an overview good enough for breaking the detailed data modeling efforts into accomplishable projects.

Where it has been done with good tools and a clearly defined methodology, fine-resolution planning, such as that in Chapter 8, has been completed in six months (less in small corporations). The eventual results from fine-resolution planning are far better than those from coarse-resolution planning. Some coarse attempts at top-down planning have been almost a waste of time because they gave insufficient guidance for detailed implementation.

On the other hand, some approaches attempt to identify too much detail in the top-down planning. This can result in the overview never being completed in a reasonable time. The top-down planning team should not normalize records or argue about the definitions of attributes. When this is done, the process can bog down in discussion of details.

DEVELOPING THE BUSINESS MODEL

The first step is the development of the enterprise model.

This can proceed in three stages, each providing an increased level of detail:

1. Develop a model showing enterprise *functions*.
2. Extend the model to show *processes*.
3. Extend the model to show *activities*.

All the methodologies described in the following chapters use *functions* and *processes*. Some do not use *activities*. In the latter case the third stage would be omitted.

ORGANIZATIONAL FUNCTIONS AND PROCESSES

Functions refer to the functional areas in a corporation, such as engineering, marketing, production, research, and distribution. One medium-sized manufacturing company listed its functions as follows:

- Business planning
- Finance
- Product planning
- Materials
- Production planning
- Production
- Sales
- Distribution
- Accounting
- Personnel

Business books contain much discussion of the functional areas in a corporation. The top management steering committee concerned with DP should agree that the list of corporate functions is complete and that the top-down data planning should encompass these functions. Sometimes the team omits one or more functions in its first look at the corporation. Completing the list of functional areas is a necessary beginning.

Each functional area carries out a certain number of processes. Figure 35.3 lists 37 typical processes in the functions listed above. Most corporations have more than this. A large, complex corporation might have about 20 functions and 150 to 200 processes.

The identification of functions and processes should be independent of the current organization chart. The organization may change but still have to carry out the same functions and processes. The identification of functions and processes should represent fundamental concern for how the corporation operates.

Many DP systems and applications have been created to provide the information needs of a specific department or organizational entity, or to provide output reports wanted by one particular manager. These become obsolete when the corporation is reorganized or management changes. The data bases created should be independent of such changes. So should the business processes identified for the purposes of top-down planning. The processes should be basic activities and decision areas which are independent of any reporting hierarchy or specific management responsibility.

The processes may be defined with simple definitions. *Inventory man-*

FUNCTIONAL AREAS	PROCESSES
BUSINESS PLANNING	Market analysis Product range review Sales forecasting
FINANCE	Financial planning Capital acquisition Funds management
PRODUCT PLANNING	Product design Product pricing Product specification maintenance
MATERIALS	Materials requirements Purchasing Receiving Inventory control Quality control
PRODUCTION PLANNING	Capacity planning Plant scheduling Workflow layout
PRODUCTION	Materials control Sizing and cutting Machine operations
SALES	Territory management Selling Sales administration Customer relations
DISTRIBUTION	Finished stock control Order serving Packing Shipping
ACCOUNTING	Creditors and debtors Cash flow Payroll Cost accounting Budget planning Profitability analysis
PERSONNEL	Personnel planning Recruiting Compensation policy

Figure 35.3 Functions and processes. A large corporation typically has 10 to 30 functions and 100 to 300 processes.

agement, for example, may be defined as "the process of controlling the receipts and withdrawals of raw materials, parts, and subassemblies from the stores, and accounting for the stock." There may or may not be a separate department to accomplish this; it is a process that may apply to multiple departments. The stores may be split or combined, *but the process goes on.*

The products and services created by an organization, and also the services needed to support them, tend to have a four-stage life cycle: plan-

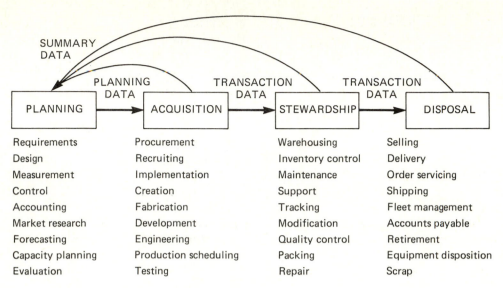

Figure 35.4   Four-stage life cycle of products, services, and resources.

ning, acquisition, stewardship, disposal. Figure 35.4 illustrates some of the types of processes at each stage in the cycle. It sometimes helps to identify the processes to think through all the stages in the life cycle of each type of product, service, or resource. This can be done with money, personnel, raw materials, parts, finished goods, capital equipment, buildings, machinery, fixtures, and so on.

The processes identified can be mapped against the executives in the organization chart. This is illustrated in Fig. 35.5. The matrix shown can then be used to identify individuals who should be interviewed about the processes. These interviews will help to establish that no processes have been omitted. The processes in which some individuals are involved are often different from those on the organization chart.

STRATEGIC PLANNING CONSULTANT:

The company has a detailed list of F&R's (functions and responsibilities). The problem is: they are not followed. Getting agreement as to who really has what responsibility, and who belongs to which data, was very difficult.

The strategic planning team should attempt to identify all of the processes in the corporation or division with which it is concerned. It should eliminate redundancies from the list of processes. It should not artificially

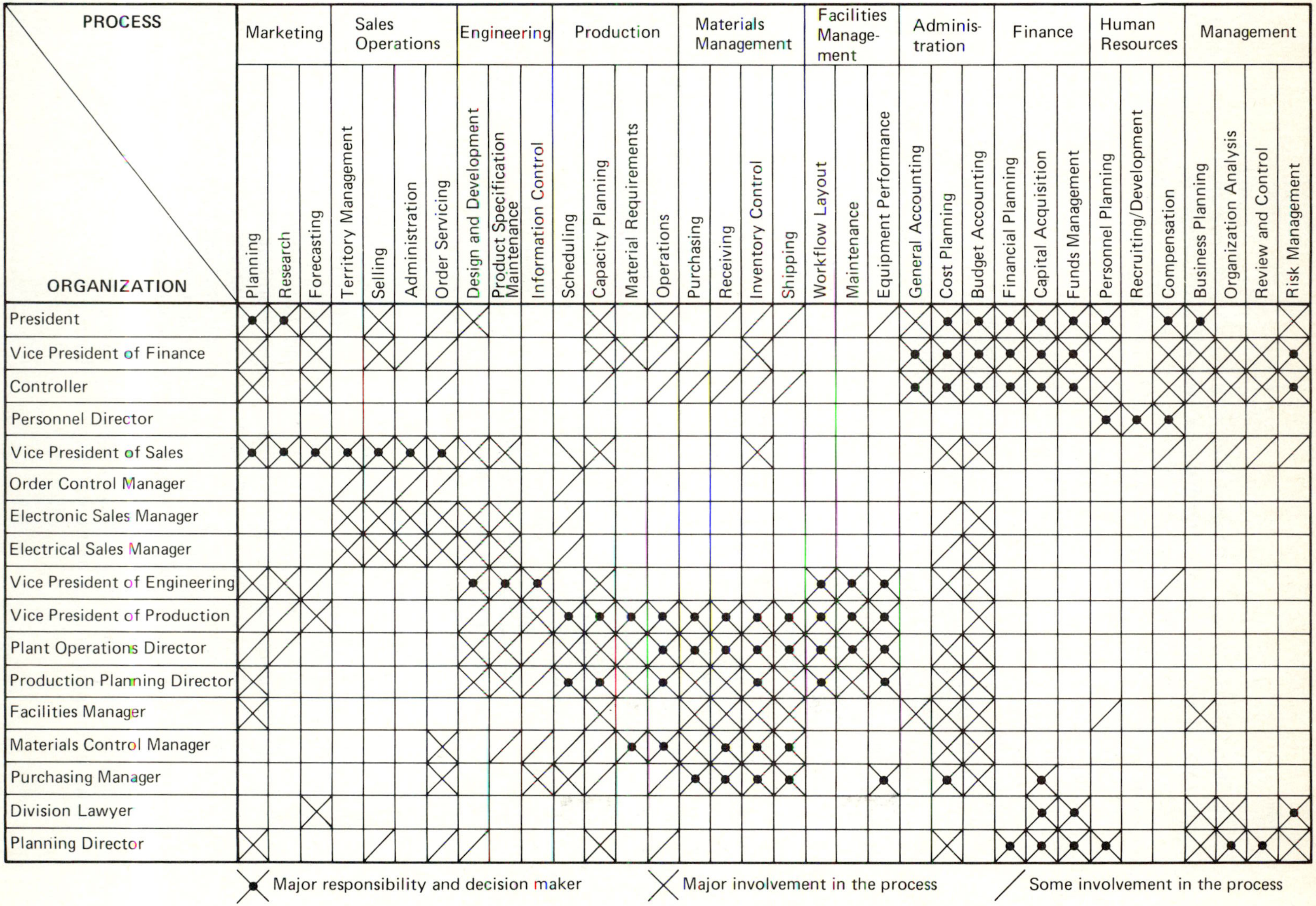

Figure 35.5 Business functions and processes mapped against the existing organization structure. (From [1].)

Legend:
- ● Major responsibility and decision maker
- ✕ Major involvement in the process
- ╱ Some involvement in the process

combine the processes to reduce their number. Often there are a hundred or more processes in a large organization. We will advocate that the planning techniques that involve manipulation of these processes should be computerized. The entire top-down plan needs to be computer-maintainable.

ACTIVITIES   In each business process a number of *activities* take place.

One of the processes in Fig. 35.3 is *purchasing,* for example. In this process, activities such as the following occur:

- Requisition for purchase
- Selection of suppliers
- Creation of purchase order
- Follow-up of delivery of items on purchase order
- Exception processing
- Preparation of information for accounts payable
- Recording supplier performance data
- Analysis of supplier performance

There are typically five to ten *activities* for each business process. There may be several hundred activities in a small corporation and several thousand in a large, complex one.

In most corporations the activities have never been charted. When they are listed, and related to the data they use, it is usually clear that much redundancy exists. Each area of a corporation tends to expand its activities without knowledge of similar activities taking place in other areas. Each department tends to create its own paperwork. *This does not matter if the paperwork is processed manually. However, if it is processed by computer, the proliferation of separately designed paperwork is harmful because it greatly increases the cost of programming and maintenance. A computerized corporation ought to have different procedures from a corporation with manual paperwork.* Most of the procedures should be on-line with data of controlled redundancy and minimum diversity of application programs.

When strategic planning lists the activities and the data they use, it should initially minimize the redundancy in the data bases or entities, but leave the redundancy in the activities. Charts mapping data against activities that use those data reveal the duplication in the activities and often suggest desirable ways of reorganizing the activities.

Top-down planning can thus move out of the realm of DP and into the realm of business management and thinking about corporate reorganization.

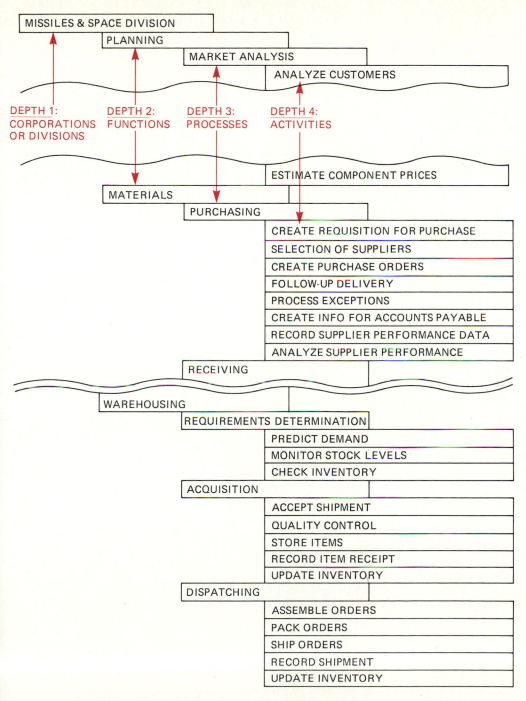

MISSILES & SPACE DIVISION

PLANNING

MARKET ANALYSIS

ANALYZE CUSTOMERS

DEPTH 1:
CORPORATIONS
OR DIVISIONS

DEPTH 2:
FUNCTIONS

DEPTH 3:
PROCESSES

DEPTH 4:
ACTIVITIES

ESTIMATE COMPONENT PRICES

MATERIALS

PURCHASING

CREATE REQUISITION FOR PURCHASE

SELECTION OF SUPPLIERS

CREATE PURCHASE ORDERS

FOLLOW-UP DELIVERY

PROCESS EXCEPTIONS

CREATE INFO FOR ACCOUNTS PAYABLE

RECORD SUPPLIER PERFORMANCE DATA

ANALYZE SUPPLIER PERFORMANCE

RECEIVING

WAREHOUSING

REQUIREMENTS DETERMINATION

PREDICT DEMAND

MONITOR STOCK LEVELS

CHECK INVENTORY

ACQUISITION

ACCEPT SHIPMENT

QUALITY CONTROL

STORE ITEMS

RECORD ITEM RECEIPT

UPDATE INVENTORY

DISPATCHING

ASSEMBLE ORDERS

PACK ORDERS

SHIP ORDERS

RECORD SHIPMENT

UPDATE INVENTORY

Figure 35.6 Enterprise chart: corporations or divisions, functions, processes, and activities.

BUSINESS CHARTS   A chart is needed which shows the business functions, processes, and activities. This chart becomes large because there are hundreds of activities—sometimes more than a thousand. It will be added to and changed throughout the study, so it is convenient to have it computer-maintainable.

Figure 35.6 shows an example of such a chart. It has four depths:

Depth 1: Corporations or divisions

Depth 2: Functions

Depth 3: Processes

Depth 4: Activities

It can be broken into smaller charts which show two of the depths, for example a corporation and its functions, functions and processes as in Fig. 35.3, or a process and its activities.

The format of this chart is the same as the chart we use for representing entities and their associations. The same software can be used for drawing and maintaining both charts, and for the logical data-base charts.

IDENTIFYING THE FUNCTIONS   The first stage—identifying the functions in a corporation—can happen quickly. It ought to involve the assistance of a senior executive or group of executives who know the entire corporation. The discussion ought to consider how the functions of the corporation might change in the future, or how they *ought* to change.

The questions should be asked:

● What are the enterprise's long-range objectives?

● What changes are planned—or are likely?

● Does the functional model created cover these objectives and future changes?

The functional model may be displayed in the form of the block diagram, with each block corresponding to a major functional area of the enterprise. Arrows between the blocks can be used to indicate the hierarchy of authority or the life cycle of products, services, and resources. Different types of organizations have different ways of representing their functional model.

BOUNDARIES OF THE STUDY   As the functions of an enterprise are charted, a decision must be made about the scope or boundaries of the top-down plan.

In a small or tightly integrated enterprise the study should encompass the entire organization. In a multicorporate organization it may proceed in one corporation at a time. The resulting plan from one corporation may be used to guide the planning process in another corporation. In a complex organization one division may be tackled at a time. In one giant aerospace corporation, for example, the Space and Missiles Divisions, themselves exceedingly complex, were tackled first.

If the scope of top-down planning is too broad and covers separate organizations, it may be difficult to control and achieve results in time to affect data-base development. On the other hand, if the scope is too narrow, the benefits of top-down planning will be partially lost. If the information resource involves heavy interaction across several divisions, a top-down study that is confined to only one division may fail to provide an adequate foundation for building the needed information systems.

The span of the strategic planning should reflect the management style of the corporation. In some corporations the divisions are truly separate and autonomous; in others they are not. Similar-sized firms in the same industry are often managed quite differently. One large insurance company, for example, has three divisions that are almost entirely separately managed, and have separate data processing. Top-down planning can be done separately for each division. Another is centrally managed and needs a top-down plan that spans the divisions.

To decide the boundaries of the top-down plan, the question should be asked: Could data structures designed for the area being studied be used or affected by any other area? If the answer is "yes," that area should be encompassed by the top-down plan. Otherwise, the boundaries of the plan should not be made unnecessarily large.

ESTABLISHING PROCESSES

When the model of the enterprise functions is established, each functional area can be tackled to establish the processes that it uses. This results in the first three levels of the enterprise chart shown in Fig. 35.6.

Identification of the processes can best be accomplished by assigned representatives of each of the functional areas. To show these representatives what is needed, a proposed set of processes may be drawn up by the nucleus team. This tentative list can then be reviewed and refined by members of the functional area, until an accurate, agreed-upon set of processes is established.

When the processes have been separately reviewed in each functional area, they can be assembled to provide a chart like Fig. 35.6 (but not yet showing activities). Anomalies and conflicts sometimes surface at this stage. Resolution of interfunction discrepancies may be handled by holding a joint meeting with the representatives in question. The overall chart may then be reviewed by top management.

The stages we have described so far have taken about a month to complete in some corporations. The methodologies we review in the following chapters differ considerably, but all of them build on the foundation of functions and processes.

DEGREE OF RESOLUTION

As we have commented, top-down planning can be done in a coarse-grained or fine-grained fashion.

The coarse-grained versions of it describe functions and processes, but not *activities* (the fourth-depth items of Fig. 35.6). They describe subject data bases rather than the entities of which these data bases are composed. We thus have levels of resolution of top-down planning, as shown in Fig. 35.7.

Chapter 36 describes coarse-grained planning with subject data bases and processes.

Chapter 37 describes finer-grained planning with entities (the *things* about which we store data) and processes.

Chapter 38 describes still finer grain planning with entities and activities.

Entities are discussed in more detail in Chapter 37 and activites in Chapter 38.

The total elapsed time for the finer-grained planning has been not much longer than for the coarse-grained planning, in most of the case histories examined, provided that a computerized tool was used and suitable help enlisted from user departments. The finer-grained planning gives much better guidelines for data-base system implementation and design. It is nevertheless important that the top-down planning should remain an *overview,* done fairly quickly, and not drown in the time-consuming detail of data attribute definition and modeling. Detailed data modeling is vitally important, but comes later and usually in smaller chunks.

DETERMINATION OF ENTITIES AND ACTIVITIES

Once the functions and processes are agreed upon, the department or group that performs each process can be contacted to identify the entities about which data are stored and possibly also the activities which each entity is associated with. A more detailed model is then assembled by the nucleus group.

A good way to organize this is to train interested end users in the different areas of the enterprise to identify the activities and entities. The analysts who identified the processes in the previous stage may go on to work with users in identifying the activities.

As the enterprise model in Fig. 35.6 comes together, the portion for each function can be distributed in that functional area for checking.

REVIEWS

The overall charts that are created are different for different methodologies. Examples of them are shown in Figs. 35.6, 36.3, and 37.9. They need to be reviewed by participants

OPERATIONS ⟍ DATA	COARSE RESOLUTION: PROCESSES	FINE RESOLUTION: ACTIVITIES
COARSE RESOLUTION: SUBJECT DATA BASES	Chapter 36	
FINE RESOLUTION: ENTITIES	Chapter 37	Chapter 38

Figure 35.7 Top-down planning can be done with coarse-grained resolution or fine-grained resolution of both the data and operations. The following chapters describe methodologies having different degrees of resolution, as shown here.

and managers in the various functional areas. The reviewers should be encouraged to examine other functional areas besides their own. This should be a thorough critique where concerns are aired and noted.

Each reviewer may examine all the functions of the chart and then work his way down into greater detail in those areas with which he is familiar. It is not feasible for any one person to understand all the detail of every function in the chart.

The tentative process of reviewing the chart and adjusting it is critical. The chart should not be "frozen" prematurely. It needs to be sufficiently accurate for guiding detailed data-base and system design. It is likely to be repeatedly adjusted and for this reason should be computerized.

REFERENCES

1. Business Systems Planning, Information Systems Planning Guide, 2nd ed., IBM Corp., White Plains, NY, 1978.

2. Manuals and information on DATA DESIGNER are available from Data Base Design Inc., 2020 Hogback Road, Ann Arbor, MI 48104.

36 SUBJECT-DATA-BASE PLANNING

INTRODUCTION   In Part I we mentioned subject data bases. A *subject data base* relates to a data subject such as customers, parts, machine tools, shipments, and so on, and is shared by multiple applications. It is the employment of *subject* data bases, as opposed to *application* data bases, that we have described in Chapter 3 as a Class III data environment.

ADVANTAGES OF SUBJECT DATA BASES   The objective of *subject data-base design* is that application development should be speeded up. The data that programmers use *should already exist* in the subject data bases. Program *data divisions* or descriptions of data should be generated automatically. In many cases data-base report generators, query languages, or high-level application development facilities should be used rather than programming languages of the level of COBOL.

DATA-BASE EXECUTIVE:

As I have looked at the unfolding of the subject data-base groupings, it has been startling how the same data have been used for many new processes. *Cash management* as we have developed it was a new requirement, but it is using very much the same data that have been available in banking for years. By representing it in data-base form and enabling access in a number of different ways, we have been able to serve our retail banking group, corporate banking group, and international banking groups.

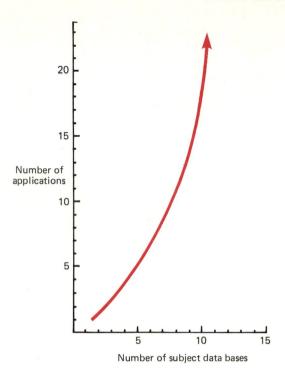

Figure 36.1 As the number of subject data bases grow, the number of applications using them grows disproportionately. Eventually, most new applications can be implemented rapidly because the data are available and the software provides tools to manipulate them. This curve was taken from a corporation with five years of subject data-base development.

As more subject data bases come into existence, the rate of application development increases in well-managed installations, as illustrated in Fig. 36.1. Increasingly, *when new applications come along the data already exist,* although possibly non-primary-key fields may be added to it. Often, application development can be done rapidly with high-level data-base languages.

SELECTION OF SUBJECT DATA BASES

Subject data bases are sometimes called *data classes.* In most installations their contents have been chosen without a formal methodology. The records relating to customers are in the customer data base; the records relating to products are in the product data bases; and so on. This sounds simple but in fact leaves much scope for argument about what subject data bases should exist and what data fit into them. Should *purchase orders* be in the *vendor* data base or the *materials* data base? In the following chapters we discuss two more formal methods for clustering entities into logical data bases. The resulting clusters are called *entity supergroups* and perform the same function as subject data bases in this chapter.

A relatively simple corporation might have about 20 subject data bases; a complex one may have as many as 60.

To identify the subject data bases the planning team may look at them from two viewpoints, and cross-reference the results.

First list the basic artifacts and organizations that the corporation works with, for example:

- Parts
- Material
- Vendors
- Subassemblies
- Work-in-progress
- Products
- Customers
- Salespersons
- Equipment
- Buildings
- Cash
- Accounts
- Shareholders
- Personnel

For each of these there may be basic records, inventory records, transactions, summary or statistical data, and planning or design data. These types of data may be written by each item on the list above. They may be thought about and written down in the life-cycle sequence of Fig. 35.4.

$$planning \rightarrow acquisition \rightarrow stewardship \rightarrow disposal$$

Thus for *materials:*

Materials: Materials planning, bills of materials, cost, purchase orders, inventory, withdrawals, statistics of usage

This is done for each basic artifact or organization and the data are grouped in 20 or more classes of related data.

A second approach is to look at the list of processes (Fig. 35.3), and write down what class of data is used as input and output to each process. This list of data classes is cross-referenced to the list above to create a joint grouping of data classes.

It is necessary to have a high-level overall perspective of a corporation in order to plan what subject data bases it should have. Such organization-wide planning needs to take into consideration not only the subject data bases but also existing or new files, and stand-alone data bases for certain applications.

This is part of the top-down or strategic planning. The detailed design and modeling of data items and records that constitute a subject (or application) data base is the *bottom-up* planning described in Part III.

In many corporations it has been discovered that a data base implemented for one process happens to serve another process, or a different area in the organization. These happy discoveries ought not to happen by chance. They ought to be planned. If they are not planned, they will often *not* happen because different areas tend to keep to themselves, be jealous of their own data, and avoid anything "not invented here."

DATA-BASE EXECUTIVE:

The *customer profile* data base was initially implemented for use internally in the operations division.

Suddenly it became of value in providing information to the commercial side of the organization as well as the retail side.

Again, once we had implemented the *demand deposit* data base for cash management in the head office, we found that its structure also served the branch network.

A BANK'S
DATA-BASE
PLAN In a large bank a plan was put together incorporating the data bases in Fig. 36.2. With these 21 data bases it was theoretically possible to run almost all of the processing in the organization.

The chart in Fig. 36.3 was drawn up mapping the data bases against the main banking processes. This was intended to be a master plan for data-base development.

On the left the processes listed were production runs, transaction processing, and simple inquiries. They represent fairly straightforward data-base usage.

On the right were information systems rather than production systems. These need complex data-base usage. Spontaneous new types of inquiries and report generation will occur once the data bases are in place and appropriate query languages are available. Some of these uses are very important in the overall management of the bank.

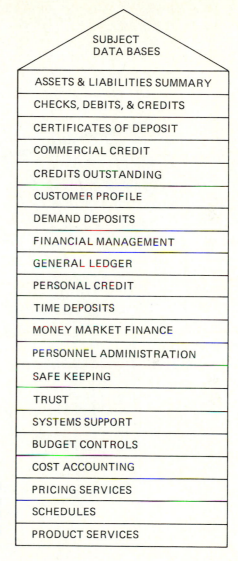

SUBJECT
DATA BASES

ASSETS & LIABILITIES SUMMARY
CHECKS, DEBITS, & CREDITS
CERTIFICATES OF DEPOSIT
COMMERCIAL CREDIT
CREDITS OUTSTANDING
CUSTOMER PROFILE
DEMAND DEPOSITS
FINANCIAL MANAGEMENT
GENERAL LEDGER
PERSONAL CREDIT
TIME DEPOSITS
MONEY MARKET FINANCE
PERSONNEL ADMINISTRATION
SAFE KEEPING
TRUST
SYSTEMS SUPPORT
BUDGET CONTROLS
COST ACCOUNTING
PRICING SERVICES
SCHEDULES
PRODUCT SERVICES

Figure 36.2 With these 21 subject data bases it would be possible to perform most of the data processing in a large bank. Figure 36.3 shows a top-down plan mapping these data bases against their prospective uses.

On the left the data are accessed by primary keys. On the right the data are accessed much of the time by secondary keys.

This represents a top-down view of the data needed to run the organization efficiently. The crosses on the chart show what banking processes and decision-making support activities use what data bases.

Before doing the planning represented by Fig. 36.3, the bank had implemented one data base—that with customer information, names,

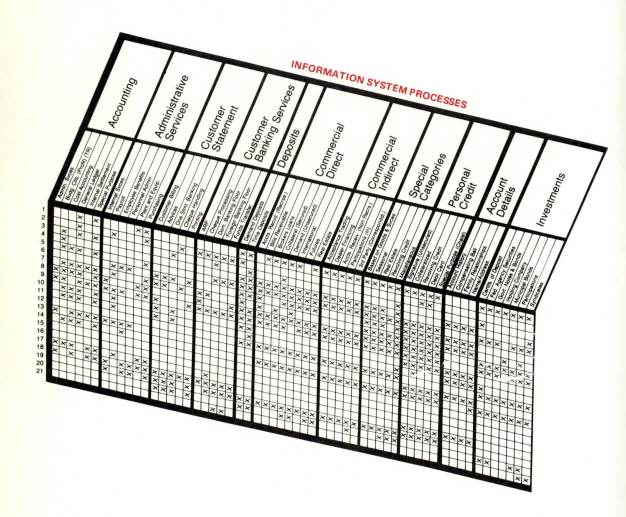

Figure 36.3　Large bank DB plan.

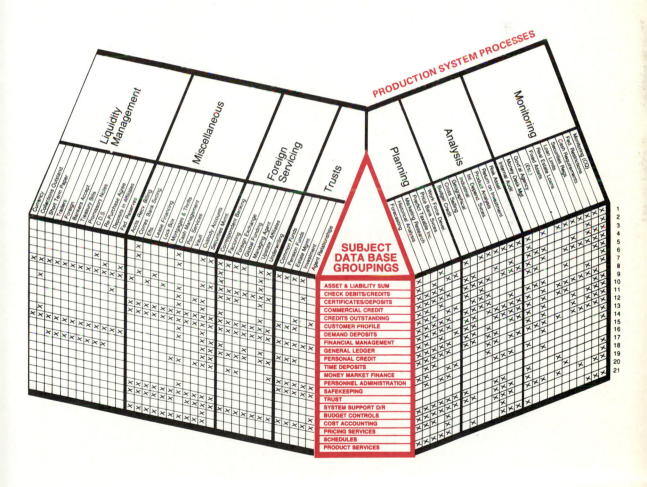

Figure 36.3 (Continued)

addresses, and customer profiles. They found that that data base was usable by applications in many areas of the organization, so they set out to plan what other subject data bases could be used organizationwide.

INTERVIEWER:

To create this chart must have needed a very thorough knowledge of how the entire bank worked. Did you have a team that understands every operation in the bank?

BANK DATA-BASE EXECUTIVE:

One person generated the chart. She does have a great deal of banking knowledge. She used the banker's handbook and talked to many people. The chart had to be verified. *All* the banking processes were included in the chart. So this person identified the business processes in which the bank was involved and how those processes do deal with essentially the same kinds of data, and then looked from the operational level to the next dimension, which was the one of decision support.

At the time of writing the data bases shaded solid red in Fig. 36.4 had been implemented. The ones shaded striped red were under consideration for implementation. Some of the others were expected to be implemented, whereas others, such as *cost accounting,* are likely to remain a collection of separate physical files.

Wherever possible it is desirable to slice up a large data-base plan into disjoint pieces because smaller, separate pieces are easier to implement.

In Fig. 36.4 the *trust* data base is separate from the others. Its use is close to being a separate business within the bank. In fact, legislative controls prevent the main part of the bank from seeing what the trust area is doing, and vice versa.

In many corporations, subject data bases have eventually been used in application areas beyond those for which they were originally intended.

The U.S. banking industry, for example, perceived the need for a cash management service during the 1970s. The need for this service arises because large corporate customers have many accounts—current accounts, interest accounts, time deposit accounts, and investment accounts. The customer has different addresses, and accounts in different branches of the bank. It is a valuable service to give the customer reports summarizing these accounts, saying how much cash is available in total and will be available in the future. The bank also needs this information about its customers. This is the cash management application.

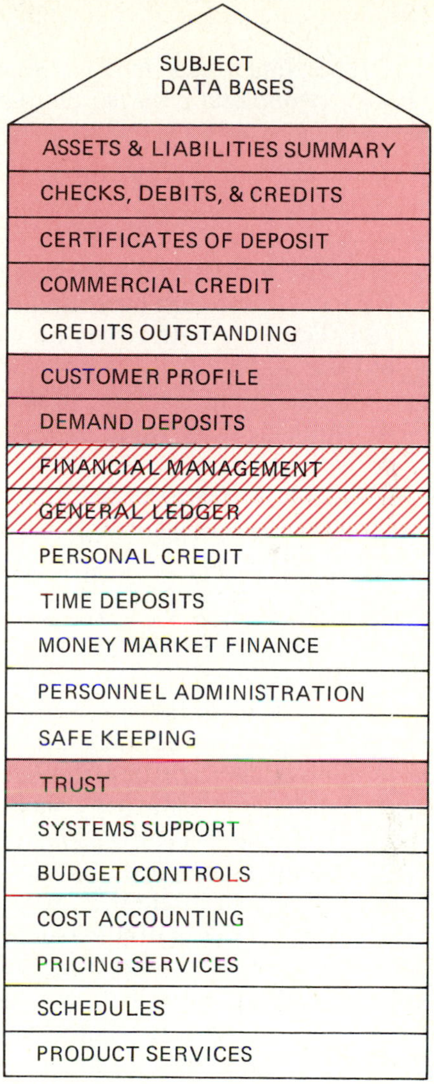

```
                SUBJECT
                DATA BASES

        ASSETS & LIABILITIES SUMMARY
        CHECKS, DEBITS, & CREDITS
        CERTIFICATES OF DEPOSIT
        COMMERCIAL CREDIT
        CREDITS OUTSTANDING
        CUSTOMER PROFILE
        DEMAND DEPOSITS
        FINANCIAL MANAGEMENT
        GENERAL LEDGER
        PERSONAL CREDIT
        TIME DEPOSITS
        MONEY MARKET FINANCE
        PERSONNEL ADMINISTRATION
        SAFE KEEPING
        TRUST
        SYSTEMS SUPPORT
        BUDGET CONTROLS
        COST ACCOUNTING
        PRICING SERVICES
        SCHEDULES
        PRODUCT SERVICES
```

Figure 36.4 Figure 36.2, showing which data bases are implemented (solid red) and which are under consideration (striped red).

BANK DATA-BASE EXECUTIVE:

Cash management is a means to pull together on-line a very complete picture of a customer's position. We use this to make certain credit decisions about the customer, and recognize when funds should be cleared under certain circumstances. At the same time it is a critical part of our customer service. We can transmit information to the customer which enables him to manage his cash portfolio. For some corporations this has become a very critical issue.

The data bases in Fig. 36.4 that are used for cash management are *checks, debits and credits, commercial credit, customer profile,* and *demand deposits.*

BANK DATA-BASE EXECUTIVE:

The *cash management process* has been one that has steadily unfolded. We have found that more and more parts of the bank are interested in it and they have new twists on what they want from an application point of view.

   The initial implementation was a matter of months. We were able to implement *demand deposit* shortly after and *commercial credit* within six months. As the cash management capability unfolded we were able to demonstrate the relationships to global credit and demand accounts. These were implemented in a much shorter time frame than could have been done in a conventional file way.

In some banks the data needed for cash management existed in several *previously implemented* data bases. In other banks cash management was an impetus toward data-base technology, and the data bases created for cash management were found also to serve the branch bank network. In one bank an on-line system for branch checking accounts was implemented using the cash management data base. Similarly, a *customer profile* data base designed to serve the internal operations division became of unanticipated value later in providing information to both the commercial and retail sides of the organization, and in identifying account relationships for cash management.

   When such unanticipated evolution occurs, there are often data-base conversion problems and other growing pains. The intent of a chart like that in Fig. 36.3 is to anticipate in what areas subject data bases will or should be used, and then the automated data modeling process can take the needs of these areas into consideration.

   It is generally essential that senior management be involved in the creation and verification of a plan such as that in Fig. 36.3. As it becomes implemented it will have a major effect on how the organization is managed.

DATA-BASE EXECUTIVE:

In the creation of a plan like this it is vital that the businessmen are involved.

INTERVIEWER:

What sort of businessmen?

DATA-BASE EXECUTIVE:

Without a doubt the people who are involved in the line operational processes. In addition, there is an important need for the people involved in corporate planning, and in the process of managing the assets and liabilities of the company. In the long run the greatest use of information services will be the one that deals with planning, analysis, product identification, market identification, and true decision support.

In many cases the business evolves and moves into new areas. It is important that the senior management who can anticipate this be involved in planning the evolution of the top-down information resource plan.

INTERVIEWER REFERRING TO THE CHART IN FIG. 36.3:

Do you expect the number of subject data bases or the types of subject data bases to change very much? Or do you think you have really identified those subject data bases you need for running a big bank?

DATA-BASE EXECUTIVE INVOLVED WITH THE CHART IN FIG. 36.3:

I think there may be more. Simply because we are getting to be more than a bank.

INTERVIEWER:

You mean your business is changing?

DATA-BASE EXECUTIVE:

Yes. As this bank holding company concerns itself with what it is to be, there will probably be more subject data groupings. Some may be distributed.

INTERVIEWER:

That really means that you want a top-level committee reviewing this chart, upgrading it, and making decisions about distribution.

DATA-BASE EXECUTIVE:

That's important. Yes. And it's vital that the businessmen participate in that process.

RESISTANCE TO THE PLAN

There is almost bound to be resistance to a plan such as Fig. 36.3 unless it is seen to have senior management backing. If this backing does not exist from the start, a plan like Fig. 36.3 is doomed to cause political fighting, and probably not enough of the plan will be implemented to make the breakthrough from conventional systems analysis to information engineering.

INTERVIEWER:

Looking back at the three years' experience in using this plan, what advice would you have for people starting to create a top-down plan for data bases?

DATA-BASE EXECUTIVE:

To get this implemented you do need a corporate top management commitment.

In the past, when we started, we were faced with a great deal of resistance both inside the DP department and outside it.

Inside the DP department we had resistance because previously, especially with tape-oriented systems, they had total control of whatever application they developed.

Outside, in the user departments, they felt that they wanted to have exclusive rights over their own data. Data base, they thought, would take away those exclusive rights.

INTERVIEWER:

So you're saying, take the broad plan to top management and get their commitment?

DATA-BASE EXECUTIVE:

More than that. Get their commitment before the plan is created. Get them involved in the creation of the plan itself. Make sure they understand it, believe in it, and say so loud and clear so that the low-level political types don't oppose it.

---

37 CORPORATE ENTITY ANALYSIS

INTRODUCTION   This chapter advocates a more finely grained top-down view in which the corporate *entities* are analyzed and charted. Working at the entity level it becomes possible to perceive harmful redundancy.

Again, working at the entity level it is possible to specify what comprises a subject data base and to put boundaries on the systems that use them.

STRATEGIC PLANNING CONSULTANT:

The BSP study gave us a list of 25 systems. However, the systems were not defined or developed to a level where they had clear boundaries. There were no defined boundaries or deliverables.

The first of these systems that they worked on was the financial system. The study gave that system number 1 priority. Work on that has been going on for three years but they can't seem to stop the system growing. It has no clear boundaries. They keep adding new areas of data.

Top-down planning can be approached at two levels: the level of subject data bases as described in the preceding chapter, and the level of entities as described in this and the following chapter.

Entities need to be gathered into clusters for practical data-base implementation. The clustering process results in what are, in effect, subject data bases. These subject data bases can then be used in the higher-level system map. Figure 37.1 illustrates this.

First-level approach

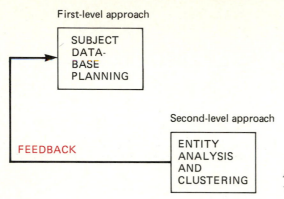

Figure 37.1 Two levels of approach to top-down planning.

CORPORATE ENTITIES

Entity analysis is a top-down attempt to identify the corporate entities.

A medium-sized corporation typically has several hundred entities. A large corporation does not have many times the number of entities of a small corporation if it is in the same business. Some large corporations are in multiple businesses, for example, both steel making and oil exploration, and these would have more entities than a single-business corporation.

The attributes that we store about an entity are kept in a record. A large corporation often has many *thousands* of types of records. However, if a good top-down analysis were done, it would be found to have only *hundreds* of types of entities. This is a situation in which much redundancy has grown because of absence of top-down planning.

The redundancy results in more application programming than is necessary, complex maintenance, difficulty in obtaining summary information for management, and lack of corporate control. Top managers often perceive the lack of control more keenly than DP management, but do not know what to do about it.

IDENTIFICATION OF ENTITIES

The identification of entities in an organization is often by user analysts who understand the business. They must be trained to recognize an entity. To do this better, it is recommended that they be trained to do first-level normalization. Usually, it is not necessary for them to put data into second, third, or fourth normal form. This can be done later in the detailed design stage.

Sometimes, top-down planners have asked users to identify something less precise than an entity. They say, for example: "Identify the information groups you work with." The foregoing definition of an entity is precise and easy to understand. It is necessary that the user analysts identify entities and associations between entities. Vaguely worded "information groups" is not adequate.

Different user analysts often identify the same entity and give it different names (e.g., "CLIENT" and "CUSTOMER"). The coordinating analyst, a DP professional with data-base training, must identify these synonyms with the help of his planning team. One name must be given to each entity. This is sometimes a problem, as different user areas want to retain their own name ("CLIENT" and "CUSTOMER"). It is often necessary to use a synonym dictionary to equate the users' names to the name selected for the entity model.

TOP MANAGEMENT INVOLVEMENT

In the experience of entity analysis which we can now examine in many corporations, it becomes clear that, as with other forms of top-down planning, the participation of senior non-DP management is needed. The quality of the results relates strongly to the quality of senior management participation.

A major reason for senior management involvement in entity analysis is to build the capability for control into the selection of entities that are used for corporate information systems.

Most corporations have never thoroughly mapped the data they use. When they do so for the first time, they discover all manner of anomalies that ought to be corrected. As we discuss in the following chapter, a by-product of entity analysis has often been corporate restructuring, which is very much the concern of senior management.

DISTINCTION BETWEEN ENTITY ANALYSIS AND DATA MODELING

It is generally impractical to build a complete data model of an entire corporation (except a small corporation). Entity analysis does something much simpler.

Data modeling is concerned with functional dependencies, as described in Chapters 10 to 12. Functional dependencies are analyzed to obtain optimal third-normal-form data structures.

Entity analysis identifies the corporate entities and attempts to avoid redundancies in the entities themselves. For example, it would recognize that a *client* and a *customer* are the same entity.

There are associations between entities. For example, one *branch office* has many *salespersons;* one *salesperson* has many *customers.* These associations are drawn with the same single-headed and double-headed arrows as in the data models of Chapter 11. Thus diagrams like Fig 37.2 are drawn.

We will refer to diagrams like Fig. 37.2 as an *entity chart.* The word

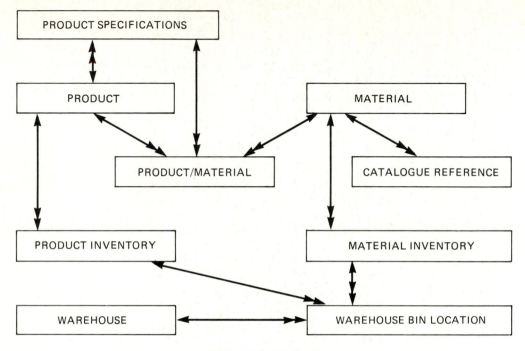

Figure 37.2   Entity chart.

"chart" is selected to distinguish it from a data "model." The data *model* has much more precision.

The detailed data model results from a thorough synthesis of end-user views, combined with stability analysis performed on the results (Box 16.1 and Chapter 17). The entity chart is merely a summary of the corporate entities. If often misses out the more complex concatenated keys.

Full data modeling takes much more time than corporate entity identification. It is too time consuming a process to hold the interest of senior management. The interest of senior management is vital, however, in doing entity analysis which reflects the true information needs of the corporation.

A common quick-and-dirty approach to data-base design has been to identify the entities about which data should be stored and write down the attributes that will be linked to them. In some cases each attribute list has been put into third normal form. This approach works in the simple environment of an academic classroom. It does not give good results with the real-life complexity of a corporation or government organization. There is no adequate shortcut for thorough data modeling.

In some cases we have had the opportunity to compare data structures designed with the facile approach of entity charting and results in the same situation designed with canonical synthesis. The results have been quite different.

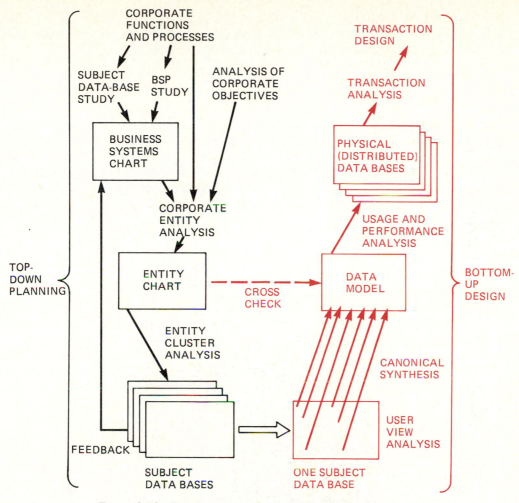

Figure 37.3 Top-down planning and bottom-up design.

Good data-base design needs *both* entity analysis, as described in this chapter, *and* data modeling, as described in Chapters 10 to 17. Corporate entity analysis is part of top-down planning; data modeling is part of bottom-up design, illustrated in Fig. 37.3.

The two approaches act as a cross-check on one another.

SPAN OF CONTROL   At the start of an entity analysis study it is necessary to determine how much of the organization is to be studied. With a small corporation it should definitely be the whole corporation. In a vast corporation it is necessary to tackle it a portion at a time.

A reason for keeping the entity analysis simple is to permit as large an area as possible to be tackled. This should be done so that commonality of entities can be detected over as broad a span as possible.

ENTITY ANALYST:

It was important to chart the entire vertical integration. This company quarries its own clay, makes its own bricks, fabricates its own window frames, grows its own forests, cuts its own timber, seasons its own joists, designs its own buildings according to customer needs, and builds them. The whole thing was about 500 entities. It took about five months to complete the analysis.

REDUNDANT PROCESSING   We have stressed that a large amount of redundant data exists in a file environment, or in a Class II data-base environment where multiple separate analysts create their own data. Somewhat less obvious is that *a large amount of redundant application code also exists* in most corporations. The redundant application code or redundant processing is not necessarily avoided when data-base techniques are used. Separate noncommunicating analysts often specify redundant uses of the same data base.

In one small textile company it was discovered that nine separate transactions existed for goods receiving. Each transaction was, in effect, doing the same set of operations, which resulted in a materials receipt record. A number of different points in the company were receiving goods. At separate times paperwork had been designed for each of these points. Application programs had been created for processing this paperwork. There were thus nine different sets of application programs where one would have sufficed. Each of these incurred maintenance costs.

The nine separate transactions appeared to be slightly different, but when the data on the documents were studied it became clear that they were essentially the same. There was no need for nine different sets of entities. This was revealed by the corporate entity analysis.

When companies grow and evolve, this duplication of functions frequently occurs. It wastes substantial DP resources. One of the objectives of corporate entity analysis should be to eliminate as much unnecessary redundancy of processing as possible.

We have stressed that in most corporations the data have become a mess which is horrifying when analyzed in a coordinated fashion. However, the logic also is a mess, with many unnecessary redundancies. Separate systems analysts (often using structured analysis) have each created their own processes without realizing that they were duplicating each other's work.

CONSULTANT PERFORMING ENTITY ANALYSIS:

Each department has solved its own particular problem. They don't usually look out to other departments and say: "Hey. Have you got the same problem?" The end result was that you found, for example, a goods receiving function into the knitting department, a goods receiving function into packaging, goods receiving into the raw materials store, and so on. They were all basically receiving raw materials.

Now, when we looked at it in terms of entity analysis, we found that *raw materials* was an entity in its own right which is common across all of those. We need *one* set of application programs, not *nine*.

DATA ADMINISTRATOR:

The plastics extrusion is a continuous process. We have a set of entities to cover that. The knitting area looks on the face of it completely different, but really it is also a continuous process and we found that the same entities could be used for it. The making of garments, on the other hand, is a bill-of-materials-type approach, so that is completely different. We have fitted the whole of production into these two broad streams. The accounting system is common to both.

Altogether we needed 110 entities for the whole factory. There were about 1000 data elements all told.

MANAGEMENT INVOLVEMENT   When non-DP managers are involved in entity analysis, it forces them to think about what entities are needed for running the corporation. What entities are needed to give them the information they would like?

DATA ADMINISTRATOR:

Doing the data definition made the management in the warehouse area think about whether they really needed bin control. Did they need a product or stock record, which simply said there are this number of units in stock, or were they really interested in the location of the stock in that warehouse?

It forced user management to make value judgments about the data they needed, and the significance of the level of detail to them in running the business. They had to really think out the benefits of having that level of detail, and whether it was really important to them to have fine control on the data.

For example, a garment is made up of a series of components, and each component is of a particular material. They had to think very carefully about the bill of materials for the garment. Did they need to identify every component in that bill of materials, or could they take a coarser approach and say that this garment has a certain *total* amount of material of each type.

It is usually difficult for DP professionals to formulate such questions. Only non-DP management know how the corporation really functions and how they might be able to improve its functioning.

Where senior management are prepared to become involved, at least for brief periods of their time, it has often been found that good communication develops between them and the DP staff. Entity analysis is common ground between them. No technical words need be used. Once non-DP managers have been taught what entities are, they can set out to identify the entities in their areas. Teaching them first-level normalization helps them to comprehend what entities are.

The non-DP people sometimes recognize when traditional thinking about physical data organization is constraining the creative processes of the DP people. The non-DP people do not have the inhibitions of traditional DP thinking.

The non-DP people, on the other hand, tend to be constrained in their thinking by existing systems. It is very necessary to put them into a creative mode. They must recognize the fundamental commonality of entities—recognize how one piece of paperwork is essentially the same as another.

ENTITY ANALYST:

The entire entity charting was easier than it seemed. It usually is, provided that you have good enough quality senior non-DP management, devoted to the task. There were only three of them, but they knew the organization inside out. Two of them were accountants (which is a higher breed of life!). A lot of chaff fell away quickly that a non-professional manager might have found himself wading through.

It is desirable to allow the business intuition of the non-DP managers to take over as fully as possible. Entity analysis gives them an opportunity to take a fresh look at how their organization works and reflect on how it might work better. The business intuition of non-DP management often results in better entity analysis than DP people alone could create.

DP ENTITY ANALYST:

The user management knew intuitively that an employee could also be a supplier, or could be an equity shareholder. I revolted against that in the design. I didn't think it ought to happen. Rubbish. It's the way the place works.

   What gets results is the intuitive knowledge of end-user management working in combination with the discipline of the technique.

THE USER ANALYST   The non-DP participant becomes, in effect, at least for a time, a new type of analyst. Some corporations have called him a *user analyst.*

   The user analyst needs no knowledge about the technology of computing. He is trained to identify and chart the data entities in his organization. He is sometimes trained to normalize data. He is selected because he has a broad knowledge of how the organization works. Often, he has a broad business background or accounting experience.

   He must be concerned with how the organization can be made to work better. How can the paperwork and its related application programs be simplified? What is common across different departments or different factories? What information is needed for controlling the organization? How can it be better controlled? What are the problems with the current organization? In some of the best entity analysis studies the whole design has been *user driven, not DP driven,* with DP acting strongly as catalysts. The users contribute a logical understanding of the business activity.

   The users can be taught in a training course of a few days. The course should omit technical jargon. It should emphasize *why* entity analysis is needed and what its advantages will be to the organization. If normalization is taught, this teaching should emphasize *why* it is needed. In some cases lack of emphasis on *why* has left users confused and unenthusiastic. It usually pays to have users return to further classes after they have had their first week or two of experience in using the technique.

COW CHARTS   Entity charts such as Fig. 37.2 can be drawn by hand when there are 20 or 30 entities. They usually become much larger than that and it is necessary to automate the chart plotting.

Some designers create hand-drawn charts which are too big to redraw quickly, and attempts to modify them create a rapidly worsening mess. The much modified chart is at last redrawn by hand and becomes regarded as a work of art—a triumphant achievement, but don't dare to modify it again!

The author has been horrified by some of the charts that data administrators keep. There is no question that these charts inhibit progress and improvement of the data structure. The data administrators will not dare to let end users propose changes to them. I suggest that we call them COW charts (Can-of-Worms charts).

Most COW-chart creators are impressed by their rococo masterpieces and pin them up on the wall.

STRUCTURED ENTITY CHARTS
Figure 37.4 shows an entity chart with 16 items. Its sphaghetti-like structure makes it difficult to work with. Real charts often have several hundred items. They rapidly become too big to draw and maintain by hand. An entity chart needs to be drawn in a clearer, more structured fashion. It

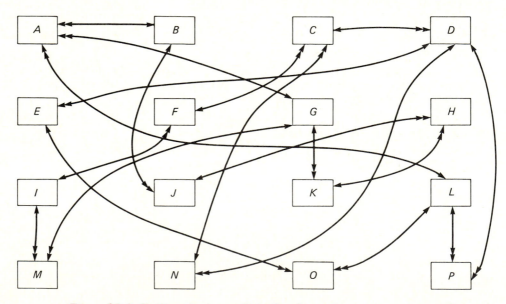

Figure 37.4 Entity charts need to be drawn in a more structured fashion than this so that they can be redrawn by computer when modifications are made. This chart has only 16 entities. Real ones often have several hundred, and modifications to them must be made frequently.

should be drawable and maintainable by computer. A procedure for this is as follows:

First, any redundant associations can be removed (at least removed for the purposes of redrawing the chart; they could be replaced in the redrawn chart).

Certain entities in the chart are *root entities. A root entity is an entity on the chart with no single-headed arrows leaving it.* It is common practice to draw a root record, segment, or entity at the top of a data-base diagram. We will refer to the root entity as a *depth 1 entity.*

A *depth 2 entity* can then be defined as an entity that has a single-headed arrow pointing to a depth 1 entity.

A *depth 3 entity* can be defined as an entity that has a single-headed arrow pointing to a depth 2 entity but no single-headed arrow pointing to a depth 1 entity.

A *depth N entity* $(N > 1)$ can be defined as an entity with a single-headed arrow pointing to a depth $(N - 1)$ entity but no single-headed arrow pointing to a lower-depth entity.

Figure 37.5 shows the depth numbers of the entities on the chart in Fig. 37.4.

The depth 1 entities are then plotted on the left-hand side of the chart. The depth 2 entities are offset by one offset distance. The depth N entities

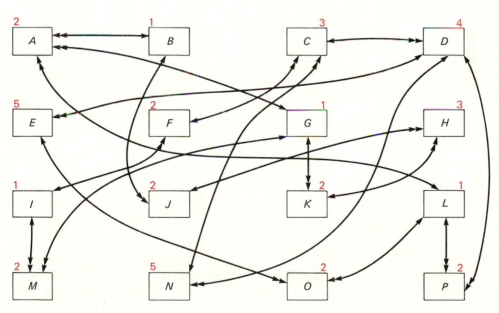

Figure 37.5 The red figures indicate the depth of each node in Fig. 37.4.

are offset by $(N-1)$ offset distances. The depth N entity $(N > 1)$ is plotted underneath the depth $(N-1)$ entity to which it points. The entities under one depth 1 entity form a cluster. Arrows that span these clusters are drawn on the left of the chart, away from the clusters, as shown in Fig. 37.6, which redraws Fig. 37.4.

The redrawing of a chart such as Fig. 37.4 begins with the identification of the depth 1 entities (no single-headed arrows leaving them). Then the depth 2 entities can be marked; then the depth 3 entities, and so on until all the entities have been given a depth number. The clusters under each root entity are drawn, and then the links spanning these clusters are added.

Sometimes a nonroot entity has a choice of parent. Entity A in Fig. 37.5, for example, is a depth 2 entity. It could be connected underneath any of three depth 1 entities: B, G, or L. Similarly, H is a depth 3 entity which could be connected underneath either of two depth 2 entities: J or K. Which is the best choice? The best choice is the strongest association, or the link most frequently used. Let us suppose that A↔B is a stronger association than A↔G or A↔L. Then A is drawn underneath B. Similarly, if J↔H is stronger or more frequently used than K↔H, then H is drawn underneath J, as in Fig. 37.6.

Similarly with a cycle:

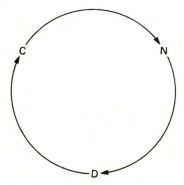

The weakest link must be temporarily broken for plotting purposes. The plotting of Fig. 37.6 assumes that C ⟶ N is the weakest link.

If the link strengths are not known, or are of equal value, an arbitrary choice is made in order to create a chart that can be redrawn automatically.

CLUSTERING INTO ENTITY SUPERGROUPS

Like the entity chart, the data-base system it represents needs to be broken up into fragments which are practical to implement. These are the subject data bases or data classes we have referred to previously. We will use the term *entity supergroup*.

We will call the hierarchical clusters of Fig. 37.6 *entity groups*. Fig.

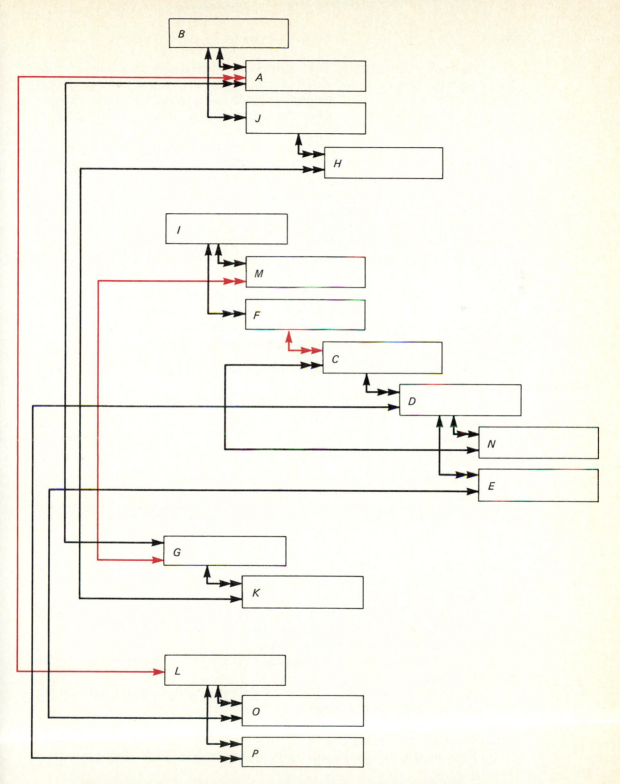

Figure 37.6 Figure 37.4 redrawn in a structured fashion showing four entity groups.

37.6 has four entity groups. The higher-level cluster, the *entity supergroup*, may contain one or more entity groups. The entity supergroup is that collection of entities that is implemented in one subject data base. It becomes the subject of detailed data modeling as described in Chapters 11 to 17.

The entities may be clustered into supergroups on the basis of how frequently the association paths between entities are used. The paths *within* a supergroup should have high usage; the paths *between* separate supergroups should have a low usage.

To this end the paths between entities may be marked as the entity analysis is being performed. They may be marked with five categories, as shown in Box 37.1, ranging from very strong associations or very frequently used links to very weak associations or very infrequently used links.

> **BOX 37.1** **Five categories of strength for the links on entity charts. These categories are used to instruct a computer about clustering the entities into supergroups.**

> 5. *Very strong* association; *must* be in the same supergroup.
>
> 4. *Fairly strong* association or frequently used.
>
> 3. *Average,* or no strong opinion.
>
> 2. *Fairly weak* association or infrequently used.
>
> 1. *Very weak* association; *must* be in separate supergroups.

Category 1 links are employed to indicate that the entities they span should *definitely* be in different supergroups. Category 5 links are employed to indicate that the entities they span should *definitely* be in the same supergroup.

This simple categorization can serve as a basis for dividing an unwieldy chart into manageable charts, or clustering the entities into supergroups. A computer algorithm can do this clustering.

Figure 37.7 shows Fig 37.4 again, but now the links are marked with the categories.

Figure 37.8 shows Fig. 37.6 divided into entity supergroups on the basis of the association categories.

The links colored red are those in categories 1, indicating that they should not be in the same subject data base. One of these, the one from C to F, is in the middle of an entity group in Fig. 37.6. This causes that

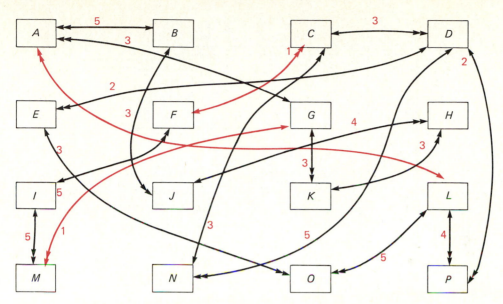

Figure 37.7 Figure 37.4, showing the links marked with their association category. The red links from A to L, M to G, and C to F are in categories 1 and 2, indicating that they should span different entity supergroups.

group to be split into two separate groups. The groups are clustered into three supergroups in Fig. 37.8.

The link categories listed above can be used for deciding to which entity group an entity belongs, where there is a choice. For example, entity A in Fig. 37.8 is drawn underneath B rather than underneath G or L. Similarly, the weak link in the cycle between C, D, and N is C ◄─►N.

Items of the same depth within a group are printed higher (i.e., closer to their parent) if their link to that parent is stronger. Thus A is above J in Fig. 37.8.

It could be worthwhile to have a more detailed weighting scheme showing with more precision the volume of use of the links. That is needed when detailed data-base design is done, but at this top-down stage the categorization described above is enough for breaking the entity chart into supergroups.

Breaking an entity chart into subject data bases should probably not be done entirely on the basis of an algorithm. Any one subject data base needs to be of a size and subject matter such that it is practical for a data administrator to carry out its detailed design within an appropriate time. This detailed design needs to take into consideration that some of the data reside in existing *files* or Class II data bases that will not be readily converted. The association categories can be used to express intuitive desires about the grouping of the entities into implementable data bases.

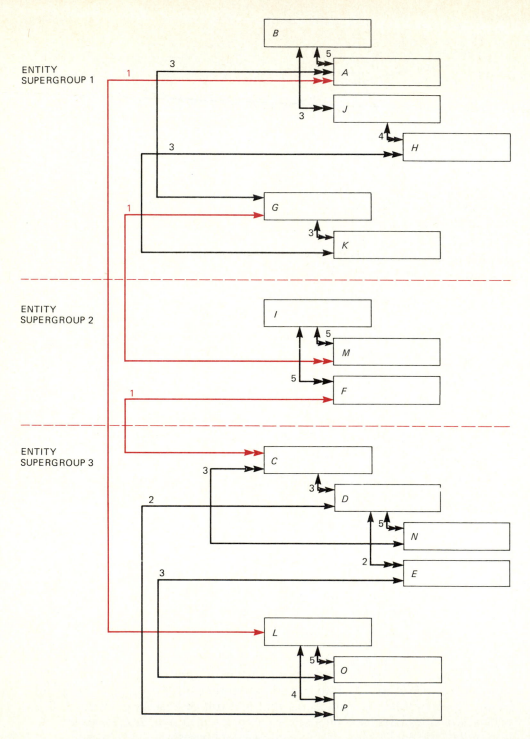

Figure 37.8 Figure 37.6 divided into entity supergroups on the basis of the association categories shown in Fig. 37.7. The categories are marked on this chart.

Using category 1 links forces a computer algorithm to split certain entities into different supergroups. Category 5 forces the clustering of certain entities into the same supergroup. Occasionally, these actions will cause the splitting of a group.

EXAMPLE

Figure 37.9 shows an entity chart from a manufacturing corporation that is fairly small on the scale of corporate data processing. It contains 95 entities. A large complex manufacturing firm might have 10 times as many.

The structured diagram helps to see visually which entities are related. To simplify the drawing, hierarchical links within an entity group have not been drawn.

Figure 37.9 is small enough to do the division into entity supergroups by hand. It helps to have a machine redraw the chart, as this is likely to be done many times.

Figure 37.10 shows a division of Fig. 37.9 into entity supergroups. These supergroups can then form the basis of a systems planning matrix such as that in Fig. 36.3.

FUNCTION, PROCESS, AND ACTIVITY

As the entities are being collected and defined, each should be associated with the function, process, and activity in which it is used, and the department in which it is used. In order to manipulate this information by computer, each function, process, activity, department and entity is given a unique identifier. The information relating to each entity is stored and redundancy between entities used in different departments and processes is eliminated as far as possible.

The result is a small data base of entities. Using a computer, questions can be asked such as: What departments use entity X? What processes use entity X? What entities are used by process Y?

Matrices can be printed mapping the entities against the processes, activities, and departments that use them. As the entities are clustered into supergroups, charts like that in Fig. 36.3 can be created automatically. Computer listings far more comprehensive than the figures in Chapter 36 can be created showing what entities are used where.

When this is done, in most corporations it is a surprise to senior management to see which data the various departments or divisions use. Often it reveals to them facts about the corporation which they had not known. Often, as we discuss in Chapter 39, it makes clear a need for organizational changes or corporate restructuring.

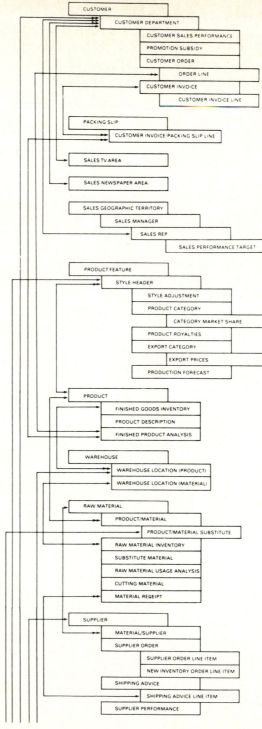

Figure 37.9 Entity chart from a manufacturing business with $40 million per year gross revenues.

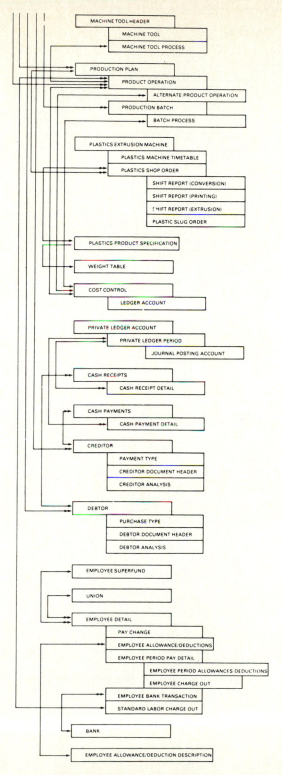

Figure 37.9   (Continued)

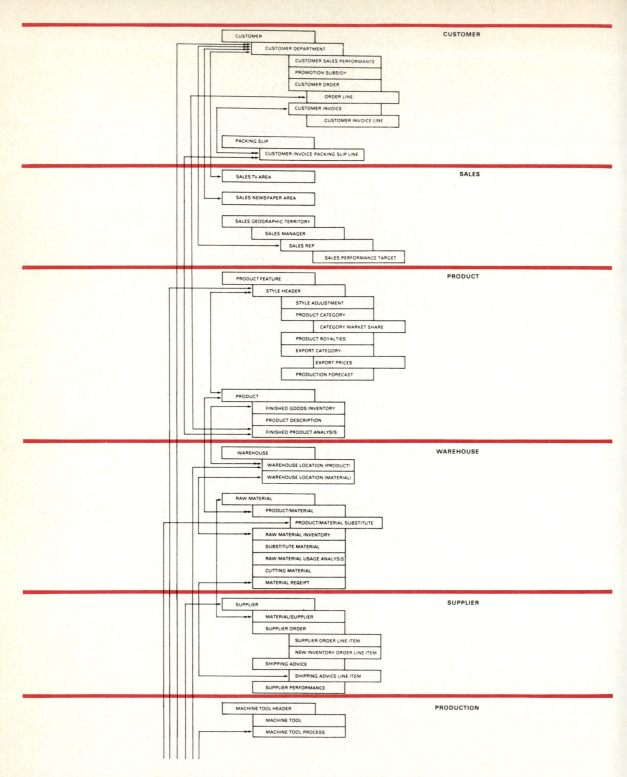

CUSTOMER

CUSTOMER
CUSTOMER DEPARTMENT
CUSTOMER SALES PERFORMANCE
PROMOTION SUBSIDY
CUSTOMER ORDER
ORDER LINE
CUSTOMER INVOICE
CUSTOMER INVOICE LINE
PACKING SLIP
CUSTOMER INVOICE PACKING SLIP LINE

SALES

SALES TV AREA
SALES NEWSPAPER AREA
SALES GEOGRAPHIC TERRITORY
SALES MANAGER
SALES REP
SALES PERFORMANCE TARGET

PRODUCT

PRODUCT FEATURE
STYLE HEADER
STYLE ADJUSTMENT
PRODUCT CATEGORY
CATEGORY MARKET SHARE
PRODUCT ROYALTIES
EXPORT CATEGORY
EXPORT PRICES
PRODUCTION FORECAST
PRODUCT
FINISHED GOODS INVENTORY
PRODUCT DESCRIPTION
FINISHED PRODUCT ANALYSIS

WAREHOUSE

WAREHOUSE
WAREHOUSE LOCATION (PRODUCT)
WAREHOUSE LOCATION (MATERIAL)
RAW MATERIAL
PRODUCT/MATERIAL
PRODUCT/MATERIAL SUBSTITUTE
RAW MATERIAL INVENTORY
SUBSTITUTE MATERIAL
RAW MATERIAL USAGE ANALYSIS
CUTTING MATERIAL
MATERIAL RECEIPT

SUPPLIER

SUPPLIER
MATERIAL/SUPPLIER
SUPPLIER ORDER
SUPPLIER ORDER LINE ITEM
NEW INVENTORY ORDER LINE ITEM
SHIPPING ADVICE
SHIPPING ADVICE LINE ITEM
SUPPLIER PERFORMANCE

PRODUCTION

MACHINE TOOL HEADER
MACHINE TOOL
MACHINE TOOL PROCESS

Figure 37.10 Entity chart of Fig. 37.9 divided into supergroups. These become the subject data bases of Chapter 36.

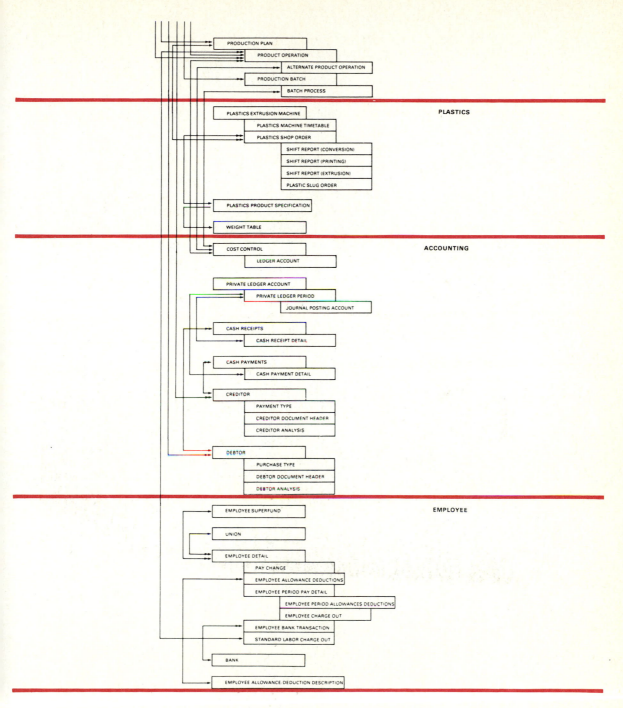

PRODUCTION PLAN
PRODUCT OPERATION
ALTERNATE PRODUCT OPERATION
PRODUCTION BATCH
BATCH PROCESS

PLASTICS

PLASTICS EXTRUSION MACHINE
PLASTICS MACHINE TIMETABLE
PLASTICS SHOP ORDER
SHIFT REPORT (CONVERSION)
SHIFT REPORT (PRINTING)
SHIFT REPORT (EXTRUSION)
PLASTIC SLUG ORDER

PLASTICS PRODUCT SPECIFICATION

WEIGHT TABLE

ACCOUNTING

COST CONTROL
LEDGER ACCOUNT

PRIVATE LEDGER ACCOUNT
PRIVATE LEDGER PERIOD
JOURNAL POSTING ACCOUNT

CASH RECEIPTS
CASH RECEIPT DETAIL

CASH PAYMENTS
CASH PAYMENT DETAIL

CREDITOR
PAYMENT TYPE
CREDITOR DOCUMENT HEADER
CREDITOR ANALYSIS

DEBTOR
PURCHASE TYPE
DEBTOR DOCUMENT HEADER
DEBTOR ANALYSIS

EMPLOYEE

EMPLOYEE SUPERFUND

UNION

EMPLOYEE DETAIL
PAY CHANGE
EMPLOYEE ALLOWANCE DEDUCTIONS
EMPLOYEE PERIOD PAY DETAIL
EMPLOYEE PERIOD ALLOWANCES DEDUCTIONS
EMPLOYEE CHARGE OUT
EMPLOYEE BANK TRANSACTION
STANDARD LABOR CHARGE OUT

BANK

EMPLOYEE ALLOWANCE-DEDUCTION DESCRIPTION

Figure 37.10   (Continued)

ENTITY ANALYSIS CONSULTANT:

It was an eye-opener to the DP steering committee to see where certain kinds of data were utilized. Senior management cannot be in touch with every area, and the data usage had simply never been mapped before.

A project manager operates largely autonomously. He is responsible for most of what goes on in a multi-million-dollar program. He defines what he needs to achieve a product. They give him the budget and let him run.

The study shows that many projects were doing the same things as other projects, and nobody realized it. They were reporting to different managers in different areas.

ENTITY ANALYST:

They had a total of eight autonomous divisions, all of whom were competing furiously with one another, all of whom were fighting tooth and nail to be top dog.

The data analysis made it clear that most of them were essentially the same. Sixty percent of the operations of each division were common. But they all had different teams of programmers who never communicated.

It became clear that they needed a thorough restructuring of the organization. Now this has happened. They are cutting the eight divisions to three.

38 ENTITY–ACTIVITY ANALYSIS

The preceding chapter referred to the use in data planning of entities, but not activities. In this chapter we discuss mapping the entities against the activities that employ them. This gives a finer-resolution chart of where the enterprise uses data and leads to a more formal clustering of the entities into subject data bases.

ACTIVITIES AND ENTITIES Figure 35.6 illustrates an enterprise model that incorporates activities.

As we have discussed, a typical enterprise might have 10 to 30 functions, and 100 to 300 processes. In coarser-resolution planning, these functions and processes are mapped against subject data bases, as in Fig. 36.3.

For each process there are certain activities that must be carried out. For example, the process PURCHASING may involve the following activities:

- Create requisitions for purchase.
- Select suppliers.
- Create purchaser orders.
- Follow up delivery.
- Process exceptions.
- Pass information to accounts payable.
- Record supplier performance data.
- Analyze supplier performance.

Typical business processes have between 4 and 15 activities.

Each activity relates to various data entities. A typical activity uses up to seven entities. It is recommended that if it uses more than seven, it should be broken into more than one activity on the business chart. An activity is intended to be performed by an employee in an efficient manner. Psychologists have demonstrated that most persons have great difficulty dealing with more than seven items or concepts at one time because the capacity of their short-term memory is around seven [1]. A human activity should therefore relate to no more than seven entities and preferably fewer than seven.

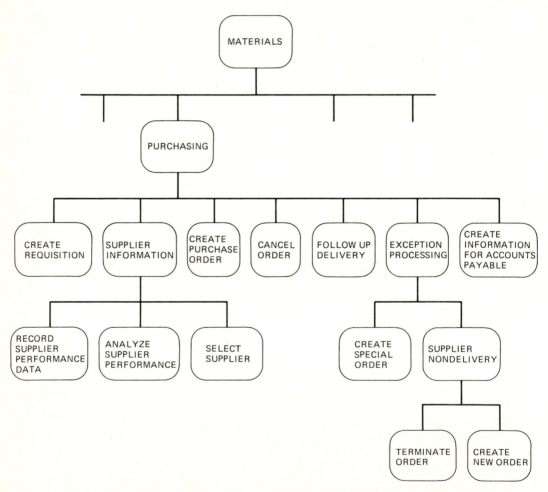

Figure 38.1 Functional decomposition: the breakdown of a function into processes and activities.

ENTITY ACTIVITY DATA BASE

The end users who assist (Fig. 35.1) need to identify the activities and entities that they use. End users are thus more involved than was the case in the preceding chapter, but in my experience this does not seem to take much longer. It may as well be done once the organization of people shown in Fig. 35.1 is set up.

The chart of entities and activities is independent of the current organization of divisions and departments. A business can be reorganized without changing the entity–activity chart. The intent of entity–activity charting is to create a stable representation of the enterprise which remains valid despite reorganizations of staff.

The data about the enterprise can be stored in a small data base. The data can then be examined in a variety of ways—for example, printing an inverted table showing the activities and processes associated with each entity.

The data base may also show the departments that carry out each activity, as well as the geographical locations of each activity. The data base can then answer such questions as: "What departments use entity X?" or "In what locations is a given activity carried out?"

As before, the entities need to be clustered into supergroups or subject data bases. When this is done, charts like Fig. 36.3 can be created automatically. Computer listings far more comprehensive than the figures in Chapter 36 can be created, showing what entities are used where.

WHAT IS AN ACTIVITY?

Where *processes* and *activities* are being analyzed, there is often some concern about what constitutes an activity.

A process is subdivided into activities as in Fig. 35.6. Some processes have a small number of activities; some have a large number. Where there are a large number of activities, it may be desirable to list higher-level activities, which are themselves broken down into lower-level activities. In other words, the tree structure of Fig. 35.6 may be extended by having more than one level of activity for those processes wherever this is helpful.

The stepping point of this breakdown is a *basic activity*. How does the analyst know when he has gone far enough in breaking down the processes into activities?

Usually, one sentence can be used to describe the purpose of a basic activity. If more than one sentence is needed, the activity should probably be reconceived.

When you ask a member of the enterprise what he is doing, often his answer will be a basic activity: for example, "I'm preparing a purchase order" or "I'm paying a vendor." A similar sentence is needed to describe each basic activity.

He usually does not say "materials planning;" this is at too high a level—or "putting a date on a purchase order;" this is too low a level.

The basic activity uses certain *entity* records. These types of entity records should be determined when the activity analysis is done and built into the entity–activity matrix. If it is not clear what entity records an activity will use, the analysis has not gone far enough.

The basic activity in the model tells us *what* is produced, not *how*. Determining *how* it functions requires much more thought and is done later, when the procedure for the activity is designed.

Sometimes there is argument over what constitutes a process and what constitutes an activity. This argument is not worth having; a process is a higher-level grouping of activities which needs subdividing into basic activities.

When the characteristics above are used to identify a basic activity, it is not worth having long discussions about the classification of basic activities or the correct stopping point of the analysis. A sense of what is "natural" is more important than mechanical adherence to rules. If further subdividing an activity promises interesting results, do it; if not, don't.

The analysis should never be regarded as being totally complete and final. There will always be some activities not discovered or new activities added later. The model can be updated later.

When a process or activity is broken down into lower-level activities, it is important to ensure that these activities are sufficient and that each of them is *necessary* to the overall purpose, no matter what reorganization or automation occurs. The modelers should feel confident that their entity–activity model will survive organizational changes. Only if the activities are *necessary* and *sufficient* will this be true. Some activities currently practiced may be found to be redundant or unnecessary. This is often the case, and entity–activity analysis sometimes leads to reorganizations of the procedures or to reorganizations of the department or management structures.

PROPERTIES OF COHERENT ACTIVITIES   After working for some time on activity analysis, Ken Winter listed the following qualities to look for in well-formed activities [2].

1. A coherent activity produces some clearly identifiable result. Its purpose is to produce this result. The result may be a marketable product, a part of a product, an idea, a decision, a sale, a set of alternatives, a paycheck, a prospect, and so on. It should be possible to identify the purpose/result of the activity in a single simple sentence. By contrast, a poorly formed activity yields no identifiable result at all, or it produces a number of unrelated results.

2. A coherent activity has clear boundaries. At a given time, one can say unambiguously who is working on it and who is not. Over time, one can identify the moments when work on the activity starts and stops. Transitions between coherent activities are well marked. Incoherent activities

overlap and blend into one another; one cannot localize when and where they are going on.

3. A coherent activity is carried out as a unit. It is done by a single person or a well-defined group of people who work as a team to produce the result. Management responsibility for the activity is similarly well defined and vested in a single person or group. An ill-defined activity may be carried out by an ill-defined group of people (i.e., it may not be clear who does it). Or it may be done by a well-defined set of people whose jobs have something in common but who do not work as a team: they do not interact, communicate, cooperate to produce the activity's result, perhaps because they are dispersed throughout the enterprise in a way that never brings them into contact with one another.

4. Once initiated, a coherent activity is self-contained—it proceeds largely independently of other activities. If an alleged activity requires intense interaction along the way with another alleged activity, consider recasting them as a single activity. Another way of putting this is that the interactions within the team that carries out a coherent activity will be rich compared to the interactions between teams working on different activities.

The following points are heuristic, not absolute requirements when forming the activity model.

Figure 38.1 shows the breakdown of a function into activities. This tree-structured diagram can be represented as a listing, as shown in Fig. 38.2.

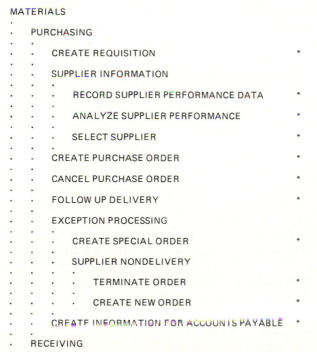

Figure 38.2   A listing containing the same decomposition as Fig. 38.1.

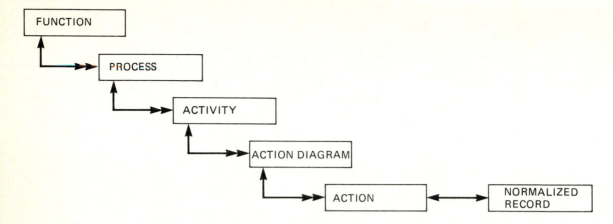

Figure 38.3 Mapping to data-base actions. (Far too detailed for top-down planning, but may be included in an implementation dictionary.)

ACTIVITIES AND ACTION DIAGRAMS
The processing required for an activity may be represented on one or more *action diagrams*.

Dictionary entries may indicate the mapping between activities and action diagrams, as in Fig. 38.3. This is much too detailed for the top-down planning process, but may help to keep track of implemented procedures.

REORGANIZING THE ENTERPRISE
Where management participates in the activity analysis, questions are often raised about what the activities *ought* to be. Some activities currently practiced may be found to be redundant or unnecessary. Certain activities may be scattered in an ill-controlled manner throughout the enterprise. There may be alternative choices of activities in the model which represent policy decisions.

Entity–activity analysis leads to a rethinking of procedures. It often leads to departmental reorganizations or to a management review committee. An appropriate question for the study team to ask is: "In what ways do you want the enterprise to be structured?" An ongoing search is necessary for ways to use data bases and terminals to improve the enterprise procedures and structures.

Often, it is a surprise to senior management to see which data the different departments or divisions use. It often reveals to them facts about the corporation which they had not known. As we discuss in Chapter 39, it also makes clear a need for organizational changes or corporate restructuring.

When the entities are mapped against processes or activities, another technique for clustering them into subject data bases becomes available.

A matrix like that in Fig. 38.4 can be computed showing the affinity that each entity has for each other entity.

Let us suppose that we have two entities, E_1 and E_2. If the two entities are never used for the same activity, their affinity will be zero. If two entities are always used together for every activity, their affinity will be 1. Many entities are used together for some activities only.

A computer can examine every activity and calculate:

1. (E_1) = number of activities using entity E_1.

2. (E_1, E_2) = number of activities using both entities E_1 and E_2.

Using these figures, an affinity factor for the two entities can be calculated. One way of defining the affinity factor is:

$$\text{affinity of } E_1 \text{ to } E_2 = \frac{a(E_1, E_2)}{a(E_1)}$$

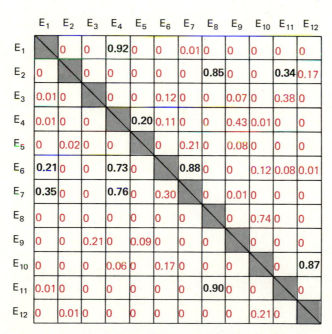

	E_1	E_2	E_3	E_4	E_5	E_6	E_7	E_8	E_9	E_{10}	E_{11}	E_{12}
E_1		0	0	0.92	0	0	0.01	0	0	0	0	0
E_2	0		0	0	0	0	0	0.85	0	0	0.34	0.17
E_3	0.01	0		0	0	0.12	0	0	0.07	0	0.38	0
E_4	0.01	0	0		0.20	0.11	0	0	0.43	0.01	0	0
E_5	0	0.02	0	0		0	0.21	0	0.08	0	0	0
E_6	0.21	0	0	0.73	0		0.88	0	0	0.12	0.08	0.01
E_7	0.35	0	0	0.76	0	0.30		0	0.01	0	0	0
E_8	0	0	0	0	0	0	0		0	0.74	0	0
E_9	0	0	0.21	0	0.09	0	0	0		0	0	0
E_{10}	0	0	0	0.06	0	0.17	0	0	0		0	0.87
E_{11}	0.01	0	0	0	0	0	0	0.90	0	0		0
E_{12}	0	0.01	0	0	0	0	0	0	0	0.21	0	

Figure 38.4 Matrix showing the computed affinity between different entities. This can be employed in the clustering of entities into subject data bases.

The affinity factor can be printed in a matrix such as Fig. 38.4.

If two entities have a high affinity, they should be in the same subject data base. If they have an affinity of zero, they definitely should not. Where is the dividing line?

A computer can group the entities into clusters based on their affinity factors. If it puts entities with affinity factor = 0 in the same cluster, there will be only one cluster. If it puts entities with affinity factor = 1 in the same cluster, there may be as many clusters as entities. It could be instructed to set the affinity factor so as to produce 20 clusters, 30 clusters, or whatever the designer decides. These clusters are then used as subject data bases.

The affinity factor above does not take into account the volumes of use of each activity. A different way of calculating affinity may take usage volumes into consideration. The method above has given good results in practice, when automatically clustering the entities into subject data bases.

CLUSTERING ALGORITHM   Suppose that we want to cluster the entities in Fig. 38.4 into data bases. The entity pairs are sorted by affinity number and we begin with the highest affinity numbers.

Entity pairs with the highest affinity form the nuclei of the clusters.

$$E_1, E_4 \quad \text{(affinity = 0.92)}$$
$$E_{11}, E_8 \quad \text{(affinity = 0.90)}$$
$$E_6, E_7 \quad \text{(affinity = 0.88)}$$
$$E_{10}, E_{12} \quad \text{(affinity = 0.87)}$$

Eventually, we arrive at an entity pair in which one of the entities is already in one of the clusters. The next entity pair we encounter is

$$E_2, E_8 \quad \text{(affinity = 0.85)}$$

E_8 is already assigned to a cluster nucleus E_{11}, E_8. Should we now link E_2 to that cluster? To determine that, we need to calculate the weighted affinity of E_2 to the cluster E_{11}, E_8.

$$\frac{(\text{affinity of } E_2 \text{ to } E_{11}) \times a(E_{11}) + (\text{affinity of } E_2 \text{ to } E_8) \times a(E_8)}{a(E_{11}) + a(E_8)}$$

Suppose that entity E_{11} is used by 3 activities and entity E_8 is used by 48 activities. Then the composite affinity of E_2 to the cluster E_{11}, E_8 is

$$\frac{0.34 \times 3 + 0.85 \times 48}{3 + 48} = 0.82$$

This is higher than any remaining affinity number in Fig. 38.4, so the cluster E_2, E_{11}, E_8 is formed.

From now on as we encounter new entities with an affinity to E_2, E_{11}, or E_8, we will compute their composite affinity to the cluster E_2, E_{11}, E_8. In this way the clusters of high-affinity entities steadily grow.

The next largest affinity number in Fig. 38.4 is the affinity of E_7 to E_4 (affinity = 0.76). However both E_7 and E_4 are already allocated to a cluster. Should these clusters be combined?

To determine that, we compute the composite weighted affinity of E_7 to the existing cluster E_1, E_4 and to a combined cluster E_1, E_4, E_6. Let us suppose that these affinity numbers were 0.55 and 0.37, respectively. These are lower than the next affinity number on the list, the affinity of E_8 to E_{10} (affinity = 0.74). This is therefore dealt with first. Each clustering decision is made in sequence by affinity number.

Some of the entities at the end of the affinity sequence may have little affinity with anything. These may be implemented as file systems or simple isolated data bases. The designer should review any remaining entities with low affinities to see whether they belong in any of the existing data bases.

MANUAL ADJUSTMENT

When any entity clustering algorithm such as this is implemented, it is likely to require some intelligent human adjustment. The algorithm may group some entities that ought to be separate for other reasons, such as reliability, protecting one type of data when another type is involved with a failure, distributed system design (discussed later), and legal considerations.

Sometimes the preservation of existing file or data-base systems may be the reason for a particular grouping. Sometimes the grouping may be adjusted so that one team can do the detailed modeling of a subject data base.

The user may run the algorithm several times, setting different affinity thresholds, or forcing the data to be split in certain ways. An entity chart may be created for each resulting subject data base so that it can be examined further.

The clustering that results from affinity analysis can act as a cross-check on the clustering that results from putting weights on the links between the associations discussed in the preceding chapter. The affinity factor matrix can be used as a reasonableness check on the formation of supergroups, shown in Figs. 37.8 and 37.10.

Again, the affinity factors can themselves be used as weights on the associations, replacing the subjective categories shown in 37.7. They could then be used for a division of the entity chart into supergroups, as in Fig. 37.8.

The overall results should be reviewed with the planning team and area representatives, and adjusted if necessary. The subject data bases that result from entity clustering can then be used for the planning of systems, as described in Chapter 4.

AN UPDATABLE TOP-DOWN PLAN   Top-down planning should not be something that happens once and is then never repeated. Most organizations change. A top-down planning methodology is needed which keeps pace with these changes and which can be updated. The methodologies described in this and the preceding chapter have that property.

As discussed in the next chapter, a corporate entity analysis usually reveals anomalies that need changing in the organization of the enterprise itself.

REFERENCES

1. E. F. Codd, "How About Recently?" (English Dialogue with RENDE-VOUS), in B. Schneiderman, ed., *Databases: Improving Usability and Responsiveness,* Academic Press, Inc., New York, 1978.

2. A project undertaken by Ken Winter of Data Base Design Inc., 2020 Hogback Road, Ann Arbor, MI 48104.

39 CORPORATE REORGANIZATION

INTRODUCTION

In many corporations entity analysis has been carried out by looking at *existing* procedures. A much more valuable approach is to be concerned with what the organization's procedures *should* be rather than what they *are*. Data-base technology provides the opportunity to substantially change the procedures in an organization as well as its information sources.

The first motorcars were called "horseless carriages" and were the same shape as a carriage without a horse. Much later it became recognized that a car should have a different shape. Similarly, the first radio was called "wireless telegraphy" without realization that broadcasting would bear no resemblance to telegraphy. Today we talk about the "paperless office" and "paperless corporation," but we build systems with screens and data bases that duplicate the previously existing organization of work. It will be increasingly realized that data bases and screens make possible different and better forms of work organization.

FUNCTIONAL ANALYSIS

Entity analysis has often resulted in a reexamination of the functions and methods in a corporation. Sometimes this approach is called *functional analysis.*

Functional analysis sets out to examine the mission and objectives in an organization. The overall objectives can be broken down into objectives for each level and each department of the organization. The questions can then be asked: "How can these objectives be measured? What data are needed for their measurement? How should decisions be made at each level so as to best achieve the objectives?"

The involvement of intelligent user management prepared to think

717

creatively in defining the data requirements of the organization often causes a questioning of existing procedures which goes far beyond DP.

ENTITY ANALYSIS CONSULTANT:

Senior functional management said they could not afford the time to participate in the entity analysis, so they gave me their senior clerks. A very senior, senior clerk, who gloried in the title "provider," learned to map data and normalize it.

One day he asked me to talk with him and the planning manager because he had something important to say. He went in and said to the planning manager, "Our OPAS meeting is wrong!"

Now OPAS is the *holy of holies* in this company. In the head office every Monday morning, the priesthood gathers—the senior functional managers who decide *what* should be *where* in the three plants, in *what proportion,* with *what priorities* and *what yield.*

This senior clerk could now see that the output of the cold reduction mill becomes feed to the slitting mill, the output of that went into the next process, and so on, and that OPAS decisions near the head of this line were screwing up export orders about 13 stages down the track.

He grabbed the planning manager and the planning manager wasn't even prepared to listen. But he wove the argument and the net and caught the manager within it. There was a draught of cold air of "Why's?" which blew all the way up to the OPAS meeting. They were questioning head office moves on the one hand and incentives on the other, and how export orders affect the planning.

All this happened because a senior clerk saw that he had a funny thing in his relational map. When he traced it through, it shouldn't have been there.

They are making sure that *that* senior clerk doesn't annoy that particular functional manager any more. They've promoted him for the first time in 20 years. He's not a "provider" any more; he's a senior production planner, which effectively removes him from harm's way.

STRATEGIC PLANNING CONSULTANT:

They have a fixed number of mailing shots per year. There is extreme competition for those mailing shots. A guy in the book division comes up with a promotion plan, and says if you'll let us do this we'll earn so many million dollars for you. A guy in the music division says: "*We* must have that mailing shot; here's what we can do."

So they set up test runs against the files they have. The files contain 50 million customers and they are constantly massaging these files, extracting, say, 10,000 customers for a test mailing for a next year's book on animals or whatever. They do extreme amounts of statistical analysis of the test samples.

Before the corporate data analysis, each individual area managed its own activities. However, the analysis shows that each area needs the same kind of entity. It's clear that the corporation needs to think about reorganizing the whole approach.

CHANGING THE ORGANIZATION

Senior management should regard entity analysis as a means, not merely of translating the *existing* organization into a data structure, but of asking how the organization should be changed or is likely to be changed by external circumstances.

User analysts have to be made to think creatively. It is easy for them to fall into the rut of documenting today's paper flow, rather than the fundamental needs of the business. They must not be constrained by today's documents. They must try to think, "What is the data that is important to us? What is it that we are going to need in the future?"

Thinking about the future is important for making the resulting data bases as resilient as possible. It is more difficult for users to put themselves into this mode. It requires senior management to have some participation in the analysis. Senior managers know what their problems are now and have ideas about the kinds of actions they would like to take to fix them. They need a tool to express that. In some corporations this has made them take an enthusiastic interest in entity analysis.

HEAD OF ENTITY ANALYSIS STUDY:

When we first started this, we thought it was a technique for examining existing procedures. We discovered, a step at a time, that it's much more than that.

First, we found that existing procedures were horrifyingly redundant. Every O&M guy in the business had invented his own bits of paper. You had numerous different forms where one computerized form would suffice. But unfortunately, each department had its own structured analyst who had cast the redundant methods into different COBOL programs. These, collectively, had become a maintenance nightmare.

Second, we found that it was more than just redundant paperwork.

The procedures and the flow of work had anomalies, sometimes weird, expensive anomalies. For the last 20 years, new procedures have kept springing up like mushrooms in the night. In some cases management had a vague sense that the anomalies were there, but they could only comprehend the trees, not the forest.

Third—and it took months before we dared to express this heresy—the management structure itself was wrong. It needed a thorough reorganization of departments and even divisions in order to get tight control and high administrative productivity. This perception could come only through a functional analysis of the entire organization.

Often the results of entity analysis surprise top management and surprise the DP steering committee.

STUDY LEADER:

The advanced systems division is really a research division. Once they bring things to a research level of operation, they are supposed to hand them over to another division for implementation. They have lately been implementing them—creating their own production facilities. Management didn't realize that that was going on. They thought it was another project. Advanced-systems people were setting up production lines, doing engineering drawings, and all the other things you need for production. Suddenly management, looking at the data matrix, said; "Why is advanced systems needing engineering test data? Oh! They're doing that? They shouldn't be doing that. We'd better think about this!"

Top management started reestablishing responsibilities, saying: "No. You can't do that. You'd better start turning that product over to the other division."

TOP MANAGEMENT INVOLVEMENT We have stressed the need for senior management involvement in top-down data planning. If that planning is likely to suggest structural changes, new procedures, or corporate reorganization, the interest of senior management is likely to be much sharper.

In most cases senior management could not care less about being involved in computerizing the existing procedures. However, if there is a threat of organizational changes, or a promise of better information sources, they usually want to know what is going on and be able to influence it. Often, what senior management takes an active interest in is the ability to make decisions about how the business should be run. Entity analysis can be presented in such a light.

ENTITY ANALYSIS CONSULTANT:

The operations manager today was talking about picking up his shop-floor reporting data in a different manner. That's something he's had as a hobby horse for some time. When we involved him in the data structure planning, he could think about what effect that should have on transaction design. Now he's got a vehicle to express the changes he thinks are necessary. He feels satisfaction in doing that.

ENTITY ANALYSIS CONSULTANT:

A number of different companies have been taken over, over the years. DP's had one hell of a job with this. Basically, there are common types of requirements in each of the companies, but each wanted its own systems. Each has its own ordering system, different types of purpose order numbers, different stock numbers. . . . The entity analysis method is a way for user managers to see the types of problems they are inflicting on themselves by not rationalizing the systems.

Entity analysis will be more fruitful *if it is accepted from the beginning that it is likely to change the corporate procedures or organization.* If this is understood, top management is likely to take more interest in the study. The study will be staffed differently and its reporting procedures will be different.

STAFFING THE STUDY
The best way to staff the study is to have a small nucleus of people assigned to it permanently for the duration of the study and a variety of people in user areas assigned on a part-time basis.

The central nucleus gives the direction, coordinates the input, creates the charts, and presents the results. This nucleus needs to be composed of excellent people and should not be too large. Four people of high quality is ideal. Large committees rarely produce excellent designs.

STRATEGIC PLANNING CONSULTANT:

The BSP committees were too large. It took a lot of people to conduct the interviews and take notes on them. These people got together in a room and brainstormed. With more than six people brainstorming, it tends to meander on. There was no strong management saying what the direction should be. A small, tough group of high quality is needed to digest the information and set the direction.

The nucleus group should not be entirely DP. An ideal mix can be two DP people with strong data-base experience and two non-DP people with experience in many areas of the corporation and a broad knowledge of how it works. The DP people give the methodology leadership and understand the software tools they can use. The non-DP people help to select user participants from other areas of the corporation. The team leader is often a data administrator (or data strategist).

Some entity analyses have been done with a much larger nucleus group. In one large steel firm, 11 non-DP staff were permanently assigned to the study. When they asked for 11 people, there was no hope that they would be given executives. No corporation could afford that number of executives to leave their normal assignments. All eleven were clerks.

It is better to have senior management involvement on a brief but carefully planned basis. Their time should be committed with top management directives before the study starts. An effective way to organize this time is in short bursts of two hours or so at intervals throughout the study. The team should do substantial preparation prior to each session with senior management.

As well as having a nucleus group which interviews key executives when needed, there should also be user analysts assigned on a part-time basis. Typically, about one day per week of their time is needed. Each user analyst operates in those areas of the corporation of which he has good knowledge. The number of user analysts needed varies with the size of the corporation. In one large aerospace corporation, 40 user analysts worked on the data analysis for one division. In small corporations, three or four user analysts have been enough.

User analysts have to be good people, not people who have been brushed aside in the organization and are doing nothing important. The study leader should tell senior management that if the user analyst is not somebody whose time they hate to give up, he is the wrong choice. Such people, however, will not be given up for more than about one day a week.

Sometimes the part-time user analysts are very senior and have a strong involvement in the project.

PROJECT LEADER:

Involved in the entity analysis we have the finance director, who is chairman of the project. He is a man close to retirement and wants to continue this activity after retirement. We have the chief accountant as a direct member of the project team, and the operations manager, who is the senior production man. The sales division was represented by a sales administration executive. He was brought in from time to time when his area was being addressed.

The group accountant found our analysis very easy to relate to because it had a systemized approach which he found easy to understand. In our early data-definition stage, he was the person who did all the data recording. We had a form on which the attributes that described each entity were listed. We did not attempt to normalize these at first. But he was enthusiastic and quickly learned normalization.

CENTRAL COORDINATION

The user analysts, each operating in their own area, map out the processes, activities, and entities that they perceive. The central group looks through this list and fits it into its overall charting of the corporation. There will be much redundancy. The central group removes the entity redundancy, reducing the entity list to as small a number of entities as is realistic. It leaves the redundancy in processes and activities. That cannot be reduced unless the corporation or work flow is reorganized.

The names that the user analysts give to the entities will often not conform to the names given by the central group. The data administrator may have the final responsibility of naming the entities. The user analysts should be allowed to keep their choice of names, at least for the time being, for clarity. The dictionary in which the entity list is kept will equate the data administrator's entity names to the names chosen by the user analysts. This is necessary because the *same* entity is often given different names by different user analysts.

The entity chart is built up a step at a time as the results come in from the user analyst. It should be redrawn *automatically* when major updates occur. This redrawing should divide it into entity groups and supergroups, for clarity. The final determination of supergroups is not done until the entire project is completed, the *affinity analysis* is performed, and various subjective, pragmatic considerations are applied to the clustering into subject data bases.

USER ANALYST EDUCATION

Particularly critical to the study is the education of user analysts. Time and time again when asked, "What would you do differently if you had it to do again?", study leaders have responded that better up-front training of user analysts is needed.

Many examples and class problems are needed to make user analysts grasp fully how to identify processes, activities, and entities. The processes in each area are often identified before the work begins and before user analysts are trained.

Some organizations have given user analysts a course on normalization of data. Others have not. Some have explained only basic normalization; some have taught third normal form (but usually not fourth normal form). The teaching of normalization helps user analysts to understand what an entity is. Apart from that, it is not strictly necessary for performing entity analysis.

TEAM LEADER:

We gave all the project members a brief course on basic normalization. Most of them had no difficulty learning it. The chief accountant quickly learned third normal form and enjoyed doing it.

The user analysts didn't *need* to normalize the data. We could quickly do that for them. But the value of it was that they got to understand what normalized data was all about. They occasionally pointed out entities on our systems map which were not fully normalized. It has become a way of life which has rubbed off on the non-DP people.

INTERVIEWER:

How long did it take you to train the users?

DP EXECUTIVE:

It varied very much from one user to another. Once they've got the concept of processes, activities, and entities, they can go away and do this until the cows come home. Some pick up the concept in no time. Others have great difficulty. One guy said after six months on the team: "I still don't really understand what an entity is." Others were experts in a week.

INTERVIEWER:

I'm surprised that anyone could take six months. What kind of user was he?

DP EXECUTIVE:

Shop floor man. Been involved with computers for several years. No college. Salt of the earth. Good knowledge of functional uses of computers. A great help in knowing what is required by the other users and in interacting with DP. But he just can't cope with abstract thought.

> We could have weeded him out early by testing the people we trained. But he was a very helpful member of the team.

It is important to understand that some highly valuable individuals have great difficulty grasping abstract concepts. Good testing following the training course is needed to find out whether they fully understand. In most cases, when individuals do not grasp the concepts, they should not be employed as user analysts.

In some cases the problem is the opposite. The users are highly intelligent and feel they have better ways of analyzing a corporation's data.

STRATEGIC PLANNING CONSULTANT:

The company is such a high-technology company. Designing systems is their big thing—prototypes, test beds, testing, and so forth.

One of the problems we ran into was self-professed experts. There were a lot of them, mostly engineers or ex-engineers. They became instant experts on entities, data base, systems, the way the study ought to be done—you name it. Eventually, we had to crack the whip and say: "Obey the rules of the methodology. Don't let this guy and that guy be presenting his philosophies to the group."

When senior managers are first involved in a study, their input often relates primarily to their current problems and whims. It is necessary to progress from this phase to a more fundamental understanding of the long-term way in which the corporation functions, and will function. By the time complex systems are implemented, there will be different management whims and problems.

DATA ANALYSIS CONSULTANT:

At the start, senior managers' input relates strongly to their current pet projects. You have to evolve from this to more fundamental statements: What are the basic units of organization? What are managers asking for? Why? What's driving them? What should they be asking for, given their objectives? What are the basic logistics of the place? The entities you get from these questions are a recognizable change from the entities you first get. When this change occurs, you recognize that you have gone through a second stage in the analysis.

INTERVIEWER:

How do you recognize that?

DATA ANALYSIS CONSULTANT:

You can recognize the differences between the urgencies of the moment and something a little more permanent, relating to a longer-term perspective.

Attempting to generate a senior management look at the future uses of data in a corporation is likely to result in fundamentally different data bases from merely conducting an examination of the current procedures.

THE BEST OF BOTH WORLDS

DATA ADMINISTRATOR:

We couldn't have done this by synthesizing user views. We simply didn't know how the users would use the data. We had to go to a fundamental analysis of the entities.

In some cases we made assumptions about usages of data based on one area and we'd go to the manager of another area and he'd say: "Hell! That's not how I run my department."

We did perform canonical synthesis, because it's automated. That served as a cross-check on the entity analysis. We believe that you must do all three forms of analysis: entity analysis, user view analysis, and analyzing the transactions. Each acts as a cross-check on the others.

What an organization needs is the best of both worlds: top-down and bottom-up design. The top-down design should be strongly concerned with *productivity*—eliminating redundant application programs and maintenance, and reorganizing the corporate procedures and structures for greater efficiency. The bottom-up design should be concerned with stability, third (and fourth) normal form design, end user languages, low maintenance, flexibility, and fast development of future applications.

The top-down entity charting and bottom-up data modeling act as a check on one another. The same design tool should be used so that data collected, or attributes identified, during the entity analysis phase are stored for the data-modeling phase.

EPILOGUE

REASONS FOR LONG-TERM DATA-BASE SUCCESSES AND FAILURES

In the mid-1970s I participated in a series of postmortems in New York reviewing the reasons for failure in the implementation of data-base systems. It became clear that the reasons were often the same in widely differing systems. Similarly, the success stories had certain factors in common.

Following this perception, I added an epilogue to my *Principles of Data-Base Management,* summarizing the reasons for failure and the reasons for success. Since then, I have surveyed or consulted on many data-base projects and have added to the summary. The following list is intended to give guidelines for long-term success in managing the data-base environment.

It is suggested that all persons involved in data-base projects go point-by-point through this list.

Reasons for long-term data-base successes and failures

Reasons for Success	Reasons for Failure or Disappointment
• Top management understanding and support of a top-level corporate data-base strategy, with a determination to make data a valuable corporate resource.	• Dissenting political factions, who prevent the integration that can maximize the value of data. Many of the best data-base plans have failed to materialize because of needless corporate politics. Such plans require support from high-level management.
• Design of data bases that relate to broadly shared data rather than being narrowly focused on one application. These shared data bases are designed to reflect the inherent properties of those data and hence be as stable as possible. They are shared by many applications. • Design of stable logical structures using the techniques of third-normal-form design (fourth-normal-form where appropriate) and canonical synthesis. • Use of stability analysis in conjunction with third-normal-form design to attempt to identify fields that could cause the need for data restructuring before the data base is implemented.	• Design of data bases to serve one application or a narrow set of applications. The data base is designed as a by-product of the functional analysis. It does not take other applications into consideration. Narrowly focused data bases then proliferate, just as files proliferate in a non-data-base environment. When the applications change, the data must change. Some systems use IMS and other data bases as little more than an access method; it is an expensive access method. A file management system would be better if the sharing characteristics of data base are not used. Many DP managers complain that data base has not lowered their maintenance costs as was originally claimed. This is usually because they did not use *shared* data bases in third normal form, designed with a technique such as canonical synthesis, using stability analysis before implementation.
• Thorough data analysis with end-user participation. A formal procedure for collecting the end-user views of data, and reviewing the logical data model with the end users and systems analysts before implementation. • Repeated iterations of the modeling process with extensive user involvement, before implementation. • Thorough cleaning up of the logical structure of the data, eliminating homonyms and synonyms. • Keeping this data-modeling process sufficiently far ahead of implementation pressures. • Use of a data dictionary and data modeling tool with end-user participation.	• Excessive application pressure. The need to have one application working quickly causes installations to not bother with data analysis, canonical synthesis, change analysis, and the building of stable future-oriented subject data bases. *Result*: before long, the data base has to be restructured and application programs which use it rewritten. To build a data base without the foundation which we describe is like building a house on sand.

728

• Inadequate tools.	• Use of analysis and design tools. —To enforce discipline in data modeling. —To handle documentation. —To enable performance comparisons of alternate physical structures. —To enforce discipline in data usage, naming, etc. —To assist in application structuring.
• Overselling "management information systems" (especially MIS for top management). However, it should be realized that some highly valuable *functional* information systems for management have grown up as a by-product of data-base systems.	• Concentration on well-specified, profitable uses of the data bases. Technical management with a business orientation.
• Ill-defined user requirements. • Terminal dialogue unacceptable to end users. • End users overly concerned about sharing data, ownership of data, and "their" data being available to other users. • End users feeling left out of the planning and installing their own facilities.	• Constant, thorough, and lucid communication with end users. Thorough end-user involvement.
• Vague attempt at data administration by committee. • Lack of support for the data administrator. —Too low in the organization. —Lacking the right skills or experience. —Reporting such that conflicts are inevitable between Developments and Operations, or between project teams. • Confusion between data administration and data-base design.	• Appointment of a technically competent data administrator who is in tight control of the logical modeling and data-base design.
• The following have been causes of major data-base catastrophes (especially with purchased systems): • Inadequate CPU power. • Inadequate main memory. • Excessively long run times. • Failure to estimate throughput. • Failure to estimate response times. • Failure to monitor usage growth. • Failure to select appropriate physical structure. All of these amount to not doing the necessary design calculations.	• Design calculations well understood. Selection of optimum data structures (access methods, CODASYL *set* clustering, DL/1 choice of physical data bases, choice of data distribution, etc.). • Skilled tuning for performance of applications written with fourth-generation languages.

(Continued)

Reasons for Success	Reasons for Failure or Disappointment
• Employment, often by end users, of powerful data-base query languages, report generators, graphics packages, application generators, and fourth-generation languages. • Doing as much application development as possible with these higher-level facilities. Thorough analysis of what user needs can be met without conventional application programming. Selection of appropriate query and development facilities for each type of user. • Encouragement of end-users to "do their own thing" with these languages and the existing data bases.	• Low-productivity application development with conventional programming only.
• Clear distinction between Class IV data management systems and the other classes. • Data in separate data management systems derived from a common data model.	• Attempts to combine fundamentally different categories of data usage (e.g., heavy-duty transaction processing and extensive data searching) in the same DBMS.
• A planned step-by-step buildup of applications of the shared data bases, each step being suitably small and easy. • Many small projects often running in parallel. • Many of the steps may be created with high-level data-base query languages, report generators, etc.	• Grandiose, all-embracing project plans.
• Corporate-wide planning by a high-level, competent, data strategist, with enough authority and top management backing. • Top-level planning of what data base *and files* should exist at what locations.	• Fragmented plans by noncommunicating groups. • The corporate-wide plan being ignored by groups who design their own data regardless.
• Adoption of a corporate-wide data description language. (The software will change, whereas the data descriptions and data model remain the same.)	• Use of multiple, separate, incompatible data-base management systems.
• Adoption of proven state-of-the-art software with both logical and physical data independence, and thorough restart-recovery capability.	• Writing your own data-base management facilities or modifying existing software. (In the long run, this is usually a disaster.)

Possible Exposures	Controls
• Selecting the wrong DBMS. • Confusion between heavy-duty DBMS and decision-support data management. • DBMS with insufficiently flexible data independence for change, maintenance, and ad hoc information generation. • Essential DBMS facilities not understood. • Competitive benchmark results in confusion (or the simplest system being selected rather than one of suitable power and flexibility). • DBMS with poor interface to data dictionary, TP monitor, and fourth-generation languages.	• Appropriate DBMS selection. • Choice of DBMS related to high-productivity application-generation languages. • Distinction between heavy-duty DBMS and decision-support data management software. Appropriate use of extractors for decision-support data.
• Uncontrolled data with the same fields represented differently by different departments. • Lack of control over using the data dictionary.	• Enforcement of data dictionary usage, preferably with dictionary software which automatically generates the programmers' description of data (COBOL Data Division, DL/1 PSBs, etc.) dictionary-driven fourth-generation languages, etc.) • Corporate-wide use of the same dictionary facilities, and standards for naming fields.
• Inadequate attention to the coexistence of the old and the new programs. • Attempts to rewrite too many old programs and convert files into a different data-base form. Often these massive conversion attempts have been abandoned. (If the old programs work, without high maintenance costs, leave them alone.)	• Conversion planning that permits the old non-data-base programs to coexist with the new. For this purpose the old files are made subschemas (logical files) of the new data bases. • Conversion facilities, which enable the old programs to continue to run correctly, are thoroughly tested.

• Casual approach to library control.	• Tight system library control.
	  Update control.
	  Version synchronization.

• Inadequate security. • Inadequate privacy controls. • Inadequate controls on embezzlement. • Unauditable systems.	• Involvement of auditors at the initial design phases.
• Inadequate data-update controls. • Inadequate data-integrity controls.	• Thorough controls on integrity and accuracy. • Data entry performed in end-user locations, locations with user management responsible for the accuracy of the data. • Real-time checks on data validity as the data are entered.

(Continued)

Reasons for Success	Reasons for Failure or Disappointment
• A comprehensive system testing plan. • Central provision of test data bases for programmers. • Establishment of a set of test procedures which vigorously apply the same checks to new and modified applications.	• Lack of a comprehensive system testing plan, including the testing of compatibility with the surviving non-data-base applications.
• Programs specifications containing full details of types and sequences of data-base accesses, thoroughly reviewed with structured "walk-throughs" with the data administrator present. This activity should relate to the logical data model and the logical access maps (LAMs) which support each procedure.	
• Thorough understanding of the options, and advantages and disadvantages of distributed intelligence, distributed files, and geographically separate data bases. • Analysis of the advantages of centralization and decentralization. Analysis of where each type of data structure ought to be located geographically. • Consideration of future development of distributed systems technology in the planning of data bases. • A top management strategy relating to distributed systems architectures and distributed data.	• Overly convoluted central structures that cause performance problems and preclude subsequent distribution.
• Distributed data administration that ensures compatibility of data at different locations, enforces common dictionary use at all locations, assists peripheral locations in data design, and deals with potential integrity problems in distributed data.	• Incompatible data at scattered locations. The same data having different bits in fields, and different fields in records.

● An appropriate mix of centralized standardization and guidance, and decentralized implementation.	● Lack of centralized control and guidance, leading to a proliferation of incompatible systems. ● Lack of agreed standards for data analysis, naming, modeling conventions, and documentation; lack of training to the project teams in these standards.
● Separation of information systems and production systems; this simplifies data structures, improves performance, and relieves scheduling problems. ● Small functional information systems implemented with special information system software (and hardware).	● Severe scheduling and response-time problems due to putting too great a diversity of usage into one system.
● Use of flexible, standard, networking software for flexible distribution of, and access to, data-base facilities.	● Clumsy, crude, or inflexible teleprocessing facilities. ● Writing your own distributed architecture software.
● Facilities that enable end users to generate their own files from existing data bases, and manipulate them in a powerful manner.	
● Careful selection of the first data-base project. The first project should be chosen to maximize the chances of success, and to act as a seed project used to develop expertise.	● First project so complex that it never succeeds or is not completed. ● First project that fails to demonstrate the value of data base.
● All persons are thoroughly educated at a level appropriate to their function.	● Lack of understanding of data-base principles or implementation requirements. ● Lack of education of application analysts, designers and programmers; these professionals often resist as they do not understand the need for change. ● Failure to educate end users.
● "Keep it simple."	● Excessive complexity. ● Confused thinking.

GLOSSARY

Note A Types and Instances

Words describing data can either refer to a *type* of data or an *instance* (or occurrence) of data. Thus we have:

Entity type	Entity instance (or occurrence)
Attribute type	Attribute instance (or occurrence)
Data item type	Data item instance (or occurrence)
Field type	Field instance (or occurrence)
Association type	Association instance (or occurrence)
Link type	Link instance (or occurrence)
Record type	Record instance (or occurrence)

Type refers to a category of data representation, independent of time or value. Instance (or occurrence) refers to a specific example of that data type. The instances of a given type differ from one another in their value. To fully describe an instance one must provide both the information that defines its type and then the values that define this particular instance.

The flight information board at an airport is designed to show certain *types* of data such as flight number, destination, departure time, and gate. If we look at the board at one instant it shows values (*instances*) of these data types.

A data model consists exclusively of *type* information. Logical data-base design is a process of discovering and defining the *types* of entities, attributes, records, associations, etc. Only when the data base is operational are *instances* created (as with the flight information board).

We often refer to data loosely without saying whether we mean a *type* or *instance*. Thus we say "record," "entity," or "attribute."

"Record" is a shorthand word which could mean either "record type" or "record instance." It might mean employee record (a type) or the record for John Jones (an instance).

This shorthand is useful in that it avoids cluttered descriptions. It should not be used unless that context makes clear whether it refers to *types* or *instances* of data.

Note B

Items in **bold** type in the Glossary are defined elsewhere in the Glossary.

ACCESS. The operation of **seeking**, reading, or writing data on a storage unit.

ACCESS MECHANISM. A mechanism for moving one or more reading and writing heads to the position at which certain data are to be read or written. Alternatively, the data medium may be moved to the read/write station.

ACCESS METHOD. A technique for moving data between a computer and its peripheral devices: for example, serial access, random access, virtual sequential access method (**VSAM**), hierarchical indexed sequential access method (HISAM), access via **secondary indices,** and **relational** accesses such a joins, projects, or other relational algebra operations.

ACCESS TIME. The time that elapses between an instruction being given to access some data and those data becoming available for use.

ACTION. Something accomplished by a single program access command when using the data base.

A *simple action* is a command that creates, reads, updates, or deletes an instance of a single record.

A *compound action* is a command that requires multiple instances of records because it performs a sort, search, join, projection, or other relational operation.

ACTION DIAGRAM. A diagram of how programs use the data base, indicating the **actions** to be taken and the control structures that relate to them.

In good structured design the action diagram is linked to a **data model** in which all records are **normalized**.

ACTIVITY. The lowest-level function on a **function chart**. The activity is a logical description of a function that an enterprise performs. A procedure (computerized or not) is designed for accomplishing that activity.

ACTIVITY RATIO. The faction of records in a file or data set which have activity (are updated or inspected) in a given period or during a given run.

ADDRESS. An identification (number, name, label) for a location in which data are stored.

ADDRESSING. The means of assigning data to storage locations, and subsequently retrieving them, on the basis of the key of the data.

ALGORITHM. A computational procedure containing a finite sequence of steps.

ALTERNATE TRACK. A track that is automatically substituted for a damaged track on a disc or other storage device.

ANTICIPATORY STAGING. Blocks of data are moved from one storage device to another device with a shorter access time, in anticipation of their being needed by the computer programs. This is to be contrasted with * demand staging, in which the blocks of data are moved *when* programs require them, not *before*.

ASSEMBLE. To convert a routine coded in nonmachine language into actual machine language instructions.

To perform some or all of the following functions: (1) translation of symbolic operation codes into machine codes; (2) allocations of storage, to the extent at least of assigning storage locations to successive instructions; (3) computation of absolute or relocatable addresses from symbolic addresses; (4) insertion of library routines; (5) generation of sequences of symbolic instructions by the insertion of specific parameters into macro instructions.

ASSOCIATION. A relationship between two **entities** that is represented in a **data model**. It is drawn as a line between the entity boxes on the data model. This line is called a *link*.

Entity A can be associated with entity B in two ways:

one-to-one   (drawn A ⟶➤B)
one-to-many   (drawn A ⟶➤ B)

The reverse association from entity B to entity A can also be of these two types.

If it is possible that there may be no instances of entity B associated with entity A, a zero may be drawn on the link by the arrowhead, thus: A⟶⊶➤ B. If there must be at least one B per A, put a "1" behind the arrowhead thus: A⟶⊷➤B.

We refer to associations between **entities**, **data items**, **normalized records**, and sometimes unnormalized records.

"Association" is a shorthand word meaning either "association type" or "association instance" (*See* Note A).

An association type may be given a name indicating the nature of the association it defines. If there are two or more association types between the same two entity types, the association types *must* be named so that one can tell which is which.

ASSOCIATION RELATION or **ASSOCIATION RECORD.** A **relation** or **record** containing information about the **association**.

The association name is sometimes stored. In more advanced forms of **data model** (e.g., **intelligent data model**) information is stored about the *meaning* of the association or rules which are applied when using the association.

ASSOCIATIVE STORAGE (MEMORY). Storage that is addressed by content rather than by location, thus providing a fast way to search for data having certain contents. (Conventional storage has addresses related to the physical location of the data.)

ATTRIBUTE
1. A descriptive property of an entity class.
2. A **data item** containing a single piece of information about an **entity**.
   Records are composed of attributes relating to a given entity.

An attribute is usually atomic, i.e., it cannot be broken into parts that have meanings of their own.

The term *attribute* is a shorthand meaning either *attribute type* or *attribute value* (*See* Note A).

All attributes of a given type have the same format, interpretation, and range of acceptable values. An instance of a record has its own (not necessarily unique) value of this attribute.

ATTRIBUTE VALUE. The number, character string, or other element of information assigned to a given **attribute** of a given **record** instance at a given time. The name, format, interpretation, and range of acceptable values of an attribute are determined by its attribute type. Within these constraints, attribute values are free to vary from time to time and from one record instance to another. The shorter term "attribute" may be used to mean attribute value, but only when the context suffices to distinguish it from attribute type.

Attribute instances can have nulls instead of values. These are of two types.
1. Value not yet known. (But there can potentially be a value.)
2. Value not applicable. (A given entity instance will *never* have a value for this attribute.)

AUTOMATIC NAVIGATION. The ability to use high-level **relational algebra** commands which are automatically executed in the use of a data base, rather than accessing records one-at-a-time.

AVAILABILITY. A measure of the reliability of a system, showing the fraction of time when one performs a function as intended.

$$\text{Availability} = \frac{\text{Time the function is performed as intended}}{\text{Total time during which the function should have been performed}}$$

BINARY SEARCH. A method of searching a sequenced table or file. The procedure involves selecting the upper and lower half based on an examination of its midpoint value. The selected portion is then similarly halved, and so on until the required item is found.

BLOCKING. The combining of two or more physical records so that they are jointly read or written by one machine instruction.

BUCKET. An area of storage that may contain more than one physical record and which is referred to as a whole by some addressing technique.

BUFFER. An area of storage that holds data temporarily while it is being received, transmitted, read, or written. It is often used to compensate for differences in the speed or timing of devices. Buffers are used in terminals, peripheral devices, storage units, and in the CPU.

CANDIDATE KEY. A **key** that uniquely identifies **normalized record** instances of a given type. A candidate key must have two properties.
1. Each instance of the record must have a different value on the key, so that given a key value one can locate a single instance.

2. No attribute in the key can be discarded without destroying the first property.

In a bubble chart, a candidate key is a bubble with one or more single-headed arrows leaving it.

CANONICAL MODEL. A **model** of data which represents the inherent structure of that data and hence is independent of individual applications of the data and also of the software or hardware mechanisms which are employed in representing and using the data.

The minimal nonredundant model is a given collection of **data items.** Neither redundant data items nor redundant **associations** exist in the canonical model.

The canonical model should correctly represent all **functional dependencies** among the data items in the model. When this is done, the model contains **third-normal-form** groupings of data items.

CANONICAL SYNTHESIS. A formal process for combining separate logical data structures into a **canonical model.**

A recommended technique for designing logical data bases, which can be automated.

CATALOGUE. A directory of all files available to the computer.

CELL. Contiguous storage locations referred to as a group in an addressing or file searching scheme. The cell may be such that it does not cross mechanical boundaries in the storage unit; for example, it could be a **track** or **cylinder.**

CELLULAR CHAINS. Chains that are not permitted to cross **cell** boundaries.

CELLULAR MULTILIST. A form of **multilist organization** in which the **chains** cannot extend across **cell** boundaries.

CELLULAR SPLITTING. A technique for handling records added to a file. The records are organized into **cells** and a cell is split into two cells when it becomes full.

CHAIN. An organization in which records or other items of data are strung together by means of **pointers.**

CHANNEL. A subsystem for input to and output from the computer. Data from storage units, for example, flow into the computer via a channel.

CHECKPOINT/RESTART. A means of restarting a program at some point other than the beginning, used after a failure or interruption has occurred. Checkpoints may be used at intervals throughout an application program; at these points records are written giving enough information about the status of the program to permit its being restarted at that point.

CIRCULAR FILE. An organization for a file of high **volatility**, in which new records being added replace the oldest records.

CODASYL. Conference of Data System Languages. The organization that specified the programming language COBOL. It now has specified a set of manufacturer-independent, application-independent languages designed to form the basis of data-base management.

COMPACTION. A technique for reducing the number of bits in data without destroying any information content.

COMPILER. A computer program which in addition to performing the functions of an assembler has the following characteristics: (1) it makes use of information on the over-all logical structure of the program to improve the efficiency of the resulting machine program; (2) its language does not parallel the actual form of the machine language, but rather is oriented toward a convenient problem or procedure statement; (3) it usually generates more than one machine instruction for each symbolic instruction.

CONCATENATE. To link together. A *concatenated data set* is a collection of logically connected data sets. A *concatenated key* is composed of more than one data item.

CONCEPTUAL MODEL. The overall logical structure of a data base, which is independent of any software or data storage structure.

      A conceptual model often contains data types not yet implemented in physical data bases. It gives a formal representation of the data needed to run an enterprise, even though only certain systems in the enterprise conform to the model.

      Some organizations prefer the term *logical model* rather than *conceptual model*, because "conceptual" might imply that the model may never be implemented.

CONCEPTUAL SCHEMA. A term used to mean the same as **conceptual model**.

      The word **schema** often refers to the logical representation of data which is used by a particular class of data-base management systems (e.g., **CODASYL**). I recommend that the word **model** be used for software independent data structures, and **schema** be used for these linked to a specific class of software.

CYLINDER. That area of a storage unit which can be read without the movement of an access mechanism. The term originated with disc files, in which a cylinder consisted of one track on each disc surface such that each of these tracks could have a read/write head positioned over it simultaneously.

DAD. *See* **Database action diagram.**

DASD. Direct-access storage device.

DATA ADMINISTRATOR. An individual with an overview of an organization's data. The data administrator is responsible for designing the **data model** and obtaining agreement about the definitions of data which are maintained in the **data dictionary**.

      The function is responsible for the most cost-effective organization and use of an enterprise's data resources.

DATA AGGREGATE (CODASYL DEFINITION). A named collection of data items within a record. There are two types: vectors and repeating groups. A vector is a one-dimensional, ordered collection of data items, all of which have identical characteristics. A repeating group is a collection of data that occurs an arbitrary number of times within a record occurrence. The collection may consist of data items, vectors, and repeating groups.

DATA BANK. A collection of on-line data.

The term **data base** is more precise than *data bank*. *Data base* implies the formal techniques of data-base management. *Data bank* refers to any collection of data whether in the form of files, data bases, or an information retrieval system.

DATA BASE
1. A collection of interrelated data stored together with controlled redundancy to serve one or more applications; the data are stored so that they are independent of programs which use the data; a common and controlled approach is used in adding new data and in modifying and retrieving existing data within a data base. A system is said to contain a collection of data bases if they are disjoint in structure.
2. CODASYL definition: A *data base* consists of all the record occurrences, set occurrences, and areas which are controlled by a specific schema. If an installation has multiple data bases, there must be a separate schema for each data base. Furthermore, the content of different data bases is assumed to be disjoint.

DATA-BASE ACTION DIAGRAM (DAD).
A diagram showing the actions used with logical records (*retrieve, create, update, delete*) in such a way as to clearly diagram the structure of a data-base application program. A structured technique especially useful with fourth-generation languages.

DATA-BASE ADMINISTRATOR.
An individual with an overview of one or more data bases, who controls the design and use of these data bases.

It is often better to use two individuals: a **data administrator** and a data-base designer who designs the physical aspects of the data base.

DATA-BASE MANAGEMENT SYSTEM.
The collection of software required for using a data base, and presenting multiple different views of the data to the users and programmers.

DATA DESCRIPTION LANGUAGE.
A language for describing data (in some software for describing the logical, not the physical, data; in other software for both).

DATA DICTIONARY.
A catalogue of all data types, giving their names and structures, and information about data usage. Advanced data dictionaries have a directory function which enables them to represent and report on the cross-references between components of data and business models.

DATA DIVISION (COBOL).
That division of a COBOL program which consists of entries used to define the nature and characteristics of the data to be processed by the object program.

DATA ELEMENT.
Synonymous with **data item** or field.

DATA INDEPENDENCE.
The property of being able to change the overall logical or physical structure of the data without changing the application program's view of the data.

DATA INDEPENDENCE, LOGICAL.
The property of being able to change the overall logical structure of the data base (**schema**) without changing the program's view of the data.

DATA INDEPENDENCE, PHYSICAL. The property of being able to change the physical structure of the data without changing the logical structure.

DATA ITEM. The smallest unit of data that has meaning in describing information; the smallest unit of named data. Synonymous with, **data element** or field.

DATA MANAGEMENT. A general term that collectively describes those functions of the system that provide creation of and access to stored data, enforce data storage conventions, and regulate the use of input/output devices.

DATA MANIPULATION LANGUAGE. The language which the programmer uses to cause data to be transferred between his program and the data base.

The data manipulation language is not a complete language by itself. It relies on a host programming language to provide a framework for it and to provide the procedural capabilities required to manipulate data.

DATA MODEL. A logical map of data which represents the inherent properties of the data independently of software, hardware, or machine performance considerations.

The model shows **data items** grouped into **third-normal-form** records, and shows the **associations** among those records.

The term "model" may be contrasted with the term "schema." A **schema** also shows a logical representation of data, but it is usually related to a type of software representation, e.g., CODASYL, hierarchical, or relational. I recommend that the term "model" be reserved for data representations which are *independent* of which class of software is used for implementation. The software choice may change, but the model remains a fundamental description of the data.

DATA SET. A named collection of logically related data items, arranged in a prescribed manner, and described by control information to which the programming system has access.

DBDC. Data-base/data communications.

DEMAND STAGING. Blocks of data are moved from one storage device to another device with a shorter access time (possibly including main memory); when programs request them and they are not already in the faster-access storage. Contrast with **anticipatory staging.**

DEVICE/MEDIA CONTROL LANGUAGE. A language for specifying the physical layout and organization of data.

DIALOGUE. A generic word for a preplanned human–machine interaction; it encompasses formal programming languages, languages for interrogating data bases, and innumerable nonformal conversational interchanges, many of which are designed for one specific application.

DICTIONARY. *See* **Data dictionary**.

DIRECT ACCESS. Retrieval or storage of data by a reference to its location on a **volume**, rather than relative to the previously retrieved or stored data. The access mechanism goes directly to the data in question, as is normally required with on-line use of data.

DIRECT-ACCESS STORAGE DEVICE (DASD). A data storage unit on which data can be accessed directly at random without having to progress through a serial file such as tape. A disc unit is a direct-access storage device.

DIRECTORY. A table giving the relationships between items of data. Sometimes a table (index) giving the addresses of data.

DISTRIBUTED FREE SPACE. Space left empty at intervals in a data layout to permit the possible insertion of new data.

DL/1. IBM's Data Language/1, for describing logical and physical data structures.

DOMAIN. The collection of **data items** (fields) of the same type, in a **relation** (flat file).

DYNAMIC STORAGE ALLOCATION. The allocation of storage space to a procedure based on the instantaneous or actual demand for storage space by that procedure, rather than allocating storage space to a procedure based on its anticipated or predicted demand.

EMBEDDED POINTERS. Pointers in the data records rather than in a directory.

ENTITY. A person, place, thing, or concept that has characteristics of interest to the enterprise. An entity is something about which we store data.

Examples of entities are: CUSTOMER, PART, EMPLOYEE, INVOICE, MACHINE TOOL, SALESPERSON, BRANCH OFFICE, SALES TV AREA, WAREHOUSE, WAREHOUSE BIN, SHOP ORDER, SHIFT REPORT, PRODUCT, PRODUCT SPECIFICATION, LEDGER ACCOUNT, PAYMENT, DEBTOR, and DEBTOR ANALYSIS RECORD.

An entity has various **attributes** which we wish to record, such as COLOR, SIZE, MONETARY VALUE, PERCENTAGE UTILIZATION, or NAME.

For each entity type we have at least one record type. Sometimes more than one record type is used to store the data about one entity type (because of **normalization**).

An entity type has one data item type or a group of data item types which uniquely identifies it.

Entity is a shorthand word meaning either *entity type* or *entity instance* (*See* Note A).

ENTITY CHART. A diagram showing entities or **entity records**, and **associations** among them.

ENTITY IDENTIFIER. A key that uniquely identifies an **entity**.

ENTITY RECORD. A record containing the **attributes** pertaining to a given entity.

EXTENT. A contiguous area of data storage.

EXTERNAL SCHEMA. A user's or programmer's view of the data. Synonymous with subschema.

See **Data item.**

A set of similarly constructed records.

FLAT FILE. A two-dimensional array of data items.

FUNCTIONAL DECOMPOSITION. Breaking the operations of an enterprise into a hierarchy of functions which are represented on a **function chart.**

FUNCTIONAL DEPENDENCE. **Attribute** B of a **relation** R is functionally dependent on attribute A or R if, at every instant in time, each value of A has no more than one value of B associated with it in relation R. (Equivalent to saying that A identifies B.)

An attribute or collection of attributes, B, of a relation, R, is said to be *fully functionally dependent* on another collection of attributes, A, of R, if B is functionally dependent on the whole of A but not on any subset of A.

FUNCTION CHART. A chart showing the *logical* operations carried out in an enterprise. A hierarchical breakdown of these operations is usually drawn. The lowest-level function in the hierarchy is called an **activity** and is the basis for the design of *physical* procedures.

HASHING. A **direct-accessing** technique in which the key is converted to a pseudo-random number from which the required address is derived.

HASH TOTAL. A total of the values of a certain field in a file, maintained for control purposes to ensure that no items are lost or changed invalidly, and having no meaning of its own.

HEADER RECORD OR HEADER TABLE. A record containing common, constant, or identifying information for a group of records that follows.

HEURISTIC. Pertaining to trial-and-error methods of obtaining solutions to problems.

HIERARCHICAL FILE. A file in which some records are subordinate to others in a tree structure.

HIERARCHICAL STORAGE. Storage units linked together to form a storage subsystem, in which some are fast but small and others are large but slow. Blocks of data are moved from the large slow levels to the small fast levels when required.

HIT RATE. A measure of the number of records in a file which are expected to be accessed in a given run. Usually expressed as a percentage:

$$\frac{number\ of\ input\ transactions \times 100\%}{number\ of\ records\ in\ the\ file}$$

HOME ADDRESS
1. The address of a physical storage location (e.g., a home bucket) into which a data record is logically assigned; as opposed to overflow address.
2. A field that contains the physical address of a track, recorded at the beginning of a track.

HUFFMAN CODE. A code for data compaction in which frequently used characters are encoded with a smaller number of bits than infrequently used characters.

INDEPENDENCE, DATA. *See* **Data independence.**

INDEPENDENCE, DEVICE. Data organization that is independent of the device on which the data are stored.

INDEX. A table used to determine the location of a record.

INDEX CHAINS. Chains within an index.

INDEX POINT. A hardware reference mark on a disc or drum; used for timing purposes.

INDEX, SECONDARY. *See* **Secondary index.**

INDEXED-SEQUENTIAL STORAGE. A file structure in which records are stored in ascending sequence by **key**. Indices showing the highest key on a **cylinder, track, bucket,** and so on, are used for the selected retrieval of records.

INDICATIVE DATA. Data that identify or describe: for example, in a stock file, the product number, description, pack size. Normally, indicative data do not change on a regular, frequent basis during processing (as in, for example, an account balance).

INDIRECT ADDRESSING. Any method of specifying or locating a storage location whereby the key (of itself or through calculation) does not represent an address: for example, locating an address through indices.

INFORMATION SYSTEM. Contrasted with *production system, to mean a system in which the data stored will be used in spontaneous ways which are not fully predictable in advance for obtaining information.

INSTANCE. (*See* Note A).

INTELLIGENT DATA BASE. A data base that contains shared logic as well as shared data, and automatically invokes that logic when the data are accessed. Logic, constraints, and controls relating to the usage of the data are represented in an **intelligent data model.**

INTELLIGENT DATA MODEL. A conventional (unintelligent) **data model** contains descriptions of **normalized records** and **associations** among them. However these data have properties inherent to them which relate to the logic, controls, and constraints which we code into programs which use the conventional (unintelligent) data base.

An intelligent data model represents the logic, controls, and constraints which should be applied whenever the data are accessed, independently of the specific application. These logic, controls, and constraints may be associated with the records themselves, or with the **associations** among records.

INTERNAL SCHEMA. The physical structure of the data. A description of the data described in the **schema** are represented on storage media. Also called **storage schema.**

INTERPRETIVE ROUTINE. A routine that decodes instructions written as pseudo-codes and immediately executes those instructions, as contrasted with a compiler, which decodes the pseudo-codes and produces a machine-language routine to be executed at a later time.

INTERSECTION DATA. Data that are associated with the conjunction of two or more **entities** or record types, but which have no meaning if associated with only one of them.

INTERSECTION OF ENTITIES. Some characteristics which are represented in **attributes** belong not to individual **entity** instances but to specific combinations of two or more entity instances. Such cases require a separate data grouping called *intersection data.*

     The intersection is represented in a logical **data model** by a normalized record type whose **primary key** is the concatenation of the keys that idenfity the entities involved, and whose other attributes represent characteristics belonging to the intersection.

     Usually an intersection relates to entities of different types (e.g., SUPPLIER and PART). Less commonly it relates to entities of the same type (e.g., SUBASSEMBLY and SUBASSEMBLY, when a product or subassembly contains multiple other subassemblies).

INVERTED FILE. A file structure that permits fast spontaneous searching for previous unspecified information. Independent lists or indices are maintained in records keys which are accessible according to the values of specific fields.

INVERTED LIST. A list organized by a **secondary key**, not a **primary key**.

ISAM. Index sequential access method.

KEY. A **data item** or combination of data items used to identify or locate a record instance (or other data grouping).

KEY, CANDIDATE. *See* **Candidate key**.

KEY, PRIMARY. A **key** that is used to uniquely identify a record instance (or other data grouping).

KEY, SECONDARY. A **key** that does not uniquely identify a record instance; that is, more than one record instance can have the same key value. A key that contains the value of an **attribute** (data item) other than the unique identifier.

     Secondary keys are used to search a file or extract subsets of it, e.g., "all the engineers" or "all employees living in Boston."

KEY COMPRESSION. A technique for reducing the number of bits in keys; used in making indices occupy less space.

LABEL. A set of symbols used to identify or describe an item, record, message, or file. Occasionally, it may be the same as the address in storage.

LAM. *See* **Logical access map**.

LATENCY. The time taken for a storage location to reach the read/write heads on a rotating surface. For general timing purposes, average latency is used; this is the time taken by one half-revolution of the surface.

LFU. Least frequently used. A replacement algorithm in which when new data have to replace existing data in an area of storage, the least frequently used items are replaced. (Contrast with **LRU**.)

LIBRARY

1. The room in which volumes (tapes and disc packs) are stored.

2. An organized collection of programs, source statements, or object modules maintained on a direct-access device accessible by the operating system.

LINK. An **association** or **relationship** between **entities** or **records.** (*See* **Association.**)

A link is drawn as a line connecting entities or records on an entity chart or data model. The word *link* is more visual than *association* or *relationship* and so is sometimes preferred when referring to such lines drawn on charts. The word *link* sometimes refers to **link relation** or **link record.**

A distinction should be made between link types and link instances (*See* Note A). This is important when the attribute instances associated with a link can change as they might in an **intelligent data base.**

LINK RELATION or **LINK RECORD.** A **relation** or **record** containing information about the link. (*See* **Association relation.**)

LIST. An ordered set of data items. A chain.

LOGICAL. An adjective describing the form of data organization, hardware, or system that is perceived by an application program, programmer, or user; it may be different from the real (physical) form.

LOGICAL ACCESS MAP (LAM). A chart showing the sequence of logical accesses to a data model used by an application. LAMs give guidelines to the designer of the program structure which employs the data base. A collection of LAMs, annotated with suitable numbers, form the input to the physical data-base design process.

LOGICAL DATA BASE. A data base as perceived by its users; it may be structured differently from the physical data-base structure. In IBM's Data Language/1, a logical data base is a tree-structured collection of segments derived from one or more physical data bases by means of pointer linkages.

LOGICAL DATA-BASE DESCRIPTION. A **schema.** A description of the overall data-base structure as perceived for the users, which is employed by the data-base management software.

LOGICAL FILE. A file as perceived by an application program; it may be in a completely different form from that in which it is stored on the storage units.

LRU. Least recently used. A replacement algorithm in which when new data have to replace existing data in an area of storage, the least recently used items are replaced. (Contrast with **LFU.**)

LVIEW. A user's view of data. Synonymous with **subschema.**

MACHINE-INDEPENDENT. An adjective used to indicate that a procedure or program is conceived, organized, or oriented without specific reference to the system. Use of this adjective usually implies that the procedure or program is oriented or organized in terms of the logical nature of the problem or processing, rather than in terms of the characteristics of the machine used in handling it.

MACROINSTRUCTION. One line of source program code which generates a program routine rather than one program instruction.

MAINTENANCE OF A FILE. Periodic reorganization of a file to accommodate more easily items that have been added or deleted. (Sometimes this term is used to refer to the process of updating a file.)

MANAGEMENT, DATA BASE. *See* **Data-base management system.**

MAPPING. A definition of the way records are associated with one another.

METADATA. Data about data, i.e., the information about data which is stored in **data dictionaries, data models, schemas,** and their computerized representation.

MIGRATION. Frequently used items of data are moved to areas of storage where they are more rapidly accessible; infrequently used items are moved to areas that are less rapidly accessible and possibly less expensive.

MODEL. *See* **Data model.**

MODULE
1. The section of storage hardware that holds one volume, such as one spindle, of discs.
2. A collection of program code that can be compiled by itself.

MULTILIST ORGANIZATION. A **chained** file organization in which the chains are divided into fragments and each fragment indexed, to permit faster searching.

MULTIPLE-KEY RETRIEVAL. Retrieval that requires searches of data based on the values of several key fields (some or all of which are **secondary keys**).

NETWORK STRUCTURE. *See* **Plex structure.**

NONPRIME ATTRIBUTE. An **attribute** that is not part of the **primary key** of a normalized record. Attributes that are part of the primary key are called **prime attributes.**

NORMAL FORM, FIRST. Data in flat file form, without any repeating groups.

NORMAL FORM, SECOND. A relation R is in second normal form if it is in **first normal form** and every **nonprime attribute** of R is fully **functionally dependent** (q.v.) on each **candidate key** of R. (E. F. Codd's definition.)

NORMAL FORM, THIRD. A relation R is in third normal form if it is in **second normal form** and every **nonprime attribute** of R is nontransitively dependent on each **candidate key** of R. (E. F. Codd's definition.)

A record, segment, or tuple which is **normalized** (i.e., contains no repeating groups) and in which every **nonprime** data item is nontransitively dependent and fully **functionally dependent** on each **candidate key.**

In other words, the *entire* **primary key** or **candidate key** is needed to identify each other data item in the tuple, and no data item is identified by a data item which is not in the primary key or candidate key.

NORMALIZATION. The decomposition of more complex data structures according to a set of dependency rules, designed to give simpler, more stable structures.

      Third normal form (q.v.) is usually adequate for a stable data structure.

NORMALIZED RECORD. A named set of **attributes** representing some or all of the characteristics of some **entity** or **intersection of entities.** One entity is represented by one or more records in **third normal form,** and an intersection of two or more entities (if that intersection has nonprime attributes) is represented by one normalized record. Every normalized record has a primary key.

      Record may be used as a shorthand for "normalized record" in contexts where there is no possible confusion with other uses of *record* that are prevalent in the field (e.g., IMS logical records or physical records). Moreover, the term *normalized record* is itself a shorthand meaning either *normalized record type* or *normalized record instance* (*See* Note A).

ON-LINE. An on-line system is one in which the input data enter the computer directly from their point of origin and/or output data are transmitted directly to where they are used. The intermediate stages such as punching data, writing tape, loading discs, or off-line printing are avoided.

ON-LINE STORAGE. Storage devices, especially the storage media they contain, under the direct control of a computing system, not off-line or in a volume library.

OPERATING SYSTEM. Software that enables a computer to supervise its own operations, automatically calling in programs, routines, language, and data, as needed for continuous throughput of different types of jobs.

OVERFLOW. The condition when a record (or segment) cannot be stored in its **home address,** that is, the storage location logically assigned to it on loading. It may be stored in a special overflow location, or in the home address of other records.

PAGE FAULT. A program interruption that occurs when a page that is referred to is not in main memory and has to be read in.

PAGING. In virtual storage systems, the technique of making memory appear larger than it is by transferring blocks (pages) of data or programs into that memory from external storage when they are needed.

PARALLEL DATA ORGANIZATIONS. Organizations that permit multiple access arms to search, read, or write data simultaneously.

PHYSICAL. An adjective, contrasted with **logical,** which refers to the form in which data or systems exist in reality. Data are often converted by software from the form in which they are *physically* stored to a form in which a user or programmer perceives them.

PHYSICAL DATA BASE. A data base in the form in which it is stored on the storage media, including pointers or other means of interconnecting it. Multiple logical data bases may be derived from one or more physical data bases.

PHYSICAL RECORD. A collection of bits that are physically recorded on the storage medium and which are read or written by one machine input/output instruction.

PLEX STRUCTURE. A relationship between records (or other groupings) in which a child record can have more than one parent record. Also called **network structure**.

POINTER. The address of a record (or other data groupings) contained in another record so that a program may access the former record when it has retrieved the latter record. The address can be absolute, relative, or symbolic, and hence the pointer is referred to as absolute, relative, or symbolic.

PRIMARY KEY. *See* **Key, primary**.

PRIME ATTRIBUTE. An **attribute** that forms all or part of the **primary key** of a **record**. Other attributes are called **nonprime attributes**.

PROGRESSIVE OVERFLOW. A method of handling **overflow** in a randomly stored file which does not require the use of pointers. An overflow record is stored in the first available space and is retrieved by a forward serial search from the home address.

PURGE DATE. The date on or after which a storage area is available to be overwritten. Used in conjunction with a file lable, it is a means of protecting file data until an agreed release data is reached.

RANDOM ACCESS. To obtain data directly from any storage location regardless of its position with respect to the previously referenced information. Also called **direct access**.

RANDOM-ACCESS STORAGE. A storage technique in which the time required to obtain information is independent of the location of the information most recently obtained. This strict definition must be qualified by the observation that we usually mean relatively random. Thus magnetic drums are relatively nonrandom access when compared to magnetic cores for main memory, but relatively random access when compared to magnetic tapes for file storage.

RANDOMIZING. An old word for **hashing**.

REAL TIME
1. Pertaining to actual time during which a physical process transpires.
2. Pertaining to the performance of a computation during the actual time that the related physical process transpires so that results of the computation can be used in guiding the physical process.
3. Pertaining to an application in which response to input is fast enough to effect subsequent input, as when conducting the dialogues that take place at terminals on interactive systems.

RECORD
1. A group of related **data items** treated as a unit by an application program.

2. **CODASYL** definition: A named collection of zero, one, or more data items or data aggregates. There may be an arbitrary number of occurrences in the data base of each record type specified in the schema for that data base. For example, there would be one occurrence of the record type PAYROLL-RECORD for each employee. This distinction between the actual occurrences of a record and the type of the record is an important one.

3. **IBM's DL/1** terminology: A logical data-base record consists of a named hierarchy (tree) of related **segments**. There may be one or more segment types, each of which may have a different length and format.

RELATION. A flat file. A two-dimensional array of **data items**. A file in **normalized** form.

RELATIONAL ALGEBRA. A language providing a set of operators for manipulating **relations**. These include PROJECT, JOIN, and SEARCH operators.

RELATIONAL CALCULUS. A language in which the user states the results he requires from manipulating a **relational data base**.

RELATIONAL DATA BASE. A data base made up of **relations** (as defined above) that uses a data-base management system has the capability to recombine the data items to form different relations thus giving great flexibility in the usage of data. If the data-base management system does not provide the functions of or equivalent to a relational algebra, the term **relational data base** should not be used.

RING STRUCTURE. Data organized with chains such that the end of the chain points to its beginning, thus forming a ring.

ROOT. The base node of a tree structure. Data in the tree may be accessed starting at its root.

SCHEMA
1. A map of the overall logical structure of a data base. (Contrast with **Data model**.)
2. **CODASYL** definition: A *schema* consists of DDL (Data Description Language) entries and is a complete description of all the **area**, **set** occurrences, **record** occurrences, and associated **data items** and **data aggregates** as they exist in the data base.

SCHEMA LANGUAGE. Logical data-base description language.

SEARCH. To examine a series of items for any that have a desired property or properties.

SEARCH KEY. Synonymous with **secondary key**.

SECONDARY INDEX. An **index** composed of **secondary keys** rather than **primary keys**.

SECONDARY KEY. *See* **Key, secondary**.

SECONDARY STORAGE. Storage facilities forming not an integral part of the computer but directly linked to and controlled by the computer (e.g., discs, magnetic tapes, etc.).

The smallest address portion of storage on some disc and drum storage units.

SEEK. To position the access mechanism of a **direct-access** storage device at a specified location.

SEEK TIME. The time taken to execute a **seek** operation.

SEGMENT. A named fixed-format quantum of data containing one or more data items. A segment is the basic quantum of data that is passed to and from the application programs when IBM Data Language/1 is used. (IBM definition.)

SENSITIVITY. A programmer may view only certain of the data in a logical data base. His program is said to be *sensitized* to those data.

SEQUENCE SET INDEX. The lowest level in a tree-structured index. The entries in this level are in sequence. Searches and other operations may be carried out in the sequence set index; those are called sequence set operations.

SEQUENTIAL PROCESSING. Accessing records in ascending sequence by key; the next record accessed will have the next higher key, irrespective of its physical position in the file.

SERIAL-ACCESS STORAGE. Storage in which records must be read serially one after the other (e.g., tape).

SERIAL PROCESSING. Accessing records in their physical sequence. The next record accessed will be the record in the next physical position/location in the field.

SET (CODASYL DEFINITION). A *set* is a named collection of record types. As such, it establishes the characteristics of an arbitrary number of occurrences of the named set. Each set type specified in the schema must have one record type declared as its OWNER and one or more record types declared as its MEMBER records. Each occurrence of a set must contain one occurrence of its owner record and may contain an arbitrary number of occurrences of each of its member record types.

SET, SINGULAR. A CODASYL **set** without owner records; the owner is declared to be "SYSTEM." A singular set is used to provide simple nonhierarchical files such as a file of customer records.

SKIP-SEARCHED CHAIN. A **chain** having **pointers** that permit it to be searched by skipping, not examining every link in the chain.

SORT. Arrange a file in sequence by a specified key.

STAGING. Blocks of data are moved from one storage device to another with a shorter access time, either before or at the time they are needed.

STORAGE HIERARCHY. Storage units linked together to form a storage subsystem, in which some are fast but small and others are large but slow. Blocks of data are moved (**staged**) from the large slow levels to the small fast levels as required.

STORAGE SCHEMA. Synonymous with **internal schema.**

SUBMODEL. A user's or programmer's view of the data.

SUBSCHEMA. A map of a programmer's view of the data he uses. It is derived from the global logical view of the data—the schema.

TABLE. A collection of data suitable for quick reference, each item being uniquely identified either by a label or by its relative position.

TERABIT STORAGE. Storage that can hold 10^{12} bits of data.

THIRD NORMAL FORM. *See* **Normal form, third.**

TRACK. The circular recording surface transcribed by a read/write head on a drum, disc, or other rotating mechanism.

TRANSACTION. An input record applied to an established file. The input record describes some "event" that will either cause a new file record to be generated, an existing record to be changed, or an existing record to be deleted.

TRANSFER RATE. A measure of the speed with which data are moved between a direct-access device and the central processor. (Usually expressed as thousands of characters per second or thousands of bytes per second.)

TRANSPARENT DATA. Complexities in the data structure are hidden from the programmers or users (made transparent to them) by the software.

TREE INDEX. An index in the form of a tree structure.

TREE STRUCTURE. A hierarchy of groups of data such that (1) the highest level in the hierarchy has only one group, called a *root*; (2) all groups except the root are related to one and only one group on a higher level than themselves. A simple master/detail file is a two-level tree. Also called a hierarchical structure.

TUPLE. A group of related fields. N related fields are called an N-tuple.

TYPE. *See* Note A.

VIRTUAL. Conceptual or appearing to be, rather than actually being. An adjective which implies that data, structures, or hardware appear to the application programmer or user to be different from what they are in reality, the conversion being performed by software.

VIRTUAL MEMORY. Memory that can appear to the programs to be larger than it really is because blocks of data or program are rapidly moved to or from secondary storage when needed.

VOLATILE FILE. A file with a high rate of additions and deletions.

VOLATILE STORAGE. Storage that loses its contents when the power supply is cut off. Solid-state (LSI) storage is volatile; magnetic storage is not.

VOLUME. Demountable tapes, discs, and cartridges are referred to as *volumes*. The word also refers to a nondemountable disc or other storage medium. It has been defined as "that portion of a single unit of storage medium which is accessible to a single read/

write mechanism"; however, some devices exist in which a volume is accessible with two or more read/write mechanisms.

VOLUME TABLE OR CONTENTS (VTOC). A table associated with a volume which describes each file or data set on the volume.

VSAM. Virtual sequential access method, an IBM volume-independent indexed sequential access method.

VTOC. *See* **Volume table of contents.**

WORKING STORAGE. A portion of storage, usually computer main memory, reserved for the temporary results of operations.

WRITE. To record information on a storage device.

INDEX

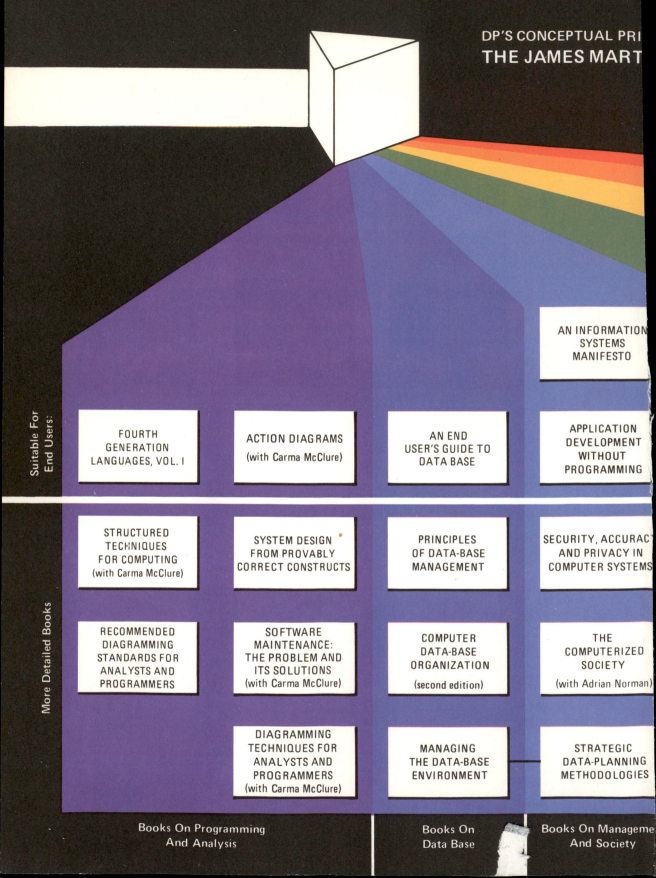